The Mirror of Great Britain

CLARE JACKSON

The Mirror of Great Britain

A Life of James VI & I

ALLEN LANE

an imprint of

PENGUIN BOOKS

ALLEN LANE

UK | USA | Canada | Ireland | Australia
India | New Zealand | South Africa

Allen Lane is part of the Penguin Random House group of companies
whose addresses can be found at global.penguinrandomhouse.com

Penguin Random House UK,
One Embassy Gardens, 8 Viaduct Gardens, London SW11 7BW

penguin.co.uk

Penguin
Random House
UK

First published 2025
001

Set in 10.2/13.87pt Sabon LT Std
Typeset by Jouve (UK), Milton Keynes
Printed and bound in Great Britain by Clays Ltd, Elcograf S.p.A.

The authorized representative in the EEA is Penguin Random House Ireland,
Morrison Chambers, 32 Nassau Street, Dublin D02 YH68

A CIP catalogue record for this book is available from the British Library

ISBN: 978–0–241–61127–2

Contents

CONTENTS

List of Illustrations

Photographic acknowledgements are shown in italics.

1. King James VI as a boy, 1574, by Rowland Lockey. Hardwick Hall, Derbyshire. _National Trust Photographic Library / Bridgeman Images._

2. Mary, Queen of Scots and her first husband, François II of France. Miniature by François Clouet, from the Hours of Catherine de Medici, c. 1573. _Bibliothèque nationale, Paris, NAL 82, folio 154 verso._

3. Armoured half-length portrait of James VI on a £20 (Scots) coin, 1576. _Stacks Bowers Auctioneers._

4. _Scene of James I at the tomb of his father, Henry Lord Darnley_ by Livinus Voghelarius, 1567. The Royal Collection Trust. _Copyright © His Majesty King Charles III, 2025/Bridgeman Images._

5. James's draft of the opening stanzas of his poem 'Ane metaphoricall invention of a tragedie called Phœnix', later published in _The Essays of a Prentice, in the Divine Art of Poesie_, 1584. _The Bodleian Libraries, University of Oxford, MS Bodl. 165 ff 36r._

6. Urn-shaped acrostic, spelling the name of Esmé Stewart, Duke of Lennox, from _The Essays of a Prentice, in the Divine Art of Poesie_, 1584. _Folger Shakespeare Library, STC 14373._

7. James VI gold 'hat-piece' coin, 1592. _Heritage Auctions/HA.com._

8. Mary, Queen of Scots, and James VI, double portrait by an unknown artist, 1583. Blair Castle, Blair Atholl, Pitlochry. _Reproduced by permission of the Atholl Estates._

9. King James VI, engraving from the Edinburgh edition of John Johnston, _Inscriptiones Historicae Regum Scotorum_, 1602.

10. King James VI, engraving from the Amsterdam edition of John Johnston, _Inscriptiones Historicae Regum Scotorum_, 1602.

11. *The Coronation of King James I at Westminster Abbey*, hand-coloured copy of an original engraving by Abraham Hogenberg, 1603. Cabinet des estampes, Bibliothèque nationale, Paris. *Raffaello Bencini/Bridgeman Images.*

12. Gilt brass and enamel table clock made by David Ramsay, 1610–15 (and later seventeenth-century alterations), with detail of the engraved base of the clock. Victoria and Albert Museum, London. *Copyright © V&A.*

13. Stone-relief portrait of James, possibly carved by Maximilian Colt, 1608. Council Chamber of the King's House, Tower of London. *Copyright © Historic Royal Palaces.*

14. James wearing the 'Mirror of Great Britain' jewel, portrait by John de Critz, after 1603. National Portrait Gallery, Edinburgh. Bequeathed by Sir James Naesmyth 1897. *National Galleries of Scotland.*

15. Queen Anna, portrait by an anonymous English artist, early 1600s. Kunsthistorisches Museum, Vienna. *Luisa Ricciarini/Bridgeman Images.*

16. Henry, Prince of Wales, large cabinet-miniature by Nicolas Hilliard, *c*.1610. National Portrait Gallery, London. *History and Art Collection/Alamy.*

17. Charles, Prince of Wales, portrait by Daniel Mytens, *c*.1623. Parham House, West Sussex. *Nick McCann/Bridgeman Images.*

18. *King Frederick V and Queen Elizabeth of Bohemia Riding near The Hague*, watercolour by Adriaen van de Venne, 1620–26. British Museum, London. *© Trustees of the British Museum.*

19. James I, statue by John Clark, 1620. Tower of the Five Orders of Architecture, Old Schools Quadrangle, Bodleian Library, University of Oxford. *Peter Wheeler/Alamy.*

20. *Dr John King preaching at Old St Paul's before James I*, painting by John Gipkyn, 1616. Society of Antiquaries of London. *Bridgeman Images.*

21. An Englishman smoking tobacco, illustration from Anthony Chute, *Tobacco*, 1595.

List of Maps and Family Trees

MAPS

FAMILY TREES

Scotland

N

Isle of Lewis

• Inverness

• Aberdeen

SCOTLAND

Dundee
Perth • • St Andrews
Lochleven Castle • • Falkland
Stirling •
Dunfermline • Burntisland
Linlithgow • Leith • Dunbar
Dumbarton • Glasgow • Edinburgh • Musselburgh
Langside • Dalkeith

Berwick-upon-Tweed

IRELAND

• Carlisle

ENGLAND

40 miles
50 kms

England and Wales

Berwick-on-Tweed

Carlisle   Newcastle

York

ENGLAND

WALES

Apethorpe   Peterborough
Fotheringhay   Huntingdon
Newmarket
Cambridge
Royston

Woodstock   Oxford
Theobalds Palace
Richmond   Greenwich
Windsor
Hampton   Eltham
Court   Dover
Salisbury   Winchester

N

100 miles
100 kms

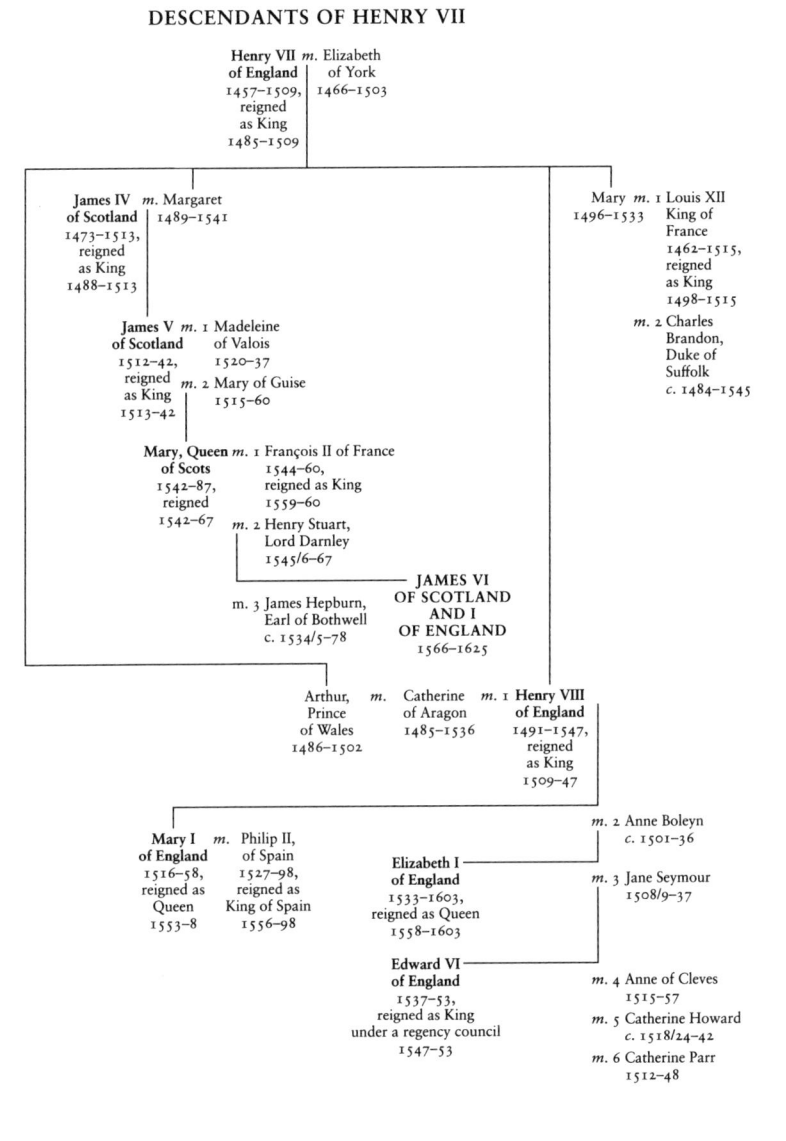

DESCENDANTS OF HENRY VII

Henry VII *m.* Elizabeth
of England | of York
1457–1509, | 1466–1503
reigned
as King
1485–1509

James IV *m.* Margaret
of Scotland | 1489–1541
1473–1513,
reigned
as King
1488–1513

Mary *m.* 1 Louis XII
1496–1533 | King of
France
1462–1515,
reigned
as King
1498–1515

m. 2 Charles
Brandon,
Duke of
Suffolk
c. 1484–1545

James V *m.* 1 Madeleine
of Scotland | of Valois
1512–42, | 1520–37
reigned | *m.* 2 Mary of Guise
as King | 1515–60
1513–42

Mary, Queen *m.* 1 François II of France
of Scots | 1544–60,
1542–87, | reigned as King
reigned | 1559–60
1542–67
m. 2 Henry Stuart,
Lord Darnley
1545/6–67

JAMES VI
OF SCOTLAND
AND I
OF ENGLAND
1566–1625

m. 3 James Hepburn,
Earl of Bothwell
c. 1534/5–78

Arthur, *m.* Catherine *m.* 1 **Henry VIII**
Prince of Aragon **of England**
of Wales 1485–1536 1491–1547,
1486–1502 reigned
as King
1509–47

m. 2 Anne Boleyn
c. 1501–36

Mary I *m.* Philip II,
of England of Spain
1516–58, 1527–98,
reigned as reigned as
Queen King of Spain
1553–8 1556–98

Elizabeth I
of England
1533–1603,
reigned as Queen
1558–1603

m. 3 Jane Seymour
1508/9–37

Edward VI
of England
1537–53,
reigned as King
under a regency council
1547–53

m. 4 Anne of Cleves
1515–57

m. 5 Catherine Howard
c. 1518/24–42

m. 6 Catherine Parr
1512–48

THE STUARTS

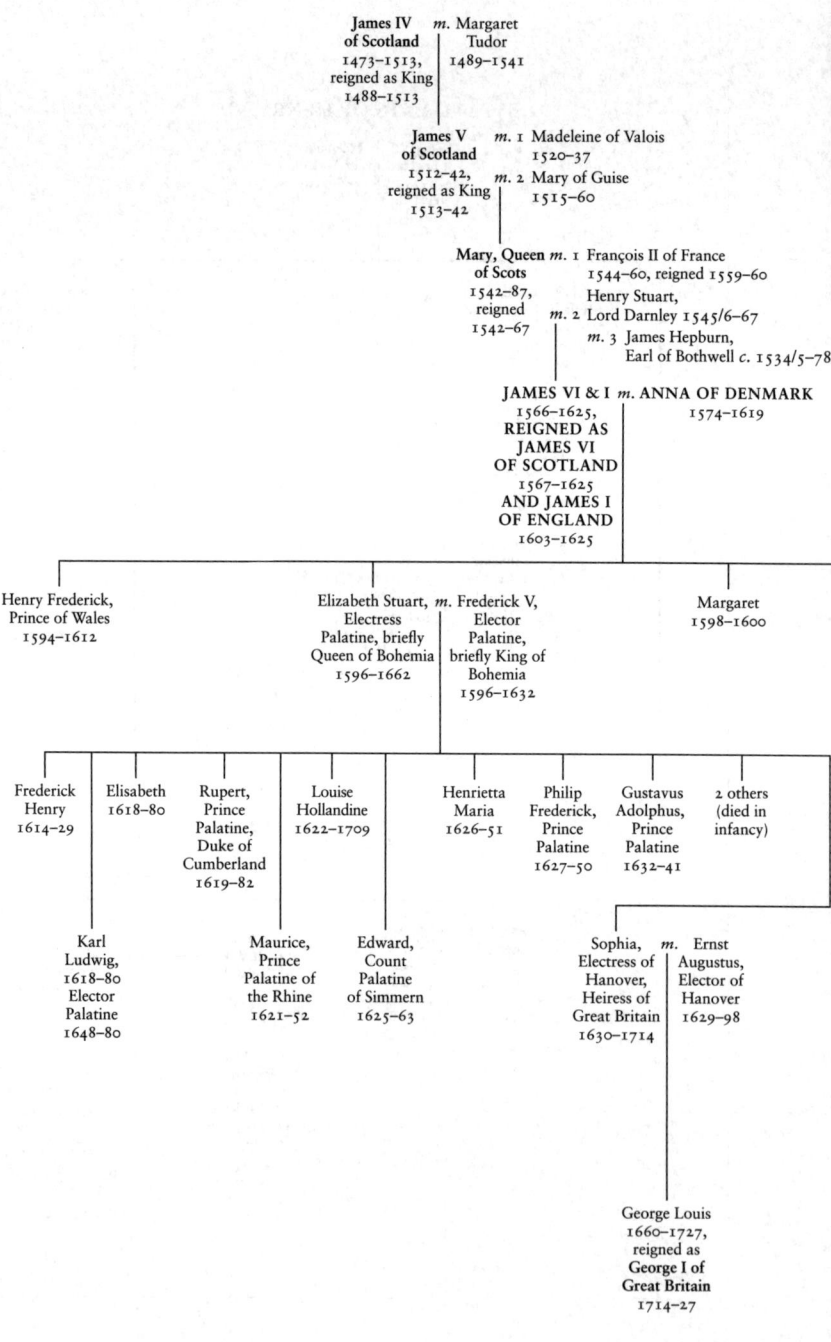

James IV _m._ Margaret
of Scotland Tudor
1473–1513, 1489–1541
reigned as King
1488–1513

James V _m._ 1 Madeleine of Valois
of Scotland 1520–37
1512–42, _m._ 2 Mary of Guise
reigned as King 1515–60
1513–42

Mary, Queen _m._ 1 François II of France
of Scots 1544–60, reigned 1559–60
1542–87, Henry Stuart,
reigned _m._ 2 Lord Darnley 1545/6–67
1542–67 _m._ 3 James Hepburn,
Earl of Bothwell _c._ 1534/5–78

JAMES VI & I _m._ ANNA OF DENMARK
1566–1625, 1574–1619
REIGNED AS
JAMES VI
OF SCOTLAND
1567–1625
AND JAMES I
OF ENGLAND
1603–1625

Henry Frederick, Elizabeth Stuart, _m._ Frederick V, Margaret
Prince of Wales Electress Elector 1598–1600
1594–1612 Palatine, briefly Palatine,
Queen of Bohemia briefly King of
1596–1662 Bohemia
1596–1632

Frederick Elisabeth Rupert, Louise Henrietta Philip Gustavus 2 others
Henry 1618–80 Prince Hollandine Maria Frederick, Adolphus, (died in
1614–29 Palatine, 1622–1709 1626–51 Prince Prince infancy)
Duke of Palatine Palatine
Cumberland 1627–50 1632–41
1619–82

Karl Maurice, Edward, Sophia, _m._ Ernst
Ludwig, Prince Count Electress of Augustus,
1618–80 Palatine of Palatine Hanover, Elector of
Elector the Rhine of Simmern Heiress of Hanover
Palatine 1621–52 1625–63 Great Britain 1629–98
1648–80 1630–1714

George Louis
1660–1727,
reigned as
George I of
Great Britain
1714–27

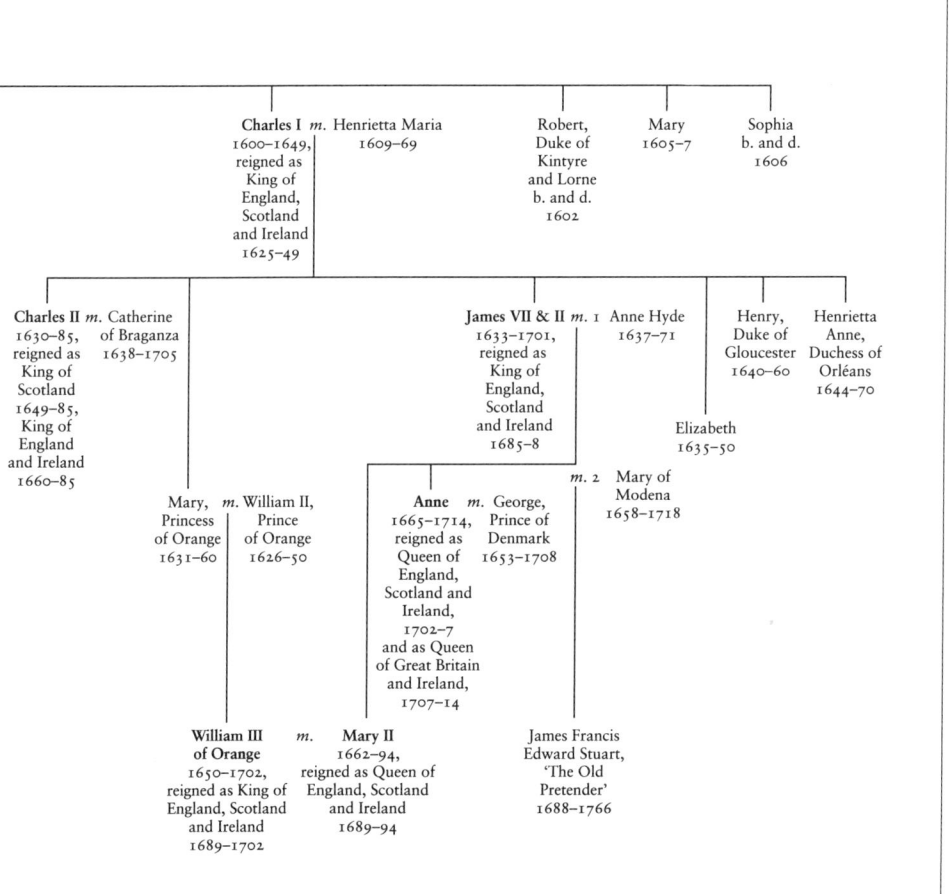

Charles I *m.* Henrietta Maria
1600–1649, 1609–69
reigned as
King of
England,
Scotland
and Ireland
1625–49

Robert,
Duke of
Kintyre
and Lorne
b. and d.
1602

Mary
1605–7

Sophia
b. and d.
1606

Charles II *m.* Catherine
1630–85, of Braganza
reigned as 1638–1705
King of
Scotland
1649–85,
King of
England
and Ireland
1660–85

James VII & II *m.* 1 Anne Hyde
1633–1701, 1637–71
reigned as
King of
England,
Scotland
and Ireland
1685–8

Henry,
Duke of
Gloucester
1640–60

Henrietta
Anne,
Duchess of
Orléans
1644–70

Elizabeth
1635–50

m. 2 Mary of
Modena
1658–1718

Mary, *m.* William II,
Princess Prince
of Orange of Orange
1631–60 1626–50

Anne *m.* George,
1665–1714, Prince of
reigned as Denmark
Queen of 1653–1708
England,
Scotland and
Ireland,
1702–7
and as Queen
of Great Britain
and Ireland,
1707–14

William III *m.* Mary II
of Orange 1662–94,
1650–1702, reigned as Queen of
reigned as King of England, Scotland
England, Scotland and Ireland
and Ireland 1689–94
1689–1702

James Francis
Edward Stuart,
'The Old
Pretender'
1688–1766

Author's Note

Dates in the text appear in 'Old Style' as per the Julian calendar, which was observed in the British Isles until 1752 and, until 1700, was ten days behind the Gregorian calendar that had been adopted in the majority of Continental European countries after its introduction by Pope Gregory XIII in 1582. Having been born in 1566, James objected to English peers and MPs in 1610 that adoption of the Gregorian calendar had sown confusion; indeed, 'I can never tell my own age; for now is my birthday removed by the space of ten days nearer me than it was before the change'. For convenience, each new year is taken to begin on 1 January, although, in England until 1752, and in Scotland until 1600, it was usual to deem each new year as starting on 25 March at the Feast of the Annunciation.

Aside from the sixth chapter considering James's interest in verse composition, the spelling and punctuation in quotations and publication titles have mostly been modernized. During the seventeenth century, the official name of the Dutch Republic was the United Provinces of the Netherlands.

I

A Mirrored Life

'Two snowballs put together, make one the greater: two houses joined, make one the larger: two castle walls made in one, makes one as thick and strong as both.'[1] Thus King James I of England exhorted sceptical members of the English Houses of Parliament in March 1607 to admit the practical benefits that would accrue by creating a united British kingdom. When united, the two formerly warring countries of England and Scotland would become a prosperous, powerful, Protestant state, with potential foreign invaders deterred by the sheer strength of Fortress Britain. Four years earlier, as King James VI of Scotland, he had succeeded to the English Crown on Elizabeth I's death in March 1603 and become the first monarch to rule both Scotland and England.

On his accession, James had assumed that closer union would inevitably follow with a single British state formed from his two separate kingdoms of Scotland and England. *Unus Rex, unus Grex et una Lex*: one king, one people and one law. But James's confidence had been misplaced; as he later conceded, 'I knew my own end, but not others' fears.' Although union commissioners held bilateral negotiations and produced a limited set of initial recommendations in 1604, the king was dismayed to observe, by March 1607, 'many crossings, long disputations, strange questions and nothing done'.[2] Only three months before James spoke in Parliament, the royal court had watched the premiere of William Shakespeare's tragedy *King Lear*, first performed at Whitehall on 26 December 1606. After having Lear call for a map of ancient Britain in order to divide his territory among his three daughters, Goneril, Regan and Cordelia, the play concluded in cataclysm. Rather than seeing father and daughters reunited and their lands preserved – as in the sixteenth-century drama *King Leir* – Shakespeare's reworking of *Leir*'s plot ended with the dying Lear cradling a strangled Cordelia and crying 'Howl, howl, howl, howl! O, you are men of stones.' The widowed, childless Duke of Albany is left to contemplate the resulting destruction of Lear's family and kingdom.[3]

Although *King Lear*'s dramatic dénouement was quickly amended to have Lear die in the (mistaken) belief that Cordelia still lived, the state of 'Great' Britain – as distinct from the smaller 'Britanny' in France – would remain a rhetorical aspiration during James's reign. Ambitious constitutional ambitions proved abortive: a bitter blow for a king who had hoped that his accession would effect 'an eternal agreement and reconciliation of many long bloody wars that have been between these two ancient kingdoms'.[4] The lessons of Shakespeare's *King Lear* only reinforced James's own convictions. In his advice manual entitled *Basilicon Doron* ('The Royal Gift') first published in 1599, James had counselled his eldest son and heir, Prince Henry, that, should he succeed to the triple Crowns of Scotland, England and Ireland, he must bequeath his territorial possessions intact, 'otherwise by dividing your kingdoms, ye shall leave the seed of division and discord among your posterity'.[5]

Half a century after James succeeded as English king, an Anglo-Scottish union ordinance was issued by the Cromwellian Protectorate in 1654 following the military subjugation of Scotland and the monarchy's abolition in England. The ordinance's provisions were, however, short-lived and ended with the collapse of the Protectorate and restoration of Stuart multiple monarchy in 1660 under James's grandson, Charles II. James's ambitions were partially realized under his great-granddaughter Queen Anne in 1707, when the Anglo-Scottish Treaty of Union created a new British state. A somewhat hybrid arrangement, the new state's unitary features included a single Westminster legislature, common currency and a single economic market, alongside more pluralistic aspects, notably the retention of separate national churches, legal systems and educational provision in Scotland and England. Having acclaimed the territorial conjunction of the two countries 'in one island, compassed with one sea, and of itself by nature so indivisible' as to render its internal borders redundant, James's unionist vision had notably been confined to mainland Britain.[6] In 1801, however, the Act for the Union of Great Britain and Ireland expanded the political state to include the island of Ireland. More than a century later, the Anglo-Irish Treaty (1921) provided for the creation of the Irish Free State – later the

Republic of Ireland – with six northern counties in Ulster remaining part of the United Kingdom of Great Britain and Northern Ireland. None of these geopolitical outcomes was quite what James had envisaged.

Becoming English king in 1603, James was no neophyte sovereign. He had been crowned King James VI of Scotland on 24 July 1567, at the age of only thirteen months, after the deposition of his mother, Mary, Queen of Scots. With political power initially vested in regents, James declared his intention to rule Scotland in his own name in 1578, aged eleven, although, in practice, his adult rule only started in the mid-1580s. The peaceful nature of James's accession to the English Crown in 1603 surprised many who had feared that, on the demise of the childless Virgin Queen, England would be plunged into a protracted and bloody war of succession between rival Protestant and Catholic claimants with French and Spanish interference. A week after Elizabeth's death, James wrote to his brother-in-law, Christian IV of Denmark, to 'acknowledge that what we have always wished has come true'.[7] A momentous juncture in British history, James's uncontested accession as English king appeared a providential fulfilment of ancient predictions, as panegyrists hailed a King Arthur *redivivus* who would gloriously fulfil Merlin's prophecy by reuniting Britain under his rule.

But by the time James again addressed MPs and peers at Westminster in March 1610, he felt himself 'now an old king' who, in addition to his decades ruling Scotland, had been in England for 'seven years [which] is a great time for a king's experience in government'.[8] On the day after his fiftieth birthday in June 1616, he summoned his English common-law judges to the Star Chamber at Westminster and recalled that, when he had arrived in London in 1603, 'I was an old king, past middle age, and practised in government ever since I was twelve years old.'[9] When James died at Theobalds Palace in Hertfordshire in March 1625, he had ruled England for twenty-two years. James was the only one of thirteen English monarchs between Henry VII and George I who lived to see a grandchild born and also the first King of Scotland to die peacefully of natural causes since Robert I ('the Bruce') in 1329.[10] His tenure of the Scottish throne for nearly fifty-eight years has since been surpassed only by Victoria and Elizabeth II.

Four centuries after King James VI & I's demise, his enlarged British snowball nevertheless looks vulnerable. Although the flag of the United Kingdom of Great Britain and Northern Ireland is nicknamed after James – the 'Union Jack' deriving from the Latin '*Jacobus*' – the polity faces an uncertain future. In *The Break-up of Britain* (1977), first published half a century ago, Tom Nairn diagnosed the multinational state of the United Kingdom as being in terminal atrophy, beset by imperial decline, an archaic constitution, and the rise of popular nationalisms in Scotland, Wales and Ireland. Dismissed by the political mainstream as pessimistic polemic, Nairn's apprehensions regarding the frailty of Britain's unreformed, asymmetrical polity now appear prescient. Two years after Nairn's book appeared, two referenda held in Scotland and Wales in 1979 failed to garner sufficient support for devolved deliberative assemblies to be established.[11] The dynamics of British territorial politics then shifted significantly when devolved administrations were created in Edinburgh, Cardiff and Belfast in the 1990s. Within Scotland, a referendum on independence in 2014 attracted a turnout of 84 per cent of the registered electorate and resulted in a majority of 55 per cent in favour of adhering to the status quo and retaining the Anglo-Scottish union.

Two years after the Scottish independence vote, a UK-wide referendum on membership of the European Union in 2016 generated a narrow majority in favour of altering the status quo, prompting negotiations that resulted in the UK's withdrawal from the European Union in 2020. The divisive and disruptive impact of 'Brexit' proved particularly acute in Northern Ireland, where commitments to avoid reintroducing either a 'hard' physical border within the island of Ireland or a customs border in the Irish Sea seemed ostensibly incompatible with simultaneously ensuring Britain's exclusion from the European Union's Single Market and Customs Union. Looking ahead, Northern Ireland's changing demographic dynamics have been interpreted as likely to yield a majority in favour of Irish reunification in a future referendum vote.[12]

In early modern Europe, dynastic agglomerates, similar to that inherited by the Stuart dynasty in 1603, were not uncommon. Today, Charles III is the head of state in fourteen sovereign countries, albeit reflecting Britain's colonial, rather than its dynastic, history. Referring to Scotland when addressing English peers and MPs in 1607, James put it simply: 'I was born there, and sworn here, and now reign over both.'[13] Inevitably, the reality was more complex as his accession as English king entailed absentee rule in Edinburgh, new forms of delegated authority, an asymmetrical balance of power, confessional tensions, overlapping and competing legal codes and a new 'British' cultural lexicon. Constitutionally, however, the mainland polity over which James ruled between 1603 and 1625 offers a plausible approximation of the situation likely to arise were Scotland once again to become an independent state: the same monarch, two independent states, two parliaments and separate national churches, currencies, economic arrangements and legal systems. Campaigning for independence in 2013, as Scotland's then First Minister, Alex Salmond reminded a public meeting in Campbeltown that 'Scotland was an independent nation for more than 100 years after the first union of the crowns. It is a phrase with a deep historical resonance in Scotland.'[14]

In 1603, James's wish to enact closer Anglo-Scottish union was a logical desire to convert the advantages of dynastic succession into territorial consolidation. Without the creation of a single British state, the link between the two formerly warring states of Scotland and England remained precarious, vested only in the persons of James and his three surviving children, Henry, Elizabeth and Charles. Following Prince Henry's unexpected death from typhoid fever in 1612, the dynastic link shrank further, leaving Princess Elizabeth – later Palatine Electress in Heidelberg with a brief tenure as Bohemian queen – and her younger brother, who succeeded James as King Charles I in 1625, but whose tenure of the British crowns led to civil war and his public execution in January 1649 by order of a radically reduced 'Rump' of the English Parliament.

Addressing the English Parliament in 1607, James remained mindful of the long history of acrimonious Anglo-Scottish relations and perennial fears of hostile incursion. As recently as the 1540s, England's failed attempt to conquer its northern neighbour had resulted in the deaths of over 10,000 Scots, the torching of numerous Scottish towns and the draining of both the English and Scots Treasuries. Those living in the traditionally lawless Border regions had, for generations, suffered endemic violence and been plagued by 'bloodshed, oppressions, complaints and outcries', standing in bleak contrast to the halcyon new world in which 'they now live every man peaceably under his own figtree'. James warned that, 'if after all this, there shall be a scissure [rift], what inconvenience will follow, judge you.'[15] Styling himself 'King of Great Britain', he sought – in parliamentary speeches and proclamations, alongside designs for a common coinage and new flag, and sponsorship of dramatic masques replete with nuptial rhetoric – to invest the idea of

Britishness with tangible psychological heft. Not without irony, it was the Scots nationalist republican, Tom Nairn, whose survey of Britain's historical evolution as a multinational state convinced him that James VI & I 'deserves greater recognition'. As Nairn acknowledged in 1997, James 'not only invented "Great Britain" but tried extraordinarily hard to make it work'.[16]

*

In a full-length portrait painted shortly after James's accession to the English throne, the king was depicted wearing a prominent hat jewel called the 'Mirror of Great Britain' (see Plate 14). Comprising three large diamonds and a ruby, the 'Mirror' offered opulent symbolic endorsement of James's vision of a united Britain, having been constituted from jewels in the English and Scottish royal collections.[17] More usually, however, mirrors reflect present realities, albeit with the capacity also to distort and deceive. Reappraising King James VI & I – as this book's title implies – can sometimes feel like entering a fairground hall of mirrors. To his subjects, especially his English ones, James often confounded popular expectations and his reputation has likewise disconcerted later generations. Mirrors, moreover, supplied James with one of his favourite verbal images. In 1626, the preacher and poet John Donne dedicated a printed sermon to the king's son and successor, Charles I, recalling that likening a king to a mirror was 'a metaphor in which your Majesty's blessed father seemed to delight'. As Donne elaborated, 'in the name of a mirror, a looking-glass, he sometimes presented himself, in his public declarations and speeches, to his people.'[18]

Addressing both Houses of the English Parliament in March 1607, for example, James sought to correct misconceptions regarding royal plans for Anglo-Scottish union and, 'with the old philosophers', had insisted 'I would heartily wish my breast were a transparent glass for you all to see through, that you might look into my heart, and then would you be satisfied of my meaning.'[19] Echoing the wish of Momus, Greek god of satire – that all humans might have a glass in their breasts to reveal their true souls – James invoked the same conceit in all subsequent English parliaments. In March 1610, he began a speech to peers and MPs 'with a great and a rare present, which is a fair and a crystal mirror . . . as through the transparentness thereof, you may see the heart of your king'. Following an address that must have lasted for the best part of an hour, the king concluded by warning that there were 'three ways ye may wrong a mirror'. His listeners might regard 'my mirror with a false light' and misunderstand his words or 'soil it with a foul breath and unclean hands', thereby conferring 'an ill meaning' on his intentions. Most serious of all, however, would be to disdain royal authority so much as to 'let it fall or break (for glass is brittle)'.[20]

Opening his next English Parliament in April 1614, James again conceived of his wishes as 'a mirror which is clear and unpolluted', hoping that his request for financial subsidy would be well received.[21] In January 1621, he likewise offered peers and MPs 'a true mirror of my mind and free thoughts of my heart', despite earlier occasions when, 'through a spice of envy', critics had spitefully attacked his words and turned them 'like spittle against the wind upon mine own face and contrary to my expectation'.[22] Finally, when opening what would be his last English Parliament in February 1624, the same metaphor was deployed to a different end when the king reminded MPs of their vital responsibilities to their constituents. James exhorted members of the House of Commons, 'be ye true glasses and mirrors of their faces, and be sure you yield true reflections and representations, as ye ought to do.'[23]

Underpinning the extensive *speculum principiis* – or 'mirror for princes' – genre of prescriptive literature offering advice to medieval and early modern rulers, mirrors supplied a metaphorical means of inculcating exemplarity and encouraging emulation. Between 1500 and 1700, four hundred works were published in England with titles including a reference to a mirror, a glass or a looking-glass.[24] In *Basilicon Doron* (1599), James urged his heir to 'let your own life be a lawbook and a mirror to your people.' By the former, 'they may read the practice of their own laws' and, by the latter, 'they may see, by your image, what life they should lead.'[25] On James's accession to the English throne four years later, the poet Alexander Craig combined the same metaphor with reference to the monarch's literary publications to warn that 'Kings be the glass, the very school, the book / Wherein private men do learn, and read, and look.'[26] In private, James wrote an anguished, if simultaneously excoriating, missive to the courtier Robert Carr, Earl of Somerset, in early 1615, citing 'things directly acted or spoken to myself' in the hope 'that ye may make good use of this little mirror of yourself' which 'lays plainly and honestly before you both your best and worst parts'.[27]

In specifying 'a fair and a crystal mirror', James was also offering MPs – metaphorically at least – the very best in vitreous technology. Imported into England from Continental Europe since the mid-1570s, crystal mirrors were not produced domestically until 1624.[28] Superior to their steel predecessors, crystal mirrors did not require regular polishing and presented images that were 'crystal clear'. Indeed, when Sir Francis Bacon (later Lord Chancellor) outlined James's preferred model of Anglo-Scottish union to MPs in April 1604, he deemed it too 'dangerous' a subject to paraphrase. Having asked the king to confirm his wishes in writing, Bacon read aloud the instructions as a 'piece of crystal, to deliver him from mistaking'.[29]

Using the metaphor of a crystal mirror, James hoped to imply maximal transparency and representational accuracy in articulating his inner thoughts, but 'definitionally, a reflection is never what it seems to be'.[30] Plane mirrors laterally invert images, while concave and convex mirrors magnify and diminish. In an era of increasing visual uncertainty, moreover, it could no longer be axiomatically assumed that, when individuals viewed an external object, everyone looking at it would perceive the same identical image, which would then pass unmediated from their eyes to their brains, and thereafter to their memories. Rather, individual vision was affected by physiological and neurological conditions as well as by the imagination's dispositional character. In 1612, Henry Peacham published an anthology of emblems inspired by *Basilicon Doron*, with each emblem matched to a quotation from James's treatise. But in a dedicatory poem to Prince Henry, the painter and herald William Segar warned of the limitless possibilities of ways in which different readers might interpret Peacham's images and the king's words:

> All eyes behold, and yet not all alike,
> Effects, and defects, both are in the eye,
> As when an object 'gainst the eye doth strike,
> The imagination straightaway doth imply
> Shapes, or what else the object doth present,
> Weaker or stronger, as the sight is bent.[31]

While the recent invention of microscopes and telescopes was dramatically expanding the range and scale of what could be perceived, simultaneous developments in artistic perspective were encouraging

increasingly sophisticated forms of optical illusion such as ana-
morphosis and *trompe l'oeil*. In the religious sphere, the Protestant
Reformation had provoked intense debates about visual delusion,
with Catholic paintings and statues of divine entities denounced as
ungodly while alleged miracles were dismissed as misreported or
visually fraudulent. Undermining all forms of religion were, moreover, diabolic forces that were widely blamed for derailing cognitive
processes by which images entered the eye or brain. In his published
dialogue, *Daemonologie* (1597), James acknowledged the Devil's skill
in deceiving the human senses to assume supernatural powers. Given
the popularity of card tricks and dice games, it was 'no wonder, that
the Devil may delude our senses, since we see by common proof, that
simple jugglers will make a hundred things seem both to our eyes and
ears otherwise than they are.'[32]

It was indeed often difficult to believe what one saw at the Jacobean court. At Whitehall, the Dutch scientist Cornelis Drebbel staged
elaborate optical displays using a camera obscura to 'present myself
as a king, decorated with diamonds and all kinds of precious stones,
and then in a moment transform myself into a beggar, all my clothing in rags, while in actual fact I am wearing only one set of clothes'.
Drebbel could likewise 'change myself into whatever creature I desire,
now into a lion, then into a bear, now into a horse, now into a cow,
a sheep, into a calf, into a pig'.[33] In 1612, Drebbel informed James
that he was devising a telescope to enable him to read private letters
from a distance of seven miles and to observe actions occurring eight
or nine miles away as easily as if they were in his royal bedchamber.
Drebbel successfully achieved the world's first submarine journey on
the River Thames, with the king among several thousand spectators
who watched for three hours in 1620, with mounting anxiety, before
Drebbel's leather vessel resurfaced, at a considerable distance from its
point of descent. So impressed was James that he reportedly demanded
that Drebbel immediately expand production from one prototype, able
to carry nine passengers, to one hundred smaller submarines for solo
individuals.[34]

The theatricality of optical illusion was also exploited on the Shakespearean stage where catoptrics – the branch of optics related to
reflection – readily veered into catoptromancy, or divination by mirrors.
In 1606, for instance, James is likely to have watched one of the first

performances of *Macbeth* in which the eponymous king consulted the 'weird sisters' in an attempt to secure his rule. Presented with a 'show of kings', Macbeth objected:

> Another yet? A seventh? I'll see no more.
> And yet the eighth appears who bears a glass
> Which shows me many more, and some I see
> That twofold balls and treble sceptres carry.[35]

In this classic 'mirroring moment', the 'glass' conjured for Macbeth images of an endless succession of future rulers, while also offering James, if he was in the audience, the opportunity to recognize himself in that descent, as ruler of Scotland and England, bearing the treble sceptred crowns of Scotland, England and Ireland.

The pre-eminent form of entertainment at the Jacobean court remained, however, glittering masques which created elaborate fictional universes and orbited around James's presiding presence as the 'Sun King'. Combining complex allegory, dialogue, music and dance, masques dazzled their elite audiences with intricate stage effects, such as those enabling performers dressed as Olympian gods to descend to the stage from hydraulic 'clouds'. Eventually writing over twenty scripts for court masques, Ben Jonson panegyrically acclaimed the cultural transcendence of James's court as a place in which 'the whole kingdom dresses itself, and is ambitious to use thee as her glass.'[36] Dazzling visual spectacles dramatically confirmed the majesty of royal power which, as the barrister Edward Forset marvelled in 1606, 'surmounts the person' of a monarch and acts 'like a brittle glass all enlightened with the glorious blaze of the sun', despite their physical body being 'as infirm and full of imperfections as others'.[37]

In reappraising James VI & I, *The Mirror of Great Britain* is as interested in the fragile and vulnerable dimensions of this king's life as in its more brilliantly gilded or sharply jagged aspects. In religious meditations published in 1624 – the year before James's death – John Donne acknowledged that divinely ordained kings occupied 'the highest ground' on earth and were its 'eminentest hills' – but still remained mortal. Although monarchs offered models for emulation, 'a glass is not the less brittle, because a king's face is represented in it; nor a king the less brittle, because God is represented in him.'[38]

*

Four centuries after King James's death, *The Mirror of Great Britain* supplies its own reflections on this remarkable king. Although it follows a broad chronological arc, its chapters are not narrative instalments, but thematic reflections on different aspects of James's life and writings. Where possible, this book brings together both the Scottish and English experiences of a king in whom, too often, the interest of historians of Scotland tends to wane after the royal court relocated to London, which, in turn, is often the cue for historians of England to interest themselves in James only as Elizabeth I's successor. While acknowledging that James's accession to the English throne was a momentous juncture in British history, events in 1603 have, too often, seemingly presented an insuperable historiographical hurdle that has encouraged biographers to produce serial volumes, restricting their focus to specific periods of James's life and reigns.[39] This book is, rather, a single-volume life of James VI *and* I. But since its structure is more thematic than chronological, a brief conspectus of James's life is helpful now, both to orientate readers unfamiliar with this era in British history and to serve as a reference point for events discussed later.

Born in Edinburgh Castle on 19 June 1566, James was the only child of the Catholic Mary, Queen of Scots, and her second husband, Henry Stewart, Lord Darnley, whom Mary had married after the death of her first husband, François II of France. When James was eight months old, Darnley was murdered by members of a faction close to James Hepburn, Earl of Bothwell, who shortly afterwards married James's mother. With Mary suspected of complicity in Darnley's murder, a group of 'Confederate Lords' took custody of the queen and obliged her to abdicate in favour of James, who was crowned King James VI of Scotland in the parish church of Stirling in July 1567, aged thirteen months. A six-year civil war ensued between a 'King's party', which promoted Protestantism and pro-English amity, while striving to uphold the infant king's fledgling authority, and a 'Queen's party', which rejected Mary's deposition as illegal. Mary herself fled to England in May 1568, where she remained under permanent house arrest, suspected of fomenting Catholic rebellion and seeking to usurp Elizabeth I, her first cousin once removed. In Scotland, a series of regents governed the country during James's minority, with the king assuming greater personal power from 1578 onwards, aged twelve. The arrival in Scotland of James's French cousin

Esmé Stuart, later Duke of Lennox, dismayed pro-English factions at court and, in August 1582, William Ruthven, Earl of Gowrie, seized the teenage king's person in the 'Ruthven Raid' and retained close control over him until James escaped ten months later. Thereafter ruling Scotland as an adult king, James agreed an Anglo-Scottish diplomatic alliance in 1585 that survived the trial and conviction for treason of his mother, Queen Mary, who was executed in February 1587 at Fotheringhay Castle in Northamptonshire, on Elizabeth I's orders. In 1589, James married the Danish Oldenburg princess Anna, with whom he had seven children: Henry (1594–1612), Elizabeth (1596–1662), Margaret (1598–1600), Charles (1600–1649), Robert (born and died 1602), Mary (1605–7) and Sophia (born and died 1606).

As King of Scotland, James faced serial challenges to royal authority from ministers in the Established Church of Scotland, who preferred Presbyterian models of church government whereby ecclesiastical authority was entrusted to representative assemblies of church elders, rather than Episcopalian models where power lay with bishops under the monarch. During the 1590s, the king also survived sporadic violent attacks on his person by refractory nobles, most prominently his older first cousin Francis Stewart, Earl of Bothwell, whose title derived from his late, disgraced uncle, who had married James's mother. In August 1600, another physical altercation involving the king – later dubbed the 'Gowrie conspiracy' – saw the death of Alexander, Master of Ruthven (whose father had led the 'Ruthven Raid' two decades earlier), while James celebrated his providential escape from another attempt at abduction or assassination.

The extinction of all lines of descent from the Tudor King Henry VIII of England and his six wives meant that James's status as a greatgrandson of Henry's elder sister, Margaret Tudor, underpinned his genealogical claim to succeed Elizabeth I and he became England's first Stuart monarch in March 1603. In the first joint coronation in England since that of Henry VIII and Katherine of Aragon in 1509, James and Anna were crowned at Westminster Abbey on 'St James's Day': 25 July 1603. The new king quickly turned his attention to addressing intra-Protestant tensions within the Church of England by convening the 'Hampton Court Conference' in January 1604 and, the following year, survived a major Catholic conspiracy when the 'Gunpowder Plot' was thwarted in November 1605. In a move aimed at isolating a dangerously radicalized minority of English Catholics from the loyalist majority, James devised an 'Oath of Allegiance' to be levied on all indicted or suspected recusants, but its denunciation of key tenets of Catholic doctrine provoked attacks from opponents across Continental Europe.

In 1609, James also oversaw the ambitious 'Ulster plantation' project, with around 3.8 million statute acres of land in the north of Ireland reassigned to new owners following the 'Flight of the Earls', when two prominent Gaelic Irish chiefs unexpectedly left Ireland for the Continent. At Whitehall, James's retention of Elizabeth I's former Principal Secretary, Sir Robert Cecil, later Earl of Salisbury, secured administrative stability, but not crown solvency. By 1618, the royal debt had risen to unprecedented peacetime levels, approaching £900,000 sterling (or approximately £188 billion in today's values, taking account of inflation).

Although James's accession saw the first functioning royal family at the English court for more than half a century, Stuart dynastic confidence was shaken when the king's eldest son and heir, Prince Henry, died from typhoid fever, aged eighteen, in November 1612. The following spring, Henry's sister Princess Elizabeth married the German Palatine Elector, Frederick V, and left England to reside in Heidelberg. But by 1618, escalating confessional tensions in central Europe led to the outbreak of what was later known as the 'Thirty Years War'. James's family, moreover, became directly involved in hostilities when Frederick V accepted an offer to become King of Bohemia, following a revolt by Protestant members of the Bohemian Estates who had rejected their Catholic king-elect.

In 1619, Queen Anna died, aged forty-four, from dropsy and consumption. Having enjoyed close relations with a succession of male favourites throughout his life, James thereafter became increasingly reliant – personally and politically – on George Villiers, later Duke of Buckingham. As a self-styled '*rex pacificus*', James resisted pressure to intervene militarily in Continental Europe on behalf of his daughter and son-in-law, who were not only ejected from Bohemia but also saw their German territories overrun by Catholic Habsburg forces. Rather, James hoped to achieve a diplomatic solution through a marriage between Prince Charles and a member of the Spanish Habsburg dynasty. But plans for a 'Spanish Match' collapsed following the rash decision of

Prince Charles and Buckingham to travel incognito to Madrid in 1623 in an attempt to conclude the marriage negotiations in person. On their return to England after a six-month stay in Spain, Buckingham and Charles instead pursued a French alliance that resulted in the prince's marriage in 1624 to the Bourbon princess Henrietta Maria. On 27 March 1625, James VI & I died, aged fifty-eight, and was succeeded by his son as King Charles I.

2

A King of Words

James had an irrepressible love of lexis and wordplay. An inventive neologist, the king is quoted over 650 times in the *Oxford English Dictionary*, with his writings cited over 200 times as the earliest recorded instance of a word being used to denote a particular meaning, and over 100 times when a word was seemingly used for the first, and sometimes only, time. According to the *Dictionary*, words inaugurated by James include 'agitate', 'Anglican', 'anorexia', 'concern' (as a noun), 'decoration', 'demonology', 'Highlander', 'impostor', 'limited government', 'meat-eating', 'polysyllable', 'preening', 'preoccupied', 'quintessence', 'turbaned' and 'weld' (as a verb). Admittedly, the *Dictionary*'s citations more accurately reflect the popularity of certain authors among its readers and lexicographers than supply definitive proof of neologisms, and the marked prominence accorded by the *Dictionary* to the Jacobean era is largely attributable to Shakespeare being cited over 30,000 times.[1]

James's locution is, nevertheless, richly distinctive and appealing. He labelled the Protestant polemicists John Knox and George Buchanan 'archibellouses [archbellows] of rebellion'; attributed the fall of the Roman Empire to 'mollities and delicacy'; and prescribed severe punishment for 'poly-pragmatic Papists'. Elsewhere, the king encouraged Prince Henry to frame carefully his 'enregistrate speech' as a permanent record, counselled him against 'orping' (fretting), and recognized his own youthful 'greening' (yearning) for fame as a poet. Aside from citations in the *Oxford English Dictionary*, a large proportion of the king's neologisms were in vernacular Scots, which remained the language of imaginative literature as well as of the government and the law in Scotland. James's reign also witnessed the peak in popularity of neo-Latin humanist culture 'with its reverence for the classical (and pagan) past', albeit 'at the exact same time as Scotland became one of the most doctrinaire Reformed countries in Europe'.[2]

'Spendidly logocentric' is how one historian has saluted the impact of this wordsmith monarch.[3] To convey the enduringly infectious character of James's logophilia, I have foregrounded his own words as much as possible, as articulated in formal publications, parliamentary speeches, royal proclamations, private letters and reported conversations. James was unique among early modern monarchs in his enthusiastic embrace of printed media, in particular, as a vehicle to enunciate the extent of his royal powers and objects of his detestation, as well as his formidable learning. Anonymously printed in Edinburgh in 1584, James's first publication, *The Essays of a Prentice, in the Divine Art of Poetry*, included a manual of poetic theory as the eighteen-year-old king sought to establish his cultural authority and to promote distinctive forms of literary creation in the Scots language. A second volume of verse, *His Majesty's Poetical Exercises at Vacant Hours*, followed in 1591, while James's *Daemonologie* (1597) examined the power of demonic forces in society, taking the form of a dialogue between Philomathes ('someone who loves to learn things') and Epistemon ('someone who understands what he is talking about') – two epithets that might just as aptly be applied to its royal author. *The Trew Lawe of Free Monarchies* (1598) cemented James's reputation as one of Europe's foremost proponents of the theory known as the 'Divine Right of Kings', while *Basilicon Doron*, published the following year, contained his contention that 'books are *vive* [accurate] ideas of the author's mind.'[4] Four days after of Elizabeth I's death in March 1603, an anglicized edition of *Basilicon Doron* was entered into the English Stationers' Register on behalf of a booksellers' syndicate, with copies available to purchase on London's streets two days later, while Latin, French, Italian, Spanish, Dutch, German, Hungarian, Swedish and Welsh translations appeared thereafter.[5]

Shortly after succeeding to Elizabeth's throne, James unleashed a printed *Counterblaste to Tobacco* (1604), lambasting the substance's recent arrival in England and asserting his royal duty – 'as the proper physician of his politic body' – to save his new subjects from toxic hellfire.[6] Following discovery of the Gunpowder Plot in London in November 1605, James turned to theological controversy in repeated attempts to deny the papacy a temporal authority that could be used by Catholics to legitimize such atrocities. Issued anonymously in 1608, James's *Triplici Nodo, Triplex Cuneus. Or an Apology for the Oath of Allegiance* was republished under the king's name the following year, with a 'premonition' reminding Protestant and Catholic monarchs alike of the papacy's record in encouraging rebellion. Although chary about meddling in the affairs of other countries, in 1615 James publicly denounced as incendiary an oration delivered in the French Estates-General by Cardinal Jacques Davy du Perron. In his determination to proscribe rebellion and bloodshed, James was confident that 'many millions of children and people yet unborn, shall bear me witness.' God had, after all, elevated him to kingship's 'lofty stage' precisely to ensure 'that my words uttered from so eminent a place ... might with greater facility be conceived'.[7] While the king's final publication took the form of a *Letter and Directions Touching Preaching and Preachers* in 1622, he also issued an unusually high number of edicts in the form of printed proclamations throughout his reign. Insisting that 'most of them myself doth dictate every word', James contended that there was 'never any proclamation of state and weight which I did not direct'.[8] He was likewise an attentive editor of other people's prose. Returning a draft document regarding the intended naturalization of Scots, for example, Sir Thomas Lake alerted the Earl of Salisbury to places where James had 'thought there was some superfluity', adding that he 'prays to be excused for playing the secretary'.[9]

James's most spectacular printed achievement was the folio edition of his collected *Works* published in 1617 that extended to over 500 pages and generated a Latin translation in 1619 and an expanded English edition in 1620. Prefacing the first edition, Bishop James Montagu of Winchester acknowledged the Bible as an inspirational model, explaining how books of scripture circulating individually had been collected together in order to constitute Holy Writ. Accordingly, James's decision to monumentalize his writings for posterity has been deemed an 'act of deliberate self-canonization'.[10] Yet if no king had previously published their collected writings, several months earlier Ben Jonson had become the first dramatist to include stage plays in a folio edition of his collected *Works*, and both James and Jonson provided precedents for the first folio edition of Shakespeare's collected *Works* (1623). Venturing into print for the first time in 1610 with his prose polemic, *Pseudo-Martyr*, John Donne had welcomed 'your Majesty's books, as the sun, which penetrates all corners'. Dedicating *Pseudo-Martyr* to James, Donne hoped that it offered reciprocal homage to a king who had 'vouchsafed to descend to a conversation with your subjects, by way of your books'.[11] A decade later, the metaphysical poet George Herbert echoed Donne's observation. James was a monarch who sought 'to be thumbed in our hands; and laying aside thy majesty, thou dost offer thyself to be gazed upon on paper, that thou mayest be more intimately conversant among us'.[12]

Clearly, if other monarchs and noble writers disdained the 'stigma of print' and eschewed its possibilities, James did not. In his preface to James's collected *Works*, Montagu acknowledged the cavils of critics who doubted that 'it befits the majesty of a king to turn clerk.' Since 'book writing is grown into a trade', it might be thought 'as dishonourable for a king to write books, as it is for him to be a practitioner in a profession'. Although writing was central to James's conception of royal authority, the very idea of a royal author disconcerted those more accustomed to royal prohibitions on free speech, as regularly enjoined by Elizabeth. As Montagu recalled, James's subjects regarded 'his Majesty's books, as men look upon blazing-stars, with amazement, fearing they portend some strange thing'. James's kingly status blurred boundaries between printed precept and official edict. It might rather be hoped, Montagu added ambivalently, that, 'if a king will needs write, let him write like a king, every line a law, every word a precept, every letter a mandate.'[13]

Subsequent British monarchs seem to have shared Montagu's wariness. Charles I's volume of devotional meditations, *Eikon Basilike*, owed its prominence to its posthumous character, being first released for sale hours after its author's public execution in January 1649. Two centuries later, when extracts from Queen Victoria's Highland journals were published in 1868, their editor hastily reassured readers that 'all references to political questions, or to the affairs of government, have, for obvious reasons, been studiously omitted.' Only the queen's impressions of Scotland's rugged scenery and its rustic inhabitants were presented. The reviewer for the London *Times* was delighted, admiring how Victoria 'takes us by the hand, she sits by our firesides, and she opens to us her heart ... she lays aside her robes of state and enters into friendly conversations with her subjects'.[14] Charles III also chose to stay within the Scottish confines of the royal family's

Balmoral Estate when, as Prince of Wales, he published a children's story, *The Old Man of Lochnagar*, in 1980, before later producing *A Vision of Britain: A Personal View of Architecture* (1989) and co-authoring *Harmony: A New Way of Looking at our World* (2010). In other words, nearly all monarchs apart from James have believed that the *arcana imperii* – the secrets of government known only to those in power – are better preserved as private credos than printed manifestos.

For the potency of print also brought potential pitfalls for royal authors. James himself believed in protecting the *arcana imperii* and his collected *Works* include a speech delivered in 1616 to England's common-law judges, making clear that any matter 'which concerns the mystery of the king's power, is not lawful to be disputed'. Prying into politics was unlawfully 'to take away the mystical reverence, that belongs to them that sit in the throne of God'.[15] Mystical reverence could not, however, prevent accidental printers' errors marring royal publications. Nor, in starting conversations with his subjects, could James deter readers from readily construing or misconstruing his intended meanings. Indeed, his final publication – a missive to the Archbishop of Canterbury in 1622 – aimed to curb debate and avoid 'unprofitable, unsound, seditious, and dangerous doctrine' emanating from England's pulpits.[16]

To his subjects, James's publishing activities self-evidently encouraged debate. Long before 'speech act theory' gained traction in the twentieth century, the Puritan polemicist Thomas Scott contended in *Vox Regis* ('The Voice of the King'), published in 1624, that James's 'words and writings are published to this end and called his *Works*, because they should be turned into works'.[17] Since James used his printed publications to accomplish political objectives, his subjects should be free to respond likewise. A generation later, the republican poet John Milton envied the authority axiomatically conferred by royal authorship as he struggled to counter the popularity of Charles I's posthumous *Eikon Basilike*. In the second edition of *Eikonoklastes* (1650), Milton ruefully conceded that the moment 'a king is said to be the author', nothing more was needed 'among the blockish vulgar, to make it wise, and excellent, and admired, nay, to set it next [to] the Bible'.[18]

There was, moreover, a compelling case to set King James's *Works* alongside the 'King James Bible'. For nowhere is the distinctive diction and syntax of the Jacobean era more enduringly resonant than in the translation of the Bible published in 1611 by the King's Printer, Robert Barker. Regarded as the 'authorized' version of Scripture on account of its royal sponsorship, its dedicatory epistle acclaimed James as 'the principal mover and author of the work'.[19] Amid celebrations of the translation's 400th anniversary in 2011, one critic pronounced its sonorous cadences and verbal climaxes as 'quite simply what English prose is, or ought to be'.[20] In 1968, half a billion people worldwide listened on Christmas Eve to a live broadcast in which astronauts aboard *Apollo 8* read aloud from the 'King James Version' to celebrate the first lunar orbit by a manned spacecraft.

Among North American Protestants, the 'King James Version' remained the best-selling translation of the Bible until the mid-1980s, with some of its most fervent adherents forming the 'King James Only' movement to insist on the Jacobean version's doctrinal superiority, deny the legitimacy of alternatives and, in some quarters, assert its divinely inspired infallibility. As the translation celebrated its quatercentenary, the literary scholar Gordon Campbell detected a defiant self-assurance among some admirers: 'Just as real men do not eat quiche, so, in a range of T-shirts sold on the Internet, "real men use a King James Version Bible".'[21] In the twenty-first century, the growth of activist translation has generated more versions, including *The Queen James Bible* (2012), whose anonymous editors justified its renaming on the grounds that 'King James was a well-known bisexual.' While retaining the 'poetic, traditional and ceremonial language' of the translation issued in 1611, *The Queen James Bible* included eight verses revised 'in a way that makes homophobic interpretations impossible'.[22]

*

Homophobia has certainly been one factor shaping James's later reputation. Contemporaries and critics alike acknowledged the intensity of the king's capacity for love. Having served as one of Queen Anna's chaplains, Bishop Godfrey Goodman of Gloucester later claimed of James that 'no man living did ever love an honest man more than he did'; Goodman had never known anyone with 'such a violent passion of love as he had'.[23] In an undated letter, probably penned in late 1622, James described to George Villiers, then Marquis of Buckingham, his desolation at their recent separation. Able to 'do nothing but weep and mourn', the king had taken a horse and ridden 'this afternoon a great way in the park without speaking to anybody and the tears trickling down my cheeks, as now they do that I can scarcely see to write'. To 'harden my heart against thy absence', James had tried to focus on 'thy defects with the eye of an enemy', but quickly recognized that 'this little malice is like jealousy . . . as it proceeds from love, so it cannot but end in love'. Hoping that his beloved might 'come galloping hither' the next day, the king insisted that 'for God's sake, write not a word again, and let no creature see this letter'.[24]

In memoirs published during the 1650s, a former courtier, Francis Osborne, blamed the mid-century civil wars on royal financial mismanagement, accounting James to have been 'like Adam . . . the original of his son's fall'. He also censured the political impact of the king's 'love, or what else posterity will please to call it' for 'his favourites or minions, who like burning-glasses were daily interposed between him and the subject, multiplying the heat of oppressions in the general opinion'. Moreover, James's readiness in 'kissing them after so lascivious a mode in public, and upon the theatre, as it were, of the world' only encouraged 'many to imagine some things done in the tyring-house [backstage], that exceed my expressions no less than they do my experience'. While Osborne left further speculation 'floating upon the waves of conjecture', subsequent critics were more sharply censorious.[25] For the historical novelist Sir Walter Scott, 'the odd familiarities which James used with his favourites' were 'to say the least, most disgusting and unseemly', while the Victorian court historian John Jesse rejected as 'hypocritical trash' James's printed dedication to Buckingham of his 'Meditation upon the Lord's Prayer' and denounced the 'gross indecency' of their private correspondence.[26]

Recent commentators are, thankfully, more sanguine. One of Buckingham's biographers has described James's love for him as 'joyful, overwhelming – the kind of love that ambushes at first sight', while dismissing as unhelpfully anachronistic 'the question of who-does-what-to-whom-in-bed'.[27] Meanwhile, the Shakespearean scholar Will Tosh has reminded readers that 'early modern queer lives weren't lived with the doctrinaire clarity of today.' Since 'few people ever found themselves labelled a "bugger" or "sodomite" as defined by law' in early modern Britain, proscribed sexual acts may well have been 'vanishingly rare in prosecution, yet an everyday activity in practice'. While Tosh judged James to have been 'no queer hero', he argues that 'Shakespeare's passionate interest in queer desire is its own answer, although his personal queerness must have been bi rather than gold-star gay.' In a stricture that applies equally to James, Tosh further insisted that 'examining Shakespeare's queer life and art doesn't mean erasing his wife or his children, just as their existence doesn't disprove his queerness.'[28]

More virulent than homophobia among Jacobean contemporaries was the vicious anti-Scottish xenophobia that greeted England's new king at his accession in 1603 and kiboshed his vision of closer British union. In his Westminster speech in March 1607, James wearily acknowledged English fears 'that this Union will be the crisis to the overthrow of England and setting up of Scotland'. Although he refused to credit claims 'that Scotland is so strong to pull you out of your houses', the king could not dispel popular panic that England would 'be overwhelmed by the swarming of the Scots, who if the union were effected, would reign and rule all'.[29] In 1604, the Scots union commissioner, Thomas Craig of Riccarton, spent several months in London and was dismayed by the extent of entrenched enmity. While Craig was convinced of the need for 'a single heart and mind in Britain both to make and to resist attack', he noted how, when English parents taught archery skills to their children, they 'encourage them to take good aim by saying, "There's a Scot! Shoot him!"'. Craig had also met an English lawyer – 'a man of some importance in his own opinion' – who had confidently denied that any 'English king had ever thought of conquering Scotland', adding that 'there were no educated men in Scotland and no universities, nor any laws other than those which had been borrowed from England'.[30] But, as Craig knew, although England had its two universities of Oxford and Cambridge, Scotland had five such establishments, following the foundations of St Salvator's College in St Andrews (1450), Glasgow University (1451), Marischal and King's Colleges in Aberdeen (1493 and 1495) and Edinburgh University (1583).[31]

If English children imagined Scots as target practice, Guy Fawkes bragged that 'his intent was to have blown them back again into Scotland' during interrogations after the Gunpowder Plot's discovery in November 1605.[32] Two years earlier, Fawkes had objected of James's court that 'near his person everyone in his Chamber are Scots – wherever there is an English official, he has placed another Scotsman', according to an intelligence report reviewed by the Spanish court.[33] Sitting in Parliament in 1610, the Nottinghamshire MP Sir John Holles likewise complained of James that 'the Scots monopolise his princely person, standing like mountains betwixt the beams of his grace and us.' Holles bore no ill-will to Scots courtiers, 'only I wish equality, that they should not seem to be the children of the family, and we the servants'.[34] Addressing Parliament four years later, the Hereford MP John Hoskins admired Canute's decision to dispense with Danish advisers when he became English king in 1016. The anti-Scottish implications of Hoskins's additional reference to the Sicilian Vespers – a rebellion in 1382 against a French-born king in which around 3,000 French settlers had been massacred by native Sicilians – were deemed so incendiary that Hoskins was detained in the Tower of London for over a year.

Yet Hoskins's hostility paled by comparison with the vitriol of a Latin mock panegyric, *Corona Regia*, published by an anonymous Catholic author in the Low Countries in 1615. Amid a volley of insults, its author denied James's legitimacy as king, attributing his capacity to 'ignore, despise, and if necessary, even kill' his mother to his having been 'a suppositious child' placed in 'the royal swaddling clothes and cradle' beside Queen Mary by heretic Protestant clerics. The tract's author likened the adult James to an oversized whale who sought to 'blast his spray high aloft' by attacking the papacy 'with a sopping quantity of words', cuttingly conceding that 'no king dared do this before, and certainly no one but you could.' *Corona Regia*'s author also mocked James's physical person, venturing 'Come on British, take heart ministers, no-one is going to fault all things curved, twisted, and wretched; by the example of the king, all things straight, level, and upright shall be banished.'[35] Regarding the latter affront, modern analyses of James's reported physical, neurological and behavioural abnormalities have since yielded a range of diagnoses including cerebral palsy and Lesch-Nyhan Syndrome.[36]

Although James directed effort and expense in trying to identify its author, *Corona Regia* was unlikely to have been widely read in Britain. But the same could not be said for the slew of savage critiques published after the English Parliament's decision to place James's son – the Scots-born Charles I – on trial for treason, leading to his execution in 1649 and the abolition of the monarchy shortly thereafter. Providing fertile fodder for generations of James's detractors, a tract entitled *The Court and Character of King James* was published in 1650, attributed to a former Jacobean courtier, Sir Anthony Weldon, who had died in 1648 after serving as a prominent Parliamentarian governor during the civil wars. Of James's physical appearance, Weldon recalled that the king's 'beard was very thin, his tongue too large for his mouth, which ever made him speak full in the mouth, and make him drink very uncomely, as if eating his drink, which came out into the cup of each side of his mouth'. Meanwhile, 'his legs were very weak' and 'his walk was ever circular, his fingers ever in that walk fiddling about his codpiece'. In an epithet that stuck, Weldon claimed that James had evidently been reputed 'the wisest fool in Christendom, meaning him wise in small things, but a fool in weighty affairs'.[37]

Two generations later, the 'Glorious Revolution' of 1688 saw James's grandson James VII & II flee from London into French exile, before suffering military defeat by his Dutch nephew and son-in-law, William of Orange, at the Battle of the Boyne in Ireland in July 1690. Jacobitism thereafter became synonymous with discredited Stuart despotism. Imitating the slanderous account of the Emperor Justinian's reign penned by the Greek historian Procopius, Walter Scott anthologized the Interregnum's hostile critiques in his *Secret History of the Court of James the First*, published in 1811. Six years later, Isaac Disraeli – father of Benjamin – was dismayed by the accrued torrent of invective and sought to restore 'the character of James the First, which lies buried under a heap of ridicule and obloquy'.[38] But the pantomime caricature had become entrenched and, by the mid-nineteenth century, the doyen of Whig history, Lord Macaulay, made clear his revulsion as he saw James 'exhibited to the world stammering, slobbering, shedding unmanly tears, trembling at a drawn sword, and talking in the style alternately of a buffoon and a pedagogue'.[39]

Over a century later, J. P. Kenyon reproduced Macaulay's reproof almost verbatim in his study of 'English [sic] kingship' entitled *The Stuarts* (1958), discerning 'an element of buffoonery in all he [James] did' and claiming that 'at dinner his vulgarity, obscenity and uproarious pedantry had full play, as he slobbered in his drink'; if not actually intoxicated, 'with his slurred speech, his heavy Scots accent and his restless, rolling eye, he must often have seemed so.'[40] A buffoon, a pedagogue – and also a persecutor. In 1921, lavish celebrations were staged in Plymouth, Massachusetts, to mark the tercentenary of New England's founding by 'Pilgrim Fathers' who had sailed from England aboard *The Mayflower* in 1620. An outdoor pageant was performed on a specially constructed stage by Plymouth Bay before audiences of up to 20,000, with honoured guests including President Warren Harding. Written and directed by Professor George Pierce Baker of Harvard University, the pageant included a scene depicting Puritan nonconformists suffering in England and the Dutch republic, with an actor playing King James 'shouting above a cacophony of bagpipes, "A Puritan is a Protestant scared out of his wits . . . I shall make them conform or I will harry them out of this land – or do worse"'.[41]

The toxically unflattering account unleashed by David Harris Willson in his biography *James VI and I* (1956) only fuelled readers' fevered imaginations. Academic critics were not uniformly enamoured, with one reviewer finding innumerable 'examples of what Dr Samuel Johnson might have called its "bottomless Whiggery"' in which an entirely incompetent, indolent and inane James could seemingly nonetheless rule as 'half a despot in England and a total one in Scotland'.[42] Indeed, Willson's biography presented an 'astonishing spectacle of a work whose every page proclaimed its author's increasing hatred for its subject', as Jenny Wormald observed in her *Oxford Dictionary of National Biography* entry for King James in 2004.[43] Two decades earlier, Wormald had herself rhetorically wondered whether James was 'two kings or one', given his starkly divergent historical reception on either side of the Anglo-Scottish border. Juxtaposing the views of two scholars of similar age and professional stature, Wormald had contrasted Gordon Donaldson's cool assessment that, as King of Scotland, James had been 'a man of very remarkable political ability and sagacity in deciding on policy and of conspicuous tenacity in having it carried out', with Lawrence Stone's shrill insistence that 'as a hated Scot, James was suspect to the English from the beginning, and his ungainly presence, mumbling speech and dirty ways did not inspire respect'.[44]

Four centuries after James's death, the depressingly common default response to mention of his name remains the glibly sarcastic dismissal that 'James I slobbered at the mouth and had favourites; he was thus a

Bad King,' as taken from W. C. Sellars and R. J. Yeatman's parodic rendering of English history, *1066 and All That*, first published in 1930.[45] A *Spectator* book review in 2021 casually referred to 'the goggle-eyed, slobbering Scottish king, James, with his peculiar penchant for shitting in the saddle while pursuing his passion for hunting'.[46] In the fictional drama *Mary and George* (2024), James appeared, to one television critic, as 'the mercurial sovereign, who veers between moments of lucidity and long stretches of what seems like madness, though it's never identified as such'.[47] As one commentator remarked at the start of the twenty-first century, 'the awkward figure of the Stuart King continues to block the recuperative efforts of history, constantly under rehabilitation but somehow never quite rehabilitated.'[48]

*

Four centuries is too long for anyone to remain in rehab. *The Mirror of Great Britain* seeks neither to valorize nor to denigrate but rather to restore appreciation of the sheer difficulty, intensity and complexity faced by James as ruler of late sixteenth-century Scotland and as the first British king. Less *The Comedy of Errors* and more *Macbeth*, James had to survive recurrent assassination threats and navigate bitter confessional conflict, religious persecution and violent vendettas. Likewise, although the lure of early seventeenth-century overseas colonial endeavours might be rendered magical through *The Tempest*'s stagecraft, their grim reality entailed commercial greed, genocide and savagery. In *Devil-Land: England under Siege 1588–1688* (2021), I characterized Stuart England as denoting an era of endemic instability and geopolitical insecurity, and such leitmotifs apply equally to James's Scottish and English reigns.

Amid the chiaroscuro contrasts, the king that emerges in the ensuing pages is intelligent, resilient, idiosyncratic, irascible, guileful and witty. No monarch in British history was keener for his subjects to know him and more intent on communicating his vision of kingship. If there was a desire for *gloire*, there was also a keen awareness of the need for self-preservation. A fortnight after the assassination of the French king, Henri IV, in May 1610, James insisted to English peers and MPs that there was 'nothing that shall concern the commonwealth, but I will be careful the people shall know it'. For 'the more the people know the reasons of my doings', the more royal power was respected. While James recognized that, ultimately, 'my glory and security stands in the love of my subjects', the veracity of this maxim would be borne out in the fate of his son and successor, Charles I.[49]

In James's early years, the very notions of royal power and the monarchical prerogative required rehabilitation, following his coronation as an infant King of Scotland by a faction that had removed his mother from power by enthusiastically extolling rights of resistance and tyrannicide. In early 1584, the seventeen-year-old James wrote to his French uncle, Henri, Duke of Guise, alarmed that 'the strength of my enemies and rebels is growing daily'. In a letter intercepted by Elizabeth I's ministers, James told his uncle that he had 'abandoned the English faction' among his advisers as he suspected the English queen of seeking 'the subversion of my state, and the deprivation of my own life, or at least my honour and liberty, which I prize more than my life'.[50] As King of England, James reiterated in 1608 that he accounted 'my reputation' to be 'ten times dearer to me than my life' in a letter to Robert Cecil, Earl of Salisbury.[51] Small wonder, then, that when he addressed the Westminster Parliament six years later, James rejected the attempts of MPs to challenge his right to levy certain taxes, by warning that he would 'die a 100 deaths before he would infringe his prerogative'.[52]

Small wonder, too, that a king of words was admired for his rhetorical dexterity, but also distrusted. After one audience with the fourteen-year-old Scottish king in 1581, Elizabeth I's envoy, Baron Hunsdon, advised her Principal Secretary, Sir Francis Walsingham, that the English queen would soon learn that 'the king's fair speeches and promises will fall out to be plain dissimulation.' When it came to dissembling, Hunsdon rued that James was, 'in his tender years, better practised than others forty years older than he'. And as Hunsdon emphasized three weeks later, Elizabeth was 'not to trust to any word or promise' made by the Scottish king, who was regarded by his advisers as 'the greatest dissembler that ever was heard of for his years'.[53]

By the time James acceded to the English throne, the resident Venetian Secretary in London identified his chief trait as a 'dissimulation' that 'constantly consisted in giving hopes to all, but never anything further to any'. Indeed, James had disarmingly defended this approach as the only means to have 'escaped the dangers he had been in when king of Scotland', believing it equally effective now he was ruler 'of a great kingdom, of which he knew neither the people, the affairs, nor the neighbours'.[54] Dissimulation created room for diplomatic man-oeuvre. For one French ambassador, James was 'a king of artifices who dissimulates above all the rest of the world', while a political maxim posthumously attributed to James was the credo that 'greater and deeper' political actions were achieved by those individuals who 'can make other men the instrument of his will and ends, and yet never acquaint them with his purpose; so as they shall do it, and yet not know what they do.'[55]

This was also the king who, at eighteen, had confidently reassured a French envoy visiting Scotland that, although he spent much time hunting, 'he could do as much business in one hour as others would in a day, because simultaneously he listened and spoke, watched, and some-times did five things at once.'[56] Fusing fatherly and royal advice, James later advised Prince Henry to remain mindful of divine judgement, 'ever learning to die, and living every day as if it were your last'.[57] Adept at working remotely, James responded to ministers' queries by return; as Salisbury admired in 1607, the king was 'quicker at a letter than the posts are with the packets'.[58] One communication from James to Salis-bury bore the holograph endorsements: 'Royston [Hertfordshire], 16 January at past eight in the night. Haste, Haste, Haste, Haste, Haste for life, life, life. Royston, 16 of January at past 10 in the night. Ware, 17 January, at one in the morning.'[59]

Having been obliged, for his own security, to remain largely within the confines of Stirling Castle for the first decade of his life, James thereafter became a restlessly itinerant king, unique in modern monarchical history for undertaking a summer progress in every year of his English reign. Between 1603 and 1625, he made around 400 visits involving at least an overnight stay, primarily to private coun-try houses but also to other royal residences, urban fortifications and episcopal palaces.[60] Shuttling around at speed, James admitted to Salisbury (then Viscount Cranborne) in 1604 that 'my last journey to London was like a flash of lightning, both in going, stay there, and returning'.[61]

His itinerant progresses rarely traversed national boundaries. After leaving Edinburgh for London in April 1603, he never set foot in either Wales or Ireland and only once returned to Scotland, for a three-month visit in 1617. Having apprised the Scottish Privy Council of his 'salmon-like instinct' to return to his native land, James travelled north with a retinue of around 1,000 attendants.[62] Upon arriving at the Scottish border, he 'lay on the ground, and proclaimed to his astonished courtiers that here was the union of England and Scotland – in his own person'.[63] Inspired by the king's journey, the poet and dramatist Ben Jonson walked with a companion from London to Edinburgh the following year, taking two months to complete their 450-mile trek.

Admittedly, a less intellectual, less energetic and less engaged monarch might have avoided notoriously well-publicized clashes with the Scots Presbyterian theologian Andrew Melville or the renowned English common lawyer Sir Edward Coke. A less intellectual, less energetic and less engaged monarch might well not, however, have facilitated wide-ranging theological discussion by convening the Hampton Court Conference in 1604, incurred the ire of the papacy and Catholic theologians across Counter-Reformation Europe through serial royal publications, initiated the immense philological achievement that is the 'King James Bible' or assumed a personal role in promoting the Ulster Plantation in Ireland. Further afield, although Virginia's name honoured the 'Virgin' queen, it was James's administration that supplied the essential state impetus needed to establish permanent settlements in North America and elsewhere. The Virginian settlement of Jamestown and the James River that flows into Chesapeake Bay bear his name. Royal endorsement also extended to sponsoring trading companies with commercial interests as far afield as Newfoundland, the Somers Islands (Bermuda) and Guinea.

Ruling three separate kingdoms, over six decades, while simultaneously sponsoring a nascent global empire, was arduous, lonely and exhausting. In December 1619, James composed a 'Meditation' on verses from St Matthew's Gospel that was published in the second edition of his *Works* the following year. As the king reflected, the account of how Pontius Pilate's soldiers had mocked the crucified Christ by placing royal ornaments about his body was described so precisely in Scripture 'that my head hammered upon it diverse times after, and especially the crown of thorns went never out of my mind'. Royal power brought 'thorny cares . . . as (God knows) I daily and nightly feel in my own person'. Having prepared *Basilicon Doron* for Prince Henry, who had since died, James now dedicated his 'Meditation' to Prince Charles, reminding his son of a 'good old Scottish proverb, that a man warned is half-armed'. Charles would not 'find the softness of a down-pillow in a crown'; a diadem was, rather, 'a thorny piece of stuff, and full of continual cares'.[64] James was speaking from long and hard-won experience: more than half a century ago, in a different country, he had undergone his first coronation as a Scottish cradle king.

3

The Cradle King

In a torrent of verse invective composed around 1622, James asked his English subjects:

> . . .Yet you, that know me all so well
> Why do you push me down to Hell,
> In making me an infidel?
> 'Tis true, I am a cradle king,
> Yet do remember everything.[1]

Having been crowned King of Scotland at only thirteen months old, the one thing that James could never remember was not being a king. The future king of both Scotland and England had been born on the morning of 19 June 1566 in a tiny, windowless room in Edinburgh Castle. Today, tourists pass into the apartment under a rusticated entrance with '1566' inscribed in gold numerals flanking the entwined initials 'M & H', denoting James's parents, Mary, Queen of Scots and Henry Stewart, Lord Darnley. On the evening of the prince's birth, artillery fusillades were fired and around 500 celebratory bonfires lit up the midsummer skies in and around Edinburgh.[2] In a Latin *genethliacum* or 'birth-poem' published to celebrate James's arrival, the lawyer Thomas Craig of Riccarton noted that the new prince had not been born in one of Scotland's recently renovated Renaissance castles, such as Linlithgow, Stirling or Falkland, but instead within 'the most glorious citadel of Edinburgh'. A fortress sitting atop an extinct volcano that 'rises threatening heaven on rocks precipitous on all sides', the Castle was a vertiginous vantage-point from whose parapets 'many raging cannons discharge their furious balls'.[3]

Visiting Edinburgh Castle in 1842, Queen Victoria noted that it was indeed 'such a very, very small room' in which the first king to rule both Scotland and England had been born.[4] But the heavily fortified location had been chosen deliberately to protect both the royal child and his mother amid a tense atmosphere of martial friction and factional violence. In later memoirs of Mary's reign, the Borders noble Lord Herries claimed that the queen had presented the newborn James to her husband and half-cousin, Darnley, observing 'he is so much your own son, that I fear it [will] be the worse for him thereafter.'[5] Since Herries was not in Edinburgh at the time, his reconstruction of events may well be apocryphal, but he accurately conveyed the nadir in relations between the infant's parents after less than a year of marriage. For, just over three months earlier, Darnley had led a group of Scots nobles and stormed Mary's private chambers at the Palace of Holyroodhouse, which lay in parkland beyond Edinburgh's fortified walls. Before a terrified queen, the intruders had seized Mary's Italian-born secretary, David Riccio, and stabbed him over fifty times. Fear of foreign papal influence, fused with personal jealousy, lay behind the fatal attack. In dispatches to London the previous autumn, the English ambassador, Thomas Randolph, had noted that Riccio was 'so great with [Mary]'; in a slur on James's paternity that would resurface during the king's life, Randolph even referred to the queen's unborn child as 'David's son'.[6]

Two nights after the attack on Riccio, Mary had detached her husband from his accomplices and, although six months' pregnant, had ridden with him to Dunbar Castle, twenty-six miles eastwards. From Dunbar, Mary had written to her cousin Queen Elizabeth I of England, describing her terror at the hands of those who had 'slain our most special servant [Riccio] in our own presence' and had threatened to hold her captive, before she had managed to escape. As Mary admitted, she had believed herself to be 'in the greatest danger, fear of our lives, and evil estate' imaginable.[7] On returning from Dunbar, Mary moved into Edinburgh Castle's protective confines before giving birth to James in June. Continuing his description of events immediately after the prince's birth, Herries reported Mary recalling how one assassin, Andrew Ker of Fawdonside, had pointed his pistol directly at her during the Holyrood attack. As Darnley beheld the safe arrival of his new son, Mary invited him to imagine, if Ker 'had shot, what would have become of him [James] and me both? ... God only knows; but we may suspect!'[8]

Like her son, Mary had also been a cradle sovereign, having succeeded as Scotland's queen when she was only six days old in December
1542 on the death of her father, James V, several weeks after he had
suffered defeat by Henry VIII's English troops at the Battle of Solway
Moss in Cumbria. In 1543, Henry tried to secure Anglo-Scottish amity
via the draft Treaty of Greenwich that envisaged a future marriage
between his only son, Prince Edward, and the infant Queen Mary –
who was also Henry VIII's great-niece, being the granddaughter of his
older sister, Margaret Tudor. But the Scottish Parliament's rejection of
the draft treaty led to a resumption of Anglo-Scottish hostilities. During
Edward VI's reign, another heavy defeat for Scottish forces at the Battle
of Pinkie in September 1547 prompted the Lord Protector, Edward Seymour, Duke of Somerset, to adopt the persona of 'the loving physician',
advising 'the mistrustful and ignorant patient'. Alliance with England
was, Somerset claimed, the only option to avert 'the destruction of the
realm of Scotland' and 'final eradication of your nation': indeed, the
Lord Protector could envisage no 'more sure defence, in the nonage of
your queen, for the realm of Scotland, than to have England patron and
garrison?'[9] Instead, James V's French widow, Marie of Guise, negotiated a different dynastic future for Mary by securing her betrothal to
King Henri II of France's eldest son and heir, François. Aged five, Mary
had left Scotland to be raised at the French court and, a decade later,
in April 1558, married François, who thereby became an absentee king
consort of Scotland.

Three months earlier, England's last continental territory, Calais,
had been captured by French forces and, in November, the country's
Catholic queen, Mary Tudor, died and was succeeded by her Protestant half-sister, Elizabeth I. In France, Henri II's death in July 1559
from injuries sustained in a jousting accident prompted the accession
of Mary's husband as King François II, whose new heraldic insignia
incorporated not only the French *fleur de lis* and Scottish lions rampant but also, controversially, English lions passant. The official styling
of François and Mary as 'King and Queen of France, Scotland, England and Ireland' – effectively arrogating Elizabeth's crown – triggered
a diplomatic crisis when the English ambassador in Paris, Sir Nicholas
Throckmorton, was served from silver dinner plates bearing the offending insignia.[10] But Stuart dynastic ambitions were soon halted when
Mary suffered, first, the death of her mother, Marie of Guise, in June

1560, followed by that of her husband, François, who succumbed to a fatal ear infection six months later.[11]

In August 1561, the widowed, devoutly Catholic Queen Mary, returned from France to Scotland to rule a country undergoing a radical Protestant reformation. Four years later, she married her younger, English-born half-cousin Lord Darnley, in a match opposed by another of Darnley's cousins, Elizabeth I. Herself unmarried, the English queen was uncomfortably aware of Mary and Darnley's merged hereditary claim to her Crown through their shared grandmother, Margaret Tudor. Before the marriage, the English ambassador in Edinburgh, Thomas Randolph, had reported 'the saying is that surely she [Mary] is bewitched' with many Scots rueful at seeing 'this queen so meanly matched'. Mary's resolve to wed Darnley despite Elizabeth's disapproval also implied that the Scottish queen was 'determined to make a divorce with England'.[12] There was little time to repent. For, after a hasty marriage, Darnley's affections soured into resentful and irascible jealousy provoked not only by Mary's closeness to Riccio but also by her refusal to grant him 'the crown matrimonial' whereby Darnley would retain the Scottish Crown if Mary predeceased him. Traces of jealousy also infused Elizabeth's reaction to news of James's birth in June 1566. Four days after riding south from Edinburgh, the Scots courtier James Melville of Halhill arrived at Greenwich Palace to find the English queen 'in great merriness and dancing after supper'. But immediately on learning of the new prince's birth, 'all merriness was laid aside for that night'. While attendees speculated as to the reason for 'so sudden a change', Melville described Elizabeth sitting down and 'bursting out to some of her ladies, how that the queen of Scotland was lighter of a fair son, and that she was but a barren stock'.[13]

*

James's role in a glorious future for Scotland seemed assured during the three days of sumptuous banquets, glittering masques, fireworks and a mock siege staged to celebrate his christening at Stirling Castle in December 1566. Inspired by the extravagant entertainments that she had enjoyed during her childhood at the French court, Mary levied the only direct taxation of her reign to mount the most magnificent Renaissance court festival ever seen in Scotland or England. In October, her Privy Councillors had recorded that, since 'some of the greatest princes in Christendom have earnestly required' that their ambassadors may 'be witnesses and gossips at the baptism', the additional expenditure was justified.[14] James's godfathers, Charles IX of France and Duke Emmanuel Philibert of Savoy, sent jewellery and an outsized jewel-encrusted fan, while his godmother, Elizabeth I, gifted a golden christening font weighing over ten kilograms.[15]

Although known as 'James', the infant prince was christened 'Charles James' in a service conducted according to Catholic rites. The accompanying court entertainments were so spectacular that even the Protestant Reformation's rabble-rouser, John Knox, admitted they 'exceeded far all the preparation that ever had been devised or set forth' in Scotland.[16] But confessional, domestic and dynastic tensions simmered. Mary had commissioned a sparkling cloth-of-gold suit for Darnley to wear, but James's father was conspicuously absent from the celebrations. The English ambassador, Francis Russell, Earl of Bedford, also absented himself from the Catholic service led by Archbishop John Hamilton of St Andrews. Over four decades later, James proclaimed his lifelong adherence to Protestantism in *A Premonition to all most Mighty Monarchs* (1609), pointing out that although he had been 'baptised by a Popish Archbishop', his Protestant godmother, Elizabeth I, had gifted 'the font where I was christened'. James's mother had, moreover, forbidden the syphilitic Hamilton from observing the traditional Catholic custom of spitting in an infant's mouth (in allusion to Christ's healing of a deaf and mute man in St Mark's Gospel). Denouncing the practice as 'a filthy and apish trick', James insisted that 'her own very words were, "that she would not have a pocky priest to spit in her child's mouth"'.[17]

Catholic ritual aside, Elizabeth's representative was also disconcerted by the ready acclaim of Prince James as a future King Arthur who would, one day, oversee Britain's reunification. Shortly before the christening celebrations, the English court had been angered by the publication in Paris of another Latin birth-poem by the Scots Protestant minister Patrick Adamson, that had rhetorically wondered of James, 'what courage does the cramped cradle with its small burden shelter?' Anticipating the imminent 'age of Merlin's prediction', Adamson had predicted that James would live 'to expand the limits of your realm, until at last you learn to unite the Britons, finished with Mars, in a single realm'. Having 'finally been chosen by the British kingdoms', James should 'cherish both Scot and Englishman with no distinction'.[18] Infuriated, Elizabeth demanded of Mary that she 'announce to the world your detestation' of Adamson's presumptuousness, protesting that 'nothing can touch my honour more, than there should be another Queen of England than myself. For as Alexander said, Carthage cannot endure two kings.'[19] In Paris, the authorities responded to Elizabeth's angry representations by imprisoning Adamson for six months.

The puissant destiny predicted for James seemed, however, unlikely, as domestic affairs in Scotland descended into a chaotic vortex. Two months after the christening celebrations, James's father was murdered when the house in which he was staying at Kirk o'Field, near Edinburgh, was blown up in a nocturnal gunpowder explosion. Darnley – who had been ill with secondary syphilis – was found lying outside, naked and strangled. On hearing of Darnley's death, Elizabeth counselled Mary 'as a faithful cousin and friend . . . to preserve your honour, rather than look through your fingers at revenge' on those responsible for her husband's murder.[20] Initially, the infant Prince James was placed in the care of Sir Alexander Erskine of Gogar, before custody was transferred in March 1567 to Erskine's older brother, John, Earl of Mar, who had accompanied Mary to France two decades earlier as a five-year-old queen. As Keeper of Stirling Castle, Mar and his family had a long history of service as royal guardians and maintained a tight security regime. Four footmen guarded the infant prince's room, 'Mar providing them with a different watchword and taking possession of all the keys of the castle each night'.[21] In formal instructions, Mary also forbade Mar from admitting any noble, Scots or foreign, to her son's presence with more than two or three companions. Ironically, Mary herself was then subjected to these restrictions in April when she visited James with the intention of taking him to Edinburgh. Obliged instead to leave him at Stirling, her visit would be the last ever meeting between the ten-month-old Prince James and his mother.

For, rather than pursuing revenge against Darnley's killers, Mary proceeded to marry the principal suspect, James Hepburn, Earl of Bothwell, in a Protestant service at Holyroodhouse in May 1567. Following a trial in which Bothwell was dubiously acquitted of involvement in the murder, it was rumoured that he had coerced Mary into marriage by abducting and raping her at Dunbar Castle. Pledging to deliver their queen from 'thraldom' and to protect Prince James, a group of Protestant Lords then formed a confederacy, fearing that 'the whole realm of

Scotland' had been rendered 'slanderous and abominable to all nations' by the shameful scandal of Darnley's murder and Mary's remarriage.[22] Mary, in turn, started raising funds by ordering the melting down of the golden font gifted by Elizabeth I for James's christening.[23] On 15 June 1567, the Confederate Lords confronted Mary and Bothwell at Carberry Hill near Musselburgh, flanked by several thousand armed supporters bearing banners depicting the naked Darnley lying dead under a tree, with his infant son quoting the Scriptural motto, 'Judge and Revenge my cause, O Lord!' Hostilities were averted by Mary's surrender and Bothwell's escape abroad. Mary was then taken to the island fortress of Lochleven Castle near Kinross, where she miscarried twins that had presumably been fathered by Bothwell.

Scotland was in crisis. In April 1567, the English Secretary of State, William Cecil, had lamented to a correspondent that the country was 'in a quagmire; nobody seems to stand still; the most honest desire to go away; the worst tremble with the shaking of their conscience.'[24] Mary's erstwhile Secretary, William Maitland of Lethington, later described the panicked decision-making that followed the queen's surrender at Carberry Hill as feeling like crossing the Firth of Forth in a ferry that caught fire: 'ye would leap in the sea, to flee the fire, and finding yourself able to drown, ye would press again to the boat'.[25] When Elizabeth's experienced diplomat Throckmorton met Maitland in July 1567, he reported that the Scot had 'smiled and shook his head' in response to English offers of mediation, advising 'it were better for us [that] you would let us alone.' Maitland had implied that the diplomatic initiative now lay with Charles IX's ambassador in Edinburgh, Philibert du Croc, who could oversee Mary's permanent withdrawal to 'lead her life in France in an abbey reclused' with Prince James 'at the French devotion', leaving Scotland to be governed by a council of French-appointed nobles and its fortresses garrisoned by French troops.[26]

Unsurprisingly, Elizabeth's ministers were determined to avoid such an outcome that would leave England sandwiched within a renewed Franco-Scottish 'Auld Alliance' at a time when England was not only facing renewed Catholic rebellion in Ireland, but French troops were also refusing to vacate Calais, despite expiry of the eight-year tenure of the territory granted to Charles IX at the Treaty of Cateau-Cambrésis (1559). Accordingly, Cecil amended draft instructions from Elizabeth to Throckmorton to indicate that 'we shall not fail but yield to her

[Mary] as good safety therein for ~~her and~~ her child as can be devised for any that might be our child born of our own body' – the deletion confirming that English sanctuary should be offered to James, but not to his mother.[27] From Edinburgh, Throckmorton advised that Elizabeth should 'leave nothing undone to get the prince in possession', but warned that any Scottish agreement to James being raised in England would require formal recognition of his hereditary right to succeed to the English throne, if Elizabeth remained childless. Without such a guarantee, the Scots would feel that they 'had put their prince to be kept in safety as those which commit the sheep to be kept by the wolves!'[28]

Events in Scotland moved apace as the Confederate Lords secured from Mary a 'voluntary' demission of her Crown and consent for her infant son to be crowned king with royal authority vested in a regent. Horrified by Mary's imprisonment at Lochleven, Elizabeth denied the Lords any right 'by God's or man's law to be as superiors, judges, or vindicators over their prince, whatever disorders they gather against her'; accordingly, 'we justly account these examples unlawful and acts of rebellion'.[29] Casuistically trying to justify the Lords' actions, the Protestant polemicist George Buchanan later contended that 'we deprived her not of liberty, but of unbridled licentiousness of evil-doing'.[30] Mary's detention at Lochleven had been, rather, an honourable rescue. For his part, Throckmorton simply wanted to return to England as soon as possible, fearing that, once James was crowned king, 'this tragedy' that had started with the murders of Riccio and Darnley would surely end with Mary meeting an unnatural death.[31]

Only seven months after the triumphant celebrations that had accompanied his christening by Catholic rites in the Chapel Royal at Stirling Castle, King James VI was crowned in Stirling's parish Church of the Holy Rood on 29 July 1567 in the first Protestant coronation in Scotland's history. With Mary's deposition widely regarded as illegitimate, no foreign ambassadors attended and many Scots nobles and clerics were likewise unsure how to respond to the rapid regime change. Although twelve Scots earls and fourteen lords had confronted Mary and Bothwell at Carberry and approved her detention at Lochleven Castle, just five earls and eight lords attended her son's coronation the following month. Four days before the coronation, the Church of Scotland's General Assembly – over which Buchanan presided as its Moderator – had passed a resolution insisting that henceforth 'all kings, princes and magistrates ... before they be crowned and inaugurated' must swear to uphold the true (Protestant) religion as currently established in Scotland via an agreement that would be 'mutual and reciprocal in all times coming'.[32] Accordingly, the infant King James was crowned only after, and not before, a rewritten and expanded version of the coronation oath was sworn on his behalf by James Douglas, Earl of Morton.

The service's Protestant credentials were confirmed by John Knox, whose coronation sermon provided a precedent for recent events by revisiting the Old Testament account in the Book of Chronicles of Athaliah, Queen of Israel, who had been killed by members of her nobility as punishment for her immorality and replaced by her seven-year-old grandson Joash, with a covenant simultaneously formed between God and Israel's virtuous nobility. The service also included a public recital of Mary's instrument of abdication as an attempt to reinforce the legitimacy of James's accession. Revolutionary rhetoric sat awkwardly alongside venerable Catholic rites that included the anointing of James's head, shoulder blades and hands with holy oil in a ritual observed at all Scottish coronations since the early fourteenth century. Just as awkwardly, the cleric who anointed the infant king was the Protestant reformist Bishop Adam Bothwell of Orkney who, two months earlier, had officiated at the controversial marriage of James's mother to James Hepburn, Earl of Bothwell.

*

Safely ensconced in Stirling Castle, the infant James was cared for by Annabella Murray, Countess of Mar, seven nurses and around a score of household servants. By twenty months, he was receiving a personal daily allocation of two capons, two and a half large loaves and a quart and a pint of ale.[33] The practical details of the king's care were approved by his mother's Protestant half-brother, James Stewart, Earl of Moray, who had been appointed as James's regent by the first Scottish Parliament of the reign that met in Edinburgh in December 1567. Seeking to minimize the radicalism of the revolution that had taken place, the parliament's commissioners recorded that James's coronation had been 'orderly done and executed', exactly as if Mary 'had been departed out of this mortal life' or, alternatively, as if she had appeared before the parliament to state her wishes.[34] During the same parliament, Mary was directly accused of complicity in the murder of the king's father,

Darnley, while draft legislation was proposed, albeit unsuccessfully, declaring that female rule was no longer approved in Scotland.[35] Several months earlier, the resident Spanish ambassador in London had reported to Philip II his conversations with Elizabeth I about recent events, alleging that Scotland's government under Moray's regency was now 'in form a republic' whose leaders 'say they hate the very name of "king", and more still the idea of being governed by a woman'.[36]

No image of James appeared on the first coinage of his reign issued in 1568. On one side was the young king's initials and an imperial crown, its closed-arch design signifying that the king's power was subject to no other earthly authority. On the other side was an upright sword with the Latin legend *Pro Me Si Mereor in Me*, abbreviating Emperor Trajan's command: 'use this for me, or against me, according as I deserve'. The injunction was not rhetorical: members of the 'King's Party' were obliged to take up swords against the 'Queen's Party' on James's behalf following Mary's escape from Lochleven Castle on 2 May 1568 before she and her supporters were defeated, eleven days later, at the Battle of Langside outside Glasgow by forces under Moray's command.

Initially, Elizabeth congratulated her cousin on escaping her unlawful detention but warned her to avoid appealing simultaneously to both England and France for support. Rather, Mary should 'remember that those who have two strings to their bow may shoot stronger, but they rarely shoot straight'.[37] In the event, Mary's impulsive decision to cross the Solway Firth into England undermined the capacity of her forces to regroup and continue fighting for her restoration. It also placed the English court in a dilemma for, although Elizabeth denied the right of subjects to rebel against royal authority, the extent to which Mary had been complicit in the murder of Darnley – an English subject – remained unclear. Detained initially in Carlisle Castle, Mary wrote to Elizabeth, admitting 'I find it strange that, coming [to England] so frankly without condition but trust in your amity, I have been kept as if a prisoner'.[38]

In an attempt to determine Mary's innocence or guilt, commissions of inquiry were held at York and Westminster during the autumn and winter of 1568–9, to which delegations from the King's Party and the Queen's Party were summoned. While Mary's representatives refused to 'acknowledge Queen Elizabeth a judge over them nor the actions of Scotland', members of the King's Party needed to prevent possible treason charges being laid against the Regent Moray by convincing

Elizabeth's ministers of Mary's involvement in Darnley's murder. Originally composed in Latin, Buchanan's *Detection of the Doings of Mary, Queen of Scots* (1571) conceded that it was 'both strange, and also for the strangeness unpleasant' for Scotland's internal affairs to be subjected to foreign adjudication, but insisted that concealing Mary's complicity would have been worse.[39] Supporting the King's Party case were the notorious 'Casket Letters': a cache of sonnets and papers that had been tampered with, if not wholly fabricated, to allege Mary's adulterous involvement in her husband's murder. Several months of hearings yielded a frustratingly inconclusive outcome, while one of the inquiry's English commissioners, the Earl of Arundel, remained apprehensive regarding the dangers attaching to suspicions that the English administration might tacitly approve a monarch's removal from power by her own people. As he warned Elizabeth, she who 'has a crown can hardly persuade another to leave her crown, because her subjects will not obey. It may be a new doctrine in Scotland, but is not good to be taught in England.'[40]

Ruling as regent on his nephew's behalf, Moray lamented the English administration's reluctance to endorse James's royal authority and objected to William Cecil in October 1569 that 'it is no time now to dissemble: uncertainty with you has bred uncertainty among us.'[41] In November, 6,000 Catholics rose in armed rebellion across northern England, while the prominent Catholic peer Thomas Howard, Duke of Norfolk – who had presided at the York commission of inquiry – was arrested and imprisoned, following discovery of his plans to become Mary's fourth husband. In February 1570, Elizabeth I's status as an international pariah was exacerbated by Pius V issuing a papal bull, *Regnans in Excelsis*, which released the English queen's subjects from allegiance to her authority and threatened excommunication on any who obeyed her orders.

Elizabeth's ministers pondered possible terms on which Mary's restoration as queen might be achieved in a way that placed Scottish affairs under English oversight with Mary's royal powers restricted by Scotland's Privy Council and Parliament. One draft settlement envisaged Mary's restoration in return for James and a dozen other Scots nobles residing in England until either Mary died or seven years had passed. Hoping that terms could be agreed, Mary wrote to James's guardian, the Countess of Mar, in June 1570, explaining that her four-year-old son 'may come here to serve for a hostage in my place, and I there in his place'. Insisting that her royal power remained intact, Mary advised the countess against obstructionism, warning that 'the day will come when I may have your son in my hands, as you have mine'.[42] Elizabeth's readiness to support Mary's restoration to power finally dissipated, however, on discovery of the 'Ridolfi Plot' during the summer of 1571. Orchestrated by a Florentine banker, Roberto Ridolfi, it envisaged Spanish troops landing at Harwich or Portsmouth to oversee Elizabeth's assassination and the installation of Mary Stuart as England's queen. Ridolfi's reckless publicization of his plans on the Continent implicated Mary's supporters in England, the most prominent of whom, Thomas Howard, Duke of Norfolk, was convicted of treason and executed in June 1572.

In Scotland, the civil war continued with Maitland fearing that James might well be left 'no kingdom at all apt for rule', but only 'a confused chaos and a country divided into two or three hundred kingdoms'.[43] Northern Scotland, much of the centre and west of the country, as well as East Lothian, were controlled by Mary's supporters. In May 1571, Lennox and other King's Party leaders had convened an assembly in the Canongate below Edinburgh in what was nicknamed 'the creeping Parliament', with members obliged to crawl around in order to dodge hostile fire from Marian supporters controlling Edinburgh Castle. That August, James made his first public appearance since his coronation at the opening of a new parliament in Stirling's Tolbooth. Dressed in miniature royal robes, the five-year-old king rode from Stirling Castle accompanied by his paternal grandfather, Matthew Stewart, Earl of Lennox, who had been appointed regent in July, after Moray's assassination in Linlithgow by a Queen's Party supporter six months earlier. Given Lennox's long residence in England, his appointment as regent had been made conditional on his swearing not to negotiate with any foreign power (i.e. Elizabeth I) and not to remove James from Scotland without agreement from the country's nobility.

Seated in the chair of honour when the Stirling Parliament opened, James delivered his first public speech which comprised sixty-four words and acknowledged that, since 'my age will not suffer me to exercise my charge myself', he was entrusting power to his grandfather and the assembled commissioners 'to administer justice ... as you will answer to God and me hereafter'. Later in the proceedings, the fidgety young king, noticing a cavity in the Tolbooth's roof, declared that 'there is a hole in this Parliament'. His comment appeared ominously prophetic when, a week later, the town of Stirling was stormed by Queen's Party forces in a nocturnal raid: the only time that the civil war's fighting directly targeted the prince's household. James was unharmed, but he may well have witnessed the fatal shooting of his grandfather, the Regent Lennox, who died shortly afterwards, on 4 September 1571.[44] The following day, the Earl of Mar – James's guardian since infancy – was appointed as the young king's third regent.

In January 1572, Elizabeth responded to Mar's appeal for English assistance to end the war by insisting that James's royal authority must be 'universally acknowledged'. Fanciful ideas of a power-sharing agreement between James and his imprisoned mother could only 'bring forth innumerable absurdities and confusions', while alternative notions of a 'neutral' governor were 'a monstrous device and a plain way to subvert and extinguish the lawful power of the ancient monarchy' of Scotland 'and the highway to coin an anarchy'. Once universal recognition of the king's royal authority was secured, Elizabeth recommended that the Scottish Parliament pass 'an Act of Perpetual Oblivion' to erase all residual animosities among James's subjects.[45]

External observers also urged the ending of internecine divisions. In October 1572, Elizabeth's ambassador in France, Sir Francis Walsingham, was alarmed by the rolling Scottish ship of state and beseeched Mar to encourage his countrymen to imitate mariners, who, 'in the time of tempest and storm, they forbear not each man to set his hand to the tacking, leaving private grudges aside in respect of a common danger'.[46] Walsingham feared a gathering Catholic storm in the form of Mary Stuart as well as bitter sectarian divisions arising from the St Bartholomew's Day massacre of around 3,000 French Huguenots in August, which he had witnessed in horror from the English embassy in Paris. Meanwhile, Mar – who had successfully negotiated a truce between the warring parties that summer – became the third of James's regents to die in office when he became fatally ill after dining at the house of James Douglas, Earl of Morton, also in October. Notwithstanding suspicions of possible poisoning, Morton succeeded Mar as James's fourth – and final – regent.

On New Year's Day in 1573, the leader of the Queen's Party, William Kirkcaldy of Grange, signalled the resumption of hostilities by bombarding Edinburgh's fish market, resulting as one eyewitness reported, in 'fish blown so high in the air that they were seen to fall on the tops of high houses.[47] In February, however, Morton signed the 'Pacification of Perth' with prominent Marian supporters from the Hamilton dynasty and, in May, English military assistance proved decisive as the fortress of Edinburgh Castle finally succumbed to sustained bombardment. Having assisted the Regent Morton in laying siege to the Castle, Thomas Cecil – son of Elizabeth I's Principal Secretary – had hoped to visit James VI, but was dissuaded as the young king was suffering a bout of smallpox in Stirling 'where almost all the youth were infected'.[48] James recovered his health and, as he approached his seventh birthday, was finally established as Scotland's undisputed sovereign.

4

Sore and Sharp Schoolmasters

In August 1605, as James was approaching forty and had ruled as England's king for over two years, he visited Oxford University, where he admired the recently opened Bodleian Library. Had he not been a monarch, James informed his hosts he should wish to have enrolled as a university scholar. On seeing the 'many books fastened with chains of iron' to the Library's shelves, he further ventured that, should he ever have the misfortune to be held captive, he would wish to be detained in the Bodleian to be chained alongside so many great authors.[1] Making the most of his time in Oxford, James surprised his hosts by hurrying out after dinner one evening to hear a fourth round of student disputations on scientific matters, including alchemy. Listening attentively, James 'many times interposed his opinion of the arguments, which were proposed very learnedly and philosophically' before spontaneously delivering 'a long discourse in Latin, which did so fill the auditors with wonder, and admiration'.[2] More than a decade later, when James returned to Scotland in 1617, the pressure of royal business prevented him from attending similar debates at the university in Edinburgh, but the king arranged for its students to hold a three-hour disputation in the Chapel Royal at Stirling Castle. According to one observer, James was 'highly delighted with the performance' in which he participated enthusiastically, 'sometimes joining the impugner and sometimes the defender; expressing himself in elegant Latin, and showing great acquaintance with the *arcana* [secrets] of philosophy'.[3]

Teaching rhetoric at Trinity College, Cambridge, in the 1610s, the poet George Herbert warmly admired the king's erudition. Rejecting the 'fluent orators, that domineered in the pulpits of Athens and Rome', Herbert instead directed his students towards 'an oration of King James, which he analysed, showed the concinnity [elegance] of the parts, the propriety of the phrase, the height and power of it to move affections', which resulted in a 'style utterly unknown to the Ancients, who could not conceive what kingly eloquence was'.[4] In a tract published in 1609, Bishop William Barlow of Rochester had likened James's dinner company to 'a little university, compassed with learned men in all professions; and his Majesty in the midst of them ... a living library, furnished at all hands, to reply, answer, object, resolve, discourse, [and] explain'.[5] Even polemical adversaries, such as the French Catholic Cardinal Jacques Davy du Perron, set aside disagreement with James's political claims to admire how he accomplished 'in his person the hope of Plato: of philosophers reigning, or of kings philosophising'.[6] After James's death, a postmortem examination was undertaken, during which physicians found 'the semyture [skull] of his head so strong as they could hardly break it open with a chisel and a saw, and so full of brains as they could not, upon the opening, keep them from spilling, a great mark of his infinite judgement'.[7]

But royal bookishness could also be belittled. In the mock encomium *Corona Regia* (1615), its anonymous author beheld James 'armed with a book and pen'. While 'other kings wore the diadem or tiara', England's king sought to 'claim for yourself the insignia and cap of a preeminent doctor'.[8] James's identification of the Bodleian Library as his prison of choice was the preference of someone who, by 1605, was the author of published treatises on poetry, political theory and demonology. It was also the preference of a king who, as a teenager, had experienced enforced detention during the 'Ruthven Raid' of 1582–3 that had amounted to a ten-month form of house arrest. James's own educational training had been both stimulating and traumatic in equal measure. The overriding priority of Scotland's governing elite had been to ensure that, for the first seven years of his life, the young king's person was securely protected from abduction or assassination within Stirling Castle while civil war raged outside its walls. A similar premium had also been placed on gaining control of James's mind, via his education, to render him a fit and godly figurehead for the victorious 'King's Party' in that war.

*

James's intellectual assuredness as an adult reflected the investment made in his education by the Scottish humanist, George Buchanan, who enjoyed a continental reputation as a neo-Latin poet before becoming a key intellectual influence within the group of Protestant Confederate Lords who had orchestrated Queen Mary's deposition. In a birth-poem composed for James in 1566, Buchanan anticipated the new prince moving beyond 'childish babbles and struggling speech' to 'learn the letters' and thereby to discern 'what clear differences separate the true from the false' and 'the sacred from the profane' in order, one day, to 'take up the reins of his nation and prosper'.[9] Before James's coronation in July 1567, it had also been Buchanan who, as Moderator of the Church of Scotland's General Assembly, had overseen the Assembly's subscription of articles stipulating that 'wise, godly, and learned men have the charge of the education of the prince' to ensure that, as James grew older, he would prove 'a comfortable instrument of God, being virtuously educated'.[10]

Having thereby 'written his future job description', Buchanan was appointed by the Regent Moray as the young king's tutor in 1569 or 1570 when James was not yet four.[11] During the 1530s, Moray had himself been tutored by Buchanan, as had James V's eldest illegitimate son, Lord James Stewart. Now in his mid-sixties Buchanan was assisted in overseeing James's education by a younger colleague, Peter Young, who had studied at Jean Calvin's academy in Geneva where Calvin's successor, Theodore Beza, had found Young to be 'uncommonly learned'.[12] Studying alongside the young James VI were classmates including John Erskine, later Earl of Mar, whose family were hereditary Keepers of Stirling Castle and whose father had been given custody of the infant James in 1567, as well as Mar's cousin Thomas Erskine, later Earl of Kellie; Thomas's young brother, George; Walter Stewart, later Lord Blantyre; and a nephew of the Countess of Mar, William Murray of Abercairney.

Buchanan and Young devised for their royal and noble charges a quintessentially humanist education that focused on the philological study of classical texts, alongside grammar, rhetoric, poetry, history, moral philosophy and Scripture. Their pedagogical approach echoed precepts set out in *The Education of a Christian Prince* (1516) written by the Dutch philosopher Desiderius Erasmus for the teenage Holy Roman Emperor, Charles V. As Erasmus had warned, educating a prince in a hereditary monarchy was 'by far the greatest and by far the most hazardous' of responsibilities. It was essential to begin 'straight away, from the very cradle', as 'the seeds of morality must be sown in the virgin soil' of a prince's infant soul to ensure that, with time, 'they may gradually germinate and mature, and once they are set, may be rooted in him throughout his whole life'. The ideal time to inculcate virtuous conduct was thus when a prince 'does not yet understand that he is the prince'.[13] Being raised in Stirling Castle free from parental influence or interference, James offered the Confederate Lords a unique opportunity to test Erasmus's teachings in practice.

Contemporary accounts suggest that James responded well to the demanding curriculum set by Buchanan and Young. The young king was clearly speaking, if not writing, in Latin before his fourth birthday in June 1570; in an oft-quoted remark, he later recalled that his tutors 'had me speak Latin before I could speak Scots'.[14] In marginalia accompanying his catalogue of the king's library, Young noted informal 'apophthegmata', or maxims, uttered by his young charge, many of which played on polyglot translations or puns. For example, a priest ('un prêtre') was, in James's view, correctly named, since he was always ready ('prêt') to act badly. Similarly, when reading Buchanan's account of the licentious life of Durstus, the eleventh (mythical) King of Scotland, the young king had burst out, 'how durst he be so evil? They might have called him "Curstus", because he was cursed, and had accursed us.'[15]

Just after James turned eight in June 1574, he was visited by Elizabeth I's ambassador, Sir Henry Killigrew, who reported to the queen's Principal Secretary, Francis Walsingham, that her godson 'speaks the French tongue marvellously well'. Killigrew had been especially impressed by James's ability to 'read a chapter of the Bible out of Latin into French, and out of French into English, so well that few men could have added anything to his translation'. The young king's linguistic proficiency was all the more remarkable since Killigrew had been invited to select any Scriptural chapter at random to ensure that the exercise had not been pre-prepared. Describing Buchanan and Young as 'rare men', Killigrew added that, although they remained keen to detach James 'from the handling of women, by whom he is yet guided and kept', he was reassured that earlier fears of clandestine attempts 'to transport the king to France' had evidently receded.[16] Equally impressed by James's precocious abilities were the Presbyterian ministers James and Andrew Melville, who also visited Stirling Castle that autumn. Watching the eight-year-old king walking with the Countess of Mar and discoursing of 'knowledge and ignorance' was, for James Melville, 'the sweetest sight in Europe that day', as he admired James's 'strange and extraordinary gifts of ingyne [wit], judgement, memory, and language'.[17]

Peter Young later supplied a more detailed account of the king's curriculum, likely to have been drawn up after James had turned twelve. Each day started with morning prayer, after which the young king 'devoted himself to Greek' by reading the New Testament, Isocrates or Plutarch. After breakfast, James turned to Latin, reading 'either from Livy, Justinian, Cicero, or from Scottish or foreign history'. Lunch was followed by composition and, 'if time permitted, he studied arithmetic or cosmography, which included geography and astronomy, or dialectics or rhetoric.'[18] By 1578, James's library numbered around 600 volumes; in his inventory, Young also listed around ninety individuals who were either donors to, or borrowers from, the royal library over a ten-year period from 1573.[19] After petitioning the Regent Morton for funds to purchase more books in 1576, Young wrote to the Lord Justice-Clerk, John Bellenden, emphasizing their mutual interest in promoting 'our Majesty's furtherance in learning'. As Young added, 'in case any person should say, as the fashion of the most part is, "what needs his Majesty so many books, has he not enough already?"', Young trusted that Bellenden 'would show them their error' and persuade Morton to approve payment.[20] Half a century later, when an English member of James's retinue expressed surprise by the ready fluency of the king's Latin interventions into the scholarly disputations at Stirling in 1617, James paid tribute to the excellence of his childhood tutors, insisting that 'all the world knew' of Buchanan's virtuoso oratory. James had, moreover, been dismayed by the mangled attempts of English scholars to speak in classical Latin or Greek. Having always followed Buchanan's pronunciation, he was 'sorry that my people of England do not the like; for certainly their pronunciation utterly spoils the grace of these two learned languages.'[21]

If James admired Buchanan's scholarship, he did not remember his schooldays fondly. Pedagogical orthodoxy regarded strict schoolroom discipline as essential to produce humble, obedient subjects. As headmaster of Merchant Taylor's School in London, Richard Mulcaster insisted in *Positions Concerning the Training Up of Children* (1581) that 'the rod may no more be spared in schools, than the sword may in the prince's hand'. 'By the rod', Mulcaster confirmed, 'I mean correction and awe': only if pupils learned to fear physical chastisement would they become loyal, dutiful citizens.[22] The courtier James Melville of Halhill later recalled that Buchanan had certainly kept the young king in 'great awe' at Stirling.[23] In his mid-sixties by the time he taught the young king, Buchanan was 'undoubtedly crabbit and dour' and 'by all accounts a cantankerous old bachelor increasingly plagued by ill-health and with an evil temper to match'.[24] In February 1582, the Spanish ambassador in London relayed reports to Philip II that the renowned poet had even 'given way to the vice of drunkenness, and is intoxicated every day'.[25] Such was the trepidation instilled that in 1622 – forty years after Buchanan's death – the Venetian ambassador in London, Girolamo Lando, reported that James had been distressed by a nightmare in which his former schoolmaster had appeared to the king in his sleep and 'predicted his fate in verse: that soon afterwards he would fall into ice, and then into fire, that he would endure frequent pain, and die after two years'.[26]

Buchanan had also been determined to mould his royal charge into a very different character from that of Queen Mary, whom he repeatedly denounced as a lascivious adulteress and murderess. In the early eighteenth century, the biographer George Mackenzie recounted an anecdote passed down by the king's classmate, George Erskine, to his grandson. On one occasion, James had evidently tried to take a tame sparrow owned by John Erskine, prompting a scuffle between the two boys that had resulted in the sparrow's death. Thereupon, Buchanan 'gave the king a box on the ear', insisting that 'that what he had done, was like a true bird of the bloody nest of which he was come'. On another occasion, after a warning from his tutor to be less rambunctious or 'he would whip his breech', James supplied a cheeky retort, prompting Mackenzie to describe how Buchanan 'in a passion ... whips the king severely'. Following an intervention by the king's guardian, the Countess of Mar, Buchanan was reported to have replied, 'Madam, I have whipped his arse, you may kiss it if you please.'[27]

While Mackenzie's tales may have been embellished, Buchanan was unambiguous in his detestation of Queen Mary and his insistence that her son be inoculated against all forms of sycophantic flattery. In 1577, Buchanan published a neo-Latin tragedy entitled *Baptistes* – which he had written in Bordeaux in the early 1540s – retelling the fate of John the Baptist in King Herod's evil hands. With Herod often understood as a lightly veiled depiction of King Henry VIII of England, Buchanan dedicated *Baptistes*, which illustrated 'the torments of tyrants and their miseries when most they seem to flourish', to the young James VI, intending his 'little book to be a witness to posterity'. Should James ever contemplate ruling tyrannically, Buchanan warned that it would 'be imputed as a failing not to your teachers, but to you, who did not obey their virtuous warnings'.[28]

In March 1578, the Regent Morton resigned his position after a coup by nobles, prompting the Scottish Parliament to announce that the eleven-year-old king had now come of age and no longer required a Regent to exercise power on his behalf. Although the coup proved premature and a Regency council was soon formed under Morton's presidency, Buchanan's daily influence over the king was receding. The following year, Buchanan dedicated another Latin tract to James entitled *De Jure Regni apud Scotos* ('The Law of Kingship among the Scots') intended to 'explain from their very cradle . . . the mutual rights or powers of kings and their subjects'. Buchanan presented *De Jure Regni* 'not only as a guide, but also as a harsh and sometimes insolent critic, to steer you, at this formative time in your life, through the reefs of flattery'. Recognizing that James possessed 'a character far above your years, eager of its own accord to strive for distinction of every kind', Buchanan nevertheless hoped that he would instinctively despise the fawnings of those who 'randomly sprinkle their conversation, as if it were seasoning, with "majesties", "lordships", "excellencies" and other terms which are even more repugnant'.[29]

Composed in the months following Queen Mary's deposition in 1567 and published when its author was in his seventies, Buchanan's *De Jure Regni* was one of the most thoroughgoing defences of popular sovereignty and rights of resistance produced in early modern Europe. Manuscript versions of *De Jure Regni* had circulated extensively since the late-1560s, with their content indicating the precepts inculcated in the royal classroom at Stirling. The tract purported to be a dialogue between Buchanan and Thomas Maitland (brother of William Maitland of Lethington, who had led the civil war 'Queen's Party'), although Thomas Maitland later insisted that the tract 'was wholly Buchanan's own invention'.[30] *De Jure Regni* opened with 'Buchanan' acknowledging that news of Mary's deposition had provoked a horrified reaction in France; in general, subjects 'approve of the murder of tyrants but are concerned at the misfortunes of kings'. 'Buchanan' nevertheless wanted to convince 'Maitland' that the actions of the Scottish political elite – in removing a monarch who was ruling tyrannically – was both morally justified and required by the Scots law of kingship. Hoping to demystify kingship's purpose, 'Buchanan' likened a monarch to a medical doctor. Even in a hereditary monarchy, 'Buchanan' insisted that, since a king's subjects 'granted him authority over themselves', they must 'be allowed to dictate to him the extent of his authority' and to take punitive action if a monarch sought to exceed such limits to their power.[31]

Buchanan himself had, after all, been in a position to dictate the limits of royal power, having used his role as Moderator of the Church of Scotland's General Assembly in 1567 to ensure that the infant James VI was crowned king only after Morton had sworn the coronation oath on his behalf. In *De Jure Regni*, the fictional character 'Buchanan' could thus supply proof of the monarch's subordinate status to Scotland's laws by explaining that, 'when our kings are publicly inaugurated', they promised to observe the rule of law and respect the country's ancient customs. Defining a king who disregarded a country's laws as a tyrant or enemy of the people', 'Buchanan' coolly proposed that 'it is the right not only of the people as a whole, but also of individuals, to kill the enemy,' to which his interlocutor, 'Maitland', meekly assented, adding – however implausibly – 'I think that almost every nation has held that view'.[32]

In reality, political elites across early modern Europe would have regarded Buchanan's endorsement of individual rights of tyrannicide as an appalling recipe for popular anarchy. But, at the same time as Buchanan was instilling theories of popular sovereignty and resistance rights into the young King James, he was also compiling a chronological account of Scottish history as ostensible proof, in practice, of his claims. In August 1582, Buchanan dedicated his *Rerum Scoticarum Historia* ('The History of Scotland') to James, explaining that, since 'chronic ill-health' now prevented him from teaching the king in person, he was sending instead 'faithful advisers from history' to provide counsel and models for emulation.[33] Invoking Scotland's past in order to justify recent actions, Buchanan's history stretched back to the mythical reign of King Fergus I in 330 BC and has since been judged 'inaccurate in fact, unbalanced in interpretation' and 'built on allegation and insinuation, half-truth and falsehood almost inextricably tangled'.[34] In his account of Mary's reign, for example, Buchanan assigned predictably lurid prominence to David Riccio's murder in 1566, alleging that, after the killing, the queen had been reassured by one of its instigators that 'what had now happened was no new thing'. Since Mary's authority 'derived from the law', Scotland's political leaders could not tolerate an Italian-born 'foreigner, hardly worthy to be a servant', subverting their sovereign. Alarmingly for James, Buchanan also claimed that, after Darnley's murder the following year, the Confederate Lords had been convinced that his mother's new husband, Bothwell, had also wanted to kill him, while a baby, in order to prevent him later seeking vengeance for his father's murder. According to Buchanan, such fears had been all the more credible, given 'manifest signs that the queen's mind did not shrink from such a crime'. Having often ventured 'that the boy would not live long', Mary claimed to have 'been told by a skilled astrologer in Paris that her first child would not live more than a year'.[35]

A month after dedicating his history of Scotland to his former pupil, Buchanan died, in September 1582. In his early eighteenth-century account, Mackenzie claimed that, when Buchanan learned, on his deathbed, that James was 'highly incensed' by publication of the *De Jure Regni* and his forthcoming history of Scotland, their author had retorted 'that he was not very much concerned about that, for he was shortly going to a place where very few kings were'.[36] Shortly after Buchanan's death, the imprisoned Queen Mary sent a ciphered request to the French ambassador in London asking to see a copy of Buchanan's history of Scotland and advising that, if the work remained in circulation, it should be banned on account of the harm inflicted on her honour, as well as that of James and their royal predecessors.[37] In Scotland, James oversaw parliamentary legislation enacted in May 1584 against 'slanderous and untrue calumnies' spread about himself and his Privy Councillors that likewise dishonoured 'his parents, progenitors, crown and estate'. The only individual named in the new legislation was Buchanan, with all owners of either his *De Jure Regni* or *Historia* threatened with fines of £200 if they failed to surrender copies to government ministers to ensure the works 'may be perused and purged of the offensive and extraordinary matters specified therein, not suitable to remain as accords of truth to posterity'.[38]

*

James VI's comprehensive rejection of Buchanan's political ideas has been characterized as 'one of the more spectacular instances of student rebellion in the early modern world'.[39] In his own published writings, James maintained that monarchs derived their authority from God alone and that inferior magistrates and individual subjects had no rights of resistance whatsoever. Often acclaimed as the pre-eminent theorist of the 'Divine Right of Kings', James insisted in *The Trew Law of Free Monarchies* (1598) that, should tyranny occur, it must be endured 'without resistance, but by sobs and tears to God' only.[40] In *Basilicon Doron* (1599), he directed Prince Henry to disregard 'such infamous invectives, as Buchanan's or Knox's chronicles'; indeed 'if any of these infamous libels remain', laws enjoining their prohibition should be enforced.[41] In labelling Buchanan and Knox 'archibellouses of rebellion', James coined a polyglot neologism that combined the Greek root of 'chief' ('archi') with the Latin word for 'war' ('bellum') to lament the survival of incendiary theories through readers having access to radical works. Moreover, by prohibiting resistance, James denied that he was silently sanctioning tyranny and claiming that 'the world were only ordained for kings', who might 'turn it upside down at their pleasure'. Rather, James exhorted all monarchs to remember that they remained solely accountable to God: 'the sorest and sharpest schoolmaster that can be devised for them'.[42]

In their education of the young king, Buchanan and Young ensured that James would have the wealth of learning, philological expertise and linguistic proficiency to publish works promoting royal power, to dispute in print with prominent continental theologians, and to conceive of the massive scholarly undertaking that produced the 'King James Version' of the Bible. Yet as an adult, James evinced a more ambivalent attitude towards royal education. He might happily have enrolled as a university scholar had he not chanced to be king. But as a king, he regarded an over-reliance on paper bullets as risky in an increasingly sectarian world in which polished rhetoric could all too easily be manipulated to the advantage of others. In *Basilicon Doron*, James advised Prince Henry to ensure that his 'language be plain, honest, natural, comely, clean, short, and sententious'. His son should not only steer clear of 'book-language, and pen and ink-horn terms, and least of all mignard and effeminate terms', but also avoid physical gestures that made him appear 'a stupid pedant'. To uphold royal authority, Henry's public statements should be short and unequivocal; lengthy reasonings should be restricted to private musing. Furthermore, James directed Henry only 'to write in your own language' for 'there is nothing left to be said in Greek and Latin' and he would soon find himself outdone by 'poor scholars' if he tried.[43]

Notwithstanding such paternal advice, James himself retained a lifelong relish for academic disputation and enjoyed a continental reputation as a learned controversialist. In 1607, the German astronomer and mathematician Johannes Kepler sent James a recent publication and hoped he might 'rule so happily over Britain that you never feel compelled to abandon philosophy because of excessive business'.[44] James's court also offered a refuge to Protestant scholars, such as the Genevan-born Isaac Casaubon, with whom the king eagerly discussed theological matters. Writing to a friend in the Paris *Parlement* in 1613, Casaubon described how James, 'great and learned as he is', often became 'so entirely taken up' with theological controversies that each recent publication 'keeps his own mind, and the minds of all about him occupied exclusively on the one topic'; 'hardly a day passes on which some new pamphlet is not brought him ... all these things I have to read and give my opinion on'.[45]

By 1613, Protestant polemicists could look to a new institution, known as 'Chelsea College', for which James had laid the foundation stone three years earlier, as well as making available the College's 28-acre site in London (via reversionary crown lands) and gifting timber from Windsor Forest. Parliamentary legislation, meanwhile, secured the College's funding via income from the water system supplying London. A generation later, a pamphleteer recalled that Chelsea College had been intended as a new type of establishment – albeit one that tacitly recognized the papacy's propagandistic success in this sphere – which would identify 'special men' who could avoid the burdens of teaching or pastoral duties required in universities and parishes. They would instead be supplied with stipends and research resources in return for producing learned publications promoting 'the truth of religion, and honour of the state' against 'the continued lies, slanders, errors, heresies, sects, idolatries, and blasphemies of our adversaries'.[46] Twenty Fellows were initially appointed and, in 1616, James wrote to the Archbishop of Canterbury underscoring the importance of further fundraising in order to fulfil the College's main purpose of defending Protestant orthodoxy.

Alas, although Chelsea College lasted through James's reign, it did not survive the civil wars. As Thomas Fuller reported in his *Church History of Britain* in 1655, the abandoned institution, despite being envisaged as 'a spiritual garrison, with a magazine of all books for that purpose', now stood 'bleak like a lodge in a garden of cucumbers'.[47] A more permanent royal legacy was created in Scotland in the King James Library at the University of St Andrews. Founded in 1612, James and his two sons, Princes Henry and Charles, sent 130 books that summer to inaugurate the new library, while around another 100 volumes were received from Queen Anna and Princess Elizabeth. But the new building remained roofless until 1618 and was only properly stocked as a library in the 1640s.[48]

Learned repositories were, however, increasingly valued by rulers as a tool of state. It was during James's reign as English king that the 'State Paper Office' was formally constituted, with its 'Keeper' the antecedent of today's Chief Executive and Keeper of The National Archives. Under Elizabeth I, Thomas Lake had assumed responsibilities later associated with the Keepership, but in an informal and unpaid capacity. On James's accession, Lake was knighted, given an annuity of £50 (sterling), and formally entrusted with 'keeping, airing and digesting' the 'records of matters of state'.[49] The premium placed on retaining a confidential record of government business was underscored in the oath imposed on each Keeper. Lake's successor, Thomas Wilson, thus swore to use his 'uttermost endeavours' to preserve the king's 'papers and records of state' from all harm, to prevent them being 'purloined, embezzled or defaced', and to withhold 'from the knowledge of others' all matters that 'shall be fit, either for reason of state or otherwise for his Majesty's service, to be concealed and kept secret'. Pressing for promotion and better remuneration in 1616, Wilson implored James to appreciate that, having been appointed to 'peruse, register, abstract and put in order, all your Majesty's papers for business of state, which I found in extreme confusion', he had spent 'ten painful years' reducing 'them into that due order and form' which the king had approved.[50] Looking ahead, Wilson contended that James should 'take more knowledge' from government records, of which 'there is not so much use made as the treasure therein hidden deserves'. Fearing that he was simply 'buried amongst dead papers', Wilson suggested that were he to become, for instance, Master of Requests, he would be ideally placed to handle petitions and appeals and 'to present unto you often times such matter out of your papers' as the king would find profitable.[51]

Since access to secret information thus conferred political advantage, James's ready sharing of bibliophile, oenophile and hunting enthusiasms with the Spanish ambassador, Diego Sarmiento de Acuña, Count of Gondomar, was distrusted. Posted to England between 1613 and 1622 (with a brief return to Spain in 1618–19), Gondomar amassed a private library at his Valladolid home, the Casa del Sol, that comprised around 6,500 items and included English and Latin editions of James's collected *Works*, a Latin translation of James's *Apology for the Oath of Allegiance* (1609), around forty histories of England (in English and Latin), and hundreds of English maps as well as printed and manuscript tracts on English geography, trade, law, politics and diplomacy.[52] In a tract published in Amsterdam in 1624, the Scots-born Puritan, Alexander Leighton, deplored the Spaniard's success in having 'so easily entered the Cabinet of our secrets' at James's court, 'where he lay so long like an old rat, feeding on a Parmesan' cheese.[53] But Gondomar's diplomatic master, King Philip IV, was delighted, claiming – a month after James's death – that his ambassador had achieved a 'total and complete knowledge' of England.[54]

When James visited Oxford University in 1605, he was among the Bodleian Library's first distinguished visitors. In an oration to the University's scholars and academics, he urged them never to 'stand at a stay, but always to go forward' in their studies, since the success of their endeavours would advance God's glory and 'make me a joyful king'.[55] (He might have been less joyful had he known that Sir Thomas Bodley had already advised his librarian, Thomas James, to acquire copies of Buchanan's *De Jure Regni* and *Rerum Scoticarum Historia*, despite both works being banned by James; if need be, Bodley advised his librarian to 'plead ignorance of any such interdiction').[56] Today, all visitors to the Bodleian Library pass in front of King James's statue, placed high above the Old Schools Quadrangle on the Tower of Five Orders (see Plate 19). From under a canopied niche, the king is depicted presenting copies of his collected *Works* to two allegorical figures: 'Fame' stands blowing a trumpet on James's right hand, with the kneeling figure of the 'University' on his left. To 'Fame', the accompanying Latin epigram reads *haec habeo quae scripsi*, and to the University, *haec habeo quae dedi* – 'these things which I have written/given'. Returning to Oxford on a dazzlingly bright summer's day in August 1619, James admired the quadrangle and the new statue that had been doubly gilded. But the figures were 'so glorious and splendid that none, especially when the sun shone, could behold them'. On the king's direction, the gilding was removed and the statue 'whitened over'; now, the figures stand in simple stone.[57]

5

The Naked Sword

More than four centuries after the event, the English annually 'Remember! Remember! The Fifth of November!' to commemorate an averted disaster. Four days after the Gunpowder Plot's dramatic discovery, James addressed both Houses of the English Parliament on 9 November 1605 to emphasize the sheer scale of the national catastrophe that had been prevented. While James likened all kings to tall trees vulnerable to 'the daily tempests of innumerable dangers', he suspected that he had been nearly felled more often than most. As he recollected, even 'while I was yet in my mother's belly', his life had been endangered by David Riccio's assassination in Edinburgh in March 1566; had his pregnant mother also been murdered, he would 'have been baptised in blood'.[1] Nearly four decades later, the Gunpowder Plot was 'a destruction prepared not for me alone', but intended to annihilate the entire political establishment at Westminster. With around 2,500 kilos of gunpowder amassed, the envisaged explosion would have unleashed sheer carnage and thousands of casualties. James characterized the conspiracy as 'a thundering sin of fire and brimstone'. Describing the horror they would have suffered, the king impressed on peers and MPs that there were three main ways by which 'mankind [may] be put to death'. If attacked by another person, one could at least defend oneself, escape, or hope that 'God may stir up in the hearts of the actors' a sense of pity. If attacked by an animal, one could likewise resist, escape, or hope that 'some pity may be had' from beasts, recalling the Biblical tale of Daniel in the lion's den. But destruction by 'inanimate things', such as fire and water, remained the 'most cruel and unmerciful' of fates, with fire the 'most raging and merciless'.[2]

James's personal safety was repeatedly threatened throughout his life, leaving him with an instinctive fear of violence. Ironically, the king's acknowledgement to peers and MPs of his repeated good fortune in surviving so many deadly threats echoed a similar observation made the previous year by the English Jesuit, Robert Persons (or Parsons). Although Persons had formerly opposed James's claim to succeed Elizabeth, he grudgingly conceded that England's new king seemed to enjoy divine protection. Admiring 'his Majesty's preservation and strange delivery from infinite dangers and most imminent perils', Persons ventured that 'neither Cyrus, nor Romulus, nor Moses himself was more strangely preserved than this king hath been since his infancy.'[3]

Perennial fears about James's physical safety were justified, as what might be termed 'terrorism before the letter' was especially pronounced between 1559 and 1628: an era when it was 'possible to *think* terrorism, even if the word did not yet exist'.[4] In 1559, the violent overthrow of Marie of Guise's French-backed regency administration ensured that 'the first shots in France's civil war were fired in Scotland', as Protestant Huguenots were inspired to take up arms against Catholic authorities in a protracted series of religious wars.[5] Thereafter Continental Europe witnessed a spate of targeted killings of monarchs and prominent nobles that were often justified along confessional lines. In 1580, for instance, Philip II of Spain issued a widely disseminated proclamation against the Dutch 'rebel' Prince William of Orange that was translated into English, offering a reward of 25,000 gold crowns to anyone, Spanish or foreign, able to 'set us and himself free from the aforesaid plague, [by] delivering him unto us quick or dead, or at the least taking his life from him'.[6] William was duly assassinated in 1584.

In England, the Ridolfi, Throckmorton and Babington Plots, devised by Catholic conspirators in 1571, 1583 and 1586 respectively, all envisaged the violent dispatch of Elizabeth I in order to facilitate her replacement as English queen by James's mother, Mary. In France, the Duke of Guise and Kings Henri III and Henri IV were murdered respectively in 1588, 1589 and 1610. On being informed of Henri IV's assassination, the French ambassador in London reported that James 'turned whiter than his shirt', while his Venetian counterpart described the king as so dazed and despairing that he was observed entering and leaving through the wrong doors to his chamber, and was 'surrounded by his bodyguard, a thing he has not been accustomed to do'.[7] Henri IV's murderer was a former monk, François Ravaillac, who justified his actions on the grounds that the French king was not only an erstwhile excommunicate and illegitimate usurper of the throne, but also sinful in his toleration of Protestant Huguenots.

For James, such vicious king-killing was the terrifying and logical upshot of subjects deciding for themselves which rulers might be considered heretical tyrants, inspired by the insistence – of his former schoolroom tutor, George Buchanan – that it was 'the right not only of the people as a whole, but also of individuals to kill the enemy'.[8] In later years, the royalist philosopher Sir Kenelm Digby recalled 'the strange antipathy which the late King James had to a naked sword', despite being 'otherwise courageous enough'. Aware that the king's 'aversion all his lifetime' was popularly attributed to the trauma that James had experienced *in utero*, Digby described how he had knelt before the king to be knighted in October 1623. In the ceremony of putting the point of a naked sword upon my shoulder', James 'could not endure to look at it, but turned his face another way, insomuch that, in lieu of touching my shoulder, he had almost thrust the point to my eyes' had not the Duke of Buckingham intervened to steer James's hand.[9] Five years later, Buckingham himself was fatally stabbed by a demobilized soldier, John Felton.

*

Acts of deadly violence punctuated James's childhood. While still a seven-month-old baby, his father, Lord Darnley, was strangled and the house in which he had been staying blown up. Three years later, James's uncle and first regent, James Stewart, Earl of Moray, was assassinated by his mother's supporters in Linlithgow. In 1571, Moray's successor as regent and James's paternal grandfather, Matthew Stewart, Earl of Lennox, was shot during a skirmish in Stirling and reportedly seen dying by his five-year-old grandson. Aged eleven, James was induced by a noble faction led by the Earls of Argyll and Atholl into accepting 'the government of his realm in his own person' in March 1578, as recorded by the Privy Council following the Earl of Morton's reluctant resignation as regent.[10] But shortly after James's authority was proclaimed in Edinburgh, his Chancellor, Lord Glamis, was shot dead in Stirling's streets amid hostilities arising from a long-running noble feud, prompting the English envoy Thomas Randolph to warn that 'all the devils in Hell are stirring and in great rage in this country'.[11] A month later, an early-morning raid was launched on James's home, Stirling Castle, by his former classmate John Erskine of Mar, who successfully dislodged his uncle, Alexander Erskine of Gogar, as the Castle's Keeper and assumed the role himself, thereby also gaining control of James. Several were killed in the skirmish, including Erskine of Gogar's son. As the English ambassador, Robert Bowes reported, the eleven-year-old king had been 'in great fear of the tumult, and tore his hair' during the raid and afterwards, 'in his sleep he is therewith greatly disquieted.'[12]

In his later published writings, James strenuously defended the authority of 'free monarchy', acknowledging that his actions had always been controlled by others during his minority. For although the young king had declared his intention to rule in his own name, a governing Council was formed and resumption of effective control by the former regent, Morton, was evident at the next parliament in Stirling Castle in July 1578. As recounted by the Presbyterian chronicler, David Calderwood, the twelve-year-old king had insisted – albeit in a 'somewhat stooting [stammering] manner' – that 'lest any man should judge this not to be a free parliament, I declare it to be free; and these that love me will think as I think.'[13] When troops were mustered in August by the rival Morton and Argyll-Atholl factions, armed followers of the latter marched with banners picturing the young King James behind a barred window and the caption: 'Captive I am, liberty I crave'.[14] Although each side attracted over 5,000 supporters, a peaceful settlement was reached with Bowes's assistance. But foul play was suspected less than a year later when the Earl of Atholl died of poisoning in April 1579, shortly after dining with Morton.

A new sphere of influence emerged when Esmé Stewart, seigneur d' Aubigny-sur-Nère, accepted James's invitation to leave his family and estates in central France and join the Scottish king's court, arriving in September 1579 with an entourage of over twenty. The Catholic nephew of James's grandfather and former regent, Matthew Stewart, Earl of Lennox, D'Aubigny was aged thirty-six, having been born in the same month as James's mother. He had acquired military experience through service in the company of bodyguards to the French king known as the 'Scots Guards' and had also been one of several hundred Gentlemen of the Chamber at Henri III's court, which had a notorious reputation for ruthless violence. As Henri of Navarre (later Henri IV) observed in the mid-1570s, the French court was 'the strangest that you have ever seen'.

Since 'we are almost always ready to cut each other's throats', courtiers carried daggers, wore chain mail and secreted cuirasses under their cloaks while 'the king is as threatened as me'; in due course, both Henri III and Henri IV were indeed assassinated.[15]

In Scotland, James was visibly delighted by the company of his older French cousin, but Protestant and Anglophile interests at court were alarmed. Only a month after D'Aubigny's arrival, the French ambassador in London, Michel de Castelnau, sieur de la Mauvissière, had heard reports that D'Aubigny 'will be declared heir of the Crown of Scotland if the said Prince [James] dies without children'. Castelnau also dismissed rumours of D'Aubigny's willingness to convert to Protestantism: 'those who want to reign, they need to know how to dissemble'.[16] After D'Aubigny was appointed governor of Dumbarton Castle and had the earldom of Lennox conferred on him by James in March 1580, Elizabeth's Principal Secretary, Walsingham, warned Bowes that Castelnau was covertly letting it be known 'that they are there in daily expectation of the transporting of the young king of Scotland into that realm [France]'. Although Bowes tried to warn James of the potential danger, the thirteen-year-old king had seemed unconcerned, prompting the frustrated ambassador to admit that anyone minded to abduct James would soon 'note in him such inconstancy, perjury, and falsehood'.[17]

In April 1580, Elizabeth I fired a shot across the bows by writing directly to Lennox to claim that, while Scotland had been 'in peace and union at his arrival', there were 'many jealousies and changes' now afoot, with observers having 'imputed the fault thereof to him as having been the chief mover and conciliator'. In response, Lennox denied wishing to subvert Scotland's religion or to undermine Anglo-Scottish amity, venturing that 'if a single point be found true of what his accusers have said, he does not ask for other mercy than to have his head cut off.' As the rumour-mongering continued, Lennox wrote again to Elizabeth in October requesting that any allegation against him be formalized in writing to James. If his detractors wished 'to maintain their talk', he declared himself 'ready to fight a duel with them in his [James's] presence and hers', envisaging an (unlikely) scenario in which the English queen and Scottish king would meet in person.[18]

Lennox's increasing domination of Scottish politics perturbed Bowes, who feared that 'the flexible nature of the king in these tender years' offered no resistance to an ambitious French noble 'who climbs so fast that some look for his sudden fall'. Incensed that control over the strategic port of Dumbarton had been entrusted to 'a subject of another prince and infected with right dangerous practices', the English ambassador regarded James's 'nobility and Council as men blinded or bewitched'.[19] By January 1581, Bowes objected that it was 'now thought as dangerous in Scotland to confer with an Englishman, as to rub on the infected with the plague, and most men openly flee the English company'.[20] After an audience with the Scottish king, another English diplomat, Thomas Randolph, admitted that, although James was still only fourteen, 'he wants neither words nor answers to anything.' In public, Randolph tried to warn a Convention of Estates at Holyrood that Lennox was seeking, 'partly by dissimulation and courting with the king', and partly by sowing divisions among the nobility, 'to make a ready way to bring strangers into the realm, and consequently to alter religion, and in the end to put the person of the king in danger, and to enable himself to get the crown'.[21] But rather than acceding to Elizabeth's offers of assistance, the Convention approved a taxation of £40,000 (Scots) 'for the resistance of foreign invasion threatened by England', while Randolph's return to England was reportedly expedited when 'he had a shot bestowed on the window of his chamber, in the place where he is wont to sit and write.'[22]

Elevated to become Scotland's only duke in April 1581, Lennox worked with the Earl of Arran to oversee the arrest and execution of former Regent Morton for complicity in Darnley's murder fourteen years earlier. Morton's fall served to shift culpability for the murder away from Mary and encouraged Jesuit missionaries – recently arrived in Scotland and England in 1580 – to seek support from the French, Spanish and Guise dynasties, as well as the papacy, to restore Mary and thereby re-establish Catholicism in Scotland. Meanwhile, Elizabeth instructed another envoy to reassure ministers in Edinburgh that 'she desires no promise or party in Scotland'; her key concerns were to preserve James's person, the Protestant religion and Anglo-Scottish amity with 'foreign servitude avoided' (evidently not regarding English involvement in Scottish affairs as 'foreign'). To her mind, Scotland seemed a 'broken state, so full of factions, [and] the king being carried away with the passion of such of the nobility there as possess him'.[23]

Had Elizabeth seen the contents of a letter sent by Lennox to Pope Gregory XIII in March 1582, she would have found her baleful diagnosis amply confirmed. Anticipating the arrival that autumn of an invasion army in Scotland of 20,000 soldiers funded by the papacy and Spain, Lennox confirmed that he would thereafter assume overall military command, while hoping for a simultaneous diversionary rebellion in Ireland. As the duke airily added, 'I did not communicate these affairs to the king since it is secret and because he is still a child.'[24] Although Lennox remained 'confident that he will come round as much in religion as in all other things as we wish', were James to 'prove stubborn' the Frenchman declared himself ready to 'act in such manner that he would not be able to harm or hinder us'.[25]

In August 1582, however, it was Scottish nobles, rather than foreign soldiers, who staged a successful coup to effect James's separation from Lennox. Later known as the 'Ruthven Raid', the coup resulted in the king being detained against his will for ten months. With Lennox and Arran at their private residences, James had undertaken a hunting trip in Perthshire and was invited by his Treasurer, William Ruthven, Earl of Gowrie, to stay at Ruthven Castle (now Huntingtower Castle). But when the king had tried to depart the next day, he was forcibly detained and, becoming tearful, was allegedly informed 'better bairns greet [cry] than bearded men'.[26]

Having taken James to Perth, the Raid's leaders issued a declaration in their capacity as Privy Councillors, disingenuously announcing that the king's unexpected presence in the town was 'in no ways forced, compelled, nor constrained for fear or terror of any man, nor that he no ways is detained here against his Highness's will, but that, as of his own free motive'.[27] A week later, a royal order commanded Lennox to leave Scotland and to dissolve any armed retinue. In London, the Spanish ambassador, Bernadino de Mendoza, heard of rewards offered 'to anyone that will bewitch, poison, or kill' Lennox, evincing the English court's determination to remove him and 'obtain possession of the king's person and the government'. Lennox thus had 'good reason to fear every dagger in Scotland, particularly as people there are not only accustomed, for slight causes, to shed the blood of private persons, but do not hesitate to kill their kings'.[28]

After being held for a month in Stirling Castle, James was escorted to Edinburgh where he effectively became a king who, although ostensibly responsible for governing Scotland and receiving foreign ambassadors, was denied any input into his Privy Councillors' decisions. To support the Ruthven regime, Bowes sought subsidies to secure its alignment with English interests, but Elizabethan parsimony left him fearing that 'this present husbandry shall at length be found like the housewifery of Calais', where an inadequate, belated English response had enabled French seizure of the strategic outpost. In Scotland, the 'greatest doubt and difficulty' for the coup's leaders was 'where and how they shall leave the king' whenever they wished to leave Edinburgh, potentially to confront anyone attempting a counter-coup to free James.[29] In late 1582, Lennox finally left Scotland, having been made aware – according to an account of 'Scotch affairs' circulating at the French and Spanish courts – that unless he returned to France, the Ruthven regime would either 'send the king to England or put him out of the way by some other method'.[30]

One ironic outcome of James's detention by the Ruthven raiders was belated recognition of his royal authority by Henri III's court, which had hitherto still regarded his deposed mother as Scotland's lawful sovereign. Since James refused to meet any foreign envoy whose credentials did not address him as king, sending a French ambassador to Edinburgh only became possible after Mary agreed to recognize her son's royal title in the hope that James might consider a future form of power-sharing or 'association'. In early 1583, two French ambassadors, Bertrand de Salignac de la Mothe Fénélon and François de Rocherolles, sieur de Maineville, met with James several times, prompting renewed alarm in London. As Walsingham warned, rumours were circulating that the Scottish king had told de la Mothe 'that though he had two eyes, two ears, and two hands, yet he had but one heart, which was French'.[31]

Sustaining parallel discussions with French and English representatives enabled James to recover some political initiative, notwithstanding his shock at learning that Lennox had become ill and died in May 1583. The next month, the king summoned James Melville of Halhill to Falkland Palace in Fife, bitterly denouncing 'his hard state and mishandling by his own subjects' and suspecting that 'he was thought but a beast by other princely neighbours, for suffering so many indignities.' As Melville recorded, James 'took up a princely courage either to put himself to free liberty or to die by the way'. Escaping from Falkland on horseback, James and Melville reached St Andrews where the king's relative, the Earl of March, offered sanctuary in the town's castle. Its buildings were soon filled with well-armed nobles 'minding again to be masters of [the] king' but, after a tense stand-off, the majority of Ruthven Raiders fled into English exile.[32]

Having regained his freedom, James issued a proclamation from St Andrews in July 1583 'to publish to the world . . . the truth of his very mind'. To avoid a repetition of recent difficulties, the seventeen-year-old sovereign was determined 'to show himself a king indifferent to all his nobility and good subjects, and not to be led or carried away by any special surnames and races or by particular men'.[33] In *Basilicon Doron*, James later drew on his experiences during the Ruthven Raid – 'the first rebellion raised against me' – to recommend especial care to ensure the loyalty of courtiers appointed in the royal household.[34] Yet, to foreign observers at least, he faced an uphill challenge in imposing royal author-ity. Sent by Mary to meet James in August 1584, for example, a French envoy, the sieur de Fontenay, confided to his brother that the Scottish king was 'for his age, the premier Prince who has ever lived', possessed of 'a marvellous mind, filled with virtuous grandeur and a good opin-ion of himself'. Yet Fontenay identified 'this one deficiency': that having been 'nurtured in fear . . . he does not very often dare to contradict the great lords', despite wanting 'to be thought bold and resolute'.[35]

*

Prominent among those 'great lords' was James's older first cousin, Francis Stewart, Earl of Bothwell, who took his title from his disgraced uncle, whose disastrous marriage to the king's mother had ended in a descent into insanity and death in a Danish prison. Bothwell's staunch Protestantism rendered him popular with Church of Scotland ministers and Edinburgh's citizenry, but his overt disrespect for royal authority infuriated James who protested that 'he would not have so many kings in this realm'.[36] In April 1591, rumours of consultation with witches led to Bothwell's detention and subsequent escape from Edinburgh Castle. In December, Bothwell attacked the Palace of Holyroodhouse with sixty armed supporters in an attempt to regain royal favour and to over-throw the authority of James's Chancellor, John Maitland. According to the English agent Roger Aston, 'the king, being almost alone, for all men were at supper, withdrew himself to the tower, and reinforced the doors and defended the place' until assistance arrived. Although James's person had not been threatened, 'his chamber door was set on fire' and the king's Master Stabler, John Shaw, had been killed.[37] Eight of Bothwell's supporters, captured during the raid, were hanged without trial, but Bothwell escaped. In a verse tribute to Shaw, James vowed that 'Thy constant service ever shall remain / As fresh with me as if thou lived again', while payment of an annual pension of £1,200 (Scots) to Shaw's sister continued into Charles I's reign.[38]

The divisions created by James's closeness to Scotland's foremost Catholic noble, George Gordon, Earl of Huntly, only deepened when Huntly ordered the brutal hacking to death in February 1592 of his territorial rival, and ally of Bothwell, James Stewart, Earl of Moray (the Protestant son-in-law of James's first regent). With Bothwell vowing vengeance on Moray's behalf, James admitted to Huntly that, following the murder, 'I have been in such peril of my life, as since I was born I was never in the like, partly by the grudging and tumults of the people, and partly by the exclamation of the ministry, whereby I was moved to dissemble.'[39] In March, Aston warned of James's suspicion that English authorities were covertly supporting Bothwell as a means of promoting Protestant interests in Scotland. If Elizabeth was intending to shelter 'those whom he so deadly hates', Aston predicted 'farewell all amity between these countries'.[40] In another raid, Bothwell and 400 supporters besieged the king at Falkland Palace for six hours in June 1592. Although the attackers were repelled, James undertook 'to hunt them the best I may' and directly exhorted the English queen 'to punish such of your own lewd subjects' as were involved, since condoning such activity set 'a perilous precedent for all princes'.[41] To the English Warden of the West Marches, Bothwell himself insisted that 'the excuse is easy': at Falkland, he had simply followed 'the self same remedy which our progenitors heretofore' had used in order to re-orientate misguided royal policy, adding that 'the raids of Ruthven, St Andrews and Stirling are recent examples, which from our enterprise differs nothing but in success.'[42]

Bothwell's popularity derived from his being perceived as a champion of godly Protestant interests and for pursuing justice for Moray's murder. When Bowes met James at Dalkeith in August, he 'earnestly moved him to provide speedily for his own safety' amid reports that Bothwell had recently stayed overnight in Edinburgh, where he had been 'seen openly in the High Street without visor or disguising, whereat the king much storms'.[43] In July 1593, obliging courtiers helped Bothwell to gain unauthorized access to James's apartments at Holyrood, where he found the king 'having his clothes not fastened about him'. In the version relayed to Bowes, a startled James had evidently feared imminent death and told his cousin that, since he preferred 'to die with honour than thus lie in captivity with shame', he 'wished them speedily to execute their intended violence against him'. But Bothwell had denied any intention to harm James and instead offered 'his own sword to the king that he might, if he listed, strike off his head, which he thrust under the king's foot and put forth his neck to the king's stroke'.[44]

Following negotiation, James permitted Bothwell to defend himself against charges of treasonable consultations with witches, of which he was acquitted the following month. Further tensions, however, led to Bowes being invited to 'loose these knots' and mediate between the king and his cousin. Tentatively suggesting that James might show greater commitment to 'reformation of the estate in matters of religion, justice and peace', Bowes admitted that 'sharp terms' were uttered. The king was implacable: he would 'suffer his hand to be cut from his arm rather than hereafter subscribe any letter or missive at their appetites'. He would, instead, 'declare himself to be captivated by them' and issue an appeal to his subjects 'to procure his delivery by force'.[45] After serial attempts at accommodation, Bothwell led several hundred armed supporters to Leith in April 1594, but was forced into retreat by royal forces. Since this latest assault had been launched from England, James conveyed to Elizabeth his outrage that the earl had 'contemptuously come and camped within a mile of my principal city and present abode', before 'being by myself in person repulsed from that place, [and] returned back in England'.[46]

Bothwell went into permanent continental exile in 1595, yet threats to James's safety continued. On 5 August 1600, he became involved in an apparently personal feud, via the so-called 'Gowrie conspiracy', after accepting an impromptu invitation by Alexander, Master of Ruthven, to Gowrie House in Perthshire with the mysterious mention of viewing a hoard of hidden treasure. After dinner, James found himself berated about the execution in 1584 of his host's father, William Ruthven, Earl of Gowrie, who had led the 'Ruthven Raid' nearly two decades earlier. According to Bowes, a physical altercation had ensued in which James, 'seeing himself alone and without weapon cried "Treason, Treason"'.[47] Alerted by the king's shouts, several courtiers had raced to his assistance, fatally stabbing Ruthven and his older brother,

John, Earl of Gowrie. Whether events at Gowrie House were a premeditated plot or spontaneous brawl remains unclear, but it gave James an excellent opportunity to publicize the perennial dangers posed to royal authority. The following month, an official account of events appeared in Scots, English and Latin tracts simultaneously printed in Edinburgh and London, with annual thanksgiving services also enjoined in all Scottish parishes.[48]

After James acceded as English king in 1603, an annual thanksgiving service on 5 August was added to the Church of England's liturgical calendar. In December 1604, the company of players recently renamed the 'King's Men' staged a new history play entitled *The Tragedy of Gowrie*, which was quickly suppressed, presumably on account of breaching protocols against depicting reigning monarchs on the stage; the play script no longer survives. But preaching a court sermon before James in August 1605, Thomas Playfere, Professor of Divinity at Cambridge University, exhorted the congregation to recall the Gowrie conspirators and to 'detest them, hate them, loath them, as a toad, or as a viper, or as some hideous misshapen monster'.[49]

When the Gunpowder Plot was then discovered in November, James directly sought to 'compare these two great and fearful Domesdays, wherewith God threatened to destroy me and all you of this little world that have interest in me'. Both the Gowrie and Gunpowder plots had occurred on the same 'day of the week, which was Tuesday' and both on the same 'day of the month, which was the fifth' of August and November. But just 'as it was the same devil that still persecuted me', James reassured English peers and MPs that 'it was one and the same God that still mightily delivered me.'[50] In 1610, Bishop Lancelot Andrewes of Chichester commemorated the tenth anniversary of the Gowrie conspiracy in a sermon preached before the king at Holdenby House in Northamptonshire. Taking as his text a hemistich from the Book of Chronicles, *Nolite tangere Christos meos* ('touch not mine anointed'), Andrewes acknowledged that the injunction comprised 'four words only'. But by upholding this divine command and preserving James's life at Gowrie House, God had 'suffered him not to take any hurt at all; anointed the shield, made it slippery, their hands slid off, their touch did him no harm'.[51] Not all divinely ordained monarchs were so fortunate. For, as well as remembering the Gowrie conspiracy,

Andrewes's sermon alluded to the recent assassination of Henri IV of France.

*

Regicide apart, royal power was further diminished by the violent deaths of a country's nobility. Accordingly, one of James's priorities as an adult king in Scotland was to eliminate feuding among nobles. A minimum figure of over 360 protracted feuds has been identified as taking place during his reign, with sometimes as many as fifty feuds simultaneously waged in a single year between the mid-1580s and 1610.[52] Local feuds could be long-running and gruesome. In 1586, for example, Lauchlan MacLean of Duart and forty clansmen were seized by a local rival, Angus MacDonald of Kintyre, while MacLean was staying with Mac-Donald. Having burned two MacLean clansmen alive, MacDonald had the remainder, apart from Duart himself, 'beheaded the days following, one for each day, till the whole number was ended'.[53]

Late sixteenth-century Scotland was also a society with a disproportionately high prominence of young men. When James turned twenty-one in June 1587, the average age of the Scottish higher nobility was around twenty-seven.[54] Initial attempts to tackle feuding among noblemen were naively well-intentioned, even fraternal, but ineffectual. In May 1587, James arranged a large banquet for his nobility at Holyroodhouse, with one diarist recording how, 'after drinking of many scols [toasts] one to another', the king 'made them after supper, who otherwise had been at great feud, take two and two by hands' and process to the Mercat Cross for more feasting. In 'a harangue' to attendees, James insisted that, having now turned twenty-one, 'he loved nothing so much as a perfect union and reconciliation among his nobility' and warned that any 'busy and seditious persons, ready to sow discord among the nobility should be rooted out and banished'.[55] In 1596, he issued a proclamation, insisting (albeit erroneously) that feuding among nobles was 'a barbarity whereunto this only country has ever been miserably subject, as an abuse not known or named in any other civil country of the world'.[56] James repeated this claim about feuds in *Basilicon Doron*, objecting that 'their barbarous name is unknown to any other nation.' He regretted the readiness of his Scots subjects 'for any displeasure, that they apprehend to be done unto them by their neighbour' to start a feud, disregarding royal and divine authority, and thereafter 'bang it out bravely, he and all his kin, against him and all his kin'.[57]

In a practical initiative aimed at ending feuds, James proposed to a Convention of Estates in 1598 a requirement for all parties presently at feud to appear before the king and Privy Council. In feuds in which no killing had yet occurred on either side, royal arbitration would be mandatory to reduce the likelihood of escalation. In feuds where killings had occurred on both sides, compensation for both parties would be agreed, but where killing had occurred on one side only, the Crown reserved the right to intervene to seek a resolution. After making 'many long and pithy harangues' to sceptical nobles, James secured majority support for the 'Act anent removing and extinguishing of deadly feuds', which received parliamentary ratification two years later.[58]

James also invested time in meeting with feuding nobles and spent entire days in 1602, for instance, resolving a dispute between Archibald Campbell, Earl of Argyll, and Ludovick Stewart, Duke of Lennox (son of Esmé Stewart). Presiding 'over the most dramatic reduction in violence in Scottish history', the king's personal interventions in acrimonious disputes have been described as 'the kind of government to which the Scottish nobles responded, and in which James was at his best'.[59] The king's determination to end feuding was also motivated by his need to rely on a united nobility, should his quest to succeed Elizabeth as England's next monarch be challenged or require armed intervention. In 1602, he dined with the Marquis of Huntly and the Earl of Argyll, and rhetorically asked 'how can ye two, being two peers of my land, either do me good service or do your nation credit, being ready to cut one another's throat?' Any attempt by James to claim the English Crown by force would be seriously undermined if his two most powerful nobles remained unreconciled. As he added, 'I will need both your helps and shall make you both dukes.'[60]

In the event, James's accession to the English throne in March 1603 was peaceful and uncontested. Henry II's twelfth-century insistence that all homicides be prosecuted in the royal courts of justice meant that English society was not characterized by what James termed 'barbarous feuds'. England's new king nevertheless encountered a different form of extra-legal violence that appeared to be escalating uncontrollably: aristocratic duelling. In *Basilicon Doron*, James had advised his son never 'to commit your quarrel to be tried by a duel', since private combat was unlawful and especially irresponsible in a monarch whose public persona meant that, with his 'preservation or fall, the safety or wreck of the whole commonwealth is necessarily coupled'.[61] Legislation enacted in 1600 by the Scottish Parliament had condemned private challenges issued 'to singular combats upon sudden and frivolous quarrels' and made it a criminal offence for anyone to engage in 'any singular combat under the pain of death' and forfeiture of their moveable goods.[62]

In England, however, the recent Italian import of aristocratic duelling was popularly observed through swashbuckling sword fights in Elizabethan and Jacobean theatres as costumed protagonists defended their disputed honour and asserted their manliness. In real life, the prerogative court of Star Chamber tried around 200 cases that involved either sending or receiving challenges to private combat or actual duelling between 1603 and 1625.[63] Admittedly, such numbers paled by comparison with Henri IV's France, where duelling between nobles accounted for around 4,000 deaths between 1589 and 1610, prompting two royal edicts against private combat to be issued in 1602 and 1609. The second edict of 1609 was quickly translated into English and relayed Henri's concern that, since kings were 'loving and gentle fathers' and responsible for their subjects' preservation, extra-legal killings were an affront to Christian teaching and undermined royal authority.[64] That same year, Chief Justice Sir Edward Coke reiterated the unlawfulness of private revenge in England, insisting that 'nothing is more opposite to monarchy, than for any man to take the sword of revenge in his hand but by lawful warrant from his sovereign'.[65] James's international image as a publicly self-proclaimed *Rex Pacificus* risked being tarnished by an apparent inability to prevent his own nobles from readily shedding one another's blood.

Violence inevitably amplified tensions between members of the Scottish and English political elites. In 1613, duelling's fatal effects touched James directly when a Scot, Edward Bruce, Lord Kinloss, challenged an Englishman, Edward Sackville, later Earl of Dorset, to a duel that resulted in Kinloss's death. The eldest son of one of the king's most trusted ambassadors and a Privy Councillor, Kinloss had met Sackville at Bergen-op-Zoom near Antwerp to avoid fighting on English soil. Recalling 'the unfortunate passage' of events, Sackville admitted that an attendant had described their determination to duel as 'butcherly and bloody' but maintained that he and Kinloss had 'wrestled for the two greatest prizes we could ever expect trial for – honour and life'.[66] In February 1614, James issued a proclamation proscribing all private challenges and combat. Not only was it unlawful for subjects to take matters into their own hands and 'rate the quality of the wrong supposed, or the satisfaction that belongs to it', but James, as a divinely ordained monarch, remained mindful of 'the precise account which we are to make in another world for the loss of so many lives'.[67] Accompanying the proclamation was *A Publication of His Majesty's Edict, and Severe Censure against Private Combat and Combatants* by Henry Howard, Earl of Northampton, whose death shortly afterwards prevented pursuit of his recommendation that a High Court of Chivalry be created to hear disputes concerning individual reputations.

Northampton's proposal had, however, been opposed by James's Attorney-General, Sir Francis Bacon, who argued that such a court would only serve to encourage duelling. Insisting that the Star Chamber remained the correct court to adjudicate cases of disputed honour, Bacon published arguments that he had advanced in court, reiterating the iniquity of subjects presuming 'to give law to themselves, and to right their own wrongs'. Demands for revenge 'cause sudden storms in court', disturbed the king, and risked the 'unsafety of his person'. They could, moreover, 'grow from quarrels, to banding, and from banding to trooping, and so to tumult and commotion, from particular persons to dissension of families and alliances, yea to national quarrels'. So long as a gentleman's sense of reputation was 'but of cobweb lawn, or such light stuff', Bacon warned that deadly violence would arise over incidental remarks; gentlemanly honour should, rather, be 'of a good strong warp or web, that every little thing should not catch in it'.[68]

Since neither proclamations nor tracts proved effective in deterring determined duellers, James chose to sit in person in a judicial capacity – for the first time in his English reign – in a Star Chamber prosecution in 1617. Two young gentlemen, Thomas Bellingham and Brice Christmas, had arranged a duel and tried to leave England to duel overseas but had been stopped at Dover. Both men had confessed their guilt, leaving the king's role as that of delivering sentence. In court, James justified his personal involvement on the grounds that it was a case that 'concerns the peace of the kingdom, which is the proper office of a king'. Since other anti-duelling deterrents had failed, he wanted 'to make such an example, as may hereafter curb the insolent minds of these duellers' and prevent the shedding of his subjects' blood.[69] Likening his royal role to that of a shepherd, he needed 'to keep and conserve his sheep from being spoiled'.[70] To underscore the case's exemplary nature, Bellingham and Christmas were each fined £1,000 (sterling) and sentenced to indefinite imprisonment; a month later, royal mercy extended to free the men and remit the fines.

Throughout his life, the naked sword hung never far from James and fuelled his repeated attempts to convince contemporaries of the terrifying regicidal threats posed by radical religious zealots, as well as the fatal effects of noble feuding and duelling. He would have been horrified to witness his son and successor, Charles I, being publicly beheaded by the common executioner in January 1649, but his political and theological writings had been animated by the fear of just such an eventuality. James would likewise have been chilled to learn that, in trying to persuade Scotland's political leaders to acquiesce in the English Parliament's decision to execute the Scots-born Charles I, Oliver Cromwell had 'entered into a long discourse of the nature of regal power according to the principles of [the Spanish Jesuit, Juan de] Mariana and Buchanan'.[71]

6

The Apprentice Poet

Sen thocht is frie, Think quhat thow will
O troublit heart to eiss thy paine
Thocht unrevelit can doe na ill
Bot words past out cumis not againe
Be cairfull ay for to Invent
the way to get thy awin Intent.

Entitled 'Song: the first verses that ever the king made', these lines comprise the opening stanza of a poem included in an anthology of James's verse compiled in the mid-1610s by the king and his son, Prince Charles, now in the British Library.[1] With three further stanzas, the poem circulated in manuscript and attracted at least one hostile rejoinder during the king's lifetime but remained unpublished for two centuries.[2] Although James readily encouraged the later anglicization of prose works, such as *Basilicon Doron*, for the English publishing market, he remained a firm advocate of verse composition in Scots; accordingly, excerpts from the king's poetry are here reproduced in their original Scots.

'Sen thocht is frie, Think quhat thow will' survives in three other manuscript versions with variant titles, one indicating that it was 'made in anno. 1583, at the Duke of Aubigny's putting out of Scotland'.[3] Composed during James's detention by the Ruthven regime in 1582–3, the poem opened with an emphatic assertion of freedom of thought, before acknowledging a 'troubled heart'. Distraught at enforced separation from his older French cousin, Esmé Stewart, Duke of Lennox, the teenage king invoked verse to distinguish between private thoughts and public utterances, and the need to devise inventive ways of achieving royal intentions. Inspiration may have come from an earlier poem, included in a collection of *Gude and Godlie Ballatis* published in 1578 and misattributed to James's fifteenth-century forebear King James I of Scotland, which opened:

> Sen wordis ar thrall And thocht is only fre
> Thow dant thy tung That power hes and May.[4]   [to dant = to tame]

Today, James I of Scotland is better known as the author of the 379-line poem, *The Kingis Quair*. Discovered and first published in the 1780s, *The Kingis Quair* was written during James's prolonged detention in England after his capture at sea by Norfolk pirates in 1406, aged eight. Imprisoned by Henry IV in the Tower of London and other locations, James I later served in Henry V's forces in France before his eventual release from prison in 1424, when he was nearly thirty.[5] While James VI may well have heard of his ancestor's interest in imaginative literature, the English detention experiences of both James I and James VI's mother, Queen Mary, also conformed to the trope of monarchs seeking private consolation by composing verse when assailed or detained by opponents.[6]

*

If James was not unusual as a monarch in writing verse, he was unique in authorizing the printed dissemination of his poetry which appeared in two publications in 1584 and 1591. The king's verse compositions were not included in the folio edition of his collected *Works* published in 1617, but when he and Prince Charles compiled their anthology of over forty manuscript works in the mid-1610s, they produced a title-page and divided the contents into 'amatoria' (love poetry), 'miscellania' and 'fragmenta'. The collection may have indicated an intention to produce a verse anthology as a sequel to the prose *Works*, but no such publication resulted.

A year after freeing himself from the Ruthven Raiders' control, James's first publication, *The Essays of a Prentice, in the Divine Art of Poetry*, appeared in Edinburgh in the autumn of 1584. Comprising original poems, a translation, and a prose manual of poetic theory, *The Essays* ran to 128 pages and was published anonymously (although a prefatory Latin 'acrostichon' by Archbishop Patrick Adamson of St Andrews revealed the name 'Iacobus Sextus').[7] *The Essays of a Prentice* was published only months after a parliamentary session at

Edinburgh in May 1584 had approved what Presbyterian critics later decried as 'the Black Acts': legislation confirming royal supremacy over all civil and spiritual matters and prohibiting the meeting of unauthorized religious assemblies. Measures were also taken to limit publicity attaching to the Ruthven Raid, which was described as 'a crime of lèse-majesté, heinous in itself, of dangerous sequel and most pernicious example'. Although James had graciously extended clemency to those involved, subjects were banned from seeking 'to justify and allow the said most treasonable incident' in speech or in writing, or to 'store any books, rhyme, act, band, or writ' implying that the Raid had been lawful.[8] But given that Elizabeth I's ministers had supported the Protestant, pro-English stance of the now discredited Ruthven regime, James's *Essays of a Prentice* could also have been deployed to serve a diplomatic purpose. Two presentation copies were specially bound in hand-decorated, orange-stained vellum for Lord Hunsdon and William Cecil, Lord Burghley. When the Earl of Arran, as Scottish Chancellor, sent Hunsdon his copy, he referred to it as 'His Highness's first proof and apprentisage in poetry', confidently predicting that 'his next shall make these fruits to seem abortive'; in the meantime, the gift betokened James's 'good inclination . . . to do well' in terms of maintaining amicable Anglo-Scottish relations.[9]

Despite its title implying the offerings of a novice, James's *Essays of a Prentice* included 'a short treatise' in prose, outlining 'some Reulis and Cautelis' to be observed when writing Scottish poetry – effectively, a set of do's and don'ts. Previous handbooks of poetic practice published in France and England had included Joachim du Bellay's *Deffence et Illustration de la Langue Française* (1549) and George Gascoigne's 'Certain notes of instruction concerning the making of verse or rhyme in English' (1575), but, as James acknowledged in regard to the Scots vernacular, 'there has neuer ane of thame written in our language.' Among contemporaries, his tract impressed the English poet Gabriel Harvey, whose marginalia averred that James had devised 'the excellentest rules, and finest art, that a king could learn, or teach, in his kingdom'. His achievement was all 'the more remarkable' and 'how worthy the pen, and industry of a king'; for Harvey, at least, James's rules were 'much better, than our Gascoigne's *Notes of Instruction*'.[10]

James's 'Reulis and Cautelis' supplied technical advice on poetic rhythm, scansion, rhyme schemes, syllable length, vocabulary, repetition, originality and translation. To resolve metrical difficulties relating to variant pronunciation, the king advised aspiring poets to listen carefully to the sound of their verse: 'your ear may be the only judge'; as with all metrical verse, 'the very touchstone whereof is music'. Regarding suitable subject matter, James offered the clear warning to 'beware of writing anything of matters of commonwealth', which were 'too grave matters for a poet to meddle in'; only rarely should poets address such topics, either metaphorically or if the subject was 'of manifest truth, openly known'.[11] The teenage king also directed aspiring poets to avoid well-worn clichés. If penning amatory verse, for example, suitors should beware describing 'your love's makdome [beauty], or her fairness', but should, rather, 'praise her other qualities, not her fairness, nor her shape'.[12] Three centuries later, George Eliot recalled this advice in *Middlemarch* (1874) when its male protagonist, Tertius Lydgate, resolved to pursue a medical career, prompting the novel's narrator to wonder if it was 'due to excess of poetry or of stupidity' that writers never seemingly wearied in 'describing what King James called a woman's "makdom and her fairnesse"' when recounting romantic love, but rarely invested equal energy in imagining other objects of passionate desire, such as professional ambition.[13]

The king's early verse was likely to have been composed collaboratively, drawing on advice and ideas from the authors of commendatory sonnets that prefaced *The Essays*, among them the English courtier and intelligencer Thomas Fowler, two English-born court musicians, Robert and Thomas Hudson, and James's declared 'master-poet', Alexander Montgomerie. Although Montgomerie was later outlawed as a Catholic conspirator, when he died in the mid-1590s James acclaimed him as 'the prince of poëts in our land', who had once been a prominent member of what the king dubbed his 'sacred brethren of Castalian band' of versifiers at the Scottish court, referring to the Castalian spring on Mount Parnassus, long regarded as a site of poetic inspiration.[14] While the term 'band' may be misleading in implying a more coherent, formal coterie than existed in practice, James illustrated strictures in his 'Reulis and Cautelis' with unattributed quotations from Montgomerie, including his contribution to *The Flyting betwixt Montgomerie and Polwart*, composed in the early 1580s.[15] 'Tumbling verse' with words 'cuttit short, and hurland ouer heuch' [cut short and hurled over a crag] was, as James explained, best suited to invective and the court entertainment of 'flyting': a war of words, presided over by the king, in which rival poets sparred with alliterative torrents of personal and scatological insults.[16] In their *Flyting*, the courtier Sir Patrick Hume of Polwarth had mocked Montgomerie's genitalia as 'a cunt, deid runt' – i.e. both a female vulva and an impotent dried-up tree stump – and demanded that his opponent 'kis ye cunt of ane kow' [kiss the cunt of a cow]. After ultimately prevailing over his adversary, Montgomerie nostalgically recalled ejecting Polwarth from the coveted bardic fireside seat while:

> [His] Highnes laughed som tym for to look
> Hou I chaist Polwart from the chimney nook.[17]

The Essays also included a work of an entirely different character: a 280-line poem entitled 'Ane metaphoricall invention of a tragedie called Phœnix'. James's anguish at forced separation from the Duke of Lennox had been compounded when he received news of Lennox's death in May 1583. In his poem, the king recounted recent events allegorically via the fate of a dazzling Arabian phoenix that arrived in Scotland, but whose brilliance incurred the envy of other birds, forcing the phoenix to flee and eventually immolate itself. The nature of James's relationship with Lennox has invited speculation among historians, ranging from a crisp assertion that it 'was an adolescent's crush on an older person . . . perfectly understandable in those terms' to the more suggestive claim that 'like the phoenix, Esmé brought colour, light, beauty and love into James's bleak world.'[18] In 1580, the Scottish Jesuit Father Robert Abercrombie, recorded how James 'converses with no-one more readily nor more often than with Lord Aubigny'. Moreover, James 'does not seem to be happy with all his nobles present if Aubigny is absent; if when only others are present, he is somewhat silent, he becomes at once merrier as soon as Aubigny enters.'[19] The duke's proximity to James was assured when the royal household was reorganized, under Lennox's direction, to imitate arrangements at the French court, with twenty-four Gentlemen of the Chamber appointed to assist James from his rising each morning until his nightly retiral. In his dual capacity as Lord Chamberlain and first Gentleman of the Bedchamber, Lennox controlled access to the king and retained the first option of sleeping in James's bedchamber.[20]

As concerns regarding James's susceptibility fused with geopolitical anxieties, one of Walsingham's contacts, Sir Henry Widdrington, reported in May 1582 that Lennox 'carries the whole sway' in Scottish politics: 'the king altogether is persuaded and led by him, for he can hardly suffer him out of his presence, and is in such love with him, as in the open sight of the people, oftentimes he will clasp him about the neck with his arms and kiss him.' Days later, Widdrington added that Church of Scotland ministers had been 'informed that the duke goes about to draw the king to carnal lust'.[21] When James was detained by the Ruthven Raiders in August, Lennox initially defied orders to leave Scotland, protesting to the king in December that he would be 'the most unhappy man in the world' if he had now been induced to think badly of him. Willing that 'my breast might be split open', Lennox insisted that only engraved vows 'of fidelity and obedience' would appear.[22] Compelled to return to France, Lennox became ill and died in Paris in May 1583, after which Walsingham learned that the duke's embalmed heart was being returned to James, although his 'widow gives out this was done without her knowledge'.[23]

Devastated by Lennox's demise, James escaped from the Ruthven lords in June, welcomed the duke's nine-year-old son, Ludovick, into residence at the Scottish court, and published the 'Phoenix' as a verse tribute the following year. Comprising forty stanzas of seven lines each, the 'Phoenix' was prefaced by an innovative pattern poem in the shape of a funeral column in which James invited readers to 'mourn with me' in the hope that, by retelling the phoenix's tale, 'I then will live in lesser grief thereby' (see Plate 6).[24] The urn-like pattern may have been the teenage king's unique invention; no similar column form appears among the fifteen geometrical figures often used by contemporary poets and listed in George Puttenham's *Art of English Poesie* (1589). The first and final letters of each line read downwards in an accompanying sonnet spelled out 'ESME STEWART DWIKE [duke]' to provide veiled identification of the allegory's subject. In the fourth stanza of 'The Phoenix', the king alluded to *The Testament and Complaint of Our Sovereign Lord's Papingo* (1530), which had been written by Sir David Lyndsay after James's maternal grandfather, King James V, had escaped detention by opponents in the Douglas dynasty. While Lyndsay's dying papingo (parrot) had spoken truth to power in advising James V to heed his councillors' advice, for his grandson the papingo was 'ane common fowle, whose kinde be all is kend [known]'. By contrast, James VI insisted that 'I lament my Phœnix rare' as an exotic 'fowl which only one at onis [once] did liue'.[25]

The poem's narrator described befriending the luminous female bird on its arrival, but when 'the countreys round about did heare' of the phoenix's wish to remain in Scotland, 'the loue they bure her, turnd into disdaine'. Among the malign birds of prey instigating intimidation were 'the rauen, the stainchell [kestrel], & the gled [kite]' – denoting the earls of Angus, Gowrie and Mar – as well as 'other kynds, whom in this malice bred'. In the twenty-fourth stanza, the narrator recounted how:

> When she could find no other saue refuge
> From these their bitter straiks, she fled at last
> To me (as if she wolde wishe me to iudge
> The wrong they did her) yet they followed fast
> Till she betuix my leggs her selfe did cast.
> For sauing her from these, which her oppresst,
> Whose hote pursute, her suffred not to rest.

But to no avail: the bird's tormenters 'spaird her not a haire', while the narrator's legs started to bleed, prompting the frantic phoenix to fly into Apollo's fiery altar and burn, as the desperate narrator dispatched messengers to learn of her fate. An envoy duly confirmed the bird's death, but also acknowledged the rebirth of a new phoenix and Apollo's recognition of the 'loue that thou her bure ... (whose name doeth end in X)', alluding equally to the fictional phoenix and Lennox.[26] Now preserved in the Bodleian Library, James's heavily edited draft version of the 'Phoenix' reveals 'the king's creased, stained, and much-thumbed working papers, mostly hidden from prying eyes' (see Plate 5).[27] But even in its published form, not all the king's readers understood his allegory. In England, Harvey evidently read James's poem after the death of Mary, Queen of Scots, in February 1587 and indicated 'the Queen executed' at the top of the page describing the phoenix's death, before identifying 'the young king her son, of most royal hope' on the next page, when the new phoenix appears.[28]

The *Essays of a Prentice* also included 'The Uranie': James's translation of a 336-line poem by the French Huguenot Guillaume du Salluste, sieur Du Bartas. Conceding that he lacked 'the like lofty and quick ingenuity' to compose verse of similar excellence, James had resorted to translation, notwithstanding his own warning against such uncreative activity in the 'Reulis and Cautelis', where he described translators being 'bound, as to a stake, to follow that book's phrases, which you translate'.[29] In *La Semaine* ('The Week'), which was first published in France in 1578, Du Bartas had produced a colossal versification of the first seven days in the Book of Genesis to re-tell the world's Creation. Du Bartas then started work on *La Seconde Semaine* ('The Second Week') – relating the successive ages of the world from the Garden of Eden to the Apocalypse – the first two days of which were published in 1584.

That same year, James's translation of 'L'Uranie', which imagined an encounter with the Christian muse Urania, and a separate translation of Du Bartas's poem *Le Judith* by Thomas Hudson were the first of Du Bartas's works to be published in either Scotland or England. Both were produced in Edinburgh by a French Huguenot printer, Thomas Vautrollier, with James explicitly seeking to promote Du Bartas's achievements by 'publishing some work of his, to this isle of Britain'.[30] Since Vautrollier maintained his shop in London's Blackfriars while resident in Edinburgh, his Scottish imprints were widely available in England, where Du Bartas's Scripture-based poetics were enthusiastically received.[31] Indeed, 'no other poem (besides those in the Bible itself) was read as widely as the *Semaines* were across early modern English and Scottish society,' eclipsing Shakespearean sonnets in popularity.[32]

In Scotland, Hudson dedicated his translation of *Le Judith* to James and recalled his rash assertion regarding the impossibility of rendering Du Bartas's poetry 'succinctly, and sensibly in our own vulgar speech', only for the king then 'to assign me *The History of Judith*, as an agreeable subject . . . to be turned by me into English verse'. With his translation thereafter 'corrected by your Majesty's own hand', Hudson directed praise for his efforts toward James, while 'default of skill, [should] be imputed to myself'.[33] Assigned by Protestants to the Bible's apocrypha, the tale of a Jewish woman, Judith, slaying the Assyrian general Holofernes – and thereby saving Jerusalem from imminent destruction – raised precisely the same question as to whether or not tyrannicide could ever be justified that was exercising late sixteenth-century French, Scottish and English minds. When Henri III was murdered in 1589, his assassin – a fanatical young monk of the Catholic League named Jacques Clément – was hailed a 'Judith'.[34]

While Hudson worked on Du Bartas's *Le Judith*, James tackled *L'Uranie* ultimately publishing his translation as 'blocking' on the recto side of every page, opposite the French original on each verso. The king's purpose was one of transparency: to enable readers to identify instances 'wherein I have erred' and allow them to 'escape those snares wherein I have fallen'. In self-deprecatory vein, James acknowledged that his rendering was 'replete with innumerable and intolerable faults', many of which, ironically, were 'forbidden in my own treatise of the art of poetry' published in the same *Essays*. At one juncture, the muse Urania extolled poetry's powerful capacity to bring its readers' understandings into alignment with that of its author:

> For as into the wax the seals imprent [imprint]
> Is lyke a seale, right so the Poët gent,
> Doth graue so viue in vs his passions strange,
> As maks the reader, halfe in author change.
> For verses force is sic, that softly slydes
> Throw secret poris, and in our sences bydes,
> As makes them haue both good and evill imprented,
> Which by the learned works is represented.[35]

In France, James's translation evidently came to Du Bartas's attention since a publication contract in July 1585 envisaged a forthcoming volume to include 'L'Uranie avec la version escoussaise faicte par le roy d'Escoce [the Scottish version of *L'Uranie*, made by the King of Scotland]' as well as a translation into French by Du Bartas of James's 'Short Poem of Time' that had appeared in *The Essays*.[36] Two years later, Du Bartas accepted an invitation from James to visit Scotland and arrived at Edinburgh Castle in May 1587, keenly expected by the king, who told courtiers that the French poet was 'the welcomest man that came to him this long time'.[37] Writing to a friend from Falkland Palace in July, Du Bartas described spending time with James hunting deer and rabbits, with the goddess Diana having temporarily displaced Calliope, the patroness of epic poetry, as his muse.[38] Maintaining their correspondence thereafter, a letter from Du Bartas to James in February 1589 lamented that 'France is going from bad to worse', with the country 'being converted little by little into a desert' through civil war, famine and pestilence. Fondly recalling 'my Scottish Apollo', Du Bartas reflected 'how much happier is Scotland which enjoys peace and repose, under a wise king.'[39]

*

In 1591, James published a second volume of verse in *His Majesty's Poetical Exercises at Vacant Hours*, this time eschewing anonymity, and including a 1,536-line translation into Scots of *Les Furies* from the *Seconde Semaine* of Du Bartas, who had died the previous year. As the king explained to his readers, he had regarded the French poet as 'a viue mirror of this last and most decreeped [decrepit] age', with 'The Furies' illustrating 'as in a glass, the miseries of this wavering world' and the vices 'over-common in this hypocritical age'. Again, James craved readers' clemency regarding likely errors and weaknesses in the *Poetical Exercises*, which partly derived from the young age at which some writings had been composed as well as, more recently, to the 'great and continual' responsibilities of kingship. For now, 'my affairs and fasherie [troubles] will not permit me, to re-mark the wrong orthography committed by the copiers of my illegible and ragged hand, far less to amend my proper errors.' James was especially concerned to guard against his 1,032-line epic poem *The Lepanto* being misconstrued. He included a prefatory note admitting the frequency with which 'the effects of mens' actions come clean contrary to the intent of the author'. Claiming that manuscript copies had been 'purchased (in truth) without my knowledge or consent', James was shocked at accusations that he had sought 'like a mercenary poet, to pen a work, *ex professo* [professedly], in praise of a foreign Papist bastard'.[40]

James's *Lepanto* supplied a topical retelling of the celebrated naval battle of 7 October 1571, when naval forces commanded by Don Juan of Austria, and involving the forces of Pope Pius V, Spain and the Venetian republic, had triumphed over the Ottoman Empire's fleet under Selim II. With around 180 Turkish ships captured, over 12,000 Christian galley slaves freed, and more than 25,000 Turkish fighters killed, the overall death toll could have been as high as 35,000. Accordingly, the poem's readers might assume its hero to be Don Juan – illegitimate son of the Holy Roman Emperor Charles V and recognized half-brother of Philip II of Spain – who followed up victory at Lepanto with punitive suppression of Protestant Dutch forces in the Netherlands, where he served as Governor of the Low Countries until his death in 1578. James insisted, however, that his intention had been to highlight the iniquity of all forms of 'cruel persecution', implying that the Holy League's resistance of Turkish aggression could be allegorically interpreted as analogous to the plight of Protestants oppressed by the Catholic League in France. As a free and independent sovereign, James did not fear censure in simply seeking 'to speak or write the truth of any' individual; any praise redounding to Don Juan was therefore 'only as of a particular man, when he falls in my way, to speak the truth of him'.[41]

By the time James published *Lepanto*, the Venetians had sued for peace independently of their allies and the Turks had regained possession of Cyprus. Nevertheless, the poem's ambiguous religious politics, together with its implied message that religious persecution was best resisted with military force, stimulated interest among Elizabeth I's ministers and English readers more generally. In June 1591, an entry in the Stationers' Company Register confirmed receipt of thirty copies of James VI's *Poetical Exercises* to be distributed by Archbishop John Whitgift of Canterbury to senior clerics and lawyers involved in English press regulation.[42] Two years earlier, one of Vautrollier's former apprentices, Richard Field, had registered rights to publish 'the furious, translated by James the Sixth, king of Scotland, with the Lepanto of the same king'.[43] Although Field did not take up the rights, he was clearly well-informed about the king's literary activities two years before the *Poetical Exercises* was published in Edinburgh.

Alongside the *Lepanto* and James's translation of *Les Furies*, the *Poetical Exercises* also included posthumous publication of Du Bartas's paraphrased French translation of James's epic poem, entitled *Lepanthe*, which simultaneously appeared in 1591 in a verse collection printed in the Huguenot stronghold of La Rochelle. Having worked from a manuscript copy of *Lepanto*, Du Bartas dedicated his translation to James, hailing him as the 'Phoenix Escossois!' – the Scottish phoenix – who possessed not only a brilliant and starry plumage, but whose 'vives & parlant' (lively and eloquent) descriptions had also tempted the Frenchman to break an earlier vow never to undertake a translation. As both authors strove to emulate the other's style, a marginal note in *Lepanthe* confirmed Du Bartas's wish to reproduce James's onomatopoeia.[44] Drawing on the multi-lingual rhetorical skills that James had learned from George Buchanan, the 'intricate intertextuality' of *L'Uranie*, *Les Furies* and *Lepanthe* presented 'a sophisticated collaborative exercise in humanist double translation', with complex and long texts translated into different languages and then back again, blurring the boundaries between French and Scots verse.[45]

Further afield, the Protestant poet-minister, Abraham van der Myl, published a Dutch translation of *Lepanto* entitled *Den Slach van Lepanten* in 1593. Van der Myl admired James as 'this wonder [that] can be seen in our days': a Scottish king 'so diligent in reading' that his literary productions 'can be read by everyone not only with great pleasure, but also profitably'.[46] On James's accession as English king, *His Majesty's Lepanto* (1603) was published in London. Thomas Murray produced a Latin verse paraphrase of *Lepanto* entitled *Naupactiados* the following year, as well as shorter Latin compositions including a martial 'schediasmata' (extemporization) addressed to England's new king. Since the island of Britain was now rendered 'one in the eyes of the whole world', Murray prophesied that James would either 'give peace also to all kingdoms, or you will, O King, conquer all kingdoms by force of arms'.[47] An allusion to *Lepanto* has also been detected in Shakespeare's play *Othello*, the earliest recorded performance of which occurred at court in November 1604. In his final speech, the play's eponymous hero recalls killing 'a malignant and a turbaned Turk' in the Cyprus wars, echoing the opening of James's *Lepanto*, which had described 'circumsised [*sic*] Turband Turkes'.[48] Since James's adjective 'Turband' was seemingly a neologism, tributes to the king were not always necessarily intended as policy endorsements or criticisms. Rather, as one critic has suggested, Shakespeare may simply have been 'complimenting him on his creative use of language'.[49]

*

By the time he acceded as English king in 1603, James's reputation as a poet was well established. In 1587, he had contributed an epitaph to a commemorative volume lamenting the death of the Elizabethan poet and soldier Sir Philip Sidney, while Sidney himself had lauded 'so piercing wits as George Buchanan' in *The Defence of Poesie*, which was posthumously published in 1595.[50] Among numerous panegyrics acclaiming James's accession, Samuel Rowlands called on English writers:

> Let every one present a flowing Quill,
> In honour of our famous Kingly Poet.[51]

The 'kingly poet' did not publish any verse as King of England, despite compiling the anthology of his manuscripts with Prince Charles in the mid-1610s. For specific occasions or individuals, James privately composed sonnets and other verse and, in 1621, remembered 'the Aprill of my dayes' when he had 'satt vpon Parnassus forked hill' in Scotland.[52] For their part, English writers also needed to navigate presentation of their bids for royal patronage alongside acknowledgement of their monarch as a published poet and critic. In an epigram 'To King James' in his *Works* (1616), Ben Jonson's approach was firmly to consign James's literary activities to his 'green' youth in Scotland, while also implying a shared equivalence of purpose with the king as a fellow poet:

> How, best of kings, dost thou a sceptre bear!
> How, best of poets, dost thou laurel wear!
> . . .
> For such a poet, while thy days were green,
> Thou wert, as chief of them are said t'have been.
> And such a prince thou art, we daily see,
> As chief of those still promise they will be.
> Whom should my muse then fly to, but the best
> Of kings for grace; of poets for my test?[53]

Certainly, England presented a different linguistic environment for James. Although he encouraged the anglicization of prose works, such as *Basilicon Doron*, for English editions, his theoretical strictures on poetry had been intended to promote composition in Scots. He was, therefore, uncharacteristically sharp in his criticism of the first 'Four Hours' of *Doomes-day*: an apocalyptic epic inspired by Du Bartas's *Semaines* published in 1614 by his fellow Scot, Sir William Alexander of Menstrie. In a sonnet dispraising such 'harsh verses after the English fashion', the king protested that although 'wee bath'd yow in Castalia's founteyns clear', Alexander had been seduced by 'your neighbours' who, 'borrowing from the raven theyr ragged quill', produced 'hard, harsh, trotting, tumbling' verse. Alluding to Alexander's silver and gold mining enterprises in Scotland, James's sonnet imagined the muses reproaching Alexander for ingratitude and his 'hurting them with his hard-hammered words, fitter to be used upon his minerals'.[54]

As James's Master of Requests for Scotland, Alexander accompanied the king on his three-month visit to Scotland in 1617, later memorialized in an anthology entitled *The Muses' Welcome to the High and Mighty Prince James* (1618), eighty copies of which were printed in Edinburgh by royal command, with forty copies remaining in Scotland and the other forty sent to London.[55] *The Muses' Welcome* comprised over 130 poems from more than sixty authors, the majority of which were in Latin, with a handful in Greek. Providing a travelogue record of James's visits to towns and cities including Edinburgh, Falkland, Dundee, Dalkeith, Stirling, Perth, St Andrews, Glasgow, Paisley, Hamilton and Dumfries, the anthology reproduced the panegyrical tributes presented and included a poem signed '*Pons Perthanus, subsidii expectantissimus*' – 'Perth Bridge, in strong expectation of financial support' – purporting to be from the city's bridge which was prone to continual flooding. 'A real work of cerebration as well as celebration', *The Muses' Welcome* illustrated 'an unselfconsciously Latinised landscape' whose writers 'rejoice to see rejuvenated by James' return'.[56]

But in England, excoriation more often eclipsed panegyric in the final years of James's reign. As one critic has noted, 'contemporaries were addicted to versifying almost everything'; convicted traitors 'spent their last hours fussing over farewell sonnets, while the despondent left suicide notes in couplets'. Enthusiasm for penning manuscript libels, invectives and ballads ensured that any 'notable event would be heralded by a verse commentary, while a serious crisis could be guaranteed a spray of poems'.[57] In the 'Reulis and Cautelis' issued in his first publication in 1584, James had warned poets against choosing political subjects for their verse compositions. Nearly four decades later, the same royal injunction was reiterated in two proclamations issued in December 1620 and July 1621, the first of which accepted the need for 'convenient freedom of speech' but warned all subjects 'from the highest to the lowest, to take heed, how they intermeddle by pen, or speech, with causes of state, and secrets of empire, either at home or abroad'. Subjects should rather preserve a 'modest and reverent regard' and recognize that such matters were 'above their reach and calling'.[58] But when proclamations seemingly proved powerless to prevent the torrent of invective, James joined the conversation and composed a 176-line poem in late 1622 or early 1623 in response to a manuscript libel (no longer extant) entitled 'The Commons Tears'. Entitled 'The Wiper of the People's Tears / The Drier up of Doubts and Fears', it opens:

> Oh stay your teares you who complaine.
> & cry as babes doe, all in vaine.
> Purblind people, why doe you prate   [prate = talk excessively]
> too shallowe for the depth of state
> . . . Kings walke the heavenly milky way
> but you by by-pathes, goe astray
> God & Kings doe passe together
> but vulgar wander light as feather
> . . . Houlde you at the publike beaten way
> Wonder at kings, & them obey.

Ironically, the king's versifying had come full circle. In Scotland, James had tried to rehabilitate royal power by proscribing caustically spiteful verse directed at him and his mother, Queen Mary, while promoting richer forms of cultural authority from the Parnassus of Holyrood. By the end of his English reign, James was still denouncing the 'railing rhymes and vaunting verse' of popular poetasters but had resorted to responding in kind. As he mused:

> Oh what a calling were a king
> if he must giue, or take no thing
> but such as you shall to him bring
> Such were a king but in a playe.[59]

Ceding to the libellers' demands would render him simply a costumed character in a stage play. In his pastoral comedy *As You Like It*, written around 1599, William Shakespeare opened one monologue with the observation that 'All the world's a stage, / And all the men and women merely players'. Composing his *Basilicon Doron* at the same time, and from the vantage-point of the Scottish throne, James had likewise drawn his subjects' attention to similarities between the theatrical majesty of royal power and imaginary kings in stage plays. He had admitted the 'true old saying, that a king is as one set on a stage, whose smallest actions and gestures, all the people gazingly do behold'. No matter how 'precise in the discharging of his office', kings were only judged 'of the substance, by the circumstances; and according to the outward appearance'.[60]

7

Mary, Elizabeth – and James

Directed by Robert Icke, a twenty-first century English production of Friedrich Schiller's play *Mary Stuart* – first performed at Weimar in Germany in 1800 – opened with the two leading actors spinning a coin to determine serendipitously which of them would play the roles of Mary, Queen of Scots, and Elizabeth I in each performance. Like playwrights, historians have long been captivated by the double-helix-like relationship of two iconic queens who never met in person, but whose interactions supplied creative inspiration to generations of novelists, composers and writers including Robert Burns, Gaetano Donizetti, Alexandre Dumas, Friedrich Schiller, Richard Wagner and Stefan Zweig. For James, Mary was the mother whom he last saw in April 1567 at the age of ten months, when his guardian, the Earl of Mar, refused to cede custody, fearing that the infant prince's life might be endangered by his mother's controversial alliance with the volatile and ambitious Earl of Bothwell. Two months later, James was crowned King of Scotland, owing his accession to the deposition of his mother who, from May 1568 onwards, spent the rest of her life detained in England on Elizabeth's orders, before her conviction for treason and execution in 1587.

Neighbouring monarchs, James and the English queen were also double first cousins, since James was related to Elizabeth through his mother's descent from the marriage of Margaret Tudor to James IV of Scotland and also via his father's descent from Margaret Tudor's second marriage to Archibald Douglas, Earl of Angus. Correspondence between the Scottish king and the English queen was sustained over twenty years, while Elizabeth also repeatedly justified intervening in James's affairs in her capacity as his godmother. Entering his thirtieth year in 1595, James admitted in one letter to Elizabeth that she might 'use me as ye list' for 'ye shall never shake me off, by so many knots am I linked unto you'.[1]

*

In their triangulated relations with James, Mary and Elizabeth variously sought to influence, persuade, counsel, flatter, hector, berate and threaten the Scottish king. From 1568 onwards, the conditions of Mary's prolonged detention in England inevitably restricted the freedom and frequency of communications with her son. When James was three, Mary was permitted to send two envoys to Stirling with letters explaining to the Countess of Mar that since it 'was now time' that her son 'began to know something of reading and writing, we have sent him an A.B.C.' and a writing manual. Describing James as 'the thing I love best in this world', Mary also suggested that, since 'we gave him the first coat that he did wear, so would we be glad he had the first doublet and hose' as a gift.[2] Having no children of her own, Elizabeth was inclined to invoke familial tropes and present herself as a metaphorical mother of her country instead. As she lamented to a French ambassador in 1569, she had 'taken great pains to be more than a good mother to the Queen of Scots', yet any child 'who uses and plots against her mother, deserves to have nothing other than a wicked stepmother'.[3] Elizabeth more often eagerly sought news of her Scottish godson. Having visited James in June 1574, just after his eighth birthday, Sir Henry Killigrew reported that he was 'well grown in body and spirit' and 'seemed very glad to hear from' the English queen, using 'pretty speeches' to acknowledge 'how much he was bound to her Majesty, yea, more than to his own mother'.[4] Instructing another envoy four years later, Elizabeth reiterated 'the comfort and great contentation' she derived from hearing propitious reports of James, having always sought 'to preserve him and his realm in quiet, with no less zeal and affection than if he had been her own natural son'.[5]

Detained in different Sheffield strongholds during the 1570s and early 1580s, Mary hoped that her restoration as queen in Scotland could be effected via scenarios that variously envisaged James being transferred to England to remain under Elizabeth's custody or his abduction from Scotland with assistance from her Guise relatives or Spanish Habsburg forces. Amid reports of Mary's involvement in plots for a foreign invasion of England, the Spanish ambassador in

London, Bernadino de Mendoza, reported a diplomatic audience in 1578 in which Elizabeth had 'loudly' referred to James's mother as 'the worst woman in the world, whose head should have been cut off years ago'.[6] When the teenage James then came under the influence of his older French cousin, Esmé Stewart, later Earl and Duke of Lennox, English security concerns fused with familial jealousy. In a draft letter in October 1580, Elizabeth warned her godson of the risks to Scottish stability if he lost her goodwill; he would quickly 'know what it is to prefer an earl of Lennox before a queen of England.'[7] Meeting James the following spring, the English envoy Thomas Randolph advised the king to heed Elizabeth's advice since he had 'found the queen of England a mother far passing her of whom he was born'. James should remain mindful that Elizabeth had 'never sought a foot breadth of the ground of Scotland, nor to hurt the liberty thereof'; she had never tried to remove James to England but had instead expended 'her treasure and the blood of her people to save Scotland'. During the civil wars, when James had been an infant, his mother detained in England and his nobility and people fighting one another, the English queen 'had means enough to have entered and conquered the country, if she had sought it'.[8]

Unsurprisingly, the growing influence of Lennox over James yielded a rapprochement between Mary and her son. In January 1581, James wrote to his mother from 'Lislebour' – a francophone name for Edinburgh – denying responsibility for returning unopened earlier letters that she had sent to him. Later that year, Lennox oversaw the treason conviction (for complicity in Lord Darnley's murder fourteen years earlier) of the pro-English former regent the Earl of Morton, who was executed in June. In London, Mendoza reported that Elizabeth had been observed sitting 'alone in a window recess', angrily denouncing to herself 'that false Scots urchin, for whom I have done so much!' She had continued to mutter frustration that, despite benefiting from Morton's efficient governance, James had ordered 'him to be arrested and his head smitten off! What can be expected from the double-dealing of such an urchin as this?'[9]

Encouraged by the promotion of francophile interests in Edinburgh, Mary liaised with her French Guise relations to devise a proposed 'association' whereby she and James would rule as joint sovereigns of Scotland. In October 1581, she requested Elizabeth to

it should never be'.[20] That July, a Convention of Estates empowered the king to conclude an offensive and defensive alliance with England, signifying a reorientation in foreign policy whereby Protestant Anglo-Scottish amity replaced the Franco-Scottish 'Auld Alliance'. Acutely disappointed, Mary continued to maintain that her son only 'held his crown as a usurper'; as her keeper Sir Amias Paulet reported to Walsingham, while Mary regretted James's refusal to pursue the proposed 'association' and had treated her unkindly, '"yet", said she, "the love of a mother is tender"'.[21]

*

For Elizabeth, a Scottish alliance offered a means of reducing England's isolation amid escalating continental geopolitical and confessional tensions. To support beleaguered Protestant interests, the English queen was supplying financial and military assistance to Dutch rebels to overthrow Spanish rule, while the secret Treaty of Joinville concluded by Philip II of Spain and the Guise leaders of the Catholic League in December 1584 had aimed to prevent the Protestant Henri of Navarre from succeeding as French king. In Scotland, however, James continued to maximize his diplomatic freedom of manoeuvre by maintaining friendly relations with his French relatives, claiming to the Duke of Guise in August 1583 that he could imagine no greater honour than to be 'so near a relative' to one 'who is universally acknowledged to be the first captain of our time'.[22] Meanwhile, despite appointing a Scottish ambassador to the French court, a promised pension from Henri III failed to materialize. Determined to dissuade James from pursuing alliances with other powers, Elizabeth reminded him during the summer of 1585 that he 'who hath two strings to one bow may shoot stronger, but never straight', repeating verbatim advice that she had given to James's mother nearly two decades earlier. Assisted by sophisticated espionage networks, she further admonished James that 'if you suppose that princes' causes be veiled so covertly that no intelligence may betray them, deceive not yourself; we old foxes can find shifts to save ourselves by others' malice, and come by knowledge of greatest secret'.[23]

Elizabeth's counsel to her godson, accompanied by presents of horses and bloodhounds, proved effective. Addressing her as 'madame and dearest sister' in June 1585, James acknowledged that her gifts, letters and envoys 'seemed rather to have proceeded from some *alter ego* than 'as I ought to do of my uncle and friend', while advising the envoy to remind Henri 'that I am a king, as he is, not comparing in greatness, but in dignity'. Free to form whatever foreign alliances he wished, 'I need no more of his consent than he hath of mine, or my predecessors, in any league that he or his predecessors had made.'[31] Also in Edinburgh was Monsieur de Courcelles – secretary to the French ambassador in London – who blamed pro-English factions at James's court for letting the king 'go so far as to imagine himself henceforth heir of England without any difficulty'.[32] Signed on 6 July 1586, the Treaty of Berwick confirmed an Anglo-Scottish alliance that was 'offensive and defensive for the causes of the true religion', with both nations undertaking to remain neutral in the event of the other being invaded. No mention was made of any financial subsidy nor of James's claim to succeed to the English throne.[33]

*

Only a month after the Treaty of Berwick's conclusion, relations between James and Elizabeth were, however, jeopardized when charges were laid against Mary of conspiring to kill the English queen via involvement in the 'Babington Plot'. Devised by a Catholic landowner, Anthony Babington, the conspiracy had envisaged a popular uprising, Elizabeth's death, and a Spanish invasion of England. Framed by English intelligence agents, Mary had been lured into supplying tacit approval of the Plot in an encrypted letter dictated to Babington in July which subsequently led to hearings at Fotheringhay Castle in Northamptonshire and a Star Chamber conviction for treason in October. When the English Parliament convened at Westminster shortly afterwards, MPs unanimously endorsed a motion petitioning Elizabeth to pass a sentence of execution against the Scottish queen. On 4 December 1586, Elizabeth issued a proclamation confirming the capital sentence against Mary but clarifying that royal consent had only been given after visitations from MPs and peers who had been obliged to fall 'upon their knees, pray, beseech, and with many reasons of great force and importance, move and press us' to pursue this course of action.[34]

Initially, James appeared relatively unconcerned. When first informed of his mother's alleged involvement in the Babington Plot, he had opined, in a conversation reported by Courcelles, that his mother 'might well drink the ale and beer which herself had brewed'. Having sworn admitted in one letter to Elizabeth that she might 'use me as ye list' for 'ye shall never shake me off, by so many knots am I linked unto you'.[1]

*

In their triangulated relations with James, Mary and Elizabeth variously sought to influence, persuade, counsel, flatter, hector, berate and threaten the Scottish king. From 1568 onwards, the conditions of Mary's prolonged detention in England inevitably restricted the freedom and frequency of communications with her son. When James was three, Mary was permitted to send two envoys to Stirling with letters explaining to the Countess of Mar that since it 'was now time' that her son 'began to know something of reading and writing, we have sent him an A.B.C.' and a writing manual. Describing James as 'the thing I love best in this world', Mary also suggested that, since 'we gave him the first coat that he did wear, so would we be glad he had the first doublet and hose' as a gift.[2] Having no children of her own, Elizabeth was inclined to invoke familial tropes and present herself as a metaphorical mother of her country instead. As she lamented to a French ambassador in 1569, she had 'taken great pains to be more than a good mother to the Queen of Scots', yet any child 'who uses and plots against her mother, deserves to have nothing other than a wicked stepmother'.[3] Elizabeth more often eagerly sought news of her Scottish godson. Having visited James in June 1574, just after his eighth birthday, Sir Henry Killigrew reported that he was 'well grown in body and spirit' and 'seemed very glad to hear from' the English queen, using 'pretty speeches' to acknowledge 'how much he was bound to her Majesty, yea, more than to his own mother'.[4] Instructing another envoy four years later, Elizabeth reiterated 'the comfort and great contentation' she derived from hearing propitious reports of James, having always sought 'to preserve him and his realm in quiet, with no less zeal and affection than if he had been her own natural son'.[5]

Detained in different Sheffield strongholds during the 1570s and early 1580s, Mary hoped that her restoration as queen in Scotland could be effected via scenarios that variously envisaged James being transferred to England to remain under Elizabeth's custody or his abduction from Scotland with assistance from her Guise relatives or Spanish Habsburg forces. Amid reports of Mary's involvement in plots for a foreign invasion of England, the Spanish ambassador in

London, Bernadino de Mendoza, reported a diplomatic audience in 1578 in which Elizabeth had 'loudly' referred to James's mother as 'the worst woman in the world, whose head should have been cut off years ago'.[6] When the teenage James then came under the influence of his older French cousin, Esmé Stewart, later Earl and Duke of Lennox, English security concerns fused with familial jealousy. In a draft letter in October 1580, Elizabeth warned her godson of the risks to Scottish stability if he lost her goodwill; he would quickly 'know what it is to prefer an earl of Lennox before a queen of England.'[7] Meeting James the following spring, the English envoy Thomas Randolph advised the king to heed Elizabeth's advice since he had 'found the queen of England a mother far passing her of whom he was born'. James should remain mindful that Elizabeth had 'never sought a foot breadth of the ground of Scotland, nor to hurt the liberty thereof'; she had never tried to remove James to England but had instead expended 'her treasure and the blood of her people to save Scotland'. During the civil wars, when James had been an infant, his mother detained in England and his nobility and people fighting one another, the English queen 'had means enough to have entered and conquered the country, if she had sought it'.[8]

Unsurprisingly, the growing influence of Lennox over James yielded a rapprochement between Mary and her son. In January 1581, James wrote to his mother from 'Lislebour' – a francophone name for Edinburgh – denying responsibility for returning unopened earlier letters that she had sent to him. Later that year, Lennox oversaw the treason conviction (for complicity in Lord Darnley's murder fourteen years earlier) of the pro-English former regent the Earl of Morton, who was executed in June. In London, Mendoza reported that Elizabeth had been observed sitting 'alone in a window recess', angrily denouncing to herself 'that false Scots urchin, for whom I have done so much!' She had continued to mutter frustration that, despite benefiting from Morton's efficient governance, James had ordered 'him to be arrested and his head smitten off! What can be expected from the double-dealing of such an urchin as this?'[9]

Encouraged by the promotion of francophile interests in Edinburgh, Mary liaised with her French Guise relations to devise a proposed 'association' whereby she and James would rule as joint sovereigns of Scotland. In October 1581, she requested Elizabeth to a nationwide Bond of Association to preserve Elizabeth's life in 1584, 'she ought to have kept her promise'. But as a trial and capital conviction appeared more likely, James revisited Mary's situation, accounting it 'the strangest that ever was heard of, the like not to be found in any story of the world'. Indeed, James asked Courcelles if 'he had ever read of a sovereign prince that had been detained prisoner so long time without cause by king or prince her neighbour', and one 'that in the end would put her to death?'[35]

To his agent in London, William Keith, James admitted that 'whole Scotland [was] incensed with this matter' and, in a spiteful swipe at Elizabeth's parentage, recalled that, even if Henry VIII was infamous for 'beheading of his bedfellow [Anne Boleyn] . . . yet that tragedy was far inferior to this'. James directed Keith to ensure that Elizabeth read the entirety of his letter in order to 'see the inward parts of my heart', where she would find 'a great jewel of honesty toward her locked up in a coffer of perplexity'.[36] Elizabeth herself wrote to James in January 1587, directly inviting him to 'transfigure yourself into my state, and suppose what you ought to do'. Given the evidence adduced against his mother, should she 'keep the serpent that poisons me?'[37] Yet James still accounted the execution of one divinely ordained and anointed monarch – as well as a woman and blood relative – by another of equal status as unthinkable. Describing the very prospect as a 'monstrous thing', James refused to credit that 'my nearest neighbour, being in straightest friendship with me, shall rigorously put to death a free sovereign prince and my natural mother, alike in estate and sex to her . . . and touching her nearly in proximity of blood'.[38]

Despite later protesting that Mary's death warrant had not been intended for immediate use, Elizabeth signed it on 1 February 1587. James's mother was beheaded at Fotheringhay Castle a week later. In the version of events presented to the outside world, Mary's execution was presented as an unfortunate 'accident' for which Elizabeth was not directly responsible; rather, her Secretary, Davison, became the regime's scapegoat, having been blamed for removing the warrant from the queen's possession. When news of Mary's death reached Edinburgh, crowds reacted angrily to the English execution of a Scottish Stuart, albeit one whose queenship they had forcibly overthrown twenty years earlier. Dispatched by Elizabeth to inform James in person, the courtier, Robert Carey, was denied entry at the Scottish border; had he 'gone in', he would 'have been murdered'.[39] In late February, James wrote to Elizabeth, sardonically indicating that he would 'not wrong you so far as not to judge honourably of your unspotted part' in his mother's death but did anticipate 'that ye will give me at this time such a full satisfaction in all respects as shall be a mean to strengthen and unite this isle'.[40] Meanwhile, Anglo-Scottish diplomatic relations were severed.

With entry into Scotland now denied to Elizabeth's envoys, Walsingham dispatched a lengthy missive to James's deputy Chancellor, John Maitland, in early March, alarmed by rumours that the Scottish king was considering an armed response to 'this remediless accident'. Walsingham supplied a detailed case for restraint based on considerations of realpolitik, insisting that James's claim to succeed as English king would be seriously weakened if he started an Anglo-Scottish war, given that 'the ancient enmity between the two nations, [was] now forgotten'. English military force would, in any case, quickly overwhelm any Scottish attack, while foreign 'princes are not so ready in these days to embrace other mens' quarrels'. With flattering references to James's 'singular judgement' and 'the excellency of his Highness's education', Walsingham trusted that he realized the futility of an aggressive response. Moreover, 'if the late queen had been innocent, revenge had been necessarily just and honourable; but being culpable, contrary'.[41] Seeming to share Walsingham's analysis, James refrained from overt action. Yet he increasingly found himself caught between the need to acknowledge his incensed subjects' demands for vengeance to defend the Stuart dynasty's honour and Scotland's independent sovereignty with a desire to preserve the recent achievement of Anglo-Scottish amity and his own claim to the English throne.

Abroad, the diplomatic rumour-mill went into overdrive. In December 1587, the Venetian ambassador in Paris relayed French reports 'that the King of Scotland, in great force, had entered England, and was burning the country', before adding that 'the English ambassador asserts positively that the news is false'.[42] Rumours of an imminent Spanish invasion of England were, by contrast, more credible, and focused attention on James's likely response. Sent to Berwick to monitor Anglo-Scottish relations, Henry, Lord Hunsdon – Robert Carey's father and a veteran diplomat – used a network of trusted intermediaries to maintain contact with James's court. In December, Hunsdon advised William Cecil, Lord Burghley, that James had let it be known that he was prepared to receive, and respond to, an overture from Elizabeth, but any missive 'must be sent to me, and I must send it in, for he is loath to have it yet known of any dealing between Her Majesty and him'.[43] Two months later, Hunsdon was dismayed at the lack of material response from the English court. Admitting that 'nothing will be done here without money', Hunsdon could not imagine 'a prince that is so far alienated from her as he [James] is'. If Elizabeth wanted to be assured of his amity, 'deeds must supply want, and he must have it either of Her Majesty or some other prince, for otherwise, he shall not be able to rule his nobility'.[44]

In August 1588, Elizabeth's envoy in Edinburgh, William Ashby, returned the same advice, reporting that James was seeking conferral of an English dukedom, an annual pension of £5,000, and a royal guard funded by England. With 'an eye to the back door' from Scotland into England, Ashby ventured that 'every pound her Majesty sends hither now will save twenty later, and many a life'.[45] Only a week earlier, however, James had reassured Elizabeth that, in the event of a hostile attack, he would 'behave myself not as a stranger and foreign prince, but as your natural son and compatriot of your country in all respects'.[46] In the failed Armada attempt launched by Philip II that same month, James adhered to his promise and remained loyal to English interests.

*

Securing the Scottish 'back door' remained critical. At the start of 1589, an English spy in Edinburgh, Thomas Fowler, advised Walsingham that, 'always, money will quench the hottest fire that they will kindle'. Outwardly at least, James seemed concerned 'not to offend the subjects of England, and boasts how well he understands the language, and can speak it, and how much he delights in English past-times of which – besides hunting – the maw is one'.[47] (Now a card game known as 'Twenty-Five', the 'maw' was evidently a current obsession for James; the previous month, another English agent, Roger Aston, apologized for cutting short a letter after being 'called for to play at the maw with the king').[48] Away from the card table, the diplomatic stakes remained high. In the spring of 1589, the English authorities intercepted letters from prominent Catholic nobles in Scotland to Philip II and his nephew, the Duke of Parma, commiserating over the Armada's failure and promising support in the event of a renewed Spanish assault on England. Writing to James in March, Elizabeth referred directly to Mary's execution in advising her godson to see, by 'late examples . . . how dishonourable it is to prolong to do by right, that [which] after they are driven to do by extremes'. Beseeching him to awake 'out of your long slumber, and deal like a king who will ever reign alone in his own', she demanded that all Armada refugees be immediately expelled from Scotland 'for your own sake, [and] not the least for mine'.[49]

Three years later, royal exasperation was re-ignited by James's apparently dilatory response when English agents intercepted another Catholic agitator, George Kerr, carrying eight blank sheets of paper signed by the same nobles which Kerr admitted were intended to agree details of Scottish support in a future Spanish invasion. Alerting James to the 'Spanish blanks' conspiracy, Elizabeth reminded him that, 'since you first breathed', she had always protected him, making 'myself the bulwark betwixt you and your harms'. In another missive, she cited reports of James 'cherishing some men for open crimes' and wished they were rather 'strange dreams' since 'at my waking, I should find them fables'. Insisting that it 'likes you to demand my counsel', Elizabeth observed 'I find so many ways your state so unjointed, that it needs a more skilful bone-setter than I to join each part in his right place'. When James later explained that, following Kerr's escape from custody, he had been advised that there was insufficient evidence to try the rebel lords for treason, Elizabeth challenged his reliance on the view of 'one lewd advocate'. Speaking from English experience where – contrary to Scots legal practice – defendants were denied access to defence counsel, the English queen admitted in October 1593 that 'it seems a paradox to me' that, in seeking to obtain justice for the Crown, an advocate could 'come in open view to plead against his master. Their office is, as to do right, so [to] do the sovereign no wrong'. In the same missive, Elizabeth then chided James for his apparent spinelessness in relation to his refractory older cousin Francis Stewart, Earl of Bothwell, blasphemously exclaiming: 'And [as] for Bothwell, Jesus!'[50] Two months later, the queen, still scolding, objected that 'it vexes me to see a seduced king' and implored him: 'for your own sake, play the king, and let your subjects see you respect yourself and neither hide nor suffer danger and dishonour'.[51] Infuriated by Elizabeth's hypocrisy in lecturing him about his timidity in suppressing opposition while simultaneously sheltering Bothwell and funding his supporters, James retorted by 'repeating the first words of your last letter, only the sex changed' to deplore, from his perspective, 'the evident spectacle of a seduced queen'.[52]

Relations between James and Elizabeth were complicated by payments made by the English Crown to the Scottish court from the mid-1580s onwards. The Treaty of Berwick had contained no reference to any regular pension and, in practice, English subsidy payments fluctuated in relation to the strategic importance Elizabeth placed on securing James's goodwill. Between May 1586 and December 1602, James received a total of £58,500 sterling from the English Crown, averaging around £3,400 sterling a year or around a sixth of his annual income.[53] Sporadically paid, the subsidy reflected the inherently asymmetrical nature of relations between the two monarchs and was underscored in the terminology by which English ministers usually referred to Elizabeth's generous 'gratuity' while James and his court were inclined to chafe if the promised 'annuity' failed to appear.[54] In December 1591, James complained to Elizabeth that her payment seemed to have 'turned from an honourable annuity to a voluntary uncertainty', obliging him to appear a weary 'suitor' in a guise unacceptably demeaning for 'one who was not born to be a beggar but to be begged at'. In brief, 'a short refusal had less displeased me than an answerless and disdainful reply'. By the time Elizabeth replied the next month, James had survived Bothwell's attack on Holyroodhouse. The English queen confessed 'I know not what to write, so little do I like to lose labour in vain.' Since James had continually failed to follow her advice in taking decisive action against refractory nobles, Elizabeth concluded, 'Well, I will pray for you, that God will unseal your eyes, that too long have been shut.' Regarding his financial requests, she added, 'I have made so reasonable answer as in reason may well content'.[55]

But in her final years, Elizabeth was confronted by challenges from her own refractory nobles, notably Robert Devereux, Earl of Essex. After learning that Essex had been corresponding with the Scottish king, Elizabeth received hot denials from James that he had been 'preparing untimeously of your funerals' in October 1600. Feigning surprise that his 'dearest sister' might also attach credence to separate rumours of communications between the Scottish court and the papacy, James claimed to wish instead that she might know 'all the secret counsels of my heart towards you'.[56] Yet that Christmas, Essex warned James that William Cecil's son, Robert, and other English ministers were 'juggling with our enemies' by promoting the succession claims to Elizabeth's Crown of Isabella, daughter of Philip III of Spain, and fomenting 'devilish plots with your Majesty's own subjects against your person and life'.[57] In an attempt to persuade Elizabeth to abandon her reliance on Cecil, Essex disastrously tried to provoke a popular rising in London in February 1601, for which he was convicted of treason and executed. Thereafter, James embarked on a covert, and likewise potentially treasonable, correspondence with several English Privy Councillors, including Cecil.[58] Following Elizabeth's death on 24 March 1603, James also quickly recast the nature of his relations with his predecessor, blithely boasting to the French ambassador in June that 'in Scotland, long before the death of [Elizabeth], he had directed her whole Council, and governed her ministers, by whom he was better served and obeyed than herself'.[59]

*

Having been laid to rest in Henry VII's chapel in Westminster Abbey in late April 1603, Elizabeth was unable to refute her godson's hubris. Nor was she permitted to rest undisturbed for, after his accession as English king, James oversaw a remarkable reconfiguration of the royal chapel that involved not only disinterring Elizabeth, but also moving the corpse of his mother from its initial resting-place in Peterborough Cathedral to the royal chapel at Westminster. After he had made James aware of the desirability of commissioning a suitably imposing tomb for Elizabeth, the queen's former Secretary, Sir Robert Cecil, now Viscount Cranborne, reported to a colleague in March 1605 that the king had responded by suggesting that 'when there was more store of money, others should be remembered, which your Lordship may guess whom he meant'.[60] While James was willing to honour his godmother with a new tomb, he also intended the same obsequies for his natural mother.

The first queen to be moved was Elizabeth, whose new tomb was completed in 1606 at a cost of £965 sterling. Initially buried in the vault under Henry VII's tomb behind the chapel altar, Elizabeth was moved to the north aisle and her coffin placed atop that of her Catholic half-sister, Mary Tudor. Elizabeth's new tomb bore a Latin epitaph – possibly composed by Cranborne or the historian William Camden – that described the late queen as 'a septuagenarian quietly freed by death' and remembered Henry VIII's daughters as 'Partners both in throne and grave, here rest we two sisters, Elizabeth and Mary, in the hope of one resurrection.'[61] Having consigned the two childless queens to the chapel's north aisle, James then reserved for his own interment the space in Henry VII's vault formerly occupied by Elizabeth's coffin, as fitting confirmation of his own double descent from Henry VII through both his mother and father.

Mary Stuart's larger tomb took longer to complete and, with eventual costs for labour and materials exceeding £1,500 sterling, cost at least £600 more than Elizabeth's. In 1612, James ordered the exhumation of his mother's body, which was brought from Peterborough and placed in the new tomb in the chapel's south aisle, between those of Henry VII's mother, Lady Margaret Beaufort, and his paternal grandmother, Margaret Douglas, Countess of Lennox. A Latin epitaph for Mary, composed by the Earl of Northampton and three times longer than Elizabeth's epitaph, included a reworking of a tribute originally devised for the twelfth-century English Empress Matilda:

> Great by marriage, greater by birth, but greatest by offspring,
> Here is buried the daughter, wife and mother of kings.[62]

Honouring Mary's marriage to the French king, the epitaph did not mention the queen's subsequent unions with Darnley and Bothwell nor clarify James's paternity. The life-size white stone effigy confirmed Mary to have been visibly younger than Elizabeth when, as the epitaph attested, she had been 'struck down by the axe, a dangerous example to kings'. But given that her grandson Charles I would be publicly struck down by the common executioner's axe in 1649, it was perhaps unfortunate that Mary's epitaph expressed the hope:

> Let it be forbidden to slay monarchs, so that in future
> This land of Britain may never flow with royal blood.[63]

8

Paterfamilias

In *Basilicon Doron*, James described marriage as 'one of the greatest actions that a man does in all his time'; it was, indeed, 'the greatest earthly felicity or misery, that can come to a man'. By the time the king committed his thoughts about matrimony to paper, he was in his mid-thirties and had been married to his Danish consort, Queen Anna, for a decade. As James explained to his son and heir, Prince Henry, marriage was triply designed to satisfy male lust, facilitate procreation, and provide a man with 'a helper like himself'. In practical terms, the king supplied three maxims for a successful royal marriage. A wife should be permitted 'never to meddle with the political government of the commonwealth' but confine herself to 'the economic rule of the house'. Secondly, since 'women are the frailest sex', ensuring the virtue and chastity of a wife's female attendants was essential. Finally, husband and wife should never be 'both angry at once': 'when ye see her in passion, ye should with reason danton [suppress] yours'. Only when an incensed wife had 'come to herself' would she be receptive to realizing 'her offence, and reverence your rebuke'. Having delineated the proper uxorial remit, James reiterated that a husband must teach his wife 'not to be curious in things that belong her not'.[1]

James had not been overly swift in embracing matrimony himself. After his marriage to Anna had been undertaken by proxy in August 1589, the twenty-three-year-old king penned an open letter 'to the people of Scotland' that October, at a time when he had yet to meet his new wife and ahead of Anna's anticipated arrival in Scotland as his subjects' new queen. As James acknowledged, 'it is manifestly known to all how far I was generally found fault with by all men for the delaying so long of my marriage'. But dynastic considerations had persuaded James to pursue matrimony. As he recognized, 'I was alone, without father or mother, brother or sister, king of this realm and heir apparent of England'. Lamenting 'my nakedness', the king's solo status had 'made me to be weak and my enemies stark [powerful]': 'one man was as no man, and the want of hope of succession bred disdain'. With such political concerns 'hourly objected', James had accepted the need 'to hasten the treaty of my marriage' but candidly admitted that 'as to my own nature, God is my witness I could have abstained longer'.[2]

By the time *Basilicon Doron* was published in 1599, James had accomplished his dynastic duty in that he and Anna had produced three children: Prince Henry (born in 1594) and two daughters, Princesses Elizabeth and Margaret (born in 1596 and 1598). Given the importance of producing healthy offspring, James also included advice in *Basilicon Doron* regarding the careful selection of a wife. His son should ensure that any prospective spouse 'be of a whole and clean race, not subject to the hereditary sickness, either of the soul or the body'. For as the king reasoned, since 'a man will be careful to breed horses and dogs of good kinds', he should be at least as concerned about 'the breed of his own loins'.[3] For kings, procreation also brought political strength. When congratulating his brother-in-law, Christian IV of Denmark, on the birth of a son in 1603, James avouched that he and Anna were 'moved both for your sake, and for the sake of the kingdom itself, over which you are ruling'. Just as 'children are a source of solace to parents, thus are they a source of support for kings; for the more children there are, the deeper are the roots and the more numerous are the supports, upon which the stability of a kingdom rests'.[4]

Marriage was, moreover, both a sacred vow and a personal commitment and its observance required fidelity and abstention. As James mused in *Basilicon Doron*, although 'fornication is thought but a light and venial sin', it was irrational to 'crave to be joined with a pure virgin, if your body be polluted'. For 'why should the one half be clean and the other defiled?' Political ramifications also attached to what the king denounced as 'the filthy vice of adultery', citing the example of his grandfather, James V, who had fathered three legitimate children as well as around eight illegitimate offspring. 'By his adultery', James claimed that his grandfather had 'bred the wreck of his lawful daughter and heir' – James's mother, Mary – since it had been James V's eldest natural son, James Stewart, Earl of Moray, who became 'that bastard, who unnaturally rebelled, and produced the ruin of his own sovereign and sister'. After his half-sister's deposition from power, Moray had served as James's first regent but was assassinated by one of Mary's supporters in 1570. The volatile repercussions then extended into the next 'unlawful generation' of the king's own cousins, as 'Bothwell's treacherous attempts can bear witness'. For James V, the dynastic 'reward of his incontinency' had been the infant deaths of two sons in 1540 and 1541, followed by the birth of Mary in 1542, 'whom he never had the hap [chance], so much as once to see or bless before his death' after the Battle of Solway Moss. James V had thus bequeathed 'a double curse' on the Scots in leaving only a female 'newborn babe . . . to reign over them'. By contrast, James VI prided himself on his 'greater continency', which had been rewarded with the births of Prince Henry and his two sisters, with hopes that further progeny would yet 'continue and increase' his dynasty.[5]

*

During James's minority, marriage plans were serially mooted on his behalf. In March 1582, Sir Francis Walsingham had sought to align Scottish interests with English policy via a Protestant match for James, suggesting Frederick II of Denmark's daughters as suitable. According to the Spanish ambassador in London, Bernadino de Mendoza, Elizabeth had, however, discouraged Walsingham from 'worrying her so much about marrying the boy "before he was out of the shell"' on the grounds 'that there would be time for that afterwards'.[6] But during James's detention by the Ruthven regime in 1583, rumours reached Elizabeth that her court favourite, Robert Dudley, Earl of Leicester, was secretly negotiating James's marriage to his step-daughter. As Mendoza reported, the queen was so outraged by this idea 'as to say that she would rather allow the king [James] to take her crown away than see him married to the daughter of such a she-wolf'. Were Leicester to persist in this idea, Elizabeth vowed to take revenge on his countess, Lettice Knollys, 'and proclaim her all over Christendom for the bad woman she was, and prove that her husband was a cuckold'.[7] At the same time, English ministers feared that James's imprisoned mother, Mary, might secure a Catholic match for James as a means of furthering her attempts to regain power in Scotland. In March 1584, for example, the Venetian ambassador in Madrid recounted discussions sponsored by Philip II that envisaged James marrying Margaret, a daughter of the widowed Empress of the Holy Roman Empire. But as the envoy explained, 'everything went wrong, for the Empress said she would rather make a nun of her daughter than marry her to a King of Scotland', much to the Spanish king's anger.[8]

There were compelling reasons for a potential Scottish–Danish match, given the Lutheran beliefs of the country's Oldenburg ruling dynasty, the fifteenth-century marriage between James's great-great-grandfather, James III, and Margaret of Denmark, and the mercantile hopes of traders with the Baltic that a Danish consort would bring commercial advantages for Scottish ships entering the Øresund. Informal discussions had taken place in 1585 and 1586, before James appointed his former tutor, Peter Young, and a judge as ambassadors to the Danish court during the summer of 1587. When asked if they should raise with Frederick II the subject of Mary's recent execution on Elizabeth's orders, James advised his envoys to 'exaggerate the fact as far as you can, but touch the names of no actors'. If asked about James's response to his mother's death, they should 'mell [meddle] not with that' and, if they encountered English diplomats in Denmark, they should behave 'coldly towards them, and dip into no purpose'.[9] But the mission ended inconclusively after Frederick pleaded indisposition through toothache while also citing concerns over the unresolved future of the Orkney and Shetland islands that had been given to Scotland in 1472 as a pledge for Queen Margaret's (unpaid) dowry, but whose restitution Frederick hoped to secure through a future marriage contract.[10] On Frederick's death in February 1588, marriage negotiations resumed with the regency government formed on behalf of his heir, eleven-year-old Christian IV.

A parallel suit was simultaneously presented at the Scottish court by James's poetic muse, the sieur Du Bartas, on behalf of Henri of Navarre's sister, Catherine of Bourbon. In February 1588, Du Bartas alluded to the desirability 'of mating her [Catherine] with a Christian prince' and enthusiastically recommended James to Henri as 'a potentate, handsome, brave, eloquent, active and discreet – in short, your own image and picture'. Writing to James later that year, the Protestant Henri celebrated 'such an affinity between our two kingdoms and churches' and flattered James by insisting that 'all Christendom looks for great things from you, and if the two nations [France and Scotland] were as closely united geographically as they are in friendship, religion and interests, our strength would be irresistible'. The following month, a French envoy to James reaffirmed Henri's admiration, averring that 'never a day passes when he does not speak of you', hoping 'that you may both meet some day and unite to chase papistry and confusion from the world'.[11] While Henri's conversion to Catholicism four years later vitiated that particular aspiration, Catherine's dynastic prestige was enhanced by her brother's accession as King of France, following Henri III's assassination in August 1589.

By then, however, James had resolved to marry the fourteen-year-old Danish princess, Anna. As the king explained to his Privy Councillors, he had spent a fortnight in seclusion seeking God's direction 'to move his heart the way' that seemed most fit, considering the physical portraits, as well as rival diplomatic benefits, of a union with either the Oldenburg or Bourbon dynasties.[12] The previous year, the English spy in Edinburgh, Thomas Fowler, had informed Walsingham that the Scottish king was instinctively 'untoward' marriage and 'never regards the company of any woman, not so much as in any dalliance'. Strenuous suits on Anna's behalf had nevertheless been made by Young and others who had seen off the French competition by hinting that the thirty-year-old Catherine of Navarre was 'old and crooked, and something worse, if all were known'.[13] In May 1589, Fowler claimed that Edinburgh's Provost, bailiffs and burgesses had marched to the home of the Scottish Chancellor, John Maitland of Thirlestane, to warn 'that if the marriage also with Denmark went not forward' – being frustrated by those who selfishly preferred to keep the king single – 'he would die for it, and all the English faction here'. To calm tensions, James had supplied assurances that, assuming suitable terms could be agreed, he was keen to accept a Danish bride which so satisfied Edinburgh's civic dignitaries that they were claiming 'by proud, boasting threats' to have accomplished the king's marriage.[14]

Formal instructions drawn up in June 1589 stipulated an immediate 'tocher' or dowry of £1m (Scots), all Scots to 'be naturalised Danish', removal of all commercial dues on Scottish ships, and mutual guarantees of armed assistance if either country suffered hostile attack. Disconcerted by the scale of James's demands, Danish negotiators eventually agreed a dowry of £150,000 (Scots) in exchange for Anna being granted properties in Scotland worth double that amount, confirmation that the Orkneys and Shetlands would remain in Scots ownership for James's lifetime, and a commitment to mutual defence, with naturalization and other requests quietly jettisoned. Although the new terms were approved by the Scottish court in July, the English ambassador, William Ashby, judged James to be 'but a cold wooer' who was 'not hasty of marriage, but will match with the Danes to please his boroughs and merchants'.[15]

A proxy marriage between James and Anna took place at Kronborg Castle in Elsinore on 20 August 1589. James was represented by George Keith, Earl Marischal, who took the king's place in the civil wedding and banquet before participating in a bedding ceremony – to provide symbolic confirmation of marriage's deferred consummation – observed by twelve nobles from Scotland and another dozen from Denmark.[16] When James was informed of his newly wedded state a week after the ceremony, Ashby observed that 'this hasty marriage makes the king half amazed'. While James 'knows not which way to turn' and had no residence suitably furnished to receive his new queen, Ashby advised Walsingham that 'his only refuge is to her Majesty' and urged English funds on the grounds that 'a penny now sent will be better accepted than a pound hereafter'. But although Anna set sail for Scotland from Copenhagen in early September, her fleet was beset by autumnal storms and westerly winds. For over a fortnight, James stayed at Seton House in East Lothian, scanning the Firth of Forth for sight of the Danish fleet. On 24 September, a public fast was ordered, and prayers were offered for the queen's safe arrival while Ashby detected a visible change in James's demeanour: he was now distraught, 'as a true lover, wholly passionate, and half out of patience with the wind and the weather'. Frustrated by the lack of news, the king 'thinks every day a year till he see his joy and love approach'.[17] Penning two sonnets in 'Complaint against the Contrary Winds' hindering Anna's arrival, James artfully presented his anguish in terms of physical pain and berated 'cruel Cupid', insisting:

> No medicine my sicknesse may asswage
> Nor cataplasme cure my wounde I see
> Through deadie shott aliue I daylie dye
> I frie in flammes of that envenomed darte[18]

Dispatched to investigate, Colonel William Stewart eventually located the Danish fleet near the island of Flekkerøy in southern Norway, which was part of the Oldenburgs' composite kingdom of Denmark-Norway. On 10 October, James's court finally received first-hand information from the Danish diplomat Steen Bille of the litany of disasters endured by Anna's party, which had included on-board explosions and fatalities, persistent gales, collisions at sea, and extensive damage to the fleet. As Fowler reported, Bille had also brought letters to the king from his new wife that were 'indeed tragical discourses, pitiful, for the said queen was in extreme danger of drowning in her own ship' and constantly seasick.[19] By unhappy coincidence, almost exactly three centuries earlier, in September 1290, the seven-year-old Margaret, Maid of Norway, had died in Orkney after setting sail from Bergen as Scotland's queen designate, thereby unleashing a protracted succession dispute and prolonged Anglo-Scottish 'Wars of Independence'.

In October 1589, James's response was to travel to meet Anna, explaining in his open letter to his Scottish subjects that he would now 'make possible on my part that which was impossible on hers'. The decision to undertake the voyage was, moreover, defiantly his alone; advisers such as Chancellor Maitland should not be held responsible 'as if I were an unreasonable creature or a bairn, that could do nothing of myself'. Initially, James had envisaged sending ships on his behalf but had found his Privy Councillors so reluctant on grounds of cost that he had been impelled 'to avow in great vehemency that', if there was no alternative, 'I should go myself alone, if it were but in one ship'.[20] Before James's departure, Fowler admitted to the English court that there was 'so extreme secrecy used in this voyage as not any nobleman in Scotland knows of his stealing away, more than by conjecture'. Predicting that 'surely here will be shortly a confused state as ever was', Fowler was especially concerned about James's unpredictable cousin, reporting that 'the earl Bothwell swears, if the king be once gone, he will enter England with fire and sword.'[21]

To James directly, Ashby expressed alarm that the king seemed 'determined secretly to embark, and to hazard your person in this fleet'. Although the English ambassador warned that such a venture 'will greatly amaze your good and faithful subjects, and make the world' account him 'rather a passionate lover than a circumspect prince', the king assured Ashby of his trust in Elizabeth's 'favourable interpretation of this our peregrination'.[22] Clearly, if James were to suffer shipwreck or other accident and die on his voyage, Scotland would be left without a ruler. But in unfinished verse, the king reiterated his political rationale for pursuing marriage and, by implication, his reasons for now seeking its consummation, while simultaneously also confirming his aversion to gynaecocracy (female rule):

> And lacking parents, brethren, bairns, or anie neare of kinn
> Incace of death, or absence to supplie my place therin
> And cheeflie in so kitle a land, where few   [kitle = difficult to manage]
>   remember can
> For to haue seene gouerning there a King that was a man.[23]

In a communication intended for his Privy Councillors after his departure, James outlined interim arrangements for Scotland's governance, indicating his intention 'to go and return in twenty days, weather favouring'. In his absence, Councillors were to reside in Edinburgh under the presidency of Scotland's most senior noble, Ludovick Stewart, Duke of Lennox (the fifteen-year-old son of Esmé Stewart), with the mercurial Earl of Bothwell as Lennox's deputy.[24] Provision was also made to manufacture a duplicate royal seal and signet since James would retain the originals.

Leaving Leith on 22 October aboard a borrowed ship, the *James Royal*, with around a hundred attendants, James arrived at Flekkerøy in southern Norway on 29 October and travelled to Oslo where he met his new wife on 19 November in the Great Hall of the Old Bishops' Palace. According to the notary David Moysie, James had 'minded to give the Queen a kiss after the Scots fashion at meeting' but his approach was declined as contrary to Danish custom; however, 'after a few words privately spoken between His Majesty and her, there passed familiarity and kisses.'[25] Since Danish sumptuary laws banned the wearing of 'sewn-on gold' except by nobles when attending court, the Scottish king's appearance was closely observed. At his first meeting with Anna and his new in-laws, James was dressed in 'a red velvet coat appliquéd with pieces of gold' forming rows of gold stars, and the next day wore 'blue velvet appliqued with pieces of gold'.[26] The marriage contract was formally signed and, on 23 November, James and Anna were married again, in person, in a service conducted in French by one of the king's ministers, before enjoying what one of Ashby's correspondents described as 'a reasonable banquet being on such an accident'.[27] The next day, James confirmed Anna's 'morning gifts' which, together with the royal palaces of Linlithgow and Falkland and a third of James's property, additionally granted Anna the Lordship of Dunfermline and its lands north of the River Forth.

Disregarding his notional three-week timetable for his journey, James reduced his entourage to under fifty and readily accepted an invitation from Christian IV and his new mother-in-law, Queen Sophia, to return with Anna to Denmark. According to an account attributed to the royal librarian, when James left Oslo with Anna on 22 December, 'he stood up in the sledge and bade all the people goodnight, not only in Scots, but also in Danish.'[28] Travelling overland, the royal party secured permission to pass through the geopolitically sensitive east–west Swedish corridor and then across the Øresund to Kronborg Castle in Elsinore. Famous as the setting for William Shakespeare's *Hamlet*, Elsinore was a strategic port with a sizeable expatriate Scots population. Generously hosted during his two-month stay at Kronborg, the Scottish king – as the Presbyterian minister James Melville recorded – simply 'made good cheer and drank stoutly till the springtime'.[29] Writing to the Presbyterian minister Robert Bruce, in Scotland, James invoked the Biblical parable of the virgins and the lamps intended to be lit for the bridegroom's return, suggesting 'I behoved to come home like a drunken man amongst them . . . which would well keep decorum to, coming out of so drinking a country as this is.'[30]

In March, the royal party moved to Copenhagen, where James heard theological and scientific discourses at the Danish Royal Academy and confirmed his appreciation to his hosts by admitting that 'since childhood', he had been '*addictus sum litteris*' – addicted to letters.[31] In Roskilde Cathedral, the king engaged in a public Latin disputation on subjects including predestination with the septuagenarian Lutheran theologian, Niels Hemmingsen, four of whose treatises had been obtained for James's schoolroom library in the 1570s.[32] The royal party also visited the laboratory complex on the island of Hven that had been built for the astronomer Tycho Brahe. Having previously received from Young a portrait of the king's former tutor, Buchanan, Brahe described how James, 'as soon as he noticed it in my study, recognised it with a smile on his face'.[33] James later composed three sonnets honouring Brahe, who had discovered a major nova in the Cassiopeia constellation and whose observational data – acquired before the telescope's invention – would inform research by Johannes Kepler and Isaac Newton. As one of the king's sonnets closed:

> Then greate is Ticho who by this his booke
> Commandement doth ouer these commanders brooke.[34]

James's final diversion before returning to Scotland was attending the wedding of Anna's older sister, Elizabeth, to Henry Julius, Duke of Brunswick-Wolfenbüttel, in the company of Danish and German royalty. Four months earlier, Ashby had suspected that James's motivation for remaining in Scandinavia had been to pursue an independent foreign policy, face to face with his new Danish relations. As Ashby reported to Walsingham, in Edinburgh it was 'now muttered in hugger mugger [secretly] that his end in enterprising this dangerous voyage was not only to bring home his queen' but also to form new confederacies and 'to strengthen himself against all occasions'.[35]

On 21 April 1590, James and Anna left Denmark in a flotilla of thirteen ships with over 200 attendants and arrived at Leith on 1 May. While the Danish entourage inspected Anna's jointure properties, plans were finalized for the first Protestant coronation of a Scottish queen consort at Holyrood Palace on 17 May. In a pomp-filled ceremony lasting seven hours, Anna received the sword and sceptre and swore an oath to uphold the true religion and work against 'all popish superstition, ceremonies and rites'.[36] With only one or two nights' notice to fulfil the commission, the Presbyterian theologian Andrew Melville produced a celebratory 315-line Latin celebratory poem entitled *Stephaniskion* that referenced James's claim to the English throne and celebrated the Scottish king as Brutus of Troy's natural successor, marvelling that:

> . . . Just as the Briton once raised kings for the world, and as many
>   kingdoms,
> So you are going to raise as many heirs to the kingdoms, you who
>   have risen from so many kings,
> You who will raise so many kings in the future with fortunate stars;
> A happy man in the sacred embraces of much-desired Anna.[37]

Two days after her coronation, Anna made a formal entry into Edinburgh, in a pageant arranged by Edinburgh's town council. Having travelled in a gold and silver coach from Holyrood unaccompanied by

James, Anna entered Edinburgh at the West Port gate, where a globe was lowered and opened, with an eight-year-old boy appearing as an angel descending from heaven, from whom Anna accepted gold keys, a Bible and a Psalter.[38] A tract entitled *The Joyful Receiving of James VI of Scotland, and Queen Anna his Wife* was published in London to describe events for English readers, while generous gifts and diplomatic ceremonial accompanied the Danish entourage's eventual departure from Scotland on 27 May.[39] Anxious to ensure that his guests were as sumptuously hosted as he had been by his Oldenburg in-laws, James was predictably exhausted by what Elizabeth's ambassador, Robert Bowes, described as 'the daily – or rather nightly – entertainment of them, as he had not leisure to rest three hours in his bed, or deliberate of any other affairs'.[40]

*

Royal marriage remained, however, first and foremost a matter of statecraft undertaken to promote the Stuart dynasty's interests via the production of healthy, legitimate heirs. Before James and Anna had even returned to Scotland, Bowes reported in mid-March that a Danish messenger in Edinburgh 'gives out very confidently that the Queen of Scots is already discovered to be with child'. Aged fifteen when she arrived in Scotland, Anna evidently suffered several miscarriages in the early years of her marriage; another pregnancy rumour circulated in November 1591 when Bowes recorded that the queen 'presently is thought to be with child . . . albeit she doth modestly deny the same'.[41] The following July, Bowes reported to Burghley that Anna seemed overwhelmed and 'inwardly grieved, as many times she falls into tears, wishing herself either with her mother in Denmark, or else that she might see and speak with her Majesty [Elizabeth]'.[42]

More insidiously, the Presbyterian chronicler David Calderwood recorded that James summoned several ministers to Holyrood in July 1593 after encoded correspondence had been seized from one of Bothwell's associates. Insisting that 'Bothwell's faction [and] the Papists . . . sought his life directly', James had showed the clerics satirical 'verses made in contempt of him, calling him David's son, a buggerer, [and] one that left his wife all the night *intactam*'. While the slur of 'David's son' cast aspersions on the king's legitimacy by alluding to his mother's closeness to David Riccio, the buggery allegation recalled some of the more salacious inferences drawn from James's attachment to court favourites, notably Esmé Stewart. Trusting in the ministers' popular credit, the king directed them 'to acquaint the people' with the libels, seemingly confident that his loyal subjects would be more outraged to hear of such insults than troubled by their content.[43]

With Queen Anna's pregnancy confirmed later that year, Prince Henry Frederick was safely delivered on 19 February 1594 and, after six successive male heirs called 'James', was named Henry Frederick in honour of the fathers of Anna, James and Elizabeth I, as well as the French king, Henri IV. The arrival of a male heir was, as Moysie put it, 'a great comfort and matter of joy to the whole people, and moved them to great triumph, wantonness, and play'; enjoying celebratory bonfires and dancing, it seemed 'as if the people had been daft for mirth'.[44] Strained Anglo-Scottish relations also improved when James oversaw formal declaration of the 'Catholic lords' as traitors by the Scottish Parliament in May, while Elizabeth's ministers stopped covertly supporting the king's cousin Bothwell, and warned the earl's followers 'in no case to seek the young Prince': i.e. abduct Prince Henry.[45] In August, Elizabeth confirmed to James her delight at being invited to become one of Henry's godparents, acclaiming 'my luck so fortunate as to be the baptiser of both father and son'.[46]

To showcase Scotland's international standing and reinforce his claim to the English throne, James staged lavish baptismal celebrations for Prince Henry in August 1594 that involved building an elaborate new Chapel Royal at Stirling Castle. Ambassadors were dispatched with invitations to courts in England, France, Denmark, the Low Countries and German duchies and, although Henri IV's court failed to respond in time, the celebrations were attended by representatives from Denmark, Brunswick, Mecklenburg-Güstrow and the Dutch States-General. (Meeting the Dutch representatives shortly beforehand, James admitted that, although their invitation as a sovereign state had caused disquiet at Elizabeth's court, the envoys should remember that the English queen was 'merely a woman and they "ought to forgive her her sex"').[47]

In the first Scottish royal baptism conducted according to Protestant rites, Elizabeth's representative, the Earl of Sussex, symbolically carried Prince Henry into the Chapel Royal. The sermon was preached by Bishop David Cunningham of Aberdeen who, Bowes noted, 'discoursed of the genealogies, alliances, leagues and amities contracted between the Kings of Scots and every one of the princes sending their ambassadors hither'; indeed Cunningham 'laboured much to make known how this prince was descended from these princes', especially 'from the kings of England'.[48] At the ensuing banquet in the castle's Great Hall, an eighteen-foot replica ship, with thirty-six guns and flags bearing the arms of Scotland and Denmark, 'sailed' across a twenty-four-foot 'sea', reimagining James's nautical voyage to meet Anna and echoing the Greek mythological heroism of Jason, leader of the Argonauts, who had retrieved the Golden Fleece, assisted by Medea. For those unable to attend, *A True Reportarie of the most Triumphant, and Royal Accomplishment of the Baptism*, published anonymously in London and Edinburgh in 1594, provided a detailed description of the celebrations. Its compiler, William Fowler, confirmed that the replica sailing ship had been James's 'own invention'.[49]

Henry's arrival had, however, provoked parental acrimony regarding arrangements for his care. To minimize the risk of abduction or other harm, James confirmed, two days after the prince's birth, that Henry would be raised at Stirling Castle by his childhood friend John Erskine, Earl of Mar, whose father and grandfather had been assigned custody 'of the sovereign princes of this realm in their young age, namely of himself, his mother and his grandfather'.[50] But raising royal children separately from their parents was not practised by the Oldenburg dynasty. Distraught at being denied care of their child, Anna waged a protracted campaign to regain custody that fomented divisive court factionalism. In June 1595, for example, the English envoy George Nicolson reported a discussion at Linlithgow Palace in which Anna, 'thinking she had the king in a good humour', asserted that it was widely known 'in Scotland, England and Denmark, that she sought to have the keeping of the young prince', and that James's refusals impugned her personal honour. While Nicolson surmised that 'the queen will never give over the motion, nor will the king ever yield', another envoy reported an exchange a month later in which James acknowledged Anna's distress but insisted that yielding to her wishes would 'be the destruction of me and my blood'.[51] The following month, Anna gave birth to a daughter – strategically named Elizabeth – followed by another daughter, Margaret, born on

Christmas Eve in 1598. Both daughters were also raised separately from their parents. Assigned to the household of Alexander, Lord Livingston, later Earl of Linlithgow, James's daughters spent their early years in the same castle, Linlithgow Palace, where his own mother had been born in 1542.

After the devastating death of Princess Margaret in March 1600, James and Anna welcomed another son, Charles, that November. Three weeks before the prince's birth, Nicolson described the performative nature of the royal couple's relationship to the English court. Admitting it was 'strange to behold', Nicolson reported that James and Anna had recently been treating one another with 'exceeding kindness', while 'the king's words used of her in secret [were] that he had the best wife of her that was in the world'; such words were 'by some wondered at, by others, suspected to be for disguising of some secret intentions'.[52] Notwithstanding the English court's suspicions, Anna gave birth to another son named Robert in January 1602, but who died four months later.

Following James's departure for England on Elizabeth I's death in March 1603, an especially distressing incident arose when the Earl of Mar – acting on royal orders – denied Anna access to the nine-year-old Prince Henry, inducing such anguish on the queen's part that she suffered a miscarriage. Thereafter persuaded to let his wife be accompanied on her journey south by their two oldest children, Henry and Elizabeth, James wrote to Anna, maintaining that 'I carry that love and respect unto you which, by the law of God and nature, I ought to do to my wife and mother of my children.' While acknowledging that 'ye are a king's daughter', James nevertheless insisted that 'whether ye were a king's or a cook's daughter, ye must be all alike to me being once my wife' and added, 'God is my witness I ever preferred you to all my bairns, much more than to any subject.'[53]

In March 1605, James anticipated another royal birth and jestingly warned Robert Cecil, now Viscount Cranborne, that 'if my wife shall not produce a fair young lion at this time', he would blame the courtiers responsible for preparing Greenwich Palace.[54] The following month, Anna gave birth to another daughter, named Mary in honour of the king's mother. The day after the new princess's birth, James wrote to his Danish brother-in-law, Christian IV, sending news of 'this child which has been so happily conceived and born', adding that 'although this is not our first child, it may nevertheless seem to be the first, since it is the first to have occurred for us after the most happy union of our kingdoms'.[55] To celebrate the first Stuart princess born in England, an elaborate christening service was held in the Chapel Royal at Greenwich at which Archbishop Richard Bancroft of Canterbury officiated, with the royal family and numerous nobles in attendance. Together with trumpet fanfares, William Byrd's anthem 'Sing Joyfully' exhorted the congregation to 'sing loud unto the God of Jacob!', overtly honouring England's new king.[56] Just two years later in September 1607, however, Princess Mary died of a fever, while James and Anna's last child, Princess Sophia, died within forty-eight hours of being born at Greenwich Palace in June 1606.

*

Compared to their two children who lived long enough to marry, James and Anna did not share the conjugal closeness that Charles I later enjoyed with Henrietta Maria or the Palatine Electress Elizabeth found with Frederick V. But by the terms James himself set out in *Basilicon Doron*, his marriage procured 'a helper' at court, generated progeny and satisfied his male lust – at least insofar as other women were concerned. When, around 1606, Cecil, now Earl of Salisbury, informed the king of accusations laid against a man for being Queen Anna's lover, James refused to be tempted into further investigation or laying charges of slander. He was not, as he put it, one of those 'unwise husbands' who 'by curious and unjust searching to discover their wife's shame, procured their own eternal infamy'. James also wished to avoid distressing Anna, 'especially at this time, when as I must confess, she uses me so kindly, in all things that if it were possible for me to love her better than ever I did before, it were my part to do it'.[57] A similarly affable tone infused a missive to Salisbury regarding travel arrangements the following year. As the Earl of Dunbar reported, 'the king says, he is not so weary of the queen that he would make a change of another wife; and therefore he will not have her to be killed with a wild, unwholesome air'; if Anna wished to join James in Salisbury sooner than planned, the king would be 'most heartily glad'.[58]

Anna also proved a 'helper' in external relations. A fluent writer in Danish, German, Latin, French, Scots, English and Italian, she regularly interceded in royal business to advance the interests of her Oldenburg family, as well as individual Danish travellers and merchants. In October 1611, the Venetian ambassador, Antonio Foscarini, reported that Christian IV's ambassador, Jonas Charisius, had 'by means of the queen' held several private meetings with James at Hampton Court achieving a mutually successful outcome, adding that 'the queen worked to this end'.[59] Letters preserved in Danish archives indicate that Anna continued a correspondence with Charisius between 1612 and 1618, writing in French and including ciphered sections for confidentiality.[60] The poet and lexicographer John Florio made her the dedicatee of the second, expanded edition of his Anglo-Italian dictionary and renamed the compilation *Queen Anna's New World of Words* (1611). A prefatory sonnet to the dictionary reassured Florio that Anna was a worthy 'protectrice of thy pains', given her illustrious reputation as a 'daughter, sister, mother, [and] wife to kings'.[61]

As queen, Anna enjoyed a degree of financial independence from her husband through jointure properties intended to generate income during a queen's marriage and, if needed, financial security in widowhood. On her marriage in 1590, Anna's Scottish jointure comprised the palaces of Falkland, Linlithgow and Dunfermline, together with a third of the lands attached to those properties and their attendant fees, leases and rents. On James's accession as King of England, complex negotiations concluded in 1606 assigned 139 possessions in twenty-nine English counties to Anna, generating an annual income of almost £10,000 sterling. James also established a new 'Queen's Court of Chancery' for all matters relating to his wife's extensive jointure.[62] In architectural terms, Anna's favoured residences – Dunfermline Palace, Greenwich Palace, Oatlands Manor in Surrey and Somerset House – were, as one critic has observed, 'united by a classical aesthetic' reminiscent of Oldenburg properties in Denmark-Norway.[63] Anna herself oversaw extensive building and renovation projects that included commissioning Inigo Jones to design the first classical building in England: the Queen's House at Greenwich. In London, Somerset House was extensively remodelled to accommodate a new suite of royal apartments looking out onto redesigned formal gardens that boasted one of the first orangeries erected in England and a tall water fountain supplied by, and visible from, the Thames.

Uxoriousness and pride in one's progeny did not, however, preclude prejudice. In his youth, James penned a love sonnet to an imaginary lady, likening himself to a marigold ineluctably following the sun, while remaining an ineluctable misogynist.[64] He was also the author of 'A satire against women' comprising ten stanzas that illustrated the defective nature of womankind, as derived from traditional Aristotelian creational biology. Lines from the king's poem asserted that 'all wemen [sic] are of nature vaine', 'ambitious all without regarde or shame' and 'sume craft they haue, yett foolish are indeede'.[65]

Commentators such as John Chamberlain noted that as King of England, James was quick in 'taking down high-handed women' – even when women offered panegyrical praise.[66] In 1616, for example, the schoolmaster Henry Reginald published a hexalingual collection of poems and epigraphs entitled *Musa Virginea*, praising James and members of his family and composed by his sixteen-year-old daughter, Bathsua, in Latin, Greek, Hebrew, Spanish, French and German. But when their young author was presented at court, the king's patriarchal put-down was instant and caustic. After Bathsua had been described as an 'English rarity' in her capacity to 'speak and write pure Latin, Greek and Hebrew', James reportedly retorted, 'but can she spin?'[67] Indeed, in a conference with English peers in the House of Lords in 1624, the king twinned women and warfare as his most fundamental aversions; both were a *'malum necessarium'* ['necessary evil'] which 'I should be loath to enter into'.[68] Several months later, he wrote to the Duke of Buckingham, anticipating their imminent meeting at Theobalds Palace and directing his favourite to 'bring all the cunts with thee (I mean both thy wife, thy mother and thy sister)'.[69]

In securing the Stuart succession, James had nevertheless achieved his key dynastic imperative. When the Danish queen, Anne Catherine of Brandenburg, died in April 1612, James wrote to Christian IV, commending 'the fact that she performed her womanly duty very well and left your family increased with numerous offspring'.[70] A year before James's death, Willem van de Passe produced an engraving entitled *The Triumphs of King James and his August Progeny* (1624), which depicted the enthroned king, surrounded by his children and grandchildren, with Prince Charles's hand resting on a copy of his father's collected *Works*. (Van de Passe also included deceased family members, including Queen Anna and Prince Henry, each holding a skull.) An updated edition of the engraving appeared in 1627, with James still centrally enthroned, maintaining his role as head of the Stuart dynasty from beyond the grave; as the accompanying caption confirmed, 'The dead father remains as the father of his family and of the kingdom.' In 1660, a third updated edition of van de Passe's engraving was published to mark the triumphant return to power of James's grandson Charles II after the mid-century civil wars.[71]

9

Slaves of the Devil

In June 1591, James took the unusual step of appearing in Edinburgh's Tolbooth, which housed the burgh's main prison, to explain to a group of jurors why he was prosecuting them for 'assize of error'. The jurors – known as assizers in Scotland – had convicted the wife of an Edinburgh burgess, Barbara Napier, of consulting a witch, while acquitting her of more serious charges that included attending a 'witches' convention' at North Berwick and participating in treasonable conspiracies that had envisaged the king's death by maleficent means. As James admitted, 'my coming hither at this time may seem strange unto you' since it was rare for kings in Scotland to attend criminal trials in person or to prosecute jurors for their verdicts. But he was determined to supply 'an example in time coming to make men to be more wary how they give false verdicts' while also seeking to curb 'the pride of these witches and their friends, which cannot be prevented but by my own presence' in court.[1] Duly chastized, the jurors changed their verdict and convicted Napier of all charges. Later that month, James wrote to his Chancellor, John Maitland of Thirlestane, directing him to obtain sworn testimony from physicians to confirm whether Napier 'be with bairn or not' and to refuse any 'delaying answer'; if she was found not pregnant, 'to the fire with her presently and cause disembowel her publicly'.[2] While no record survives of Napier's eventual fate, it is likely that she was executed later that year and, in common with other women convicted of witchcraft, probably burned alive.

Six years later, the king's publisher in Edinburgh published an eighty-page tract entitled *Daemonologie, in Form of a Dialogue* (1597) with a title-page displaying the royal standard and lion rampant and a preface signed by 'James Rex'. The only work on demonology to be written by an early modern monarch anywhere in the world, *Daemonologie* was suffused with a vivid sense of immediacy as the king sought to alert his 'beloved reader' to 'the fearful abounding at this time in this country, of these detestable slaves of the devil, the witches or enchanters'. James's aims in writing the treatise were twofold: to endeavour 'so far as I can, to resolve the doubting hearts of many, both that such assaults of Satan are most certainly practised', and to insist that those involved in such activities 'merit most severely to be punished'.[3] Entered into the English Stationers' Company Register in March 1598, *Daemonologie* was republished in two London editions in 1603 on James's accession as English king. That same year, two different Dutch translations appeared in Amsterdam and Dordrecht, one of which formed the basis of a Latin translation published in the Hessian city of Hanau in 1604. Other seventeenth-century editions were printed in Hanover and Frankfurt, and *Daemonologie* was included in the king's collected *Works* of 1617. For just as James claimed unique authority as an experienced monarch to write about the theory and practice of kingcraft, personal experience also informed his understanding of diabolic witchcraft and its political implications. A decade into James's reign as king in England, an investigation was undertaken in 1613 into the reported bewitchment of one of the king's courtiers, Robert Devereux, Earl of Essex. Reminding the Archbishop of Canterbury, George Abbot, that satanic destruction was continually fostered through new diabolic stratagems, James rebuked the primate for sceptically doubting the reality of witchcraft and directed him to 'look [at] my *Daemonologie*'.[4] And yet, the king was no rabidly obsessive witch-hunter. By the end of his life, James's reputation 'among his contemporaries as an exploder of false accusations of witchcraft was equal to his reputation as a demonologist'.[5]

*

In post-Reformation Scotland, Protestant keenness to promote moral reform was fuelled by a resolve to eliminate residual Catholic reliance on superstitious practices, such as exorcism. Three years before James was born, the Scottish Parliament passed a Witchcraft Act in June 1563, literally applying the Biblical text from Exodus 22:18 – 'Thou shalt not suffer a witch to live' – to put under pain of death anyone engaging in acts of witchcraft, sorcery or necromancy, or seeking 'help, response or consultation' from practitioners.[6] By contrast, the Witchcraft Act passed by the English Parliament five months earlier in January 1563 had contained no capital sanctions. In 1565, Elizabeth's ambassador in Edinburgh, Thomas Randolph, vouched for the credibility of rumours emanating from Queen Mary's court of 'consultations with witches . . . to know times and years of some folks' lives'.[7] Two years later, after the queen's controversial third marriage to James Hepburn, Earl of Bothwell, another English envoy reported that the queen's wayward conduct 'confirmed her real character as a witch, in common parlance also a poisoner, by trying to poison her son James in an apple . . . and in a sugar loaf'.[8] Polemical literature justifying Mary's deposition in July 1567 presented the queen as 'this fatal Medea': the evil enchantress in Greek mythology who murdered her sons. In *The Detection of the Doings of Mary, Queen of Scots* (1571), George Buchanan pointed out that, in the controversial 'Casket Letters' allegedly written to Bothwell, Mary 'partly compares herself with Medea, a bloody woman, and a poisoning witch'.[9]

But not all references to supernatural forces in James's youth were necessarily malevolent or menacing. The opening passage of Alexander Montgomerie's *The Flyting betwixt Montgomerie and Polwart* – performed as court entertainment in the early 1580s – invoked folkloric belief in an annual elfin fairy cavalcade at Hallowe'en and was cited by James as an example of alliterative anapaestic metre suitable for emulation in his *Essays of a Prentise*. In the autumn of 1590, however, witchcraft became a matter of immediate and personal alarm for James when he received reports that a group of witches in East Lothian had confessed to plotting to kill him by maleficent magic in a conspiracy apparently involving the king's notoriously capricious cousin Francis Stewart, Earl of Bothwell. Addressing the jurors in Barbara Napier's case in June 1591, the king confirmed that 'I have been occupied these three-quarters of this year for the sifting out of them that are guilty herein.' Although James denied fearing death in a personal capacity, since he was still only in his mid-twenties and childless, he feared the destabilizing impact that his untimely murder would have on his subjects. As he wondered rhetorically, 'if such troubles were in breeding whilst I retained life, what would have been done if my life had been taken from me?'[10]

The witchcraft allegations arose directly from the storms that Queen Anna and her entourage had experienced when trying to reach

Scotland by sea during the autumn of 1589. The commander of Anna's ill-fated fleet, Admiral Peder Munk, sought to deflect allegations of mismanagement by blaming inadequate maintenance of the Navy's ships on the head of the Danish Treasury, Christoffer Walkendorf. Danish authorities cleared Walkendorf of wrongdoing in July, but by that time rumours were rife that the storms had been caused by human imprecation. In April 1590, a woman named Ane Koldings had confessed – after interrogation under torture – to have practised witchcraft to ensure that Queen Anna 'would not reach Scotland on the first attempt'.[11] Koldings was convicted of witchcraft and burned at the stake in June, having implicated another nine Copenhagen women, of whom at least three were convicted and executed, including the wife of a former mayor of the city who had once been involved in a physical fracas with Munk. In his memoirs, the Scots courtier Meville of Halhill recalled the storms that had beset Anna's fleet as well as another maritime disaster in which a ship sailing from Burntisland in Fife to Leith in September 1589 had sunk, losing a cargo of wedding gifts for James and Anna and drowning passengers who included Melville's sister-in-law, Lady Jean Kennedy, intended as one of the new queen's ladies-in-waiting. As Melville recorded, the storms and gales were 'alleged to have been raised by the witches of Denmark', provoked by 'a cuff or a blow which the Admiral of Denmark gave to one of the bailies [aldermen] of Copenhagen', whose wife then consulted with 'her associates in that art, [and] raised the said storm to be revenged upon the said Admiral'.[12]

One of the most notorious witch-hunts in Scottish history then ensued between late November 1590 and May 1591, when over 100 suspects were examined in and around Edinburgh and East Lothian and over 300 individuals were alleged, in one way or another, to have engaged in acts of diabolism. The trials started when a bailie-depute in Tranent, David Seton, became suspicious about the nocturnal healing activities of one of his servants, Geillis Duncan. In an early examination, Duncan claimed to have met someone from Copenhagen 'in the midst of the Firth' and 'after they had gotten her name they commoned [talked] together'. Duncan also implicated a middle-aged midwife and healer from Haddington, Agnes Sampson, who confessed to meeting the Devil, both in human and animal form, who had told her that 'it should be hard to the king to come home and that the queen should never come except the king fetched her.' When Sampson asked if James would have heirs, the Devil had 'answered that he should have lads and then lasses'.[13]

After the claims were brought to royal attention, Sampson was questioned again in James's presence at the palace of Holyroodhouse on 4 and 5 December, initially about her methods of curing sick individuals and livestock. Fragmentary Justiciary Court records of the examination indicate that, having identified contradictions in her account, 'his Majesty charged straightly [severely] to confess the truth, which she did.' Sampson repeated the Devil's claims about the queen's difficulties in reaching Scotland, James's likelihood of having sons before daughters, as well as the Devil's prediction that 'the ministers would destroy the king and all Scotland, but if he would use his counsel, he should destroy them', although it is unclear whether, by 'he', Sampson meant James or the Devil. Sampson also admitted that, when first arrested, she had intended to remain silent and, even when her interrogation had started, had still 'resolved never to confess, were [it] not his Majesty's speeches that had moved her' to do so and, repenting before God, was now mindful of her sins.[14]

As Elizabeth's ambassador, Bowes, confirmed to Lord Burghley, James had thereby 'by his own especial travail' induced 'Sampson, the great witch, to confess her wicked doings, and to discover sundry things touching his own life', including attempts to procure one of the king's shirts or other laundry 'for the execution of their charms'.[15] Following further interrogation, Sampson was tried and convicted of witchcraft on 27 January 1591 and executed the following day. A month later, as questioning of other suspects continued apace, Bowes sent Burghley a summary of Sampson's revelations, confirming that 'of the 102 articles of her dittay [indictment], she confessed fifty-eight' and promising that 'the king will have their examinations printed soon after they are ended.' Disconcerted to learn that his name had featured in interrogations, Bowes observed that 'many things are told to please the examiners – chiefly the king – to win grace, and that are far more strange than true.' Among the more fantastical claims was an (erroneous) description of 'the English ambassador, being a little black and fat man with black hair . . . as I am informed' who, after James had departed for Norway, 'had been with them in a cellar and given them gold to hang up and charm a toad for the hurt of the king in his life, and to hinder the issue to come of his body'.[16]

Fortunately for Bowes, scant credit was seemingly given to rumours of his dabbling in maleficent magic, but details from the confessions of Sampson, Duncan and others appeared in a pamphlet entitled *News from Scotland*, three versions of which appeared in Edinburgh and London in late 1591 and 1592. Printed anonymously, the tract's preface affirmed the veracity of its contents, since all evidence reported was 'taken and uttered in the presence of the king's Majesty'.[17] The tract's royal endorsement can also be inferred from James's direction, in an early manuscript version of *Daemonologie*, that curious readers should consult 'their confessions that have been at this time apprehended which all are to be set forth in print'.[18]

Presenting a shocking narrative, *News from Scotland* revealed that those questioned had described around 200 people gathering at North Berwick church on All Hallow's Eve 1589 for a Sabbath, attended by the Devil 'in the habit or likeness of a man'. Directed to 'kiss his buttocks in sign of duty to him; which being put over the pulpit bare, everyone did as he had enjoined them'. Thereafter, the Devil 'did greatly inveigh against the King of Scotland' and, asked why he loathed James VI so much, had replied 'by reason the king is the greatest enemy he hath in the world'.[19] The pamphlet also relayed Sampson's confession that the whole group 'together went to sea each one in a riddle or sieve . . . with flagons of wine, making merry and drinking'.[20] *News from Scotland* further revealed that, during James's journey to Norway and Denmark, Sampson had attached the bones of a dead man to a cat that was cast into the Firth of Forth, thereby causing the ship carrying Lady Jean Kennedy and the wedding gifts to sink in September 1589. On the king's return to Scotland the following April, Sampson had raised another storm directed only against James's ship, 'which thing was most strange and true, as the king's Majesty acknowledged; for when the rest of the ships had a fair and good wind, then was the wind contrary and altogether against His Majesty'. James had nevertheless withstood the witches' attempts to harm him because 'he is the Lord's anointed, and they but vessels of God's wrath.' 'So long as God is with him, he fears not who is against him.'[21]

The author of *News from Scotland* was probably the minister of Haddington, James Carmichael, who belatedly reminded the king in 1615 that he was still owed payment of an allowance granted for attending 'fifteen months upon the examination of diverse witches'.[22]

In one remarkable passage, the pamphlet's author explained why James seemed to shift from an initially sceptical stance to one of frightened credence as he listened to Sampson's 'miraculous and strange' revelations. When the king pronounced 'they were all extreme liars', Sampson had objected and:

> ... taking his Majesty a little aside, she declared unto him the very words which passed between the king's Majesty and his queen at Oslo in Norway the first night of their marriage, with their answer each to other; whereat the king's Majesty wondered greatly, and swore by the living God that he believed all the devils in Hell could not have discovered the same, acknowledging her words to be most true; and therefore gave the more credit to the rest which is before declared.[23]

While corroboration of this extraordinary exchange does not survive in other records, the tract's author was unlikely to have risked royal wrath through fictional invention. This was the moment when 'a hitherto sceptical king changed his mind – and was clearly terrified'.[24]

*

If James had been disturbed by Sampson's revelations at Holyrood, he was even more unnerved by claims made after her execution. In May 1591, one Janet Stratton gave evidence as a witness that Sampson had attended another witches' convention at Acheson's Haven, near Prestonpans, on the previous Lammas Eve (31 July) at which she had produced a wax image of James, intending 'to wrack [destroy] him for my Lord Bothwell's sake and for the gold and silver that he has promised and should give us, with victual to me and my bairns'. Another hexagenerian witness likewise attested that 'the thing was sought to be done for my Lord Bothwell', amid expectations that 'the gold would shortly be gotten out of England', despite one attendee, Robert Grierson, opining 'that it would be long or [a long time before] the gold came out of England'. In June, another witness, Janet Kennedy, was apprehended in England and brought to Scotland for examination before the king. Kennedy confirmed that Bothwell had attended the witches' convention when Sampson had roasted the image of James 'and desired the said Agnes to make the fire bolder', before Sampson had admitted that 'all was in vain they assayed against the king for nothing of their craft' proved effective.[25]

The levels of coercion applied to secure confessions was indicated in a postscript added by Bowes in a letter to Burghley on 15 April 1591, reporting that Grierson had died that day 'as it is thought by the extremity of the tortures applied to him', although he had 'confessed little'.[26] The next day, Bothwell was summoned before James and his Privy Councillors and imprisoned in Edinburgh Castle. According to Bowes, the earl admitted to consulting a suspected witch named Richard Graham but denied any treasonable conspiracy against the king and had even volunteered to undergo torture in order to prove his innocence. When Bothwell asked James directly about the offence of which he was suspected, the king had replied 'with practice to have taken his life'.[27]

Bothwell's reported involvement transformed the East Lothian witch-hunt into a treasonable conspiracy at the centre of James's court. For as well as being the king's first cousin, Bothwell was the country's Admiral and responsible for the ships sent to Norway and Denmark. Bothwell was also known to Barbara Napier and the daughter of a judge, Euphame MacCalzean, who was convicted of witchcraft and burned alive on Edinburgh's Castle Hill on 25 June 1591. Four days before MacCalzean's execution, Bothwell escaped from Edinburgh Castle, prompting the Privy Council to issue a proclamation condemning the earl as a 'declared rebel, traitor, and enemy to God, his Majesty, and this his native country' and subjecting his estates to forfeiture. As the proclamation continued, Bothwell had 'given himself over altogether into the hands of Satan', directly intending to harm James's person through 'consultation with necromancers, witches, and other wicked and ungodly persons'.[28] Bothwell was, however, supported by a number of Presbyterian ministers, one of whom penned an anonymous letter 'to the nobility' insisting that the witchcraft charges were politically motivated. Denying that the testimony of an alleged necromancer such as Graham should be preferred to an earl's protestations of innocence, the author warned other nobles that 'if he [Bothwell] shall die because they fear him, then neither shall your lives be safe, for you also give them terror.'[29]

Bothwell remained at large for six months before breaking into

Holyrood Palace on 27 December 1591 in an attempt to seize James and kill Chancellor Maitland. Although several accomplices were apprehended and executed, Bothwell fled, prompting James to dispatch Melville of Halhill to the English court a week later. As James insisted, Elizabeth needed to hear a full eyewitness account of 'the dangerous and most treasonable attempt, the barbarity whereof we abhor to remember, never to be enough wondered in all ages and posterity to come' to deter her from sheltering Bothwell.[30] When the Scottish Parliament convened the following May, James opened proceedings with 'a harangue, wherein he laid to Bothwell's charge that he sought his destruction, first by witchcraft' and 'next, by violence'.[31] In July 1593, Bothwell again appeared unexpectedly in the Palace of Holyroodhouse where, having caught James unawares, he denied any wish to harm the king, but demanded to undergo a formal trial on the original witchcraft charge.

On 10 August 1593, Bothwell was acquitted of any involvement in witchcraft after a nine-hour trial with James in attendance. In London, Burghley received an eyewitness report recounting the allegations made in court that 'the earl Bothwell should have a poison delivered [to] him, made of adders' skins, toad skins, and the hippomanes [birth materials] in the forehead of a young foal' to be mixed together and 'laid where the king should come, so as it might drop upon his head'. Other charges related to Bothwell devising an image of James from 'wax mingled with certain other things, which should have consumed and melted away in time, meaning the king should consume as it did', and attempts to render James 'enchanted to remain in Denmark, and not return into Scotland'. The original charges of diabolical conspiracy had been made by Richard Graham who – despite guarantees of royal protection in return for testifying – had been executed eighteen months earlier on a witchcraft conviction. Graham's brother, however, testified in court that his brother had 'many times protested to him that he was forced to accuse the Earl Bothwell for fear of maiming with the boots and other tortures'.[32] Since Bothwell continued to command extensive support among the nobility and Church of Scotland ministry, it would have been unthinkable for James to pursue his jurors for wilful error in returning their verdict of acquittal as he had done two years earlier in Napier's case. Nevertheless, James banished Bothwell from Edinburgh and, following further rebellious acts by the earl, the presbytery of Edinburgh excommunicated him in February 1595. The following month, Bothwell went into continental exile, dying in Naples in 1612 in poverty and, once again, suspected by the local authorities of dabbling in necromancy.

In Scotland, another large-scale series of witchcraft investigations and trials occurred in 1597, coinciding with a period of fraught Church–State relations, outbreaks of plague, harvest failures and famine. Although sparsely documented, around 400 cases are estimated to have arisen in Aberdeenshire, Fife, Perthshire, Glasgow and Stirlingshire between March and September that year, with the main instigator 'not a witch-hunting king, but the witch-haunted Kirk'.[33] Alarmed at the rapid escalation of prosecutions, James intervened in one case to halt proceedings against a mother and daughter in Aberdeen who had consulted a midwife, describing their visit as a matter of 'ordinary comfort and supple [help]' and no different from those regularly undertaken by 'women of all estates in the country'.[34] While most allegations arose from local community tensions, echoes of the earlier witch-hunt emerged in the testimony of one man who, as Bowes reported in August 1597, confessed to a conspiracy 'to have drowned the king in his passage over the water at Dundee' when James had travelled to the Church of Scotland's General Assembly the previous May. With other suspects confessing to designs on the life of the young Prince Henry, James was, as Bowes put it, 'pestered and in many ways troubled in the examination of the witches which swarm in exceeding number and (as is credibly reported) in many thousands'.[35] Observing how 'the king has his mind only bent upon the examination and trial of sorcerers', one of Bowes's informants reported in September that James had summoned four ministers to Falkland Palace 'to preach in his presence' on 'the essential power of Satan', with another twelve ministers from Angus and Fife invited to attend in order to debate the subject.[36]

It was against this background that James published *Daemonologie*, vehemently asserting the reality of diabolical activity but seeking to 'sail surely, betwixt Charybdis and Scylla' to avoid the twin dangers of excess scepticism 'lest that draws us to the error that there is no witches' and excess credulity entailing 'innumerable absurdities, both monstrously against all theology divine, and philosophy human'.[37] A manuscript draft of *Daemonologie* reveals that, when countering assumptions that all witches were manic or melancholic, James had observed that individuals convicted of the crime were actually 'rich and worldly-wise', 'fat or corpulent', and 'altogether given over to the pleasures of the flesh', inserting marginal references 'EM', 'RG' and 'BN' to refer, respectively, to Euphame MacCalzean, Richard Graham and Barbara Napier.[38] Comprising a dialogue between the inquisitive 'Philomathes' and the knowledgeable 'Epistemon', *Daemonologie* was divided into three books considering ritual magic, witchcraft and sorcery, and the nature and operation of spirits. In devising a dialogue format, James's intention was that his tract would be 'pleasant and facile [easy]' for readers.[39]

Approaching demonology in terms of contrarieties, James insisted that 'since the devil is the very contrary opposite to God, there can be no better way to know God than by the contrary'.[40] Diabolic activities on earth proved God's ontological existence – and the divine right of kings – by inverse corollary. In the tract's preface, James described 'God as the first cause, and the Devil as his instrument and second cause'. In his subordinate role as 'God's hang-man', the Devil tempted ordinary individuals into becoming his sworn followers and withdrawing their allegiance from God. Hence it was the responsibility of monarchs, as God's chosen lieutenants on earth, to root out all forms of satanic activity; failing to punish severely 'so odious a fault and treason against God' was both unlawful and sinful. For when witches were confronted by the godly magistrate, they lost their occult power. Asked by 'Philomathes' why 'there are twenty women given to that craft, where there is one man', 'Epistemon' supplied the 'easy' answer: women were 'frailer' than men and more susceptible 'to be entrapped in these gross snares of the Devil' as proven 'by the Serpent's deceiving of Eve' in the Book of Genesis.[41]

As James elaborated, much diabolic practice presented a parodic aping of godly worship. The Devil often appropriated churches for his conventions and only admitted those bearing the Devil's mark to confirm their rejection of the baptismal cross. But compared to divine miracles such as Moses's rod turning into a serpent in the Book of Exodus, the Devil's acts involved counterfeit imitations: 'deluding of the senses, and no ways true in substance'. Accordingly, the king was keen to suggest alternative hypotheses for apparent manifestations of diabolic activity. Asked by 'Philomathes' about werewolves, for example, 'Epistemon' suggested that lycanthropy was provoked by 'a natural superabundance of melancholy' whereby individuals experienced such intense levels of mental distraction 'that they have thought themselves very wolves indeed at these times' and have thus 'counterfeited their actions – in going on their hands and feet, pressing to devour women and bairns, fighting and snatching with all the town dogs', becoming in effect 'beasts by a strong apprehension'. Asked about transvection as the means by which witches travelled to attend diabolic conventions, James again inferred an inverted imitation of Scripture – specifically the angelic transportation of Habakkuk to Daniel in the Apocrypha – to grant that witches might travel 'either above the earth or above the sea swiftly', but only for 'short bounds' that lasted as long as a natural breath.[42] Uncovering deception thus remained as important a royal duty as locating witches. Evidently referring to an instance of fraudulent claims, James congratulated Prince Henry on 'the discovery of yon little counterfeit wench' in an undated letter and hoped that his son 'may be my heir in such discoveries'. Moreover, since Henry knew James's view that 'most miracles nowadays prove but illusions', it was essential to observe strict judicial procedure, given 'how easily people are induced to trust wonders'.[43]

*

After James's accession as English king, a new Witchcraft Act was passed by the Westminster Parliament in 1604 that attached capital sanctions to the crimes of conjuring evil spirits or seeking to kill another person by maleficent means. Responsibility for the Act's drafting and legislative passage lay not with James but with the Chief Justice of the Court of Common Pleas, Sir Edmund Anderson, who in 1602 had warned a London jury hearing a case of alleged demonic possession that 'the land is full of witches; they abound in all places' and, unless prosecuted diligently, 'will in a short-time over-run the whole land'.[44] Anderson's perspective was, however, unrepresentative. While reported instances of witchcraft were fairly common in England, it was not regarded as a religious crime. Differences between English and Scottish criminal procedure – notably the strict prohibition on torture as a means of extracting confessions in England – also meant that the comparable proportion of individuals accused, convicted and executed for witchcraft in early modern England was markedly lower than in Scotland and Continental Europe. Put simply, 'a Scottish woman in the seventeenth century was twelve times more likely than her English counterpart to be executed for witchcraft.'[45]

In both countries, however, the onus to extirpate witches could nevertheless be harnessed as a means of promoting religious reform by those keen to find evidence of residual popery and superstition. More sceptical members of the clerical establishment were unsettled by such endeavours. A week before Elizabeth's death, the chaplain to Bishop Richard Bancroft of London, Samuel Harsnett, entered a tract entitled *A Declaration of Egregious Popish Impostures* into the Stationers' Company Register. As well as attacking 'seduced Catholics', Harsnett denounced zealous Puritan 'devil-finders, and devil-puffers, or devil-prayers' whose dabbling in dispossession rendered them as likely to find 'a devil in a lane, as soon as a hare in Waltham Forest'.[46] In retaliation, one of the named 'devil-puffers', John Swan, took advantage of James's accession to the English throne to object, in another pamphlet, that Harsnett's strictures 'gives a most dishonourable counter-buff to your Highness's treatise which handles that argument'.[47]

As king in England, James combined his keen interest in reported instances of supernatural occurrences with a strident insistence on stringent investigation. He echoed Harsnett's hunting trope when he admitted having been 'ever kept so busy with hunting of witches, prophets, Puritans, dead cats, and hares' while staying in Hertfordshire in early 1605.[48] In January, the king examined two women in Royston, Hertfordshire, and referred them for further investigation at Cambridge University, where the 'two maids suspected to be bewitched' remained until May when a diagnosis of natural hysteria was accepted instead.[49] In April, James summoned to court a Salisbury physician, Richard Haydock, who had gained renown for preaching brilliant sermons including passages in Greek and Hebrew when asleep, despite claiming no knowledge of either language or any recollection of his orations when awake. After being interrogated several times by James, Haydock admitted to simulating sleep-talking. Claiming that 'none can more condemn me, than I do myself' for his fraud, the repentant Haydock prepared an oneirological treatise that included a chapter enumerating 'His Majesty's arguments that there can be no reasonable discourse in sleep'. Haydock eventually abandoned hopes of publication after learning of 'His Majesty's displeasure' regarding the potential for 'dangerous sequels ... in other ill-disposed instruments of the Devil, who might dissemble and counterfeit the like ability', thereby disseminating 'what heresies in religion, and Machiavellian plots in the commonwealth they pleased'.[50]

During the summer of 1605, James also spent the first day of his visit to Oxford University in August interviewing a woman, Anne Gunter, who for over a year had been manifesting symptoms of demonic possession that included vomiting or excreting hundreds of metal pins at a time. Two local women, blamed by Gunter and her family for the affliction, had been tried for witchcraft and acquitted at the Abingdon assizes. Having placed Gunter under the care of Bancroft – now Archbishop of Canterbury – and his chaplain, Harsnett, James held three further meetings with Gunter that autumn at Whitehall and near Windsor during which she confessed to having simulated her symptoms, on the orders of her father Brian, as part of a long-running dispute with neighbours including the women acquitted of bewitching her. Three days after confirming Haydock's hoax, James reassured the Earl of Salisbury that Gunter 'finds herself perfectly cured' of her 'pin-pranks' and other symptoms and confirmed 'that she was never possessed with any devil nor bewitched'.[51] While discovery of the Gunpowder Plot thereafter diverted James's attention, Star Chamber legal proceedings were initiated against Gunter and her father in February 1606, and although there is no surviving record of the case's outcome, Brian Gunter was evidently still in prison two years later. Meanwhile, Guy Fawkes's failed attempt to blow up the English Houses of Parliament gave the Jacobean court a shocking reminder of the power of destructive diabolism. Preaching a thanksgiving sermon five days after the disaster was averted, Bishop William Barlow of Rochester described the unrepentant Fawkes as 'the Devil of the vault'.[52]

Nowhere is the concatenation of demonism, witchcraft, necromancy and treason brought together with more terrifying intensity than in Shakespeare's *Macbeth* (c. 1606), the opening scene of which sees a trio of witches (or 'weird sisters') pronouncing 'Fair is foul, and foul is fair: / Hover through the fog and filthy air'. It has been noted that the weird sisters speak more often in seven-syllable lines than any other length of line combined, creating 'memorable acoustic force' in lines such as 'When shall we three meet again?', 'When the battle's lost and won' and 'Fair is foul, and foul is fair'. Suitably fitting their demonic characters, lines with odd numbers of syllables tended to be regarded by Shakespeare's contemporaries as stylistically deformed – 'anatomically mangled and misshapen' – and James himself had advised aspiring poets always to ensure that the number of syllables 'in every line be even and not odd' in his 'Reulis and Cautelis' of poetry, published in 1584.[53] Although the weird sisters' contribution was later expanded by Shakespeare's collaborator, Thomas Middleton, the plot's focus remained the terrible tale of an ambitious tyrant, Macbeth, resolving after an encounter with witches to commit the highest form of treason and seize royal power by murdering a good king, Duncan, in Macbeth's own home. As Macduff exclaims in horror on learning of Duncan's death, 'Confusion now hath made its masterpiece!'

10

Textuaries of Kingship

Suffering serious illness in the autumn of 1598, James became keenly aware of his own mortality. That October, the English agent George Nicolson confided to Sir Robert Cecil that he had been told 'in great secret' that the thirty-two-year-old Scottish king had been 'troubled in his chamber in his sleep' and now feared Elizabeth I would outlive him. Accordingly, James had written 'an apology and rule how his son shall be brought to succeed' as England's next sovereign 'and how all shall be governed for the attaining thereunto'.[1] Entitled *Basilicon Doron* – meaning 'the king's gift' – James's treatise was prepared for 'my dearest son, and natural successor', Prince Henry. Acknowledging that 'the hour of death is uncertain to me, as unto all flesh', James directed that the tract should be regarded 'as my Testament and latter will'.[2] After the 'King James Version' of the Bible, *Basilicon Doron* would become the work for which the king is now best known.

*

The first publication of James's *Basilicon Doron* in 1599 was indeed a 'great secret'. A small print run of seven presentation copies was produced in Edinburgh by the royal printer, Robert Waldegrave, using high-quality paper to display the text within wide margins, in a lavish italic script and adorned by numerous printers' embellishments. Accidental printing errors were carefully hand-corrected, as evidenced in two surviving copies in the British Library and the National Library of Scotland. But as rumours of *Basilicon Doron*'s covert publication leaked from James's court, Robert Cecil learned in London that the king had 'distributed the books of his last will' to Prince Henry, Queen Anna, Adam Newton (Prince Henry's tutor), Lord John Hamilton and the 'Catholic earls' of Angus, Huntly and Errol, all of whom had 'sworn not to divulge this book during his [James's] lifetime, and shall perform the same to their power after his death'.[3] Secrecy was, however, breached after the king's employment of an amanuensis led to a manuscript copy being seen by James's main Presbyterian antagonist, Andrew Melville, who extracted eighteen 'Anglo-pisco-papistical conclusions' from its content and submitted a request to the Synod of Fife for *Basilicon Doron* to be reviewed in its entirety at the forthcoming General Assembly of the Kirk.

Although James intervened to prevent the General Assembly discussing his text in 1599, interest in the king's secret testament persisted. In January 1600, a French envoy in Edinburgh informed Henri IV that the Scottish king had composed '*trois livres du gouvernement*' ('three books of government'), claiming – erroneously – that the third book taught his son '*comme il faut traciter les Anglois*' ('how one needs to negotiate with the English').[4] When James prepared a new edition to be published in Edinburgh and London in 1603, he added an extensive preface. Echoing claims made more than a decade earlier in 1591 to accompany publication of his poem *Lepanto*, James insisted that publication of *Basilicon Doron* was 'contrary to my intention and expectation'. The king insisted that his track had been conceived as a 'secret councillor and faithful admonisher' for his son. But he found himself effectively compelled to publish an official version as a means of correcting 'the false copies that are already spread, as I am informed'. James also asserted that unauthorized digests of *Basilicon Doron* – albeit 'lacking both my method and half of my matter' – were circulating in a work bearing the objectionable title *The King's Testament*, 'as if I had eiked [added] a third Testament of my own' to the Old and New Testaments in Scripture.[5] Although no copies of a work bearing that title survive, in October 1602 the London newsletter-writer John Chamberlain had learned that the Scottish king was 'printing a little piece of work christened with a Greek name in nature of his last will or remembrance to his son', precisely to correct versions that had 'gone abroad, subject to many constructions and much depraved by many copies'.[6]

The fortuitous timing of *Basilicon Doron*'s publication in both Edinburgh and London also generated a much larger readership for the tract than James might have anticipated, since its publication was entered into the Stationers' Company Register in London to a syndicate of booksellers on 28 March 1603, four days after Elizabeth I's death. While the Venetian Secretary in London reported that James's tract was 'sent to press here within an hour of the queen's death', London booksellers were certainly selling copies of *Basilicon Doron* by 30 March, with between 13,000 and 16,000 copies estimated to have been printed in eight editions before an outbreak of plague disrupted production in mid-April.[7] For English readers, there could be no more direct way of learning about their new king. Emphasizing 'the integrity of the author' over any 'perfection in the work itself', James insisted that *Basilicon Doron* revealed 'the true image of my very mind, and form of the rule, which I have prescribed to myself and mine'. Its content yielded 'a discovery of that which may be looked for at my hand, and whereto even in my secret thoughts, I have engaged myself for the time to come'.[8] Coinciding with James's accession as England's new king, *Basilicon Doron*'s publication in affordable quarto editions also meant that large numbers of his subjects could quickly share in what had originally been a tightly guarded royal secret; 'each copy was not merely the cheap product of the press, but "the kingly gift"'.[9]

The publication of *Basilicon Doron* was presented as the divulging of mysterious secrets of state (the *arcana imperii*) and precious personal confidences. But above all, *Basilicon Doron* was a manual of kingcraft: a means through which Henry should 'study to know well your own craft, which is to rule your people'. In his earlier *Daemonologie* (1597), James had sought to demonstrate God's existence by acknowledging the reality of diabolic power. In *Basilicon Doron*, the king again approached his subject in terms of contrary positions by maintaining that the best way to understand virtuous kingship was to recognize vicious tyranny as its inverse. Accordingly, he advised Henry to remain ever mindful of the 'true difference between a lawful good king, and a usurping tyrant'. Citing the Latin maxim '*contraria iuxta se posita magis elucescunt*' ('opposites placed next to each other become more apparent'), James averred it was 'easy then for you (my son) to make a choice of one of these two sorts of rulers'.[10]

Throughout *Basilicon Doron*, James illustrated theoretical precepts with insights from his own experiences as king. As explained in the new preface added in 1603, he had sought to identify 'the particular diseases' in Scottish society as well as their 'best remedies', having learned 'both the theory and practice thereof'. As the country's ruler, he was better placed to provide explanations 'than any simple school-man, that only knows matters of kingdom by contemplation'. Throughout *Basilicon Doron*, the king adopted the dual personae of a *paterfamilias* to provide a permanent *vade mecum* for his young son and heir, as well as a *pater patriae* to make himself better known to all Scots and his new English subjects. His intentions remained pedagogic and, if readers criticized his style of instruction as 'too particularly plain', he was unapologetic. He was, however, careful to confirm that the kingly advice he had prepared four years earlier only applied to Scottish governance; he would 'speak nothing of the state of England, as a matter wherein I never had experience'. Although his long-standing hope that either he or Henry would, one day, succeed as English king was evident in *Basilicon Doron*, James denied any wish 'to be a busybody in other princes' matters, and to fish in other folks' waters, as the proverb is'.[11]

*

For his Scots subjects, James had, moreover, already produced a work of political theory. In the same year that he composed *Basilicon Doron*, he published *The Trew Law of Free Monarchies* (1598), albeit adopting a Greek pseudonym 'Philopatris' (a 'lover of his country') to sign its preface. Issued by the royal printer, Waldegrave, *The Trew Law* was modest in its physical appearance; although only a third the length of *Basilicon Doron*, it was produced on relatively cheap paper with narrow margins framing the text. Addressing 'my dear countrymen', the king assumed the guise of a patriotic commentator whose long-standing concern regarding the future of 'this our so long disordered, and distracted commonwealth' had 'compelled me at last to break silence' to demonstrate the iniquity of previous rebellions against royal authority in Scotland.[12]

While *Basilicon Doron* was republished in numerous editions and foreign translations during James's lifetime, it was *The Trew Law* that first publicly disseminated his strictures on how Scots should act as 'honest and obedient subjects to your king in all times coming'. On James's accession as English king, *The Trew Law* was reprinted at least four times in London in 1603 and included in the king's collected *Works* in 1617. Its royal author equipped readers with a storehouse of arguments against the dangerously seductive 'siren songs' of those who claimed that monarchs remained subject to human laws and, in the event of misrule, should be resisted, deposed or killed. Recent Scottish history demonstrated all too graphically that such questions were not solely matters of abstract speculation. James's own accession to power in 1567, at just over a year old, had been effected by a group of subjects whose forcible deposition of his mother, Queen Mary, had supplied a vivid instance of the type of rebellious disobedience that *The Trew Law* vigorously denounced as sinful. More recently, 'the superstitious rebellion of the [Catholic] Leaguers, who upon pretence of heresy' had unlawfully tried to prevent the (then) Protestant Henri of Navarre from succeeding as French king, had resulted in 'the great desolation of their whole country'.[13]

Following a tripartite structure, *The Trew Law* first presented the case for dutiful obedience in terms of Scriptural exegesis, before turning to Scots fundamental law and natural law. Struck by its opening claim that 'Monarchy is the true pattern of Divinity', later generations of readers have often regarded *The Trew Law* (and *Basilicon Doron*) as archetypal expositions of divine-right theory. Certainly, had James openly proclaimed his authorship of *The Trew Law* rather than using a patriotic pseudonym, his quotation of the verse from Exodus (22:28) – 'Thou shalt not rail upon the judges, neither speak evil of the ruler of thy people' – would have appeared more a royal command than Biblical counsel. Equally authoritarian assumptions underlay *The Trew Law*'s explanation that Scottish monarchs retained ultimate overlordship over their subjects: as 'master over every person' in his lands, kings had 'power over the life and death of every one of them', while the rights of buried treasure hoards and estates of intestate individuals likewise reverted to a monarch as 'over-lord over the whole lands'.[14]

But focusing solely on the potentially oppressive aspects of *The Trew Law* would be misleading. For while James presented an 'apology for kings', he was keen to reassure readers he was not thereby implying that 'the world were only ordained for kings, and they without controlment to turn it upside down at their pleasure'. Suffusing his directives regarding royal power was an emphasis on benevolent paternalism as James likened the selflessness of parenthood to a monarch's responsibility for their subjects. By 1598, the Scottish king was father to two young children, Henry and Elizabeth, with another daughter, Margaret, born on Christmas Eve that year. For James, a monarch not only served as God's lieutenant on earth, but he was also 'a loving father, and careful watchman' to his subjects; just as a parent believed that their 'earthly felicity and life stands and lives more' in their offspring than themselves, 'so ought a good Prince [to] think of his people'.[15]

Extending to around 10,000 words, *The Trew Law* was similar in length and appearance to published sermons. Around a third of the tract comprised Scriptural exegesis, with the king's text taken from the Book of Samuel (8:9–20) where the prophet advised the Israelites of the implications of their request to be ruled by a temporal monarch. Adopting his favoured role as knowledgeable teacher and authoritative guide, James insisted that if readers 'consider the very words of the text in order, as they are set down, it shall plainly declare the obedience that the people owe to their king in all respects'.[16] Confident instruction did not always, however, entail textual fidelity, prompting one modern critic to warn of 'the extent to which James's manipulations of Scripture at times amount to misrepresentations'.[17] For at the outset of *The Trew Law*, James cited Psalm 82 to aver that 'Kings are called Gods by the prophetical King David, because they sit upon God his Throne in the earth, and have the count of their administration to give unto him.'[18] Yet while the quotation's opening is correct, the construction 'because' was James's gloss since the psalm reads:

> I have said, Ye are gods; and all of you are children of the most High
> But ye shall die like men, and fall like one of the princes.

James's Scriptural exposition sought to demonstrate that, just as the Israelites declared themselves willing to endure whatever iniquities wicked kings, such as Saul, might inflict in order to receive royal protection, Scots should likewise recognize that any monarch might rule tyrannically. But since prophets such as Samuel, David and Elias did not advocate 'uproars & rebellions against these wicked kings', it was unlawful now for 'seditious preachers' of any sectarian denomination 'to stir up rebellion, under cloak of religion'. Rather, James repeated the advice to persecuted Christians in the early days of the Church: *preces, & lachrymæ sunt arma Ecclesiæ* ('prayers & tears are the weapons of the Church'). Since God alone was responsible for judging a king, dutiful Scots should simply pray 'for his continuance, if he be good; for his amendment, if he be wicked', obeying all lawful commands, but 'eschewing and flying his fury' regarding unlawful edicts.[19]

Having demonstrated the Scriptural warrant for royal power in *The Trew Law*, James turned to the fundamental laws of Scotland where he set about rewriting George Buchanan's *Rerum Scoticarum Historia* (1582) regarding the authority wielded by the country's supposed first king, Fergus I, around 330 BC. According to Buchanan, when the ancient Scots had feared attack from the Picts and Britons, they resolved to 'procure both foreign auxiliaries, and a foreign prince', prompting Fergus to travel from Ireland to assist in successfully repelling the attackers; thereafter Fergus had returned to Ireland and 'the Scots confirmed the kingdom to him and his posterity by an oath'.[20] By contrast, James insisted that Fergus had arrived in a 'scantily inhabited' Scotland with an armed force and had made 'himself master of the country, by his own friendship, and force', as the Scots 'willingly fell to him'. Accordingly, James declared it 'plainly proved, that a wise king coming in among barbarians' first established the form of government; the institution of royal power pre-dated any meetings of estates and the Scottish Parliament was 'nothing else but the head court of the king and his vassals'.[21]

Although deducing radically divergent political theories, both James and Buchanan adhered to the same ancient constitutionalist history of Scotland that maintained (however implausibly) that Scotland had been ruled by an unbroken succession of monarchs for over two millennia, as described in Hector Boece's *Historia Gentis Scotorum* (1527). As James started to assume more personal power as Scotland's king, in 1579 his Privy Council approved the design of a new gold coin worth forty shillings, to be known as the 'Scots Crown'. On one side, the coin's motto would read *hactenus invicta miserunt* ('thus far have they gone unconquered') and, on the other, *ad te centum et quinque proavi* ('a hundred and five ancestors to you').[22] At Elizabeth I's court, Henry Howard (later created Earl of Northampton by James), penned a work admiring how, after the ancient Scots solemnly swore allegiance to Fergus I, 'till this present from 333 years before Christ, excepting . . . certain bastards, none but the right offspring of King Fergus has governed'.[23] On his return to Scotland in 1617, James was welcomed to Perth by a city merchant who lauded his country's unique fortune in having 'continued these 2,030 years bypast under the government of 107 kings, all lineally sprung from Fergus I'.[24] In the early 1680s, James's grandson Charles II commissioned a Dutch artist to give visual realization to this tradition by producing a full-size painting of Fergus I, followed by portraits or busts of Charles II and all his 111 putative royal ancestors to be displayed, as they remain today, in the Palace of Holyroodhouse in Edinburgh.[25]

For James, royal power was inherently patriarchal, with monarchs occupying the same hierarchical role over the body politic as the head over a physical body. While the sub-title of The Trew Law addressed 'the reciprocal and mutual duty betwixt a free king and his natural subjects', James conceived such reciprocity in terms of the dual responsibilities of monarchs to rule virtuously and wisely and the parallel duty of subjects to obey. Quite different was Buchanan's contractual account of monarchy whereby royal power was entrusted to rulers on a conditional basis that permitted active resistance which, in the event of misrule, was even acclaimed as virtuous. Accordingly, James was intent on dispelling the 'very deceivable argument' that positive outcomes might justify the means; in all instances, 'evil should not be done, that good may come of it'. Aside from its inherent unlawfulness, popular resistance invariably entailed the commonwealth's destruction by encouraging 'bare men to set up themselves, and fly with other mens' feathers, the reins being loosened to all the insolences that disordered people can commit'.[26] Only one non-Scriptural authority was cited in The Trew Law, which was the view of James's erstwhile friend and poet the sieur Du Bartas, in lines from La Seconde Sepmaine that remained unpublished until 1600: 'Better it were to suffer some disorder in the estate, and some spots in the commonwealth, than in pretending to reform, utterly to overthrow.'[27]

*

Returning to Basilicon Doron, James again devised a tripartite structure for his tract, advising Prince Henry first on his 'duty towards God as a Christian', before turning to 'your duty in your office as a king' and appropriate conduct 'in indifferent things' that were not inherently right or wrong but only became so if 'rightly or wrongly used', such as table manners, dress, sleeping patterns and recreational pastimes.[28] Couched in straightforward prose, Basilicon Doron combined a proliferation of aphorisms drawn from classical sources, extensive Scriptural quotation, and James's personal glosses on such precepts, as informed by his practical experiences as king. Basilicon Doron would, accordingly, have been familiar to contemporary compilers of commonplace books who were accustomed to extracting short sententiae from compendious volumes, often returning to re-read selected maxims for their enduring prescriptive value.

In *Basilicon Doron*'s first section on 'a king's Christian duty towards God', James provided his son with a succinct reference guide to Scripture, asking, for example: 'Would ye then know your sin by the Law? Read the books of Moses containing it.' Although the king designated the Books of Proverbs and Ecclesiastes 'so full of golden sentences, and moral precepts' that Henry could find no better instruction elsewhere, his father counselled him to approach Scripture patiently, to 'read with delight the plain places, and study carefully to understand those that are somewhat difficult'. The king thus hoped that Henry might ultimately become 'a good textuary, for the Scripture is ever the best interpreter of itself', with the *Dictionary of the Older Scots Tongue* crediting James with the first use of the French loan-word 'textuarie' to denote an authoritative interpreter of Scripture.[29] Since prayer was best undertaken in quiet solitude, Henry should seek to be 'neither over-strange with God, like the ignorant common sort' who relied on set printed prayers, 'nor yet over-homely with him, like some of the vain Pharisaical Puritans, that think they rule him upon their fingers'. To James's mind, prayer was, after all, 'nothing else, but a friendly talking with God'.[30]

As his caustic aside regarding 'Pharisaical Puritans' suggested, James distinguished between fatherly advice regarding private prayer and Bible study and the ways in which his son, once king, should interact with members of the clerical estate. In 1598, some of the king's determination to 'break silence' and publish *The Trew Law* had been fuelled by his increasingly antagonistic relations with prominent Church of Scotland ministers. In the second book of *Basilicon Doron*, addressing Henry's future duties as a king, James warned that different estates were 'subject to some special vices', not least the lamentable 'pride, ambition, and avarice' that regularly afflicted clerics everywhere. More particularly in Scotland, the Protestant Reformation had been 'extraordinarily wrought by God, wherein many things were inordinately done by a popular tumult and rebellion', in regrettable contrast to countries such as England and Denmark whereby religious change had occurred 'proceeding from the Prince's order'. Following the death of Marie of Guise in 1560 and the removal from power in 1567 of James's mother, Queen Mary, 'fiery spirited men in the ministry' had started 'to fantasy to themselves a democratic form of government'. As James explained, he was thus 'often calumniated in their popular sermons, not for any evil or vice in me, but because I was a king, which they thought the highest evil'. Factious ministers 'would sometimes snapper out well grossly with the truth of their intentions' to try to persuade parishioners that monarchy was inconsistent with the freedom of the Established Church.[31]

James's frustration with overweening clerics prompted his denial that even notoriously incorrigible Highlanders or 'Border-thieves' were capable of 'greater ingratitude, and more lies and vile perjuries' than Presbyterian clergy. Indeed, the only rationale for his son Henry to tolerate such 'fanatic spirits' in his commonwealth might be in emulation of Socrates, who had deliberately chosen the ill-tempered Xanthippe as his wife simply to render all his other human relations more pleasurable. To promote godliness over sectarian division, James recommended that his son 'cherish no man more than a good pastor' and 'hate no man more than a proud Puritan'. A divinely ordained monarch should act as 'a loving nourish-father to the church' to ensure that it flourished 'in piety, peace, and learning' under careful royal custodianship. James also invoked a familial trope to warn his son against nobles' 'feckless arrogant conceit of their greatness and power'. As king, he was dismayed to observe members of the nobility 'drinking in with their very nourish-milk' a proclivity to oppress social inferiors as well as pursuing mutually destructive feuds at the slightest provocation.[32]

*

In preparing *Basilicon Doron* for publication in Edinburgh and London in 1603, James undertook some damage limitation to try to obviate likely reaction to his colourful invective. In a new preface, he acknowledged 'the sharp and bitter words' used in the tract's 1599 edition when characterizing the 'humours of Puritans and rash-heady preachers'.[33] James likewise presented himself as an instinctive conciliator who would 'equally love and honour the grave men' of all opinions, so long as religion was not used as a pretext for disobedience or schism. Alongside his captious asides about Puritans, James also worried that readers might suspect he entertained 'a vindictive resolution against England', given his exhortations to Henry to honour the memory of his ancestors, one of whom – Queen Mary – had been executed on Elizabeth I's orders. But as James hastily explained, he bore no ill-will towards English subjects, none of whom could be envisaged as acting treasonably in this regard, since they had not been his mother's subjects.[34]

The concurrent timing of James's accession as England's new king and *Basilicon Doron*'s publication also kindled extensive interest outside Britain. In May 1603, the English ambassador in Paris, Sir Thomas Parry, commissioned an authorized French translation of the treatise from Jean de Hotman de Villiers, who had undertaken a diplomatic mission to Edinburgh in the 1590s and whose father was the Huguenot polemicist François Hotman.[35] That same month, Parry also reported to Sir Robert Cecil that he had halted an unauthorized translation which he feared was unlikely to convey accurately 'the energy of the words and pithiness of the phrase' in the king's original. Cecil responded by acknowledging that, since 'even the best writings in the world' might be poorly translated, so long as Parry believed a translation had been undertaken in good faith, he should not prevent publication.[36] Five French editions of *Basilicon Doron* were published in Paris during James's lifetime.[37] Different French editions were also produced in Rouen, Lyon and the Hessian city of Hanau in 1603 and 1604 and other unlicensed editions reported in Poitiers and Sedan. While the king's literary reputation in France originated from Du Bartas's translation of *Lepanto*, *Basilicon Doron* became 'the first prose work in the vernacular of Great Britain which could be read by Frenchmen who knew no language but their own'.[38]

In the Dutch republic, the States-General recorded a translation of the 'book written by the King of Scotland' on 12 June 1603, indicating the speed with which Vincent Meusevoet had produced his vernacular translation of *Basilicon Doron*, which was reprinted at least once that year. Although *Lepanto* and *Daemonologie* had been published in Dutch editions, no attempt had been made to translate *The Trew Law*, perhaps reflecting uncertainty attaching to James's authorship and the extent to which its strident denunciation of rebellion may have resonated uncomfortably with Dutch readers, anxious to uphold the legitimacy of their recent revolt against Spanish rule. Separate German translations of *Basilicon Doron* were published at Speyer and Hamburg in 1604, followed by a Swedish edition in Stockholm in 1606. Undertaken by a University of Heidelberg student, György Szepsi Korotz, a Hungarian translation was published in the Palatinate town of Oppenheim in 1612.[39] Most foreign translations, such as Korotz's, were based on one of the four Latin translations published in London, Hanau and Prague between 1604 and 1607. Within two years of his accession as English king, therefore, James's works were printed in at least eleven different cities, in Latin and in a range of vernacular languages, facilitated by an extensive network of printers and publishers meeting at trade events such as the Frankfurt and Leipzig book fairs.[40]

In Rome, the English Jesuit Robert Persons (or Parsons) prepared his own Latin version for Pope Clement VIII in 1603. After reading aloud his translation to the pontiff, Persons claimed that Clement 'could scarcely hold tears for comfort' in hearing the new English king's exhortations to virtue and had acknowledged that 'I do highly admire many things in that book.' Although Clement hoped that James might yet become 'a Catholic, for he would be a mirror to all princes', papal esteem proved insufficient to prevent *Basilicon Doron*'s later inclusion on the Catholic Church's Index of Prohibited Books.[41] In 1603, however, another Italian reader, also likely to have been a Catholic cleric, was intrigued by the work's secrecy topos. In his *Discorso del libro del Re di Scotia* ('Discourse of the Scottish king's book'), the author identified 'many parts in this work that make me believe that his original intention was to keep it secret'. James's candid admission of his intentions regarding the English succession 'could possibly be counted "*inter arcana imperii*"', while its author admired how the Scottish king 'pungently and really well narrates the vices and deficiencies of all the said estates' represented in his country's Parliament.[42]

In *Basilicon Doron*, James cited the Horatian maxim '*Quia nescit vox missa reverti*' ('because a word which has been sent out cannot return').[43] On arriving in England in 1603, he quickly heard his own writings cited by his new subjects in panegyrical tributes. The previous year, one of Elizabeth I's godsons, Sir John Harington, had composed a manuscript tract enumerating the Scottish king's strengths as the queen's successor, noting 'his writings (*indices animi* [indicators of intention]) that pass among us though but scatteringly, and as it were by stealth'.[44] Following his accession, James was welcomed to the City of London at Stamford Hill on 7 May 1603 by the barrister and MP Richard Martin, and was specifically thanked for the 'certain knowledge' that derived from observation of his 'forepast actions, and some books now fresh in every man's hands, being (to use your Majesty's own words), the *vive* ideas or representations of the mind'.[45] That same year, the Hereford poet John Davies published a 6,000-line poem entitled *Microcosmos* that rhetorically asked James:

> How came I with thee to be so acquainted
> That so I should describe each part of thee?
> Thy book wherein so lively thou art painted
> . . . And if the books compiled by us, do bear
> The image of our minds (as thou do'st say)
> Then in that book that image doth appear
> Bright as the sun (in virtue's best array)
> To light all kings to keep their king's highway:
> No sentence, line, clause, word, or syllable
> Therein contained, but doth pure thoughts betray.[46]

Elsewhere, the rector of Ruskington in Lincolnshire, William Willymat, produced a parallel English and Latin versification of the (abridged) text which he dedicated to Prince Henry. Having obtained a copy of *Basilicon Doron*, Willymat explained how 'my wits were so ravished therewith at the first reading, that I again and again read it over', before rendering its main precepts into 169 English and Latin rhyming sestets. Beseeching the nine-year-old prince to accept his tribute amid the cacophony of 'busy bawling barkers, curious cavillers, [and] saucy sycophants', Willymat signed off by bidding:

> Farewell, young imp of British soil the stay,
> Read, see, and tread your father's chalked way.[47]

En route from Scotland to London, James had stayed at Hinchingbrooke House in Huntingdonshire, where he met a teacher from Kimbolton Grammar School, Henry Peacham, who later gained renown for his manual of polite conduct, *The Compleat Gentleman* (1622). As Peacham recalled, after presenting the new king with several emblematic drawings, he was encouraged to devise an emblematized rendering of *Basilicon Doron* by James Montagu, Master of the recently founded Sidney Sussex College in Cambridge and later editor of James's collected *Works*. Structuring his manuscript volumes in the same tripartite form as the king's treatise, Peacham created 109 emblems pairing each with a quotation from *Basilicon Doron* and a Latin motto and epigram. Dedicating one volume to James, Peacham described how, 'exulting in my new enthusiasm or rather boldness' after their encounter at

Hinchingbrooke, he had 'ventured indeed to turn your Royal Gift into emblems', notwithstanding the challenges of schoolteaching, 'where everywhere there is children's noise and chatter ... and one is not even permitted a half-hour's leisure'.[48] In 1612, Peacham published a selection of his emblems entitled *Minerva Britanna* [sic], *or A Garden of Heroical Devices.*

*

In the event, Prince Henry – the dedicatee of both *Basilicon Doron* and Peacham's *Minerva Britanna* – did not live to apply his father's precepts on kingly rule as he died of a fever in November 1612, aged eighteen. Several years later, *Basilicon Doron* appeared in a popularized version entitled *The Fathers Blessing* (1616), which expanded key points from James's text to create a book of general paternal counsel. Entered into the Stationers' Company Register in October 1615, *The Father's Blessing* was seemingly published shortly before another book of family advice, *The Mother's Blessing*, was entered into the same Register four months later.[49] Published posthumously, *The Mother's Blessing* (1616) was the work of a Puritan, Dorothy Leigh, who had dedicated her tract to James's staunchly Protestant daughter Elizabeth. Immensely popular, *The Mother's Blessing* went through at least nineteen editions before 1604 and, in one edition published in the 1620s, was bound together with *The Father's Blessing* to form a comprehensive handbook for seventeenth-century parents.[50]

In 1619, James suffered another period of illness and, mindful of his mortality, indicated his intention 'to set down at large ... the whole principal points belonging to the office of a king' the following year.[51] Such a work never materialized, but the king did publish *A Meditation* on verses from St Matthew's Gospel which he dedicated to his son Prince Charles, who, in turn, compiled his own set of meditations in late 1648, intended for his eldest son (and James's grandson), also Prince Charles. By that time, Charles I had spent a decade fighting his own subjects during the civil wars and now faced the prospect of being indicted for treason by members of the English Parliament.

Entitled *Eikon Basilike* – 'the Image of the King' – the title of Charles I's work paid homage to *Basilicon Doron* and, like James's treatise, offered his subjects 'sight into my most retired thoughts'. *Eikon Basilike*'s striking frontispiece drew parallels between Christ's passion and crucifixion and Charles's predicament, and depicted the king holding a crown of thorns. Hoping that his eighteen-year-old son and heir would become 'an anchor, or harbour, rather, to these tossed and weather-beaten kingdoms', Charles exhorted him to 'seriously consider the former, real or objected, miscarriages, which might occasion my troubles, that you may avoid them'. James's precepts were echoed in his son's denunciation of 'this mask of religion on the face of rebellion', as well as in his hope that his own son might, in turn, restore peace by 'keeping the middle way between the pomp of superstitious tyranny, and the meanness of fantastic anarchy'.[52] To the alarm of England's new republican rulers, *Eikon Basilike* was released for sale on the afternoon of Charles I's execution on 30 January 1649. It went through at least thirty-nine English editions that year alone and also appeared in seven Dutch, six French, four Latin translations and one Danish translation.

11

This Triangle Monarchy

After going to bed at Holyrood Palace on the evening of 26 March 1603, James was wakened by the unexpected arrival of the Northumberland landowner and MP, Robert Carey, who kneeled and acclaimed him as King of England, Scotland, France and Ireland. Earlier that year, Carey had observed first-hand the deterioration in Elizabeth I's health and had written to James, undertaking that should the English queen die, 'I would be the first man that should bring him news of it.' When Elizabeth died at Richmond Palace in the early hours of 24 March, aged sixty-nine, Carey defied courtiers' attempts to stay his unauthorized errand and risked making a reality of the idiom 'breakneck speed' by leaving London between 9 and 10 o'clock on that Thursday morning to reach Edinburgh by late Saturday evening. As Carey later recalled, he had hoped to arrive at supper time, but sustained 'a great fall' from his horse who 'gave me a great blow on the head, that made me shed much blood', forcing him to reduce his pace on the final leg of his three-day journey. He also took with him 'a blue ring from a fair lady' (a sapphire jewel belonging to his sister, Philadelphia) that had evidently been agreed as a code, prompting James to pronounce 'you are a true messenger'.[1] Albeit bloody, dishevelled and exhausted, Carey had fulfilled his promise of being the first to inform James that, after decades of anxious fretting over the succession, he was indeed, at the age of thirty-six, King of England and Ireland, as well as Scotland, with the euphemistic addition of France in his royal title now only nominal, following the loss of Calais in 1558.

In England, a proclamation was read aloud at Richmond Palace an hour after Elizabeth's death, confirming that James VI of Scotland was 'by law, by lineal succession and undoubted right' now King of

England, Scotland, Ireland and France. Enjoining the loyalty of local officials, the proclamation warned that measures would be taken to prevent any 'word or deed, against the public peace' or any attempt to impugn 'our only undoubted dear Lord and sovereign that now is, James the first king of all the said kingdoms'.[2] The same proclamation was read at 10 a.m. at Whitehall, St Paul's, Ludgate, Cheapside and Cornhill in London, amid tightened security that included alerting the English Navy, closing the nation's ports, detaining prominent Catholics in the localities, withholding troop consignments intended for the Dutch republic, and placing the Crown Jewels and royal silver collection under special guard. In the evening, a specially convened 'Great Council' met at Whitehall to confirm James VI of Scotland's succession as King James I of England and dispatched official messengers – who arrived in Carey's wake – to inform the Scottish king of Elizabeth's death and of his accession as England's new monarch. Thereafter, John Chamberlain observed a northbound exodus of ambitious individuals, quickly setting off on 'their own errand, as if it were nothing else but first come, first served, or that preferment were a goal to be got by footmanship'.[3]

*

The death of any long-reigning sovereign inevitably generates an atmosphere of liminal uncertainty, but the mood in England was especially apprehensive in the spring of 1603. Amid fears of a sudden coup attempt, arms and munitions were stockpiled and food prices soared. Over a decade later, John Donne recalled the sense of panic that had gripped Londoners at the time: 'every one of you in the City were running up and down like ants with their eggs bigger than themselves, every man with his bags, to seek where to hide them safely.'[4] A week before the queen's death, Robert Carey's brother, John, who was Deputy Governor of the Border stronghold at Berwick-on-Tweed, had written to Elizabeth's Principal Secretary, Sir Robert Cecil, wondering if he should travel to London 'to see her Majesty rather than remain with these terrors and fears of mind'. Carey feared the prospect of not knowing 'how or for whom to keep this place', given Berwick's location 'in the Devil's mouth, a place that will be first assailed'.[5] Much of the pervasive perturbation reflected the long-standing ban imposed on all discussions of Elizabeth's eventual successor. More than three decades earlier, legislation enacted in 1571 had rendered it a treasonable offence to discuss the royal succession in terms of 'any such claimer, pretender, usurper, utterer, declarer, affirmer, publisher or not-acknowledger'.[6]

For his part, James had long sought in vain to persuade Elizabeth to affirm publicly that he possessed the strongest hereditary right to succeed her and that his hereditary claim had not been impaired by his mother's conviction for treason. Denied formal endorsement, James had been obliged to promote his claim to succeed as English king without provoking the ire of its queen. But tensions sporadically surfaced: after Elizabeth had learned of his correspondence with her erstwhile favourite, the Earl of Essex, for instance, James suggested in September 1600 that she seemed 'to charge me with the preparing untimely of your funeral'. Given how often he had given his godmother 'full satisfaction in that point', he affected surprise that 'your ears should yet be so open to such as goes about'.[7] Six months later, the king wearily advised his envoys in London to remind the English queen of her longstanding undertaking to avoid acting in any way that might impair his claim to succeed her, always assuming that 'she be not to endure as long as the sun and the moon'.[8]

In *Basilicon Doron*, James repeatedly hoped that Prince Henry 'shall be king of more countries than this'.[9] In his pseudonymously authored *The Trew Law of Free Monarchies*, James had also upheld the inviolability of hereditary succession, insisting on the dual obedience that subjects owed not only to their ruling sovereign, but also in perpetuity to that sovereign's lawful heirs and successors. But the principles governing succession to the English throne were unhelpfully ambiguous.[10] In James's case, his hereditary claim risked being compromised by the common-law prohibition on foreigners inheriting property in England, while a fourteenth-century statute passed by Edward III excluded anyone born outside the monarch's allegiance from the line of succession. Moreover, in testamentary wills from 1544 onwards, Henry VIII had addressed the risk that none of his children (Edward VI, Mary Tudor or Elizabeth) would leave direct heirs by confirming the hereditary rights attaching to the offspring of his younger sister, Mary, Duchess of Suffolk, and ignoring those of his older sister – and James VI of Scotland's great-grandmother – Margaret.

While scrutiny of different successors' claims was prohibited in England, a purportedly objective adjudication was made in *A Conference about the Next Succession to the Crown of England*, compiled, solely or collaboratively, by the English Jesuit Robert Persons (or Parsons) and published in Antwerp in 1595. Enjoying an unusually large initial print run of 2,000 copies, the *Conference* warned readers of the dangers posed by popular ignorance of the unsettled succession.[11] Reviewing earlier English succession crises, Persons denied that the Crown had always passed to the strongest hereditary claimant and judged John of Gaunt's right to have succeeded Edward III in 1377 as more compelling than that of Richard II. Constituting 'an extended exercise in genealogical complication, indeed obfuscation', Persons' *Conference* also included dynastic tables to indicate that Philip of Spain's daughter Isabella Clara Eugenia was a descendant of Philippa, oldest child of John of Gaunt, and his first wife, Blanche, whereas James VI of Scotland's Lancastrian heritage only dated back to the illegitimate children of John of Gaunt's third wife, Catherine Swynford.[12] The *Conference* likewise evaluated the rival claims on behalf of James's English cousin Arbella Stuart (great-granddaughter of Henry VII's eldest daughter, Margaret Tudor) and Catherine Grey (granddaughter of Margaret Tudor's younger sister, Mary). Despite its ostensibly neutral stance, Persons' tract concluded by identifying the Catholic Infanta Isabella Clara Eugenia as the most likely 'to bear it away', after vigorously denying that any significant benefits would accrue to the English polity from the Scottish king's accession. As Persons warned, large numbers of Scots would seek 'the commodities and riches of England' without offering reciprocal assets. Any attempted Anglo-Scottish union would be short-lived, given the Scots' 'aversion and natural alienation' from their English neighbours and their ancient alliances with the French and Irish.[13]

For hopeful Catholic readers, Persons's claim that the Spanish Infanta had the strongest claim to succeed Elizabeth suggested that imminent regime change in England could yet bring confessional reversal. But in Britain, once an explicitly pro-Catholic author impugned James VI's claim, the ensuing Protestant backlash only strengthened it. The more emphasis placed on the dangers of a Catholic alternative – endorsed by the Jesuits, Spain and the papacy – the more James's attractions could be appreciated as a legitimate, male, Protestant sovereign who had male and female heirs, and the possibility of more offspring. James himself was keen to produce such counter-arguments. In February 1597, Sir Robert Cecil's father, William, Lord Burghley, learned that one of his contacts in Edinburgh had been loaned a copy of Persons' *Conference* for 'a night and half a day', but during that 'time it was sent for thrice by the king'.[14] Two months later, James remained visibly agitated about the succession and to Elizabeth's ambassador, Robert Bowes, made a 'solemn protestation that, to gain the Crown of England, he would not wish the shortening of her Majesty's reign or days or justly grieve or offend her during her life'. A shocked Bowes instantly stopped the king in his tracks by making clear that the succession was 'so holy' a matter that 'I durst not let my ears, tongue or hands be touched therewith'; Bowes knew, however, that 'publicly at his table and privately in his bed-chamber' the king 'used oftentimes like speeches and protestations'.[15]

In November 1597, James took the unusual step of translating into Scots, and preserving in the Privy Council register, the letter sent to him by Elizabeth a decade earlier, in which the English queen had under-taken never to permit any action that might diminish 'any right or title that may be due' to him.[16] The next month, an English agent informed Cecil that James had delivered a great 'oraison' (oration) in the Scottish Parliament, denouncing Elizabeth's 'false, malicious, envious dealing against his own person and state'. He had also described her inten-tion to leave the question of her successor 'in suspense', or covertly to favour another claimant, as 'no longer sufferable'. Scotland's most senior judge had then asked each parliamentary estate for its view on the best way 'to provoke' Elizabeth into nominating 'the king as her apparent successor'. Stimulating international support for James's claim was widely supported and the burghs had pledged £100,000 (Scots) to subsidise embassies 'to all his foreign friends and brother kings and princes to complain', and matching amounts had been promised by the other estates.[17]

While discussion of the royal succession was banned in England, at the royal court in Edinburgh, the Dublin-born poet Walter Quin composed sonnets, anagrams and dialogues in English, Latin, French and Italian championing James's claim. Recited aloud and circulating in manuscript, Quin's compositions endorsed James as 'the nearest heir, sure and virile, the issue of an English father, native to this very island'. Was Elizabeth really willing, as Quin put it, to let the 'crowd of wolves, foxes and donkeys' at her Council Table, 'bray and yell from their prophane mouths' to deny the Scottish king's right by denounc-ing him as a foreigner?[18] Moreover, Elizabeth's ministers learned that

James hoped to publish a Latin tract by Quin 'concerning the king's title to England that it may be dispersed to foreign princes', despite resistance from his English-born printer, Robert Waldegrave, who had fled to Scotland to evade prosecution for involvement in the Puritan 'Marprelate' controversy in the late 1580s. Waldegrave did, however, print two posthumous works on the English succession by the Puritan MP Peter Wentworth, who suffered serial imprisonment for publicly discussing the succession before dying in the Tower of London in November 1597. With their contents smuggled into Scotland, perhaps via the diplomatic bag, Wentworth's tracts regarded the royal refusal to settle the succession as supremely irresponsible. As Wentworth warned Elizabeth, should she die with the matter unresolved, 'there will be as many kings proclaimed, as there will be competitors . . . four or five at the least'. Accordingly, 'your executors will be so busied to set up a new king' and adjudicate the competing claims 'that they shall not possibly have one hour's leisure to attend, nor once think of your burial, or will', leaving Elizabeth's corpse to 'lie upon the earth unburied, as a doleful spectacle to the world'.[19]

If few of Elizabeth's subjects matched Wentworth's candour, there was residual apprehension that, so long as the succession remained uncertain, the queen's death risked plunging England into the type of turmoil suffered during the fifteenth-century Wars of the Roses, or the sectarian strife that had recently convulsed French society. In 1601, one of Sir Robert Cecil's associates, Thomas Wilson, assessed the health of the English body politic by first taking the country's pulse in relation to 'the point of succession'. With the subject 'straightly prohibited to Englishmen to discuss', Wilson warned that 'herein indeed the pulse beats extremely', given that he could name 'twelve competitors that gape for the death' of Elizabeth.[20] Following the Earl of Essex's disastrous coup attempt in February 1601, James instructed his two envoys in London – John Erskine, Earl of Mar, and Edward Bruce – to promote his claim to succeed as king by various means, seeking 'to walk surely betwixt these two precipices of the Queen and the people', trying 'to secure the hearts of as many noblemen and knights as ye can' and obtaining information regarding the general state of military preparedness across England. At all costs, James wanted to ensure that 'my enemies have not the whole commandment of the armour and my friends only be unarmed'.[21]

The Caledonian charm offensive seemingly worked. In 1602, one of Elizabeth I's godsons, Sir John Harington, composed a manuscript tract upholding James's succession claim and recalling how the Earl of Mar and the Scottish delegation had 'demeaned themselves in all things so gallantly, conversed with us so kindly, feasted us so lovingly, [and] embraced us so affectionately'. Notwithstanding the long-held Scotophobia of Londoners, 'you should hear them in shops openly commend their persons, their fashions, their face, their activity, and compare the Earl of Mar to their darling, that they do yet mourn for, the Earl of Essex'.[22] Further afield, at a meeting of the Spanish Council of State in December 1602, it was reluctantly recognized that Persons's preferred candidate – now Archduchess Isabella Clara Eugenia of the Spanish Netherlands – was not interested in claiming the English throne. With no universally supported Catholic alternative, the Spanish court did not relish the prospect of the Scottish king's succession. In the view of Philip III's chief adviser, the Count of Olivares, James presented 'the worst solution of the question for us'. Not only would the dominions of the English monarch be enlarged significantly by his accession, but the Scottish king was 'personally to be distrusted', having always 'exhibited in all his actions a false and shifty inclination' while 'not a single good quality appears to counterbalance the evil known of him'.[23]

Ironically, however, it was precisely James's skills as a dissembler and his success at subterfuge that assisted his accession as English king. For after the Earl of Essex's downfall in 1601, the Scottish king started a clandestine correspondence with several of Elizabeth's closest associates, including Sir Robert Cecil. Known to only half a dozen individuals, the correspondence was conducted via secret letters placed in the ordinary diplomatic post for the unsuspecting English agent George Nicolson – nicknamed 'the pigeon' – with return missives from the Scottish court addressed to French Huguenot nobles in London.[24] In an early encoded missive, Cecil admitted to James that 'the subject itself [succession] is so perilous to touch among us, as it sets a mark upon his head forever that hatches such a bird.' He counselled the king not to fret that 'everything we do is not hourly made demonstrative to you'; what mattered was that Elizabeth's ministers had 'found in you a heart of adamant in a world of feathers'. In a later letter, Cecil likewise reassured James that 'your ship shall be steered into the right harbour without cross of wave or tide that shall be able to turn over a cockboat', with many more of Elizabeth's subjects 'fitter pilots' to assist than they seemed at present.[25]

*

The accession of a Scottish Stuart king to the English throne raised the prospect of a reconfigured British mainland. In his pamphlet *1603. The Wonderful Year*, Thomas Dekker amended slightly the timing of the queen's demise to rejoice that James, 'at seven of the clock wert a king but over a piece of a little island, and before eleven the greatest monarch in Christendom'.[26] On 26 March, Cecil wrote to James, predicting that his accession would inaugurate a new and 'glorious empire' that 'may pass happily with all acclamation by the name of Great Britain or Britannia Major'.[27]

Such confident assertions reflected wider interests in rehabilitating vatic prophecies that had predicted the eventual restoration of the British mainland's territorial integrity and reunification of its inhabitants. Reviving the ancient name of 'Britain' invoked the legendary account of the island's first settlement by Brutus in the aftermath of the Trojan War, and his entrusting of England, Scotland and Wales to his three sons, Locrinus, Albanactus and Camber. James's accession likewise stimulated revived interest in myths popularized in Geoffrey of Monmouth's twelfth-century *History of the Kings of Britain* and its vivid recounting of the legendary King Arthur's defeat of Saxon invaders and his successful rule over a united Britain. More recently, the Scots historian John Mair's *Historia Maioris Britanniae, tam Angliae quam Scotiae* (1521) had publicized the term 'Great Britain' and asserted that '*omnes in Britannia natos Britannos*' ('all who were born in Britain are Britons').[28] In England, the antiquarian William Camden drew on George Buchanan's *Rerum Scoticarum Historia* (1582) when embarking on an 'endeavour for several years to search out the most ancient British people and the origin of the English'. Published in 1586, the first edition of Camden's *Britannia* provided Elizabethan readers with a chorographical, Latin account of the different *gentes* (peoples) who had settled the island and their later consolidation into territorial boundaries. In the same year, William Warner's 'historical map of the same island', entitled *Albion's England* (1586), claimed that 'our whole island [was] anciently called Britain, but more anciently Albion.'[29] Hence, although the origins and extent of 'Britain' and 'Albion' remained unclear and controverted, they were not novelty terms. As James journeyed south from Edinburgh in April 1603, the Venetian Secretary in London relayed reports that the new king was evidently 'disposed to abandon the titles of England and Scotland, and to call himself King of Great Britain'. Emulating 'that famous and ancient King Arthur', James sought 'to embrace under one name the whole circuit of one thousand seven hundred miles' of coastline as a single 'United Kingdom now possessed by His Majesty, in that one island'.[30]

Although the creation of dynastic agglomerates was not uncommon in early modern Europe, rulers who acquired new territories usually remained in their original royal seat. In 1603, however, James's accession as English king saw the royal court relocate from Edinburgh to London, with Scotland becoming an absentee monarchy. In verse entitled 'Scotland's Tears', Alexander Craig bewailed the injury inflicted on his country, asking:

> What art though Scotland then? No Monarchie allace,   [allace = alas]
> A oligarchie desolate, with straying and onkow face,   [onkow = strange]
> A maymed bodie now, but shaip some monstrous thing,
> A reconfused chaos now, a countrey, but a King.[31]

At Sunday service in Edinburgh's St Giles church on 3 April, James addressed the congregation, recognizing that his imminent move to England was simultaneously an occasion for joy and sorrow. As recorded by the Presbyterian historian David Calderwood, James nevertheless exhorted his listeners to conceive of Scotland and England as one entity, with 'no more difference between London and Edinburgh, yea, not so much, as between Inverness or Aberdeen and Edinburgh', given less rugged English terrain. Under his kingship, the peoples of both countries were now 'joined in wealth, in religion, in hearts, and affections'. James also reminded the congregation that, since 'I have a body as able as any king in Europe . . . I shall visit you every three years at least', so his Scots subjects may 'see and hear me, and from the meanest to the greatest, may have access to my person, and pour out your complaints in my bosom'.[32] Before leaving Edinburgh two days later, the king wrote to nine-year-old Prince Henry, warning him that excitement arising from his father's accession to the English throne should not 'make you proud or insolent, for a king's son and heir was ye before, and no more are ye yet'.[33] Entering England for the first time on 6 April, its new king stayed overnight at Berwick-on-Tweed, where he climbed the town's fortified walls and fired a cannon 'so fair, and with such sign of experience' that 'the most expert gunners there' were impressed.[34]

Before Elizabeth's death, James had deemed it 'dangerous to leave the chair long empty', since 'the head being so far distant from the body may yield cause of distemper to the whole government'.[35] As Londoners keenly awaited the new king's arrival, Dekker described how 'all men's eyes were presently turned to the north, standing even stone-still in their circles, like the points of so many geometrical needles', awaiting 'his Majesty's more near and nearer approach'.[36] James, however, deliberately delayed arriving in London until all formal obsequies were over, since court etiquette required the burial of a former monarch before public appearances of their successor. He spent the day of Elizabeth's funeral on 28 April 1603 at the Huntingdonshire home of Sir Oliver Cromwell, who had been part of the English delegation attending Prince Henry's baptism celebrations in Stirling a decade earlier. At Sir Robert Cecil's Hertfordshire home of Theobalds, James chaired his first English Privy Council meeting on 3 May, with five Scots added to its membership, including the king's relative Ludovick Stewart, Duke of Lennox, and his childhood companion (and previous envoy in England) the Earl of Mar.

On 7 May, James was welcomed to the City of London. After several nights' residence in the Tower of London, the royal entourage moved to the relative safety of Greenwich since the new king's arrival coincided with one of the worst outbreaks of plague in early modern England. From Greenwich, James issued a proclamation on 19 May after receiving reports of unrest on the Anglo-Scottish border, where 'certain disordered and wicked persons' were 'pretending ignorance' of his intention to unite the two kingdoms. To remove any doubts, the king confirmed that the dynastic union achieved via his accession to the English throne was the precursor to closer political, religious, economic and legal unity. While God had endowed him with 'power and force sufficient' to further those plans, James also claimed to have found 'in the hearts of all the best-disposed subjects' in both realms 'a most earnest desire, that the said happy union should be perfected'. Meanwhile, subjects in England and Scotland should regard the two countries 'as one realm and kingdom' and consider themselves 'as one people, brethren and members of one body'.[37]

As a divinely ordained monarch, James believed that he possessed sufficient power and force to rule without further confirmation of his royal title. But not all his new subjects were so easily persuaded. Judicial examinations revealed what became known as the 'Bye Plot', which envisaged a large number of Catholics assembling at Greenwich on Midsummer Night in June 1603 in order to kidnap James and imprison him in either the Tower of London or Dover Castle until a guarantee of religious toleration for Catholics could be extracted. In a separate 'Main Plot', plans were hatched to install James's English cousin Arbella Stuart on the throne in a conspiracy that necessitated, as one plotter admitted, destruction of 'the king and his cubs'.[38]

It was against this destabilizing background of serial attempts to seize his throne that James finalized arrangements for his English coronation at Westminster Abbey, selecting the date of 25 July 1603 for the ceremony to coincide with St James's Day (see Plate 11). By then, he had been joined in England by Queen Anna who, together with Prince Henry and Princess Elizabeth, had arrived at Windsor on 30 June.[39] In the first joint coronation in England since that of Henry VIII and Katherine of Aragon in 1509, James and Anna were crowned in a ceremony that adhered to the ritual prescribed in the fourteenth-century manuscript 'Liber Regalis'. The coronation service would nevertheless have sounded very different as James insisted that it be conducted entirely in English rather than Latin. Other innovations included issuing admission tickets to control the number of attendees. (In a proclamation, the king had acknowledged the comfort that his new subjects would derive from 'the sight of our person, of the queen our dear wife, and of our children', but explained that allowing crowds of spectators would make his coronation 'a means not only of increasing the infection within our city, but of dispersing it into all places of this realm'.[40] Another notable ceremonial deviation was omitting the traditional practice of presenting a new English monarch to the congregation for acclamation and 'enquiring their will and consent'; instead, James was declared 'the rightful inheritor of the crown of this realm', with the congregation simply 'required to make acknowledgement of their allegiance to his Majesty'.[41]

*

While James was determined to negate all notions of election attaching to his tenure as English king, residual uncertainty remained regarding the likely geopolitical implications of what one manuscript author called 'this triangle monarchy'.[42] While the plague outbreak necessitated postponing the meeting of James's first English Parliament, he wrote to his Scottish Privy Councillors in January 1604, directing that measures to promote British union be debated in the Edinburgh legislature. Since Scotland and England were now united under his rule 'in one isle disjointed from the great Continent of the world', James reiterated his desire for subjects in both countries to 'join and coalesce together in a sincere and perfect union, and, as two twins bred in one belly, love one another as no more two, but one estate'.[43]

When James opened his first Westminster Parliament on 19 March 1604, he reminded peers and MPs of his hereditary descent from Henry VII of England and presented himself as bringing peace 'in a double form'. First, he was descended from a king who had ended England's internal division between the rival Houses of Lancaster and York by uniting them in marriage; that union had produced James's great-grandmother, Margaret Tudor, whose marriage to James IV of Scotland had now resulted in James VI's English accession. Secondly, natural logic now dictated the union of England and Scotland, which James described as 'two countries being separated neither by sea, nor great river, mountain, nor other strength of nature, but only by little small brooks, or demolished little walls, so as rather they were divided in apprehension, than in effect'. Envisaging a new state of Great Britain that dissolved current borders, the king explained that, just 'as little brooks lose their names by their running and fall into great rivers', so too vanished 'the very name and memory of the great rivers swallowed up in the ocean'. Geopolitical ambition was recast in the language of holy matrimony, as James warned that 'what God hath conjoined then, let no man separate. I am the husband, and all the whole isle is my lawful wife.' The king's marital imagery nevertheless remained notably Protestant, with 'the whole island' denoting mainland Britain, to the exclusion of Catholic Ireland.[44]

But among a vocal number of England's political representatives, the king's manifesto for union unleashed emotive fears that the creation of Britain signalled the eradication of separate English and Scottish identities, religious worship, laws and influence. When James returned to

Westminster on 20 April, he reminded peers and MPs that England and Scotland were united in 'one allegiance, and loyal subjection, in me and my person, to my person and my posterity forever'. To James's mind, his accession to the English throne was part of a providential plan, whereby a remarkable number of pre-existing similarities between the two countries required 'finishing'. Frustrated by their negative response, James then wrote to English MPs in a letter that was read aloud in the Commons on 1 May, indicating that he 'had given over wrangling upon words with you'. Reminding MPs that Anglo-Scottish union was a divine blessing, the king warned that, to disregard 'God's benefits so freely offered unto us, [is] to spit and blaspheme in His face by preferring war to peace, trouble to quietness, hatred to love, weakness to greatness and division to union'. To avoid appearing overly prescriptive, James approved the appointment of bilateral English and Scottish Commissioners to pursue the matter and allowed those commissioners to 'be your own cooks, to dress it as ye list'.[45]

Two days later, Robert Cecil wrote to James's relative the Duke of Lennox explaining parliamentary recalcitrance. No matter how much peers and MPs might 'wish the union with all their souls', they could not approve the 'common name of Britain' until necessary measures had been agreed by union commissioners and parliaments in both England and Scotland, ensuring 'the laws may be so compounded as the island may not have two forms of government, which will keep several parliaments still on foot.' To proceed otherwise, Cecil warned, would mean 'all our laws are dissolved, as soon as the name is given; which, though it seem strange, yet is it certain.' Preferring to proceed instead by 'quiet conference', Cecil doubted that 'any man [can] be so stupid' as to obstruct the opportunity 'God's providence has offered us for the mutual peace and felicity of both realms'.[46]

James's proposal to adopt a new royal style of 'King of Great Britain' had also been resisted by several English judges who had warned that its introduction would entail 'an utter distinction of all the laws now in force ... all processes, all writs, all executions of justice, yea, the very recognition of the king in this parliament'.[47] In 1616, James dismissed this opinion as 'a foolish quirk of some judges' and, over four centuries later, a monarch's prerogative right to adopt their own regnal style was upheld in *McCormick v. Lord Advocate* (1953), in response to objections that the designation 'Elizabeth II' was, in Scotland, historically inaccurate.[48] In 1604, however, fears that England's vaunted liberties faced imminent extinction prompted a bill seeking confirmation of Magna Carta's provisions to be placed before the Commons in March, while a 'Form of Apology and Satisfaction' – purporting to explain the English Parliament's customary privileges to a foreign king – was read aloud in the Commons in June, but not formally presented to James.[49]

On the day scheduled for the first meeting of union commissioners, 20 October 1604, James simply announced the formal change in royal style to 'King of Great Britain' by proclamation, insisting that 'the blessed union, or rather reuniting of these two mighty, famous, and ancient kingdoms of England and Scotland, under one imperial crown' was God's will. The union of the two kingdoms had not been 'enforced by conquest and violence, nor contracted by doubtful and deceivable points of transaction', but it derived naturally from the conjunction of James's dynastic claim to both crowns, 'being lineally descended from the blood of both through the sacred conjunction of wedlock'. With England and Scotland now constituting, territorially, 'a little world within itself', James defended proposals to 'perfect' the union as measures 'which justly and safely we may by our absolute power do'. Accordingly, in replacing the names of England and Scotland with that of Great Britain, he contended that 'we do not innovate or assume to us any new thing, but declare that which is and hath been evident to all.'[50]

Days earlier, James had also authorized a new coinage for both England and Scotland, maintaining that the 'reducing of the gold and silver of both the said kingdoms to one perfect equality' was an essential preparation for closer union. English 'sovereign' coins were renamed 'unites' and bore a Latin legend from Ezekiel that promised 'I will make them one nation.' As one MP confirmed during a Commons debate, 'if we put our hand in our purse, and can feel a twenty-shilling piece of gold, we may perceive on it, *Faciamus eos in gentem unam*' ('Let us make ourselves into one people'). Larger silver coins – 'half-unites' – presented James's union project as dynastic destiny with the non-Scriptural legend '*Henricus Rosas Regina Jacobus*' ('[As] Henry the roses, [so] James the kingdoms'). Silver shillings bore a text from the Gospel of Matthew (19:6), '*Quae Deus Coniunxit Nemo Separet*' ('What God has joined together, let no man put asunder').[51]

Over six weeks between October and December 1604, forty-eight English and thirty-one Scots commissioners agreed a limited set of proposals that were formalized as an 'Instrument' of union, recommending the abolition of mutually hostile laws, new administrative and judicial arrangements for the Anglo-Scottish Borders, measures to promote free trade, and suggested clarifications regarding mutual naturalization. The Scots commissioners included the lawyer Thomas Craig, who recalled being astonished to find so many in England 'so little informed upon their past history'. When Craig marvelled that Anglo-Scottish union was now being negotiated as a result of a peaceful dynastic accession, he had been 'flatly contradicted' by assertions that no English monarch had ever contemplated conquering Scotland, which instead owed 'her security solely to her cold climate, her poverty, mountains and bogs'.[52]

Beyond Westminster, proposals for closer Anglo-Scottish union generated a torrent of printed pamphlets, manuscript memoranda, sermons and poems, as well as detailed Latin commentaries extending over hundreds of pages. In one such commentary, Craig likened Stuart dynastic expansion to successful Habsburg aggrandizement noting how, over centuries, 'the kings of Spain bent all their energy' to uniting the Iberian peninsula into a single state; now 'Spain is known simply as Spain' and the names of former kingdoms, such as Castile, Aragon, Leon and Portugal, were subsumed within the Habsburg superpower.[53] In a manuscript tract, John Doddridge – who became English Solicitor-General in October 1604 – suggested creating 'a common parliament for both kingdoms, for the general causes which shall equally concern both people'. The 'Helvetians and Swiss' convened such an assembly with representation from 'all the cantons or confederate states', while 'every estate particularly have nevertheless their proper and peculiar parliament'.[54] Elsewhere, in his *De Unione Insulae Britannicae* ('Concerning the Union of the British Island'), published in 1605, the Scots Presbyterian David Hume of Godscroft recommended creating a new 'Supreme Council' of Britannia, comprising an equal number of Scots and English representatives who could oversee regional councils in London, York, Lancaster, Edinburgh and possibly Aberdeen, with a new bicameral British Parliament meeting in York. Measures to promote integration could include compulsory exchange systems between the five Scottish universities and Oxford and Cambridge. For Hume, British public service was self-evidently preferable to provincialism: as he put it, 'who in his right mind does not prefer to be the hundredth at Rome, or even in London or Edinburgh, than first in our Auchterarder?'[55]

Countering such enthusiasm, however, was pervasive scepticism regarding the benefits to be gained from closer union, alongside barely veiled xenophobia. Scrutiny of Scotland's political sovereignty only served to rehabilitate medieval claims of English suzerainty over its northern neighbour. Since the English population of around four million was four times larger than Scotland's, it was argued that closer union risked opening England's floodgates to greedy, penniless Scots. Removing trade barriers would likewise harm the English economy, while jealousy was also directed to long-standing commercial and naturalization privileges enjoyed by Scots in France through the 'Auld Alliance'. Moreover, James's repeated allusion to 'conquest' – both as the historic basis of royal power in Scotland and the process by which the state of England had itself been formed from the earlier Anglo-Saxon heptarchy – landed badly with English common lawyers, who preferred to locate the origins of their law in 'time immemorial' and to deny the impact of the Norman invasion in 1066.

Privy Councillors in Scotland also objected to the first union flag – later known as the 'Union Jack' – introduced to be flown at sea in April 1606, since it displayed the English cross of St George superimposed upon the Scottish cross of St Andrew, or saltire. Between James's accession and the new flag's introduction, British ships had been obliged to fly both national flags from the same mast which, unfortunately, implied that some sort of hostile encounter had occurred in which the flag flown higher had triumphed. Heraldically, the new union flag was intended to denote the parity of both states, for, although the cross of St George overlay the saltire, the colours of Scotland's patron saint lay nearest the hoist, in the most honourable quarter of the flag. But, as the Privy Councillors explained, fragmenting the cross of St Andrew while leaving that of St George entire was 'very prejudicial to the freedom and dignity of this estate, and will give occasion of reproach to this nation'.[56] Two designs were therefore approved, with English ships using the original design and Scottish ships flying a reverse arrangement (with the saltire superimposed upon the cross of St George). Both designs remained in use until the nineteenth century.

*

Discovery of the Gunpowder Plot and other parliamentary priorities delayed discussion of the union commissioners' 'Instrument' for a year. In the autumn of 1606, however, English MPs not only denied closer union to be necessary, useful or likely, but also clamoured to denounce James's countrymen as 'beggarly Scots' and 'the most base, peasant-like, perfidious people of the world'.[57] In February 1607, Sir Christopher Piggott unleashed a vituperative attack, the 'outrageousness' of which – 'both in words and actions' – put MPs 'into an astonishment', was withheld from the parliamentary record, and led to Piggott's detention in the Tower of London.[58] Meanwhile, the MP for Stockbridge in Hampshire, Sir Edwin Sandys, devised a cynically effective means of opposing any recommendation, however minor, by speciously claiming that discussion should instead be directed towards achieving an entire and perfect union between the two kingdoms, clearly aware that such an aim was unrealizable. Writing to Philip III, the Spanish ambassador, Pedro de Zúñiga, observed James's agitation over the lack of progress towards union as Westminster MPs 'keep speaking out freely and hostilely against the Scots'. With James claiming that 'those wretches not only do not want to enact the union, but they would like to kill me', Zúñiga judged it 'unbelievable how much ill-will the English have for him, and the harm he would like to do them'.[59]

Trying to expedite matters, James addressed both Houses of Parliament in March 1607, frustrated at 'finding many crossings, long disputations, strange questions, and nothing done'. By contrast, as he pointed out, when foreign envoys had congratulated him on his accession as English king in 1603, they had 'saluted me as monarch of the whole isle' with 'much more respect of my greatness' than as a ruler of only one realm. Everyone could also now see 'Irish, Scottish, Welsh and English, diverse in nation, yet all walking as subjects and servants within my court'. James reiterated the national security advantages that would accrue from union and also reassured MPs that England would naturally remain the dominant partner in a British union. Invoking his favoured rhetoric of conjugal concord, he explained that 'you are to be the husband, they the wife: you conquerors, they as conquered, though not by the sword, but by the sweet and sure bond of love'. But since 'union is a marriage', it was illogical to seek 'perfect', entire union while refusing the limited proposals recommended in the 'Instrument'. Pursuing the nuptial metaphor, James asked, 'would he not be thought absurd that, for furthering of a marriage between two friends of his, would make the first motion to have the two parties laid in bed together' to achieve its consummation?[60] Since a marriage was preceded by mutual sight and acquaintance, discussion of the nuptial contract, agreement of any dowry or jointure and other preparatory works, Anglo-Scottish union was likewise a matter to be approached reverently, discreetly, advisedly and soberly.

Returning to the Commons on 2 May, James hoped that his address 'had not fallen into stony or sandy hearts'; where legitimate concerns remained, he wanted to play 'the part of a good gardener, to prune, and dress, and take away the weeds and brambles, that may hinder the springing and budding of this good plant'. Regarding the extent of union, James objected that 'because I spoke of an absolute union, to say, or think I wished nothing in the meantime, were absurd'. As the king carefully clarified, 'at the beginning, when I first craved a union, my desire was to have a perfect union.' But English MPs 'drew back' at his ambition and declared it a matter to be 'entered into by little and little'; hence 'when I would have had a more full and liberal commission' for the bilateral negotiations in 1604, 'you bounded it yourselves.' Nevertheless, James remained ready to accommodate whatever MPs requested in order to expedite union. As he suggested, 'I will stay one year in Scotland, and another here; as some other kings do, that have several kingdoms'; alternatively, he could 'keep my court nearer Scotland, at York' or 'some place thereabouts', so at least 'you and Scotland shall be both alike *procul a fulmine*' ('far from his thunderbolt').[61] As the resident Venetian envoy inferred, James was 'now forced to desire the union, not only because it is useful, but also for his own reputation's sake. Like all great minds, opposition fires him.'[62]

*

Compliance with royal wishes was more forthcoming in the Scottish Parliament, where members approved most of the Instrument's provisions in August 1607, including naturalization of both *post-* and *ante-nati*, with the caveat that naturalized subjects in Scotland could not hold royal, judicial or parliamentary appointments without royal dispensation. In a letter to the king, the parliamentary Estates acknowledged their concern to ensure 'a true and friendly union' as opposed to a situation in which Scotland became 'a conquered and slavish province to be governed by a viceroy or deputy, like such of the King of Spain's provinces', to which James had alluded in speeches at Westminster. As members of the Edinburgh Parliament insisted, union 'must be a joyful marriage and a happy love-knot' in which Scotland and England became 'one loving and humble body politic to so gracious and glorious a head'. Admitting, too, their 'hope to be often refreshed by your Majesty's presence', the commissioners suggested that James might devise a means to enable his person 'as well as your heart be equally divided between us'.[63]

Although the Westminster Parliament grudgingly approved legislation to remove mutually hostile laws between England and Scotland, it rejected the Instrument's recommendations regarding naturalization. James sought to resolve that matter via a legal test case whereby an English estate would be conveyed to a Scots child born after 1603 and thereafter forcibly possessed by another party, prompting a recovery action by the child's parents. Assuming the defendant would claim that, as an alien, the plaintiff was ineligible to plead, a judicial ruling to confirm the child's status would be needed. Two estates in London were duly transmitted to Robert Colvill (also known as 'Calvin') in October 1607, prompting cases submitted to the Courts of King's Bench and Chancery that were then transferred to the Exchequer Chamber. In the ensuing argumentation, James's Solicitor-General, Sir Francis Bacon, cited Ireland as an example of a separate jurisdiction whose inhabitants, although technically aliens, were treated as English subjects and did not require patents of denizenization. To Bacon's mind, 'the case of Scotland is as clear as that of Ireland, and they that grant the one, cannot deny the other'.[64]

By a majority decision, the judges hearing *Calvin's Case* in 1608 agreed and determined that a subject's allegiance was owed to the sovereign as a natural person, rather than as a distinct political body. James's view that monarchs ruled by a law of nature superior to common or municipal law was upheld. Those born in Scotland after James's accession as English king in March 1603 – the *'postnati'* – owed their allegiance to the sovereign of England, as well as of Scotland, and were to be regarded as natural-born English subjects and could inherit English land. By contrast, those born before James's accession as English king – the *'antenati'* – thus only owed allegiance to James as King of Scotland, retained alien status in England law, and could only become naturalized English citizens by statute. By this ruling, James achieved for his '*post-nati*' subjects a different type of 'birth'.

With no major parliamentary debates on union after 1607, James's plans for closer British union have often been dubbed 'abortive'. Yet *Calvin's Case* was a deceptively momentous decision. For the jurist Sir Edward Coke, it was 'the shortest in syllables' but 'the longest in substance ... both for the present, and for all posterity'.[65] Nearly a century later in 1706, the Presbyterian pamphleteer George Ridpath opposed revived plans for an incorporating Anglo-Scottish union and argued that all envisaged benefits would be better secured by returning to *Calvin's Case* and ensuring full implementation of all *post-nati* rights. Untroubled by 'modern distinctions of federal, incorporating, complete and entire unions', James VI & I's subjects had seemingly 'solved all those difficulties' and 'cut the Gordian knot by a General Act of Naturalisation'.[66] The Anglo-Scottish union enacted in 1707 under James's great-granddaughter, Queen Anne, ultimately fell short of 'complete and entire' union. Although a new British state was created with a single Parliament at Westminster, the distinct legal and educational systems, as well as national churches, of Scotland and England were preserved.

12

Bodily Constitutions

Opening his first English Parliament on 19 March 1604, James acknowledged that its meeting had necessarily been delayed as the nation
awaited God's merciful tempering of 'his devouring angel against the
poor people of this city'.[1] London had just experienced its worst outbreak of plague since the fourteenth century. Lasting from March 1603
until the following February, the epidemic eventually accounted for the
lives of around 30,000 people. In his account of *1603. The Wonderful
Year* – with 'wonderful' denoting strange and unusual – the playwright
Thomas Dekker recounted how popular dismay at Queen Elizabeth's
death had been instantly transformed into joy by news of James's accession before citizens then confronted 'this mortal and pestiferous battle'.[2]
Another pamphleteer, James Godskall, recommended the best course as
being to 'fly and shun the infected and corrupted air, and to depart unto
a wholesome and purer air'. The three rules were '*cito, longè, tardè*:
depart speedily, far off and return slowly.'[3]

On arriving in London in May 1603, James's court quickly relocated to Greenwich and, aside from a brief return to Westminster for
the coronation in July, spent that summer and autumn on an extended
progress around England's southern counties. Temporarily installed in
Winchester in September, Sir Robert Cecil admitted to a correspondent that the court would stay in Hampshire 'so long as the plague
can escape us, which drives us up and down so round as I think we
shall come to York'. Aware that the disease was likely to be spread
by the influx of foreign ambassadors arriving in England to congratulate James on his accession, and by court followers and royal servants,
Cecil admitted that 'once a week one or other dies in our tents' in the
encampment servicing the makeshift court. But while Cecil objected

that the local surroundings had 'no savour but of cows and pigs', the king remained in good health.[4]

James was no stranger to plague's mortal dangers. During an epidemic in Fife in July 1585, the Scottish Privy Council had taken measures to disperse 'the confluence, great repair and resort of rascal people' around Falkland Palace, where the nineteen-year-old king was staying. Anyone found in the town of Falkland without valid occupation or royal permission would be given six hours to leave the town 'under the pain of death'.[5] During another epidemic in August 1597, the burgh council in Edinburgh provided a daily allowance of 16d (Scots) to indigent individuals placed in isolation on account of the plague and also covered the accommodation and food costs of children separated from their families by enforced isolation.[6] During the London outbreak of 1603–4, Elizabethan Plague Orders formulated in 1579 were reissued and given new statutory authority, requiring the houses of infected individuals to be identified with a painted cross and sealed for quarantine periods of between twenty-eight and forty days.

*

As James's thankful observance to the English Parliament confirmed, contemporaries adhered to a theodicy of plague that regarded the onset of disease as evidence of divine wrath. A serious outbreak of plague coinciding with his accession could be interpreted as an ill omen for a monarch who regarded himself as a sovereign physician. As James had contended in *The Trew Law of Free Monarchies*, 'the proper office of a king towards his subjects, agrees very well with the office of the head towards the body'. The head exercised judgement and directed all other bodily movements; accordingly, just as 'the head cares for the body, so does the king for his people'. If members of the political body were afflicted with an infirmity, kings had a duty to 'care and provide for their remedy, in case it be curable', but if incurable, they were equally obliged to 'cut them off for fear of infecting of the rest'.[7] Infectious diseases threatening the commonwealth could be pathological, such as plague, or existential, such as rebellion.

James also invoked corporeal analogies to explain British union. As he outlined to English MPs in May 1607, 'when a child is in the mother's womb, though it hath all the lineaments and parts of a body, yet it is but an embryo, and no child; and shall be born in his due time.'

Likewise, when a baby is born, 'though it then be a perfect child, yet it is no man; it must gather strength and perfection by time. Even so is it in this case of union.' Accordingly, James dismissed as invalid the objections of MPs in relation to the limited provisions recommended by the 'Instrument', insisting that preliminary measures towards closer union were 'no more unperfect . . . than a child, that is born without a beard'. British union remained 'perfect in my title and descent; though it be not an accomplished and full union; for that time must ripen and work.'[8]

In England, sovereign physicians could also be perceived as sanctified physicians able to cure their subjects' ailments. Indeed, no attribute underscored the quasi-divine character of English and French monarchy more than the purported gift of 'touching for the king's evil' as a means of healing the painful, disfiguring glandular condition known as 'scrofula'. Among contemporaries, the royal touch was regarded as an effective cure, although the tendency for the condition to flare up intermittently meant that receiving the royal touch could plausibly coincide with natural periods of remission.

On his accession as English king, James initially appeared chary of involvement, citing Protestant objections that the age of miracles had passed. In September 1603, however, he participated in a royal-touch ceremony for the first time while on progress in Woodstock. Delivering an *ex tempore* speech, James denied that he was personally capable of curing scrofula sufferers, 'for that were to attribute more to myself than belongs unto any man, for miracles are ceased, and God doth work by ordinary means'. But since he was duty bound to pray for his subjects, he invited all attendees 'to pray with me for this diseased child' in the hope that God would accede to their invocations. James was keen that he should 'not refuse to satisfy my peoples' desires' regarding the royal touch and had satisfied himself that he was freed 'from all the superstition hereof'. After the king had concluded his speech, one eyewitness observed that he then looked 'towards the Scots ministers around him, as though he expected their approval of what he was saying, having first conferred with them'.[9] Observing a similar royal-touch ceremony three years later, James Melville – former Moderator of the Church of Scotland's General Assembly – confirmed that James's participation was 'not for healing (which was only in God's hand), but for prayer and alms towards the poor diseased'. 'Political reasons' also explained the Scottish king's initial opposition and subsequent change of mind. Given the ceremony's popularity in France, if James abstained from involvement, it might weaken 'some of the substance' of his royal power regarding the 'title which he had to the kingdom and crown of France'.[10]

In 1604, James also confirmed his role as 'proper physician of his politic body' in the first published tract he specifically composed for an English readership. Initially issued anonymously, *A Counterblaste to Tobacco* acknowledged that, just as all human bodies suffered 'some sorts of diseases or infirmities', so too were all political commonwealths, no matter how peaceable or well-governed, susceptible to 'popular errors and naturally inclined corruptions'. In England's case, the king had been dismayed to observe the widespread popularity of tobacco smoking after its introduction in the last half-century from Spanish America (see Plate 22). Venturing that 'a man cannot heartily welcome his friend now, but straight they must be in hand with tobacco', James despised smoking as 'a custom loathsome to the eye, hateful to the nose, harmful to the brain, [and] dangerous to the lungs', with tobacco's 'black stinking fume' resembling 'the horrible Stygian smoke of the pit that is bottomless' – i.e. Hell.[11]

While James acknowledged the potential for tobacco to possess curative medicinal properties if responsibly prescribed, he claimed that post-mortem examinations more often revealed that tobacco 'makes a kitchen' of a smoker's internal organs, 'soiling and infecting them, with an unctuous and oily kind of soot'. The king particularly objected to smoking during mealtimes and judged it 'a great iniquity' that husbands who smoked either persuaded their wives to share the habit and thereby corrupted their 'sweet breath' or obliged them to live 'in a perpetual stinking torment'. James further denied that few individuals ever wished to start smoking but only did so 'because they were ashamed to seem singular' in refusing. Nevertheless, once they had started, tobacco's 'bewitching quality' soon rendered them addicts and even if smokers' deaths could be formally attributed to other causes, tobacco remained a contributory factor. Chronic smokers in denial resembled 'old drunkards' who 'never remember how many die drowned in drink before they be half-old'.[12]

Adopting an approach emulated by generations of modern policymakers, James's anti-smoking strategy focused on increasing significantly tobacco's purchase cost. Having established a commission to consider tobacco taxation, in 1604 the king increased the duty levied on imported tobacco from 2d per pound to 6s 8d – a rise of 4,000 per cent – at a time when tobacco imports averaged around 25,000 pounds annually.[13] Mindful of crown indebtedness, James thereafter faced the dilemma of personally despising a habit that generated lucrative crown revenue. In December 1619, a proclamation further protected royal customs duties by banning the domestic cultivation of tobacco on the grounds that samples of the crop grown in England were found to be 'more crude, poisonous and dangerous' than imports from 'hotter climates'.[14] In Scotland, James initially pursued a different approach by imposing an outright smoking ban in May 1616 whereby both the importation and sale of tobacco were forbidden. As James's Scottish Privy Councillors explained, the king had been 'credibly informed that the use, or rather abuse, of taking tobacco' had become so widespread that 'all young and idle persons are in a manner bewitched therewith', distracting them from employment, encouraging them to waste money, and provoking violent quarrels with 'youths of good birth and parentage'.[15] By 1622, however, difficulties of enforcement led to abandonment of the prohibition policy in Scotland and James instead permitted the granting of import licences in return for customs-duty receipts.[16]

*

Accompanying his paternalistic care for the body politic, James also sought to be his own 'proper physician'. It had, after all, been the onset of serious illness in 1598 that encouraged him to compose *Basilicon Doron* for Prince Henry, wherein he emphasized the need to pursue a regimen designed to make 'your body strong and durable for travel at all occasions, either in peace or in war'. Eating sensibly would ensure that 'your diet may be accommodated to your affairs, and not your affairs to your diet'. James thus advised his son to eschew excessively rich cuisine and repeated late nights to avoid becoming accustomed 'to over-great softness and delicacy in your sleep, more than in your meat; and specially in case you have ado with the wars'. Regarding regular physical exercise – to make a king's body 'able and durable' – James recommended 'running, leaping, wrestling, fencing, dancing, and playing at the catch or tennis', together with archery and a precursor of croquet known as *palle maillé*. At the same time, the king warned Henry against 'all rough and violent exercises', such as football, which seemed as likely to injure as to benefit players. Also to be avoided were acrobatics and the sort of 'tumbling tricks' practised by comedians and street-dancers 'to win their bread with'.[17]

Physically active throughout his life, James never took good health for granted. Within two years of acceding to the English throne, he had reorganized the court timetable to enable him to spend significant periods of each year away from London, preferably hunting. As he explained to Privy Councillors in January 1605, a 'lack of open air and exercise brings with it present indisposition'.[18] The following July, James declined to apologize to his brother-in-law, Christian IV of Denmark, for sending a letter devoid of startling or significant news. As James conceived, there 'can never be too numerous or frequent on either side, the letters which announce the good health, welfare, safety and prosperous affairs of friends!' Being offered an unexpected opportunity to dispatch a messenger to the Danish court, he was simply delighted to report that 'we are in very good health; that all our children are well; and that all our affairs are fine.' The same upbeat tone infused a missive sent by James to Christian the following month, discussing geopolitical tensions in the Holy Roman Empire but concluding with reassurances that 'we and our wife and children are enjoying excellent health and prosperous affairs'.[19]

Physical strength, stamina and military preparedness ostensibly run counter to conventional images of James as the archetypal 'rex pacificus'. But as the king himself acknowledged in his *Meditation upon the Lord's Prayer* (1619), he had never known 'by what fortune, the dicton [aphorism] of *Pacificus* was added to my title, at my coming in England; that of the lion, expressing true fortitude, having been my dicton before.'[20] In Scotland, a new coinage issued in 1575 had included a £20 (Scots) coin that became the largest hammered gold coin ever struck for circulation in the British Isles. Bearing the first minted portrait of James, the gold coin had depicted the nine-year-old king dressed in armour, holding a large sword in one hand and an olive branch in the other (see Plate 3). Shortly after arriving in England in 1603, James issued his first sterling coinage, in which he chose to be presented in armour and likewise selected similarly martial attire for his portrait on the new Great Seal and different versions of his first English coinage. To his new subjects, James's martial appearance in armour, sometimes on horseback with a drawn sword, was not necessarily 'innately aggressive or bellicose', but confirmed his military readiness.[21] For as James had indicated in *Basilicon Doron*, Henry must 'fail never in times of wars to be galliardest [smartest] and bravest, both in clothes and countenance'.[22] Military armour was, however, only one presentational style. Shortly before Queen Elizabeth's death, two different engravings of James were included in variant editions of an album of neo-Latin verses entitled *Inscriptiones Historicae Regum Scotorum* ('Historical Inscriptions of the Kings of Scotland') describing all Scots monarchs since 330 BC. Published in Amsterdam and Edinburgh in 1602 and London the following year, 'possibly purchasers could take their choice' of preferred royal image, with one variant presenting James in full body armour and the other including an engraved image of the king in court dress with a high hat and ruff (see Plates 9 and 10).[23]

Compared to the celebrated portraiture of Henry VIII and Charles I, James engaged no equivalent of Hans Holbein or Anthony van Dyck to render his physical appearance instantly recognizable to later generations. Among the king's new English subjects, Henry Peacham – who created emblematized versions of *Basilicon Doron* – complained that he could 'never find any true picture of his Majesty', while one modern historian has suggested that 'of all the early modern kings and queens, James I is the ruler least recognised or visually imagined'.[24] The Dutch artist Adrian Vanson has been admired for achieving, in a portrait painted in 1595, an 'unflinching presentation of the king's character – intelligent, wary, single-minded' – in his depiction of James in court dress, wearing a doublet, cloak and tall, dark sugar-loaf hat with a large jewelled 'A' signifying his marriage to Queen Anna.[25]

Distinctive jewellery was also the focal point of James's first official full-length portrait as English king, which was painted around 1606 by his Antwerp-born Serjeant Painter, John de Critz, and copied in multiple versions by members of Critz's workshop and by his Flemish brother-in-law, Marcus Gheeraerts the Younger. Compositional differences variously attired James in a jewelled silver cape or dark fur cape, and presented him either standing or reclining, but the common feature to all versions of Critz's portrait was the conspicuous 'Mirror of Great Britain' jewel which the king wore in his hat (see Plate 14).[26] Incorporating jewels from both the Scottish royal collection and that of Elizabeth, the 'Mirror' comprised three diamonds and a large ruby combined into a rhombus shape, with two large pearls and a pendant drop of the renowned fifty-five carat 'Sancy diamond', which was the largest known diamond at the time. Later decried as epitomizing 'the encrusted vulgarity of the Jacobean court', the 'Mirror of Great Britain' supplied vividly spangling symbolic confirmation of the king's British vision.[27]

One version of Critz's depiction of James wearing 'The Mirror of Great Britain' is known to have been painted for the Florentine Grand Duke, Ferdinando I de Medici. More often, foreign states were obliged to rely on descriptive pen-portraits from envoys. After visiting Edinburgh in 1602, for example, the English diplomat Henry Wotton described James to Ferdinando's Secretary as being of medium stature with '*una certa bonta naturale tirando al modesto*' ('a certain natural kindness, inclining to modesty') detectable in his eyes and general visage.[28] The following year, a papal spy, Giovanni Degli Effetti, joined the French entourage sent to London by Henri IV to congratulate the new English king on his accession. Degli Effetti shared Wotton's observation that James had:

> . . . a fine countenance, noble and genial; he is pale and very fair; he wears a longish square-cut beard; has a small mouth, blue eyes, fine and aquiline nose; he is jovial, neither too fat, nor too thin; well-made in body; rather above the average size.[29]

Another delineation was supplied by the Venetian republic's Secretary, Giovanni Carlo Scaramelli, who joined an audience of foreign dignitaries crowded into Greenwich Palace in May 1603 where he observed James wearing 'a chain of diamonds round his neck, and a great diamond in his hat', estimating the jewel in the king's hat to be worth around 200,000 crowns. By contrast, Scaramelli suggested that 'from his dress', James 'would have been taken for the meanest among the courtiers', which was 'a modesty he affects'.[30]

Modesty and restraint in raiment were maxims that James indeed sought to inculcate, reminding Prince Henry in *Basilicon Doron* of the threefold reason that God had instituted clothing: to 'hide our nakedness and shame', 'make us more comely', and 'preserve us from the injuries of heat and cold'. Henry should thus ensure that his attire was not 'over-superfluous like a debauched waster, nor yet over-base, like a miserable wretch; not artificially trimmed and decked, like a courtesan, nor yet over-sluggishly clothed, like a country clown; nor yet over-lightly, like a Candie [Cretan] soldier or a vain young courtier; nor yet over-gravely, like a minister'. Advising his son to follow a 'middle form' of dress between judicial robes and military fatigues, James further counselled that monarchs should wear their clothes nonchalantly, 'in a careless, yet comely form'. Above all, Henry must avoid appearing 'effeminate in your clothes, in perfuming, preening or such like', and 'make not a fool of yourself in disguising or wearing long hair or nails, which are but excrements of nature'.[31]

The king's strictures on appropriate dress reflected sartorial signi-fiers prescribed in Scotland's sumptuary legislation that remained on the statute book until 1701, albeit irregularly enforced. To preserve social hierarchies, in 1581 the Scottish Parliament enacted a law which insisted that, since 'God has granted to this realm sufficient com-modities' to clothe its inhabitants, 'subjects of the mean estate' were forbidden from 'presuming to copy his Highness and his nobility' by wearing garments made from silk, linen or cambric, or with gold, silver, silk or woollen trimmings 'made and brought from other foreign coun-tries'.[32] Meanwhile, members of the nobility took their own action to curb extravagant spending on dress that they feared risked making them appear 'uncomely and unhonest'. In May 1593, a group of four-teen nobles (including Ludovick Stewart, Duke of Lennox) pledged a bond to forswear acquiring new clothing that was 'laid over or smeared' with any form of ornamental braid, trimmings or passementerie. While the signatories permitted themselves to 'wear away our clothes already made', anyone breaking the undertaking in regard to new apparel agreed to host a banquet for the whole group and to donate the offend-ing 'garment to the use of the first fiddler that can espy it'.[33]

James, however, remained a 'clothes conscious and elegant' king whose signature style has been characterized by one historian of dress as consisting of 'eye-catching colour, enhanced by the general applica-tion of trimmings, and jewellery'.[34] In 1596, the king celebrated the birth of Princess Elizabeth by ordering a purple velvet suit and a cloak of 'rose peach' velvet. A similar palette informed a later order, as English king, of 'a doublet of pinked carnation silk grosgrain and hose of uncut carnation velvet trimmed with embroidered silk lace'.[35] Suits of doublet and hose were the mainstay of James's wardrobe, with sixty-five new suits purchased in 1603–4. Meanwhile, the king's linen requirements in

England amounted to an annual purchase of 'seventy-two fine holland shirts edged with bobbin lace . . . along with forty-eight day ruffs, twenty-four night ruffs, 192 handkerchiefs, and twenty-four night caps'.[36] A pair of elbow-length, gauntlet-like leather gloves has been attributed to James's ownership: lined with crimson silk, their exterior purple satin panels are richly embroidered in silver-gilt thread, depicting foliage, grapes and pomegranates. Having thrown a party in 1769 at his castellated Twickenham home, Strawberry Hill – so lavish he feared the expense 'will almost mortgage it' – the writer and connoisseur Horace Walpole greeted his guests wearing these gloves, together with an extraordinary limewood cravat that had been carved by Grinling Gibbons around 1690 to mimic, in wood, the delicacy of needlepoint lace.[37]

Ostentatious and opulent, the extravagance of 'Stuart style' belied James's exhortations to demure modesty in *Basilicon Doron*, while conspicuous consumption of any sort invariably invited censure. During the king's first Westminster Parliament, all extant sumptuary legislation in England was repealed, not from a conviction that sartorial restrictions were undesirable, but rather from MPs' refusal to entrust the Crown with sole responsibility for their regulation.[38] In parish churches, an Elizabethan homily continued to remind congregations that everyone should dress 'according to his degree, as God hath placed him', which should see many 'compelled to wear a russet-coat, which now ruffles in silks and velvets'.[39] Attacking luxury foreign imports in his play, *The Seven Deadly Sins of London* (1606), Thomas Dekker protested that 'an Englishman's suit is like a traitor's body that hath been hanged, drawn and quartered'. As he elaborated, one might find 'the collar of his doublet and the belly in France; the wing and narrow sleeve in Italy; the short waist hangs over a Dutch butcher's stall in Utrecht; his huge slippers speak Spanish; Poland gives him his boots', leaving the traitor's block a fitting resting-place for one whose 'head alters faster than the felt-maker can fit him'.[40]

Nowhere was sartorial suavity and emblematic jewellery more in evidence than at masques. During the Jacobean court's Twelfth Night festivities in 1604, Queen Anna danced the part of Pallas Athena (goddess of war) in *The Vision of Twelve Goddesses*, prompting a junior courtier, Dudley Carleton, to note the performers' debt 'to Queen Elizabeth's wardrobe' for their costumes, while the shortness of the new queen's skirt revealed that 'a woman had both feet and legs, which I never knew before'.[41] While portraiture captured sitters' likenesses, masques offered a dynamic way to appreciate physical bodies in three dimensions. Attending a court masque in 1618, the Catholic chaplain to the Venetian embassy, Orazio Busino, admired the audience's opulent finery: 'the splendour of their diamonds and other jewels was so brilliant that they looked like so many stars'. But after several hours' entertainment, James evidently found the masque's plot wearisome and, as Busino described, 'being naturally choleric, got impatient and shouted aloud, "Why don't they dance? What did they make me come here for? Devil, take you all, dance!"' While the king's new favourite, George Villiers, gracefully obliged and order was restored, Busino noted it was not until 'half past two in the morning' that 'half-disgusted and weary, we returned home'.[42]

*

Flamboyant fashion runs counter to conventional caricatures of James as physically ungainly and graceless. But despite suffering a range of physical disabilities, the king was no valetudinarian. Observing James aged eighteen, a visiting French envoy, Monsieur de Fontenay, had ventured that 'he has a weak body, but is in no ways delicate'.[43] Nearly forty years later, the king's own doctor, the Genevan-born Huguenot, Sir Theodore Turquet de Mayerne, admitted that James 'laughs at medicine and regards physicians as not only unnecessary, but positively useless', dismissing their diagnoses as 'based on mere conjectures, which are uncertain and therefore invalid'.[44] To ailing associates, the king dispensed dry wit. Following a bout of toothache in February 1614, the Bishop of Bath and Wells, James Montagu, relayed to his mother: 'the king tells me that if my head ache, I must cut it off the next time, but I tell him I will leave that for him to do.'[45]

In December 1623, Mayerne compiled a meticulously detailed psychosomatic report on the king, intended to inform other court physicians while he undertook a visit to Switzerland. In his Latin 'labyrinth of the royal anatomy' – which remained unpublished until the twentieth century – Mayerne listed James's physical symptoms, daily habits and past afflictions as well as recommended remedies and cures. As Mayerne's biographer has observed, so comprehensive is this record that 'we know not only the liver and the spleen, the gout and the diarrhoea, the medical history and the dietary habits, but also the personality and the mind of one of the most elusive of our kings'. For alongside James's ailments, Mayerne enumerated the king's 'human weaknesses and eccentricities, his lability, his disorderly habits, [and] his resentment of discipline'.[46]

Ascribing to the king 'the most exquisite sensibility', Mayerne acknowledged that, when in pain, 'his mind is tossed by the most violent motions and the bile surges around his heart, aggravating instead of soothing the evil'. The physician also reported James's dislike of having plasters applied to his skin, 'which is so thin and tender that it itches very easily'. The same observation was made by Sir Anthony Weldon in a polemical tract posthumously published in 1651: James's skin was 'as soft as taffeta sarsnet, which felt so, because he never washed his hands, only rubbed his finger-ends slightly with the wet-end of a napkin'.[47] Weldon's further claims that James had been unable 'to stand at seven years of age' and that 'his walk was ever circular' were corroborated by Mayerne's reference to a permanent weakness in the king's legs and his irregular gait.[48] Meeting James in 1584, Fontenay had likewise observed how the eighteen-year-old monarch 'never stops in one place, taking a singular pleasure in walking, but his gait is bad, composed of erratic steps, and he tramps about even in his room'.[49] Aware of his own habit of walking in circles while engaged in discussion, in 1604 James admitted to the Earl of Northampton that his allusion to '"deambulatory councils" and such-like satiric tricks did a little chafe me'. But as James conceded, it would be Sir Robert Cecil who had 'best cause to complain' of this trait, 'for I will oft-times walk so fast roundabout and about with him that he will be like to fall down dead upon the floor'.[50]

James's circumambulatory tendencies were more spitefully stigmatized by the anonymous author of *Corona Regia*, published in 1615. Observing how 'you do not proceed in a straight line with distinct footsteps; instead, you pace in a circle round and round', the mock encomiast speculated as to whether James's irregular gait derived from excess alcohol or, alternatively, some 'heavenly motion', given that 'nothing is more beautiful and perfect than the circle, nothing more divine, and nothing worthier of a king'. Caustically affecting to admire James's unusual physique, the tract's author noted how 'your body does depart from the basic principles of nature' with 'more in your shins than your thigh, buttocks, belly, chest, neck and head can match proportionately', enabling the king to 'carry around your well-kept little body and its burgeoning paunch'.[51] As one critic has observed, the author of *Corona Regia* 'portrayed James as a physically deformed sodomite, connecting his disordered rule to his disorderly desires and disordered body'.[52]

Although *Corona Regia*'s attack on James was unusually ferocious in its malice, the king's Secretary, Cecil, was only too aware that 'the fashion of the court and London is to laugh at all deformities,' as he had admitted to his sister-in-law in the late 1590s.[53] Caused by scoliosis, the hunchbacked shortened stature of Cecil – later Earl of Salisbury – was mercilessly mocked in manuscript libels, both during his lifetime and after his death in May 1612. Drawing parallels with Richard III, one poetaster asked 'Richard or Robin, which is the worse? / A crookback great in state is England's curse', while another versifier celebrated Salisbury's death by claiming that 'The Devil now hath fetched the ape, / Of crooked manners, crooked shape'.[54] In late 1612, James's Attorney-General, Sir Francis Bacon, published a collection of essays, in one of which – entitled 'Of Deformity' – John Chamberlain reported that 'the world takes notice that he paints out his late little cousin to the life'.[55] Consumed by jealousy at Salisbury's success and convinced that his relative had regularly frustrated his own advancement, Bacon savagely suggested that 'deformed persons' were often 'void of natural affection' and 'extremely bold'. Bacon further posited that 'deformity is an advantage' to promotion, since a disabled individual's determination 'to rescue and deliver himself from scorn' was frequently underestimated, leaving 'their competitors and emulators asleep'.[56]

Cruel caricatures aside, no bodily function of a monarch, however intimate, escaped scrutiny. The Jacobean court adhered to the Eltham Ordinances drawn up by Henry VIII in 1526 ensuring that, for all English kings, it was only the Groom of the Stool who was permitted 'to follow us into our secret or privy room, when we go to ease ourself'.[57] Conscientiously relaying royal motions to Salisbury in October 1610, Viscount Fenton was thus concerned that 'His Majesty has been a little loose since his coming to Royston, but not in the extremity, and he does not lose his meat.'[58] As Mayerne noted in 1623, James did indeed suffer '*Diarrheae per totam vitam obnoxius*' – obnoxious lifelong diarrhoea – that was exacerbated by periods of acute anxiety, including the weeks directly following the deaths of Prince Henry in 1612 and Queen Anna in 1619.[59]

Courtiers likewise noted James's recurrent emesis. In May 1586, an English envoy reported to Queen Elizabeth's court that the nineteen-year-old Scottish king had recently suffered 'a great looseness of his body, and withal had a very great vomit', followed by a twenty-four-hour period of illness at Dalkeith. Thereafter, James had pronounced himself recovered and rushed to Falkland to inspect a consignment of deer recently gifted to him by Elizabeth, despite 'disguised and feigned' excuses that the journey to Fife was to discuss political matters.[60] Nearly three decades later, *Corona Regia*'s author disingenuously acclaimed as 'supernatural' the king's ability 'to regurgitate food whenever it is a burden', affecting to admire how 'it is as easy for you to vomit from off a horse as to load up at the table'. Contending that James's 'life consists in a feast', the mock panegyricist drew attention to royal eating habits, acknowledging to the king that 'you do not eat your food, you gulp it down' and likewise 'do not drink, but with a loud noise you slurp your wine, and so to speak, inhale it'.[61]

More recently, contemporary comments on the king's health and bodily habits have been used to inform attempts at retrospective diagnosis. In an article published in *History of Psychiatry* in 2012, clinicians and academics enumerated a range of symptoms observed in James, including his delayed childhood ability to walk; persistent lower-limb weakness; lifelong movement and behaviour disorders; difficulties in swallowing and speech, with an over-sized tongue; delicate, itchy skin; recurrent renal colic; gouty arthritis; and a proneness to 'hypochondriac melancholy' at stressful junctures.[62] Entered into a database containing information relating to 2,500 neurological syndromes and able to generate differential weighted outcomes, the king's symptoms produced a speculative diagnosis suggesting that James may have suffered one of three (relatively mild) forms of Lesch-Nyhan syndrome, as well as other possible musculo-skeletal disorders, such as Charcot-Marie-Tooth disease. A rare inherited disorder, Lesch-Nyhan syndrome occurs today in around 1 in 380,000 live births and almost entirely affects males, resulting in neurological and behavioural abnormalities and an over-production of uric acid, while Charcot-Marie-Tooth disease encompasses a range of hereditary sensory and motor neuropathies that damage peripheral nerves. The article's authors also noted Chamberlain's report that James had, for several days in 1613, been 'ill-disposed by the falling down of his uvula', which potentially indicated 'one of the orofacial clefting syndromes', while the king's physician, Mayerne, identified a restriction in James's gullet that appeared to be a hereditary condition, suffered also by the king's mother and grandfather, James V.[63] In 2003, a different team of clinicians writing in the *Journal of Gerontology* suggested that James may have suffered vascular dementia in later life, having identified a reduction in the syntactic complexity of his correspondence after a period of severe illness in 1618–19.[64]

*

If James experienced difficulties eating, he did not let it detract from the importance he attached to public dining as a projection of royal sociability. In *Basilicon Doron*, he identified 'manner of refection at his table, and his behaviour thereat' as one of a king's most visible actions that observers 'especially strangers, will narrowly take heed to'. James thus recommended public, rather than private, dining and fewer, rather than more, dishes to remove suspicions of 'the vice of delicacy, which is a degree of gluttony'. Food served at the royal table should be 'simple, without composition of sauces; which are more like medicines than meat', while Henry should avoid appearing 'like a dainty dame; but eat in a manly, round and honest fashion'.[65] Having visited Edinburgh in 1602, Henry Wotton described the royal court as '*piu all francese ch'all'inglese*' – more French in style than English. Wotton had been especially struck by the convention that anyone could enter while the king was eating, allowing James to converse with everyone around him. When the king retired after mealtimes, he was accustomed to '*sentendo burle et motti; di che ne piglia gran gusto*' ('hearing jokes and mottos, which he enjoys very much').[66]

Despite James's exhortations to culinary restraint, special occasions were celebrated with sumptuous fare. In the spring of 1598, for example, Queen Anna's younger brother, Ulric, Duke of Schleswig-Holstein, made a surprise visit to Edinburgh, prompting festivities which led the English-born courtier Roger Aston to lament that 'the god Bacchus is a great guider among us at this time'.[67] In May, Edinburgh Town Council helpfully covered the £1,100 (Scots) cost of a banquet held in Ulric's honour in a private residence in the city's Lawnmarket that required two puncheons (casks) of wine and five gallons and a quart of claret, with another seven quarts of wine needed for 'hypocras': a precursor of mulled wine. As well as a tun of English beer and four barrels of ale, the

Council also arranged a 'mutchkin' (three-quarters of an imperial pint) of perfumed rose water. As for food, James donated venison from the royal larder while the Council ordered wild and tame fowl, 'Brissel fouls' (probably turkeys), five 'stones' of butter, five dozen eggs, twenty-five apples, thirty oranges, raisins, cinnamon and saffron.[68]

As English king, James continued to combine dining with informal discourse, while also enacting measures in 1604 that sought to reduce the number of dishes served by the royal kitchen, curb an endemic theft of silverware, and reduce the number of free meals provided by the court.[69] While James and the royal family hosted sumptuous banquets to honour visiting foreign dignitaries, they also enjoyed lavish hospitality as guests. In May 1607, for example, the Merchant Taylors' Guild hosted an opulent banquet for James and Prince Henry after the king had dined with the rival Clothmakers' Company the previous month. As well as commissioning new celebratory songs from Ben Jonson, the Merchant Taylors purchased victuals including '224 tongues from various unfortunate animals; fifty-nine pikes; seventeen swans; 417 chickens; ten owls; 1,300 eggs; 360 pounds of butter; 446 pounds of sugar; fourteen and a quarter gallons of cream; twenty-eight barrels and a tun of beer and ale; about 441 gallons of wine; twenty-four pounds of prunes; twenty pounds of currants; three gallons of gooseberries; sixty pounds of potatoes; 120 artichokes and fourteen pickled lemons.'[70]

Such exorbitant feasting formed a stark contrast with the popular hunger and distress that led to riots breaking out the following month across Leicestershire, Northamptonshire and Warwickshire. Lasting for six weeks, 'the Midlands Revolt' saw local populations angrily register their desperate frustration at rising food prices, corn dearth and the relentless enclosure of communal land, which reduced access to grazing and fishing. Defending the government's repressive prosecution of recalcitrant rioters, James issued a proclamation on 28 June 1607 that restated his role as sovereign physician and confirmed he would 'follow the course which the best physicians use in dangerous diseases, which is by a sharp remedy applied to a small and infected part, to save the whole from dissolution and destruction'.[71] By July, however, the king was offering royal pardons to any offenders still at large and, in August, he appointed a royal commission of inquiry which duly revealed that, in Northamptonshire alone, over 27,000 acres had been enclosed by private landlords, resulting in the destruction of more than 350 farms and the eviction of almost 1,500 individuals from eighteen villages. By June 1608, corn prices were also found to have increased by 30 per cent over the previous year, prompting James to issue 'dearth orders' to enable crown regulation of the grain market.[72]

'Fat King, Lean Beggar' remained, however, as much a default reality as a Shakesperean trope.[73] Returning from his extended progress to Scotland in August 1617, James stayed overnight at Hoghton Tower in Lancashire, where he was served a two-course dinner comprising thirty dishes for the first course with another twenty-seven for the second (including an entire pheasant for the king). That evening, the king's two-course supper extended to twenty-five first-course dishes, followed by another eighteen second-course dishes that included 'herons', 'ducks' and 'red deer pie'.[74] So lavish was the hospitality bestowed on the royal party at Hoghton that James was reported to have spontaneously knighted a lion of beef 'Sir-Loin', thus giving rise to subsequent speculations regarding the naming of the cut of meat known as 'sirloin'. As Samuel Johnson explained in his *Dictionary* of 1755, for example, 'sirloin' was 'a title given to the loin of beef, which one of our kings knighted in a fit of good humour'.[75] Culinary ingenuity combined with informal bonhomie likewise infused celebrations of Prince Charles's eighteenth birthday in November 1618 when James hosted a supper party at Newmarket in Suffolk to which all guests contributed a dish. As one observer noted, while 'some strove to be substantial, some curious, and some extravagant', the winner was judged to be Sir George Goring's imaginative rendering of a 'carriage and horses' made from 'four huge brawny pigs, piping hot, bitted and harnessed with ropes of sausages, all tied to a monstrous bag-pudding'.[76]

Even kings cannot, however, live on meat alone and James himself was especially fond of fresh fruit which, as Mayerne noted, he ate at all times of day or night, as well as sweetened orange, lemon or pomegranate juice.[77] The greater availability of citrus fruit in early seventeenth-century England reflected a fashion for including orangeries when developing aristocratic estates. At the banquet held in August 1604 to celebrate the Anglo-Spanish Treaty of London, James presented the Constable of Castile with 'a melon and half a dozen of oranges on a very green branch, telling him that they were the fruit of Spain transplanted into England', with the fruit likely to have been cultivated on Sir Francis Carew's estate in Surrey.[78] The following year, the king thanked the Earl of Salisbury for sending him 'fine peaches and grapes', and when the Duke of Buckingham fell ill in 1624, James sent his favourite fruit cordials and fresh cherries, melons, grapes, peaches, strawberries and raspberries.[79] Meanwhile, whenever the court's spicery chief, Mr French, sought to herald the arrival of each season's new strawberry crop with a brief speech, 'the king never had the patience to hear him one word, but his hand was in the basket.'[80]

But even if James failed to exercise self-control when it came to strawberries, sheer force of royal willpower more usually rendered the sovereign physician a formidable patient. As the king once told Mayerne, 'he found anything easy when he had once decided that it had to be done.'[81] In his *Meditation upon the Lord's Prayer* (1619), James rejected the excuses of 'tobacco-drunkards, who cannot abstain from that filthy stinking smoke, because, forsooth, they are bewitched by it'. Smoking and drinking were no different to any other vice and all sinners continued sinning not 'because they cannot leave it; but the truth is, because they will not leave it'.[82]

13

The Reins of Government

The timetable and location of the Jacobean court was dictated by 'the chase': i.e. hunting. In September 1620, the Venetian republic's ambassador, Girolamo Lando, despaired of the English court's readiness to 'lose all diligence over foreign affairs'; an international crisis rarely disrupted 'the delights of their daily and incessant hunting'. On this occasion, Lando wanted to discuss with James the likelihood of English support against threats to Venetian interests posed by growing Spanish Habsburg influence in northern Italy. Delighted to have been granted an audience – after the king had declined interview requests from Lando's Spanish and French counterparts – the ambassador eventually located James and his entourage in 'narrow, one might almost say poor, quarters' in Havering in Essex. 'In the midst of his beloved forests, full of great herds of stags and deer', the king was 'hunting with enthusiasm and with incessant application'. Having outlined the urgency of Venetian concerns about Habsburg aggression at a time of escalating conflict across Continental Europe, Lando reported that James had responded with 'a rigmarole of phrases', clearly seeking 'to afford me the utmost satisfaction, and by studious language, to disappoint me as little as possible'.[1]

Alongside cramped conditions, hunting's sanguinary rituals incurred Venetian distaste. Two years earlier, the embassy's chaplain, Orazio Busino, had described the 'ceremony with which they close the chase'. After hounds had killed the quarry, James would arrive, whereupon he 'cuts its throat and opens it, sating the dogs with its blood, as the reward of their exertions'. With 'imbrued hands', the king would then 'regale some of his nobility by touching their faces', with the daubed blood 'unlawful to remove or wash off' representing, as it did, 'a certificate of his sovereign's cordial goodwill'. Hispanophobia only compounded

Lando's anxieties at the royal favours extended to his Spanish counterpart, Diego Sarmiento de Acuña, Count of Gondomar. As Lando sourly observed in January 1620, Gondomar readily 'tries to conform in all things to the inclination and taste of the king' and 'vies with him in putting his hands in the blood of bucks and stags, and doing cheerfully everything that his Majesty does'. By such amenability, 'chiefly, has he acquired his favour'.[2]

Lando had another reason to be frustrated by James's field sports: for the self-styled *rex pacificus*, they served as a substitute for actual martial engagement. In September 1622, the ambassador compiled a detailed report on English affairs, observing that James's dual devotion to academic study and the chase had 'rendered him the best scholar and hunter ever known among his equals'. For 'though hating real war, he loves the exercise which is its image'.[3] Indeed, it was this aspect that James had himself extolled in his *Basilicon Doron* two decades earlier, when he enthusiastically recommended hunting *par force de chiens* – in which hounds pursue a deer by scent and run it to death – as 'the most honourable and noblest sort' of the sport. By contrast, it was 'a thievish form of hunting to shoot with guns and bows', while greyhound hunting was 'not so martial a game'. James was likewise lukewarm in his endorsement of hawking – whereby hawks were thrown directly from the fist at quarry such as rabbits, hares, pheasants and partridges – on the grounds that it did not 'resemble the wars so nearly as hunting does'.[4]

Hunting was, moreover, to be championed as an excellent form of physical exercise. As James advised Prince Henry, it denoted an essential part of good government since it was 'most requisite for a king to exercise his engine, which surely with idleness will rust and become blunt'.[5] In December 1604, Edward Somerset, Earl of Worcester, confessed to a friend that he was managing only two hours' sleep each night while accompanying James on a hunting trip near Huntingdon. 'On horseback by eight' each morning, they continued 'in full career from the death of one hare to another, until four at night', after which, royal correspondence required attention. Aged over fifty, Worcester felt 'never better in health', while James likewise insisted that benefits from hunting enabled him to discharge his constitutional duties.[6]

In a proclamation issued in 1609, James acknowledged to his English subjects 'how greatly we delight in the exercise of hunting, as well for our recreation, as for the necessary preservation of our health'.[7] As the king became increasingly debilitated by gout in his fifties, the London newsletter-writer John Chamberlain reported in June 1619 that James had recently observed a marked improvement in his legs and feet after learning of 'a very good expedient'. He would 'bathe them in every buck's and stag's belly in the place where he kills them, which is counted an excellent remedy to strengthen and restore the sinews'. On James's fifty-eighth birthday in June 1624 – the last he would celebrate – Chamberlain recounted how the king had 'gone a-hunting early this morning' on horseback at Wanstead, in Essex, accompanied by the mother and sister of his favourite, the Duke of Buckingham.[8] Indeed, for James, time itself could be measured by the amount of quarry killed; as he concluded one letter in March 1605, 'so going to bed, after the death of six hares, a pair of fowls and a heron'.[9]

*

Girolamo Lando was by no means the first foreign envoy to grumble about the king's priorities. When the French envoy, Monsieur de Fontenay, had been sent by James's mother to Scotland in August 1584, he had noted that the eighteen-year-old king 'loves the chase above all the pleasures of this world, living in the saddle for six hours on end, running up hills and down dales with loosened bridle'. In Fontenay's view, James was 'too addicted to his pleasure, principally that of the chase'; this might be 'pardonable in one of his youth, but there is a fear that it will become a habit'.[10] By then, however, it had already been several years since James's first hunting expedition, which had taken place, near Stirling, a week before his thirteenth birthday in June 1579. To celebrate the king's 'first passing to the fields', Patrick Hume of Polwarth had published *The Promine* (1580): a panegyric that acclaimed James as a 'maist maikles mirrour' [most matchless mirror] and 'the maist imperiall king / That is, or was, or in the world sall ring'.[11]

The Scottish king's hunting habit was one shared with the majority of early modern royalty, whether undertaken for private recreation and recuperation or staged as major court ceremonial. During Elizabeth I's final summer progress in Buckinghamshire in August 1602, it was reported that 'the queen hunts every second or third day, for the most part on horseback, and shows little decay in ability'.[12] Before marrying

James, Anna had also participated in her father's 'Great Hunt' in 1587, the logistics of which rivalled a complex military campaign, involving thousands of conscripted beaters. Likewise, the seasonal hunt around Skanderborg Castle that was led in 1593 by Anna's sixteen-year-old brother, Christian IV, 'killed over 1,600 stags, other deer, wild swine and smaller game'.[13]

In July 1606, Christian visited his sister and brother-in-law in the first state visit to England since the Holy Roman Emperor, Charles V, had met Henry VIII in 1522. After arriving at Tilbury, Christian and James spent six of the Danish king's first nine days in England hunting at Eltham, Greenwich and Waltham Forest.[14] With the two kings joined in the field by twelve-year-old Prince Henry, the royal party attracted crowds of spectators who enthusiastically ran after the hunt, keen 'to behold so rare and excellent a sight, two kings and a prince', embodying the physical robustness and assured future of England's new Stuart dynasty.[15] Journeying south from Scotland in 1604, Henry's younger brother, Charles, had also 'been initiate in the sports of hunting', when staying in Nottinghamshire, having 'taken pleasure in viewing the quarries of deer killed'.[16] The princes' sister, Elizabeth, was likewise a keen huntswoman who, many years later – approaching her thirty-fifth birthday and pregnant with her thirteenth child – described being in the Rhineland, 'hunting as hard as we can: I think I was born for it, for I never had my health better than now'.[17]

It was therefore not only in Scotland and England that the prolonged pursuit of prey disrupted and dictated court timetables. Serving as James's ambassador in the Spanish capital of Valladolid in 1605, for example, Sir Charles Cornwallis complained that 'if there be a bird to be shot at in the wood, a hare in the field, or rabbit in the burrow, the papers lie dead', no matter whether current business concerned 'the life or soul of the poor, or the greatest good whatsoever of the commonwealth'.[18] Sent as the first English ambassador to Mughal India, Sir Thomas Roe encountered a ruler equally obsessed by hunting; indeed, even James might have struggled to match Emperor Jahangir's claim in 1617 that, since the age of twelve, he had personally hunted 17,167 animals.[19] Back in England, James also happened to have succeeded as king in what later was acclaimed as a golden age for the chase. Reviewing centuries of English history, the late seventeenth-century antiquarian

John Aubrey nostalgically recalled James's reign, and the early years of his son's rule, as 'a serene calm of peace': a uniquely tranquil era when 'hunting was at its greatest height that ever was in this nation.' By contrast, English rulers had been distracted by rebellions and tumults from the Roman invasion onwards, while the country's deer stocks were irreparably depleted by the mid-seventeenth-century civil wars, prompting an eventual shift towards fox-hunting. Hence, as Aubrey rued, it was in the early 1640s that 'the glory of the English hunting breathed its last'.[20]

*

Whereas Elizabeth I had only participated in the principal hunting season between early July and mid-September each year, James hunted all year round. In January 1605, the king wrote to his English Privy Councillors to explain that, since 'lack of open air and exercise brings with it present indisposition', he was prescribing future arrangements to be observed whenever he was not in London. Privy Councillors should formally meet once a week 'in such places as our dearest wife shall keep her court' to enable subjects to know when and where they might approach ministers.[21] In another communication, James reassured his advisers that if his absence diminished their 'authority or respect, one word shall bring me home and make me work till my breath work out'. But he doubted such recourse be 'needful if ye make not mountains out of molehills'.[22] Reporting the king's decision to his diplomatic masters, the Venetian ambassador, Nicolò Molin, added a ciphered explanation that James was evidently finding 'this sedentary life very prejudicial to his health' and an unwelcome contrast to his life in Scotland where he had been accustomed 'to spend much time in the country and in hard exercise'. In London, enforced 'repose robs him of his appetite and breeds melancholy and a thousand other ills'.[23] This pattern of devolved government continued throughout James's reign. In July 1620, for example, the king sought 'to wind up the clock, for this great vacation', before his summer progress, by identifying fourteen action points requiring the attention of Privy Councillors and stipulating specific days on which the Council was to meet.[24]

Accordingly, a new court timetable evolved whereby the king usually spent Christmas in London and, when Twelfth Night festivities had ended, moved to hunting lodges at Royston in Hertfordshire and

Newmarket in Suffolk, then returned to London to celebrate his accession day and Easter. Thereafter, he normally resided at Greenwich, before undertaking summer progresses to different parts of England. Most of each autumn was spent in Royston and Newmarket, with short return visits to London for state occasions, such as the opening of Parliament, and to mark anniversaries such as the Gunpower Plot's discovery each November. Between 1605 and 1609, James purchased new residences in Newmarket and Royston, as well as a mansion at Holdenby in Northamptonshire and a house in the Norfolk town of Thetford. In May 1607, James also gained ownership of the Earl of Salisbury's residence at Theobalds, in Hertfordshire, which he had visited at least nine times before a formal exchange of properties was agreed, whereby Salisbury received the formerly royal estate of Hatfield. The transfer documentation confirmed that Theobalds was a property to which 'his Majesty hath taken great liking', being 'a place so convenient for his Majesty's princely sports and recreation'.[25] Meanwhile, the king divested crown properties at Dartford, Canterbury and Charing in Kent and at Woking in Surrey.

Ensconced in his rural retreats, James relished rusticity and seclusion. In October 1605, he wrote to Salisbury, apologizing for adding more instructions to the Privy Council's already overflowing in-tray, which seemed as pointless as trying 'to spur a free-running horse'. But from his 'hunting cottage', the king also offered Salisbury a series of parodic prognostications inspired by a recent solar eclipse, styling himself as similar to 'the troglodytes of the Nile that dwelt in caverns, the shepherds of Arcadia dwelling in little cabins, [and] the Tartars harbouring in their tents like the old patriarchs'.[26] Occurring only weeks after a partial lunar eclipse, the total solar eclipse of October 1605 featured in Shakespeare's *King Lear* (1606), when Edmund rejects his father's gloomy portends by decrying 'the excellent foppery of the world' that sought to blame 'our disasters' on 'the sun, the moon, and stars, as if we were villains by necessity'.[27]

Alongside the benefits of physical exercise, James obtained different perspectives on state matters by distancing himself from the country's capital city. The proximity of Royston and Newmarket to Cambridge University facilitated regular book-borrowing requests by James to different libraries, as well as payments to the university to supply clerics to preach before the king whenever 'he should lie within twelve miles of Cambridge'.[28] Such an arrangement assisted in recruiting new royal chaplains and lent a seminary atmosphere to rural hunting lodges. As a young chaplain to James's last Lord Keeper, John Hacket later claimed that Privy Councillors were – in terms of political business – 'held to it closer, and sat up later in those retirements, to make dispatches, than at London'. Hacket likewise recalled the learned conversations that accompanied hunting-lodge mealtimes when the king 'was ever in chase after some disputable doubts; which he would wind and turn about with the most stabbing objections that ever I heard.' As Hacket described, James was 'as pleasant, and fellow-like in all those discourses, as with his huntsmen in the field'.[29]

Hacket's invocation of the language of the chase echoed James's fondness for hunting metaphors. Addressing the Westminster Parliament in March 1607, the king recalled the warmth of his arrival in England four years earlier when 'I was received with joy, and came as in a hunting journey.'[30] That October, he reviewed the Privy Council's plans to improve crown finances and avoided thanking each Councillor individually for 'the parts you acted in that comedy', but from 'this hunting residence of mine' at Royston, 'I cannot say that this hound or that hound only ran well, but that it was a good kennel and they all ran well and in a full cry.'[31] The following year, Sir Thomas Lake described the king's satisfaction with the new working arrangements; James maintained that 'he had kept his word with his Council, by being parsimonious, and not troubling them with directions', while his Councillors 'had performed their part by leaving him quietly to his sports'.[32]

Hunting terminology also inspired James's long-standing nickname for the Earl of Salisbury, whom he saluted as 'my little beagle' in thirty-five surviving letters, with variations including 'my little cankered beagle' and 'my patient beagle'. Partly affectionate, but also alluding to his Principal Secretary's physical deformity, Salisbury was both the beagle skilled at tracking the scent of prey to sniff out and hunt down and 'the little beagle that lies at home by the fire, when all the good hounds are daily running in the fields'.[33] James did not doubt, however, the burden borne by Salisbury and the key importance of his Secretariat in ensuring the flow of information and efficient dispatch of business. As the king marvelled to Salisbury in August 1608, 'ye sit at your ease and direct all' government in Scotland and England. 'News from all the parts of the world comes to you in your chamber' and 'the king's own resolutions depend upon your posting dispatches.' In hunting language, James ventured that Salisbury could even 'with one call or whistling in your fist' summon the king to his presence.[34]

But not all James's subjects or foreign commentators were so sanguine. In Edinburgh, Thomas Fowler was only one of sundry English observers to report suspicions among Scottish subjects that their king 'cares more for his hounds than his state', as Fowler put it in December 1588.[35] Less than two months after James's accession as English king, the Venetian Secretary in London deplored the new monarch's readiness to rely entirely on his predecessor's ministers, suggesting that James 'seems to have almost forgotten that he is a king except in his kingly pursuit of stags, to which he is quite foolishly devoted'.[36] When Archbishop Matthew Hutton of York wrote to Sir Robert Cecil, then Viscount Cranborne, in December 1604, suggesting that James might show 'more moderation in the lawful exercise of hunting', Cranborne promptly rebuked the primate, pointing out that, as the Roman emperor, Trajan, had been commended for 'such manlike and active recreations', Hutton should likewise admire 'our king of so able a constitution' and his young heirs. James's presence in the saddle of English government had 'freed our minds from all those fears which had besieged this potent monarchy, for lack of public declaration of his lineal and lawful succession to the same' under Elizabeth. For his part, James dismissed Hutton's objections as 'the foolishest letter that ever he read'.[37] But as the Venetian ambassador, Zorzi Giustinian, griped – or groused – in May 1606, 'this perpetual occupation with country pursuits, though possibly not distasteful to those who hold the reins of government, is extremely annoying to those who don't.'[38]

It was not only James's apparent neglect of constitutional duties that disturbed critics. Hunting posed clear dangers to a king who had, after all, been on hunting expeditions when he had been detained by the Ruthven Raiders in 1582 and surprised by the 'Gowrie conspiracy' in 1600. Only a month after discovery of the Gunpowder Plot in 1605, James went hunting in Richmond, despite courtiers' fears that, 'lured on by the pleasure of the chase, [he] should stay out late into the evening, thus offering an easy occasion for any who desires to injure him to do so'.[39] The following spring, Giustinian related an incident when James had been 'out hunting in the country' while, in a nearby village, local constables had tried to arrest a man for a minor offence. When the suspect fled, the constables had pursued him, shouting 'Traitor! Traitor!', prompting locals to assume that the man must have attacked James. Messengers 'set off at full speed for London to tell the queen and Council that the king was dead'. While 'the uproar was amazing', James was then surprised when tearful villagers fell to their knees with relief on seeing him alive, which 'made the king think that something serious had happened in London'.[40] Only a few months later, the royal court received details, via an informer, of a conspiracy to assassinate James while he was hunting with his Danish brother-in-law, Christian IV. Two Italians had outlined 'their plan to kill the king', acknowledging that they only needed 'good pistols and a swift horse' and intending that 'the deed should be done in the country, while the king was at the chase'.[41]

Even if James was not violently attacked, he remained quite capable of injuring himself accidentally. Meeting the new English king for the first time in May 1603 'amid upwards of ten or twelve thousand persons' at Greenwich Palace, the Venetian Secretary, Scaramelli, observed that James had 'his arm in a white sling, the result of a fall from his horse when out hunting'.[42] On other occasions, it was the horses that paid the penalty for royal (over)exertions. In May 1609, James and Prince Henry chased one deer for so long that the prince's horse died from exhaustion; unable to return to Greenwich, the king and the prince were obliged 'to sleep at a village cottage' while 'the queen and the court were in great anxiety that night'.[43] Four years later, it was Anna who 'shooting at a deer, mistook her mark and killed Jewel, the king's most principal and special hound'. As Chamberlain described, although James 'stormed exceedingly a while', on learning his wife was the culprit, he 'was soon pacified, and with much kindness wished her not to be troubled with it, for he should love her never the worse, and the next day sent her a diamond worth £2,000 as a legacy from his dead dog'.[44]

Among the king's subjects, hunting was socially divisive and locally disruptive. In James's first English Parliament in 1604, new game laws were introduced to update the original fourteenth-century values for lesser gentry whose titles did not confer automatic hunting rights; henceforth, members of the lesser gentry or below who wished to hunt lawfully needed to own freehold land worth at least £40 sterling.[45] The royal right to demand purveyance – purchasing provisions and carts at less than market rates – was resented by local populations with strained resources, while farmers suffered the trampling and destruction of their crops. When James stayed at Royston in December 1604, one of his favourite hunting dogs, Jowler, was stolen and returned the following day with an anonymous message tied around its neck, requesting him to speak to the king 'for he hears you every day'. Jowler was to ask 'his Majesty to go back to London, for else the country will be undone; all our provision is spent already, and we are not able to entertain him longer'.[46] The Norfolk town of Thetford earned lasting royal obloquy after a frustrated farmer was so incensed by James 'riding over his corn, in the transport of his passion', that he 'threatened to bring an action of trespass against the king'.[47] Similar objections could, however, be equally deployed by the king against unauthorized hunt followers. In 1619, James issued a royal order permitting spectators to watch the departure and return of royal hunting parties, but warning individuals who thereafter tried to follow the hunt that they would be speedily escorted to the nearest jail for detention at his Majesty's pleasure. James denounced 'the bold and barbarous insolence of multitudes of vulgar people' who had disrupted previous hunts and 'ride over our dogs, break their backs, spoil our game, run over and destroy the corn', not to mention endangering the king and Prince Charles 'by their heedless riding and galloping'.[48]

Subversive strains of criticism also distrusted the more private and homosocial aspects of hunting. Hailing James as a new 'Actaeon who takes great pleasure in the hunt', the anonymous author of the mock Latin encomium, *Corona Regia* (1615), described the king pursuing 'attractive and graceful' prey for whom 'you use a different kind of spear, you search through a different kind of underbrush, and you capture different kinds of pleasure'.[49] As George Villiers's control of Jacobean politics intensified in the early 1620s, manuscript libellers derived plentiful punning opportunity from the king's pursuit of buck in the field and his evident closeness to Villiers, later Duke of Buckingham, at court. Entitled 'To the duke', one verse read:

> The Kinge loves you, you him
> Both love the same.
> You love the king, he you,
> Both Buck-in-game.
> Of you the king loves game,

Of Game the Buck.
Of all you, why you?
Why he the Luck.[50]

In the final years of James's reign, apprehensions also emerged that Buckingham's sway over both James and Charles had extended to such an extent that the duke and the prince were seeking to sequester the king in one of his hunting lodges in order that they might control all state business unimpeded. In April 1624, two Spanish ambassadors and their confessor arranged a secret meeting with James, with neither Charles nor Buckingham present. The confessor, Don Francisco de Carondolet, warned an aghast king that he seemed to be 'a prisoner, or at least besieged, so as no man could be admitted to come at him', likening James's situation to that of the French king, John II, who had been imprisoned in London during the 1350s.[51] The Spanish allegations prompted a temporary estrangement between the king and his favourite, whereupon Buckingham became ill. A distraught James sent him food and medicines, as well as 'the eyes, the tongue and the dousets [testicles] of the deer he killed in Eltham Park'.[52]

*

The idea of an ageing king kept captive by his favourite and his son was entirely antithetical to the image of the proud lion rampant that had adorned the personal banner of every Scottish monarch since the thirteenth century. As a precocious child, James had once countered his tutors' counsel that he 'should never be angry' by objecting that, if so, 'I should not wear the lion in my arms, but rather a sheep.'[53] A Scottish coinage issued in 1584 included a gold 'noble' coin worth seventy-five shillings that depicted a lion serjeant holding a sword and sceptre in its forepaws, while a £4 (Scots) gold coin issued in 1592 presented the lion serjeant in profile, holding in its paw a sceptre raised to the heavens as a form of 'lightning conductor' to draw divine blessings down upon the Scottish king (see Plate 7).[54] Two years later, James dressed up as one of three 'Christian knights' and participated in a tiltyard tournament at Stirling Castle during Prince Henry's baptismal celebrations. The Scottish king's shield displayed a heraldic *imprese*, or device, of a lion's head, with open eyes, accompanied by the Ovidian motto, '*Timeat et primus et ultimus orbis*' ('May he fear worlds both near and far').[55]

1. In this portrait by Rowland Lockey, the eight-year-old King James VI is depicted with a sparrowhawk on his gloved hand.

2. Mary, Queen of Scots, and her
first husband, François II of France.
Miniature by François Clouet, *c.* 1573.

3. Armoured half-length portrait of
James on a £20 (Scots) coin issued in
1575 and 1576. The largest hammered
gold coin ever struck for circulation in
the British Isles, it shows the ten-year-
old king holding a sword in his right
hand and an olive branch in his left.

4. *Memorial of Lord Darnley* by Livinus Voghelarius (1567) was commissioned by Darnley's parents, the Earl and Countess of Lennox, who are depicted kneeling in grief by their son's tomb, with their surviving son and Darnley's infant son, James. The inset shows Mary's surrender at Carberry Hill in June 1567.

Phœnix   1

The diuers fallis that fortoune giues to men
quhilk by turning ouire hir quheile to their aney
quhen i do heir thame grugge althocht thay kno
that olde blinde dame infalset to ledyt
of all seis hir use quhilk i dois conuoy
hir quheile bydges not huiking to the richt
bot still turnis up that paire quhilt is toliche

thus quhen i hard sa mony did complaine
sum for the losse of uardlie uelth & geir
sum deith of freindis quha can not cume againe
sum losse of health quhilk unto all is deir
sum losse of fam quhilk still uit his dois beir
ane griefus to thaim quha meritis it indeid
yit for all thir appeiris thayre sume remeid.

for as to geive that chance sybill maide you tantit
restore you may the same againe or maire
for losse deith of freindis althocht thay same i grantit
can nocht returne; yit men are nocht sa raire
bot ye may gett the lyke: for seik nes faire
youre health may cume or to ane bettir place
ye must: for fame gud deidis uill mend disgrace.

5. James's draft of the opening stanzas of his poem 'Ane metaphoricall invention of a tragedie called Phœnix', later published in *The Essays of a Prentice, in the Divine Art of Poesie* (1584).

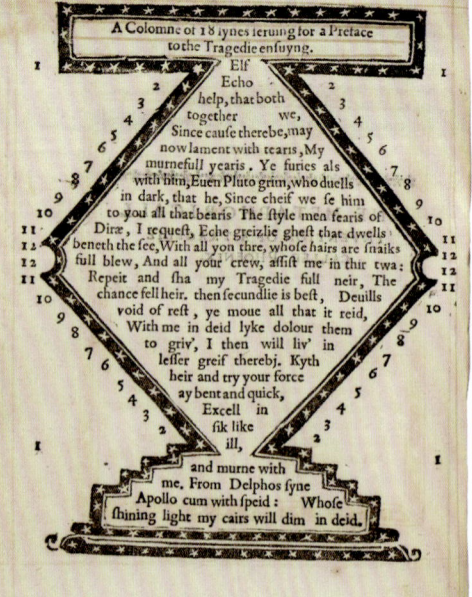

A Colomne of 18 lynes seruing for a Preface to the Tragedie ensuyng.

Elf
Echo
help, that both
together we,
Since cause therebe, may
now lament with tearis, My
murnefull yearis. Ye furies als
with him, Euen Pluto grim, who duells
in dark, that he, Since cheif we se him
to you all that bearis The style men fearis of
Diræ, I request, Eche greizlie ghest that dwells
beneth the see, With all yon thre, whose hairs are snaiks
full blew, And all your crew, assist me in thir twa:
Repeit and sha my Tragedie full neir, The
chance fell heir. then secundlie is best, Deuills
void of rest, ye moue all that it reid,
With me in deid lyke dolour them
to griv', I then will liv' in
lesser greif therebj. Kyth
heir and try your force
ay bent and quick,
Excell in
sik like
ill,
and murne with
me. From Delphos syne
Apollo cum with speid: Whose
shining light my cairs will dim in deid.

6. Inviting readers to 'mourn with me', James devised this urn-shaped preface to introduce the 'Phœnix': his verse tribute to Esmé Stewart, Duke of Lennox.

7. Gold 'hat-piece' coin, worth £4 (Scots), issued in 1592. James wears a tall hat, while the obverse shows a crowned lion holding a sceptre, with a cloud and the Hebrew word for Jehovah. The Latin motto translates as 'Thee alone do I fear'.

8. Although Mary last saw James as a ten-month-old baby in April 1567, in this double portrait painted in 1583 by an unknown artist, mother and son are imagined as joint sovereigns, with the Scottish crown floating between them.

IACOBVS. VI REX SCOTORVM,

IACOBVS VI REX SCOTORVM.

9. and 10. Engraved images of James included in *Inscriptiones Historicae Regum Scotorum* (1602), describing all Scots monarchs since Fergus I. Purchasers may have been able to choose between variant editions that presented James either in court dress or in full body armour.

11. *Left:* Etching by the German artist Abraham Hogenberg of James's coronation as English king in June 1603 at Westminster Abbey. James appears twice – entering the choir and holding a sword at the altar – while Anna is in the procession on the left side.

12. *Below:* Table clock made by the Dundee-born David Ramsay, who became royal 'Watchmaker and Constructor of Horologes' in 1613. On its sides are images of the four Evangelists, while concealed on its underside is an engraving depicting James and his two sons holding Pope Paul V's nose to a grindstone, being turned by two English bishops.

13. Portrait of James, commissioned for the Council Chamber of the King's House at the Tower of London by the Tower's Lieutenant, Sir William Waad (or Wade), in 1608. Possibly by the Flemish carver Maximilian Colt, the stone relief accompanied a marble memorial commemorating the failure of the recent Gunpowder Plot.

Leonine images were not solely confined to emblematic depictions. In 1584, James authorized payments for a lioness and a leopard to be transported in a cage with rope tows from Edinburgh Castle to Holyroodhouse. Twelve years later, his Danish brother-in-law, Christian IV, sent a lion as a gift to the Scottish court, together with its own German lion-keeper.[56] Reflecting on tropes conventionally associated with leonine might, in *Basilicon Doron* James advised his son on circumstances in which a wise monarch might be magnanimous as opposed to taking revenge. Warning that 'the wrath of a king, is like to the roaring of a lion,' James was echoing the Scriptural text from Proverbs 19:12: 'The king's wrath is as the roaring of a lion; but his favour is as dew upon the grass.'[57] James's subjects were equally quick to apply the Scriptural analogy. When, for instance, English MPs learned that their new king wished to intervene in order to adjudicate disputed elections to the House of Commons in April 1604, there was 'amazement, and silence' before one MP 'stood up, and said, the prince's command is like a thunderbolt; his command upon our allegiance, like the roaring of a lion: to his command, there is no contradiction.' But as the MP added, 'the question' was crucially 'how, or in what manner, we should now proceed to perform obedience'.[58]

MPs were wise to be cautious. For according to the humanist curriculum that had constituted James's education, too close an identification with puissant wild animals risked encouraging tyrannical misrule. As Desiderius Erasmus had warned in his *Education of a Christian Prince* (1516), 'if you are looking for what corresponds to the tyrant, think of the lion, the bear, the wolf, or the eagle, who live by mutilation and plundering.'[59] By James's reign, however, counter-arguments articulated by Niccolò Machiavelli in *The Prince* – first published in 1532 – had gained traction, including the controversial insistence that all rulers 'must know how to act like a beast'. As Machiavelli counselled, wise leaders should learn to imitate both 'a fox to recognise traps, and a lion to frighten away wolves'; those who traditionally relied 'merely upon a lion's strength do not understand matters'.[60] Opening a new English Parliament in 1621, James directly echoed this language by identifying 'two sorts of speakers which I would inhibit' as likely to foment disloyalty in debates. The first were 'lion-like speakers that dare speak of anything that appertains to princes' and the second were those orators who were 'fox-like that seem to speak one thing and intend another, as to bring the king in dislike with his subjects'.[61]

As Christian IV's gift of a lion indicated, the presentation of live animals was an integral aspect of the culture of gift-giving at early modern royal courts. When James turned seven in June 1573, the Regent Morton had presented him with a falcon as a gift.[62] From George Keith, Earl Marischal, James received an otter in 1584, which he evidently intended to walk like a hound, having purchased a set of leashes.[63] Consignments of English deer were sent to cement the Anglo-Scottish alliance concluded with Elizabeth I two years later, together with huntsmen and footmen that, as the envoy Thomas Randolph confirmed, could 'whoop, holler and cry' so loudly 'that all the trees in Falkland will quake for fear'.[64] Soon after moving to England, James wrote to Christian IV admitting that his missive was not 'burdened with matters of great importance and weight', but asking if his brother-in-law might send a consignment of hawks. After many years of enjoyment hawking with Danish birds, James now wished to 'test whether your hawks delight more in the English or Scottish sky'.[65] For hunting purposes, the king also reintroduced wild boar, imported from France and Germany, at Windsor and in the New Forest.[66]

New World settlement further stirred James's interest in exotic fauna. In 1609, Henry Wriothesley, Earl of Southampton, let James's Principal Secretary know that, in a recent conversation with the king, 'by chance I told him of the Virginia squirrels which they say will fly', upon which James 'very earnestly asked if none of them was provided for him'. Knowing how much he was 'affected to these toys', Southampton felt obliged to alert Salisbury.[67] A decade later, Sir Thomas Roe returned from a four-year term serving as James's ambassador to the Mughal court, principally based in Ajmer. At an audience at Hampton Court, Roe presented the king with 'two antelopes, a strange and beautiful kind of red deer, a rich tent, rare carpets, certain umbrellas and such like trinkets from the Great Mogul'.[68]

Exotic gifts of live animals likewise served to promote dynastic diplomacy. In 1611, Savoyard attempts to secure a double marriage involving both Prince Henry and Princess Elizabeth saw the arrival in London of four horses and 'a tame leopard of great beauty' that followed James 'like a dog' and willingly dispatched 'any deer, red or fallow, that the king shall point out', to the great delight of its new owner.[69] In October

1623, Charles and Buckingham returned to England with a gift of forty-six horses, having spent six months at Philip IV's court in Madrid trying to secure the prince's marriage to the Spanish Infanta. Three months earlier, the Spanish king had gifted five camels and an elephant to James's court, prompting the Venetian ambassador to wonder cattily if the elephant's arrival in London 'comes as an earnest of the Infanta or instead of her'?[70] With its keeper allocated an annual budget of £270 sterling for upkeep, the elephant was housed in St James's Park and given a gallon of wine to drink daily.[71] Another new post in the royal household was the 'Keeper of His Majesty's Cormorants, Ospreys and Otters', and the Italian chaplain, Busino, reported of James and his cormorants in 1618 that 'this very day he was to fish with them in the Thames from a boat'.[72] Following a Chinese technique thought to have been introduced into England via the East India Company, cormorants dived underwater to catch prey which they were then prevented from swallowing by laces tied around their throats.

James pursued his interests in anthropomorphic observation by organizing animal-baiting encounters at the Tower of London, which had housed lions since the thirteenth century. Two days before his ceremonial entry into London in March 1604, the king requested the Master of the Bear-Garden, Edward Alleyne, to procure three mastiffs that were introduced to 'the lustiest lion' in ascending order of ferocity. Confronted by three pugnacious dogs 'and contrary to the king's expectation, the lion fled into an inward den', from which James deduced that the lion 'exceeded the dog in strength, but nothing in noble heart and courage'. In another encounter devised by the king in 1605, a group of cockerels were quickly devoured by the lions, but a single lamb 'went unto the lions, who very gently looked upon him, and smelled on him, without sign of any further hurt', thereby supplying evidence of the leonine kindness recounted in the Old Testament story of the prophet Daniel emerging unscathed from the lion's den.[73] As king, James oversaw extensive remodelling of the lions' enclosure at the Tower, with a new viewing platform installed that, by the end of his reign, had been expanded into a gallery, more than ninety feet wide, to entertain distinguished guests and foreign dignitaries.[74] In one spectacle watched by the royal family in June 1609, the Tower's lions were presented with a fierce bear which had recently killed a child, but the bait descended into chaos when the lions declined to attack the bear, prompting a horse and dogs to be introduced, only for the dogs to attack the horse, which then required rescuing by three bear-keepers 'while the lion and bear stared upon them'. On James's orders, the bear was then baited to death on stage a fortnight later, while the dead child's mother was 'given twenty pounds out of part of that money which the people gave to see the bear killed'.[75]

Finally, just as James received faithful service from his 'little beagle', the Earl of Salisbury, so did a succession of canine companions provide steadfast loyalty. Before he was twenty, James had been dismayed by the bitter divisions that erupted between Scottish Episcopalians and Presbyterians over subscription to new ecclesiastical articles in 1585. Returning from a hunting expedition one day, he was observed raising a toast 'to all his dogs, and, above the rest, to one of his dogs, called Tell-True'. As the king had acknowledged, 'I drink to thee above all the rest of my hounds; for I will give thee more credence, nor either the bishop or Craig,' having become exhausted by the exorbitant levels of support for and opposition mounted, respectively, by Archbishop Patrick Adamson and John Craig to the new articles.[76]

Throughout his life, James remained keenly interested in the extent to which empirical observations of animal behaviour challenged traditional distinctions between rational humanity and instinctive bestiality. During a royal visit to Cambridge University in 1615, a philosophical disputation was staged before James to debate 'whether dogs could make syllogisms'. Drawing on arguments from the third-century BC Stoic philosopher Chrysippus, the proposer of the motion envisaged a hound trying to locate a hare and, losing its scent, establishes that 'she is not gone that way, and follows the conclusion, "Ergo", this way, with mouth open'. The proposer's claim was countered by the answerer who granted that 'dogs might have sagacity, but not sapience, in things especially of prey, and that did not concern their belly'. Dogs had the ability to smell, but not the capacity to reason. At this point in the proceedings, however, James intervened to object to the debate's moderator that he was unsatisfied by the arguments articulated thus far. From his own observations, James 'did believe a hound had more in him than was imagined'. The king then described his experience of watching a dog, separated from its pack, pick up a fresh scent but decline to pursue it alone. Instead, the dog 'observes the place and goes away to his fellows, and by such yelling arguments as they best understand, prevailed with a party of them to go along with him, and bringing them to the place' enabled the pack to pursue the scent to its quarry. For James, since such behaviour supplied proof of canine reasoning capacity, he directed the debate's moderator either to 'think better of his dogs or not so highly of himself!' While the debate's proposer was keen to 'pursue the king's game', the disputation was hurriedly brought to a close by the moderator – who acknowledging that James's 'dogs were able to outdo him' – announced that the king had 'ye better' of the debate and James 'went off well pleased with the business'.[77] He was, however, less pleased to be presented with a specially illustrated copy of John Caius's history of Cambridge University, *De Antiquitate Cantabrigiensis Academiae* (1584). Knowing that Caius had also published a detailed description of English dog breeds, James looked askance at the weighty tome and asked the University authorities, 'What shall I do with this book? Give me rather Caius's *De Canibus*!'[78]

14

God's Silly Vassal

Resident in Geneva, the Calvinist theologian Theodore Beza found much to admire about James VI's Scotland. In 1596, he congratulated a colleague, John Johnston, on returning to a post at St Andrews University in a country where the 'purity and unspotted sincerity' of the national Church prospered in 'a blessed and peaceable state', uniquely fortunate in its godly and erudite king. Having formerly taught James's childhood tutor Peter Young, Beza ventured that the Scottish king possessed 'so great and exact knowledge' of the Christian religion 'that the Lord, it seems, has made His Majesty both a prince and preacher to his people'.[1]

Beza's Latin encomium was published in Edinburgh in 1597, but its depiction of Scottish Church–State relations as 'peaceable' might have elicited a wry grimace from James as he faced sharp criticism from Kirk ministers, English agents, and a laity concerned about his apparent laxity in suppressing prominent Catholic nobles, notably George Gordon, Earl of Huntly. After Huntly surreptitiously returned to Scotland from continental exile in the summer of 1596, commissioners from the Church of Scotland's General Assembly sent a delegation to James at Falkland Palace that included Johnston's colleague Andrew Melville, Principal of St Mary's College in St Andrews. According to Melville's nephew, James, the king responded in a 'most crabbit [bad-tempered] and choleric manner' to hearing that the commissioners had met without his permission, whereupon Andrew Melville – in an exchange often glibly assumed to epitomize Kirk–State relations throughout the reign – informed the king that he was but 'God's silly vassal' (with 'silly' denoting of lowly significance). Seizing the king's sleeve, Melville insisted that there were 'two kings and two kingdoms in Scotland. There is Christ Jesus the king, and his kingdom the Kirk, whose subject King James the Sixth is, and of whose kingdom, not a king, nor a lord, nor a head, but a member!' Two decades older than the king, Melville advised him that 'when ye were in your swaddling-clothes, Christ Jesus reigned freely in this land', adding more baleful warnings 'with great liberty and vehemence'.[2]

While James's tempestuous exchanges with Andrew Melville provide a background to the king's comments regarding 'fiery spirited men in the ministry' in *Basilicon Doron*, his relations with the Established Church in Scotland and, after 1603, its English counterpart, were complex and fluctuating.[3] In Scotland, James owed his accession as an infant king to the Kirk's involvement in deposing his Catholic mother, and his championing as a future 'godly prince' had been key to the King's Party securing English support and emerging victorious in the Marian civil war. In England, James was the first adult monarch to accede to the throne since Henry VII whose reign was not accompanied by a radical change in religious policy. In both countries, significant segments of society variously sought to further or reverse changes arising from the sixteenth-century Protestant Reformation, including relations between secular and ecclesiastical power, the remit of institutions such as Parliament, the General Assembly and Convocation, the status of different forms of religious ceremony and liturgy, doctrinal content, and the practical organization and funding of the national churches.

*

In 1572, a new oath of supremacy required all Scottish clergy to recognize six-year-old James VI as the 'only lawful and supreme governor of this realm, as well in things temporal as in the conservation and purgation of religion'.[4] That same year, the Regent Mar oversaw the Convention of Leith's reinstatement of the office of bishops in Scotland's thirteen dioceses; the restored bishops remained subject to the General Assembly in ecclesiastical matters and to the Crown in secular matters, with most diocesan revenues remaining with lay patrons. Anti-episcopal sentiment nevertheless remained strong among many Kirk ministers and, as James Melville recounted, the new prelates were derided as 'Tulchan' bishops, nicknamed after the Highland practice of using 'tulchains, that is, calves' skins stuffed with straw' to deceive cows into producing milk.[5] But their post-Reformation reintroduction was supported by many nobles who, as Melville's uncle, Andrew, explained to Beza in 1579, 'complain that, if the pseudo-episcopacy be abolished, the state of the kingdom will be overturned; if presbyteries be established, the royal authority will be diminished; [and] if the ecclesiastical goods are restored to their legitimate use, the royal treasury will be exhausted.'[6]

Once a pliable infant prince became a determined seventeen-year-old king, tensions inevitably arose. James had resented the Kirk's open support for his detention by the Ruthven Raiders in 1582–3, before being obliged to repel another coup attempt by the same faction at Stirling Castle in February 1584. In May that year, a slew of legislation – later calumniated by Presbyterians as 'the Black Acts' – was passed by the parliament in Edinburgh. Prefaced by censure of 'treasonable, seditious and contemptuous speeches uttered' against James, his predecessors and Councillors 'in pulpit, schools and otherwise', the legislation established a permanent royal guard, emphasized Parliament's authority, and reaffirmed royal supremacy over the Kirk. Since an unlicensed meeting had sought 'to justify and authorize the fact perpetrated against his Highness's person and estate at Ruthven', all unauthorized convocations of clergy were now banned as illegal, aside from parochial kirk sessions.[7] Further legislation in August required 'all beneficed men, ministers, readers, masters of colleges and schools' to subscribe obedience to these enactments, with any refusal resulting in an individual's loss of benefice, living and stipend, with provision made for a successor 'as if they were naturally dead'.[8]

Reaction to the 'Black Acts' was swift and aghast. In his diary, James Melville 'could scarcely a long while believe myself that the devil dared so soon and plainly utter himself in Scotland', describing 'the absolute power' claimed by the Scottish king as 'a monster never heard of in any just government'.[9] Several ministers refused subscription and fled to London, while Baron Hunsdon relayed to the English court James's fear that 'other princes think him irreligious'. Musing alone with an English huntsman, James had also admitted 'with water in his eyes' his distress at persistent slurs 'that he is not the king's son, but David's, which, says he, comes from these men' who maliciously resuscitated salacious speculation regarding his mother's relationship with her murdered Italian secretary, David Riccio.[10] In December 1584, James confronted one outspoken minister, James Gibson of Pencaitland, who informed him that 'so long as ye maintain the wicked acts against God and the liberty of his Kirk, ye are a persecutor'. Gibson further admitted to having likened James to the persecutory king in Scripture, Jeroboam, and to having delivered even more critical sermons, prompting the king to expostulate 'I will not give a turd for thy preaching!'[11] Two years later, an English agent in Edinburgh compiled a report on 'the state of Scotland' in which he commended the twenty-year-old king's 'care to give good example to others by sometimes resorting on Sundays to the ordinary sermons in Edinburgh church, and his patience in hearing himself publicly reproved there by the preachers'.[12]

James's attempts to increase royal control over the Kirk was, ironically, undermined by English clergy concerned to neutralize Puritan challenges to episcopal authority in the Church of England. Given his recent support for the Elizabethan regime in repulsing the Spanish Armada, James was incensed to receive reports of a belittling sermon preached in February 1589 by the Lord Chancellor's chaplain, Richard Bancroft, from London's most prominent pulpit, Paul's Cross, in the grounds of St Paul's Cathedral. Bancroft had described Scotland as a country in which, even in its 'best reformed places, as in Dundee, St Andrews, Edinburgh and sundry other towns', the power of Kirk ministers regularly put 'the king in great danger, and fear of his life by their lordly discipline'. Were such Presbyterian models to be introduced in England, Bancroft had warned 'the wonderful pride and insolence' of Scotland's clergy showed that 'instead of one Pope, we should have a thousand, and of some lord bishops in name, a thousand, lordly tyrants in deed, which now do distain the name'.[13] The following summer, Queen Elizabeth likewise warned James of the dangers posed by 'a sect of perilous consequence, such as would have no kings, but a presbytery' and urged him to 'staple the mouths, or make shorter the tongues' of Scottish clergy who publicized the fate of Puritan dissidents detained in England. Even if James was willing 'to bear with their audacity towards yourself', Elizabeth refused to 'receive that indignity at such caterpillars' hands'.[14]

In trying to uphold the royal supremacy while seeking common ground among Protestants, James steered a *via media* that resisted the more theocratic visions of radical Presbyterians, on the one hand, while avoiding sustained persecution of loyal Catholics on the other. Rather than yielding to English pressure, James repaid Bancroft's slights by appointing Robert Waldegrave – responsible for illegally publishing incendiary Puritan pamphlets known as the 'Martin Marprelate' tracts – as his royal printer in October 1590, after Waldegrave had escaped prosecution in England by fleeing first to the Huguenot city of La Rochelle and then to Edinburgh. The following June, James boldly appealed to Elizabeth to release from prison two English clerics: the Puritan Hebraist John Udall, who had preached before James at a General Assembly meeting in 1589, and the Presbyterian, Thomas Cartwright. Despite the detained ministers' vocal opposition to episcopacy, James urged the sincerity of their intentions in articulating alternative interpretations of Scripture and declared himself determined to defend 'such as are afflicted for their conscience in that profession'.[15] Alarmed at the potential damage to Protestantism's international image by the persecution of nonconformists without evidence of criminality, the king was also seeking to fulfil the self-styled role he had announced for himself on the title-page of his Scriptural *Meditation* in 1588: the 'most Christian king, and sincere professor, and chief defender of the truth'.[16] While Udall later credited the Scottish king's intervention for staying his execution, he died in prison in 1592; Cartwright was released into house arrest that year and lived for another decade.[17]

The English episcopate was predictably alarmed by James's apparent rapprochement with Kirk ministers. When the General Assembly met in Edinburgh in August 1590, the Scottish king delighted attendees by concluding his speech with thanks to God 'that he was born in such a time, as in the time of the light of the Gospel, to such a place to be king, in such a Kirk, the sincerest Kirk in the world'.[18] Serving as Moderator of the same Assembly, James Melville nevertheless took the opportunity to remind ministers of the 'sharp, two-edged sword' to be deployed against poor sinners, as well as 'binding of kings in chains, and the most honourable princes in fetters of iron'. The Kirk should also guard against 'these Amaziahs, the belly-god bishops in England' who, 'by all means and money, were seeking conformity of our Kirk with theirs'.[19] In April 1592, the Scottish Parliament enacted legislation that retained the royal supremacy and reserved to the king the right to name the dates and venues for General Assemblies. But the so-called 'Golden Act' also reversed some provisions of the 'Black Acts' by endorsing the rights of kirk sessions, presbyteries, synods and

General Assemblies, and omitting any mention of bishops.[20] After serving as a Privy Councillor for over two years in the early 1590s, James Melville later reflected that, while he had sought 'to win the king' to the Kirk, the king had also succeeded 'in winning of me to the court', although – when agreement eventually proved elusive – 'we relented and fairly retired'.[21]

Closer co-operation between James and Kirk ministers was derailed by the 'Spanish blanks' affair when a Catholic agitator, George Kerr, was arrested on the Scottish west coast in late 1592 carrying eight blank sheets of paper, signed by the earls of Angus, Errol and Huntly. Under torture, Kerr admitted that the 'Spanish blanks' had been intended to confirm details of Scottish support in a future Spanish invasion. James's failure – yet again – to be seen to take decisive action against dissident Catholic nobles prompted the synod of Fife to excommunicate the three earls and, although James reversed the sentence, they suffered parliamentary forfeiture of their estates in March 1594. Two months later, the English ambassador, Robert Bowes, learned of a sermon preached in St Johnstone in Perth that 'affirmed the king to have been a reprobate, a traitor and rebel to God, and a fine hypocrite and dissembler', drawing attention to James's connections to the French Guise dynasty, who were noted 'persecutors of God's church'.[22] In January 1595, Bowes learned of a foiled Catholic conspiracy in which signatories had undertaken 'deprivation of his Majesty, coronation of the Prince [Henry], murder of sundry courtiers, and distribution of the offices of estate and Session to Papists'.[23]

Popular anxieties regarding Catholic infiltration swelled amid rumours that another Spanish Armada was being assembled by Philip II – even larger than the fleet vanquished by 'Protestant winds' and storms in 1588. In Scotland, the death of James's Chancellor, John Maitland, led to the appointment of eight exchequer commissioners (known as the 'Octavians'), who included Scotland's most senior judge, Alexander Seton, President of the Court of Session. Since Seton was a suspected papist, mistrustful minds suspected he might offer a conduit for Spanish funds to restore Catholicism in Scotland. James's decision to entrust custody of Princess Elizabeth, born in August 1596, to the Catholic wife of a courtier only compounded ministers' anxieties, which had been stoked by Huntly's furtive return to Scotland earlier that summer. While Melville decried James as 'God's silly vassal' at Falkland in September, the Privy Council questioned a St Andrews minister, David Black, the following month, about a sermon in which he had insisted that 'all kings were the devil's children, [and] the devil was in the court', denounced Elizabeth I as 'an atheist', and claimed that 'the religion that was professed there [in England] was but a show of religion, directed by the bishops' injunctions'.[24] While Elizabeth thanked James for censuring 'the frantic man', Black produced a 'declinature' denying that the king and Council had the right to judge anything said in a pulpit. When the General Assembly's commissioners then endorsed Black's 'declinature' as official church policy in November, James ordered the commissioners to leave Edinburgh within forty-eight hours.

Matters came to a head on 17 December 1596 when a group of Edinburgh's ministers and peers met in the 'Little Kirk' of St Giles and sent a deputation to the king – meeting in the adjacent Tolbooth with his Court of Session judges – to demand that any Octavian suspected of Catholicism be removed and that the banished Kirk commissioners be recalled. An armed crowd surrounded the Tolbooth, besieging James and the judges; as an English agent confirmed, 'we who were with him, presently closed the doors and manned the same. It was very dangerous for a while, in their fury.'[25] Eventually, the royal party returned to Holyroodhouse, with burgesses' wives lining Edinburgh's streets and chanting – not very catchily – 'Put away the papist lords, make us quit of Huntly and all his faction, the favourers of the Spaniards.'[26] The following morning, James left for Linlithgow and issued a proclamation ordering closure of the Court of Session, with an envisaged relocation to St Andrews. In the court's absence, the Kirkcudbright minister, John Welsh (son-in-law of John Knox) preached a sermon in Edinburgh, maintaining that, since the king was 'possessed with a devil ... the subjects might lawfully rise, and take the sword out of his hand'.[27]

But the ministers' resistance thereafter lost momentum as noble support failed to materialize and Edinburgh's Town Councillors feared the loss of lucrative revenue were the Court of Session's business to be lost. James reasserted control and entered Edinburgh on 1 January 1597, accompanied by a small army. Presbyteries and synods were henceforth banned from meeting in Edinburgh and, in a visitation to St Andrews in July, Andrew Melville was removed from his post as university Rector and theology students and staff were prohibited from attending presbytery meetings. As the king admitted of Kirk ministers in a letter to Huntly that year, while he would 'protest before God in extremity' to 'love the religion they outwardly profess', he hated 'their presumptuous and seditious behaviour'.[28] When the General Assembly met at Dundee in March 1598, James 'made a harangue', reminding attendees of the 'great care he had to adorn and accommodate the Kirk', which he was ready to expand further by enabling its reintroduction as a parliamentary estate. While not seeking 'to bring in Papistical or Anglican bishopping', James believed church leaders should be able to vote on ecclesiastical matters and 'not to stand always at the door, like poor supplicants, despised, and nothing regarded'.[29]

In 1600, three bishops were appointed by royal command to sit in the Scottish Parliament, creating a precedent whereby, once James became King of England, he (and not the General Assembly) would determine Scottish episcopal powers, and by 1602 two bishops had been appointed as Scottish Privy Councillors. Accordingly, James could scarcely believe being subsequently accused, by continental Catholic writers, of having been 'a Puritan in Scotland'. In a published attack on the Jesuit cardinal Robert Bellarmine in 1609, the king protested that he had been 'persecuted by Puritans there, not from my birth only, but even since four months before my birth', referring to Riccio's murder. In 1584, he had 'erected bishops, and depressed all their popular parity, I then being not eighteen years of age'. Indeed, 'if the daily commentaries of my life and actions in Scotland were written (as Julius Caesar's were)', James ventured there 'would scarcely a month pass in all my life', since he had turned thirteen, in which Kirk ministers had not attempted 'some accident or other'.[30]

*

A tumultuous experience of Church–State relations thus informed James's depictions of Scottish ministers in *Basilicon Doron* as he recalled being 'often-times calumniated in their popular sermons, not for any evil or vice in me, but because I was a king, which they thought the highest evil'. The king, moreover, mistrusted 'the preposterous humility' of 'proud Puritans' who claimed 'we are all but vile worms' but refused to be judged by any earthly power.[31] In the new preface that accompanied the London edition of *Basilicon Doron* in 1603, James claimed that his 'description of the humours of Puritans, and rash-heady preachers' had been misinterpreted, with the term 'Puritan' apparently only intended to refer to a small sect of Anabaptists. But either en route from Edinburgh or shortly after acceding as English king, he was presented with the 'Millenary Petition', ostensibly bearing the signatures of over a thousand English ministers and calling for a conference to consider moderate reforms, such as lifting requirements for ministers to wear surplices and dispensing with the sign of the cross at baptism, while also calling for initiatives to expand clergy numbers and prevent non-residence.[32] In October, James issued a proclamation warning that his readiness to address alleged 'corruptions' within the English Church had been 'misconstrued by some mens' spirits, whose heat tends rather to combustion than reformation' and who had resorted to 'public invectives' and 'gathering subscriptions of multitudes of vulgar persons to supplications'.[33]

In January 1604, James summoned prominent reformers and selected bishops to the Hampton Court Conference and opened proceedings by contrasting his recent experiences as the Church of England's supreme governor with his earlier struggles to assert authority over refractory Kirkmen. James thanked God for 'bringing him into the promised land, where religion was purely professed, where he sat among grave, learned and reverend men; not, as before, elsewhere, a king without state, without honour, without order'.[34] Comprising three all-day sessions, the first was reserved for the king, Privy Councillors and bishops whose resistance to reform was articulated by Archbishop John Whitgift of Canterbury and Bishop Richard Bancroft of London (whose denigration of the Kirk had angered James fifteen years earlier). On bended knee, the primates begged James to avoid altering the Church of England's government or liturgy for fear of offering Puritans and Catholics alike an opportunity to claim oppression since the Reformation. The king, however, denied the soundness of reasoning which implied that 'because a man had been sick of the pox forty years, therefore he should not be cured at length'.[35]

During the conference, James drew on his Scottish experiences to warn English bishops about Presbyterian challenges to their hierarchy: 'if once you were out, and they in place, I know what would become of my supremacy. No Bishop, No King.'[36] While this *obiter dicta* quickly became shorthand for royalist insistence on the mutual support of monarch and episcopate, 'No Bishop, no King' assumed ominously prophetic overtones under Charles I when bishops were abolished in Scotland in 1641, eight years before abolition of the monarchy in England. When clerical vestments were discussed, with support expressed for the 'Canterbury cap' or biretta, James acknowledged to the English bishops that 'you may now safely wear your caps, but I shall tell you, if you should walk in one street in Scotland, with such a cap on your head, if I were not with you, you should be stoned to death with your cap.'[37] With lay baptism among the more controversial subjects discussed, an unofficial account of events recorded how, to one bishop's claim that an early Church Father had used sand for the sacrament, the king had riposted by giving 'a turd for the argument: he might as well have pissed on them, for that had been more liker water to sand'.[38]

The conference ultimately concluded with a notable agreement to sponsor a new translation of the Bible, together with reforms including amendments to the Book of Common Prayer, changes to the operation of ecclesiastical courts, measures to expand the preaching ministry in specific areas of England and Ireland, curbs on the importation of popish publications, and tighter enforcement of legislation requiring parishioners to take Communion at least once annually. Reviewing proceedings, James was understandably upbeat; as he put it to the crypto-papist, Henry Howard, Earl of Northampton, he was relieved to have 'kept such a revel with the Puritans here these two days'.[39] Accustomed to intense theological sparring with Kirkmen, he had been surprised by the Puritan representatives' apparent tractability.

In the event, Puritan hopes were disappointed by new canons later agreed by the Church of England's Convocation that retained controversial practices, such as the sign of the cross in baptism. Addressing the House of Lords in March 1604, James admitted that 'Puritans and Novelists [innovators]' did 'not so far differ from us in points of religion', but he regarded as problematic 'their confused form of policy and parity, being ever discontented with the present government, and impatient to suffer any superiority, which makes their sect unable to be suffered in any well-governed commonwealth'.[40] As in the aftermath of the 'Black Acts' passage in Scotland in the mid-1580s, adoption of the new English canons was followed by a concerted campaign to secure conformity, led by Bancroft, who became Archbishop of Canterbury in November 1604.

James thereafter found his hunting trips in eastern England disrupted by presentations of petitions on behalf of local ministers who refused subscription. Confronted by a petition signed by around 200 yeomen in Royston, with rumours of 3,000–4,000 more signatures forthcoming, James wrote to Sir Robert Cecil, now Viscount Cranborne, warning that he had 'daily more and more cause to hate and abhor all that sect, enemies to all kings and to me only because I am king'.[41] Indeed, the king's determination to enforce expulsion of nonconformist ministers may have been stiffened after being serially accosted by delegations of Puritan clergy in Huntingdonshire, Cambridgeshire and Hertfordshire, as 'his passion for hunting arguably served better to educate him about the nature, and the limitations, of Puritan aspirations than ever the Hampton Court Conference had done.'[42]

Between seventy-three and eighty-three beneficed clergy – or one per cent of English ministers – lost their livings for not subscribing conformity to the new canons during the early months of 1605.[43] James himself readily acknowledged the dilemmas posed by scruples of conscience in religious matters but brooked no exceptions regarding the political obedience signified by conformity. Presented with another 'Northamptonshire petition' urging abrogation of penalties suffered by nonconformists, the king spent eight hours one Sunday in February discussing Church–State matters with his Privy Councillors and reportedly acknowledged that 'he could hazard his crown, but he would suppress those malicious spirits.' As he 'most bitterly inveighed against the Puritans', James reminded Councillors that far-reaching revolutions in Scotland and the Low Countries had originated with petitions for religious reform, and he lamented that both 'his mother and he, from their cradles, had been haunted with a Puritan devil, which he feared would not leave him to his grave'. The king directed even harsher censure towards Catholics, proclaiming 'his utter detestation of their superstitious religion'. So firm was James's hostility that 'if he thought his son and heir after him would give any toleration thereunto, he would wish him fairly buried before his eyes.'[44]

The Gunpowder Plot's discovery in November 1605 provided justification for those who regarded papist conspiracy as a greater threat than Puritan nonconformity, but, by then, the number of ministerial deprivations had subsided. Endorsing the conformist drive, one of the king's chaplains, William Wilkes, denounced 'Newfanglists' as 'bewitched with strong enchantments' in withholding obedience solely on account of specific ceremonies. In *Obedience or Ecclesiastical Union* (1605), Wilkes condemned hot-headed zealots determined to 'make religion their stalking-horse, under whose belly they shoot at what their appetites do most affect'.[45] Exhortations to conformity also extended beyond the pulpit, since Wilkes was quoting almost verbatim from the tragicomedy *The Malcontent*, written and staged the previous year by his son-in-law, John Marston, in which the villain 'Mendoza' had warned:

> Beware a hypocrite;
> A churchman once corrupted, O avoid!
> A fellow that makes religion his stalking-horse,
>
> > [Shoots under his belly]
>
> He breeds a plague.

Earlier, the eponymous malcontent Malevole informed Mendoza that he might emulate the hotter sort of Protestants, imagining how he might 'live lazily, rail upon authority, deny kings' supremacy in things indifferent, and be a Pope in my own parish'.[46]

As James drove conformity in England, anti-episcopal sentiment increased in Scotland. In July 1605, nearly thirty ministers attended an abortive, unauthorized General Assembly in Aberdeen, with several thereafter convicted of treason, which bore a capital sentence that could be commuted to banishment. Postponing passing sentence on the convicted ministers, James invited eight Kirk leaders to London in September 1606 to discuss Scottish church affairs, convening a series of meetings, services and entertainment that, as James Melville recorded, left 'our brains full of wine and music, and our stomachs empty of victuals'. After hearing a sermon in which Bishop John Buckeridge of Rochester – through 'ignorance or malice, or both' – repeatedly yoked 'the presbytery with the Pope, as though the one had been joined in the same judgement with the other', the Scots ministers joined James, Prince Henry, Archbishop Bancroft and other English clerics and courtiers to discuss 'whether the Assembly last held at Aberdeen was a lawful General Assembly or not?' As his nephew described, Andrew Melville spoke first, 'talked all his mind in his own manner, roundly, soundly, fully, freely, and fervently, almost the space of an hour', before his colleagues also defended their brethren who had met in Aberdeen, 'most reverently on knees, but therewith most freely, stoutly, and plainly, to the admiration of the English auditory, who were not accustomed to hearing the king so talked to, and reasoned with'.[47]

Unfortunately, James Melville learned that the king and Bancroft 'had their spies, who, under colour of friendly visitation, reported both our speeches and actions' in private. Summoned before the king, Andrew Melville admitted to composing satirical Latin verses about the Anglican liturgy, provoked by the 'vanities and superstition' he had observed. When Bancroft remonstrated, Melville 'took occasion, plainly in his face, before the Council, to tell him all his mind, which burst out as enclosed fire in water!' In a gesture reminiscent of his altercation with James at Falkland in 1596, Melville seized Bancroft 'by the white sleeves of his rochet [vestment]', shook them and 'freely and roundly called them "Romish rags, and a part of the Beast's mark"!'[48] While all eight Kirk ministers were initially barred from returning to Scotland and entrusted to the custody of English bishops, Andrew Melville was convicted of the seditious crime 'scandalum magnatum' and imprisoned in the Tower of London between 1607 and 1611, before going into permanent exile in France as a professor of theology in the Protestant principality of Sedan.

In Scotland, a visit to Edinburgh in June 1608 by George Home, Earl of Dunbar, and his chaplain, George Abbot (later Archbishop of Canterbury), sought 'to persuade the Scots that there was no substantial difference between the two realms', as the Presbyterian chronicler David Calderwood put it. According to Dunbar and Abbot, 'it was his Majesty's will, that England should stand as he found it, and Scotland as he left it'.[49] In practice, however, James evidently regarded the Church of England as a more suitable model for British convergence; he had, after all, insisted at the Hampton Court Conference, 'I will have one doctrine and one discipline, one religion in substance, and in ceremony.'[50] In 1606, the Scottish Parliament restored bishops fully to their temporal estates with all thirteen bishops entitled to sit in Parliament. When the General Assembly met in June 1610, two new courts of High Commission were created in Scotland, modelled on their English counterparts, with powers to investigate breaches of ecclesiastical order.[51] James also oversaw the restoration of apostolic succession to Scotland to continue the uninterrupted transmission of spiritual authority held to date from the days of the Apostles. That October, John Spottiswoode was consecrated as Archbishop of Glasgow, alongside the bishops of Brechin and Galloway, at a ceremony in London that was presided over by several English bishops but without archiepiscopal involvement to avoid suspicions of Anglican superiority. In 1612, the Scottish Parliament ratified the General Assembly's conclusions, thereby restoring the episcopate to full jurisdictional competence.

*

A significant threat that James encountered as King of England was renewed Protestant heterodoxy. Traditional Calvinist beliefs in predestination – whereby God bestowed salvation on 'elect' individuals – were challenged by the arguments of a Dutch theologian, Jacobus Arminius, who gained notoriety by promoting a theory of 'conditional' election, maintaining that God gave salvation to individuals whom He believed would retain a permanent belief in Christ, with such individuals free to resist God's gift of grace if they wished. Although Arminius died in 1609, James addressed soteriology, or divergent theories of salvation, in a private meeting with a Dutch delegation sent to London the following year to discuss fishing rights. According to a Dutch attendee, the king explained that 'he had studied this matter as much as anyone else, and had found that no-one should be too confident that their view was the correct one'. Given the complexity of arguments, he 'would bet that his opinion on the topic was best, but that he would not base his salvation on it'; he had, moreover, 'scarcely dared to touch upon' such matters in his own publications.[52] But in August 1611, Abbot sent James a copy of *Tractatus Theologicus de Deo* ('Theological Treatise on God'), written by a German follower of Arminius, Conrad Vorstius, who was shortly to become professor of theology at Leiden University. Directly after reading Vorstius's *Tractatus*, James instructed his ambassador in The Hague, Sir Ralph Winwood, to inform the Dutch authorities 'how infinitely we shall be displeased, if such a monster receive advancement in the Church.' Less than a fortnight later, Winwood addressed the States-General in a speech published in Dutch translation. Although James had no desire 'to stick his nose into someone else's affairs', Winwood warned that Vorstius's appointment threatened Anglo-Dutch amity and that the king 'will not compromise his religion for friend-ship'. Informed by Winwood in April 1612 that James, if he wished, could render Leiden's magistrates compliant with his demands, the Secretary of the States-General, Johan van Oldenbarnevelt, angrily retorted that 'he was born in liberty and therefore could not "digest" such kind of language', adding that even the Spanish king 'did never speak in so high a style'.[53]

A 'Defender of the Faith' for British and continental Protestants, James deemed it his duty to confront heresy wherever it appeared. Politically, irreconcilable divisions among Dutch Protestants risked undermining the new state of the United Provinces and potentially facilitating reassertion of Catholic control by Spain. James was equally concerned about the likely export of theological divisions into neigh-bouring polities. In that same month of April 1612, a Staffordshire draper, Edward Wightman, became the last individual to be executed for heresy in England when he was burned at the stake in Lichfield. Wightman had earlier prepared an anti-Trinitarian treatise for James that rejected the three main Apostles', Nicene and Athanasian creeds. In presenting 'the entire framework of Christian orthodoxy as a mass of unscriptural accretions', Wightman's beliefs have been character-ized as 'a kind of hypertrophied Puritanism, a species of separatism run amok'.[54]

Three weeks before Wightman's execution, another anti-Trinitarian, Bartholomew Legate, became the last man to be burned at the stake in London, after prolonged imprisonment and serial interviews with James regarding his theological views. In February 1612, the English ambassador in Venice, Sir Dudley Carleton, learned that Legate had been 'long forborne and mildly dealt with', amid ambiguity attaching to the legality of executions for heresy. While some lawyers argued that such prosecutions could only be initiated by the court of High Com-mission, James had allegedly said of Legate that 'if he be so desperate to deny Christ to be God, he will adventure to burn him with a good conscience'.[55] That same month, the Venetian ambassador in London, Antonio Foscarini, relayed reports that Vorstius had left Leiden to join his numerous supporters in The Hague, observing that 'this news has greatly disturbed the king's mind, which was not quiet before'. Foscarini then discussed Legate's case, since James 'insists that the execution shall take place as soon as possible, for the position of this man is very similar to that of Vorstius'.[56]

As theological divisions in the United Provinces persisted, James recommended to the States-General in April 1617 – in a letter published in French and Dutch translation – that a National Synod should be called if the 'evil is found to be already so strong and enrooted among the population that it cannot be quickly and easily pulled out'.[57] The resulting Synod of Dort that met in 1618–19 attracted over one hundred international delegates, including a quarter from outside the Dutch republic. The clerical delegation dispatched to Dort by James included a Scot, Walter Balcanquhall, specifically tasked with representing church interests in James's northern kingdom. In later years, Balcanquhall acknowledged various divisions of doctrinal opinion among the British delegation, but insisted that 'the directions of our blessed Peacemaking king kept us from kindling new fires; where we had work enough to quench the old.'[58] Regarding Vorstius, James's demands were finally met in June 1619 when the States of Holland removed the theologian from his position at Leiden and Vorstius was banished from the Dutch republic by the States-General.

By the summer of 1619, however, James had become mired in ecclesiastical difficulties in Scotland over his attempted introduction of what became known as the 'Five Articles of Perth'. Promoted during James's visit to Scotland in 1617, the Articles enjoined kneeling to receive communion, private communion, private baptism, episcopal confirmation, and observance of five holy days (Christmas, Good Friday, Easter Sunday, Ascension and Pentecost). Dissuaded from submitting the Articles to Parliament during his visit, James was 'highly incensed' when they subsequently failed to gain approval at a General Assembly meeting in November. As Calderwood recorded, James intended to 'let the Kirk of Scotland know, what it is to have ado with an old king, or to abuse his lenity'.[59] Although approval was secured at the next General Assembly in Perth in August 1618, an armed guard was stationed outside the meeting and all votes were closely recorded for royal inspection. Preaching to the Perth Assembly, Archbishop Spottiswoode admitted that 'I would, if it had been in my power, most willingly have declined the receiving of these articles.' But, as matters stood, 'the evil of disobedience' to the royal will was a greater sin than adopting ceremonial changes which, although 'new this day, with a little use, will become familiar and old'.[60]

But as Spottiswoode feared, Assembly approval did not ensure automatic observance. Resistance was primarily directed towards the fifth article enjoining kneeling at communion, which was widely rejected as an unacceptable posture of adoration and equivalent to accepting the Catholic doctrine of transubstantiation. Opponents argued that ministers and parishioners should instead take the sacrament seated together at a table, in imitation of Christ's Last Supper with his disciples. Amid a flurry of publications on kneeling, Bishop Buckeridge of Rochester – whose yoking of Presbyterians with Papists had infuriated Andrew Melville and his colleagues a decade earlier – attached a tract enjoining kneeling to publication of his Passion Sunday court sermon preached in 1618. Buckeridge lambasted Puritans as 'these *elephanti*, elephants that have no joints in their knees', who 'have sworn and vowed that they will not kneel to God, and his Christ', esteeming 'their own fantasy more than they do the oath of God'.[61] In his own *Meditation* on verses from St Matthew's Gospel published the following year, James likewise criticized 'our foolish, superstitious Puritans, that refuse to kneel at the receiving of the blessed Sacrament'.[62] Reflecting on the Lord's Prayer, the king also admired its divine entreaty to reverence, in contrast to those who 'love to sit Jack-fellow like with Christ at the Lord's Table, as his brethren and comrades'.[63]

Although the Perth Articles received parliamentary ratification in July 1621, non-compliance persisted. In August, James exhorted his Scottish bishops to proceed vigorously against nonconformists, warning that 'if any or all of you be false or faint-hearted we are able enough . . . to put others in your places, who both can and will make things possible, which ye account so difficult'. For James, religious ceremonies were not a matter of conscience, but of loyalty. Since 'papistry is a disease of the mind, and Puritanism is in the brain', the 'only true remedy and antidote' was 'a grave, settled, uniform and well-ordered Church, obedient to God and their king'.[64] Yet rather than settled obedience, refusal was so widespread that 'to kneel or not to kneel became the defining religious act for a generation of Scots in certain key localities'.[65] The physical contortions to which the septuagenarian minister at St Giles in Edinburgh, Patrick Galloway, put himself in an attempt to display compliance but avoid kneeling during the Easter service in 1622 epitomized the Church of Scotland's internal tensions by the end of James's reign. A former General Assembly Moderator who had preached Queen Anna's coronation sermon in 1590, Galloway was observed taking communion, having 'bowed the one leg, had the sole of his other foot upon the ground, and sat withal upon the firm [bench]'.[66]

15

The King James Version

One of Rudyard Kipling's last short stories, 'Proofs of Holy Writ' (1934), imagined Ben Jonson and William Shakespeare supplying covert assistance to the new translation of the Bible published in 1611, widely known as the 'King James Bible'. Relaxing in Shakespeare's back garden in Stratford one September afternoon, the playwrights were interrupted by a messenger bearing proofs of five verses from the Old Testament Book of Isaiah. Shakespeare explained that one of the official 'Translators' of this new edition of the Bible, Miles Smith from Brasenose College, Oxford, after admiring *Macbeth*, had started sending him passages for emendation 'when direct illumination lacked, for a tricking-out of his words or the turn of some figure', prompting Jonson to observe, 'they never called on me.' Thereafter, however, Jonson read out the relevant verses from earlier Latin and English Bibles while Shakespeare improved Smith's draft translation. Returning the proofs to Oxford, Jonson wondered, 'Who will know we had part in it?' to which Shakespeare replied, 'God, maybe – if He ever lay ear to earth.'[1] Kipling's tale captured the collaborative approach that facilitated the new translation, as well as the care for sonorous cadences in a keenly oral culture accustomed to hearing Scripture read aloud. Half a century after 'Proofs of Holy Writ' was published, the opening of Anthony Burgess's novel, *Enderby's Dark Lady* (1984), reversed Kipling's fantasy by imagining Jonson as the Bible translators' secret contact who entrusted Shakespeare with revision of the Psalms.

Setting aside fictional re-imagining, the 'King James Bible' came into being as the result of an unexpected intervention during the second day of the Hampton Court Conference's debates regarding Church of England reform in January 1604. When the Puritan President of Corpus

Christi, Oxford, John Rainolds, suggested that 'there might be a new translation of the Bible', Bishop Richard Bancroft of London had quickly objected that 'if every man's humour should be followed, there would be no end of translating'. But James was more receptive, acknowledging that 'he could never, yet, see a Bible well translated in English'. Pursuing Rainolds's proposal, the new English king moved that a concerted effort be made towards achieving 'one uniform translation', undertaken 'by the best-learned' at the universities of Oxford and Cambridge before being reviewed by the Church of England's bishops, Privy Councillors and James himself.[2]

Seven years later, in 1611, the new translation was published. Known thereafter as the 'King James Bible', it remains the most influential and widely sold English-language work ever produced. Two years before James's accession as English king, a similar aspiration had been mooted in Scotland. When the General Assembly met at Burntisland in Fife in May 1601, members of the Kirk had moved that errors in existing translations of the Bible should be corrected and that a metrical translation of the Psalms be prepared. As Archbishop John Spottiswood later recalled, James had responded enthusiastically to calls for a new translation of the Bible 'and did urge it earnestly', envisaging the 'glory' that would redound to the Church of Scotland by its accomplishment. By instantly identifying controverted passages and reciting psalms from memory, the king had also demonstrated 'that he was no less conversant in the Scriptures than they whose profession it was'.[3]

Members of the English Church's hierarchy were no less impressed at the Hampton Court Conference three years later. As Bishop William Barlow of Rochester recounted, he and his fellow bishops could scarcely contain their 'astonishment' that James – 'brought up among Puritans, not the most learned men in the world' and having governed 'a kingdom, full of business, and troubles' – should 'in points of divinity show himself as expedite and perfect as the greatest scholars, and most industrious students there present, might not outstrip him'. By the end of the Conference's second day, James's 'singular readiness, and exact knowledge' of theological matters had so awed attendees that one prelate declared himself 'fully persuaded, his Majesty spoke by the instinct of the spirit of God'. For Barlow, James was, indeed, 'a living library and a walking study', echoing the epithet conferred on the first-century BC classical philosopher Cassius Longinus by the Greek rhetorician Eunapius.[4]

James had, after all, been the precocious eight-year-old who had once impressed an English ambassador by his facility in translating randomly selected passages from Scripture, from Latin into French and then into English. When the king was nineteen, Queen Elizabeth wrote to confirm how much she did 'both admire and rejoice to see your wise paraphrase, which far exceeds their text', alluding to the *Paraphrase on the Book of Revelation*, a copy of which James had evidently sent to the queen but which remained unpublished until 1617.[5] In his early twenties, James did, however, publish two interpretations of Scripture: *A Fruitful Meditation* (1588) providing a commentary on verses from Revelation and *A Meditation* on verses from Chronicles (1589). James opened the latter *Meditation* by disingenuously claiming that its publication was not motivated by belief in 'my ability to instruct' readers, but rather to provide posterity with 'a certain testimony of my upright and anefauld [honest] meaning in this so great and weighty a cause'.[6] Prefaced by commendations from Kirk ministers, the Scottish king's exegeses positioned him as a prominent 'Defender of the (Protestant) Faith', as ready to confront the Papal Antichrist in print as on the battlefield. Published just after the Spanish Armada's defeat, James's *Fruitful Meditation* warned readers of 'armies amassed . . . in France against the [Protestant] saints there; in Flanders for the like; and in Germany', alongside 'what is prepared and come forward against this isle'.[7] By the time he acceded as English king, an anglicized version of James's *Fruitful Meditation* was being sold in London, while French, Latin and Dutch translations were published in Amsterdam, La Rochelle, Basle, Halle and Jena.

*

After the Hampton Court Conference, the practical challenge of undertaking a new translation of the Bible was addressed by appointing around fifty 'Translators', organized into six sub-committees or 'Companies' and later known, from their geographical locations, as the Oxford, Cambridge and Westminster Companies, each of which was responsible for translating different sections. Production of the King James Bible thus represented a major collaborative achievement, with the term 'Company' evoking not only the troupes of actors who performed in London playhouses and received royal patronage from King James, Queen Anna and Prince Henry, but also the commercial organizations established to promote colonial expansion overseas, such as the Muscovy Company founded in 1555 and the more recent East India Company established in 1600. Writing to the heads of Cambridge colleges in July 1604, Richard Bancroft explained that 'you will scarcely conceive how earnest his Majesty is to have this work begun', claiming that James 'rejoices more' about the new translation of Scripture than the peace treaty recently concluded between England and Spain. The following month, Bancroft admitted to Cambridge University's Vice-Chancellor and Master of Trinity Hall, John Cowell, that he had 'written so many letters about this matter of translation, as keeping no copies of them, I do confound myself, forgetting what, and to whom, I have written'.[8]

Having been elevated as Archbishop of Canterbury in November 1604, Bancroft assumed default responsibility for the project's organization. That same month, insight into the workings of the First Westminster Company, tasked with translating the Old Testament book of Genesis through to the books of Kings, was supplied by the Dean of Westminster, Lancelot Andrewes, who sent apologies for missing a meeting of the Society of Antiquaries into which he had recently been elected. As Andrewes explained, 'this afternoon is our translation time' and it was especially important that he attend since 'most of our Company are negligent'.[9] Ten months later, Andrewes's concern was echoed by John Rainolds – who had first called for a new translation – when he apologized to King James's Principal Secretary, the Earl of Salisbury, for absenting himself from court, having 'received commandment from the king to take pains about their translation of the Bible, all other business set apart'. Although Rainolds's First Oxford Company was meant to meet in 'conference three days weekly', recurring poor attendance meant 'that, if he were absent, there would not be a major part to prosecute it' and progress would stall.[10] While Andrewes and Rainolds occupied divergent positions within the Church of England's spectrum of opinion regarding church government and ceremonial observance, their combined erudition was remarkable. Andrewes spoke fifteen modern languages, and could read Latin, Greek, Hebrew, Chaldee, Syriac and Arabic, while the Puritan-inclined Rainolds had earlier delivered a series of 250 lectures arguing that the Biblical Apocrypha were non-canonical, although he would not succeed in preventing the Apocrypha's inclusion in the King James Bible.[11]

Royal instructions mandated that the translation costs of the new edition were to be borne by the Church of England's bishops, who were to identify vacant church livings valued with an annual income of at

least £20 for any unbeneficed Translators. Bancroft also circulated fifteen 'rules' to be observed by Translators, including the injunction that
the version of Scripture in the so-called 'Bishops' Bible' produced in
1568 was to be 'as little altered as the truth of the original will permit'.[12]
Modern scholarship has shown that this advice was, however, disregarded, with greater textual reliance placed on the earlier Geneva Bible
of 1560, despite this being denounced by James as 'the worst of all'
translations.[13] Since the king particularly objected to the polemical
character of some of the Geneva Bible's marginal commentaries, Bancroft's rules banned all marginal notes in the new translation, aside
from glosses of single Greek or Hebrew words that resisted translation
into English. (While the absence of marginal notes in the King James
Bible was one reason for its later popularity on non-denominational
grounds, it is ironic that James inserted marginal notes in his own *Meditation upon the Lord's Prayer*, one of which regretted 'every ignorant
woman, and ordinary craftsman, taking upon them to interpret the
Scriptures').[14] Another rule stipulated retention of 'the old ecclesiastical
words', specifically confirming that 'church' was not to be translated as
'congregation'. For when William Tyndale had produced the first English translation of the New Testament in 1526, Sir Thomas More had
seen in his rendering of '*ekklēsia*' as 'congregation' a covert attempt to
promote ecclesiological reform.[15]

In the Jacobean era, the sheer scale of the new translation prompted
recurrent fears regarding feasibility. In June 1607, Oxford University's
Vice-Chancellor, Henry Airay, wrote to members of the Second Oxford
Company (responsible for translating the Gospels, Acts and Revelation)
urging more meetings in order to progress the translation, 'lest further
delay of that business bring great displeasure both from his Majesty'
and Bancroft, 'who is very earnest for the finishing of that work'.[16]
After its publication, the legal scholar John Selden admired the 'excellent way' taken by Translators in entrusting specific sections to scholars
with particular linguistic expertise, before 'they met together, and one
read the translation, the rest holding in their hands some Bible, either
of the learned tongues, or French, Spanish, Italian etc. If they found any
fault, they spoke; if not, he read on.'[17]

As Selden's account indicated, regular recourse was made to continental scholarship and, in January 1611, a diary entry by the Genevan-born
Protestant classicist Isaac Casaubon described one Sunday afternoon at

Whitehall during which the Bishop of Bath and Wells, James Montagu, read aloud the marginal notes accompanying a recently published Catholic Bible printed at Douai, provoking comments of censure by James to which Andrewes, Casaubon, Bishop Richard Neile of Durham and others responded.[18] Such discussions evidently took place just as final portions of the new English Bible were being sent to press, since the translation was finally published, in folio format and weighing over twenty pounds, by the king's printer during the summer of 1611. The title-page confirmed that this edition of the Bible was 'newly translated out of the original tongues', with existing translations 'diligently compared and revised by His Majesty's special commandment'.[19]

Dedicating the new edition to the king, the Translators claimed – with some hyperbole – that, since the idea of a new translation had first arisen, James 'did never desist, to urge and to excite' the project's completion with the assiduity and perseverance that 'a matter of such importance might justly require'.[20] Acclaiming him 'as the principal mover and author of the work', the dedication's invocation of the phrase 'mover and author' underscored the divinely ordained nature of James's kingship, drawing parallels between royal authority and God's power as 'the first mover'.[21] The Translators further hoped that royal sponsorship would confer some degree of protection, fearing imminent censure and criticism for their efforts. On the one hand, they anticipated being 'traduced by popish persons at home or abroad', who begrudged all attempts to 'make God's holy truth to be yet more and more known unto the people, whom they desire still to keep in ignorance and darkness'. Among Protestants, on the other hand, they would 'be maligned by self-conceited brethren', prepared to accept 'nothing, but what is framed by themselves, and hammered on their anvil'.[22]

The new edition's dedication to James was followed by a preface from the 'Translators to the reader', extending to over 11,000 words and penned by Miles Smith – the Translator who would later feature in Kipling's short story. In this preface, Smith explained that the Translators had 'never thought from the beginning, that we should need to make a new translation, nor yet to make of a bad one, a good one'. Rather, they had sought 'to make a good one better, or out of many good ones, one principal good one', building on the reformist shoulders of earlier scholars, such as Miles Coverdale, Archbishop Matthew Parker and William Tyndale, and harnessing their own collective linguistic, lexical and philological expertise. Tribute was paid to all earlier translators who 'break the ice' and lay foundations for later scholarship, while readers were also reminded of the many revisions and translations through which the original sources of Scripture had already passed, in languages including Hebrew, Greek and Latin. Regarding the delights of rendering Scripture into the vernacular, Smith insisted that 'translation it is that opens the window, to let in the light; that breaks the shell, that we may eat the kernel; that puts aside the curtain, that we may look into the most Holy place; that removes the cover of the well, that we may come by the water'.[23]

Translating Scripture was, however, no ordinary task since the text originated 'from heaven, not from earth; the author being God, not man'. Given the centrality of God's Word to Protestant worship, the Translators saluted James's courage in promoting the new translation, thereby setting 'himself upon a stage to be gloated upon by every evil eye'. Even though he had metaphorically cast 'himself headlong upon pikes, to be gored by every sharp tongue', the Translators confirmed that James had nevertheless stood 'resolute, as a statue immovable' in his commitment to the enterprise. In any case, the divinity of Scripture's content could not be compromised by imperfect and defective translation. For just as a speech of King James's 'which he uttered in parliament, being translated into French, Dutch, Italian, and Latin, is still the king's speech, though it be not interpreted by every translator with the like grace, nor peradventure so fitly for phrase, nor so expressly for sense, everywhere'.[24]

Although the new edition's title-page indicated that it was 'appointed to be read in churches', unlike every edition of the Bishops' Bible produced since 1568 it was not 'authorised and appointed to be read'. Perhaps on account of Bancroft's death in November 1610, no Privy Council order regarding authorization was made; accordingly, 'the Bible known in England as the Authorized Version seems not to have been authorized'.[25] Yet even if the term 'Authorized Version' only started being used to denote the King James Bible from the 1820s onwards, the new edition was quickly taken up by contemporaries, with around 140 smaller and cheaper (non-folio) editions produced between 1611 and 1640. Initially, use of the new translation was confined to England. In 1610, the royal printer in Edinburgh had produced a new folio edition of the Geneva Bible (known as the 'Geneva-Tomson-Junius' edition), despite James's disparagement of its polemical editorial glosses. Since this edition was the first republication of the Geneva Bible in Scotland since its original printing in 1579, its appearance was presumably a pre-emptive move ahead of the new edition's publication in London the following year. It was not until after James's death in 1625 that the first edition of the King James Bible was published in Scotland, in octavo format in 1633, to coincide with Charles I's delayed coronation in Edinburgh, three years before a new set of church canons required every Scottish parish church to possess a copy.[26]

Much of the new edition's popularity undoubtedly derived from the even and rich quality of its prose as collaboratively agreed by the Translators. Sonorous rhythm structures generated memorable phrases. When Adam informed God of Eve's sin in Genesis (3:12) – 'she gave me of the tree and I did eat' – the verse's iambic pentameter echoed many Shakespearean lines.[27] The new edition's luxuriant lexicon also reflected the varied and cosmopolitan experiences of different Translators. For instance, Lancelot Andrewes's first Westminster Company, which was responsible for describing the lushness of the Garden of Eden in the opening Book of Genesis, included a Greek and Hebrew scholar, John Layfield, who had nearly drowned while serving as a chaplain on an expedition to the West Indies in 1598. Visiting Puerto Rico, however, Layfield had waxed lyrical about the abundance of delicious fruit: guavas, pomegranates, figs, grapes, limes and pomecitrons that 'grow to so huge greatness' that one horse could only carry three or four, together with pineapples that Layfield could best compare 'to very ripe strawberries and cream, the rather if a man has already eaten almost his belly full'.[28]

Approved by committee, the text of the new edition has been dubbed 'the King James steamroller' for the manner in which it 'flattened differences between Hebrew, Aramaic, and Koine Greek into a single dignified amalgam'.[29] Nor was that amalgam apolitical, as seen by Bancroft's insistence on 'church' over 'congregation'. Unsurprisingly, the 'King James Bible' also confirmed the robustness of monarchical rule, with the term 'prince' appearing over 350 times and used as the equivalent of fourteen different Hebrew terms.[30] Yet the text of the 'King James Bible' also 'exerted a steady gravitational pull on the ordinary speech, not to mention poetry, of future English.[31] Countless everyday modern idioms, not to mention numerous titles for novels, derive from its lyrical phraseology. The Book of Psalms avers that 'out of the mouth of babes and sucklings has thou ordained strength because of thine enemies' (8:2), while the opening chapter of Ecclesiastes declares that 'the thing that hath been, is that which shall be; and that which is done is that which shall be done: and there is no new thing under the sun' (1:9). Rhetorical questions abound, including those from the Old Testament Book of Jeremiah, 'can the Ethiopian change his skin, or the leopard his spots?' (13:23), and the New Testament Gospel of St Luke, 'can the blind lead the blind? Shall they not both fall into the ditch?' (6:39). Some oft-quoted sentences are models of pithy precision, such as the line from St Matthew's Gospel, 'for many are called, but few are chosen' (22:14).[32] Other lines are simply earthy, such as the half-dozen instances of individuals urinating via the phrase 'pisseth against the wall'.[33]

*

James's designation as the 'principal mover' of what became known as the 'King James Bible' was fitting acclaim for a monarch whose delight in hearing the Word of God explained his elevation of sermons above other aspects of religious worship. In Reformation Scotland, the injunction from Romans, 'faith cometh by hearing' (10:17), had been reflected in the prioritization accorded to the Word of God, over the sacraments and religious discipline, in the Confession of the Faith adopted by the Scottish Parliament in 1560. For John Knox, it was not 'the chanting or mumbling over of certain psalms' or reading set lessons and homilies 'that feed the souls of the hungry sheep', but injunctions by Christ, the Apostles and St Paul 'all commanding us to preach, to preach, and that to preach Christ Jesus crucified' that demonstrated the 'efficacy' of 'the living voice above the bare letter read'.[34] Indeed, the sub-title of *A Fruitful Meditation* (1588), which James published in his early twenties, explained that it was 'in form of a sermon'. A preface by the minister, Patrick Galloway, confirmed that the king's *Meditation* was a work 'which God's spirit did utter by our sovereign'.[35]

In England, James doubled the number of sermons preached at the royal court by adding weekly sermons on Tuesdays, as well as Sundays, to commemorate the Gowrie conspiracy that had occurred on Tuesday 5 August 1600, with all Privy Councillors expected to attend on both days. James's accession also marked a change in the public face of royal religious observance. Whereas Elizabeth had conscientiously attended all court sermons during Lent, and sporadically on Sundays and feast days, she had been present for the whole of each service. By contrast, James continued his Scottish practice of believing that 'his entrance was a cue to start the sermon – with an anthem as a bridge, during which the preacher made his way into the pulpit'.[36] Once the sermon had concluded, five psalms were sung before the king departed. To deliver the expanded rota of court sermons, James recruited a larger pool of court clerics, which resulted in his being attended by forty-eight royal chaplains at his death in 1625, in contrast to the seventeen in post when Elizabeth died. After James's death, the Chancellor of York Minster, Phineas Hodson, extolled the late sovereign's stamina by calculating that, during his twenty-two-year reign as English king, 'he heard more sermons, than all the princes before him in two hundred'.[37]

Contemporaries acknowledged James's keen delight in encouraging the highest standards of pulpit oratory. Writing to the English ambassador in The Hague, John Chamberlain described how the king had been so eager to see the notes from which Lancelot Andrewes had preached his Christmas Day court sermon in 1609 that he had obtained a copy before departing for Royston 'and says he will lay it still under his pillow'.[38] Notwithstanding the enduring fame of Shakespeare and Ben Jonson, 'James VI and I did not sleep with a copy of *Macbeth* – much less *The Golden Age Restor'd* – under his pillow.'[39] In the 1920s, T. S. Eliot admired how 'Andrewes takes a word and derives the world from it'; his exegetical method involved 'squeezing and squeezing the word until it yield a full juice of meaning which we should never have supposed any word to possess'.[40] Sharing James's enthralment with lexis, Andrewes regularly preached at court on major festivals including 24 March 1611: an Easter Sunday that coincided with the eighth anniversary of James's accession as English king. Andrewes's selected verse was taken from Psalm 118 – 'The stone, which the builders refused, the same stone, is become, the head of the corner' – to explicate the resurrection in terms of the rejected stone (Christ) being later raised as the Church's cornerstone. Punning on James's accession as king of the 'Angli' in 1603, Andrewes noted that he had thereby become 'head of the angles' and thus also a metaphorical cornerstone: England's very name 'hath affinity, and carries an allusion to the term, *anguli*, in the sound of it'.[41]

In the north of England, conscientious commitment to Calvinist ideals of a preaching ministry was epitomized by Tobie Matthew, who preached over 2,000 sermons in forty years as both Dean and Bishop of Durham, before becoming Archbishop of York in 1606. Even when aged over eighty, Matthew was commended in 1625 by a Leeds vicar for still preaching 'more sermons in a year' than all the 'Popes since Gregory the Great's days'.[42] In a posthumous tribute to Bishop John Williams of Lincoln – who preached James's funeral sermon in 1625 – John Hacket likewise recalled how Williams had often insisted 'that the way to get the credit from the nonconformists was to out-preach them'. Since most nonconformists 'were covetous, cross-grained, half-witted and distractious', they had 'nothing but much preaching to make them plausible and popular'.[43] But other clerics opposed Puritan tendencies to prioritize the pulpit and sermons on the grounds that it diminished the importance of private prayer and the sacraments. A year before being appointed as a chaplain to James in 1607, Richard Meredeth had preached a court sermon criticizing 'a certain new-fangled, and over-licentious opinion' that the chief points of Christian worship lay in reading Scripture, attending lectures and listening to sermons. Hoping to see England's churches become 'oratoria, not auditoria', Meredeth had extolled the value of prayer, recalling how earlier generations had worshipped 'with knees as hard as camels' hooves, with continual praying'.[44]

James powerfully exemplified his divinely ordained duty to interpret Scripture in the folio edition of his collected *Works* that was published in 1617 by the same royal printer, Robert Barker, who had been responsible for producing the folio edition of the new edition of the Bible in 1611. James's *Works* included a frontispiece engraving by Simon van der Passe that showed him seated on a throne, holding an orb and sceptre under the canopy of state, with the Bible to his right, bearing the title '*Verbum Dei*' ('the Word of God'). A verse underneath the engraving ended with the line 'But knowledge makes the King most like his maker', promoting parallels between James and God, indeed with 'King' capitalized, rather than 'maker'.

The first item in the *Works* was James's 'Paraphrase' on the twenty-two chapters of the Book of Revelation, which, as the last text of the Bible, could be seen as implicitly suggesting that the king's *Works* sought to continue the exegetical achievements of the new translation of the Bible published six years earlier. 'Paraphrase' now appeared in print with a prefatory 'Epistle to the whole Church Militant, in whatsoever part of the Earth'. Readers may, however, have been puzzled by the king's apparent reticence that someone 'of my age, calling, and literature, should have meddled with so obscure, theological, and high a subject'.[45] No contextual information was offered to explain that the 'Paraphrase' had been James's first prose work, composed in the mid-1580s before he turned twenty; by the time the king's collected *Works* were published, he had an international reputation as a published author and prominent religious controversialist.

The king's use of prosopopoeia in the 'Paraphrase' – the rhetorical device whereby writers communicate with their audiences by speaking as another person – enhanced the extent to which James's writings could be read as a temporal rendition of divine wisdom. For whereas the Bible explains, at the outset of the Book of Revelation, that Jesus sent the Revelation 'by his angel unto his servant John' (Revelation 1:1), James's paraphrase adopted the first-person singular in describing how Jesus sent 'an angel or minister, to me John his servant, and by him to reveal unto me certain things' that would take place, in order that 'the chosen may be forewarned by me'. In the prefatory epistle, James suggested that he had designated St John as speaker for reasons of simplicity and brevity; he was not 'so presumptuously foolish' as to imagine that his paraphrase of Revelation was 'the only true and certain exposition of this epistle, rejecting all others'. The king's paraphrase was nevertheless significantly longer than the original and accompanied by subjective glosses and polemical interpolations, despite insisting that he had 'used nothing of my own conjecture, or of the authority of others'. According to James, he had only 'interpreted it, in that sense which may best agree with the method of the Epistle, and not be contradictory to itself'. While the Book of Revelation ends with warnings about the miseries awaiting anyone who inserted additions or removed words from its text (22:18–19), the king's paraphrase amplified such threats by maintaining that any future copyist, translator or interpreter who 'wittingly strays from the true meaning of it ... to follow the fantastical invention of man, or his own preoccupied opinions' would be cursed 'as a perverter of the truth of God and his Scriptures'.[46] Since James's injunction could equally be read as extending to his own paraphrase, what has not escaped critical notice is how consistently the king 'tries to claim authority both as writer and as reader, while disallowing *his* readers any such authority'.[47]

For those hearing – rather than reading – Scripture, church pulpits became the source of increasingly outspoken attacks on James in the latter years of his reign, especially in relation to his perceived failures to defend Protestant interests in Continental Europe. In response, the king issued a proclamation 'against excess of lavish and licentious speech of matters of state' in 1620, followed by another edict the following year prescribing severe punishments for those failing to control 'the boldness of audacious pens and tongues'.[48] In August 1622, James specifically targeted sermon content by issuing six *Directions Touching Preaching and Preachers* to the Church of England's bishops, which restricted the frequency of preaching and banned anyone less senior than a bishop or dean from discussing 'the deep points' attaching to predestination, election, and other aspects of soteriology. Nor should there be any attempt to 'declare, limit, or bound out' the 'power, prerogative, jurisdiction, authority, or duty of sovereign princes, or otherwise meddle with those matters of state'. Preachers should, rather, 'confine themselves for those two heads: faith and good life'.[49]

In a letter of explanation accompanying the *Directions*, Archbishop Abbot hoped that clergy would not assume an 'ill construction to that, which may receive a fair interpretation'. The next month, the newsletter-writer Joseph Mead anticipated attending a sermon by John Donne at Paul's Cross, intended 'as the Londoners talk, to teach men how to preach hereafter'.[50] Tasked with defending the *Directions* in London's most prominent outdoor pulpit, Donne encouraged his listeners to read the directive for themselves in order to appreciate the king's desire to distinguish 'grave, and solid, from light and humorous preaching'. Rather than curbing sermons, Donne claimed that the *Directions* sought to promote edification by encouraging better preaching. For as he pointed out, if James 'had affected ignorance in himself, he would never have read so much; and if he had affected ignorance in us, he would never have written so much, and made us so much the more learned by his books.'[51]

Six months earlier, Donne had preached a sermon on Easter Monday at the capital's other major outdoor pulpit, St Mary Spital, in north London, describing the interdependence of sermons and sacraments as 'a powerful thunder, and lightning, that go together'. Preaching was 'the thunder, that clears the air, [and] disperses all clouds of ignorance', while communion was 'the lightning, the glorious light, and presence of Christ Jesus himself'. The combustible character of sermons not-withstanding, Donne decried congregations with 'such itching ears, as come to hear popular and seditious calumnies and scandals, and reproaches, cast upon the present state and government'. He also denied any necessary preoccupation with 'points of controverted doctrine'. For Donne's congregation in 1622 was in a very differ-ent confessional world from that into which James had been born in 1566, only six years after Protestantism had been established in Scot-land. Most in Donne's audience were, rather, 'persons born since the Reformation of religion': they were 'not naturalised by conversion, by transplantation from another religion to this, but born the natural children of this Church'.[52]

While the image of King James choosing to sleep with one of Lan-celot Andrewes's sermons tucked under his pillow dilutes conventional claims regarding drama's centrality to Stuart court culture, stage and pulpit had a shared theatricality. Inspiring Jacobean audiences and con-gregations made significant demands of actors and clerics alike. After delivering his Easter Monday sermon at the Spittle in 1622, Donne com-plained that 'his voice was enfeebled through sheer weariness'.[53] In the twenty-first century, virtual reality and acoustic-modelling technology have facilitated reconstruction of the auditory experience of listening to an actor deliver the two-hour Gunpowder Day sermon that Donne preached, later that year, at Paul's Cross.[54]

Throughout his life, James not only regarded the Word of God as cen-tral to divine worship, but also felt it was incumbent on him to use his divinely ordained powers as monarch to reveal God's mysteries to his subjects. Publishing his *Fruitful Meditation* on verses from Revelation as a young king in 1588, it had been the 'armies amassed' against Prot-estants in 'this isle' that had convinced him it was 'due time for revealing of this prophecy'. In militant, apocalyptic tone, James had insisted that 'we are threefoldly besieged': spiritually, by heresies of the Antichrist; physically, as 'members of that Kirk' being persecuted; and, particularly, by 'this present army' sent by Philip II of Spain.[55] But such confessional militancy had melted by the time James published his *Meditation upon the Lord's Prayer* in 1619; in his early fifties, the king was now pursu-ing a controversial dynastic marriage for his son, Prince Charles, with Philip II's granddaughter the Infanta María Ana. As James himself reflected, he was indeed the author of exegetical reflections that ranged from 'wading in these high and profound mysteries in the Revelation, wherein an elephant may swim' to considering 'the plain, smooth and easy Lord's Prayer, that every old wife can either say or mumble'. Ironically, his interest in devotional writing mirrored that of his erstwhile Jesuit adversary Cardinal Robert Bellarmine, who was now publishing 'a short meditation every year', having evidently 'given over his bickerings in polemics and controversies, wherein he was bred all his life'.[56]

16

A 'Catholic Christian' King

Addressing his first English Parliament in March 1604, James reassured peers and MPs that he was 'no stranger to you in blood, no more am I a stranger to you in faith, or in the matters concerning the House of God'.[1] Just as Queen Elizabeth had presided over a Protestant state, so would Protestantism remain the country's established faith under his kingship. To peers and MPs at Westminster, James described himself as a cradle king who had 'sucked the milk of God's truth, with the milk of my nurse' – albeit a portrayal that risked reminding his listeners that God's truth could be imbibed in different ways. After being baptized in a Catholic ceremony in 1566, James's upbringing had been overseen by staunch Presbyterians. In 1603, his accession to the English throne not only made him Supreme Governor of the Episcopalian Church of England, but also King of Ireland, where the majority population remained Catholic.

Throughout his life, James regularly offered his subjects insights into his own religious credo, usually in ways that emphasized unity and common ground over sectarian division. As he elaborated to English peers and MPs in 1604 – in a speech that was quickly published – he was 'never violent nor unreasonable' in his religious beliefs and was determined to avoid 'persecution, or thralling of my subjects in matters of conscience'.[2] Adhering to the Nicene Creed's conception of 'one holy Catholic church', James held his Protestant faith to be part of Christ's universal Church, as distinguished from the 'Church of Rome', which Protestants believed had despoiled the Church's catholicity. More concessive Protestants (later termed 'Anglo-Catholics') regarded the Church of England as part of a family of national churches over which the pope remained the notional spiritual head, albeit firmly denied any temporal power. Accordingly, in his parliamentary speech in 1604, James confirmed that he recognized 'the Roman Church to be our Mother Church, although defiled with some infirmities and corruptions'. He also admitted his heartfelt wish 'that it would please God to make me one of the members of such a general Christian union in religion' that differences could be jettisoned and Protestants and Catholics 'might meet in the midst, which is the centre and perfection of all things'.[3]

Not all James's subjects shared his inclinations towards Christian unity and, in the later years of the king's life, confessional warfare across Continental Europe led to a sharp polarization of religious opinion that undermined ecumenical ideals. By the time James came to address what would be his last English Parliament in April 1624, he regretted the lengths to which he had gone in repeatedly restating his personal religious beliefs, lamenting that no 'king suffered more by ill tongues than I have done'.[4] Preaching at the king's funeral the following year, Bishop John Williams of Lincoln described how, four days before his death, James had asked to receive the sacrament of Holy Communion. Reciting articles of the Church of England's creed, he confirmed that 'he believed them all, as they were received and expounded by that part of the Catholic Church which was established here in England.' 'With a kind of sprightliness, and vivacity', the king had added that, 'whatever he had written of this faith in his life, he was now ready to seal with his death'.[5]

Some Protestant clerics felt less sprightly. In 1623, one of James's chaplains, Matthew Wren, had returned from spending six months with Prince Charles in Spain, voicing more confidence in the prince's commitment to 'the doctrine and discipline and right estate of the church' than that of his father, who was generally viewed as 'so much inconstant in some particular cases'.[6] Certainly, throughout James's English and Scottish reigns, doubts about royal constancy were expressed by Presbyterians, Puritans, Catholics, Calvinists and Episcopalians alike. Avoiding narrow, exclusive commitments in religious matters not only preserved maximal room for political manoeuvre, but also reflected James's lifelong love of debate and disputation – both in printed tract and private conversation – as a means of pursuing greater theological understanding.

An account survives of a debate in May 1622 between James and the prominent Jesuit priest John Percy (alias 'Fisher') that addressed points of contention between Protestants and Catholics, including papal deposition theories, Catholic image-worship, and Christ's real presence in the Eucharist. The debate was one of several arranged by James, also involving a number of Anglican clerics, in (unsuccessful) attempts to prevent the Catholic conversion of the Marquis of Buckingham's mother, before whom the debates were held. Three years younger than James, Percy had converted to Catholicism aged around fourteen and, as a Jesuit priest, had endured decades of clandestine ministry, imprisonment and continental exile before being granted regular prison furlough in the mid-1610s. While Percy's narrative respected James's wish that the contents of their four-hour debate should remain private, he recalled how he had felt he 'could not freely speak' as much as he had wished, 'thinking it no good manners to interrupt his Majesty'. Percy had also avoided expanding responses beyond the time allowed by James, which was 'often so short, as I could say little before he would assault me with some new argument, or pass over to another, and from that to another point'. At other junctures, the king had asked a question, but had not let Percy respond, 'making the answer himself'. But when their debate had ended around 10 p.m., Percy recalled having kneeled before James 'and craved pardon of my earnestness in defending my case', to which 'his Majesty answered, I like thee the better, and so went away from me'.[7]

*

Rather than promoting ecumenism, most committed Puritans, Presbyterians, Calvinists and Catholics hoped, prayed and petitioned the king to move the national Church more decisively in their preferred direction. Among Catholics agitating for confessional reversal, the English Jesuit Robert Persons (or Parsons) advised his Superior-General in October 1581 that 'the greatest hope we have lies in Scotland, on which country depends the conversion not only of England, but of all the lands in the north.' Persons was optimistic that the fifteen-year-old James VI could be induced to return to the Catholic faith in which he had been baptized as a means of strengthening his bid to succeed Elizabeth, fulfilling his filial duty to his imprisoned mother, Queen Mary, and gaining Catholic support to foil the 'plots against his own life, so often initiated by the heretics'. But the window of opportunity was small: 'the two years to come appear to be the critical period for gaining Scotland'.[8]

Accordingly, the political dominance speedily achieved by Esmé Stewart, Duke of Lennox, in the early 1580s alarmed Protestants who suspected him of acting as an *agent provocateur* for James's relations and allies of Spain, the French Guise dynasty. Although James encouraged his older relative to convert to Protestantism, Lennox publicly refused to 'play the hypocrite' unless convinced in conscience to change his religion.[9] To allay Protestant fears, James and members of his household (including Lennox) signed *A Short and General Confession of the True Christian Faith and Religion* in 1581, later known as the 'Negative Confession', due to its denunciation of doctrines and practices rejected by the Kirk. Disseminated for public subscription, the oath confirmed that its adherents 'abhor and detest all contrary religion and doctrine, but chiefly all kind of papistry' and 'especially we detest and refuse the usurped authority of that Roman antichrist upon the Scriptures of God upon the Kirk, the civil magistrate and conscience of man'.[10]

Although Lennox's ascendancy was dismantled by the Ruthven Raid, large regions of Scotland were controlled by Catholic magnates throughout James's reign. Around one-third of the Scots peerage is estimated to have been Catholic between 1587 and 1625, providing James with strategic counterweight to pro-English, Protestant influences at court.[11] James remained close to prominent Catholics, notably George Gordon, Earl of Huntly, who enjoyed more access and reward from the king during his Scottish reign than any other court favourite (Lennox excepted) and whose uncle was a Jesuit priest. As James set about re-establishing his authority after escaping the Ruthven Lords' control, the seventeen-year-old king received at court a delegation from the presbytery of Edinburgh in July 1583, dismayed at the number of practising or suspected Catholics. While James protested that 'there was no king in Europe would have suffered the things that he had suffered', one minister, David Ferguson, responded 'I would not have you like any other king in Europe . . . ye have been otherwise brought up'. The Presbyterian chronicler David Calderwood duly recorded James's retort: ' "I am catholic King of Scotland" said the king, "and may choose any that I like best to be in company with me." ' Warning him that 'ye are in greater danger now than when ye were rocked in the cradle,' another cleric denied that there had ever been anyone 'in chief authority, that ever prospered after the ministers began to threaten them', at which 'the king smiled headingfully [scornfully]'.[12]

Determined to forge new alliances, James wrote to Pope Gregory XIII in February 1584, imploring him to 'keep very secret the communication

I thus open with you' for fear of seeing 'my state utterly ruined'. In a missive intercepted by the English authorities, James expressed his belief that he had more reason to expect 'aid and succour from your Holiness than from any other prince'. He recounted the Ruthven Raid, describing how his own subjects had 'banded themselves against me, with the aid and countenance of my neighbour, the queen of England, who has always held out her hand to all their bad enterprises undertaken with the object of utterly ruining me'.[13] James likewise re-established contact with his French relations after Lennox's death. He summoned the duke's eldest son, Ludovick, aged eight, to Edinburgh on whom he confirmed his late father's Scottish titles, appointed him chamberlain to the royal household for life, and symbolically recognized him as heir to the Scottish Crown by entrusting him to carry the crown at Parliament's opening session in May 1584. Four years later, James oversaw the marriage of Ludovick's older sister, Henrietta, to Huntly, who delighted the king in making a show of nominal conformity to Protestantism by signing the Negative Confession. Referring to Henrietta as 'his daughter and beloved of his blood', James stood in for the deceased Esmé Stewart and acted as father-of-the-bride at the nuptials, supplied the commendatorship of Dunfermline Abbey as the bride's dowry, and hosted the wedding celebrations at Holyroodhouse for which he wrote his only (incomplete) masque.[14]

Publicly, James's presentation of his Protestant faith verged on the militant by the time the Spanish Armada prepared its attack on England in 1588. The king's *Fruitful Meditation* on verses from Revelation identified the pope as Antichrist and predicted destruction of his 'false and hypocritical Kirk' in a lake of fire and brimstone. In the meantime, Protestants needed to confront Jesuits as a new, 'most pernicious vermin', and repulse the military threat of 'what is prepared and come forward against this isle'.[15] But only a few months later, English intelligence agents intercepted ciphered letters sent in January 1589 by Huntly and other Catholic peers to Philip II of Spain's nephew the Duke of Parma, regretting the Armada's recent defeat and affirming Scottish support in the event of a renewed attempt. As captain of the royal guard, recently established to protect the Scottish king, Huntly reassured Parma that he had 'such credit' with James that 'I shall ever be able to be master of his person.' He would thus be able, with 'your aid on arriving, to despoil the heretics by his authority, in order therewith to fortify and support

your enterprises'. Huntly added that his recent subscription of the Negative Confession had been 'not at all from the heart', but a pragmatic
expedient after being 'menaced on all sides'.[16]

James's seeming timidity in confronting the treachery of the 'Catholic
lords' elicited a predictably irate response from Elizabeth I, who admonished her godson in March 1589 that 'your behaviour is so exasperating
that if I did not love you better than you deserve, I should not mind to
see you ruined'.[17] But the king was moved to action when Huntly and his
associates started an armed rising the following month at the Brig o'Dee
near Aberdeen, as part of a long-running feud with the Chancellor, John
Maitland. Publicly pledging to pursue the Catholic lords 'to the furthest
part of Scotland, or else to reduce them to his obedience', James led a
force of 2,000 men to the Brig o'Dee, where he confronted Huntly, who
declined to take up arms against the king in person, surrendered, was
fined and temporarily detained.[18] As an English agent informed Walsingham, 'the king's too much affection to Huntly' remained disturbing.
With the earl ostensibly a prisoner in Edinburgh Castle, James 'went
to the castle to dinner, where he entertained Huntly as well and kindly
as ever, yea he kissed him at times to the amazement of many'.[19] Elizabeth's administration knew that pro-English inclinations at the Scottish
court could not be taken for granted. In May 1589, James received
a £3,000 sterling subsidy from the English government, followed by
another payment of the same amount in September.

Yet financial subsidies could also come from other sources and,
throughout the 1590s, Catholics continually speculated as to the likelihood of conversion by a king who had been baptized as a Catholic,
was the son of an unofficial Catholic martyr, and had never suffered
papal excommunication. In December 1593, Persons received reports
that James had been so 'moved and exasperated' by the effrontery of
the Kirk's ministers as 'to say that if the Spaniards would not come of
themselves, himself would go to fetch them'.[20] The following summer, a
ship docked in Aberdeen carrying Huntly's Jesuit uncle, a papal agent,
significant amounts of gold and papal letters offering James an annual
pension of 10,000 ducats if he converted to Catholicism. Despite the
civic authorities seizing the ship and its cargo and detaining its passengers, when Huntly threatened to raze the town by burning, the prisoners
and cargo were released. With the court's attention focused on Prince
Henry's christening celebrations the next month, an English informant

claimed that it was 'openly spoke in Council, that the Catholic lords increase so fast in their forces that they may, some morning, carry away from Stirling the king and young prince without great impediment'.[21]

Aside from the possibility of forced abduction, some feared that James might undergo a strategic change of faith to gain foreign support, following Henri IV's conversion to Catholicism in 1593 in order to secure the French throne. But as one English agent observed, the Scottish king publicly railed that, even if he agreed 'to hear and know the devices of the enemy, yet he shall never consent to them'. He would not 'change his religion and do as the French king has done to gain any kingdom or save his own [kingdom] or yet his own life'.[22] Queen Anna was, however, rumoured to be, as Persons put it, 'very well inclined to the Catholic religion'. Having been invited by James to give her opinion of 'the Calvinists' communion', the queen 'answered that she could very aptly liken it unto a tavern breakfast'.[23] Later described as a consummate 'church papist' for combining outward conformity to the Church of England with private Catholic worship, Anna's regular attendance at Church of Scotland services enabled her to deflect enquiries from the English ambassador in 1596. Declining 'to reveal the names of the practisers' of any other faith among her attendants, Anna nevertheless averred her 'full resolution' to the Established Church.[24]

Anna was thus well-placed to take over covert correspondence between the Scottish court and the papacy after Elizabeth's ministers intercepted a letter sent by James to Pope Clement VIII in 1599 in which the Scottish king had signed himself '*obsequntissimus filius*' – 'most submitting son'. Such epistolary ceremonial clearly contrasted with James's published diatribes against the Antichrist a decade earlier. But while, outwardly, James hotly insisted to the English court that the letter must be a forgery, Anna's use of the royal 'we' afforded convenient ambiguity. In 1601, the Scottish queen instructed an envoy to Rome to confirm her conversion to the papal authorities and to explain that 'if we, prompted by danger to our present state, are attending the rites of heretics, let it not be attributed to our desire, but to the hostile times which we are compelled to endure.'[25] In a report sent to the Jesuit Superior-General that same year, however, the Scottish king and his Privy Councillors were described as 'overawed and corrupted by the power and the gold of England'. James's sole concern was to secure 'the crown of England, which he would gladly take, to all appearance, from the hand of the Devil himself, though Catholics and heretic ministers were all ruined alike, so great is his longing for this regal dignity'. If conversion to Catholicism seemed likely to further this aim, such considerations 'might some day make him a hypocrite; but only a great miracle of God's power, and an extraordinary inspiration, will ever make him a Catholic in reality.'[26]

*

In the event, James's peaceful accession to the English throne was cautiously welcomed by most Catholics whose spokesmen were equally as proactive as their Puritan counterparts in submitting petitions seeking redress of grievances. Anticipation regarding the potential re-establishment of Catholicism or the institution of religious toleration was also rife among foreign observers. In May 1603, the Venetian Secretary, Scaramelli, met James's envoy, Lord Kinloss, who affirmed the king's gratitude to Clement VIII, 'spoke of him as truly Clement', for not having obstructed his accession and resisting calls for his excommunication. But to Scaramelli's enquiry regarding the potential reorientation of religious policy, Kinloss had retorted, 'No! beyond a doubt this will never happen; our bow which hitherto had two strings will have but one for the future.' James hoped, rather, that the papacy might 'summon a General Council' of all Christian churches whereby 'abuses would be removed on all hands, and a sound decision would put an end, perhaps forever, to the discords in the Christian faith'.[27] In November, James directed his ambassador at the French court to inform the papal nuncio, Monsignor Innocenzo del Bufalo, of his hope that the papacy might convene 'a General Council, justly and legitimately declared and assembled, by which all contentions and controversies could be settled and composed'. A single service of worship might even be agreed for Protestants and Catholics: 'common and uniform in all things, not thoroughly defiled by the corruptions of men, nor repugnant to the divine laws'.[28]

Inspired by ecumenical gatherings such as the Council of Constance (1414–18), James's calls for a council to heal sectarian divisions were, for a Protestant sovereign, unusual in their insistence that such a council needed papal leadership and organization to have a realistic chance of practical success. But the papacy remained sceptical, citing numerous divisions among Protestants and preferring instead to pray for the English king's straightforward conversion. From an envoy in Rome,

James learned in early 1605 that Clement VIII had nevertheless met with twelve cardinals to discuss 'what was meetest to his Holiness to do in that which concerned your Majesty and your dominions' in the first formal papal meeting about English religious affairs for nearly half a century. The previous September, del Bufalo relayed second-hand reports from England of James's repeated insistence 'that he recognised the Roman Church as the Mother Church, and the Pope as the universal bishop of the whole Church, with spiritual authority over all'. Although the English king also professed that he would 'gladly be reunited with the Roman Church, and would take three steps in that direction if only the Roman Church would take one', his simultaneous protestations of inability to amend anti-Catholic legislation explained the papacy's tepid response. Reading del Bufalo's account of James, Clement VIII endorsed the letter: 'these are things which make doubt that he believes anything'.[29]

Catholic disillusionment reflected the lack of significant change signalled in the new king's public pronouncements. On his accession, James had suspended temporarily the recusancy fines levied on individuals who refused to attend Church of England services and appointed crypto-Catholics, such as Henry Howard, Earl of Northampton, as Privy Councillors. But in February 1604, a proclamation objected to the number of seminary priests and Jesuits 'abounding in this realm' and acting freely, apparently 'upon a vain confidence of some innovation in matters of religion to be done by us, which we never intended, nor gave any man cause to expect'.[30] Catholic clergy illegally in England were ordered to leave the country by 19 March – the day on which James's first English Parliament was due to open – and, after a year's suspension, recusancy fines were reintroduced. In response, the priest John Colleton presented *A Supplication to the King's Most Excellent Majesty* (1604) pleading for formal toleration and accusing Puritans 'of a more presuming, imperious, and hotter disposition and zeal' in seeking to 'bring the kingdom, especially the ecclesiastical state, to a parity or popular form of government'. Despite the loyalty of Catholics to James's mother and to her son, theirs was the faith that 'is despised, trodden under foot, maligned, punished, and must be, alas, by all violence abolished'.[31] With partisan relish, Persons relayed reports that when the king had started to read Colleton's tract, he 'fell into great passion' and, uttering a stream of furious oaths, threw it down, stamped on it, but 'yet, after, took it up again and perused it'.[32]

In June 1605, the Rutland courtier Sir Everard Digby – whom James had knighted two years earlier – learned that the government intended to pursue 'hard terms with our English Catholics'. James had delivered a speech 'three hours long' to his enrobed judges before they left for their summer circuits, comprising 'a most straight charge to enquire of all recusants' in the localities.[33] In October, Digby became one of the last recruits to Robert Catesby's Gunpowder Plot, which was dramatically discovered on the night of 4 November 1605. Alerted by a tip-off, the Palace of Westminster's authorities discovered Guy Fawkes in a cellar underneath the House of Lords, with thirty-six concealed barrels of gunpowder to be detonated when James opened his second session of Parliament the following day. Fawkes was part of a militant group of Midlands-based English Catholics whose dejection at James's seeming determination to maintain the statutory framework of Elizabethan penal legislation had led them to attempt mass murder. On 8 November, the group's charismatic ringleader, Catesby, was killed in a dramatic shoot-out in Staffordshire that resulted in the death or arrest of most remaining Plotters. A proclamation issued the day before had, however, made clear James's refusal to regard the Plot as evidence of axiomatic Catholic disloyalty. Confident that the vast majority of his subjects, of whatever religious persuasion, 'do as much abhor this detestable conspiracy as ourself', the king also exonerated foreign powers from suspected involvement on the grounds that no 'prince, of what religion soever, could give ear to so savage and barbarous an imagination'.[34]

On 9 November, James addressed both Houses of Parliament, proroguing the session on account of the national emergency. To the peers and MPs who would have perished in the carnage alongside the royal family, James confirmed that the venue had been deliberately chosen. Under interrogation, Fawkes had disclosed that, since Parliament was where England's anti-Catholic laws had been framed, the Plotters had resolved that 'both place and persons should all be destroyed and blown up at once'.[35] Writing to his Danish brother-in-law Christian IV, James described the Plot as 'the most horrid and detestable of all treasons either undertaken anywhere in the world within the memory of man, or conceived in thought and mind'.[36] Days after its discovery, the Venetian ambassador described an audience in which James's younger son, Prince Charles, now Duke of York and 'about five years old, came into the chamber', prompting the king to marvel that 'this poor boy's innocence' and that of other intended targets, had prevailed with God to thwart the Plotters' 'perfidious malignity'.[37] While James and his sons would have perished, intelligence revealed that the Plotters had envisaged exploiting the ensuing chaos to abduct Charles's sister, nine-year-old Princess Elizabeth, from Coombe Abbey in Warwickshire, hoping to marry her to a Catholic consort and install a second Queen Elizabeth as a puppet sovereign to rule over a re-Catholicized England.

The Plot's discovery unleashed predictable demands for more stringent anti-Catholic measures. In May 1606, the Westminster Parliament passed legislation permitting the royal seizure of land owned by recusants and levying a new oath on indicted or suspected recusants, as well as any adult who had not taken Anglican communion at least twice within the previous year. Comprising seven clauses, the 'Oath of Allegiance' did not require from swearers denial of the pope's spiritual authority, but obliged them 'from my heart [to] abhor, detest and abjure as impious and heretical this damnable doctrine' that heretical or excommunicated sovereigns 'may be deposed or murdered by their subjects or any other whatsoever'. Swearers were also required to confirm that they took the oath 'without any equivocation or mental evasion or secret reservation whatsoever' in an attempt to deflect the doctrine of equivocation devised to protect Catholics from imperilling their consciences if interrogated by heretics.[38]

Two months earlier, the deceptive danger of equivocation had been prominently rehearsed at the trial of the English Jesuit Superior-General Henry Garnet, who was convicted of treason, having failed to disclose his prior knowledge of the Gunpowder Plot on the grounds that his information had been acquired under the confessional seal. At Garnet's indictment, Attorney-General Sir Edward Coke had acknowledged the priest as 'superior to all his predecessors in devilish treason ... a doctor of Jesuits, that is, a doctor of five DDs, as dissimulation, deposing of princes, disposing of kingdoms, daunting and deterring of subjects, and destruction'.[39] In Shakespeare's *Macbeth* – thought to have been first performed in the second half of 1606 – the practice of equivocation was framed more comically, by having the Porter at Inverness Castle, on hearing Macduff and Lennox knocking at the gate, ask:

> Knock, knock. Who's there, in th' other devil's name? Faith, here's an equivocator that could swear in both the scales against either scale, who committed treason enough for God's sake, yet could not equivocate to heaven.[40]

Whereas James later insisted that the Oath was designed to differentiate between 'civilly obedient papists, and the perverse disciples of the powder-treason', Pope Paul V issued a breve to all English Catholics in September 1606, ordering them to desist from swearing it on the grounds that 'it contains many things which are flat contrary to faith and salvation'.[41] The following January, James's Privy Councillors learned from the English ambassador in Spain that local preachers were swelling their 'sermons with declarations against the cruelties of England, some of them affirming that much easier it was for the Christians in the days of Diocletian'.[42] For as well as demanding allegiance to James as temporal monarch, the Oath required Catholics to confirm as impious, heretical and damnable the doctrine of papal deposing power long endorsed by theologians and popes. Among modern critics, the Oath's introduction has been variously interpreted as a means of isolating subversive promoters of papal temporal authority (as James claimed); of expanding the spiritual authority attaching to the English monarch's role as Supreme Governor of the national Church; of promoting an ecumenical agenda to bring Protestants and Catholics closer; or, finally, of constituting 'possibly the most lethal measure against Romish dissent ever to reach the statute book'. By the last view, the 'poisonous potential' of the Oath's content was the inevitable creation of myriad divisions among Catholics.[43]

In England, the effective leader of England's recusant community, Archpriest George Blackwell, refused to distribute Paul V's brief and swore the Oath, regarding acceptance of James's temporal authority, albeit as a 'heretic' ruler, as compatible with adherence to Catholicism. Detained in the Gatehouse prison at Westminster Abbey, Blackwell wrote to fellow priests in July 1607, urging his brethren to swear the oath to 'shake off the false and grievous imputations of treason, and treacheries' and prevent seizure of their estates.[44] In what James deemed unacceptable interference in civil affairs, Paul V sent a second breve to English Catholics in September 1607, denouncing as craven the misguided motivations of recusants who swore the Oath, while Blackwell was removed as archpriest. Observing James's fury, the Dean of the Chapel Royal, James Montagu, confirmed to the Earl of Salisbury that, over four days in December 1607, the king had penned twenty-four sheets rebutting the pope's interference. Punning that James was embracing a new sport of (papal) 'bull'-fighting, Montagu ventured that now 'he should neither speak of hawking nor hunting'.[45]

In February 1608, James anonymously published his *Triplici Nodo, Triplex Cuneus. Or an Apology for the Oath of Allegiance*, which defended the Oath of Allegiance's rationale as simply seeking to 'make distinction between the sheep and goats in my own pasture'. Also translated into French and Latin, the king's *Triplici Nodo* protested that he had treated English Catholics more leniently than Elizabeth and had avoided sustained persecution, while conferring knighthoods on 'known and open recusants' and offering royal access 'to both sides, bestowing equally all favours and honours' on Protestants and Catholics alike. James particularly resented his adversaries' failure to appreciate that, unlike the Elizabethan Act of Supremacy (1558), the Oath of Allegiance introduced in 1606 had not denied the pope's spiritual authority over Catholics. Incensed by Paul V's attempt to sow differences between his Catholic subjects and their king, James rhetorically asked, 'as for the Catholic faith, can there be one word found in all that Oath tending or sounding to matter of religion?' Although London and Rome did not maintain formal diplomatic relations, James blamed the papacy for having 'broken the rules of common civility and justice between Christian princes' in 'accounting me a persecutor' and seeking 'to meddle between me and my subjects . . . in matters that merely and only concern civil obedience'.[46] Predicting that *Triplici Nodo* 'will attract many replies', the French ambassador in London, Antoine Le Fèvre de la Boderie, assured Henri IV's court that polemical rejoinders 'will only put the author in his element, for this is the science of which he knows the most and in which he most delights'.[47]

Boderie was correct: James's restrictive interpretation of the Oath was not universally accepted. In July 1608, the Spanish ambassador in London approvingly reported to Philip III that the Jesuit Cardinal Robert Bellarmine, Persons and others were countering the English king's arguments in print 'by indicating his mistakes fully, but without offending him in sharp words, since he has the world's biggest temper'.[48] Adopting the pseudonym 'Matthaeus Tortus' (after his chaplain, Matteo Torti), Bellarmine published a *Responsio* to the king's book in 1608. James then commissioned a reply from Bishop Lancelot Andrewes of Chichester, which was published in 1609 under the punning title, *Tortura Torti* ['Tortus twisted/confuted']. In a sermon preached at Whitehall on the third anniversary of the Gunpowder Plot in November 1608, John King had also alluded to the slippery character of his Catholic adversaries – these 'chameleons, these *Mattheus Tortus*' – decrying their casuistical 'meanderings, turnings and windings, their mental reservations, their amphibolous, amphibious prepositions'. Just as some creatures live 'part in the land, part in the water', so did papists speak 'half in the lips, half in the heart and conscience'.[49]

As the 'Oath of Allegiance debate' escalated, Montagu later recalled reading aloud to James at his hunting lodges in Royston and Newmarket 'the four tomes of Cardinal Bellarmine's controversies' – presumably in selected extracts, given their voluminous length. While 'his Majesty took fresh air and weighed the objections and answers of that subtle author', James also 'sent often to the libraries in Cambridge for books, to examine his quotations'.[50] Bellarmine's response was especially alarming since it made public James's letter to Clement VIII in 1599 that had been written as part of the Scottish king's campaign to garner international support for his claim to succeed Elizabeth I. With no option but to order an investigation, James admitted to his Privy Councillors that Bellarmine's allegation was potentially as damaging to his 'reputation as any one that ever happened unto us in all our life'.[51] A scapegoat was, however, found in the king's former Scottish Secretary, the Catholic Sir James Elphinstone, who conveniently confessed to having asked James to sign such a letter in 1599 without necessarily making him aware of its content.

Stung by the sharp attacks mounted against *Triplici Nodo*'s anonymous author, James sought to reclaim royal dignity by admitting his authorship in the work's second edition, produced in 1609. Quickly translated into Latin, French, Dutch and German, this edition was accompanied by a 'Premonition' to the Holy Roman Emperor, Rudolf II, and other continental princes regarding the papacy's record of encouraging rebellions against temporal monarchs. James also commissioned special velvet-bound presentation copies for his fellow rulers, adorned with solid-gold corners stamped with images of a rose, thistle, lion and (French) lilies. By rendering their subjects' loyalty always dependent on the pope's will, James exhorted sovereigns in Catholic states 'to consider and weigh, what a feather he pulls out of your wings': at any point could 'ye be removed as scabbed sheep from the flock, if so be the Pope think you to be, though your skin be indeed never so sound'. At the same time, James reiterated his eschatological assertions regarding the identity of 'the Antichrist, which I am sure I can better fasten upon the Pope, than Bellarmine can do his pretended temporal superiority over kings'.[52] Rejecting the label of 'heretic', James provided readers with another confession of his religious upbringing and beliefs, insisting that 'I am such a Catholic Christian' who upheld the three main Apostles', Nicene and Athanasian creeds and respected ecclesiastical hierarchies. He would, moreover, 'with all my heart, give my consent that the Bishop of Rome should have the first seat': James further mused on the irony of having been attacked for writing 'ten times more bitterly' of his Protestant Puritan critics than of Catholics, as indicated by the 'long apologetic preface' to *Basilicon Doron*'s second edition in 1603.[53]

*

James's worst fears regarding the incendiary effects of papal theories of excommunication and deposition were realized when Henri IV was assassinated in May 1610. The French king had survived at least twenty-three previous assassination attempts when his coach was detained by Parisian traffic, a knife-wielding Catholic extremist, François Ravaillac, leapt onto a wheel of the stationary coach and fatally stabbed him twice in the chest. Addressing the English Parliament a week after the murder, James insisted that, among the regicidal Catholics from whom Henri's assassin had emerged, 'their aim was not at him alone, but at other princes too, whereof I assure you I was one.'[54] In June, the English state's unequivocal rejection of Catholic deposition theory was confirmed in a proclamation condemning 'the papists' bloody doctrine, that make martyrs and saints of such as kill their own kings' and observing in Henri's murder 'that butcherly theory and practice so linked together'.[55] New measures to enhance royal security included barring all Catholics from living within ten miles of London, ordering all priests and

Jesuits to leave the country within a month, and confirming that the Oath of Allegiance would now be levied on all adults, rather than only on suspected or convicted recusants. In effect, all Catholics remaining in England were now identified as potential terrorists. On the tenth anniversary of the Gowrie Plot that August, Bishop Andrewes referred to Henri's assassination in a court sermon that punningly execrated the papacy's readiness, in regard to kings, to 'depose them and to dispose of them', first through excommunication and thereafter by sanctioning their murder.[56]

By 1610, James's claim – made to English peers and MPs six years earlier – that 'my mind was ever so free from persecution, or thralling of my subjects in matters of conscience', rang somewhat hollow. The appearance of cassocked priests on scaffolds facing gruesome execution shifted attention away from their convictions for treason to their conscientious refusal to swear a particular oath. In December 1610, the Welsh-born Benedictine monk John Roberts insisted before a crowd of around 3,000 people at Tyburn, that he had 'never said, nor will I ever say, any evil against the king' and proceeded to bless James, the royal family, Privy Councillors and the judges 'that condemned me'. It did not save him from the gallows. In Roberts's view, it was 'not the king who is the cause of my death', but the English state's insistence that he take an Oath 'so mixed with matters of religion'.[57] The previous night, the Spanish noblewoman and missionary Luisa de Carvajal y Mendoza had hosted a dinner in Newgate Prison for Roberts and another condemned secular priest, Thomas Somers, and, after their deaths, oversaw the grisly retrieval of their mutilated bodies from a communal pit of executed criminals. Writing to the marquis of Caracena, Carvajal confirmed that 'Father Roberts, minus one leg' and one 'half' of Somers were now temporarily installed in her Barbican home. Admiring how the priests' quartered remains 'stood up straight like pieces of armour', Carvajal sent to the English Jesuit Joseph Creswell 'a piece of his [Roberts's] holy flesh', trusting in the thaumaturgic properties of Roberts's relic.[58]

A proclamation issued in June 1610 had reiterated royal insistence that the Oath of Allegiance was framed as 'an act of great favour and clemency towards so many of our subjects, who, though blinded with the superstition of popery, yet carried a dutiful heart towards our obedience'.[59] James's various claims as to the Oath's intended meaning could not, however, alter its content. Prosecuted for refusing to take the

Oath in 1612, Edward, Lord Vaux, pleaded that 'he thought it better to swear, from his heart, his true allegiance to the king, than to swear to a matter of the which he in his conscience had some doubt'. To this end, Vaux confirmed his willingness to take the Oath 'after the king's book, which he had with him', but this offer was rejected by the Attorney-General, who dismissed such a caveat as undermining royal authority by erroneously implying 'that the king hath a particular exposition of this statute to himself'.[60] Although Vaux was sentenced to indefinite imprisonment and loss of his property, when moves were made to prosecute his wife and two Jesuits arrested in her home, James indicated 'that he had already been too forward to take blood' and would take 'no more'.[61] That autumn, Carvajal was surprised when, in London, 'the bells were pealing as if they were about to crack' in accompaniment to the procession taking Mary Stuart's body to Westminster Abbey for reburial. As Carvajal observed to a correspondent at the Spanish court, 'the Protestants keep quiet and pretend not to know'. But as James had issued instructions for the dignified interment of his Catholic mother, Carvajal ventured that he 'has done an excellent thing, I believe for the first time in his life'.[62]

In France, James's late mother was remembered as a queen consort on whom unofficial martyrological status had been conferred after her execution on Elizabeth I's orders. Although a Protestant, her son was admired for his public denunciations of papal deposition theory by Gallican factions within the French Catholic Church who sought to restrict the papacy's power to spiritual affairs. When the French Estates-General met for the first time in more than a quarter of a century in 1614, the Third Estate requested Louis XIII's regency government to confirm, as 'a fundamental law' of France, that there was 'no power on earth whatever, spiritual or temporal' that could deny the sacred nature of French kingship nor absolve subjects from loyal obedience to its monarch.[63] But the request was rejected, having been opposed at length by the erstwhile Huguenot-turned-Cardinal Jacques Davy du Perron, who insisted that the proposal had 'come by sea and swum from England'.[64]

James's ambassador in Paris made representations at Louis XIII's court that were published in both French and English. On a personal level, James had been 'greatly offended' by du Perron's stated belief that the French did not live 'under a king that makes martyrs', effectively implying that 'the King of Great Britain is so cruel and unmerciful, as he takes pleasure in the effusion of the blood of innocents'. But James also sought to counsel France's fourteen-year-old king, thereby 'opening your eyes to see and apprehend ... the scandal, danger, and pernicious consequence' of endorsing papal deposing powers. As the ambassador explained, James had enjoyed a 'hearty and sincere amity' with Louis's father, Henri IV, with whom he had made an 'amiable accord, and brotherly agreement' that, when the first of them died, 'the survivor should undertake as father and protector of the children of the prede-ceased'. Accordingly, it was James's duty to warn Henri's son that his throne remained 'continually in danger' if du Perron's doctrines were not repudiated.[65]

Back in England, the king's official watchmaker, the Dundee-born David Ramsay, created a remarkable gilt brass and enamel square table clock – now in the Victoria and Albert Museum – the sides of which dis-played images of the four Evangelists: Matthew, Mark, Luke and John (see Plate 12). Concealed on the clock's underside, however, was an engraving depicting James and his two sons, Henry and Charles, hold-ing Pope Paul V's nose to a grindstone that was being turned by two English bishops, while a Catholic cardinal and three friars looked on in dismay.[66] By the time Bishop Montagu came to prepare the king's col-lected works for publication in 1617, he admitted that James's decision openly to challenge Paul V, Bellarmine and other Catholic authorities had resulted in 'scarce a people, language or nation in Christendom' abstaining from the controversy.[67] James's determined defence of royal power had placed Stuart England firmly on the map of international polemic.

17
More Ado with Ireland

There is an oft-quoted anecdote that when James was taken on a tour of the newly established State Papers Office at Whitehall in March 1619, he was taken aback by the sheer bulk of paperwork relating to Irish affairs. As the king remarked to the Keeper of the Records, Sir Thomas Wilson, 'there was more ado with Ireland than all the world besides'.[1] As Wilson later confirmed, there were 120 bound volumes of documentation relating to 'Hibernia', compared to twenty-three 'great books' on France and three volumes relating to the Holy Roman Empire and German principalities.[2] Much of the paper mountain had been generated by royal enthusiasm for a predominantly Protestant, Anglo-Scottish plantation in the northern Irish counties of Ulster that had started a decade earlier, in 1609. Controversial in its eventual transformation of Ireland's physical, political, demographic, religious, economic and cultural landscape, the Ulster Plantation has been seen as providing a prototype for future imperial expansion globally. Between 1603 and the outbreak of the Irish Rebellion under Charles I in 1641, approximately 100,000 English and Scots are estimated to have settled in Ireland, including around 30,000 Scots in Ulster. By comparison, only around 6,000 individuals emigrated to Massachusetts over the same period, and around 8,000 to Virginia.[3]

Despite a long-standing interest in its affairs, James never set foot in Ireland. When *Basilicon Doron* was first published in 1599, he counselled Prince Henry that, should he accede to more crowns than solely that of Scotland, he must ensure 'once in the three years to visit all your kingdoms' to hear subjects' complaints directly and to have 'the principal matters ever to be decided by yourself when ye come in those parts'.[4]

While James himself disregarded such advice (and never visited Wales either), fulsome tribute to his oversight of Irish affairs was supplied by his combative Irish Attorney-General, Sir John Davies, who insisted in *A Discovery of the True Causes why Ireland was never entirely subdued* (1612) that 'all the defects in the government of Ireland' had been 'fully supplied' in the nine years since James's accession as English king. In less than a decade, Davies averred that more had been achieved 'in the work and reformation of this kingdom' than in the preceding 400 years since Henry II's Anglo-Norman invasion and attempted conquest of Ireland in 1172.[5] Even when beset by a refractory English Parliament demanding large-scale military deployment on the Continent in the early 1620s, James still referred to Irish policy in notably personal, often proprietorial, terms. In April 1621, he insisted to MPs in the English House of Commons that Ireland was 'never in so great prosperity as now'.[6] But in a move to avert an extended parliamentary debate on Irish affairs, Lionel Cranfield – who became Lord Treasurer three months later – reassured MPs that the king 'will have ears his open' when receiving individual petitions, but nevertheless 'wishes to have this work wholly left to himself, that he may make it his masterpiece'.[7]

*

Only twelve miles separate Torr Head in County Antrim from the Mull of Kintyre on the Scottish mainland. As King of Scotland, James's efforts to extend the reach of central government were often tested in remoter regions on the country's western seaboard. Royal authority competed with traditional clan attachments, obligations and alliances in the region where the quasi-independent MacDonald Lordship of the Isles had once stretched from the Western Isles to County Antrim until its forfeiture in 1493. That same year, James's great-grandfather, King James IV, led an expedition to the Western Isles, followed by another in 1495, while his son, James V, set out in 1540 – as George Buchanan put it – 'to circumnavigate Scotland and reduce the fierce spirit of the islanders to the obedience of the laws'.[8] Unlike his great-grandfather and grandfather, James VI did not circumnavigate the isles, despite declaring an intention to do so in 1596, 1598 and 1600.[9]

A centuries-old seasonal trade also subsisted whereby West Highland and island Scottish clansmen provided mercenary forces for Gaelic Irish leaders. Accordingly, the North Channel offered James a key strategic means of exerting leverage over Elizabeth I, especially once her administration became militarily and financially stretched by the Irish rebellion started in 1592 by Hugh O'Neill, Earl of Tyrone, and later known as the 'Nine Years War' (1593–1603). Scotland and England were, however, formally allies as a result of the Treaty of Berwick, concluded in July 1586. Accordingly, James braved domestic unpopularity by acceding to an English extradition request in 1591 and arresting a fugitive Gaelic lord from Leitrim, Brian O'Rourke. In Glasgow, a hostile crowd derided royal officers as 'Queen Elizabeth's knights' and alleged 'that the king was bought with English angels [ten-shilling coins]'.[10] Meanwhile, the English regime needed to secure a judicial ruling in favour of extra-territoriality to proceed with O'Rourke's treason trial in London for alleged crimes committed in Ireland, for which he was duly convicted and executed. For his part, James regularly reminded Elizabeth of her reciprocal obligations to surrender Scots fugitives in England, including his rebellious cousin the Earl of Bothwell. In June 1593, he also directed an envoy to request the loan of several English warships to assist in suppressing rebellious clansmen in the Western Isles. Pacifying Scotland's western seaboard would 'make the north parts of Ireland much more obedient and profitable to our said dearest sister', which was 'a matter thought of, and especially provided in the league betwixt us'.[11]

As Tyrone's rebellion escalated, Elizabeth sent James the names of Scots suspected to be in Irish pay in October 1594, demanding – primarily 'for the world's satisfaction' – that he take action. Despite being 'the subjects of a king, our friend', if Scots fighters in Ireland were detained by the English authorities, they would receive the same treatment as that 'which we shall be forced to do to our own rebels'.[12] James effectively delegated responsibility for halting the mercenary trade in Scottish soldiers to the teenage Archibald Campbell, Earl of Argyll, who reportedly declined Tyrone's offer of annual payments of £10,000 (Scots) in return for supplying 2,000 men.[13] The following summer, the English government also learned of an expeditionary force of around 5,000 Highlanders and one hundred ships that intended to reassert Scottish claims to the Isle of Man, regarded as an English dependency since the mid-fourteenth century. Although stormy weather diverted the Highland force to Lough Foyle on the north coast of Ireland, in late 1595, the Highland chief Angus MacDonald of Dunivaig 'dealt very earnestly' with James 'that he might be suffered to invade the Isle of Man to force it to the king's obedience', but he was directed by the king that he 'should not meddle therewith', on the grounds that 'he would never offend her [Elizabeth I] as long as she lived'.[14] As English forces struggled to prevail over Irish insurgents, the presence of powerful Highland leaders undermined James's protestations of innocence. In May 1598, the Irish Secretary of State, Sir Geoffrey Fenton, warned that the Scottish king was 'a secret supporter of these Irish rebels', notwithstanding his proclamations prohibiting the supply of men and arms 'and many other fair shows'.[15]

But by the late 1590s, James was belatedly realizing that he risked jeopardizing his chance of succeeding Elizabeth if his support for royal authority in Ireland seemed lukewarm. He had, after all, advised Prince Henry in *Basilicon Doron* 'to do as ye would be done to: especially in counting rebellion against any other prince, a crime against your own self.'[16] In November 1601, a proclamation condemned any Scots travelling to fight for Tyrone in Ireland for 'preferring their naughty gain and particular commodity [benefit] to his Highness's honour and obedience'.[17] Those Scots would, moreover, be joining traitorous rebels who had effectively switched allegiance from England to Spain, following the landing of Philip III's troops in southern Ireland the previous year. In December 1601, English forces led by the Lord Deputy, Lord Mountjoy, achieved a decisive victory at the Battle of Kinsale and the war finally ended when Tyrone – unaware that Elizabeth had died six days earlier – surrendered and concluded terms with Mountjoy at the Treaty of Mellifont on 30 March 1603.

In Dublin, James was proclaimed as King of England, Scotland, France and Ireland on 11 April, and his accession was largely welcomed by Ireland's majority Catholic population, who hoped their new king – as son of the unofficial Catholic martyr Mary Stuart – might grant freedom of religious worship. Genealogists enthusiastically traced James's Gaelic descent, on his mother's side, from King Fergus I and, on his father's side, from Corc, the fifth-century king of Munster, as well as other dynastic connections to the kings of Connacht and Leinster.[18] The bardic poet Eochaidh Ó h'Eódhasa acclaimed James's accession as tantamount to the transformative Ovidian 'Metamorphoses'.[19] From Rome, Pope Clement VIII wrote to James confirming that he was now King of England, Scotland and Ireland '*potentissimus et nomineris et existas*' – most powerful in both name and fact.[20]

Reflecting the optimism generated by James's accession, a 'recusancy revolt' spread across towns and cities in the south and west of the country, drawing support from the Gaelic Irish population and the 'Old English' community, who were predominantly Catholic descendants of Anglo-Norman immigrants. Large religious processions were staged and Protestant Church of England cathedrals and churches were spontaneously taken over by Catholics and subjected to hasty redecoration and reconsecration as Passion Week and Easter approached. As Mountjoy reported, the mayor of Tredagh in County Louth had sought to mitigate citizens' conduct by asserting that they wished 'to declare their religion to his Majesty and the world in that time between two reigns, wherein they suppose it lawful or less dangerous', while in southern Ireland, Kilkenny's inhabitants also insisted that it was 'not against the law, to profess their religion publicly till the king's coronation'.[21] From Wexford's mayor, Mountjoy learned of the warm reaction to the accession of 'their most mighty and undoubted King James that now is, whose Majesty, by common judgement of all men here, few excepted, is thought to be Catholic'.[22] By May, however, Mountjoy had suppressed all Catholic resistance with armed force.

Regarding Jacobean Ireland's future governance, irreconcilable differences seemed inevitable between, on the one hand, vengeful veterans of the Nine Years War intent on re-establishing English authority and enforcing Protestant worship and, on the other, Old English communities accustomed to enjoying considerable civic autonomy and retaining covert adherence to the Catholic faith. The post-war situation was further complicated by James's readiness to reach pragmatic accommodation with controversial powerbrokers, as evidenced in Scotland by his closeness to the Catholic Earl of Huntly. Later that summer, Tyrone was invited to accompany Mountjoy on his return to the royal court at Whitehall, where Tyrone was pardoned for past actions in return for his submission at the Treaty of Mellifont. As Tyrone joined James on hunting expeditions, the welcome extended to 'that damnable rebel' provoked resentment among war veterans, including the courtier Sir John Harington. To seek 'that knave's destruction', Harington recalled having 'adventured perils by sea and land, endured toil, was near starving, ate horseflesh at Munster; and all to quell that man, who now smiles in peace at those that did hazard their lives to destroy him.'[23]

James's ecumenical instincts also inclined him to favour the peaceful promotion of Protestantism over violent attempts to extirpate Catholicism. In January 1604, English Privy Councillors emphasized to the President of Munster, Sir George Carew, that fostering 'a zealous and learned clergy' was a priority for 'the king, who knows well that true religion is better planted by the word than by the sword'.[24] But just as Puritan elements pressured the new king to enforce stricter anti-recusancy measures in England, increased stringency was likewise advocated for Ireland. A proclamation issued in July 1605 firmly disabused James's Irish subjects of any 'untrue suggestion and report' that he intended 'to give liberty of conscience or toleration of religion to his subjects in that kingdom'; not only was the rumour false, but it also implied that the king was 'more remiss or less careful in the government of the Church of Ireland than of those other churches whereof he has the supreme charge' in England and Scotland.[25] Priests were given until 10 December to leave Ireland and subjects forbidden from sheltering Catholic clerics.

Anti-recusancy measures received predictable impetus with the Gunpowder Plot's discovery in London, while Mountjoy's replacement as Lord Deputy – another military veteran, Sir Arthur Chichester – suggested in October 1605 that 'the king shall more strengthen and confirm his estate, better content his subjects, and leave a more honourable memory behind him in the reformation and making civil of Ireland than in regaining France'.[26] Accordingly, Chichester started issuing 'mandates' to prominent Old English aldermen, who were then fined, imprisoned and removed from office if they refused to swear the Elizabethan Oath of Supremacy or failed to attend Church of Ireland services. From Whitehall, Privy Councillors again urged caution in January 1606, reminding Chichester that, since Ireland had only recently been pacified after extensive rebellion, 'a main alteration in religion is not suddenly to be obtained by forcing against the current, but gaining by little and little'. The Dublin administration should, rather, pursue 'a temperate course between both extremes, neither yielding any hope of toleration of their superstition, nor startling the multitude by any general or rigorous compulsion'.[27]

Enforcement of anti-recusancy measures was accompanied by the imposition of English property law and creation of a royal 'Commission for Defective Titles' in 1606 requiring all Irish landowners to produce valid documentary title to their lands on pain of fine or forfeiture. In

Ulster, Tyrone faced challenges to parts of his vast estates from lesser lords, as well as predatory attempts to reclaim former church lands by Bishop George Montgomery of Clogher, Derry and Raphoe. In August 1606, a senior courtier, Sir Thomas Lake, confirmed to the Earl of Salisbury that James was 'now so well informed' about Irish matters that 'men may know it is his own judgement of his affairs that guides his tongue and not infusions from private persons'. Regarding challenges to Tyrone's lands, Lake relayed the king's concerns about relying wholly on 'strictness of law ... in a country where their evidence and records are so ill kept'.[28] Worried that the courts potentially offered a partisan avenue to settle old scores, James recommended that Tyrone's grievances instead be set out in writing for royal review in London. In a report prepared for Salisbury, Sir John Davies described recently travelling around Ulster with Lord Deputy Chichester, and had found that 'these Irish lords appear to us like glow-worms, which afar off seem to be all fire; but, being taken in a man's hands, are but silly worms'. Tyrone had also given out 'a false alarm' that he and his wartime ally, Rory O'Donnell, Earl of Tyrconnell, 'were going into Spain, a common and poor Irish policy ... to amuse the state with rumours, that are utterly false'.[29]

But confronted by a summons to Whitehall to adjudicate pending land disputes, Tyrone became apprehensive and, accompanied by Tyrconnell, headed a party of around ninety that left Rathmullen in County Donegal for the northwestern Spanish port of La Coruña in September 1607. Diverted by storms and obliged to land instead at Quillebeuf in Normandy, the earls travelled overland through the Spanish Netherlands and eventually to Rome, presenting themselves as religious refugees, forced to flee their estates on account of religious persecution. Furious that the earls' actions risked damaging his international reputation as a religiously tolerant monarch, James was also keen that his recent reorientation of English foreign policy in a pro-Spanish direction should not be jeopardized. A proclamation simultaneously issued in English and Latin described the earls as 'contemptible creatures so full of infidelity and ingratitude'. Foreign powers should not grant them asylum since the earls had 'withdrawn themselves for matter of religion – a cloak that serves too much in these days to cover many evil intentions'.[30]

*

In Irish history, the 'Flight of the Earls' has been seen as a watershed moment resulting in the permanent demise of Gaelic culture in Ulster, but a more unstable and ambiguous legacy is also discernible.[31] The term 'Flight of the Earls' was coined by Lord Deputy Chichester ten days after the event, simultaneously conveying a sense of fearful culpability and – by emphasizing the fugitives' noble status as 'earls' – disloyal ingratitude. The flight was also assumed to be a temporary expedient to secure Spanish or other assistance, enabling the earls' return to Ulster with a foreign armed force and foreign funds. To secure the region against external incursion, Chichester thus urged the speedy granting of the earls' lands to existing inhabitants, former Elizabethan soldiers, and new Scots and English landowners. Deeming plantation 'the best of all' options, Chichester reminded English Privy Councillors that, before the wars of the 1590s, the earls' estates in Ulster 'like the kingdom of China were inaccessible to strangers'.[32]

The 'Flight of the Earls' offered James's administration an unexpectedly long-term opportunity to promote 'British' integration and seek to defray rising costs of around £100,000 sterling per annum required to maintain order in Ireland. Following an intense flurry of surveying and mapping, a remarkably ambitious scheme to redistribute all confiscated lands from the estates of Tyrone and Tyrconnell was agreed by the English Privy Council in January 1609.[33] Nearly 3.8 million statute acres of land in the counties of Armagh, Cavan, Coleraine, Donegal, Fermanagh and Tyrone would be distributed to English and Scots 'Undertakers' (so-named on account of conditions they undertook to fulfil), former soldiers, Protestant clergy, members of Trinity College Dublin, and to around 300 'deserving natives'.[34] Representatives from London's merchant guilds would be given the whole county of Coleraine, with additional baronies in Tyrone and Antrim to create a new county of Londonderry. There would be no massive seigneuries – the largest undertaker's portion would be 3,000 acres – and all settlers would be within a day's journey of one of dozens of new market settlements envisaged in this remodelled landscape.

In framing his Ulster plantation policy, James drew on success in the 'Hamilton-Montgomery' plantation in eastern Ulster where former O'Neill lands in the Ards had recently been allocated to two Scots, Hugh Montgomery and James Hamilton, thereby reversing English policy under the Tudors that had aimed at removing Highland Scots from Ulster. As King of Scotland, James had also sponsored plans, from the mid-1590s onwards, to extend royal control over the country's remoter regions by – as one English observer reported – seeking 'to erect new towns and castles of strength there and constitute new colonies of habitations as the Romans did'.[35] In 1597, the Scottish Parliament had passed legislation requiring all landowners in the Highlands and islands to travel to Edinburgh and present documentation demonstrating valid title deeds to their lands in an attempt to investigate suspiciously low rents and crown revenues returned from those regions. In *Basilicon Doron*, James offered a starkly dichotomous dissection of Scottish society that later informed his understanding of Ireland's inhabitants. In the tract's first edition, he differentiated between Highlanders residing on the mainland – who were 'barbarous, and yet mixed with some show of civility' – from those living in the isles, who were 'utterly barbarous' and more like 'wolves and wild boars'.[36] By the time *Basilicon Doron* was revised for its London edition in 1603, the king had toned down his bellicose rhetoric and removed the reference to wolves and boars. In all remoter regions, James recommended 'planting colonies' of Lowlanders to 'reform and civilise the best inclined among them' while also, if necessary, 'rooting out or transporting the barbarous and stubborn sort'.[37]

Practical realizations of this policy took effect in three attempts between 1598 and 1609 to plant the island of Lewis after the clan chief of the MacLeods of Lewis, Torquil MacLeod, failed to produce documentation confirming his landholding rights, prompting his estates on Lewis, Ronalewis, the Shiant Isles and Trotternish in Skye to revert to crown ownership. Observing the Scottish Privy Council's approval in August 1598 of plans to dispatch intrepid Lowland 'adventurers' from Fife in the first Lewis plantation, Elizabeth's ambassador in Edinburgh advised the English court that James's scheme seemed 'a good platt [plan] for her Majesty to subdue our Ireland with'.[38] But in spring 1602, the new settlement was destroyed by Niall and Tormod MacLeod in an attack that killed at least fifty Lowland planters. In a proclamation, James vigorously denounced 'the detestable and barbarous behaviour' and 'beastly and monstrous cruelties' of the native population. The islanders' unruliness was all the more inexcusable given that Lewis was 'the most fertile and commodious part of the whole realm.'[39]

Following the 'Flight of the Earls', lush descriptions were soon extolling similar riches to be derived from cultivating Ulster's verdant pastures and exploiting the plentiful salmon-fishing in the rivers Bann and Foyle that bordered the new county of Londonderry. At the start of 1609, the king was presented with a literary 'New Year's Gift' by his English Solicitor-General, Sir Francis Bacon, who celebrated James's personal role in promoting and overseeing the Ulster Plantation. As Bacon urged, 'the more strongly and fully your Majesty shall declare yourself in it, the more shall you quicken and animate the whole proceeding.' Moreover, since the Ulster Plantation was 'not a flash, but a solid and settled pursuit', it was a project fit 'for pulpits and parliaments and all places to ring and resound of it'.[40] To Bacon's mind, the possibilities afforded by Anglo-Scottish union and plantation in Ulster were twin, heaven-sent gifts to James and entirely unlike unhappy Tudor precedents in Ireland, where plantation had been forcibly imposed via a rhetoric of settler superiority, resulting in bloodshed. Bacon also rejected parallels between James's promotion of plantation in Ulster and colonial ventures in Virginia simultaneously being undertaken for commercial profit by mercantile companies.

Several months later, a tract entitled *Motives and Reasons to induce the City of London to undertake the plantation in the north of Ireland* (1609) was circulated to all of London's livery companies, presenting the newly established towns as central to a lucrative international mercantile network connecting Ireland with England, Scotland, Spain and the New World. In 1609, James also co-authored a set of *Orders and Conditions* to be observed by plantation undertakers. Published simultaneously in London and Edinburgh, the *Orders and Conditions* emphasized how much the king had disregarded 'his own profit' by redistributing the confiscated lands to third parties; his sole concern was 'the public peace and welfare of that kingdom [Ireland]'.[41] That summer, James confirmed to Chichester that he was prosecuting no project 'with greater earnestness than the plantation of Ulster' since he knew that achievements on the ground were critical to his royal reputation. As he admitted, 'foreign states do cast their eyes upon it, and the ill-affected at home and abroad, will be ready to take advantage of anything omitted or neglected therein'.[42] James's keenness to secure progress in Ulster was, moreover, stoked by the effective stalling of his plans for closer Anglo-Scottish union. The hope was now to see droves of ambitious Scots and English flooding into Ulster to assume owner-ship of new estates.

Aware that James's administration was keen to broadcast quick suc-cess, Sir John Davies's *Discovery of the True Causes why Ireland was never entirely subdued* (1612) confirmed that the Ulster Plantation had been 'projected and prosecuted, by the special direction and care of the king himself'. The Irish Attorney-General credited James with avoiding the mistakes of previous English rulers who had gifted unmanageably large estates to court favourites. Similarly, while native inhabitants had been excluded from earlier land redistributions, Davies lauded James's 'master-piece' as having 'made a mixed plantation of British and Irish, that they might grow up together in one nation'. As he celebrated, 'the clock of the civil government is now well set, and all the wheels thereof do move in order'.[43] Yet Davies's rosy rhetoric was undermined by serial reports of insufficient new settlers arriving in Ulster, inadequate capital being raised, and a lack of local leaders willing to spearhead progress on the ground.

Given the inauspicious history of Tudor plantation in Ireland, not everyone was initially enthusiastic. Having served in Ireland since the 1570s, the Essex-born soldier Barnaby Rich published a *New Descrip-tion of Ireland* in 1610 which claimed that, on a recent visit to London, he was asked about 'sixteen several times' in less than a week about the realistic prospects for adventurers to Ulster. Londoners wondered what 'could save their throats from cutting, or their heads from being taken from their shoulders' by local inhabitants? Even if a new settlement was built, 'why might not the Irish do then as they had done before, in one night to lay waste and consume all with fire and sword?'[44] Another deterrent to potential adventurers were concerns regarding security of land tenure, given sporadic rumours regarding Tyrone's imminent return to reclaim his former estates with armed support from Spain or the papacy. To obtain statutory confirmation of Tyrone's forfeitures, James thus summoned the first Irish Parliament to meet since 1585 and also demanded from Chichester an exact survey of progress in the Plan-tation in December 1612. As James made clear, the survey was to be undertaken without any 'fear to please, or ill-please, or displease, any of our subjects, English or Scots, of what quality soever'.[45]

James's first Irish Parliament was also the first to draw representa-tion from the whole island. With Ulster now under royal control, forty

new two-member borough constituencies were created in areas designated for plantation, resulting in disputed elections as well as the first
Protestant majority, with Catholics now outnumbered by 132:100 in
the Commons. When the parliament opened in Dublin Castle in May
1613, Catholic concerns about gerrymandering descended into farci-
cal chaos. The government's nominee as Speaker, Sir John Davies, was
challenged by Old English MPs who instead installed a Catholic former
judge, Sir John Everard, in the Speaker's Chair, only for the corpulent
Davies to be lifted up by supporters and forcibly placed on Everard's
lap. Everard's ejection then prompted a walkout by Catholic MPs and
peers. When recusant peers refused to return to the chamber for fear
they would 'be blown up by gunpowder', their concerns were dismissed
by Chichester, 'seeing that he himself and the other Lords were to sit
along with them'.[46] By early June, the escalation of divisions was generating rumours in London that Irish Catholics were plotting a rebellion
similar to 'that horrible bloody plot of the massacre in Paris' – i.e. the St
Bartholomew's Day massacre of French Huguenots in 1572.[47]

A delegation of Old English MPs travelled to Whitehall that autumn,
bypassing the Dublin executive in order to present their religious and
civic concerns directly to James. Describing his parting encounter with
the king at Royston in October, one of its spokesmen, Sir James Gough,
claimed that although James had denounced their disruptive conduct in
Parliament, he denied any wish to force men's consciences. He had thus
warned the MPs against further recalcitrant acts, adding that 'kings
have long ears, and be assured that I will be inquisitive of your behaviour'.[48] True to his word, James was incensed to learn that his private
reassurances were quickly canvassed in Dublin as a firm undertaking
to confer religious toleration. As the king protested to Lord Deputy
Chichester in early 1614, he could not recall specifically discussing the
forcing of individual consciences. His key concern had, rather, been to
forbid the Irish MPs from making further appeals over the Lord Deputy's head. Since 'he expressly inculcated that into their brains', it was
vexing that the MPs had seemingly focused on toleration, rather than
'the main thing which he then sought to beat into their ears'.[49]

Dramatic entertainment at James's court offered another arena onto
which Irish political tensions could be projected. During the Christmas season in 1613, Ben Jonson's *Irish Masque at Court* included an
anti-masque section describing the disrupted journey of twelve Irish

'imbashators' (ambassadors) who were played by six English and six Scots courtiers, mirroring the Anglo-Scottish balance James was hoping to achieve among plantation landowners. Having lost their fine masqueing clothes in a storm crossing the Irish Sea, the ambassadors were forced to dance in traditional mantles before the character of a bard, extolling King James's policies in Ireland, promised that, if they 'will stoop but to the music of his peace', they will 'come forth newborn creatures all'.[50] Removing their mantles, the ambassadors then found their fine masqueing clothes miraculously preserved, underscoring the benefits of loyal submission to royal authority.

At Whitehall, although investigation into the grievances of Old English MPs identified instances of malpractice, James resented their temerity in challenging his right to create new parliamentary boroughs. Having summoned the MPs back to London in April 1614, the king unleashed a tirade, rhetorically asking, 'what if I had made forty noblemen and 400 boroughs? The more the merrier.' Deploring the obstructionism of Old English MPs as 'rude, disorderly, inexcusable and worthy of severe punishment', the king warned that they risked appearing 'but half-subjects' who 'have an eye to me one way and to the Pope another way'.[51]

Rather than unleashing harangues in London, James might have followed his own advice to Prince Henry by prioritizing regular visits to his different kingdoms in order to hear the complaints of his subjects directly. By his own lights, James's failure to visit Ireland was unfortunate, obliging him to rely on partial and partisan information. John Speed's *The Theatre of the Empire of Great Britain* (1612), for example, endowed the king's unionist aspirations with cartographic support as the first atlas to present the islands of Great Britain and Ireland in a single folio publication. Speed's atlas was dedicated to James as 'most learned defender of the faith; enlarger and uniter of the British Empire; restorer of the British name; establisher of perpetual peace, in church and commonwealth.' But since, like the king, Speed never set foot in Ireland, his depictions relied on second-hand information. In the case of Ulster, Speed included images of Elizabethan fortifications but retained sixteenth-century landownership arrangements and disregarded the recent reconfiguring imposed by plantation. The absence of accurate and accessible maps and surveys yielded advantages to the Dublin administration in avoiding scrutiny when redistributing land, remodelling the parliamentary franchise, and levying taxation. But with no attempt to update Speed's atlas, either in later editions or the publications of rival mapmakers, it remains remarkable that, 'for the first 75 years of its institutional lifetime, the Ulster plantation did not cartographically exist.'[52]

Documentary reports evaluating plantation's progress on the ground, meanwhile, remained sombre. From a survey undertaken in 1611, the former President of Munster, Sir George Carew, observed Old English and native Irish communities finding increased common ground, prompting concern that 'the next rebellion, whensoever it shall happen, threatens more danger to the state' than any earlier uprising. If any foreign power sent 10,000 soldiers to Ireland, Carew warned that 'all the modern English and Scots would, in an instant, be massacred in their houses'.[53] In time, Carew's predictions were realized with the outbreak of the Irish Rebellion in 1641. Surveying the Londonderry plantation in 1614, Josias Bodley – younger brother of the Oxford librarian, Thomas – also described the settlement's poor fortifications, poverty and under-population. As Bodley reported, too many absentee adventurers preferred to instruct agents remotely, with the result that 'they have neither built the number of houses required; nor fortified their towns as they ought; nor planted the country as the very name itself of plantation enjoins them.'[54] In 1615, Barnaby Rich's 'Anatomy of Ireland' likewise disputed the paean of progress presented in Attorney-General Davies's account. Acknowledging the risks borne by all whistleblowers, Rich presented his critique directly to James. While Rich primarily blamed 'this canker, that is crept in by popery' for Ireland's ills, he also accused English administrators of widespread embezzlement, observing that if anyone sent from England was potentially 'a bribe-taker, the Irish will corrupt him'. Moreover, royal authority was little esteemed: 'words that in England would be brought within the compass of treason ... are accounted with us in Ireland for ordinary table-talk.'[55]

*

Amid claims of administrative malpractice and financial corruption, King James recalled Sir Arthur Chichester after a decade-long tenure as Lord Deputy in 1616. Leaving Ireland, Chichester admitted to Carew that 'the government of this kingdom is chargeable in the entrance into it, painful in the continuance, and dangerous in the end'.[56] Regarding charges, by 1616 around £60,000 sterling had been raised (albeit reluctantly) by London's livery companies via compulsory levies for the Londonderry plantations; although a sizeable sum, it was dwarfed by the £1.63 million of private revenue raised the following year via the East India Company's second joint-stock issue.[57] Moreover, although the Earl of Tyrone's death in Rome in 1616 removed the danger of the sexagenarian earl's imminent return that had haunted the Dublin administration for a decade, the threat of foreign invasion through Ireland never receded.

James's residual anxieties about strategic security were only exacerbated by the outbreak of what later became known as the 'Thirty Years War' in 1618 and involved James's son-in-law, the Elector Palatine Frederick V, being ejected as King of Bohemia in 1620 and seeing his ancestral Palatine territories overrun by Catholic Habsburg troops. As confessional conflict escalated, a reconvened English Parliament in January 1621 saw MPs lobbying for large-scale continental military deployment to support Protestant forces seeking to recapture the Palatinate. But James remained mindful of Ireland. As the Venetian ambassador, Girolamo Lando, reported, the king 'seemed to fear that if once he unsheathed the sword against the Spaniards, they would begin to harass him in his own dominions, especially in Ireland, recalling what took place under Queen Elizabeth and in the time of the Earl of Tyrone'.[58] By contrast, MPs and ministers seemed unconcerned, hubristically confident in the apparent pacification achieved by recent plantation.

In 1619, Thomas Wilson, as James's Keeper of the Records, had suggested to the king that 'the multiplicity and mass of business' relating to Irish affairs offered an ideal opportunity to compile an updated history to complement Davies's *Discovery of the True Causes why Ireland was never entirely subdued*. Deeming it 'a great pity' that 'such a treasure should be always hidden', Wilson proposed drawing on the state papers and interviewing individuals involved in the plantation. In Tacitean vein and via idiosyncratic Latin, he envisaged a history of Irish affairs undertaken '*sine ira aud odirunt absentandi libidine uscham sine amore, alio quam veritatis* [without anger, hate, lust or love, but truthful]'.[59] But by the early 1620s, James's freedom of manoeuvre to direct Irish policy – as well as his capacity to receive objective information – had become compromised by his political and emotional dependence on George Villiers, later Duke of Buckingham, whose rapid rise as court favourite entailed a domination of Irish patronage, a proliferation of peerages and pensions, and a predatory policy of land seizures across the country.

Following a series of attacks on corruption and malpractice in the English House of Commons in 1621, a wide-ranging commission of inquiry was sent to Ireland the following spring, tasked with reviewing all aspects of Irish governance in Church and State since 1615. One commission member – Richard Hadsor, an Old English lawyer with long experience as crown counsel for Irish affairs at Whitehall – privately compiled a trenchant distillation of failings in Irish governance based on his own supplementary investigations after the other commissioners returned to England. Citing a litany of 'heavy oppressions, and extreme courses', Hadsor blamed dishonest local officials who 'fleece and rob under the pretence of his Majesty's title though little to his benefit really'. Hadsor recommended establishing a standing commission on Irish affairs to meet weekly in Whitehall and review all proposed transactions, alongside deployment of 'special men of trust' in all Irish shires who would imitate successful Venetian practice by supplying 'private intelligence' and identifying discrepancies between transactions on the ground and official returns.[60]

Although the formal Commission identified numerous reasons for the plantation's failure to match original ambitious aspirations, it found consensus only in insisting that overall responsibility for Irish policy still lay with the king. For James, the Commissioners' report revealed '(as in a clear glass) the true state of that kingdom; by which we see, how much our goodness, and bounty, hath been abused; our intentions, and directions eluded; and many things done, that must be reformed'.[61] Goodness and bounty may have infused James's original intention to foster peace, prosperity and Protestantism in Ireland, but significant reform seemed unlikely for as long as the country's patronage and profits remained within Buckingham's purview. In September 1622, the Venetian ambassador, Girolamo Lando, acknowledged to the Venetian Doge and Senate that Ireland remained a tempting entry route to the British mainland for hostile powers. Accordingly, James's subjects in England and Scotland 'would be better without it', while the Irish themselves 'seem always disturbed in mind, if not in deed, his Majesty tending to remain the enemy of all'. As Lando bluntly opined, 'Ireland is such that it would be better for the king if it did not exist and the sea alone rolled there.'[62]

18

The King in Parliament

In one of the reign's more dramatic confrontations, James summoned his English Privy Councillors, six judges and the House of Commons clerk to Whitehall on 30 December 1621 to witness him ripping out from the official Commons record a 'Protestation', submitted twelve days earlier by MPs. Preserved today in the National Archives, the 'Torn Journal' is a vivid physical reminder of a heated constitutional dispute. The offending 'Protestation' comprises just over 250 words, registering MPs' insistence that 'the liberties, franchises, privileges, and jurisdictions of Parliament, are the ancient and undoubted birthright and inheritance of the subjects of England'. With Parliament being the designated forum to discuss 'arduous and urgent affairs' concerning king, commonwealth, church and national security, MPs upheld their entitlement to freedom of speech in debates, together with 'freedom from all impeachment, imprisonment, and molestation' unless ordered by the House of Commons itself. But to his Councillors and judges, James objected that, since it had been passed in a late-night sitting with less than a third of members present, the 'Protestation' was 'fit to be razed out of all memorials, and utterly to be annihilated'.[1] A week later, a proclamation was issued announcing Parliament's dissolution.

In early 1622, James published a *Declaration* explaining his decision to dissolve the recent parliament and reproducing transcripts of messages sent between his court at Newmarket and Westminster. On 11 December, he had responded to a petition from MPs, dismissing concerns that he was misinformed about Commons debates and reminding them that he was 'an old and experienced king, needing no such lessons' in political communications. He did, however, correct the MPs' reference to their 'ancient and undoubted right and inheritance' by confirming that all parliamentary privileges remained royal gifts; he would, nevertheless, remain as careful to preserve MPs' liberties as they should be to respect his royal prerogative.[2] But in the Commons, James's response had alarmed the former Attorney-General and Chief Justice, Sir Edward Coke – now sitting as MP for Liskeard – who objected that 'when the king says he cannot allow our liberties of right, this strikes at the root. We serve here for thousands and ten thousands.'[3] But following the assembly's adjournment, Coke was imprisoned in the Tower of London where he remained from late December until the following August, when he was released after being cleared of charges of defrauding the Crown of monies relating to his private estates.

For historians seeking a 'high road to civil war' – the origins of the military conflict that would break out between the king and Parliament in 1642 – this confrontation between James and House of Commons MPs in 1621 appeared symptomatic of irreconcilable divisions between defenders of Stuart absolutism and parliamentary liberties. James's published reasons for dissolving the parliament were intended to portray his critics as a minority faction whose views were untypical of those elected to Parliament. Having first addressed a Scottish Parliament at the age of five, James's description of himself as 'an experienced king' in parliamentary affairs was proven when he dissolved its English counterpart half a century later. He was also a monarch who appeared more often in the English Parliament than his Tudor predecessors, opening new sessions in person as well as delivering speeches and attending debates. Indeed, before its dissolution in 1621, James had acknowledged that, 'in former times kings sat not in the parliament by representation but [by] person, as I do now', adding that 'I may much more come personally when I will' to attend Westminster sessions.[4]

James's responses to parliamentary proceedings were thus often couched in personalized terms. Confronted by English MPs in May 1607, speciously claiming that interim measures to foster closer Anglo-Scottish union could not be approved on the grounds that they did not achieve 'perfect' union, the king warned 'I am a man of flesh and blood, and have my passions and affections as other men.' MPs should 'not too far move me to do that which my power may tempt me unto' – i.e. prevent their meeting.[5] But when James dissolved the same Parliament, over three years later in December 1610, he denied to his

Privy Councillors that any 'House, save the House of Hell, could have found so many' grievances as those vented in the Commons, advising that 'such bold and villainous speeches ought ever to be crushed in the cradle'. The king protested that, having left Scotland seven years earlier 'with an unstained reputation and without any grudge in the people's hearts'; if 'we have misbehaved ourselves here, we know not nor we can never yet learn.' But as he objected, his royal 'fame and actions have been daily tossed like tennis balls' among MPs whose ceaseless criticism and obstructionism had 'perilled and annoyed our health, wounded our reputation, emboldened all ill-natured people, encroached upon many of our privileges, and plagued our purse with their delays'.[6]

*

James was correct to contrast his Scottish and English parliamentary experiences, given the different structural organizations and institutional cultures of the two legislatures. Before the opening of the purpose-built 'Parliament House' in Edinburgh in 1639, the unicameral Scottish parliament met in different venues with its members, known as commissioners, valuing their ethos of free assembly. In 1578, for instance, objections had been lodged to the twelve-year-old King James and Regent Morton that a parliament convened in Stirling Castle 'was not a free Parliament being held within a strong castle'.[7] The number of Scottish parliamentary commissioners varied, but division lists generated by the assembly held in July 1621 recorded just over 140 voting members.[8] By that date, parliamentary business in Scotland was also managed by a committee of crown appointees, known as the 'Lords of the Articles', through whom all legislative initiative was channelled.

During James's Scottish reign, sixteen parliaments were held before his accession as English king in 1603, followed by another seven before his death in 1625. Between 1578 and 1603, James evidently attended every Scottish Parliament as well as around sixty 'Conventions of Estates' that met between November 1585 and the relocation of the royal court to London in 1603.[9] Over the latter period, the average time between conventions of estates was four months, but after 1603, only five further conventions were held in James's lifetime. Attracting around fifty members, conventions could be convened quickly without a forty-day plenary summons. Although terminology varied between 'conventions of the estates', 'conventions of the nobility' or simply 'conventions', they usually drew representatives from the traditional 'three estates' of clergy, nobility and burgesses, and they had powers to levy taxation and enact administrative orders that could, if needed, later be converted into parliamentary statutes.

As well as attending parliaments and conventions of estates, James significantly expanded the Scottish Parliament's membership by regularizing the position of lesser barons or 'lairds'. At the parliament convened in Edinburgh in July 1587, a new estate of shire commissioners was created on the grounds that James and his ministers needed 'to be truly informed of the needs and causes pertaining to his loving subjects in all estates, especially the commons of the realm'.[10] In return for a tax of £40,000 (Scots) from lairds, each shire would annually elect two commissioners from its resident barons to stand ready to attend the next parliament.[11] Approving 'an avalanche of statutes', the same parliament in 1587 passed more acts (136) than any of its predecessors and was dignified by formal opening and closing ceremonies. Royal concern regarding 'the decay of the form, honour and majesty' of Scottish parliaments since James V's reign was reflected in legislation intended to restore their 'ancient order, dignity and integrity' by imposing fines of £200 and exclusion on any parliamentary commissioner not attired in appropriate 'apparel in seemly fashion'.[12] Five years later, the English ambassador, Robert Bowes, was disconcerted to arrive in Edinburgh to find that Parliament – officially adjourned until 1 June 1592 – had actually started on 29 May. Having been told 'that this was a running Parliament to take beginning at the king's pleasure', Bowes sought an audience with James and went to the city's Tolbooth where, as he reported to London, 'the King in Parliament hath expended the most part of all the days in this week', with the frenetic pace maintained until a 'long oration' by James marked Parliament's close on 5 June.[13]

In June 1592, the progress of parliamentary business was expedited by three conventions of estates that had met in March, April and May. The political mood was febrile after the audacious raid on James's apartments in December 1591 by the king's cousin the Earl of Bothwell, followed by popular outrage at the brutal murder of Bothwell's ally the Earl of Moray in February 1592. Throughout the parliamentary sitting, 'the council of Edinburgh mounted a watch at Holyrood and on the spire of St Giles' looking for signs of riot or disturbance.[14] In the pulpit at St Giles, a local minister, Walter Balcanquhall, used the anniversary of the

Regent Morton's execution on 2 June to berate the king and his advisers for neglecting Kirk affairs. When Balcanquhall was summoned before James and the Lords of the Articles committee, the king rebuked his temerity in criticizing royal policy and directed the committee to devise 'an act against such liberty of speech' that gave 'commission to some special magistrates, to pull the ministers out of the pulpits when they speak after that manner'. When Edinburgh's Lord Provost refused, James 'chafed, and that night at supper railed against the ministers', as recorded by the Presbyterian chronicler David Calderwood.[15] Three days later, Presbyterians celebrated passage of the so-called 'Golden Act', which confirmed the rights of kirk sessions, presbyteries, synods and General Assemblies, with no mention of bishops. A silver lining for the king nevertheless lay in the legislation, being the first time that the civil power had ratified specific internal arrangements within the post-Reformation Scottish Kirk.

If James's physical presence in the Tolbooth attending the Scottish Parliament or its committees seemed a full-time occupation in 1592, the 'king in parliament' was nevertheless an occasional event. In an age of personal monarchy, most government business was executed by Privy Councillors who met approximately every three days throughout the year. While James maintained a 'remarkably assiduous attendance' at Privy Council meetings between 1595 and 1603, responsibility for much of the workload was assumed by officers of state, most prominently the Chancellor.[16] An insight into James's hands-on approach to the dispatch of Scottish government business is vividly illustrated in a tirade fired off to the Clerk-Register, Alexander Hay, in December 1591. Worth quoting at length, the king's diatribe covered a range of current preoccupations including household affairs, legal reform and Queen Anna's 'tocher' (dowry), part of which had been loaned to Edinburgh's burgh council as an investment:

> Because the Chancellor is occupied in his dispatches, I must address my complaint to you. I have been Friday, Saturday and this day waiting upon the direction of my affairs and never even one man is coming. Those of the Exchequer who were ordered to take the accounts – never one awaits. The tasks of the household should have been settled this day – no man comes down. I sent for the Advocate on both Friday and Saturday – neither meeting nor answer. Similarly for the bailies of this town, for the matter of the tocher – the like answer. I ordered, as you

heard, a certain number to make proposals for reforming the Session – no such thing is contemplated. I ordered the Treasurer to have charges made about the horners [outlaws] – I have heard nothing of that as yet. In short, no appointment or meeting is kept. What is spoken late tonight is forgotten in the morning. In the morning, I see nothing spoken of but to girn [complain] about; seeing none of the work done, while I am earnestly waiting upon it. And when I am compelled to rest myself, then to lay the blame upon me: a pretty trick.[17]

At a time when much political communication comprised verbal exchanges at court, the frustration of the twenty-five-year-old king at apparent ministerial lassitude was powerfully laid bare.

In constitutional terms, James accorded the Scottish Parliament a subordinate place. As he outlined in *The Trew Law of Free Monarchies* (1598), since the institution of monarchy pre-dated the formation of any estates, the country's Parliament was 'nothing else but the head court of the king and his vassals'.[18] The logical inference, as elaborated in *Basilicon Doron*, was that prudent kings would 'hold no parliaments, but for necessity of new laws, which would be but seldom'.[19] The right to sit as a parliamentary commissioner was also a royal favour that remained revocable. At a Convention of Estates in June 1600, entrenched opposition from burgh and shire representatives obliged the king to abandon proposed new fiscal duties on sales of grain, cattle and sheep. Dismissing the Convention, James acknowledged support from noble and clerical representatives, but warned the lairds and burgh commissioners that 'he should remember them and be even with them'. Recalling the expansion of parliamentary representation achieved in 1587, the king also reminded the defiant lairds that 'he gave them vote and made them a fourth estate, which he should undo again'; if he wished, he could 'call a parliament and displace them of vote in parliament and convention'.[20]

*

An entirely different constellation of parliamentary customs and expectations confronted James when he acceded as English king in 1603. Simply in terms of magnitude, as he reminded the House of Commons in 1614, 'there is not in the world so great a counsel as yours'.[21] Indeed, during James's reign, Commons membership increased from 462 in 1601 to

477 by 1621 through new burgh enfranchisements and conferring the right on the universities of Oxford and Cambridge – described in the letters patent 'as the very eyes and souls of our kingdom' – to return two members each to Parliament from 1604 until their separate franchise was abolished in 1948.[22] Accommodated in St Stephen's Chapel in the former medieval palace at Westminster, the Commons chamber (at just under twenty metres long and almost ten metres wide) only had seating for around half of all MPs, leaving standing room on the floor or in upstairs galleries in key debates. Lack of physical capacity was thus another reason adduced in opposition to James's plans for Anglo-Scottish parliamentary union; as one MP insisted in 1607, an influx of additional Scots members was unthinkable since 'already this House is as great as one Speaker can moderate, as one room can contain, as we can hear one the other speak'.[23] With three-hour sittings usually scheduled each morning, the Commons chamber had no fire and was cold in winter but, during the summer, MPs were so dazzled by sunlight flooding in through an enormous east window that exterior awnings were erected as a way of 'keeping out the sun' in 1621.[24] Despite MPs outnumbering peers threefold, the Lords met in a chamber of comparable size that had a fire, was hung with tapestries commemorating the Elizabethan defeat of the Spanish Armada, and had a canopied throne for the monarch.

Initially, James planned to convene an English Parliament directly after his coronation but was obliged to wait until March 1604 when the outbreak of plague in London had receded. In January, he issued a proclamation describing the Parliament's purpose as 'merely and only to consult and resolve with our loving subjects of all those things, which may best establish the public good'; he had 'nothing to propound for satisfaction of any private desire, or particular profit of our own'. Given Parliament's involvement in laws regulating religious affairs, the king nevertheless enjoined 'that there be great care taken, to avoid the choice of any persons either noted for their superstitious blindness one way, or for their turbulent humours other ways', in veiled reference to Catholics and Puritans respectively.[25]

Among the MPs elected to James's first Westminster Parliament in 1604 was the common lawyer John Doddridge, whose historical researches had convinced him that the institution's origins could be traced back to the era of the ancient Druids. Such claims ran counter to James's assertions that, since the institution of monarchy pre-dated the formation of political estates, all parliamentary privileges were gifts from the king. Doddridge accepted, however, that evolution of the English Parliament's membership, organization and authority had been shaped by successive rulers, some of whom – notably William I – had come to power by conquest. Notwithstanding, Doddridge was proud that 'there is no king in the world, nor no subject of any king, that have a greater and more binding, and yet a freer counsel, than this our parliament in England'.[26] Nor did the English Parliament's antiquity necessarily preclude future alteration. Later appointed as one of the bilateral union commissioners, Doddridge suggested that successful Anglo-Scottish union would require creation of an additional 'common parliament for both kingdoms, for the general causes' without derogating from the proper business of each country's existing Parliament.[27] Accordingly, although Doddridge claimed that druidical parliaments existing before monarchy was established, the institution itself supported, rather than rivalled, royal power. As he explained, 'the king himself (*jure Regio*), as a Flower of the Crown, hath the absolute power of calling and dissolving it'.[28]

Once his first parliamentary session started, however, James soon learned that not only did English monarchs have little control over legislative initiative, but different techniques of parliamentary management were required in a bicameral legislature. Moreover, he could not rely on traditional royal methods of exerting conciliar control over the Lower House on account of his recent keenness to confer peerages on his Privy Councillors, thereby rendering them ineligible to stand as MPs. In the Commons, MPs showed little enthusiasm for closer Anglo-Scottish union, although – as the Venetian ambassador, Nicolò Molin, observed in May – James did not 'cease to labour, argue, plead, but all, as yet in vain'. Molin also described as 'mistaken' his failure to control the Commons, which was 'full of seditious subjects, turbulent and bold, who talk freely and loudly about the independence and the authority of Parliament in virtue of its ancient privileges, which have fallen into disuse, but may be revived'.[29]

By the time James came to prorogue the English Parliament's first session on 7 July, he shared Molin's diagnosis. For while the king thanked peers in the House of Lords for having 'carried yourselves with discretion, modesty, judgement, care and fidelity', he acknowledged to MPs that there were 'well-affected' individuals, but also 'idle heads, some rash, some curious, some busy informers'. Whereas in Scotland 'I was heard not only as a king, but [also] . . . as a counsellor', it seemed that at Westminster there had been 'nothing but curiosity from morning to evening to find faults with my propositions'.[30]

A similar warning accompanied James's speech to the English Parliament on 9 November 1605, four days after discovery of the Gunpowder Plot. Thankful for their collective deliverance, the king conceded that, had the Plot succeeded, at least posterity would know that he had not 'died ingloriously in an ale-house, a stews [tavern], or such vile place', but rather in Parliament, which was the 'most honourable and fittest place for a king to be in'. Now, however, he needed to prorogue Parliament on account of the national emergency. Not only did his government need to focus on investigating the conspiracy, but an unknown number of Plotters remained at large and MPs were needed in their localities to deter further atrocities. The king also took this opportunity to remind peers and MPs that the English Parliament was 'nothing else but the king's great Council'. Accordingly, its members 'should be ashamed to make show of the quickness of their wits here, either in taunting, scoffing, or detracting the prince or state in any point, or yet in breaking jests upon their fellows, for which the ordinaries [inns] or ale-houses are fitter places'.[31]

Breaking jests – and also breaking wind. Little better illustrates the ribald wit of unruly English MPs that so unnerved its new king than a genre of poems recounting the 'Parliament Fart'. On 4 March 1607, the Wiltshire MP Henry Ludlow farted just after a House of Lords messenger had interrupted a long and heated Commons debate on Anglo-Scottish union. The incident inspired multiple verse improvisations, extending from 40 lines to over 225 lines, with reactions ascribed to at least 113 different MPs; satirically scatological, the poems also confirmed the unpopularity of the king's cherished union project. With the popularity of 'Parliament Fart' verse continuing well after James's death, one scribal miscellany, probably compiled in Cambridge in the 1640s, recalled:

> And thus the [1607] Parliament, in mens' opinion
> Hath turned to a fart the matter of union!

In another version, MPs debated how best to respond to parliamentary flatulence:

Quoth Sir Thomas Lake, if this House be not able
To censure this fart, I'll have it to the Council table,
Quoth Sir George More, I think it be fit
That we this fart, to the serjeant commit
Not so, quoth the serjeant low on his knees,
Farts will break prison, but never pay fees.[32]

Angered by what he regarded as intemperate and disrespectful debates, James's frustration was compounded by little progress in regard to either Anglo-Scottish union or parliamentary approval of significant financial supply. Addressing peers and MPs on 31 March 1607, James described himself as 'the eldest Parliament man in Scotland', who had 'sat in more parliaments than any of my predecessors'. Contrasting his very different experiences, he described how, in Scotland, if any member made 'any seditious or uncomely speeches, he is straight interrupted and silenced by the Chancellor's authority'. By contrast, at Westminster, MPs evidently believed there was a 'liberty for any man to speak what he list, and as long as he list'. With most Scottish parliamentary sessions lasting less than a fortnight, James also suggested, since 'the English Parliaments are so long, and the Scottish so short, that a mean between them would do well'.[33] Having encountered 'the nearest thing to a filibuster to be found in any Stuart parliament ... James made not one inch of progress' during the Westminster session that sat for 112 days between November 1606 and July 1607.[34]

*

At the next session of James's first Parliament in February 1610, James tasked his Lord Treasurer, the Earl of Salisbury, with explaining the urgent need for increased crown revenue at the assembly's opening. James himself waited until 21 March to address Parliament, when he described himself as 'now an old king' who had ruled Scotland for thirty-six years before completing 'my apprenticeship of seven years here; and seven years is a great time for a king's experience in government ... I must not be taught my office'. With geopolitical tensions raising the possibility of continental warfare, James recognized that funds 'cannot be supplied out of the air or liquid elements, but must come from the people'; nevertheless, he advised against responses that might undermine his domestic or foreign reputation.[35]

Perhaps predictably, English MPs proved no more docile than previously. In a debate in May about whether additional duties on imports, known as impositions, might be levied by the Crown alongside normal customs duties, the City of London MP, Nicholas Fuller, observed that, although James was 'in truth very wise', he was also 'a stranger to this government'. The previous day, the king had angrily berated MPs for challenging his prerogative right to levy impositions which 'all your kings have ever had, which two women have had and exercised', and which was automatically assumed by monarchs in France, Spain, Sweden and Denmark. Reiterating precepts articulated in *The Trew Law of Free Monarchies*, James warned English MPs that they had no right to question or to resist royal power. If they considered themselves ill-governed, '*preces et lachrimae* (prayers and tears) were ever their arms'. With disarming frankness, James denied that any subject could 'clip the wing of greatness. If a king be resolute to be a tyrant, all you can do will not hinder him.' James further insisted to MPs that 'many things I may do without parliament, which I will do in parliament, for good kings are helped by parliament' and, jointly enacted, 'may seem more glorious'. But MPs should know that 'the more wayward you shall be, I shall be the more unwilling to call you to parliament, for such behaviour will make me the seldomer' to seek their counsel and co-operation.[36]

By late May 1610, the newsletter-writer John Chamberlain found little to report of the parliamentary session, 'seeing they have sat now [for] fourteen weeks to so little purpose'. Hearing the language of 'monarchical power and regal prerogative strained so high', Chamberlain feared that – were such rhetoric to become reality – 'we are not like to leave to our successors that freedom we received from our forefathers'.[37] James's apparent inability to work with parliaments had encouraged recourse to other mechanisms and, two months later, a petition from MPs voiced concern that royal reliance on proclamations seemed likely 'to bring a new form of arbitrary government upon the realm'.[38] In numerical terms, MPs had reason to be alarmed, for whereas Elizabeth had never issued more than eighteen proclamations in any year of her reign, her successor issued thirty-two in his first nine months as king and a total of 267 during his twenty-two-year English reign.[39]

During the summer of 1610, James responded to the concerns of MPs by commissioning a panel of judges to investigate. In what became known as *The Case of Proclamations* (1610), Sir Edward Coke denied that proclamations could 'create any thing to be an offence which was not an offence before against the laws of this realm'.[40] Since Coke's opinion was only posthumously published in 1656, the matter was not openly resolved in 1610 but, in September, James revoked all but one of the orders objected to in the MPs' petition, albeit by issuing another proclamation.[41] But when Parliament reconvened the following month, Salisbury's bid to resolve the Crown's financial difficulties through a scheme known as the 'Great Contract' failed to gain approval. To Salisbury, James protested that, although he had 'received more disgraces, censures, and ignominies than ever [a] prince did endure' from Westminster MPs in his seven years as English king, he did 'not have asinine patience; he is not made of that metal'.[42] Accordingly, James adjourned his first Parliament in December and dissolved it two months later.

Regarding the Scottish Parliament, the royal court's relocation to London meant that James was thereafter represented by an appointed commissioner. Acting as James's representative during the parliament which met in July 1604, John Graham, Earl of Montrose, took a calculated risk in allowing an 'Act in favour of the Kirk' to be introduced, passed and ratified without James's knowledge in order to secure the union commissioners' appointment. Despite the king's insistence that both countries enact legislation that was identical 'word by word', the Scottish legislation thereby excluded ecclesiastical affairs from the commissioners' remit.[43] In the financial sphere, however, Scottish commissioners proved equally as reluctant as English MPs to approve significant increases in crown revenue. At the parliament held at Edinburgh in October 1612, James's commissioner, Thomas Hamilton of Drumcairn, successfully secured ratification of General Assembly acts facilitating the full restoration of episcopacy in Scotland, but the Crown's demand for £800,000 (Scots) in taxation provoked 'very contentious controversy'. Threatened with dissolution, parliamentary commissioners eventually agreed a sum of £260,000.[44]

Aside from difficulties of parliamentary management in London and Edinburgh, James's first Irish parliament, meeting in Dublin Castle in May 1613, was adjourned shortly after its opening amid disputed elections and a walkout by Catholic Old English MPs. The following spring, the English Attorney-General, Sir Francis Bacon, advised James to avoid simultaneous meetings of the English and Irish legislatures for, by keeping the Dublin parliament adjourned, its 'unsettled business' might encourage English MPs to approve financial supply. Meanwhile, 'the loving and frank proceeding' of James and the Westminster Parliament should, in turn, 'daunt the ill-affected part of the parliament of Ireland'. Moreover, when a new English Parliament met, Bacon counselled James to avoid framing his opening speech 'in the language of an accountant by setting forth the particulars of his debts, charge and revenue, or in the language of a merchant by crying of his royalties to sale, or in the language of a tyrant' by threatening sanctions in the event of non-compliance. Instead, the king should confirm his aim in calling Parliament was simply that 'he might know his subjects better and his subjects likewise might know him better'.[45]

Duly advised, when James opened a new English Parliament on 5 April 1614, he readily granted that its members 'know the state of the country that live there better than I do'. With no better forum than Parliament for members to 'speak so freely and safely, and have means to lay open the just complaints and griefs of his subjects', James ventured that 'this parliament, I hope, shall be called the parliament of love.' Although MPs thereafter gave readings to over a hundred bills, they refused to sanction royal requests for financial supply without receiving reassurance regarding the legality of fiscal imposition levied by royal prerogative. The following month, Sir Edwin Sandys – one of the most outspoken opponents of closer Anglo-Scottish union a decade earlier – acknowledged the 'very gracious and full' action taken by the king to address concerns about extra-parliamentary measures, but constant vigilance was essential 'as in a garden clean weeded, weeds next year. So here, by new patents, proclamations' and other instruments. A fortnight later, Sandys denied it was the monetary value of impositions that was disputed but, rather, James's insistence that he might levy such taxes without parliamentary consent: MPs simply could not allow 'the liberties of the House to run through our fingers'.[46]

Amid escalating Commons rhetoric, Thomas Wentworth MP – whose father, Peter, had incurred Elizabeth's wrath for urging debate about the royal succession in the 1590s – quoted Scriptural texts from Daniel and Ezekiel to warn of the fatal ends that befell monarchs who levied excessive taxes. Helpfully observing how a mighty monarch like Henri IV had 'died like a calf that had his throat cut by a butcher', Wentworth hoped that James might avert such a fate. On 3 June, the Tamworth MP, Sir Thomas Roe, feared that imminent dissolution would be 'the ending, not only of this, but of all parliaments' and, four days later, the king dissolved the assembly; having sat for only forty-three days, it was later dubbed 'the Addled Parliament'.[47]

Following Parliament's dissolution, James candidly vented his frustration to the Spanish ambassador in London, Diego Sarmiento de Acuña, later Count of Gondomar, describing the English House of Commons as a rambunctious and unmanageable body whose meetings comprised only 'cries, shouts and confusion'. Surprised 'that my ancestors should ever have permitted such an institution to come into existence', James admitted, 'I am a stranger, and found it here when I arrived, so that I am obliged to put up with what I cannot get rid of.'[48] Reporting to Philip III's court, the ambassador confirmed that the king had 'started to become upset and to show distress, as if feeling embarrassed' when discussing MPs' actions. Having evidently read up on English parliamentary procedure, Sarmiento had reassured James that 'he still had one great prerogative and privilege over parliament, which was to be able to call it and disband it in whichever way he wanted.' 'Greatly relieved', the king had agreed, adding that 'anything done and said in parliament turned to nothing without his approval.' Sarmiento also relayed a witticism that the king had 'found amusing': namely, 'that the Catholics might have tried to use the powder and the wick to blow the last parliament [in 1605], but that the Puritans had, in effect, blown it now'.[49]

*

Following the collapse of the 'Addled Parliament', James did, however, 'get rid' of English parliaments – at least in the short term. The period between June 1614 and the next time he opened a Westminster Parliament in January 1621 was the longest without an English Parliament since 1515. In financial terms, given the abortive nature of the 'Addled' Parliament, the most recent parliamentary subsidies had been approved in 1610, meaning that James had effectively embarked on a decade-long 'Personal Rule' that set a controversial precedent for the more notorious eleven-year 'Personal Rule' of his son, Charles I, between 1629 and 1640.

A three-week session of the Scottish Parliament was nevertheless convened in Edinburgh in June 1617. Held during the king's three-month visit to Scotland that summer, James resumed his former practice of assiduous attendance and spent twelve days sitting with the Lords of the Articles committee. But royal attempts to increase the committee's proportion of state officers failed and James was also obliged to abandon draft legislation giving the Crown power to order all the Church of Scotland's ecclesiastical and liturgical arrangements, effectively removing the need for General Assemblies. Serving as James's ambassador in Brussels, William Trumbull learned of ministerial hopes in London that the Scottish Parliament's surprise opposition to royal proposals 'will cause his Majesty to rise speedily and to hasten his retreat' south. Moreover, 'the English will get this profit by it, not to be held the only refractories of the world in accommodating their sovereign's desires.'[50] But from a member of the king's retinue in Edinburgh, Bacon was informed that, after the Scottish session ended, James had professed himself satisfied that – presumably unlike his experiences in Westminster – 'nothing was gotten by shouldering or wrestling, but by debate, judgement, and reason without any interposition of his royal power in anything'.[51]

Facing a renewed crisis in royal finance and with Continental Europe convulsed by large-scale warfare, James called a new English Parliament, which opened on 30 January 1621. Amid February temperatures so cold that the River Thames had frozen over, two financial subsidies worth around £160,000 (sterling) were approved in less than three weeks. During the parliament's first session, between January and June 1621, Prince Charles attended over two-thirds of its sittings in the House of Lords and conveyed messages between James and his Westminster representatives. Addressing peers in late March, James ventured that 'never any king hath done so much for the nobility of England, as I have done' and, in numerical terms at least, the membership of the Lords expanded significantly from seventy-five peers in Elizabeth I's last parliament in 1601 to 144 peers by 1628. With royal support for the Lords confirmed 'by my own presence, coming diverse times among you', alongside that of his son, James was confident that 'ye, with him, shall have the means to make this the happiest parliament that ever was in England.'[52]

Moves were also made that year to summon a new Scottish Parliament, after a convention of the nobility the previous autumn had declined to grant significant financial assistance without parliamentary endorsement. Dispatched to London to recommend the summoning of Parliament, Archbishop John Spottiswoode of St Andrews raised the possibility of securing a sum of £1.2 million Scots (£100,000 sterling).

From James's perspective, however, it was 'not so much the importance of the sums which you are able to contribute that we respect, as the trial of your affections, your straining of yourselves to your uttermost abilities'; such determination 'may give example to your neighbours of greater wealth, to do the like in their due proportion'.[53] At what would be James's last Scottish Parliament, commissioners meeting in Edinburgh in July 1621 voted £400,000 (Scots) of supply in four annual instalments as well as a new levy on interest payments and annuities.

As popular pressure mounted on James to deploy military forces in support of his son-in-law's attempts to recover the Palatinate from Spanish Habsburg forces, a new Council of War estimated that it would cost £200,000 sterling to raise an army and £190,000 a year for maintenance.[54] But when English peers and MPs reassembled for a second parliamentary session on 20 November 1621, deliberations became derailed by disagreements between MPs in London and James's court in Newmarket. Believing that they had encouragement from the king's favourite, the Marquis of Buckingham, MPs' draft petitions urged James to declare war in alliance with German Protestant princes and to abandon his hopes of regaining the Palatinate through diplomatic means and, more specifically, by securing a Spanish Habsburg wife for Prince Charles. After several peppery exchanges between Westminster and Newmarket, MPs drew up the short 'Protestation' that was forcibly torn from the Commons Journal by James in December, shortly before the parliament was dissolved.

Continental military tensions and domestic divisions had only deepened by the time James opened what would be his final English Parliament on 19 February 1624, but the royal tone remained buoyant. Describing himself as 'your own kindly king', James insisted that he 'had rather maintain your liberties than alter them in any thing'. Three weeks later, he confirmed that he was 'so desirous to forget all rends in former parliaments' that he might be thought 'in love with parliaments, and call them often'. Intent on communicating as 'freely and clearly' as possible, James reminded peers and MPs that, although he had 'broken the neck of three parliaments, one after another', he still hoped that this would prove 'a happy parliament, and make me greater and happier than any king of England ever was'.[55] Sitting until late May 1624, the assembly approved seventy-three statutes and a grant of around £300,000, albeit with the caveat that all monies spent be approved by a Council of War accountable to Parliament. The loyalty of MPs remained distinctly conditional. As the member for Portsmouth, Sir Benjamin Rudyerd, had acknowledged in the Commons in March, while he welcomed the king's 'declared inclination to parliaments', he advised James against being 'over-curious and ingenious in our own overthrow; for I assure you, Sir, we may blow up the House without gunpowder, we may do it with our own passions'.[56]

19

This Canker of Want

Throughout his life, James occupied an unenviable and discordant position: perennially impoverished but pedalling a rhetoric of kingly prerogative. Financial largesse axiomatically denoted royal power; penury implied frailty. Describing the Scottish court at Holyrood in March 1589, the English spy Thomas Fowler reported that James 'is not able to live like a king. He borrows often of his towns, and never pays.' He possessed 'neither [silver] plate nor stuff to furnish one of his little half-built houses, which are in great decay and ruin'. Since James 'never thinks of money, nor how it shall be gotten', Fowler conceded that Elizabeth I should at least know that 'he is neither ambitious, malicious nor covetous.'[1] Once King of England, James had little option but to think constantly about money and different ways of obtaining it. Writing to his Principal Secretary, Sir Robert Cecil, now Earl of Salisbury, in October 1605, he was willing to 'confess that it is a horror to me to think upon the height of my place, the greatness of my debts, and the smallness of my means'. Insufficient revenue was compounded by James's ready admission that 'my heart is greater than my rent'; instinctively munificent and generous, he lacked wherewithal. Since Salisbury had, however, 'perfectly used the first part of a physician's office' in diagnosing the malady, James directed his Privy Councillors 'to cure me' and relieve his anxiety by 'letting me see how my state may be made able to subsist with honour and credit'.[2]

But successive sessions of the English Parliament ended in acrimonious failures to obtain financial supply. Following another unsatisfactory sitting in July 1607, James wrote to his Privy Councillors from Royston, identifying 'this eating canker of want' as being 'the only disease and consumption which I can ever apprehend as likeliest to endanger me'.

Derived from the same etymological root as 'cancer', a 'canker' was a sore that, left untreated, spread around a body. As James admitted, were it not for his financial difficulties, 'I could think myself as happy in all other respects as any other king or monarch that ever was since the birth of Christ.' Vowing, once again, to be a diligent patient who would abide by whatever financial remedy was prescribed, the king reminded his Councillors that devising ways of ensuring royal solvency was 'the only subject whereupon ye break your brains all this time of my absence'.[3]

Money was one sphere in which James's natural articulacy deserted him. When the English Parliament next met in February 1610, it was Salisbury, as Lord Treasurer, who delivered a speech at the assembly's opening, seeking to impress on peers and MPs the urgent need to increase crown revenue. Addressing Parliament several weeks later, James was ready to 'confess I am less naturally eloquent, and have greater cause to distrust my elocution in matters of this nature, than in any other thing'.[4] In 1622, the Venetian ambassador in London, Girolamo Lando, compiled a report on English affairs that emphasized the clear discrepancy between royal penury and the king's lavish instincts. As Lando explained, James 'has not accumulated money, but rather debts', being accounted 'rich in jewels only'. Nonetheless, his 'liberality and munificence flow like rivers and seas and continually fatten his favourites'. Domestically, 'all payments are delayed for years, making things very hard', while 'the Council usually discusses nothing else'. To Lando's mind, the dilemmas of English crown finance seemed intractable since 'the aims of his Majesty and of the parliament are diametrically opposite': the king 'leans to absolute monarchy' while his parliament 'lean to liberty'. Successive failures to secure financial supply had left James determined to call parliament only 'when absolutely compelled and to avoid doing so with all his might'.[5]

*

When James acceded as king in 1567, Scotland's outdated fiscal structure involved assessments of land values in terms of their pre-war 'old extent' (referring to the fourteenth-century wars of independence against Edward I of England), while valuations of church properties derived from thirteenth-century assessments intended for the papacy. The Convention of Royal Burghs imposed levies on royal burghs, while tenants on crown lands were liable to feu duties (the monetary replacement for traditional military service).[6] In general, however, Scotland was lightly taxed, with Queen Mary levying only one direct taxation in her reign – £12,000 (Scots) in October 1566 – to fund entertainments celebrating James's christening that December. In her capacity as dowager queen of France, Mary's income was supplemented by up to 50 per cent via revenues amounting to around £30,000 (Scots) annually, although in practice she rarely received the full amount.[7] Indirect taxes were also levied via customs duties, but attempts to impose direct taxation were generally resisted unless raising monies for a specific purpose. As in Elizabethan England, the default expectation was that monarchs would 'live of their own' income. Revenues from crown lands were, however, decreasing in value as inflation eroded the value of fixed feu duties. James's personal expenditure also steadily increased, as he gained his majority, established a royal household, and acquired a wife and growing family.

In contrast to England, there was no central financial department of Scottish government. A permanent Exchequer was created in 1584, initially entrusted with auditing royal accounts and overseeing revocations of crown lands leased during royal minorities. A Comptroller handled the royal household's revenue from crown lands, burghs and customs, while the Lord High Treasurer received feu dues and 'casualties': taxation proceeds and profits from justice intended to cover the monarch's personal expenses. Although the offices of Comptroller and Treasurer were combined in 1610, since all direct taxation was separately approved by conventions or parliaments, the office of Tax Collector remained separate. Scottish financial officers were, moreover, personally liable for debts incurred on the Crown's behalf. Before instigating the pro-English 'Ruthven Raid' in August 1582, James's Treasurer, the Earl of Gowrie, had become alarmed by significant rises in court expenditure, attributed to policies instigated by Esmé Stewart, Duke of Lennox. Obliged to 'wadset' (mortgage) some of his own estates in return for short-term interest-bearing loans, Gowrie's personal debts had risen to £67,488 (Scots) by May 1583.[8]

As James tried to extricate himself from the Raiders' control, the English court learned that ambassadors sent to Scotland by Henri III of France were hoping to draw James away from English influence by offering him an annual pension of 100,000 crowns, while also supplying Gowrie with 'ready money' of 10,000 crowns, a yearly pension of 2,000 crowns, and repayment of all his debts incurred as Treasurer.[9] (In Elizabethan England, a 'crown' was worth five shillings and deemed equivalent in value to a French *écu*, or crown.) Although a French-sponsored settlement did not prevail on this occasion, royal indebtedness underlined the importance of the subsidies James received from Elizabeth after the Treaty of Berwick in 1586. With James's annual income from all domestic sources estimated at around £150,000 (Scots) in the mid-1580s, the fact that English subsidies between 1586 and 1602 averaged around £30,000 per year denoted a considerable injection of funds, despite the studied vagueness that Elizabeth deliberately attached to the size and regularity of their payment.[10]

James's marriage to Queen Anna yielded a Danish 'tocher' (dowry) of which £108,000 (Scots) returned to Scotland in 1590, where it was deposited with larger Scottish burghs that returned interest payments to the Crown at a rate of 10 per cent.[11] Despite suggestions that the dowry should remain a permanent reserve, regular withdrawals to meet current expenditure exhausted the capital by the late 1590s, leaving James's ministers obliged to request direct taxation from conventions of estates. In April 1588, a levy of £100,000 had been agreed to cover expenses related to the king's marriage and another convention in January 1594 agreed the same sum to finance celebrations for the anticipated arrival of his first child.[12] The sumptuous baptism celebrations staged for Prince Henry at Stirling Castle in August yielded generous gifts including 'two standing cups of pure gold' valued at £1,200 sterling from the Dutch States-General, who also conferred an annual pension of £500 on the prince.[13] The courtier James Melville was, however, dismayed to learn that the Dutch goblets were 'soon melted and spent' in partial repayment of the king's debts; in Melville's view, the gold cups should have been 'kept in store to the posterity'.[14] (A generation earlier, Queen Mary had raised over 5,000 crowns by melting down the golden font received from Elizabeth for James's christening in 1567.)

In January 1596, James appointed eight individuals to act collectively as commissioners of the Exchequer, following the death of his Chancellor, John Maitland of Thirlestane. As the English agent George Nicolson observed, the king 'was very merry, saying he would no more use [a] Chancellor or other great men' to handle his financial affairs, 'but such as he might convict and were hangable', in a darkly humorous reference to hanging as a form of execution usually only meted out to

THE MIRROR OF GREAT BRITAIN

non-nobles.[15] Including James's former tutor Peter Young and the President of the Court of Session, Alexander Seton, the group was dubbed 'the council of our Octavians' in a report to the English court.[16] But despite the Octavians' renewed focus on maximizing crown revenue and reducing royal expenditure, the court's credit-driven difficulties continued. By early 1598, James was reliant on loans received from private individuals such as the Treasury commissioner, the goldsmith Thomas Foulis, who, together with a merchant named Robert Jowsie, amassed debts of £160,522 (Scots) to creditors, equating to around a year's gross crown revenue from all sources. Although Foulis and Jowsie received legal protection for their Scottish debts, Jowsie was imprisoned in England in 1599 for debts contracted on James's behalf south of the border.[17] The impossibly bleak state of royal finances was only underscored when the Comptroller, Sir George Home of Wedderburn, absconded in February 1599, unable to continue provisioning the royal household from his own income at the same time as facing large demands from creditors.[18] In *Basilicon Doron* published that year, James advised Prince Henry to 'choose honest, diligent, mean, but responsible men, to be your receivers in money matters'. Believing that 'mean' financial officers would be less tempted to engage in sharp practice when acting on the Crown's behalf, James identified 'this oversight ... [as] the greatest cause of my mis-thriving in money matters'.[19]

*

The chronic problems of Scottish crown finance improved after James's accession as English king and the royal court's permanent relocation to London. As in Scotland, however, traditional orthodoxy held that an English king should 'live of his own' and meet normal expenditure via revenue from crown lands, profits from justice, customs duties, and feudal dues such as 'wardship' (whereby the Crown assumed temporary guardianships of estates if the tenants-in-chief were minors). The final years of Elizabeth's reign had, moreover, placed severe strain on government finance amid inflation, harvest failures, and the escalating costs of waging war against Spain and suppressing Tyrone's rebellion in Ireland. Four months before the queen's death, Sir Robert Cecil had despaired of rising costs in Ireland, admitting that 'all the receipts are so short of the issue, as my hair stands upright to think of it'.[20] Hence, as well as acceding to Elizabeth's Crown in 1603, James also inherited English royal debts of around £420,000 sterling.

Although direct fiscal levies were more common in England than Scotland, when the Elizabethan and Jacobean reigns are compared, the proportion of English crown revenue received from parliamentary-approved direct taxation fell from over 16 per cent between 1560 and 1602 to just over 9 per cent between 1603 and 1625.[21] As King of England, James received around £900,000 sterling in grants from the English Parliament over the course of his reign, averaging around £41,000 per year. Meanwhile, the English Crown paid £708,000 between 1604 and 1619 (or a yearly average of around £47,000) into the Irish Treasury alone, to cover the country's civil establishment and a small military force.[22] Accordingly, when James objected to English peers and MPs in January 1621 that 'I have had less supply from my people than every king or queen had, I know not for many hundred years,' he had reason to feel aggrieved.[23] By contrast, the radical transformation of state revenue effected during the mid-century civil wars – including the introduction of monthly assessments and excise duties – would see the proportion of finance raised by the English Parliament exceed 90 per cent during the 1640s.[24]

Royal largesse nevertheless remained an essential means for monarchs to secure and reward loyalty. To regulate the endless flood of requests for royal gifts and pensions, the Scottish Parliament had passed legislation in 1592, restricting approval of all such requests to Privy Councillors and forbidding anyone from seeking 'to present any to his Majesty or to urge him to subscribe them'.[25] With no such restrictions operating in England, James issued a proclamation from Cecil's Hertfordshire estate in May 1603, reassuring his new subjects that all petitions would be carefully considered, but requesting that they 'forbear all assembling and flocking together in multitudes' to ensure that requests were presented 'without numbers, without clamour, or any other kind of disorder'.[26] He also suspended all patents of monopoly conferred by Elizabeth, pending conciliar review. Formally welcoming James to the City of London, the barrister and MP Richard Martin hoped that the new reign would thus be one in which industrious individuals would no longer suffer having their 'marrow sucked with most odious and unjust monopolies' and 'unconscionable lawyers, and greedy officers shall no longer spin out the poor man's cause' to enrich themselves.[27]

Despite James's injunctions exhorting restraint, some of his new English subjects showed remarkable persistence in submitting direct requests to the king. In late 1604, for instance, James recounted to Cecil a protracted encounter with the veteran naval captain and President of the Council of the North, Edmund, third Baron Sheffield. Having received the new king's standard offer of an annual pension of £1,000 sterling, Sheffield had objected that 'this would do him no good' since he was already £10,000 in debt. In response, James had indicated that 'my liberality ought not to be measured by his want, for I was bound to be no man's banker'. Unmoved by Sheffield's claims of lengthy royal service, James admitted to Cecil that, before acceding as king, 'I never knew that there was a Lord Sheffield living in England'. When Sheffield further 'reckoned that I had repaired the ruins of every nobleman's estate in England except his', James had retorted by pointing out that, even as King of Scotland and 'heir to this crown', he had received around £3,000 yearly from Elizabeth – i.e. only three times what Sheffield was being offered – with the king willing to wager that he 'had been thrice more steadful [loyal] to the state' than Sheffield.[28]

In practical terms, one of the first challenges that the new king's retinue encountered on its journey to London was discovering that Scottish coins could not be used to purchase supplies in England. Accordingly, James had authorized a proclamation from Whitehall on 8 April 1603 legalizing use of Scottish currency in England on the grounds that both countries were now 'united and incorporated together' under his rule.[29] After arriving in London, James issued his first sterling Mint indenture in May, retaining Elizabethan coinage denominations, but now showing the Scottish and Irish coat of arms incorporated with the English, alongside an image of James in decorated armour with the legend *Tueatur Unita Deus* ('May God guard these [kingdoms] united') on the reverse of smaller gold denominations.[30] In another proclamation issued in November 1604, James announced a new common British coinage that would display 'our picture on horseback' and reminding subjects that 'nothing is more appropriate to the sovereign dignity of princes than the ordering of their monies'.[31] By this edict, James also addressed a disparity in the rating of gold and silver coins by confirming that the common international bimetallic standard of 12:1 used in

Scotland when valuing gold coins against silver coins would replace the English ratio of 10.75:1 that had left English gold coins undervalued in terms of intrinsic metallic content. As for currency exchange, a 'British crown' was also deemed to be worth £6 (Scots) or 10d. (sterling), while the ratio of valuing £12 Scots as equivalent to £1 sterling remained in place until after the Anglo-Scottish union of 1707.[32]

James also faced currency complexities in Ireland following recent devaluation of the country's coinage. During Tyrone's rebellion, the English government had sought to prevent the importation of arms into Ireland by issuing a proclamation in May 1601 that withdrew sterling from circulation and obliged the country's inhabitants to rely instead on debased 'mixed money': silver coins and copper tokens that had been demonetized in England, but were now reintroduced to Ireland.[33] The response was a widespread refusal to accept debased coins, rapid inflation, food shortages and popular resentment. Accordingly, James quickly sought to restore confidence in the Irish coinage to boost trade and uphold his royal authority. By September 1603, base coins had been revalued at tariffs consistent with their silver content and a new Irish coinage issued in denominations of a shilling and a sixpence with a portrait of James on the obverse and a crowned harp on the reverse. Four years later, English sterling was proclaimed as legal tender in Ireland and the former Tudor exchange rate of 3:4 reinstated.[34]

When James's first English Parliament convened in March 1604, the subject of crown finance quickly surfaced, as MPs called for the abolition of traditional prerogative rights such as wardship and purveyance – the latter denoting the Crown's right to purchase provisions and secure carriage for the royal household at below-market rates.[35] Throughout successive sessions of this first Jacobean Parliament which lasted until 1610, MPs considered serial proposals for alternative arrangements whereby the Crown might receive some form of regular payment, or composition, if traditional dues including wardship and purveyance were surrendered. The only financial support actually received, however, were three subsidies, worth around £450,000 over three years, agreed when Salisbury successfully exploited national security fears in his addresses to the parliament which reconvened in January 1606, following the Gunpowder Plot's discovery two months earlier. As the Venetian ambassador observed in May that year, 'the populace make this shrewd remark, "Three subsidies, much evil, no redress".'[36]

Without regular parliamentary subsidies, James resorted to following Tudor precedents to pursue different ways of supplementing crown revenue. Despite his temporary suspension of patents of monopoly in May 1603, over 150 commercial projects were reviewed during James's English reign. These encompassed proposals to regulate alehouse licences, fine usurers, grow mulberry trees for silk production, and manufacture soap, pins, starch and steel, with the majority of projects including some form of monopoly patent that, in return for a proportion of revenue returned to the Crown, conferred protection from competition on so-called 'Projectors' in relation to specific inventions or industries. Ministers thus considered restricting trade solely to the monarch in certain domestic products such as 'cloth, lead, tin, alum, iron ordinance, wine and salt', while 'foreign imports such as Spanish pepper and quicksilver, French salt, Florentine corn and Italian alum' also offered potentially lucrative future revenue options.[37]

Among other infrastructure projects, the king keenly endorsed domestic silk manufacture following patents granted to French importers of mulberry trees. In 1607, James issued a circular letter to the Deputy Lieutenants of counties in southern England, directing landowners to buy and plant trees available at subsidised cost. Adding royal endorsement to a published pamphlet on silk manufacture, James highlighted the success with which Henri IV had 'won to himself honour, and to his subjects a marvellous increase of wealth' through the promotion of sericulture; similar riches might be reaped by the English, 'now the way is showed them by us their sovereign, as these of France have been'.[38]

Parallel attempts were also made to overhaul management of crown lands in the hope of increasing revenue by investigating sundry 'concealments' and defective land titles, as well as collecting unpaid rents from newly drained lands and illegal 'assarts' (parts of royal forests that had undergone unauthorized clearing and cultivation). Ministers needed, however, to reassure peers and MPs not only that such initiatives were legitimate, but also that additional revenue was urgently required. As swarms of surveyors started inspecting ancient deeds and titles, the Northampton MP, Henry Yelverton, objected to the Commons in March 1606 that 'it is the Devil's walk to tread over England and Wales, and full it is of danger to have it known what land the realm contains; and how much every man has in possession'.[39] But in Scotland, the jurist and union commissioner Thomas Craig of Riccarton was enthused by the potential for feudal land tenures to foster bonds of loyalty and gratitude. In his *Jus Feudale* – composed around 1605 – Craig penned a dedication to James, extolling the benefits that could accompany a revitalized system of crown tenures in which 'no matter how far the subdivision of the soil of Britain were carried, every acre would be held of your Majesty in fee ... and the possession of every holding would carry with it the obligations of a faithful servant.'[40] Although Craig's British vision was unfeasibly ambitious, decades of local resistance were eventually overcome in 1617 when a central Register of Sasines (land titles) was created with all Scottish land disputes thereafter referred to the Court of Session for resolution.

Initiatives to maximize crown revenues were accompanied by regular exhortations to economy and retrenchment. Having become Lord Treasurer in 1608, Salisbury insisted to James that royal finances could not be restored 'when the garden of your Majesty's treasure shall be made a common pasture for all that are in need, or have unreasonable desires'. James needed to realize that it was simply 'not possible for a king of England, much less of Great Britain ... to be rich or safe, but by frugality'. Compared to its continental neighbours, England 'may certainly be counted potent, but not opulent'.[41] Salisbury's initial review of royal finances revealed that, by 1608, James's debts had risen to £600,000 sterling, while his annual expenditure was running at £375,000 from annual income of around £300,000.[42] In July that year, the Spanish ambassador in London, Don Pedro de Zúñiga, advised Philip III that 'the time is opportune for any undertaking, for the financial difficulties and diversity of troubles of the English have thrown their government into a state of confusion and despair.' Rising costs in Ireland ensured that 'there is not a penny left in their Treasury'; as Zúñiga described, Salisbury was 'tearing his hair out in despair and telling his friends how bitterly he regrets having accepted that office; he said it will kill him and ruin his honour and reputation.'[43]

In 1610, Salisbury attempted to solve the dilemma of chronic royal penury by asking the English Parliament for a one-off sum of £600,000 to pay the king's debts, together with an annual direct taxation of £200,000 thereafter. At the assembly's opening in February, Salisbury sought to impress on peers and MPs the sheer scale of royal debt and necessary expenditure. Acknowledging the risk of 'some suspicion that the truth of my relation might be doubted', Salisbury protested 'before

God, I will not willingly speak an untruth' and denied undue inflation of the sums cited. He had earlier reminded peers and MPs that 'for a king not to be bountiful were a fault', while allowing that James's 'three first years were his Christmas'.[44] The following month, James himself suggested that MPs might pause before claiming to 'mislike me for my liberality, since I can look very few of you this day in the face, that have not made suits to me, at least for something, either of honour or profit'. While conceding that his accession to the English Crown in 1603 had been accompanied by initial profligacy, James made clear 'that Christmas and open tide is ended'. As he recalled, 'I made knights then by hundreds, and barons in great numbers, but I hope you find I do not so now, nor mind not to do so hereafter.'[45] Returning to the Commons in May 1610, James insisted that 'the supply of the king is the good of the people, and there is no more division between the king and the people than between the head and the body.' Reminding MPs that 'I was born to be begged at, not to beg,' James also emphasized the need to strengthen national security in the wake of Henri IV's murder that same month. Given that 'in time of peace, it is fit to provide for war', only making financial 'provision after time is like mustard after dinner'.[46]

In debates over what became known as the 'Great Contract', MPs continued to insist that any agreement regarding a regular subsidy required a reciprocal relinquishment by the Crown of its right to dues such as wardship and purveyance, as well as its prerogative claim to levy impositions (a form of customs duty) without parliamentary approval. The amounts requested by the Crown were also deemed exorbitant, with one MP claiming – albeit hopelessly inaccurately – that an annual levy of £200,000 would amount to 'the eighth part of all the kingdom's possessions'.[47] Scotophobia undoubtedly compounded the reluctance of MPs. By 1610, James had awarded Scottish members of his Bedchamber over £10,000 sterling in annual pensions, over £88,000 in cash gifts and over £133,000 to pay off historic debts.[48] In November, the Hereford MP, John Hoskins, objected to his colleagues that since 'the royal cistern had a leak', until 'it stopped, all our consultation to bring money into it was of little use'. Insisting that 'this fault could not be personal but national', Hoskins conspicuously exonerated the Irish, English or Dutch, silently isolating the Scots as culpable.[49]

For his part, Salisbury regarded as unrealistic MPs' grudging agreement of around £107,000 sterling from one subsidy and one fifteenth (referring to a fourteenth-century tax amounting to a tenth of the value of a lay individual's moveable goods in towns with parliamentary representation and a fifteenth for rural inhabitants). As he had objected to the House of Lords in July 1610, the amount 'given by the Lower House is so small, being but one subsidy and one fifteen as I esteem but a drop in a cistern of water'.[50] Several months earlier, a similar analogy had been invoked in an audacious double-entendre directed towards the lavish gifts bestowed by James on his male favourites, both English and Scots. The outspoken MP for Oxford, Thomas Wentworth, had asked why MPs should agree a substantial subsidy 'to draw a silver stream out of the country into the royal cistern, if it shall daily run out thence by private cocks'? In the same debate, the City of London MP, Nicholas Fuller, recalled James's own strictures in *Basilicon Doron* wherein Prince Henry was advised to be 'careful not to impoverish his subjects' because 'the riches of the subject is the best treasure of the king.'[51] Since the king maintained his right to levy impositions at will, if MPs agreed a regular sizeable annual subsidy, incentives for future monarchs to summon Parliament might thereby be removed. Following protracted debate, the 'Great Contract' failed to receive parliamentary approval, prompting an exasperated king to lambast the House of Commons as 'the House of Hell' in December 1610.[52]

*

Opening a new session of the English Parliament more than a decade later, in January 1621, James reiterated 'that I mean not to make every day Christmas'.[53] By then, however, Christmas had ironically come to James's subjects, who escaped financial exactions as a result of parliamentary refusals to grant supply. As one modern critic has observed, the Great Contract's failure in 1610, followed by the collapse of the 'Addled Parliament' four years later, 'literally made the decade a golden one, as local gentlemen never had subsidy commissioners disturb their financial calculations'.[54] Denied parliamentary subsidies, ministers necessarily pursued alternative avenues. In 1611, for example, a new vendible title of baronet was devised by the Privy Council whereby gentlemen with an annual worth of £1,000 could pay, in three yearly instalments, £1,095 for a new title that could be passed to descendants but did not carry a right to sit in the House of Lords. At a time when finance was desperately needed to promote plantation in Ulster, the price for such titles had been calculated as sufficient to keep thirty foot soldiers in Ireland for three years, at the daily rate of 8*d*. With eighty-eight new baronets created in 1611 alone, the cash for these honours generated over £96,000 sterling.[55]

Ministers had likewise been concerned to curb practices that potentially defrauded the Crown of licit revenue. In May 1611, James became the first English monarch for over a century to preside over 'the trial of the pyx' at the Royal Mint: the annual ceremony – still held today – whereby the coinage's metallic content is tested and verified. Accompanied by Prince Henry, Lord Treasurer Salisbury and other Privy Councillors, James 'searched and examined the abuses of the commonwealth practised by very many persons upon all sorts of monies' with 'kingly care and prudence'.[56] Nine days after the royal visit, a proclamation prohibited anyone not employed by the Mint from seeking 'to melt, or otherwise to alter' any coin in an attempt to suppress the illegal practice of 'culling out': withdrawing specie from circulation and melting it down into ingots for export.[57]

Salisbury's anxieties regarding crown finance were, moreover, exacerbated by fears that James's heir, Prince Henry, seemed just as 'like enough to prove an unthrift' as his father, with the prince's annual expenditure exceeding £50,000 sterling by May 1612.[58] Following Salisbury's death that same month, James drew on his Scottish experiences with the Octavians and put his financial affairs into commission. Observing the appointment of James's Attorney-General, Sir Francis Bacon, and others as commissioners required 'to devise projects and means for money', John Chamberlain observed that 'the world thinks it a strange choice, since most of them are noted, for not husbanding and well governing their own estate'.[59]

No matter how entrepreneurial the range of initiatives considered, expenditure constantly outstripped income; the Treasury commissioners were operating 'within a political milieu that raised £22,000 for Princess Elizabeth's aid and spent £115,000 on her wedding and related festivities' in 1613.[60] In March 1614, the Spanish ambassador, Sarmiento, gained access to detailed information about James's revenue and expenditure that enabled him to submit a report to Philip III outlining 'the amount and quality of this king's finances', correctly presuming that 'procuring particular information about this was of a useful curiosity'.[61] A month later, James flatly denied pleading penury in order to expand his prerogative right to levy taxes and impositions, protesting to peers and MPs, 'I never meant it.' As the king knew, 'he that overmuch strains and blows his nose will cause blood. So, if a prince should stretch his prerogative, it would cause his people to bleed.'[62] In an attempt to identify all potential revenue streams, James also ordered an investigation into government record-keeping, complaining in 1616 to the Lord High Treasurer, Thomas Howard, Earl of Suffolk, that 'great abuses have crept into the Exchequer, by the accounts being kept in the hands of the auditors, and passed without due examination', as well as 'other misdemeanours'. Accordingly, the king directed Suffolk to review all receivers' accounts since Mary Tudor's reign in the mid-1550s, ensure that all rent rolls and court rolls were 'properly deposited', and compile 'a table of Exchequer offices'.[63]

Envious eyes looked overseas for inspiration, recognizing the Dutch republic's success in processing English raw materials for profitable re-export as finished goods. To this end, the Governor of the Eastland Company, Alderman William Cockayne, proposed annual returns to the Crown of around £47,500 sterling if he was granted a monopoly to finish woollen cloth for continental export. But following proclamations that banned the export from England of unfinished cloth and woollen yarn in July and November 1614, Cockayne's scheme backfired disastrously when clothiers and dyers struggled to finish sufficiently large amounts of cloth while the Dutch republic retaliated by prohibiting imports of all English cloth, thereby leaving the domestic cloth industry in long-standing recession.[64] The Dutch also took opportunistic advantage of James's desperation to raise funds without summoning Parliament by instructing their ambassador in London, Sir Noel Caron, to suggest to James a sum of £250,000 to redeem the two 'Cautionary Towns' of Brill and Flushing that had been entrusted to England during the Elizabethan wars against Spain. Although the Dutch debt to the English Crown stood at around £600,000, Caron's proposal was sufficiently tempting for the towns' sale to be agreed in May 1616 at the suggested Dutch price, thereby removing England's final continental toeholds.

Among government ministers, confidence continued to be placed in speculative projects on the grounds that 'these things will yield money with time. In the meantime, to borrow.'[65] In early 1617, the City of London and the 'merchant strangers' community lent the Crown

£120,000, while the royal debt had reached £900,000 by September. Between 1618 and 1620, however, 160 merchant strangers and several London goldsmiths were indicted in several Star Chamber cases in which the goldsmiths were accused of privately supplying vast quantities of gold and silver coin and bullion to the merchant strangers which was then smuggled abroad, facilitating profits made by arbitrage via the differential precious-metal content of imported specie and local coinage. While Attorney-General Sir Henry Yelverton suggested in November 1618 that as much as £7 million sterling worth of gold had been exported from England since James's accession, Lord Chancellor Bacon anticipated that successful prosecution of the merchant strangers would 'demonstrate also that Scotland is not the leech (as some discoursers say), but the Netherlanders that suck the realm of treasure'.[66] While the Crown eventually obtained around £23,000 in fines from individuals convicted of illegal bullion export, it was rumoured that the merchant strangers had offered James potential compensation of £100,000 to abandon the prosecutions. Meanwhile, the struggle to make ends meet continued; following Queen Anna's death in March 1619, the king reluctantly sold some of his late wife's jewels in order to generate a short-term cash injection of £18,000 required to fund that summer's royal progress to Hampshire and Surrey.[67]

After years of risking valuable political capital in desperate attempts to raise funds, James's appointment of the London merchant Lionel Cranfield as Master of the Court of Wards in 1619 and Lord Treasurer from 1621, was accompanied by a retrenchment programme that started to bring royal income and expenditure into alignment. When the English Parliament reconvened in January 1621, investigations into alleged abuses arising from monopolies and patents also offered James and MPs an unexpected opportunity to find common ground in exposing financial malpractice. As the king admitted to the House of Lords in March, MPs' interest in alleged embezzlement was so keen that he found himself 'so troubled with complaints in this kind at Newmarket, as they were brought into me when I was in my bed'. For his part, James insisted that 'I have been always a hater of projects and projectors.'[68]

Draft legislation prohibiting monopoly grants to individuals received Commons support, but failed in the Lords. In December, James again addressed peers and declared himself 'ashamed (and it makes my hair stand upright) to consider, how in this time my people have been vexed and polled by the vile execution of projects, patents, bills of conformity, and such like; which besides the trouble of my people, have more exhausted their purses, than subsidies would have done.'[69] Meanwhile, Lord Treasurer Cranfield's austerity drive was yielding results. In December 1621, the Marquis of Buckingham informed him that James thought it 'a great mystery that whereas at Hampton Court there was talk of pawning jewels' to pay for royal progresses, 'now without any such shift he is removed and his servants paid and yet money remaining'.[70]

Military and diplomatic expenditure nevertheless continued to escalate and, in April 1622, James was obliged to request another year's grace to repay a sum of 200,000 imperial thalers loaned by his brother-in-law, Christian IV of Denmark, to assist with attempts to recover the Palatinate. Bemoaning his perennial penury two years later, James reminded the House of Lords that 'I have incurred a great debt to the King of Denmark which I am not yet able to pay.'[71] By way of context, Christian IV's personal fortune was greater than any other European sovereign, having been amassed through lucrative investments, toll revenues from the Baltic Sound, and access to the extensive treasury of his mother, Queen Sofie, who was a member of the Mecklenburg-Güstrow dynasty. Eleven years younger than James, Christian lent large sums to lesser Danish nobles at favourable interest rates, while his personal wealth gave him considerable freedom in policymaking, enabling him to wage international war if he wished, without seeking conciliar consultation or approval.[72] The contrasting financial positions of James and his brother-in-law could not have been starker.

20

Dynastic Diplomacy

With minimal parliamentary financial supply forthcoming, dynastic diplomacy was potentially an alternative route to crown solvency. In the late 1580s, one compelling reason for James choosing to marry the Oldenburg princess, Anna, over Catherine of Navarre, had been the certainty of receiving a dowry from the Danish court at a time when the French court was preoccupied with waging war. In June 1589, James had instructed his ambassadors to Denmark to seek, alongside commercial concessions for Scots merchants, a dowry of 'ten hundred thousand pounds Scots', supplied 'at once and delivered really into our hands immediately after the completing of the marriage'.[1] Although James's initial suggestion of a £1 million Scots dowry proved wildly optimistic, a generation later, in October 1612, his ambassador in Paris, Sir Thomas Edmondes, relayed private assurances that the French court was willing to offer a settlement of 800,000 crowns if James's heir, Prince Henry, married Marie de' Medici's second daughter, Christine.[2] Equivalent to around £240,000 sterling (or £2.8 million Scots) in 1612 – over £52 million in today's values – such a sum would have been the largest marriage settlement ever proposed by the French court. Since James's Chancellor had, only five months earlier, calculated the royal debt as standing at £500,000 – and the English Crown's annual deficit at £160,000 – significant financial and geopolitical dividends could potentially be reaped from successful dynastic diplomacy.

*

As James had advised Prince Henry in *Basilicon Doron*, marriage not only facilitated procreation but could also bring 'beauty, riches, and friendship by alliance'.[3] By 1603, the English court had not known a functioning royal family for over half a century, and James's credentials to succeed as English king had been strengthened by having three surviving children, Henry, Elizabeth and Charles, and the prospect of Queen Anna bearing yet more heirs. Progeny not only assured dynastic security but also diplomatic potential. As James's ambassador in Madrid, Sir Charles Cornwallis, observed in 1608, contemporary political wisdom admired 'princes with large posterity' for 'as many children as any king has, so many more baits they have' to tempt prospective partners in an exacting and highly restricted international marriage market.[4]

In Spain, Philip III responded to news of James's accession in April 1603 by resurrecting ideas of a future Habsburg–Stuart marriage alliance.[5] The following month, during a banquet held at Greenwich Palace, Henri IV of France's envoy, the Marquis of Rosny, confessed surprise when James 'told me softly' that he would drink a toast to 'the double union, which he meditated between the royal houses', envisaging a double marriage between Prince Henry and Princess Elizabeth and two of Henri IV's children. Not only had James 'never till now said a single word to me about this', but Rosny was well aware that Philip III had already 'applied to him upon the same subject'.[6]

French mistrust was warranted for, at another Whitehall banquet in August 1604 to celebrate conclusion of the Anglo-Spanish Treaty of London, James placed a diamond ring on the finger of the chief Spanish Habsburg representative, the Constable of Castile, to signify the new 'marriage' between the two countries.[7] By December, the Venetian ambassador in London was reporting 'a rumour is rife that there will be a match between the Prince of Wales and the Infanta, who will bring the Low Countries as her dower.'[8] For not only was the Infanta Ana María heiress to the Spanish throne – before the birth of her younger brother (later Philip IV) the following spring – but should Archduke and Archduchess Albert and Isabella die childless, rule over the Spanish Netherlands would also revert to Philip III. Following the return visit by English dignitaries to ratify the Treaty of London at Valladolid in 1605, Cornwallis dismissed rumours of an alternative Anglo-Florentine match for Prince Henry as insufficiently prestigious, insisting that James esteemed his heir 'worthy of the best fortune in marriage that this world can yield'.[9]

James's accession as English king in 1603 attracted a large international gathering of ambassadors; indeed, 'for a brief period, the chief ministers of the Netherlands, France and Britain were all in London, engaged in face-to-face negotiations over the future of their relationship.'[10] Elizabeth's death had occurred at a critical juncture in Spain's long-running war with the Dutch republic: although France and Spain had concluded a separate peace at the Treaty of Vervins in 1598, neither the Habsburg Archdukes nor the Dutch leaders could be sure that English financial and military assistance would continue under her successor. While James's instinctive disapproval of republican rebellion initially augured ill for the Dutch, after private meetings with the new king, both French and Dutch diplomats reported that James 'seemed to awake as if from a profound sleep' upon realizing 'the condition in which England would stand if the King of France or the King of Spain achieved peaceful possession of all seventeen provinces of the Netherlands'.[11]

During Elizabeth's reign, there had, moreover, been no resident Spanish diplomatic presence in London to compete with the French embassy for precedence at court entertainments. With diplomats constantly calibrating their treatment by host courts as indicative of underlying foreign-policy preferences, perceived favours or snubs could easily escalate. In January 1604, for instance, Queen Anna invited Philip III's envoy, the Count of Villamediana, to attend the Twelfth Night court performance of Samuel Daniel's masque *The Vision of Twelve Goddesses*, in which Anna herself danced the part of Pallas Athena, goddess of war. But as Villamediana reported to the Spanish court, the resident French ambassador, the comte de Beaumont, 'believed he had managed to score a hit against me' by inveigling a spontaneous invitation to the same event from James only to have it quickly rescinded thereafter.[12]

In Spain, Cornwallis hoped that the new Anglo-Spanish amity might be strengthened further through a marriage alliance. Writing to James's Principal Secretary, the Earl of Salisbury, in January 1607, the ambassador identified a Habsburg–Stuart match as 'the only sovereign medicine for the sick estate of this garboiled world': 'a composition of their pearl of Spain with our diamond of England'.[13] A year later, when she attended the performance of Ben Jonson's *The Masque of Beauty* at Whitehall, Queen Anna gave visible expression to Cornwallis's jewelled metaphor by conspicuously donning the dazzling diamond and gold collar gifted by Philip II to Mary Tudor on their marriage in 1554. Not only was Anna's jewellery choice clearly intended to compliment one of the court's distinguished guests – the resident Spanish ambassador,

Don Pedro de Zúñiga – but the failure to extend the same invitation to Zúñiga's French counterpart, Antoine Le Fèvre de la Boderie, provoked renewed outrage. Despite receiving a separate invitation to a private dinner with the royal family, as Boderie protested to Henri IV's court, since 'one is a private action, and the other a spectacle and public solemnity', observers 'would publish it throughout the whole of Christendom' were he to accept the inferior invitation.[14]

Having performed as a cupid in *The Masque of Beauty*, Prince Henry had moved centre-stage by the Jacobean court's Twelfth Night festivities in 1610 to assume the lead role in a masque scripted by Ben Jonson, with set designs by Inigo Jones. In *Prince Henry's Barriers*, Henry played 'Meliadus – Lord of the Isles', alluding to the medieval legend that had celebrated James as a new King Arthur, fulfilling Merlin's prophecy through the reunification of Britain. Five months later, Henry's parliamentary installation as Prince of Wales on 4 June 1610 denoted the first investiture of a Prince of Wales in England since the future Henry VIII's installation in 1504 and prompted lavish celebrations funded by a loan of £100,000 from the City of London.[15] Together with a tilting contest and a fireworks display, a mock naval battle took place on the River Thames in which 'Turkish' naval aggressors simulated an unsuccessful attack on 'English' merchant ships. A similar form of waterborne entertainment had been staged in Edinburgh in May 1562 by James's mother, Queen Mary, but the sea battle celebrating Henry's installation was the first to be held in London.[16]

The prince's parliamentary installation occurred less than a month after the shocking assassination of his godfather, Henri IV, by François Ravaillac, in May 1610. Ravaillac later defended his actions on the grounds that, as an erstwhile excommunicate, Henri was not only an illegitimate usurper failing in his divine duties by tolerating heretic Protestant Huguenots but had been about to compound his sinfulness by forming a cross-confessional alliance – involving England and the Dutch – to attack imperial and Spanish Habsburg forces in the religiously mixed Rhineland territories of Cleves-Jülich. Following Henri's assassination, however, militant Protestant hopes were transferred to his Stuart godson, who was often painted in armour and depicted alongside images of pikes and muskets.

Critics of James's pacifist rhetoric thus saw in Prince Henry a future military leader who would one day lead a crusade against England's

Catholic neighbours. In a Latin birth-poem written to celebrate Henry's arrival in 1594, the Scots Presbyterian Andrew Melville had predicted that the new prince, 'born of a Scoto-Britannic king', would 'press under your foot the triple crown of the papacy' and, with 'thunderbolts drive down ... the thrice cursed Pope, and the Italian, and the Iberian as well'.[17] At the English court, Henry became the focus for militant Protestant aspirations and, in 1608, was presented with a set of brief, but bellicose, 'Arguments for War' by his advisers. Concerned that the English nation might 'grow wanton through too much wealth and idleness', the tract's authors advocated overseas expansionism to generate 'honour, as the style of our kings, by confluence of so many titles increased; and by accession of so many territories'. In response, James commissioned a detailed rebuttal from the antiquarian scholar Sir Robert Cotton, which reviewed English military engagements and concluded by advising that 'it is the best for safety, and the most for honour, to remain as we were, arbiters of Europe, and so by neutrality sway still the balance of our mightiest neighbours'.[18] But safety and honour could also serve as euphemistic shorthand for penury. Writing to James's ambassador at The Hague, Sir Ralph Winwood, in June 1608, one of Winwood's agents remained pessimistic about continued English military support for the Dutch republic, acknowledging not only that 'his Majesty [is] a lover of Peace', but also that he was 'miserably poor, having not wherewithal to maintain his ordinary expenses, much less to feed a war'.[19]

Henri IV's assassination only intensified the martial expectations of James's heir. One French-born author, George Marcelline, acclaimed Prince Henry as 'the honour and ornament of your age' and 'a comet of dreadful terror' to England's enemies. Henry was, moreover, descended from an unbroken Stuart line of Scottish kings, as 'ever more royal eagles do produce imperial eagles, eagles that have continually made war with dragons, with foxes, and (above all) with serpents.' For Marcelline, Henry seemed 'a warrior already, both in gesture and countenance'.[20] Among over a hundred works dedicated to the prince was *The True Ancient Roman Catholic* (1611) by Robert Abbot, Master of Balliol College, Oxford, published in the same year that Abbot's younger brother, George, became Archbishop of Canterbury. Anticipating that Henry's 'princely name may more and more grow great, and may be a terror to that self-exalting kingdom and monarchy of the great Capitolian priest', Robert Abbot prayed that God would 'strengthen your arm, and give edge to your sword to strike through the loins of all of them that are the supporters of that Antichristian and wicked state'.[21]

*

In terms of dynastic diplomacy, it nevertheless remained the case – as James had admitted to Henry in *Basilicon Doron* – that 'the number of any princes of power and account, professing our religion, be but very small'.[22] The most lucrative marriage offers, rather, attached to Catholic brides. In 1611, a double Catholic marriage proposal was mooted by Duke Charles Emmanuel of Savoy, whereby the duke's eldest son, Victor Amadeus, would marry James's daughter, Princess Elizabeth, and Prince Henry would wed the duke's third daughter, Maria. The duke's envoy, the Count of Cartigiana, was dispatched twice to London to confirm the Savoyard offer of 700,000 crowns (around £210,000 sterling) if Henry married the Infanta Maria.[23] Although the double marriage proposal had been conceived by Duke Charles Emmanuel as a means of avoiding geopolitical isolation after the death of his main ally, Henri IV, James indicated to the English ambassador in Venice, Sir Henry Wotton, that he preferred to match Prince Henry 'and his sister severally than in one place' in order better to serve 'ourself and our posterity with many branches of alliance'.[24]

The premium deriving from multiple 'branches of alliance' was only underscored by the surprise announcement of the Franco-Spanish Treaty of Fontainebleau, concluded in April 1611. Ironically, the initial effect of Henri IV's assassination had been to reduce geopolitical tensions, as his widow and new Queen Regent, Marie de' Medici, swiftly reversed French foreign policy by opening secret negotiations with Philip III's court. As the first Franco-Spanish treaty of mutual assistance for a century and a half, the Treaty of Fontainebleau committed the erstwhile enemies to a ten-year defensive pact against foreign and domestic adversaries and ended mutual frontier disputes. The treaty also agreed preliminary arrangements for a double marriage between Philip's eldest daughter, the Infanta Ana Maurici, and the future Louis XIII, alongside a union between Marie de' Medici's eldest daughter, Elisabeth, and the future Philip IV. To confirm that these were held to be marriages between powers of equal status, identical dowries were agreed and both princesses renounced their rights of inheritance to avoid potential inequities posed by Salic law that barred the French Crown being transmitted through the female line.[25] Such a dynastic alliance had the potential radically to reconfigure European geopolitics, shifting the balance decisively in favour of Catholic powers. The proposed double Habsburg–Bourbon marriage was indeed an unexpected humiliation for James; as the ambassador representing the Spanish Netherlands in London reported, it was 'the rudest blow that this state could receive'.[26]

Having received indications that Philip III's ministers remained interested in a future Habsburg–Stuart alliance, James nevertheless had little option but to court Spanish greatness himself. Sent to Madrid in 1611, his ambassador, Sir John Digby, was soon perturbed by the Spanish court's evasiveness and – with the eldest Infanta already promised to the French Crown – was unconvinced that her six-year-old sister, the Infanta María Ana, offered a suitable match for Prince Henry, aged seventeen. Spanish deception extended further to fabricating rumours regarding a potential marriage between Henry's sister, Princess Elizabeth, and Philip III after the king's consort, Margaret of Austria, died in childbirth in September 1611. To suspicious colleagues in Madrid, Digby rejected reports that Philip intended to 'demand the Lady Elizabeth' as Spanish courtiers tried 'to blind the world' by confidently insisting that James's daughter would convert to Catholicism to facilitate the marriage.[27] But James consistently refused to consider any alliance for Princess Elizabeth that failed to guarantee free exercise of her Protestant faith – even if it came with an offer 'to make her Queen of the World'.[28]

Amid an apparent consolidation of confessional coalitions, in March 1612 James signed a defensive alliance treaty with the Protestant Evangelical Union, now led by the Palatine Elector Frederick V, who had succeeded his father two years earlier. Simultaneously, James also entertained proposals, advanced by the prominent Huguenot, Henri de La Tour d'Auvergne, Duke of Bouillon, of a marriage between Princess Elizabeth and Frederick, who had been raised in Bouillon's household in the Protestant principality of Sedan. By May, marriage terms had been agreed for Elizabeth and Frederick, who – unusually for early modern royal marriages – were the same age, having been born within days of each other in August 1596. The marriage treaty stipulated that James would pay a settlement of £40,000 sterling within two years of the marriage and would also commit, with Frederick, to provide regular contributions to cover the future expenses of Elizabeth and her retinue.[29]

Later that summer, Prince Henry concluded the annual progress season by hosting a lavish banquet for his father, mother and sister in a

14. A half-length painting derived from a full-length portrait by the Flemish-born artist John de Critz, painted shortly after James's accession as English king. In his hat, the king wears the 'Mirror of Great Britain', which incorporated jewels from the Scottish and English royal collections to symbolize the new regal union.

15. Queen Anna, painted in the early 1600s by a member of the 'English School'.

16. Henry, Prince of Wales, by Nicolas Hilliard, c. 1610; the prince is depicted wearing a suit of gilt armour in the imagined setting of a military encampment.

17. Charles, Prince of Wales, by Daniel Mytens, painted shortly after the prince's return from Spain in 1623.

18. Frederick V and Elizabeth lived in Dutch exile after their ejection as king and queen of Bohemia. In this watercolour by the Dutch artist Adriaen van de Venne, James's son-in-law and daughter are showing riding near The Hague in the early 1620s.

19. Statue of James by John Clark, carved in 1620 and erected on the Tower of the Five Orders of Architecture in the Old Schools Quadrangle of the Bodleian Library, University of Oxford.

20. 'Paul's Cross', in St Paul's churchyard in the City of London, was the most prominent public pulpit in Jacobean England. Painted in 1616, John Gipkin's depiction was part of a diptych that showed James and Anna listening to a sermon from a raised gallery. Smoking chimneys from houses built against the cathedral's nave waft the caption: 'View, O king: how my wall-creepers / Have made me work for chimney-sweepers'.

21. Engraving of Pocahontas by the Dutch artist Simon van der Passe, published posthumously in *Baziliωlogia: A Book of Kings* (London, 1618).

22. The first known illustration of an Englishman smoking tobacco appeared in Anthony Chute's *Tobacco* (1595); James's first publication as king of England was *A Counterblaste to Tobacco* (1604).

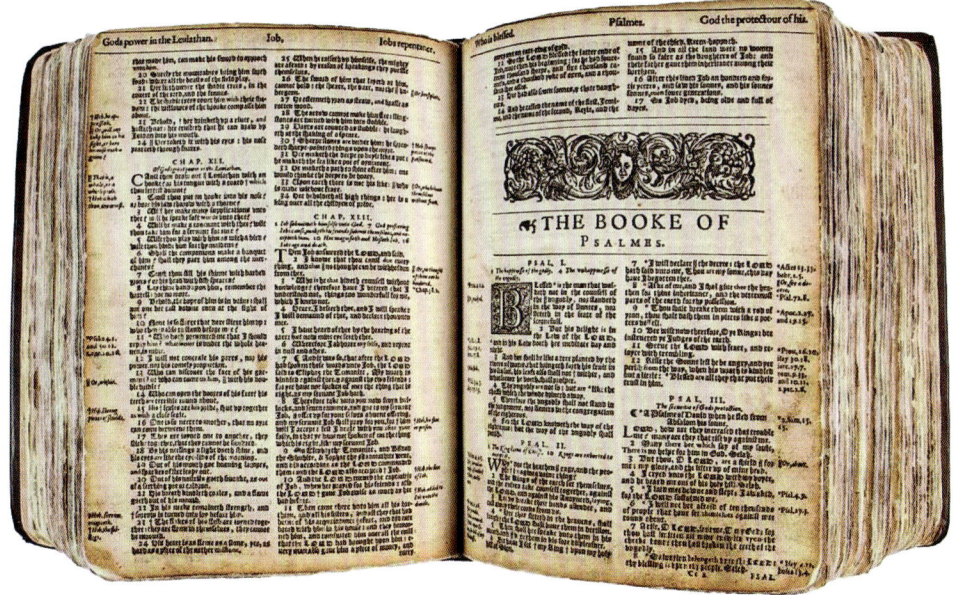

23. An edition of the 'King James Version' of the Bible, published in 1620 and brought to North America by the English cooper and settler John Alden, who travelled aboard the *Mayflower*.

24. *Above left:* Undated letter from George Villiers to James. After receiving serial missives from the king, Villiers ventures that he has 'made a hundred answers to them in my mind'.

25. *Above right:* Miniature heart-shaped portrait of James, undated, attributed to Lawrence Hilliard.

My onlie sweete & deare chylde notwithstanding of youre desyring me not to wryte yesterdaye, yett hadde I written in the evening, if at my coming in out of the parke, suche a drowsie headache had not comed upon me, as I was forced to sitt in my chaire, halfe an houre & could not contente my selfe withowte sending to yow, praying god that I maye have a ioyfull & comfortable meeting with you, & that wee maye make this christenmasse a newe marriage, ever to be kept heareafter, for god so love me, as I desire only to live in this worlde for youre saike, & that I hadde rather live banished in anie pairte of the worlde with you, then live a sorrowefull widowes lyfe without you, & so god blesse you my sweete chylde & wyfe & grante that ye maye ever be a comforte to youre deare dade & husbande

James R

26. *Left:* Letter from James to Villiers, now Duke of Buckingham (December 1623 or 1624), hoping that they might make 'a new marriage ever to be kept hereafter' and admitting that 'I desire only to live in this world for your sake'.

27. *Above:* Painted before October 1621, Anthony van Dyck's racy double portrait presented Villiers and his wife, Katherine Manners, as 'Venus and Adonis'.

28. Portrait of James holding an orb and sceptre and wearing his coronation robes and the collar and badge of the Order of the Garter. Painted in 1620 by the Flemish artist Paul van Somer, its backdrop was the new Banqueting House, designed by Inigo Jones and commissioned by James the previous year. When construction was completed in 1622, architectural details on the building's façade differed from those imagined by van Somer.

timber banqueting house erected in the gardens of his newly acquired Oxfordshire residence, Woodstock Palace. In a halcyon display of cultural creativity, the food was served in reverse seasonal order, starting with meat for winter, pies for autumn, fruit for summer and concluding with spring water for diners to rinse their hands. After Christmas dances, the post-prandial entertainment comprised an autumn 'antic of drunkards', a summer 'country dance of haymakers or reapers' and springtime Morris-dancing.[30] Being 'so much amazed at the sight' of his son's sophisticated hospitality at Woodstock, James reportedly conceded that he had 'never seen the like before all his lifetime, and that he could never do so much in his own house'.[31]

Meanwhile, James continued to receive flattering offers in the dynastic marriage market. To outbid his Savoyard counterparts, the Grand Duke of Tuscany, Cosimo II, proposed his sister, Caterina de' Medici, as a bride for Prince Henry, together with a settlement of a million crowns. While the Savoyards fretted that, despite the lack of dynastic prestige, James's notorious penury might incline him to accept a more lucrative offer from their Tuscan rivals, Queen Anna – who was, after all, the daughter, sister and wife of different kings in her own right – objected that, as a prospective daughter-in-law, 'she would prefer a Princess of France without a dower to a Florentine Princess with any amount of gold they might offer.'[32] It was at this juncture that James was informed by his ambassador in Paris, Sir Thomas Edmondes, that Marie de' Medici was considering a sum of 800,000 crowns as a settlement were Henry to marry her second daughter, Christine. In September 1612, Edmondes wrote to Henry, relaying James's wish to 'hear what your Highness's free opinion is of this particular compared with the others'. Replying to his father, Henry indicated that 'betwixt France and Savoy, if your Majesty look to the greatness of the dowry, then it is likely you will make choice of Savoy', but if he considered 'which of these two will give the greatest contentment and satisfaction to the general body of Protestants abroad', the French suit seemed preferable. Excusing his apparent indifference, Henry explained his wish to defer to James 'to resolve what course is most convenient to be taken by the rules of state'; as things stood, 'my part to play, which is to be in love with any of them, is not yet at hand'.[33]

Disaster struck, however, when Henry became ill – probably suffering from typhoid fever – and died on 6 November 1612, aged eighteen. Writing to his Danish brother-in-law the following day, James struggled to articulate 'the grief which we can scarcely express out loud'. Aware of his duty to inform Christian IV promptly of his nephew's death, James admitted that 'we are still so confused by the distress and sorrow from this most serious and unexpected misfortune that we could scarcely collect our thoughts for the brief moment while we were communicating about what had to be made known to you.'[34] Henry's distraught sister, Princess Elizabeth, refused food for several days and Queen Anna was grief-stricken. The Venetian ambassador, Antonio Foscarini, observed an anguished King James trying to continue with royal business, but 'even in the midst of the most important discussions, he will burst out with "Henry is dead, Henry is dead."'[35]

For a month after his death, Henry's encoffined body lay in state in St James's Palace, where his corpse was attended by ten courtiers at a time with the 'same service and order of meals as when he was alive'.[36] On 7 December, funeral ceremonies were simultaneously held in Bristol, Cambridge and Oxford, while a procession of 2,000 mourners, led by Henry's twelve-year-old brother, Prince Charles, accompanied the prince's coffin to Westminster Abbey, alongside a fife and drums which were normally reserved for military heroes who had died in action. While both James and Anna absented themselves from their eldest son's funeral, the solemnities were described by one eyewitness as conducted 'truly with much magnificence but with more grief than any was these many hundred years'.[37] One diplomat, Isaac Wake, confessed to never having 'seen such a sight of mortification in my life' nor known such shared sorrow among spectators 'whose streaming eyes made known how much inwardly their hearts did bleed'.[38]

Henry's sudden death encouraged inevitable conjectures as to the spectacular – if speculative – renaissance of cultural splendour and military dominance confidently forecast to have accompanied his future reign as Henry IX. As Foscarini described to the Venetian Doge and Senate, since 'many predictions centred around his person, and he seemed marked out for great events', Henry's posthumous memory became a palimpsest for others' ambitions, hopes and expectations, exacerbated by the prince's deathbed order to destroy his private papers. Being 'athirst for glory if ever any prince was', Henry's 'whole talk had been of arms and war'; consequently his 'death will certainly cause great changes in the course of the world'.[39]

In London, the Spanish noblewoman and missionary, Luisa de

Carvajal y Mendoza, surveyed James's remaining progeny and advised her cousin-in-law Don Rodrigo Calderón (secretary to Philip III's favourite, the Duke of Lerma), that 'all there is left here is a half-consumptive child [Prince Charles] and the sister is no better than the old Queen Elizabeth.' Insisting that 'despite everything, there is time to prevent the marriage' of James's daughter to the Palatine Elector Frederick V, Carvajal was alarmed that the 'Palatine, a bad chip off the old Calvinist block, is as close as he can be to becoming King of England'. Mindful of her recent efforts to recover as relics the mutilated bodies of Catholic priests executed on James's orders, Carvajal feared that if such persecution was taking place under 'a prince who right now is so weak, how is it to be sorted out with one who is much stronger?'[40] More immediately, Henry's death also meant that hopes for an imminent and lucrative marriage dowry evaporated, underscoring the seriousness of James's financial woes. As John Chamberlain admitted, a fortnight after the prince's demise, there was now no means of 'helping ourselves by his marriage, and stopping the gap of our wants for the present by that way, so that we must of necessity have recourse to a Parliament'.[41]

*

But James did not believe that death should derail dynastic diplomacy. Just over a month after Henry's demise, the king admitted to Edmondes that it seemed 'a very blunt thing' to continue negotiations with Marie de' Medici's ministers about 'marriage, the most contrary thing that could be to death and funerals'. Since the twelve-year-old Prince Charles made a better suitor than Henry for the six-year-old Bourbon princess, Christine, James thus directed Edmondes to approach the subject in such a way as simultaneously to avoid conveying any impression 'that we are become greedy in urging it' or that the French might be deterred by 'our slowness and averseness in it'.[42] Meanwhile in London, the newly arrived Palatine Elector Frederick was accorded a prominent place behind Prince Charles in the funeral cortège for Prince Henry before being made a Knight of the Garter at a private ceremony in December. Investing a German Elector into England's highest knightly order not only supplied confirmation of James's determination to uphold the Protestant Palatine alliance, but also provided the foreign-born Frederick with a symbolic compliment of the type denied to James by Elizabeth I during the 1590s when, as King of Scotland, he had persistently hoped for elevation to an English dukedom or commensurate title of honour.

Official mourning for Prince Henry ended just before Princess Elizabeth's marriage to Frederick was publicly solemnized in the royal chapel at Whitehall on St Valentine's Day, 14 February 1613, following the couple's private marriage in the Banqueting House the previous month.[43] Promising a pan-Protestant bulwark against Catholic Habsburg domination, Elizabeth and Frederick's marriage was invested by militant Protestants with eschatological significance after Henry's death had dramatically docked the line of succession. Given that James's own health was doubtful and Prince Charles was known to be physically frail, there was – as Carvajal had recognized – a plausible prospect that the princess might, one day, reign as Queen Elizabeth II. With her husband Frederick's Imperial electoral dignities and Palatine territories, the couple could rule a single Protestant state with territories strategically situated in the centre of the Holy Roman Empire with Atlantic, colonial and maritime access. Six weeks before the wedding, Carvajal had made a sarcastic swipe at the king's sexuality by warning Calderón that James 'likes the son-in-law so much that they have got one bed between them already'. A month after the nuptials, she reported James's apparent determination 'to make the Palsgrave a king'; when asked by courtiers to name a suitable territory, James reportedly suggested – with unnerving prescience – 'Bohemia'.[44]

The first royal wedding to be staged in England since Mary Tudor had married Philip II of Spain in 1554, Elizabeth's marriage to Frederick was celebrated with courtly entertainments including banquets, masques, fireworks displays and mock naval battles on the Thames exceeding in scale those devised for Prince Henry's parliamentary installation three years earlier. The resident French ambassador, the sieur de Buisseaux, described how spectators lined the banks of the River Thames to watch over twenty simulated sea battles between 'Christians' and 'Turks', with the former sailing in 'twenty-five or thirty well-equipped ships bearing the flags of England, Scotland, Ireland, Venice and the Palatinate'.[45] In a published account of the festivities, the Thames waterman-cum-poet John Taylor explained that, while these mock encounters were meant to recall the famous Christian victory at the Battle of Lepanto in 1571, fought in similar 'bloody manner was the memorable battle betwixt us and the invincible (as it was thought) Spanish Armada in the year 1588'.[46]

Providential significance was indeed attached to the timing of Elizabeth's marriage, which coincided with the twenty-fifth anniversary of the English victory over the Armada secured by the princess's godmother, Elizabeth I. Fortunately perhaps, the resident Spanish ambassador in London, Don Alonso de Velasco, had declined his invitation to the festivities, refusing to attend any event at which the Dutch republic's representative might be present since Spain did not recognize the Dutch state's sovereignty. By excusing his absence on the grounds that the public wedding date fell within Lent – at least according to the Gregorian calendar – Velasco also avoided the decorations adorning the temporary structure erected for dinner guests: gigantic Delft-woven tapestries celebrating the Armada's defeat, which had been commissioned in the 1590s by the Navy's Lord High Admiral, the Earl of Nottingham, and acquired by James for the royal collection in 1612, but were later destroyed by the Palace of Westminster fire in 1834. Deeming the décor an outrageous insult, Carvajal objected to the tapestries' depictions of Englishmen 'killing Spaniards and triumphing over them ignominiously . . . how nice of them to invite the Spanish ambassador to eat there!'[47]

Ceremonial spectacle aside, the primary objective of royal marriages was to secure dynastic succession. Accordingly, on the morning after the wedding, Chamberlain reported James's visit to the two 'young turtles that were coupled on St Valentines' Day', where he addressed Frederick and 'did strictly examine him whether he were his true son-in-law, and was sufficiently assured'.[48] More eloquent was John Donne, whose ingenious *Epithalamion*, or 'marriage-song', for Elizabeth and Frederick celebrated the suitability of Valentine's Day for a marriage, being the day on which birds choose their mates. Donne conjured the newlyweds not as two larks, doves, goldfinches or sparrows, but as two phoenixes, sidestepping the mythological constraint whereby only a single phoenix can ever exist at one time by seeing the consummation of Frederick and Elizabeth's marriage as creating a united whole. Donne imagined the Palatine Elector approaching 'first her sheets, then her arms, then anywhere' while courtiers outside the royal apartments laid wagers as to 'whose hand it is / That opens first a curtain, hers or his'.[49]

As Elizabeth and Frederick prepared to depart for Heidelberg, Foscarini observed that James 'seemed to feel their departure keenly, and said he hoped to see them soon again, and with offspring', musing that his daughter and new son-in-law 'were both born in the same year and in the month of August, and had not yet finished their seventeenth year. All this he said with great tenderness.'[50] In mid-April, as Elizabeth waited in Canterbury for a westerly wind to set sail, James received one of the most affectionate epistles that he ever received from any of his children. Writing in French, the new Electress acknowledged that 'I shall possibly never, as long as I live, again see the flower of princes, the king of fathers, the best and most gracious father under the sun.'[51]

Correct in her prediction, Elizabeth never saw James, her mother or brother again. But pan-Protestant dynastic hopes were fulfilled when she and Frederick produced a son, Prince Henry Frederick, on New Year's Day 1614, named in honour of his deceased uncle, German father, and Danish grandfather, Frederick II. Opening a new English Parliament that April, James acknowledged to MPs and peers that, although God had taken Prince Henry from him, 'he has given me now, not long after, a grandson'. Moreover, in a startling reversal of his earlier published pronouncements regarding the transcendent capacity of hereditary claims to trump any statutory provision regarding the English succession, James directed Parliament to confirm the naturalization and succession rights of Elizabeth, Frederick and their heirs. For should Prince Charles die without issue, James insisted that his daughter 'and the issue male of her body are to succeed in this imperial crown'.[52]

Although James had hoped that the parliament opened in April 1614 might become known as the 'Parliament of Love', it lasted only forty-three days before being dissolved. On the last day of its meeting, one MP, John Dackombe, had urged members to approve financial supply for the Crown, given James's 'power to match his son, so as he shall not want [supply]'.[53] Denying James financial assistance would leave the king little option but to pursue a lucrative – and Catholic – match for Prince Charles. The previous year, a new, charismatic Spanish ambassador had arrived in England – Don Diego Sarmiento de Acuña, later ennobled as the Count of Gondomar – with instructions to tempt James's court away from a Bourbon marriage settlement by resuscitating plans for a Spanish match, assisted by 'such quantity of gold as should please His Majesty', claiming that Philip III was 'willing to give four times as much dowry' as the French.[54] Sarmiento was confident that a Habsburg bid could gain traction, given English opposition to a French bride; as he reported in

January 1614, a majority of Privy Councillors 'cry out' against an agreement with Paris, believing that 'the Scots, by this match (being so favoured in France), will be preferred in authority and favour before them'.[55]

Attempts were also made in Paris, by James's ambassador, Edmondes, to dissuade Louis XIII from realizing the double Bourbon–Habsburg marriage agreed with Spain in 1612. In a representation to the French court in June 1615, later published in French and English, Edmondes relayed the British king's concern that the fourteen-year-old French king had not yet reached 'that maturity of years and judgement, requisite and necessary for your direction in the choice of your wife and associate'. To James's mind, Louis was being 'precipitated into the yoke of marriage, to the manifest prejudice of your health, and (maybe) of your contentment and affairs'. While the French king's regency government retained only a fragile control of internal affairs, a Bourbon–Habsburg dynastic union would alienate France's long-standing allies and risk 'a general combustion throughout all Christendom'.[56] That November, however, Louis fulfilled the terms of the Treaty of Fontainebleau by marrying Philip III's daughter, Ana, while his sister, Elisabeth, wed the future Philip IV of Spain. The double nuptials took place on pontoons symbolically erected in the middle of the Bidasoa River on the Franco-Spanish border.[57]

*

Although dynastic diplomacy thereafter continued intermittently on Prince Charles's behalf, the prospect of a Catholic queen consort presented inescapable difficulties. Notwithstanding his various attempts to secure prestigious matches for his sons, James himself had advised Prince Henry in *Basilicon Doron* that he would 'rather have you to marry one that were fully of your own religion; her rank and other qualities being agreeable to your estate'. While 'disagreement in religion brings ever with it, disagreement in manners' when a royal couple were known to adhere to different faiths, difficulties also inevitably arose over the education of their children and religious divisions among their subjects were implicitly encouraged.[58] During the king's progress to Scotland in 1617, his Secretary of State, Sir Ralph Winwood, confided to the Venetian Secretary his belief that James could readily secure significant financial supply from Parliament if he instead pursued a domestic, Protestant alliance for his son. Winwood ventured that 'neither Spain nor France can give so large a dower to the prince in ready money as these people will provide if he takes one of themselves'. Marriage to a suitable noblewoman would further ensure that 'the door will be shut upon all the disadvantages' likely to arise 'by the introduction of a foreign woman'.[59] Winwood's death five months later removed one of James's most vocal opponents to a Spanish Habsburg match for Charles, but the prospect also found little favour with the prince's uncle, Christian IV, whose ambassador relayed the Danish king's concern 'that it was sacrificing the prince to marry him to Spain'. As Queen Anna related 'in great confidence' to a Venetian envoy, her brother's intervention had 'greatly offended' James whose riposte had been that 'he chose to dispose of his children according to his own fancy.' By 1618, however, Anna distrusted serial Spanish over-tures as strategic temporizing and resented 'the immense sums of money' distributed by Gondomar who, 'being vastly sagacious and crafty, had spoiled and corrupted the whole court'.[60]

The queen's scepticism was shared by the Keeper of the State Papers, Sir Thomas Wilson, who was tasked with reviewing government records relating to previous royal marriages. To James, Wilson was careful to present his findings neutrally, insisting that his research was 'a child of my pains, rather than of my brains, and a work of my pen in transcrib-ing, collecting, and abstracting, rather than of my judgment in devising and contriving'. To James's ambassador in Paris, however, Wilson was clear that Spanish marriage diplomacy only ever sought 'to divert us from France by amusing us with great offers which in the end will prove *parturiunt montes* [a pointless labour]'.[61] Pursued to achieve particular strategic objectives, Habsburg dynastic diplomacy was just as quickly abandoned if those priorities shifted. Moreover, even when secured, as in the case of Mary Tudor's marriage to Philip II in 1554, Wilson contended that Spain's sole motivation had been to avert an Anglo-French alliance.

The outbreak of continental war in 1618 inevitably heightened the stakes of dynastic diplomacy. Although serial marriage discussions between London and Madrid had created well-worn channels for dip-lomatic communication, Frederick V's decision to accept the crown of Bohemia – jestingly suggested by James six years earlier – led to the invasion of his Palatine territories by Spanish Habsburg forces and, following defeat at the Battle of White Mountain in 1620, his expul-sion, with Elizabeth, into Dutch exile. Although James continued to suggest that pursuing a Spanish marriage for Prince Charles offered a diplomatic route to secure restitution of the Palatine territories to his son-in-law and daughter, the king's subjects were more sceptical. In September 1621, the Venetian ambassador Girolamo Lando reported that James often inveighed against the Spanish: 'as usual, he cries out against them and afterwards caresses them', while likewise 'exclaims almost constantly against the Palatine [Frederick] although, in this, his manner of speaking and writing changes every hour'. Lando also relayed rumours that James had displayed 'great agitation and passion in his bedchamber recently, swearing and declaring that everyone was betraying him and adding that he would never believe anyone again'.[62]

In 1623, the impromptu decision of Prince Charles and the king's favourite, the Marquis of Buckingham, to travel to the Spanish court ultimately served to liquidate, rather than expedite, Stuart–Habsburg marriage negotiations. Returning to London from their six-month sojourn in Madrid with neither a Spanish bride nor lucrative dowry, Charles and Buckingham thereafter promoted an increasingly bellicose policy that favoured a French royal marriage with potential access to Louis XIII's sizeable army as a means of confronting Habsburg aggression in central Europe. In London, the Venetian ambassador accounted James to be, by May 1624, 'a poor old man who once knew how to rule, but now knows nothing about it'.[63] In quantitative terms, the perceived worth of a Stuart prince as a marriage partner nevertheless remained unchanged. According to the treaty concluded in Paris in November 1624, Louis XIII agreed a dowry of 800,000 crowns for Charles to marry Princess Christine's younger sister, Princess Henrietta Maria. Five weeks after James's death, Charles I and Henrietta Maria were married in a ceremony at Nôtre-Dame in Paris on 1 May 1625, with the new king's kinsman, the Duke of Chevreuse, acting as his proxy.

21

It Will Cause Scandal

In a biography of James entitled *The Wisest Fool*, published in 1958, William McElwee recounted the well-known anecdote in which a young Scots courtier, Robert Carr, injured himself when falling from his horse during an Accession Day tilting contest in March 1607, instantly captivating his middle-aged king. James's infatuation with his new court favourite saw Carr quickly elevated to become, by 1614, Lord Chamberlain, Keeper of the Privy Seal, a *de facto* Secretary of State and son-in-law to the Lord High Treasurer, Thomas Howard, Earl of Suffolk. As McElwee judged – somewhat hysterically – 'thus, by James's folly, in one afternoon the whole pattern of English politics and of English history was changed, immeasurably for the worse.'[1]

Although the long-term course of English history may not have been irredeemably derailed by the king's involvement with Carr, James himself was devastated when their intimacy soured. Writing to Carr in early 1615, James bewailed his 'fiery boutades [outbursts]' which were 'coupled with a continual dogged sullen behaviour towards me; especially shortly after my fall' – a riding accident the previous autumn in which the king's horse had landed on him – that contrasted so starkly with the solicitous care that the king had shown 'after your fall and in all the times of your other diseases'. James insisted that he had never suffered such intense anguish, protesting before 'Almighty God that I have borne this grief within me to the uttermost of my ability'. Indeed, the king hoped that Carr's changed affections would not result in the 'hastening of his death, through grief' of someone who had 'many a time prayed for you, which I never did for no subject alive but for you'. Such was the depth of James's despair that he had felt suicidal and risked 'committing an unpardonable sin against God in consuming myself wilfully'. But as

James knew, his death would seriously endanger his subjects' security and 'even the estate of religion through all Christendom, which almost wholly under God lies now upon my shoulders'.[2] His personal torment could not be detached from inescapable royal responsibilities.

Notwithstanding the outwardly smooth transfer of power that had accompanied James's accession as English king in 1603, Carr's meteoric rise – and equally swift fall – revealed significant differences between Tudor and Stuart governance. The Elizabethan court had maintained a clear separation between state business conducted in the Privy Chamber and the predominantly female sphere comprising the queen's privy lodging. On Elizabeth's death, the English acquired a male adult monarch accustomed to presiding over a relatively informal Scottish court, with similarities to its French counterpart in offering relatively free and open access to courtiers and senior nobles. At Whitehall, James created a new Bedchamber department, staffed entirely by Scots, which became key to facilitating royal access, shaping political patronage, and determining policy. As the Venetian Secretary, Scaramelli, observed as early as May 1603, Elizabeth's erstwhile ministers were quickly accused of 'having sold England to the Scots, for no Englishman, be his rank what it may, can enter the Presence Chamber without being summoned, whereas the Scottish Lords have free *entrée* of the Privy Chamber, and more especially at the toilette', where state and other matters were easily and privately discussed with James.[3] While the Earl of Salisbury continued the model of an Elizabethan bureaucrat minister of state who liaised closely with Privy Councillors, his death in 1612 saw the axis of Jacobean politics shift decisively thereafter towards James's Bedchamber 'favourites', notably Carr between 1612 and 1615, followed by George Villiers, later Duke of Buckingham. Viewed through the prism of the king's relationship with Carr, the destabilizing politics of court scandal and its repercussions on Jacobean politics during the 1610s are revealed.

*

Born in Scotland in the mid-1580s, Robert Carr was the youngest son of a Border laird, Sir Thomas Ker of Ferniehirst, who had supported the Marian cause during the civil wars, but died in 1586 after being detained for reported involvement in the death of an Elizabethan courtier. Several years earlier, James had intervened to prevent Robert's older sister, Anne Ker, from marrying his close ally George Gordon, Earl of Huntly, to ensure that Huntly instead married Henrietta Stewart, daughter of Esmé Stewart, Duke of Lennox, thereby avoiding the creation of a new and potentially threatening Highland-Border dynasty.[4] Having joined the household of George Home, later Earl of Dunbar, Robert Ker travelled south with the royal court in 1603, anglicized the spelling of his surname from Ker to Carr, and obtained a courtier's position as a Groom of the Bedchamber in 1604.

Following his tiltyard accident in March 1607, Carr was knighted on Christmas Eve and, in March 1608, received from James 'a tablet of gold set with diamonds, and the king's picture' for which a payment of £300 sterling was recorded in the state papers.[5] In his *Traditional Memoirs* of James's reign published in 1658, Francis Osborne noted the lucrative gifts and estates that Carr received from James and described how Salisbury, having received 'a peremptory warrant' to make £20,000 sterling as a gift for Carr, 'laid the former mentioned sum upon the ground in a room through which his Majesty was to pass: who, amazed at the quantity, as a sight not impossibly his eyes never saw before, asked the Treasurer whose money it was'. When Salisbury replied that the money had been James's before being gifted to Carr, 'the king fell into passion, protesting he was abused, never intending any such gift: and casting himself upon the heap, scrambled out the quantity of two or three hundred pounds, and swore he should have no more'. But since Carr was 'the king's minion', the Treasurer dared 'not provoke him further than by permitting him only the moiety [half]'.[6] In March 1611, Carr was elevated as Viscount Rochester and Baron Winwick, thus becoming the first Scot to receive an English title, conferring a right to sit in the House of Lords. As one observer grumbled to James's ambassador in Venice, the new favourite 'hath broken the ice', so 'who and what will follow, God knows.'[7]

What followed in May was Carr's installation as a Knight of the Garter, filling the place of his former patron, the Earl of Dunbar, who had died in January. In April 1612, Carr, as Dunbar's protégé, became an English Privy Councillor, prompting a Council clerk to describe him as 'the bright sun of our firmament, at whose splendour or glooming, all our marigolds of the court open or shut'.[8] He was evidently also a fragrant lodestar who secured from James's physician 'a concoction of roses, coriander, aromatic reeds, musk, amber and civet' as a means of counteracting the odour that the viscount claimed was generated by diamond necklaces on his clothes.[9]

Rochester's ascendancy coincided with the emergence of a significant power vacuum at James's court with the death in 1611 of Dunbar, followed the next year by that of Salisbury, who had simultaneously served as Principal Secretary, Lord Treasurer, Master of the Court of Wards and *de facto* head of the Privy Council. In written reflections on his role, Salisbury had acknowledged that, lacking formal remit or commission, 'the place of a Secretary is dreadful, if he serve not a constant prince'. Secrecy and mutual trust were paramount. As Salisbury conceived, so long as a monarch and Secretary could be confident that all political matters were discussed entirely confidentially, their working relationship was comparable 'to the mutual affection of two lovers, undiscovered to their friends'.[10] After Salisbury's death, James entrusted English Treasury responsibilities to six commissioners led by Henry Howard, Earl of Northampton, but the king seemed disinclined to appoint a new Principal Secretary immediately. As John Chamberlain observed, despite 'the multitude of competitors for the Secretaryship', the king 'makes no haste to nominate any, but says he is pretty skilled in the craft himself, and till he be thoroughly weary, he will execute it in person'.[11]

Within James's administration, the crypto-Catholic Northampton headed one faction of influence that believed the Crown's financial difficulties were best addressed by promoting lucrative projects and securing a sizeable Spanish dowry for Prince Charles through a Habsburg–Stuart marriage alliance. Staunchly opposed to such views was a rival grouping of disaffected magnates, including the earls of Southampton and Pembroke, who instead advocated restoring good working relations with the English Parliament to secure financial supply. Political rivalries became conflated with personal affections when, by 1613, it emerged that Rochester sought to marry Northampton's great-niece Frances Howard, whose earlier marriage in 1606 to Robert Devereux, third Earl of Essex, had been overseen by James in an unsuccessful attempt to reconcile antagonistic court factions. While Northampton now identified his great-niece as 'that dainty pot of glue' able to effect a potent alliance between his family and Rochester, the liaison was bitterly resented by another courtier, Sir Thomas Overbury, who was a long-standing friend of Rochester's, described by one contemporary as his 'bedfellow, minion and inward counsellor'.[12]

With both the king and Overbury increasingly dependent, emotionally, on Rochester, Overbury incurred royal displeasure when he declined the offer of a royal embassy, potentially to Muscovy, Brussels or Paris. Privately, Chamberlain inferred that the king wanted to dispatch Overbury overseas to remove his sway over Rochester: it was unconducive to royal majesty 'that the world should have an opinion that Rochester ruled him and Overbury ruled Rochester'.[13] For refusing the royal embassy, Overbury was imprisoned in the Tower of London, from where he sent threatening missives to Rochester. Having assisted Rochester in his courting of Frances Howard, Overbury was furious to observe how he 'fell in love with that woman, as soon as you had won her by my letters' and now intended 'a marriage with that woman'. Alluding to their own relationship, Overbury charged Rochester with being seemingly ready to 'forget him betwixt whom was nine years' love, and such secrets of all kinds have passed'.[14]

Meanwhile, although James warmly supported his favourite's desire to marry 'that woman', it required nullification of the earlier Howard–Essex union. Accordingly, a commission of senior clerics was appointed to hear Howard's request that the marriage be annulled on the grounds of non-consummation. When the Archbishop of Canterbury, George Abbot, proved reluctant to pronounce Howard a virgin and Essex impotent, James intervened, rejecting as 'preposterous' the objection that a nullity could not be granted without specific Scriptural warrant. As James insisted, similar claims might be made in regard to 'many points betwixt the papists and us [Protestants]' concerning matters 'never mentioned by the Fathers, because they could never have dreamed that such questions would arise'. For his part, James supported Howard's claim that Essex could plausibly be suffering selective impotence – evidenced only in relation to his wife – as a result of *maleficium* or bewitchment. Directing Abbot to 'look [at] my Demonology' to learn more about how new forms of witchcraft emerged, James also warned that refusing the nullity would leave Howard and Essex 'forcibly kept together . . . forced to live in perpetual scandal or misery, or both'.[15]

Given the commission's need to establish whether consummation had occurred, Chamberlain invited a correspondent to imagine senior Church of England clerics 'in open audience demand' of Essex 'whether he had affection, erection, application, penetration, ejaculation with a great deal of amplification upon every one of these points'.[16] Following the addition of more pliant prelates to the clerical commission, the nullity was granted on 25 September 1613, ten days after Overbury had died, while still a prisoner in the Tower of London.

In November, James elevated Rochester further by naming him Earl of Somerset and Baron Brancepeth. A month later, Somerset and Frances Howard were married in the royal chapel at Whitehall, on 26 December 1613, in the same venue and by the same celebrant (Dean James Montagu) who had married Howard and Essex nearly eight years earlier. A fortnight of seasonal festivities concluded with a performance of the anonymously authored *The Masque of Flowers* at the Banqueting House, paid for by James's new Attorney-General, Sir Francis Bacon. The only time that a real garden appeared on the Jacobean stage, *The Masque of Flowers* celebrated James as the 'great sun of our firmament' whose divinely endowed omnipotence enabled the magical appearance of a magnificent spring garden in the midst of winter.[17]

By 1614, Somerset was at the peak of his political dominance. After the death in June of his wife's great-uncle the Earl of Northampton, Somerset received Northampton's former offices of Lord Privy Seal and Warden of the Cinque Ports before succeeding his father-in-law as Lord Chamberlain when the Earl of Suffolk was appointed Lord Treasurer. With Somerset controlling all royal patronage and his father-in-law determining all monetary rewards, James rhetorically asked, 'do not ye two, as it were, hedge in all the court with a manner of necessity to depend upon you?'[18]

As the 'Howard faction' exerted growing sway over Jacobean politics, covert negotiations resumed for a 'Spanish match' for Prince Charles. With the new Spanish ambassador in London, Diego Sarmiento de Acuña, enthusiastically welcoming the prospect of a separate Stuart–Habsburg match, James and Somerset avoided consulting other Privy Councillors but directed the English ambassador in Madrid, Sir John Digby, to devise provisional marriage conditions to be considered by the Spanish Council of State, its theological junta and the papacy. When Digby returned proposed terms in early 1615, James declared himself indifferent to the need for papal approval and suggested that Philip III should 'procure what dispensations he pleases, as may suit his conscience, it being a thing with which I have nothing to do'. To the Spanish insistence that all religious members of the Infanta's household in England be permitted to wear their clerical habits, however, James pithily retorted 'it will cause scandal.'[19]

*

Potential scandal, however, lay much closer to home as James's personal relationship with Somerset started to deteriorate. Marriage to Frances Howard may have prompted a change in the earl's affections, together with resentment at James's interest in a likely new favourite, George Villiers, whom the king had first met while staying at Apethorpe Palace in Northamptonshire in August 1614. Villiers's introduction had been contrived by a group of Somerset's opponents including Archbishop Abbot who, in memoirs penned in 1627, admitted trying to find measures to alleviate a 'kingdom groaning under the [inter-related] triumvirate of Northampton, Suffolk and Somerset'. As Abbot recalled, Queen Anna had also wished to reduce Somerset's sway by introducing a rival, but had presciently warned Abbot of the likelihood that Villiers would, in time, prove just as dominant as Somerset if his introduction to the king went well. As the queen had reflected, 'I know your master better than you all.'[20] Ironically, Somerset's unpopularity at court only confirmed the sapience of James's own strictures. In *Basilicon Doron*, he had specifically directed Prince Henry to 'use not one [individual] in all things, lest he wax proud, and be envied of his fellows'.[21]

In the letter sent by James to Somerset in early 1615, the king sought to avoid arguing with his favourite in terms, as he put it, of '"he said" and "she said"'. Denying that Somerset had any reason to doubt his continued devotion, James was nevertheless dismayed to observe how 'of late ... this strange frenzy took you, so powdered and mixed with strange streams of unquietness, passion, fury and insolent pride', compounded by 'a settled kind of induced obstinacy' that 'chokes and obscures' all his attractive qualities. Among a litany of hurts, James objected to Somerset's outbursts 'being uttered at unseasonable hours and so bereaving me of my rest', which the king suspected was done 'of purpose to grieve and vex me'. Moreover, 'in many of your mad fits', Somerset had intimated that he intended 'not so much to hold me by love hereafter as by awe', confident 'that I dare not offend you or resist your appetites'. James then moved paraliptically to 'leave out of this reckoning your long creeping back and withdrawing yourself from lying in my chamber, notwithstanding my many hundred times earnest soliciting you to the contrary'. Nor had their quarrels been a private matter. As the king lamented, it was now 'known to so many that ye have been in some cross discourse with me'. Their differences were only too evident to others, aware of 'your long being with me at unseasonable hours, loud speaking on both parts, and their observation of my sadness after your parting, and want of rest'. Looking ahead, James sought 'your entire heart, but softened with humility'. If ever Somerset might 'think to retain me by one sparkle of fear, all the violence of my love will, in that instant, be changed into as violent a hatred'.[22]

James's reproof supplies a rare and unflinchingly direct insight into a monarch's inner turmoil. Royal liaisons were just as keenly observed four centuries ago as today by palace servants and popular readerships across Continental Europe. In his mock encomium published in 1615, the anonymous author of *Corona Regia* admitted that he was 'prying into your secrets', knowing that England's king 'would prefer that the repute of these matters rest within your private sphere'. But discussing such matters might also be considered fair game, given the extent to which James 'would publicly declare your amorous passions and enticements, which you cannot or will not withdraw from the eyes of all'. Seeing how the king set about 'inciting desire with immodest words, caressing cheeks, stealing a kiss', the author feigned admiration of James's 'charming, cheerful, and uninhibited' demeanour. Invoking St Matthew's injunction to 'suffer little children to come unto me', *Corona Regia*'s author watched James 'summon boys – the very fair ones in particular' with faux cheer and encouraged him to 'carry on, dearest king, continue to behave as you do, proceed to stun all mortals with wonder.' Aware of favours serially conferred, the anonymous author named Somerset among the king's favourites, as well as 'a young man of incomparable beauty, George Villiers', known to have been 'introduced by the queen herself into your chamber'.[23]

In September 1615, Somerset's fortunes went into steep reversal when James received evidence to suggest that Overbury's death in the Tower of London, two years earlier, had been the result not of natural causes but of deliberate poisoning. In a written statement, the Tower's Lieutenant, Sir Gervase Elwes, reported he had successfully thwarted repeated attempts to harm Overbury while in his custody by, for example, discarding 'tarts and pots of jelly' supplied by the Countess of

Somerset that Elwes believed had been adulterated.[24] Writing to Philip III's favourite, the Duke of Lerma, the Spanish ambassador, Sarmiento, relayed rumours that Overbury had also been prescribed medicine 'which produced sixty or more stools till he expired', explaining that Elwes 'did not then dare to speak because so great persons were touched by it'.[25] Coincidentally – or not – Somerset had recently obtained from James a royal pardon for 'all minor offences, as frauds, conspiracies, extortions, contempts &c.', albeit not extending to 'any other offence affecting life or limb'.[26] But Somerset had subsequently failed to secure a general pardon under the Great Seal. As Samiento recounted, despite the king's support for the earl's request, Lord Chancellor Ellesmere had refused to sign any such pardon, 'saying that its clauses were general, and without a single precedent'.[27] In October, Ellesmere joined the Chief Justice of the King's Bench, Sir Edward Coke, and other senior courtiers on a commission established by James to investigate the circumstances surrounding Overbury's death.

Confronted by Somerset's demands to abandon the investigation, James remained implacable. Disappointed that the earl should 'have bestowed so much scribbling and railing covertly against me and avowedly against the Chancellor', James made clear that his actions, in such a serious matter, must be governed by 'my conscience before God, and next my reputation in the eyes of the whole world'. Accordingly, it was inconceivable that 'I should suffer a murder (if it be so) to be suppressed and plastered over to the destruction both of my soul and reputation'. If Somerset's conscience was clear, he had nothing to fear. James further regretted that both Somerset and his father-in-law – Lord Treasurer Suffolk – had 'ever and at all times behaved yourselves' in ways that seemed unhelpfully obstructive.[28] In October 1615, Somerset was placed under house arrest at Whitehall, while his wife was detained at Blackfriars.

In the ensuing scandal, James was not only implicitly involved through his closeness to Somerset, but also implicated on account of Overbury dying while in royal custody. Consequently, when Coke indicted the Tower of London's Lieutenant, Elwes, before a grand jury, he relayed the king's stated alarm that, since Overbury had been his 'prisoner, shall I be made the instrument to effect their cruelty? A stalking horse for murder and poison?'[29] As Attorney-General Bacon later reminded George Villiers, Overbury was 'the first prisoner murdered in the Tower, since the murder of the young princes by Richard III, the tyrant'.[30] In the Dutch

'Cautionary Town' of Flushing, the English governor, Viscount Lisle, was warned by his deputy, Sir John Throckmorton, that news of Overbury's murder had prompted the local populace to 'speak afresh of the brave Prince Henry' – who had died suddenly in 1612 – 'as though they would call a doubt of his being poisoned also'. Writing to Lisle again the next day, Throckmorton was appalled to observe 'not only Flushing, but all the world far and wide' was now inclined 'to brand-mark us with that hideous and foul title of poisoning one another, and ask if we be become Italians, Spaniards or of what other vile, murderous nation?'[31]

Back in London, Overbury's keeper at the Tower, Richard Weston, was tried and, despite initially refusing to enter a plea, convicted of administering the fatal poison and executed in October 1615. The following month, Weston's former employer, Anne Turner – also a confidante of the Countess of Somerset – was tried and convicted of murder, as were the Tower's Lieutenant, Elwes, and an apothecary from Maidstone, James Franklin, who had helped to procure the fatal poison. Before his trial, Weston was reported to have articulated his hope that the authorities 'were not making a net to catch the little fish and let the great ones break through'.[32] Those bigger fish included Somerset's wife, who gave birth to a daughter in late 1615, while still under house arrest. Meanwhile, an inventory of Somerset's belongings compiled in November 1615, on Chief Justice Coke's orders, listed opulent domestic furnishings, paintings, tapestries, ceremonial robes, twenty-five cloaks, and nearly fifty doublets and hose, embroidered with satin lace, silk grogram, and 'black taffeta, cut upon tinsel', in flamboyant gold, silver, pink, crimson, 'seagreen' and 'ashcoloured' hues.[33]

James hoped that Somerset might follow his wife's example and confess to involvement in Overbury's murder, thereby avoiding the need for a public trial. But after the earl refused several inducements to confess, the king wrote secretly to the Tower of London's new Lieutenant, Sir George More, acknowledging his fear that Somerset might consider 'laying an aspersion upon myself of being an accessory to his crime'.[34] Tasked with preparing the prosecution against the Somersets, Attorney-General Bacon was keen to remove any chance of the king being traduced in open court and reassured James that if the earl 'should break forth into any speech of taxing the king', he would be interrupted, silenced and, if necessary, removed from the courtroom with all evidence thereafter heard in his absence. Were this to happen, however, Somerset would be made aware that 'it shall not be in the king's will to save his life, the people will be so set on fire'.[35]

On 24 May 1616, Bacon led the arraignment against the Countess of Somerset and drew attention to James's insistence that the rule of law must always prevail. To the multitude of paying spectators crammed into Westminster Hall, Bacon emphasized that, under such a wise and fair king, 'there is no respect of persons; that his affections royal are above his affections private; that his favours and nearness about him are not like popish sanctuaries, to privilege malefactors.'[36] After the countess was convicted on the basis of her confession, Somerset was tried the following day, with Bacon acknowledging to the peers sitting in judgement that the earl 'is yet of your number, a peer as you are; so as you cannot cut him off from your body but with grief'. Bacon underscored Somerset's formerly close relationship with the murder victim, alleging that he had routinely passed on royal letters, sometimes unopened, to Overbury, who had 'perused them, copied, registered them, made tables of them'. So comprehensive was Overbury's involvement in Somerset's affairs that 'Overbury knew more of the secrets of state than the Council-table did.'[37] After a trial lasting around thirteen hours, Somerset was convicted of being an accessory to Overbury's murder and a capital sentence was pronounced. Popular anticipation that Somerset and his wife would follow Weston, Turner, Elwes and Franklin to the scaffold was, however, disappointed. Although James formally pardoned the countess in July 1616, the couple were detained in the Tower of London until January 1622 and, in return for an undertaking never to return to court or Parliament, the earl was pardoned in 1624.

*

The Somersets' scandalous involvement in Overbury's death tarnished the image of the Jacobean court and undermined royal authority. Disagreements over crown finance and dynastic diplomacy had been compounded by suspicions of endemic deviance and corruption, alongside more salacious rumours of diabolism. On the eve of Somerset's trial, Throckmorton had penned a letter from Flushing reporting (erroneously) that the earl was to be charged with 'procuring by sorcery to inveigle the king's heart, so as he should have no power to deny him anything'.[38] Somerset's countess, Frances Howard, was likewise denounced as 'a wife, a witch, a poisoner and a whore', embodying the transgressive threat that overly ambitious women in general were deemed to pose.[39] Erasure of the couple's influence was reflected in the hasty renaming of royal residences. As John Chamberlain reported in March 1617, when James dined with Queen Anna on Shrove Tuesday at her London residence of Somerset House in the Strand, the property 'was then new christened, and must henceforward be called Denmark House'.[40]

Somerset's trial had also been delayed by demands for an investigation into whether the earl's interactions with the Spanish ambassador, Sarmiento, had been potentially treasonable. Certainly, the pro-Spanish inclinations of James and his former favourite were not shared by other Privy Councillors. In November 1616, six months after Somerset's trial, Sarmiento alerted Philip III to deteriorating Anglo-Spanish relations and counselled the resuscitation of long-standing Spanish plans to invade England should hostilities break out. Citing the experiences of the Romans, Danes, Saxons and Normans, Sarmiento reminded Philip that 'every nation that has ever made war to England, when managing to put their foot in the island, it has been successful in conquering it'. But Sarmiento advised against traditional assumptions that the entry route to England lay via France or Flanders. Rather, the ambassador's recommendation was 'to disembark an army in Scotland, using protected ports close to England where we would not find any resistance (actually assistance)'. Regarding such a plan as 'the only course for the conquest of England', Sarmiento explained that 'the road from Scotland to England is an easy one'.[41]

Oblivious to Spanish interest in Scotland as a potential launch-pad to invade England, James embarked on an extended progress to his northern kingdom during the summer of 1617. Further court scandal followed in his wake. For after being removed from his post as Chief Justice of the King's Bench the previous autumn, Coke saw a potential marriage between his fourteen-year-old daughter, Frances, and George Villiers's older brother, John, as a likely means of returning to royal favour. Such a match was, however, vigorously opposed by Frances's mother, Lady Elizabeth Hatton (who retained the surname of her first husband, Sir William Hatton, after marrying Coke). In July, she removed Frances to an address in Oatlands, whereupon Coke secured a warrant to remove his daughter but evidently went 'further than his warrant and broke open diverse doors before he got her'. Hatton thereupon appealed to James's Privy Councillors, who expressed concern that this domestic incident denoted the first instance of 'riot and disturbance' since the king's departure for Scotland. But James returned a response that unequivocally supported Coke's right, as a father, to determine his daughter's affairs. Moreover, James countered that 'the first breach of that quietness which hath ever been kept since the beginning of our journey was made by them that committed the theft' – in other words Hatton, who was placed under house arrest while Frances was returned to her father's house.[42] Thereafter, Hatton declined the invitation to attend the sumptuous wedding at Hampton Court in September 1617, at which James himself gave Frances Coke away to John Villiers, prompting Chamberlain to comment that the bride's mother had 'done herself a great deal of wrong, in kicking against the prick, and by indirect courses to hinder that which lay not in her power'.[43]

Ostensibly, the Coke–Villiers union sought to restore patriarchal norms on James's return from Scotland. But further marital disharmony and unwelcome echoes of the Overbury poisoning scandal soon resurfaced at the heart of James's court in the family woes of Sir Thomas Lake, who jointly shared, with Sir Ralph Winwood, the responsibilities of the Secretary's role once discharged by Salisbury. In 1616, Lake's daughter, Anne, married one of Salisbury's descendants, William Cecil, Lord Roos, who was also first cousin to Frances Coke. Within a short time, however, the couple were living apart. In early 1618, Lady Roos publicly accused Frances Cecil, Countess of Exeter, of not only conducting an adulterous affair with her husband, but also of twice attempting to murder her, first with a poisoned enema and then with a poisoned syrup of roses. Having fled to Italy – where he died shortly afterwards – Lord Roos wrote directly to James in June 1618, describing his mother-in-law as 'satanical' and 'diabolical', and denouncing his wife as a 'younger imp of hell', an 'impudent whore' and a 'shameless brat of hell'.[44]

After a Privy Council investigation of Lady Roos's claims proved inconclusive, the Earl and Countess of Exeter sued the Lake family for slander, prompting counter-suits by the Lakes. When the case came to court, James resolved to hear *Earl of Exeter v. Lakes* in person and presided over the five-day hearing in the Star Chamber in February 1619. In a decisive victory for the Exeters, Sir Thomas Lake, his wife and daughter were found guilty of forgery, slander and suborning witnesses, and were fined and imprisoned in the Tower of London and Lake was removed from his Secretaryship. Declaring the court's judgement, James likened the case as equivalent to the second Fall of Man, presuming that his erstwhile Secretary had been 'seduced by his Eve, but as it saved not Adam's turn' to blame 'the woman thou gavest me, but he was made to sweat for it, so I think it just that Sir Thomas should smart for it'.[45] The previous month, James's Treasurer, Thomas Howard, Earl of Suffolk, had meanwhile been suspended from his position and, together with his wife, was found guilty of numerous corruption charges after an eleven-day hearing in the Star Chamber in November.

Behind the successive court scandals, charges and counter-charges lay unsettled personal and political scores that centred around failed bids for positions in James's Bedchamber, as well as political divisions over foreign policy, royal revenue, and relations between Crown and Parliament. In February 1618, Chamberlain had reported the unsuccessful attempt of Suffolk and other members of the Howard dynasty to 'recover their fortunes by setting up this new idol' – a young man named William Monson – taking 'great pains in tricking and pranking him up, besides washing his face every day with posset-curd'.[46] While the king had responded by banishing Monson from court, George Villiers's anger at the Howards' blatant attempt to dislodge him from James's affections prompted him to draw royal attention to suspected financial malpractice by the Lord Treasurer. Another public trial thereafter became inevitable when Suffolk refused to admit any wrongdoing.

While the full extent of crown losses incurred through Suffolk's embezzlement is unclear, Coke estimated that they could amount to approximately £51,000 sterling. The Suffolks were also suspected of stealing around £140,000 worth of crown jewels entrusted to their care shortly after James's accession. Although Suffolk's son-in-law, Somerset, had failed in 1615 to obtain a general pardon under the Great Seal that would have averted his later felony conviction, prosecution of the Suffolks' suspected theft was precluded by an 'acquittance' issued in 1607 protecting them from any losses incurred while the jewels were in their custody.[47] Regarding the other corruption charges, however, Sir Francis Bacon – recently promoted as Lord Chancellor – concluded the prosecution's case by dismissing the Suffolks' protests regarding regular gifts on the grounds that 'new year's gifts did not last all the year.' Sitting in judgement was Coke (restored as a Privy Councillor), who insisted that 'the king's treasure was the soul of the commonwealth' and those who destroyed it were 'guilty of civil murder'.[48] But with Somerset, Suffolk and Lake, together with Suffolk's eldest son, Theofilus Howard, Lord Walden, all detained at His Majesty's Pleasure in the autumn of 1619, Chamberlain jestingly suggested that an alternative Privy Council meeting could be convened at the Tower of London, since its prisoners now included 'a Lord Treasurer, a Lord Chamberlain, a Captain of the Pensioners and a Secretary'.[49]

22

Sitting in Royal Judgement

When James pronounced judgement in *Earl of Exeter v. Lakes* in the court of Star Chamber in February 1619, this was the last time that an English or Scottish monarch personally sat in judgement on any of their subjects. (By contrast, James's son Charles I became 'rather more notable for having his subjects sit in judgement on him' in 1649.[1]) James's decision to act in a judicial capacity – determining liability and prescribing punishment – had not been taken lightly. The case itself took five days to hear, with the king arriving in court just after 7 a.m. on some mornings.[2] Nearly ninety witnesses were named in the court papers after the king's Secretary of State, Sir Thomas Lake, adduced numerous claims and counter-claims against his daughter's in-laws, the Earl and Countess of Essex.[3] As one observer feared, 'all the Star Chamber days of the term would be too few' to hear the case, given that 'the books on both sides contain 19,000 sheets' of evidence.[4] While some matters were adjudicated at pre-trial hearings, the Star Chamber case assessed the submitted evidence and ruled decisively in favour of Exeter. A written confession by the Countess of Essex purporting to admit intent to murder Lady Roos was deemed a forgery, while Lake was found to have abused his powers as a Privy Councillor by imprisoning two servants from whom false testimonies had been extracted.

Comprising the monarch's Privy Councillors and the Chief Justices, the court of Star Chamber sat twice weekly during law terms to hear criminal cases usually involving violence. In his history of the court prepared in 1621, the barrister William Hudson recalled how James had delivered his judgement in *Exeter v. Lakes* 'with more than Solomon's wisdom'. Indeed, the king 'pronounced a sentence more accurately eloquent, judiciously grave, and honourably just' than 'any of his royal progenitors' cited in the court's records. As Hudson elaborated, the judges in Star Chamber normally embodied the stars that adorned the court's star-spangled ceiling, reflecting the solar light of royal power as they acted in the monarch's stead. But when James had sat in judgement, 'the shining of those starts is put out', for 'representation must needs cease when the person is present.'[5]

Dispensing righteous judgement was central to James's conception of divinely ordained kingship. His decision to intervene personally in *Exeter vs. Lakes* was presumably motivated by the case's notoriety. A year before it was heard, John Chamberlain was relaying rumours that the families' dispute involved 'so foul scandals of pre-contracts, adultery, incest, murder, poison and such like peccadillos'.[6] The case also directly involved one of the king's two Secretaries of State, who was duly found to have abused his powers as a Privy Councillor to pervert the course of justice. During the Overbury scandal in 1615, James had refused to be pressured into abandoning a judicial investigation. As King of Scotland, he had likewise recommended in *Basilicon Doron* that Prince Henry should 'be a daily watch-man over your servants, that they obey your laws precisely: for how can your laws be kept in the country, if they be broken at your ear?' A just king should be seen 'punishing the breach thereof in a courtier, more severely, than in the person of any other of your subjects'.[7]

James's conjuring of the case as a second Fall of Man also reflected a more gender-specific disquiet concerning the crimes of Lady Lake and Lady Roos. Addressing the court on the first day of the trial, James invoked the Book of Kings and explicitly 'compared himself to Solomon that was to judge between two women', albeit adding that he only intended to 'parallel them as women' since the Scriptural tale of a custody dispute concerned two women conventionally regarded as prostitutes.[8] Among James's ministers, Lady Lake's domineering demeanour had led to her being likened to Socrates's spirited wife, Xantippe, while evidence adduced in *Exeter v. Lakes* revealed that she had been engaged in questioning and pressuring witnesses involved in the dispute.[9] As John Chamberlain learned, James had thereafter directed 'all his Secretaries or that stood to be Secretaries not to impart matters of state to their wives'. Another commentator reported that the king had also 'charged the judges to beware of papists, especially of women, who are the nourishers of papistry'.[10] For although Sir Thomas Lake's younger brother, Arthur, had become Bishop of Bath and Wells in 1616, Sir Thomas's family remained covert Catholics who lived next door to the Venetian embassy in London. That same year, the ambassador, Antonio Foscarini, confirmed that the Lake family attended Mass in the embassy chapel and that Sir Thomas and his wife sometimes entrusted him with 'devotional things, to take care of them, when they were afraid that the house might be searched'.[11]

James's intervention in *Exeter v. Lakes* thus sought to underscore royal impartiality in the face of alleged wrongdoing among his own courtiers and to send a strong message regarding the need to re-establish Protestant orthodoxy and patriarchal order. But even after the case was formally adjudicated, witchcraft joined its heady concoction of gynae-cocracy, popery and scandal. In February 1620, a former schoolmaster, Samuel Peacock, was detained in the Tower of London for, as Chamber-lain reported, 'practising to infatuate the king's judgement by sorcery' during *Exeter v. Lakes*. Despite the fact that Peacock was 'hanged up by the wrists' and interrogated by the Lord Chancellor, Attorney-General, Solicitor-General and others, Chamberlain denied 'that they have wrung any great matter out of him'.[12]

*

The identification that James drew with the Israelite King Solomon as the administrator of divine justice, when presiding on the first day's hearing of *Exeter v. Lakes*, was not an isolated allusion. Four dec-ades earlier, when he had made his first official entry into Edinburgh in October 1579, the first tableau that James encountered at the city's West Port was a re-enactment of Solomon's Biblical judgement between the two mothers.[13] In the mid-1590s, James had made Stirling Castle a showcase of Scottish Renaissance splendour to host Prince Henry's baptism by overseeing construction of a new Chapel Royal designed to the same precise proportions as the Temple of Solomon described in the Scriptural Books of Kings and Chronicles.[14] In *Basilicon Doron*, James acclaimed Solomon as 'the wisest king that ever was' and ventured that Prince Henry would not find 'so rich a storehouse of precepts of natural wisdom' anywhere as in the Books of Proverbs and Ecclesiastes, attrib-uted to Solomon's authorship.[15] Preaching at Paul's Cross in London three days after Elizabeth I's death in March 1603, the rector of St Mary Woolchurch, John Hayward, anticipated James's imminent arrival in the English capital by quoting Solomon's dictum that 'a king sitting in the throne of judgement drives away all evil with his eyes.' Eschewing simple flattery, Hayward's optimism was evidenced by James's record of governing Scotland and being admired by those who 'peruse his writings'.[16] Over two decades later, following James's own death in 1625, Bishop John Williams of Lincoln entitled the king's funeral sermon *Great Britain's Solomon* and denied that there had ever been 'two kings more fully paralleled among themselves, and better distinguished from all other kings'.[17]

Although the occasions on which James sat in judgement in civil or criminal cases were rare, they denoted junctures in which he deemed a particular case to have significant wider resonance. Writing to James's ambassador in Brussels in December 1618, Archbishop George Abbot of Canterbury observed of *Exeter v. Lakes* that 'the matter is held so exemplary and of consequence that the king himself intends to be present.'[18] Nearly thirty years earlier, James had identified a similar onus when he intervened in Barbara Napier's trial for witchcraft in June 1591. After the assize, or jury, had returned its verdict of acquittal, James had indicated that he intended to prosecute the assizers for wilful error, having become alarmed that 'common assizes' were generally not as inclined to 'condemn the guilty as clear the innocent, which are alike abominable before God, as Solomon teaches'. As he had explained to the court convened in Edinburgh's Tolbooth, he was intervening 'not because I am James Stuart, and can command so many thousands of men, but because God hath made me a king and judge to judge righteous judgement'. In Napier's case, her suspected diabolism was also alleged to have been part of a larger treasonable conspiracy to kill the king that had been orchestrated by James's cousin Francis Stewart, Earl of Bothwell. Accordingly, royal involvement in Napier's case was essential, 'because I see the pride of these witches and their friends, which cannot be prevented but by mine own presence' in court. Threatening Napier's assizers with prosecution would, James hoped, serve as 'an example in time coming to make men to be more wary how they give false verdicts, not only in this cause but in all other causes'.[19]

As Scottish king, James only intervened directly in a handful of cases, but he regularly acted as a mediator or an arbitrator in noble feuds and disputes, and he attended numerous Privy Council meetings at which judicial decisions were taken. During the 1590s, the king also attended hearings in Scotland's Court of Session for an average of around twenty-five days a year to observe the general conduct of business and inform his responsibility for making judicial appointments.[20] As James advised his son in *Basilicon Doron*, Henry should 'delight to haunt your Session, and spy carefully their proceedings', being vigilant to spot 'any bribery ... among them, which cannot over-severely be punished'. While a king should sit there 'only for doing of justice' and not to influence outcomes, James acknowledged that a royal presence could serve to secure 'expedition of justice' for poorer subjects who might otherwise be 'debarred by mightier parties'.[21]

Royal determination to dispense righteous judgement nevertheless risked undermining judicial independence. In March 1599, the English court's agent in Edinburgh, George Nicolson, described James's fury after the Court of Session's judges had agreed to hear a case submitted by the outspoken Presbyterian minister Robert Bruce, who was suing for recovery of his stipend in a dispute involving local landowners in Angus and the Commendator of Arbroath Abbey. After James had 'persuaded the voting against Mr Robert, and in a manner commanded it', the Earl of Dunfermline, as Lord President, had objected that, if the king was seeking to direct the bench to ignore their judicial oaths and dictates of consciences, he would decline to vote. As Dunfermline explained, he intended to vote in favour 'not for Mr Robert's sake, being of little acquaintance with him', but on the merits of his claim. Another judge, Lord Newbattle, addressed James directly, protesting 'that it was said in the town – to his slander and theirs – that they durst not do justice, but as the king commanded them'. Undeterred, Newbattle insisted that he and his colleagues 'would vote against him, in the right, in his own presence', whereupon 'the king reasoned much and very earnestly, sometimes persuading, sometimes taunting and chiding'.[22]

After the judges had then voted to allow Bruce's case to be heard, Nicolson reported that 'the king raged marvellously and is in great anger' with the judges. Moreover, on learning that one judge, Lord Blantyre, had breached court protocol by communicating with Bruce's counsel during deliberations, James ordered Blantyre's detention in Edinburgh Castle and his resignation as Lord Treasurer, which Blantyre refused until he received debt repayments exceeding £18,000 (Scots) owed him by the Crown. Meanwhile, Dunfermline resisted further royal pressure and, as Nicolson confirmed, upheld the court's judgement, which he 'says he will pen in Latin, French and Greek to be sent to all the judges of the whole world to be approved, and that by his vote it shall never be reversed. And so say the whole Session.'[23] James's eventual retreat denoted a victory for judicial independence.

In addition to asserting his prerogative right to determine which cases should be heard in Scottish courts, James also intervened to demand specific punishments and even came 'close to creating a new crime on his own authority' in 1601.[24] Granting a judicial commission to Lord Roxburgh to prosecute one Peter Nairn for conspiracy to murder an unidentified Englishman, James acknowledged that there was 'no law made against practisers and conspirators of a murder unexecute, and this fact, nakedly considered, will not appear punishable to the death'. To instil 'terror' in others, however, James directed Roxburgh 'of our own absolute authority and power' to deliver a capital sentence if Nairn was convicted.[25] Although the outcome of Roxburgh's investigation is unknown, that same year an English agent advised Elizabeth's court that James had become 'a great "justicer" having executed a Douglas, a Maxwell, a Johnstone and two other gentlemen' for the crimes of stealing and counterfeiting money.[26]

In *The Trew Law of Free Monarchies* (1598), James also made clear that, however prudent it may behove wise monarchs to observe the rule of law, he had 'at length proved, that the king is above the law'.[27] Sovereigns must retain the power to intervene in instances where a country's law appeared unclear, outdated, or excessively harsh, being mindful of the Ciceronian maxim *summa ius, summa inuiria* – that law pushed to extremes may become injustice. The first compilation of all Scottish statutes enacted from the time of King James I's Parliament in 1424 had been published in 1566 – the year of James VI's birth – with the majority of statutes appearing in print for the first time.[28] James's positive attachment to statute as the pre-eminent source of authority in Scots law was also shared by his tutor George Buchanan, who had pronounced in his *Rerum Scoticarum Historica* ('History of Scotland') in 1582 that the Scots 'have no laws but their acts of parliament'.[29]

For James, little independent authority thus attached to allegedly 'fundamental' laws for, if the Scottish Parliament was 'nothing else but the head court of the king and his vassals', all 'laws are but craved by his subjects' and were only given legal force by the royal sceptre. In *The*

Trew Law of Free Monarchies, James had also emphasized the role of conquest in English history, rhetorically asking, 'when the bastard of Normandy came into England, and made himself king, was it not by force, and with a mighty army?' In 1066, William the Conqueror 'gave the law, and took none, changed the laws, [and] inverted the order of government', as reflected in the continued use of French law by English lawyers, which saw Elizabeth I's subjects still governed by laws 'written in his language and not in theirs'. In both Scotland and England, therefore, 'the kings were the authors and makers of the laws, and not the laws of the kings.'[30]

*

By the time James succeeded to the English throne in 1603, erstwhile Elizabethan ministers and courtiers were aware of his involvement in Scottish legal cases, while his strictures on the law were also widely disseminated via the large print runs of *Basilicon Doron* produced in London that spring. The previous year, a courtier and godson of Elizabeth I, Sir John Harington, had been unsettled by reports of James ordering the summary execution of a pickpocket caught red-handed among crowds attending the royal progress in Newark-on-Trent. Suggesting that such action seemed to betoken a casual disregard for due process, Harington mused that 'our new king hath hanged one man before he was tried; 'tis strangely done: now if the wind blows thus, why may not a man be tried before he hath offended?'[31] (While Harington was more alarmed by the lack of trial than the king's involvement, it later emerged that the same thief had already received royal pardons from James on two occasions, with execution only ordered for his third offence.[32]) Once installed in London, the new king was reminded of his royal duties to dispense righteous justice in the sermon preached at his coronation by Bishop Thomas Bilson of Winchester. As Bilson explained, kings 'are gods by office; ruling, judging and punishing in God's stead'. On God's behalf, monarchs were obliged to repress 'adultery, incests, rapes, robberies, perjuries, conspiracies, witchcrafts, murders, rebellions, treasons, and such like heinous and impious enormities'.[33]

In May 1603, James had directed that his English Privy Councillors should devote Tuesday afternoons to hearing private legal suits, although the volume of private legal business adjudicated by the Council is unknown since the Council register for the years between 1602 and

1618 was destroyed in a Whitehall fire in 1619. A surviving register of royal answers to private petitions indicates, however, extensive personal involvement: 'in the first year alone, James appears to have handled some 466 private disputes.'[34] Assisted by the Master of Requests, royal intervention usually involved referring cases to different courts or submitting cases to external arbitration.

More publicly, James's vision of closer Anglo-Scottish union provoked English and Scots lawyers alike to undertake searching reviews of the grounds of authority underpinning their respective laws. On 13 April 1604, James confirmed to English peers and MPs that, 'at his death, his wish, above all things' was to see '1. one worship to God, 2. one kingdom entirely governed. 3. one uniformity in laws.'[35] But a fortnight later, Sir Edwin Sandys, as MP for Stockbridge, objected that 'we can give no laws to Britain', since the Houses of Parliament were only competent to legislate for England; moreover, 'the king cannot preserve the fundamental laws by uniting, no more than a goldsmith' could forge a single crown without destroying the originals.[36] When the Scottish Parliament met at Perth in July, its members proclaimed themselves 'ravished in admiration with a so fortunate beginning' and appointed commissioners to secure 'that constant love and perfect amity between both nations so tenderly wished by his most excellent majesty'. The Scots commissioners' remit was, however, carefully circumscribed to ensure that provision for closer union in no way derogated from 'any fundamental laws, ancient privileges, offices, rights, dignities and liberties of this kingdom'.[37]

That August, James employed the MP for Ipswich, Sir Francis Bacon, as 'learned counsel' for advice on matters being considered by the union commissioners. Warning James that achieving 'an entire and perfect union' of the laws would be 'a matter of great difficulty and length', Bacon deemed it prudent instead 'to proceed by parts': prioritize the most urgent areas for unification and 'leave the rest to time.' Creatively reimagining the geography of mainland Britain, Bacon identified the Anglo-Scottish Borders as the region where 'the healing and consolidating plaster should be chiefly applied' and proposed establishing a new court at Carlisle or Berwick, with jurisdiction extending 'part into England and part into Scotland' and proceeding not 'precisely or merely according to the laws and customs either of England or Scotland, but mixtly'. On a supranational level, Bacon suggested that James might – as the '*commune vinculum*' (common bond) of both English and Scots legal systems – 'erect some court about your person, in the nature of the Grand Council of France' and thereby 'draw causes from the ordinary judges of both nations' as the French king received cases from different *parlements*.[38]

On the same day that the union commissioners met in October 1604, James confirmed his change in royal style to 'King of Great Britain' by proclamation and reiterated that 'this union is not enforced by conquest and violence, nor contracted by doubtful and deceivable points of transaction.' Since his accession as English king was, rather, the natural product of a dynastic marriage, James further asserted that 'immediately upon our succession, diverse of the ancient laws of this realm are *ipso facto* expired', citing escuage (feudal payments in lieu of military service) and the naturalization of Scots as examples. More generally, James claimed to observe 'a greater affinity and concurrence between most of the ancient laws of both kingdoms, than is to be found between those of any other two nations'.[39] In late November, James wrote from Royston to Sir Robert Cecil, recently created Viscount Cranborne, approving the commissioners' draft regarding the abolition of mutually hostile statutes, removal of certain trade restrictions, and naturalization of the *post-nati*, with a similar intention declared for the *ante-nati*, subject to office-holding restrictions. Directing Cranborne to 'bestow a good dinner upon your northern neighbours' and to drink 'a health to your common and indifferent master' (himself), James nevertheless insisted that the final phraseology be amended to confirm that 'working in this errand shall never be left off till it be fully accomplished, I mean specially by the uniting of both laws and parliaments of both the nations'.[40]

Initially, parliamentary discussion of the union commissioners' recommendations was delayed by investigation of the Gunpowder Plot and other pressing business. In February 1607, however, the Commons committee tasked with reviewing the proposals acknowledged the multi-dimensional complexity of union, being a 'matter of common law, matter of civil law, matter of *ius gentium* [law of nations], matter of state, matter of story [history]'.[41] Although frustrated by the lack of progress, when James addressed both Houses of Parliament in March he claimed to have found 'that the grounds of the common law of England are the best of any law in the world, either civil or municipal, and the fittest for this people'. Closer Anglo-Scottish union neverthe-less offered an opportunity to 'let your laws be looked into' in order to provide clarity in areas where the common law was unclear and to reduce judges' reliance on case law and precedent at a time when 'the variation of cases and mens' curiosity, [are] breeding every day new questions'. James also clarified that, in calling for legal union, he had never intended 'the abolishing of the laws, but only the clearing and the sweeping off the rust of them'.[42] Speaking in the Commons four days earlier, Bacon – shortly to be promoted as Solicitor-General – had welcomed the opportunity for comprehensive law reform, deeming it 'indeed a work (rightly to term it) heroical' for England's new king to initiate.[43]

To its critics, the prospect of closer Anglo-Scottish legal union risked making English common law appear an awkwardly narrow, provincial obstacle. Among the most vocal opponents of legal union in the Com-mons was the Gray's Inn barrister, Puritan and City of London MP, Nicholas Fuller, who warned in February 1607 that 'God hath made people apt for every country; some for a cold, some for a hot climate'; none too subtly, he added, 'all grounds be not fit for one kind of grain, some for oats, some for wheat.'[44] That summer, Fuller objected to the title of a proposed bill 'for the continuance and preservation of the blessed union' on the grounds that no such union had yet occurred; provision to abolish mutually hostile statutes was duly renamed an 'act for the utter abolition of all memory of hostility'.[45]

Fuller's parliamentary opposition to Anglo-Scottish union coincided with his attempts to protect the jurisdiction of English common law from encroachment by prerogative institutions. Defending religious nonconformists pursued by the court of High Commission, Fuller chal-lenged the court's statutory powers to imprison, put to oath or fine subjects. Having drafted measures to restrict the court of High Com-mission's remit, Fuller was imprisoned when Parliament adjourned in July 1607. In a published tract, he acclaimed England's judges as 'the more careful, judicious and jealous preservers of the laws of England'; by contrast, when confronted by the court of High Commission's prac-tice of withholding standard common-law protections from suspects, 'it seemed to him, that he was in a new world, or other commonwealth'.[46] After Fuller secured a writ enabling a High Commission case to be transferred to the court of King's Bench, in October, James wrote to

Cecil – now elevated as Earl of Salisbury – denouncing Fuller as 'the villain'. As the king ominously warned, 'whensoever the ecclesiastical dignity, together with the king's government thereof, shall be turned in contempt and begin to vanish in this kingdom, the kings hereof shall not long after prosper in their government, and the monarchy shall fall to ruin'.[47]

Heated consultations at court ensued, as James suspected attempts to undermine the authority of the crown-appointed ecclesiastical court by common lawyers. In his posthumously published Twelfth Report, Coke included his account of the *Prohibitions del Roy* ('prohibitions of the king'), recounting how, as Attorney-General, he had publicly denied assurances made to James by the Archbishop of Canterbury, Richard Bancroft, that English monarchs might decide any case they pleased, since 'the judges are but the delegates of the king.' On the contrary, Coke had insisted that, although James's royal authority was present in all tribunals, 'judgements are always given *per curiam* (by the court)' and 'no king after the [Norman] Conquest assumed to himself to give any judgement in any cause whatsoever'. Coke had also ventured that, although James possessed 'excellent science, and great endowments of nature ... his Majesty was not learned in the laws of his realm of England'. Matters concerning his subjects' lives, inheritances, goods and fortunes were 'not to be decided by natural reason, but by the artificial reason and judgement of law' which 'requires long study and experience'.[48]

In the event, the King's Bench judges deemed the court of High Commission competent to pursue individuals on charges of heresy and schism. As Salisbury reassured James in November 1607, the judges had gratifyingly added that, since they regarded themselves as 'one of the king's strong arms', they respected the dignity of other tribunals and had not intended to imply suspicion of encroachment by the court of High Commission's officers.[49] That same month, James took another opportunity to insist on his royal duty to deliver judgement. Debating the jurisdictional remit of the Council in the Marches of Wales with the same King's Bench judges, he reiterated that the monarch was 'the supreme judge' and 'inferior judges his shadows and ministers'. Hence 'the king may, if he please, sit and judge in Westminster Hall in any court there, and call their judgements in question.'[50]

*

In Sir Edward Coke, James encountered a brilliant jurist whose prodigious research into the origins of English common law would be celebrated in the epitaph adorning his tomb in St Mary's Church at Tittleshall in Norfolk. An 'inerrant oracle of the laws', Coke was remembered as 'a river, torrent, and flood of eloquence' and 'singular priest of persuasion'. Coke had been 'a living library', as well as 'father of twelve children and thirteen books'.[51] In terms of irascible temperament, moreover, Coke had also been James's equal. In 1609, a third-party account of one exchange described how, aggravated by Coke's opposition, 'his Majesty fell into that high indignation as the like was never known in him, looking and speaking fiercely with bended fist, offering to strike him', at which point Coke 'fell flat on all fours, humbly beseeching his Majesty to take compassion on him and to pardon him' if the king felt that his zeal was excessive. While James 'continued his indignation', Salisbury had intervened, braving the king's bafflement as to why he should offer assistance by explaining that Coke was married to his niece.[52]

Coke was also equally as sensitive to any perceived attempt to undermine the authority and dignity of common law. He resented, for example, the enthusiastic royal reception accorded to George Ruggle's play *Ignoramus*, which was performed before the king, Prince Charles and 2,000 spectators at Trinity College in Cambridge in March 1615. Cleverly circumventing an earlier royal order that had sought to suppress student rowdiness by banning any play in English from being performed within five miles of the city, Ruggle's neo-Latin farce lasted six hours in duration and mercilessly satirized common lawyers for their cack-handed linguistic contortions. 'Quota est clocka nunc?' was, for example, how one character – likened to both Coke and the city's unpopular Recorder, Francis Brakyn – asked the time.[53] While James demanded a repeat performance and returned to Cambridge in May, Chamberlain observed Coke evincing 'much bitterness' about Ruggle's play, which 'hath so nettled the lawyers that they are almost out of all patience', evidently appearing 'to think themselves so *sacrosancti* that they may not be touched'.[54]

Coke was likewise fiercely ready to defend judicial independence and, having been appointed Chief Justice of the King's Bench in 1613, clashed with his replacement as Attorney-General, Bacon, over the monarch's right to solicit judicial opinions before a trial. In December

1614, for example, an elderly Somerset preacher, Edmund Peacham, was arrested after sermon notes attacking James and his state officers were found in his house. But since no sermon had been delivered or published, it was unclear whether the notes alone constituted grounds for treason and, despite being interrogated 'before torture, in torture, between torture, and after torture', Peacham himself refused to elaborate. When James then directed Bacon to consult individually with the judges, Coke had refused on the grounds that 'judges were not to give opinions by fractions' and – casting an allusive slur on Catholic sacraments – had warned that 'this auricular taking of opinions, single and apart, was new and dangerous'.[55]

James, meanwhile, produced his own commentary on the case in March 1615, insisting that Peacham's compilation of the sermon notes was an explicit act that encompassed his own death. There might be grounds for mitigation if Peacham had 'spewed forth all the venom ... either in drunkenness' or through 'sudden passion or discontentment'. But Peacham's notes had contained 'all the injuries that the hearts of men, or malice of the devil, can invent against the king, to disable him utterly, not to be a king, not to be a Christian, not to be a man or reasonable creature, not worthy of breath here, nor salvation hereafter'. If penning such a vicious attack was not deemed treasonable, James inferred that his judges were 'caring more for the safety of such a monster, than the preservation of a crown'.[56] Eventually tried and convicted for treason, Peacham escaped execution but remained in jail in Taunton, where he died in 1616.

Debates about the royal prerogative also featured prominently in the acrimonious rivalry between Coke and Thomas Egerton, Baron Ellesmere (Lord Chancellor since 1596), over the court of Chancery's right to hear cases after judgements at law had been pronounced in other tribunals. In what Coke dismissed as 'dangerous and absurd opinions', Ellesmere maintained that, since his role as Lord Chancellor rendered him 'keeper of the king's conscience', he was solely responsible to James and 'whatsoever the king directed in any case he would decree accordingly'.[57] To resist what he regarded as dangerous encroachments on the authority of common law, Coke started approving writs of *habeas corpus* to release individuals imprisoned for contempt when they had ignored summons by Chancery after their cases had been determined in common-law courts. Coke was also suspected of tacitly hinting to individuals to consider alleging *praemunire* (the criminal offence of maintaining an alternative, formerly papal, jurisdiction in England) against Chancery officials who, by issuing injunctions, appeared to impugn the finality of common-law judgements. Among Ellesmere's papers are the notes of an eyewitness who observed Coke's fury after a grand jury declined to endorse two indictments for *praemunire* in February 1616. Denying the right of anyone who 'shall set his hand to a bill into any English court after a judgement at law', Coke had warned 'we must look about, or the common law of England will be overthrown.'[58]

It was thus a weary king who summoned his twelve common-law judges to the Star Chamber on the last day of the legal year in June 1616, before they departed for the summer assize circuits. Exhorting them to show 'brotherly love one toward another', James lamented the relentless multiplication of lawsuits that encouraged subjects to attend court 'only out of curiosity, to hear questions of the jurisdictions of courts disputed' and to see 'what court is like to prevail above the other', whereby 'pleas are turned from court to court in an endless circular motion, as upon Ixion's wheel'. James recalled visiting Denmark a quarter of a century earlier in 1590. Since Danes were 'governed only by a written law', there were no additional advocates: 'the parties themselves plead their own cause,' after which 'a man stands up and reads the law, and there is an end, for the very law-book itself is their only judge. Happy were all kingdoms if they could be so.'[59]

In a strenuous assertion of the royal prerogative, James reminded his judges that their office was *ius dicere*, not *ius dare*: to articulate law, not to make it. Judicial prying into the 'absolute prerogative of the crown' was 'no subject for the tongue of a lawyer, nor is it lawful to be disputed'. He especially resented the idea of invoking *praemunire* as 'a foolish, inept and presumptuous attempt, and fitter for the time of some unworthy king'. Since the English had, in James, 'a king of reasonable understanding, and willing to reform', alleged miscarriages of justice were for him alone to remedy. Direct appeal to the monarch remained 'the high way' and disgruntled litigants should not 'go the other way, and back way, in contempt of our authority'. Recalling that he had sworn by his coronation oath to uphold the rule of law, James concluded his speech by vowing 'in point of justice, to keep myself unspotted all the days of my life', confident that 'the world will know, that I came hither this day to maintain the law, and do justice according to my oath'.[60]

Commending James's 'most excellent and learned speech' in Star Chamber, one Gray's Inn barrister, Richard Hutton, recorded in his diary that 'we have cause to rejoice for his love to religion and to the common law.'[61] By contrast, another Gray's Inn barrister, Timothy Tourner, was deeply alarmed by James's assertions and blamed successive Lord Chancellors for having 'insinuated with the king' that the royal prerogative eternally trumped all other authority. So long as such views prevailed, Tourneur feared that 'the liberty of the subjects of England will be taken away and no law practised upon them but prerogative'; indeed, England's body politic 'will in a short time die in all the parts' amid rumours 'that no Parliament will be held in England again'.[62] In the short term, further altercations led to James dismissing Coke as Chief Justice in November 1616. As Chamberlain surmised, 'four Ps have overthrown and put him down, that is Pride, Prohibitions, *Praemunire* and Prerogative.'[63]

By the time James faced the prospect of the first Westminster Parliament to be called since 1614, his frustrations with the legal profession were palpable. In a proclamation issued in November 1620, the king bluntly warned constituents across England and Wales to select as MPs experienced representatives who would participate constructively in debates rather than 'curious and wrangling lawyers, who may seek reputation, by stirring needless questions'.[64] When James addressed the House of Lords the following March, he acknowledged that his English judges were 'men of great understanding and gravity, but for common lawyers, they are wind instruments, their tongue being their pipe'. Moreover, 'a bagpipe is a greater noise than a viol, although a viol hath better music and heavier.'[65] In the Commons, it was indeed the most curious and wrangling lawyer of all, Coke – sitting as MP for Liskeard in Cornwall – who assumed leadership of a vocal opposition faction that successfully revived medieval practices of parliamentary impeachment to ensure that charges of corruption were laid against Coke's longstanding nemesis, Lord Chancellor Bacon. To avoid a public trial, Bacon resigned and confessed in writing in April 1621 that 'I do plainly and ingenuously confess that I am guilty of corruption; and do renounce all defence,' for which he suffered three days' imprisonment in the Tower of London and permanent debarment from public office.[66]

Thereafter, James shocked observers by appointing, in Bacon's place as Lord Chancellor, a senior cleric, John Williams, to the equivalent office of Lord Keeper. As Chamberlain inferred, James had evidently 'resolved to have no more lawyers (as men so bred and nousled [reared] in corruption that they could not leave it)'.[67] Throughout his life, James had firmly believed – as he reminded English peers and MPs in 1607 – that in any instance 'wherein no positive law is resolute, *Rex est Iudex* [the king is judge], for he is *Lex Loquens* [a speaking law], and is to supply the law, where the law wants'.[68] Practical tensions arising from judicial comity and professional rivalries led James to become an unusually active and interested *Lex Loquens*. More broadly, chronic congestion in the courts and confused relations between different courts encouraged, from 1621 onwards, the revival of the House of Lords as both a first instance and appellate judicature, from litigants doubtful that definitive judgement was obtainable in either the common law or equitable courts. It would be another 250 years before the Judicature Act (1873) reorganized England's higher court structure and ended serial internecine disputes by fusing the administration of law and equity and abolishing common injunctions. James would thus have relished the resonances of Charles Dickens's fictional Chancery suit, *Jarndyce v. Jarndyce*, as described in the first chapter of *Bleak House* (1853):

Jarndyce and Jarndyce drones on. This scarecrow of a suit has, in course of time, become so complicated, that no man alive knows what it means. The parties to it understand it least; but it has been observed that no two Chancery lawyers can talk about it for five minutes, without coming to a total disagreement as to all the premises ... [Meanwhile] the little plaintiff or defendant, who was promised a new rocking-horse when Jarndyce and Jarndyce should be settled, has grown up, possessed himself of a real horse, and trotted away into the other world.[69]

23

A New Britain in Another World

Before returning to North America to take up his appointment as Governor of Virginia, George Yeardley was invited to the royal court at Newmarket in November 1618 where he was knighted by King James. After accompanying the king, Prince Charles and the Marquis of Buckingham to church, Yeardley attended dinner 'where for a long hour and a half', James 'reasoned with him alone, and only of Virginia'. As one eyewitness observed, the king asked about 'the number and increase of cattle' in the colony, as well as the religious inclinations of the native population, and directed Yeardley 'and all the planters to deal gently and favourably with the Indians' in order 'to induce them to Christianity and not to tyrannise over them like the Spaniards'. James was also concerned to ensure that religious ministers arriving in Virginia were not 'authors of novelty or singularity' and that the colony's churches were not 'built like theatres or cockpits, but in a decent form, and in imitation of the churches in England'. Regarding economic subsistence, he emphasized the need for diversification to avoid over-reliance on tobacco cultivation, observing that, just as 'our Saviour Christ in the Gospel says man lives not by bread alone, then I may well say, man lives not by smoke alone'. Accordingly, the king 'much delighted in hearing the description of the silkgrass, and of the several uses it might be converted to', prompting discussion of cordage as an essential component in shipping materials and a royal reminder 'not to neglect the planting of vines' as an attractive stimulus to 'good company to come and live there'. Enthused by his conversation with Yeardley, James rose from dinner and publicly pronounced that 'this is the first day that ever I began heartily to love Virginia, and from this day forward I will ever protect it and defend it.'[1]

Fortified by royal encouragement, Yeardley returned to Virginia in the spring of 1619 and set about implementing the reformist agenda agreed by the London-based Council of the Virginia Company. As well as overseeing the abolition of martial law and regularizing private land-holding, he summoned the first meeting of the General Assembly of Virginia that July, comprising Yeardley as governor, a Council of State and twenty-two elected burgesses. Later acclaimed as the first repre-sentative self-governing body to meet in the Americas, the Assembly resolved at its inaugural meeting that English common law would be instituted in Virginia and 'that no injury or oppression be wrought by the English against the Indians whereby the present peace might be dis-turbed and ancient quarrels might be revived'. Common-law provision extended to the local Chickahominy tribe unless contrary directions were received from London or 'they do provoke us by some new injury.'[2] The same eyewitness who recounted Yeardley's conversation with James at Newmarket the previous autumn had celebrated the export of English common law to Virginia, identifying one of the Company's directors and prominent MP, Sir Edwin Sandys, as 'our Solon and Lycurgus' in a reference to the legendary lawgivers of ancient Sparta and Athens. The colony's laws and ordinances were, moreover, 'not to be chested, or hidden like a candle under a bushel', but 'in form of a Magna Charta, to be published to the whole colony', extending equal legal protection to all social ranks.[3]

Back in Newmarket, and less than two months after meeting Yeard-ley, James had written to the Virginia Company's Treasurer (and leader), Sir Thomas Smythe, objecting to having 'been troubled with diverse idle young people' converging around the royal court. While James directed Smythe 'at the next opportunity to send them away to Virginia', Smythe, in turn, requested London's Lord Mayor, Sir Wil-liam Cockayne, to oversee the vagrants' removal from Newmarket and their detention at Bridewell prison until the next transatlantic voyage departed.[4]

James's impromptu announcement in November 1618 of his renewed interest in Virginia's affairs echoed the personal, and often proprietor-ial, terms in which he had presented plantation policy in Ireland. For although the royal charters granted to individual proprietors or trading organizations, such as the Virginia Company, conferred considerable autonomy regarding the practical management of colonial affairs, the Stuart Crown retained ultimate oversight and remained ready, if necessary, to recall charters or revise specific privileges. More generally, the English Crown retained a legal, as well as a strategic, obligation to supervise its overseas territories at a time when other European powers were ready to challenge for control.[5] Published in 1620, the Virginia Company's *Declaration of the State of the Colony and Affairs in Virginia* confirmed that all measures proposed by the colony's General Assembly were submitted 'first to his Majesty's view and approbation, it being not fit that his Majesty's subjects should be governed by any other laws, than such as receive the influence of their life from him'.[6] Two years later, the Company's Council reminded Yeardley's successor as governor, Sir Francis Wyatt, of royal financial interests: if the colony prospered, crown revenue would increase through customs duties and other levies.

Yeardley's discussion of Virginian affairs at Newmarket in November 1618 thus occurred at a pivotal moment in the colony's early history. Indeed, the day before the meeting, John Chamberlain had enthusiastically suggested to the English ambassador at The Hague, Dudley Carleton, that 'if you would ever begin a plantation – now is the time'.[7] The Virginia Company's debts that year were estimated to amount to £8,000–£9,000 sterling and its settler population only numbered around 400, but colonist numbers had increased to around 1,000 by the following spring. Through Yeardley's reorganization of older landholdings four new boroughs were created and named in honour of James and his children: Jamestown, Charles City, Henrico and Kecoughtan (soon changed to 'Elizabeth City').[8]

*

Authorizing settlement of lands 'not now actually possessed by any Christian prince or people', the royal charter granted to the Virginia Company in April 1606 was issued by James less than a year after final ratification of the Anglo-Spanish Treaty of London, which notably neither permitted nor prohibited English trading rights in the Spanish Indies.[9] A 'Plymouth group' of financiers and merchants from south-west England was directed towards lands lying between latitudes of 38° and 45° north, along over 400 miles of coastline in what later

became known as 'New England'. A settlement was established at Sagadahoc on the Maine coast in autumn 1607, but abandoned a year later,
after a sharp winter and hostile encounters with the local Etchemin
inhabitants.[10]

At the same time, James's charter had also encouraged a 'London'
group of investors and adventurers to settle territory between the
latitudes of 34° and 41° north, extending from North Carolina to the
Chesapeake region, which led to the establishment of 'James Fort'
in May 1607. Renamed 'Jamestown', it became the first permanent
English settlement in the Americas. As the motto underneath the
Virginia Company's coat of arms ambitiously proclaimed: '*En Dat
Virginia Quintam*' ('Behold, Virginia gives us a fifth dominion'),
joining England, Scotland, Ireland and France as territories under
James's rule. In March 1609, one of the king's chaplains, Richard
Crakanthorpe, celebrated the sixth anniversary of James's accession
to the English throne in a sermon sponsored by the Virginia Company and preached at Paul's Cross. Denying that any king in British
or continental history had rivalled James's 'learning, judgement and
memory' or his 'justice, clemency and wisdom', Crakanthorpe also
extolled the rich opportunities awaiting emigrants to Virginia 'to see
a new Britain in another world'.[11]

The geographical precision attaching to territories identified in the
Virginia Company's founding charter reflected James's hope to avoid
conflict with neighbouring continental powers, notably Spain and Portugal. For after Christopher Columbus's exploration of North and
South America, Pope Alexander VI had issued a papal bull in 1493,
establishing an imaginary line of demarcation running through the
eastern part of present-day Brazil, with American lands to the west and
east of this border granted to Spain and Portugal respectively. But since
English exploration was undertaken by chartered Companies rather
than centrally directed by the Crown, James could conveniently resort
to plausible deniability, if needed. In September 1607, for instance, he
feigned ignorance when pressed about the Virginia Company's activities
by the Spanish ambassador in London, Pedro de Zúñiga, protesting –
as Zúñiga put it – that 'he was not informed as to the details of what
was going on, so far as the voyages to Virginia were concerned'. Notwithstanding James's dismissive description of merchant adventurers as
'exasperating people', Zúñiga scorned the 'shabby deceit' by which the

English state pursued its overseas ambitions. As he advised Philip III, direct Spanish intervention in Virginia would ensure that 'the few who are there should be finished outright' and their forcible expulsion would 'cut the root, so that it would not sprout again'.[12] The following June, James's ambassador in Madrid, Sir Charles Cornwallis, warned that, although Spanish 'tongues use silence' in regard to Virginia, he observed 'their hearts and their eyes much fixed upon that plantation' and predicted an imminent 'endeavour to pull it up by the roots, as they did that of the French in Florida'.[13] While there was no direct attack against English settlements in the region, a Spanish prisoner in Virginia in 1613 likewise urged Philip to act swiftly and 'stop the progress of a hydra in its infancy, because it is clear that its intention is to grow and encompass the destruction of all the West'.[14]

As well as fears of hostile attack, natural disasters disrupted colonial communications and supplies. In July 1609, Sir Thomas Gates sailed in the *Sea Venture* with Admiral Sir George Somers, to serve as the acting Governor of Virginia, ahead of Thomas West, Baron De La Warr, who sailed for the colony in April 1610, and arrived in June. Encountering a hurricane en route, Gates and Somers were shipwrecked on the island of Bermuda, almost six hundred miles east of the North Carolina coast. Remaining on Bermuda while two new ships were constructed, Gates and Somers eventually arrived in Virginia in May 1610 to find the colony on the point of extinction, having suffered famine and Powhatan attacks; there were just 'sixty persons, most famished and at the point of death'.[15] Although Gates and Somers had resolved to evacuate Jamestown and return to England, the settlement's abandonment was forestalled by the arrival, in June, of De La Warr – after whom the state of Delaware would later be named. Back in London, promoting the discovery of lushly abundant resources in the twenty square miles of Bermuda (or 'Somers Island') offered a helpful distraction from the desperation of Virginia's 'Starving Time'. A vivid narrative of the *Sea Venture*'s voyage, penned by Gates's secretary, inspired Shakespeare's *The Tempest*, which was first performed before James's court in November 1611. By the time James issued letters patent creating the 'Somers Island Company' nearly four years later, Bermuda had a population of around 600 colonists, which was more than twice the number in Virginia.

*

In England, James's discussion of Virginian matters with Yeardley at Newmarket in November 1618 occurred only a month after the execution of the explorer and erstwhile courtier, Sir Walter Ralegh. In 1603, Ralegh had been convicted of treason for his involvement in the 'Main' plot that had envisaged a popular rising, with possible Spanish intervention, to remove James from the English throne in favour of his English cousin, Arbella Stuart. Thereafter, Ralegh had been detained in the Tower of London until his release in 1616 to lead an expedition to Guiana in search of gold and silver mines near the Orinoco River. Although royal permission was granted on condition that Ralegh avoided hostile encounters with the Spanish, forces led by his lieutenant, Lawrence Keymis, had stormed the settlement of San Thomé in an assault that proved fatal for its Spanish governor, and Ralegh's elder son, Walter. With his voyage a fiasco, Ralegh had returned to England where he was arrested for breaching royal orders and executed in October 1618.

Thereafter, James oversaw publication of a tract describing Ralegh's prosecution, which volunteered that, although kings were only obliged to account for their actions before God, he had 'always been willing to bring them before sun and moon', rather than 'let them pass in uncertain reports'. In this instance, Ralegh had not only 'so enchanted the world' with promises of an (elusive) gold mine in Guiana, but had also directly given 'many vehement asseverations' to James that 'he never meant or would commit any outrages or spoils upon the King of Spain's subjects'.[16] Ralegh himself had previously objected that his venture had been sabotaged from the outset by 'that braggadocio, the Spanish ambassador', who had prevailed with James to obtain, from Ralegh, detailed written confirmation of his intended route and the numbers of men and amount of ordnance on each of his ships. Such information had then been passed to the Spanish ambassador and onwards to Madrid, ensuring that Philip IV had been fully apprised of the expedition 'before my departure out of the Thames'.[17]

Mercantile interest in the region nevertheless remained strong and a commander involved in the San Thomé attack, Roger North, sufficiently convinced James of his loyalty to issue prospectuses for a new Amazon Company enumerating Guiana's plentiful 'rich dyes, medicinable drugs, sweet gums, cotton wool, sugar canes, choice tobacco, precious woods, nutmeg trees, and other spices, useful plants and pleasant fruits'.[18] In September 1619, James granted the Amazon Company a royal charter, which predictably incensed Spanish interests in London, most notably the Count of Gondomar, who immediately set about ensuring the new Company's liquidation on his return to England as ambassador in spring 1620. Outraged that around a fifth of James's Privy Councillors had invested in the venture, Gondomar maintained that the Amazon region belonged to Philip III 'by virtue of discovery, demarcation and possession', comprising lands to which the Spanish king's title was comparable to that of James's in regard to Scotland and Ireland. Insisting that embarking on English settlement in the Amazon was tantamount to declaring war on Spain, Gondomar dismissed claims of *terra nullius* ('land belonging to no one') on the grounds that, just as he owned a modest estate with areas of uninhabited land, English Privy Councillors would judge it wholly unacceptable if commissions were issued in Spain for colonists 'to settle the vacant places which they had in their estates'.[19]

To Gondomar, James evidently declared himself 'the unhappiest king in the world'; as the Spaniard reported, 'everybody assured me that they had never seen him so aroused' by his Councillors' involvement in the new Amazon Company. Meeting with Gondomar at Whitehall, James had protested that the ambassador's distress in the matter 'had pierced his heart', telling him 'three or four times that he beseeched me to have pity on him, and to console him, and help him to take remedies'. Although James duly cancelled the Amazon Company's patent, North's expedition left for the Orinoco River without permission. On his return to England in February 1621, North was arrested and his cargo of 28,000 pounds of tobacco and other goods was seized as rightfully belonging to the Spanish king. With North detained in the Tower, Gondomar reminded Philip that 'the English thieves' dens in Virginia and Bermuda' were 'a matter which requires a very considered and effective remedy'.[20]

Coincidentally, in September 1619, James also held an audience at Hampton Court with Sir Thomas Roe who, nearly a decade earlier, had commanded an expedition to Guiana that had reached as far as the Oyapoc River. The Hampton Court meeting, however, marked Roe's return to England after serving as James's ambassador to the Mughal Court in India, from where Roe had written to Prince Charles in October 1616, accounting Emperor Jahangir to be, in terms of jewels, 'the Treasury of the world, buying all that comes, and heaping rich stones as if he would rather build than wear them'. In his journal, Roe described attending Jahangir's birthday celebrations and admiring the emperor 'clothed, or rather laden with diamonds, rubies, pearls and other precious vanities, so great, so glorious!'[21]

The ruler of around 100 million subjects, Jahangir drew on an annual revenue estimated to exceed the equivalent of £54 million sterling: an eye-watering amount for the perennially penurious Stuart monarchy. Indeed, after Roe had presented his diplomatic gifts on arriving at the imperial court – which included a musical instrument known as a 'virginal' and a gilded horse-drawn carriage – he informed the East India Company's directors that Jahangir had apparently questioned aloud 'whether the King of England were a great king, that sent presents of so small value'.[22] Thereafter, Roe failed to fulfil his mission of securing permanent East India Company trading monopolies in Gujurat and elsewhere amid entrenched local perceptions of the English as 'a base people' that 'dwell in a little island'.[23] In response, James resolved to send more impressive gifts to Jahangir and, in 1622, informed East India Company Councillors of his intention to dispatch royal representatives to present 'inventions', including Cornelis Drebbel's newly devised submarine that might assist with pearl-fishing in the Indian Ocean, as well as Drebbel's novel mechanisms for air conditioning, which would be 'a great cooling and refreshing in these extreme hot countries, and a benefit much desired by the Mogul'.[24] Received sceptically by Company Councillors, James's plans proved abortive and no English ambassador was sent to India for another eight decades until Sir William Norris's embassy to the court of Jahangir's grandson, Aurangzeb, in 1699.

By the time of Norris's embassy, the English East India Company was celebrating a centenary of activity, having been founded by Elizabethan charter in 1599. After James's accession as English king, it was restructured as a joint-stock company in 1609 and raised over £400,000 sterling when the first stocks were released in 1613, followed by an astounding £1.6 million from a second issue four years later. Considerable overlap in personnel subsisted within London's mercantile organizations. Sir Thomas Smythe's tenure as the East India Company's first governor – lasting from 1600 until his resignation in 1621 (aside from a short break in 1605–7) – coincided with his election as Treasurer of the Virginia Company from its creation in 1606 until Sandys's election in 1619. In December 1609, James, Anna and Prince Henry had travelled to the Thames dockyard at Deptford to launch two new Company ships: the *Trades Increase* at nearly 1,300 tons, and a smaller pinnace, the *Peppercorn*, with 'the names being given his Majesty' as confirmed by the royal shipbuilder, Phineas Pett. But an unfortunate combination of adverse tides and technical problems arising from the sheer size of the *Trades Increase* frustrated the successful launch of either vessel which, as Pett noted, 'did somewhat discontent his Majesty'. Later given command of the *Peppercorn*, Nicholas Downton recorded the day as one 'wherein all things failed and nothing was effected'.[25] Three years later, the *Trades Increase* sank ignominiously in the Bay of Banten in Indonesia after a failed attempt at careening to repair damage suffered by repeated groundings on account of the vessel's unusually deep draft.

Much more successful was the East India Company's 'Eighth Voyage', which lasted from 1611 to 1614 and not only secured the first trading rights for English merchants in Japan, but also returned a profit of 211 per cent to its investors. In the first diplomatic contact between the two countries in 1613, James received from Japan's military ruler, Shōgun Tokugawa Hidetada, ten gilded and painted folding screens and two suits of armour, one of which remains in the Royal Collection and is unusually light and flexible, being constructed from individual pieces of lacquered and laced iron.[26] Free access to all Japanese ports was granted in a letter sent to James by Tokugawa Ieyasu, who had retired as shōgun but had been sent gifts from the English king that included a silver-gilt telescope nearly two metres in length. As Ieyasu had confirmed, although 'separated by 10,000 leagues of clouds and waves, our countries are, as it were, close to each other' and, if James's subjects arrived in 'any part or port of my dominion . . . they shall be most heartily welcome'.[27]

Inspired by benefits accruing to mercantile companies 'trafficking in the East Indies, Greenland, Muscovy and such like remote places', James encouraged his Scottish subjects to emulate such success. While in Scotland in May 1617, he issued letters patent under the country's Great Seal to create a Scottish East India Company, which was granted 'all power and freedom to trade to all those countries which the English [East India] Company previously earlier has been privileged'. The Company's founder and governor, Sir James Cunningham of Glengarnock, started preparations for a whaling voyage to the island of Spitsbergen in northern Norway, but in March 1618 the English Privy Council declared the Scottish Company's patent invalid on the grounds that it infringed the privileges of the East India and Muscovy Companies. Although

Cunningham received £5,000 sterling in compensation from the latter Company, the readiness of an English institution to declare invalid a patent granted under the Great Seal of Scotland was ominous.[28]

*

James's frustrated hopes for a Scottish East India Company echoed the outspoken opposition that, a decade earlier, Sandys and other MPs had mounted against royal proposals for closer Anglo-Scottish Union. In the late 1610s, Sandys's sharp criticism of the king's pro-Spanish foreign policy prompted James to try to obstruct his re-election as the Virginia Company's Treasurer in 1620, evidently advising Company members to 'choose the Devil if you will, but not Sir Edwin Sandys'.[29] While the Earl of Southampton thereafter stood as Sandys's proxy to become leader of both the Virginia and Somers Island Companies, Sandys also incurred royal suspicion through his correspondence with another group of James's critics: a congregation of Puritans who had emigrated to Leiden from Nottinghamshire in 1607–8 in search of greater religious free-doms. Informed that the separatists now wished to move to America, James was reported to have approved their intention to subsist via fish-ing on the grounds that it was 'an honest trade, 'twas the Apostles' own calling'.[30] Arriving near Cape Cod aboard the *Mayflower* in Novem-ber 1620, the prayers offered by the new arrivals in gratitude for their safe passage is annually remembered at American Thanksgiving. Decid-ing to settle in Plymouth – but lacking documentation to settle outside Virginia – the erstwhile separatists drew up the 'Mayflower Compact' in which they described themselves as 'loyal subjects of our dread sov-ereign Lord King James' and thereafter presented themselves as the English king's representatives when negotiating a treaty of mutual sup-port with a local leader, Massasoit Ousamequin.[31]

In November 1620, James granted new letters patent authorizing the Council for New England, which was granted territory between 40° and 48° north, extending from present-day Philadelphia to St John's, Newfoundland. Yet not all colonial officials were convinced by the con-stant oversight of parent Companies. The previous month, Bermuda's governor, Sir Nathaniel Butler, heard reports that Company directors in London were claiming to 'have every day spent twelve hours in studying the courses that concern the plantations'. As Butler objected to one of the largest shareholders in the Somers Islands Company, Sir Nathaniel Rich, 'more true understanding of the condition and state of these islands every way will be attained by six months' sight and experience here than by thousands of your discoursative courts in England'. In August 1620, the first meeting of Bermuda's General Assembly had taken place in St George, comprising Governor Butler, his Council, bailiffs, and two elected burgesses from each of the island's eight parishes. As Butler proudly opined, the Assembly meeting had produced 'fifteen statutes, passed by us in four days' that would have taken 'fifteen years with you'. In their 'continual brangles and perpetual disputes', Company courts in London resembled cockpits, in which 'you conclude nothing, but rather seek to cross one another, than to find out the truth'. Accordingly, Butler disdained numerous instructions received from Company Councils that 'by their equivocations, contradictions, oppositions, and defective expressions seem rather to ensnare than inform me'.[32]

By the time James summoned the English Parliament in January 1621 for its first meeting in nearly seven years, he was over £900,000 sterling in debt and seeking financial assistance to intervene militarily in continental hostilities. After securing two subsidies worth £150,000, James and his Treasurer, Lionel Cranfield, exacerbated the Virginia Company's financial difficulties by unexpectedly abolishing its right to run fundraising public lotteries. First licensed in 1612, the 'bewitching lotteries for Virginia' – as one London observer described them eight years later – had proven popular in provincial English towns, offering individual prizes as well as philanthropic donations to local institutions.[33] But amid a nationwide depression and demands for armed intervention to retrieve the Palatinate for James's daughter Elizabeth and son-in-law Frederick V, the large sums of money generated by the lotteries for the Company's coffers were resented. As Cranfield put it, he would thus 'let Virginia lose, rather than England'.[34] James and Cranfield were, moreover, frustrated by the Company's reluctance to pay duties on tobacco imports at a time when the annual crop being produced in Virginia amounted to around 50,000 pounds in weight. As criticism of James's alliance with Spain intensified, relations between the king and certain Virginia Company directors only deteriorated. In June 1621, both Sandys and Southampton were arrested and detained for several weeks, suspected of being 'too busy and industrious to trouble His Majesty's service both at home and abroad'.[35]

Further anguish ensued in March 1622 when between 500 and 600 men from an alliance of local Algonquian communities launched a surprise attack on Virginia's settlers, killing at least 347, which amounted to around a quarter of the colony's inhabitants. Another 500–600 hundred colonists succumbed to famine and disease, while a blast furnace at Falling Creek, fledgling glassworks, and the educational College at Henrico were destroyed. After traumatized refugees returned to England from Virginia aboard *The Seaflower* in July, the Company Council wrote to Governor Wyatt announcing 'a perpetual war without peace or truce'. Wyatt was directed to extirpate the native population by 'surprising them in their habitations, intercepting them in their hunting, burning their towns, demolishing their temples, destroying their canoes, plucking up their [fish] weirs, carrying away their corn', and sparing only Indian children to be recruited as labourers.[36] Yet only four years earlier, when King James had met Wyatt's predecessor, Yeardley, at Newmarket, he had urged gentle and favourable treatment of the indigenous population. Hence, amid recriminations provoked by a Powhatan attack in March 1622, colonists quickly retaliated when Company directors tried to 'pass so heavy a censure upon us as if we alone were guilty'. As Virginia's colonists reminded Council directors in London, the 'instructions you have formerly given us' had been 'to win the Indians to us by a kind entertaining them in our houses, and if it were possible to cohabit with us' as the best means of maximizing security.[37]

Such ideals of native assimilation had also been boosted by the well-publicized, Company-funded visit to London of the Jamestown planter John Rolfe, his Algonquian wife, Pocahontas, and their infant son, Thomas. Traditional accounts have focused on the Rolfes' attendance at a Twelfth Night court performance at Whitehall of Ben Jonson's masque *The Vision of Delight*, in January 1617, but in reality, 'the trip was expensive and risky, a last-gasp effort to support a colony that was not yet a decade old.'[38] A daughter of the Powhatan chief, Wahunsonacock, Pocahontas had been abducted by Virginia's settler community as a child and converted to Christianity before marrying Rolfe and taking the name 'Rebecca', redolent of the text from Genesis: 'two nations are in your womb'. After her appearance at the court masque, she was depicted by the Dutch artist, Simon van der Passe, in an engraved portrait that preserved aspects of her indigenous features, while presenting her in stiff Jacobean fashion with an ostrich-feather fan, tall hat, pearl earrings and starched lace ruff (see Plate 21). The portrait's caption referred to the sitter by her Algonquian birth name, 'Matoaka' (rather than her childhood nickname Pocahontas, denoting 'playful' or 'mischievous one'), and included a pedigree confirming her father as 'the mighty Prince Powhatan' and her status as a 'converted and baptised' anglicized American.

Pocahontas was accompanied to England by her sister Matachanna and brother-in-law, Uttamatomakkin, who was *de facto* successor to Wahunsonacock. In his *General History of Virginia* published in 1624, the erstwhile Jamestown colonist John Smith recounted re-establishing contact with Pocahontas during her visit. 'Not seeming well contented', Pocahontas had recalled Smith's arrival in Virginia in 1607 and his initial reassurances to her father as Powhatan chief that 'what was yours should be his, and he the like to you'. But Pocahontas now surmised that 'your countrymen will lie much', while her brother-in-law was equally disillusioned. Lamenting the lack of reciprocity evidenced during his visit to England, Uttamatomakkin observed that Smith had once given 'Powhatan a white dog, which Powhatan fed as himself, but your king gave me nothing, and I am better than your white dog'.[39] While her royal status was emphasized by her inclusion in *Baziliωlogia: A Book of Kings* (1618) – which presented 'true and lively ettigies of all our English kings from the conquest to this present' – Pocahontas ultimately succumbed in England to illnesses to which she had no immunity.[40] Too ill to make the return voyage to Virginia she died, probably of pneumonia, at Gravesend in March 1617.

Following the Powhatan attack on English settlers in March 1622, the Virginia Company's directors, led by Sandys, publicly presented the event as a 'massacre' that justified a reorientation of policy towards the local Chesapeake population. The Company's original aims in settling the territory would be realized more effectively by reassertion of Company control over colonial officials. In August, the Company Secretary in London, Edward Waterhouse, published an updated *Declaration of the State of the Colony and Affairs in Virginia*, reassuring prospective settlers and investors that the 'treachery and cruelty' of the Powhatans would only redound on themselves; the attack 'must needs be for the good of the plantation after, and the loss of this blood to make the body more healthful'.[41] In November 1622, John Donne, as Dean of St Paul's, admitted to becoming 'an adventurer, if not to Virginia, yet for Virginia', after accepting the Company's invitation to preach, with a subsequent 'commandment' to publish his address. Taking his text from the Acts of the Apostles, Donne referred to the Powhatan attack, advising that 'though you see not your money, though you see not your men, though a flood, a flood of blood have broken in upon them, be not discouraged.'[42] Having become a Company shareholder in June, the philosopher Thomas Hobbes is known to have attended Donne's sermon, which also warned against any 'who seek to establish a temporal kingdom' in Virginia that derogated from James's authority.[43] As Donne elaborated, if settlers 'propose to themselves an exemption from laws, to live at their liberty, this is to be kings, to divest allegiance, to be under no man' in the same way as attempts to discover 'a sudden way to be rich' and achieve levels of self-sufficiency that 'need no man'. Since 'liberty and abundance, are characters of kingdoms', Donne reminded the Company that 'the Apostles were not to look for it, in their employment, nor you in this your Plantation.'[44]

*

At the time of Jamestown's original settlement in 1607, Philip III's ambassador in London, Pedro de Zúñiga, had observed fears among Virginia Company officials that, if their plantation failed, 'they will put the king [James] in the position of taking it in his own hands.'[45] By the early 1620s, Zúñiga's prediction had proved correct, amid rising calls for closer royal involvement. At the end of Sir Nathaniel Butler's tenure as Governor of Bermuda, petitions were presented from the islanders, their Council and Butler himself, which criticized, *inter alia*, the perennial factionalism and 'anarchy' of the Somers Island Company Council. As the petitioners explained, the difficulties experienced in Bermuda were a direct result of the 'multiplicity of voices in the Somers Islands courts in England' with factional agendas frustrating practical proposals. Moreover, 'this course, as being in itself full of confusion and error, is directly contrary and opposite to the noble government of a monarchy, under which we have been born and bred, and desire always to live'.[46] In autumn 1622, Butler visited Virginia, where he encountered pervasive starvation and unburied corpses lying in the streets. On his return to London, Butler presented a devastating indictment – entitled 'The Unmasked Face of our Colony in Virginia' – to the Privy Council in April 1623, objecting that, although there had been 'no fewer than 10,000 souls transported thither', mismanagement by the London Company meant that only around 2,000 were 'at the present to be found alive, many of them also in a sickly and desperate estate'. Without speedy intervention 'by some divine and supreme hand' in Virginia's affairs, 'instead of a plantation, it will shortly get the name of a slaughterhouse and so justly become both odious to ourselves and contemptible to all the world.'[47]

Undertaking such intervention, James ordered a royal commission of investigation led by a judge, Sir Richard Jones. By terms agreed in May 1623, commissioners were empowered to subpoena all documentation dating back to the Company's creation in 1606, audit its financial affairs, examine witnesses under oath, and pursue enquiries in Virginia as well as in London. That same month, James wrote to the Somers Island Company Council to denounce the practice whereby 'of late, in a confused manner, the two Companies of Virginia and the Somers Islands have been wont to meet together at one time and place, which we by no means like'. Councillors were instead directed to 'appoint some fit and convenient place for your own Company to keep their courts by themselves' and forbidden from electing into office Sandys and four others (Lord William Cavendish, Sir John Danvers, and John and Nicholas Ferrar) – 'being in the nature of delinquents' – who had been suspended from their Virginia Company roles and were under house arrest.[48] In his later memoirs, one 'delinquent', Nicholas Ferrar, blamed the Count of Gondomar for suggesting to James that the Virginia Company's meetings were 'a seminary for a seditious parliament', being run by 'deep politicians' who 'had further designs than a tobacco plantation'.[49]

As internal divisions between Sandys and other Virginia Councillors deepened, Nathaniel Rich's submission described Sandys's determination to dispatch thousands of colonists between 1619 and 1623 – with insufficient provisions and against advice from colonial officials – as a reckless 'means to cast away the lives of many of his Majesty's subjects'.[50] In July, an argument between Cavendish and Rich's cousin the Earl of Warwick provoked a challenge to duel, whereupon Warwick disguised himself as a merchant and travelled to Ghent in order to meet Cavendish on foreign soil, while his adversary was intercepted by royal officials and prevented from leaving Shoreham.[51]

When a new English Parliament convened in spring 1624, James wrote to MPs in the House of Commons in April to confirm, as Chamberlain put it, that he would 'rid them of a thorny business touching Virginia and the Somers Islands'. Aware that investigations into colonial affairs were 'followed on both sides with much eagerness and animosity', the king 'resumed and reserved the whole course to his own hearing'.[52]

After the Jones commission's findings confirmed the Virginia Company's operational dysfunctionality and precarious finances, the court of King's Bench issued a decree confirming the Company's formal dissolution. Responsibility for the colony's affairs reverted to the Privy Council as Virginia became England's first crown colony. A body known as the 'Commissioners of Virginia' was created, chaired by the Privy Council President, Henry, Viscount Mandeville, which held its first meeting in July 1624 at Sir Thomas Smythe's City house in Philpot Lane – which was where the first meeting of the Virginia Company had taken place nearly two decades earlier.[53] That same month, James wrote to Governor Wyatt, reaffirming his personal involvement in the colony's affairs and insisting that 'we were and are still resolved to proceed to the perfecting of that work which we have begun for the good of the said plantation'. Confident that Virginia would become 'a lasting monument of our most gracious and happy government', James trusted that the colony could yet produce 'diverse goods and staple commodities, though in the sixteen years' government past it had yielded few or none'.[54]

Pending such diversification, the viability of colonial society depended on tobacco, which served as both an export crop and a form of domestic currency. In 1619, Virginia's General Assembly had declared tobacco to be legal tender, with the governor, burgess representatives and government clerks all receiving their salaries entirely in pounds of tobacco, which were recorded as credits in individual ledgers.[55] Five years later, James issued a proclamation in September 1624 acknowledging Virginia and Bermuda to be 'part of our dominions', governed by 'our royal authority' and now 'added to the rest of our empire', albeit 'in their infancy'. Tobacco production was also recognized as the most likely means by which such colonies would 'be brought to maturity and perfection'. Notwithstanding the 'dislike we have ever had of the use of tobacco in general', Virginia and Bermuda were granted a monopoly on all tobacco imports into Britain.[56] Following James's death the following spring, his son issued a proclamation in May 1625 declaring the territories of Virginia, the Somers Islands and New England 'to be a part of our royal empire', and confirming 'that the government of the colony of Virginia shall immediately depend upon ourself'. For as Charles I explained, although mercantile companies might legitimately be entrusted with overseeing trade and commercial affairs, it could never 'be fit or safe to communicate the ordering of state affairs' to such organizations.[57]

24

I am an Old King

When James returned from Scotland in the late summer of 1617, George Villiers, Earl of Buckingham, warned the Lord Keeper, Sir Francis Bacon, that the king was still angry at Bacon's initial opposition to the marriage arranged between Buckingham's brother John and Frances, daughter of Sir Edward Coke. Attempts by Bacon to explain his conduct had been judged by James 'confused and childish', while his English Privy Councillors should expect 'a kingly reprimand' for 'their ill behaviour'.[1] Summoned to Hampton Court in September, the Councillors were calmly informed by James – in a speech reported by the Spanish ambassador, the Count of Gondomar – that he was 'neither a god nor an angel, but a man like any other' who would 'act like a man, and confess to loving those dear to me more than other men'. With Buckingham present, the king wanted his other Councillors to 'be sure that I love the Earl of Buckingham more than anyone else, and more than you who are here assembled'. Furthermore, James confirmed his 'wish to speak in my own behalf, and not to have it thought to be a defect, for Jesus Christ did the same, and therefore I cannot be blamed': 'Christ had his John, and I have my George.'[2]

The focus of James's affections in the last decade of his life, Buckingham first met the king at Apethorpe Palace in Northamptonshire in August 1614. As James recalled seven years later, 'he came to me as poor George Villiers' but was quickly appointed a royal cupbearer, before being knighted and made a Gentleman of the Bedchamber the following year.[3] In January 1616, Villiers became royal Master of the Horse, was created a Knight of the Garter in April, elevated to a viscountcy in July, and appointed Lord Lieutenant of Buckinghamshire in September. That same year, it was Villiers who had sought advice from Bacon, then

Attorney-General. Despite demurring that he 'rather studied books than men', Bacon had offered detailed counsel, acknowledging that Villiers was 'now the king's favourite': 'the whole kingdom hath cast their eye upon you, as the new rising star, and no man thinks his business can prosper at court, unless he hath you for his good angel.' While Bacon hoped that the new favourite's tenure would endure and that 'you shall not be a meteor, or a blazing star, but *stella fixa*', he warned Villiers to 'remember then what your true condition is.' As the king's favourite, 'you are his shadow' and, since divinely ordained monarchs remained above criticism, if events miscarried 'you may be offered as a sacrifice to appease the multitude.'[4]

In 1617, Villiers was created Earl of Buckingham and appointed as both an English and a Scottish Privy Councillor; he was then elevated to a marquisate the following year and appointed Lord Admiral of the Navy in 1619. Following conferral of a dukedom in 1623, Buckingham became the first duke to be created for nearly a century who was not a blood relative of the monarch; the only other dukes then in England were the king's son, Prince Charles (Duke of York), and the king's cousin Ludovick Stewart, Duke of Lennox.[5] Following his marriage to Katherine Manners, daughter of the Earl of Rutland, in May 1619, Buckingham also provided James with a new extended family of whom the king was visibly fond. That Christmas, the Puritan diarist Sir Simonds D'Ewes described a snug scene at court involving Prince Charles playing cards with Buckingham and the marquis's wife, mother and father-in-law. As D'Ewes recorded, 'the king looking on, he openly professed: "here is a father and son (meaning himself and the prince), a father and daughter (meaning Rutland and his daughter) and a son and mother (meaning Buckingham and his mother). The Devil on me if I know which I love best."'[6]

Born as a younger son of a minor gentry family in Leicestershire, Villiers had just turned twenty-two when he first met James in 1614. The king nicknamed him 'Steenie' after the martyr Saint Stephen, who had 'the face of an angel' (Acts 6:8). Regarding Buckingham's physical beauty, one of the king's chaplains, John Hacket, recalled that 'from the nails of his fingers, nay, from the sole of his foot to the crown of his head, there was no blemish in him'; it was his graceful carriage and 'every stoop of his deportment' that 'were the beauty of his beauty'.[7] The recipient of lucrative pensions and jewels alongside titles,

Buckingham became a knowledgeable connoisseur and a skilful self-fashioner. Today, visitors to London's Banqueting House can admire Peter Paul Rubens's ceiling painting, *The Apotheosis of James I*, which depicts the king ascending to the heavens on the back of Jupiter's eagle with his foot resting on a globe. But visitors to Osterley Park in west London could also – until its destruction by fire in 1949 – admire a remarkably similar ceiling canvas by Rubens that showed Buckingham being celestially conveyed to the Temple of Virtue by Minerva and Mercury (the deities of wisdom and communication), while repelling attempts of a figure, personifying Envy, trying to pull the duke back down to earth.[8]

As royal favourite, Buckingham expected and experienced envy, alongside veneration. In an early biography, the diplomat Sir Henry Wotton deployed a horticultural metaphor to describe the duke's 'germination' and rapid rise from obscurity, observing that 'surely had he been a plant, he would have been reckoned among the *spontes nascentes*, for he sprung without any help'. Since James was 'a king [that] could peruse men as well as books', Wotton emphasized the tutelage conferred by a paternalist monarch who had found his new favourite 'susceptible of good form' and moulded him 'by degrees, as great architects use to do, in the workmanship of his regal hand'.[9] During James's absence in Scotland in 1617, Sir John Holles – who supported Frances Coke's mother in opposing the planned marriage to John Villiers – grumbled to the king's disgraced former favourite, the Earl of Somerset, that Buckingham's sway over court patronage was such that 'we are all reeds, we bow with every breath, not oaks which withstand the most tempestuous winds'.[10] It was, however, precisely in gratitude for 'your continual attendance upon my service, your daily employments in the same, and the incessant swarm of suitors importunately hanging upon you' that James dedicated his *Meditation upon the Lord's Prayer* to Buckingham in 1619. For although 'you were not bred a scholar', the king recalled how 'diverse times before I meddled with it, I told you, and only you, of some of my conceptions upon the Lord's Prayer, and you often solicited me to put pen to paper'.[11] Joining the ranks of supplicants petitioning Buckingham for preferment in August 1621, John Donne undertook to 'lie in a corner, as a clod of clay, attending what vessel it shall please you to make of' his available talents; two months later, Donne became Dean of St Paul's Cathedral.

Among foreign observers, the Venetian ambassador Girolamo Lando reported resentment at the extent to which Buckingham had become, by September 1622, 'the sole access to the court, the sole means of favour, in fact, one might say, the king himself'. James had 'given him all his heart' and would 'not eat, sup, or remain an hour without him, and considers him his whole joy'.[12] That same year, D'Ewes noted the king's effervescent mood, observing how James, 'hugging him one time very seriously' then 'burst forth, "Begot man, never one loved another more than I do thee, and let God leave me when I leave thee."'[13]

For his part, Buckingham reciprocated by recognizing, in an undated letter, his fortune 'for so great a king to descend so low' as to care so intensely for one of his subjects; James was 'my purveyor, my good fellow, my physician, my maker, my friend, my father, my all'. As Buckingham elaborated, their relationship was one of 'more tenderness than fathers have of children, of more friendship than between equals, of more affection than between lovers in the best kind, man and wife'. In another missive, Buckingham defiantly declared himself ready to stand *contra mundum*, insisting that 'I naturally so love your person ... that were not only all your people, but all the world besides, set together on one side, and you alone on the other, I should, to obey and please you, displease, nay despise all them.' The key verb was 'to obey'. In Buckingham, James received the same personal devotion, combined with conscientious political capability, that he had treasured as a teenager from his older French cousin Esmé Stewart, Duke of Lennox. As Lennox had protested in 1582, were his breast to be slit open, the only words to be found there would be 'fidelity and obedience'. Four decades later, Buckingham styled his service to James in the form of canine constancy, regularly signing himself 'your Majesty's humble servant and dog'. In another undated letter, he wondered aloud whether James loved him more now, or 'at the time which I shall never forget at Farnham, where the bed's head could not be found between the master and his dog'.[14]

*

If Buckingham had become the 'blazing star' of James's court, alarming auguries were inferred when a real blazing star, or comet – nearly double the size of the moon – appeared in the skies in the autumn of 1618. Although the king himself disliked popular tendencies to interpret celestial phenomena as divine prognostications, he could not deny the constellation of geopolitical, as well as personal, challenges confronting him in the last years of his life. But in his *Daemonologie* (1597), James had denounced astrology – 'preaching of the stars' – to be part of 'the Devil's school', deeming it 'utterly unlawful' for rational Christians to try to infer, from unusual stars or planets, 'what commonwealths shall flourish or decay ... what way, and of what age shall men die; what horse shall win at match running'.[15] Two decades later, James remained just as contemptuous, with one court observer noting that 'concerning the blazing star, his Majesty, they say, swears it is nothing else but Venus with a firebrand in her arse.'[16] In verse that circulated extensively in manuscript, the king asked:

> Ye men of Britain, wherefore gaze ye so
> Upon an angry star?
> ... Misinterpret not with vain conceit
> The character you see on heaven's height:
> Which though it bring the world some news from fate,
> The letter is such as none can it translate:
> And for to guess at God Almighty's mind
> Were such a thing might cosen all mankind.[17]   [cosen = to deceive, trick]

Notwithstanding royal reassurances, anxious doomsayers in London did not have long to wait before a large fire at Whitehall Palace destroyed the Banqueting House in January 1619. Since the expanding collection of state papers had been recently relocated to a new repository at Holbein Gate, their Keeper, Sir Thomas Wilson, could only exult at the timely providence that had secured their survival. Recalling James's role in foiling the failed Gunpowder Plot in 1605, he insisted that 'since his Majesty's prophetical presage of the blow in the powder-treason, there was never such a prevention of so great a mischief as this would have been'. Although Wilson claimed that there had been 'not so much hurt sustained as the worth of a blank paper' in the fire, this was incorrect: documentation destroyed included the register of the Privy Council between 1602 and 1618.[18]

Two months later, on 2 March 1619, the Jacobean court suffered another blow with the death of Queen Anna at Hampton Court from consumption and dropsy, at the age of forty-four. The previous November, the Venetian envoy, Antonio Donato, had reported that popular portents attaching to the 'large and long comet' over London's skies included fears 'that the queen will not much longer'.[19] In another unpublished poem, addressed to Anna, the king alluded to recent sightings of the comet to acknowledge how:

> Thee to invite the great God sent a star
> Whose friends and kindred mighty princes are,
> For though they run the race of men and die,
> Death serves but to refine their majesty.
> So did the queen from hence her court remove
> And left the earth to be enshrined above.
> Thus she is changed, not dead, no good prince dies,
> But like the day star, only sets to rise.[20]

On the day that Anna died, James wrote to her brother, Christian IV of Denmark, reassuring him that 'many tokens of both her love and her virtue remain after her life, whence a great desire remains for her remains in us.' Describing the queen as 'this heroine, your sister, by whose marriage our affinity was established', James hoped that Britain's diplomatic amity with Denmark would not weaken on account of her demise.[21]

James himself was also seriously ill that spring, with John Chamberlain reporting in April that the king had 'prepared to settle things as if he were to leave all', being attended by his son, Buckingham, the Duke of Lennox, and other nobles. The previous month, Chamberlain had been heartened to see 'the world so tenderly affected toward' the king, apprehending 'what a loss we should have if God should take him from us'.[22] In early May, James's daughter, Elizabeth, was cheered to receive news in Heidelberg of her father's recovery, acknowledging her gratitude to God for mercifully not seeking to 'overwhelm me with two such great losses at the same time'.[23] James did not, however, attend Anna's state funeral held in Westminster Abbey on 13 May 1619, leaving Prince Charles to lead the cortège of over 1,300 mourners. With the king's motto – *Beati Pacifici* ('blessed are the peacemakers') – adorning the queen's hearse, embroidered banners and gilded escutcheons confirmed Anna's extensive armigerous alliances that encompassed the Protestant kingdoms of England, Scotland, Denmark, Norway and Sweden, together with the duchies of Saxony, Mecklenburg and Pomerania, and additional smaller territories and historic Danish tribes.[24] By the time

James returned to London in early June, he was recovered from illness and dressed in a suit of pale blue satin 'laid with silver lace, with a blue and white feather', astride a horse in a matching caparison. To Chamberlain, 'so gallant' a king seemed 'more like a wooer than a mourner'.[25]

All blessed peacemakers were, however, soon confronted by escalating confessional tensions across Europe amid the outbreak of what would later be known as the 'Thirty Years War', eventually accounting for around five million war-related deaths in the Holy Roman Empire alone.[26] James's family was centrally involved. In August 1619, his son-in-law, the Palatine Elector Frederick V, was invited to become King of Bohemia by Protestant members of the country's Estates who had led a revolt and deposed their Catholic king-elect, Ferdinand of Styria, who shortly afterwards became Holy Roman Emperor. Receiving the Bohemian invitation to become their king on his twenty-third birthday, Frederick had written to Elizabeth doubting 'that this will remain a secret for long', but 'struggling to resolve what to do'.[27]

James's lifelong political philosophy firmly upheld the rights of legitimate rulers and rejected all forms of resistance as illegal. He had also already attempted to mediate in the dispute between Ferdinand and the Bohemian Estates by dispatching an envoy, James Hay, Viscount Doncaster, to central Europe the previous spring. But writing to Doncaster in September, James protested that, although the Bohemian Crown had now been 'taken from one head and set up another', he had been 'utterly ignorant' of this envisaged outcome. Determined to ensure that 'there may not rest the least blemish or stain' attaching to him personally, James disingenuously downplayed his delayed responses to Frederick's repeated requests for advice and instead wondered aloud, 'who would imagine that our son-in-law would ever have entertained such a thing, and not at first acquainted us with it, and taken our counsel?'[28]

At home, James refused to recognize the new titles of his daughter and son-in-law as rulers of Bohemia and denied permission for celebratory bonfires, bell-ringing, or other forms of thanksgiving. By contrast, the Archbishop of Canterbury, George Abbott, was delighted to learn that Frederick had accepted the Bohemian Crown, interpreting events in apocalyptically Protestant terms. To Secretary of State Sir Robert Naunton, Abbot admitted, 'methinks I do in this . . . foresee the work of God, that by piece and piece, the kings of the earth that gave their power unto the Beast . . . shall now tear the whore, and make her desolate, as St John in his Revelation hath foretold'.[29]

In October 1619, Frederick and Elizabeth left their Palatine home in Heidelberg for the Bohemian capital, Prague, with their progress enthusiastically acclaimed as a quasi-confessional crusade by the Protestant pamphleteer John Harrison. As he watched James's daughter 'march forward: showing herself like that Virago at Tilbury in 1588, another Queen Elizabeth for so now she is', Harrison breathlessly predicted that future military successes would 'run along still, like a train of gunpowder, till at length, we hear the final report, of the sudden downfall of that great city Babylon [Rome] even to the ground'.[30] In London, however, the Venetian ambassador Girolamo Lando observed of the royal court that, even by late December, 'at least in appearance, they still pretend not to know anything about the coronation' in Prague.[31] Meanwhile, in central Europe, Catholic Habsburg forces challenged Frederick's acceptance of the Bohemian Crown, and started a military campaign to regain the throne for the intended successor, Emperor Ferdinand.

Disregarding calls to mount a military intervention to support his daughter and son-in-law, as well as Protestant interests more generally, James instead focused – seemingly counter-intuitively – on negotiations pursued intermittently since 1614 for a marriage between Prince Charles and Philip III's daughter, the Infanta María Ana. Accordingly, James was delighted by the Count of Gondomar's return to England as Spanish ambassador in March 1620. Recounting his first royal audience to Philip III, Gondomar described how James had 'said in a loud voice to those who were standing around, that I looked like an excellent gentleman, a great friend of his', to which 'I answered as loudly', confirming his joy in renewing the king's acquaintance. With public opinion resolutely Hispanophobic, James had recalled the anti-Spanish inclination of his now deceased former Secretary of State, Sir Ralph Winwood, observing 'the malice of these people so increased that he had now three hundred Winwoods in his court and palace.'[32] During the audience at Theobalds', the floor of a hall collapsed, plummeting courtiers and visitors into the storey beneath. Although Gondomar escaped injury by jumping into a nearby doorway, he reported to Madrid his fears 'that the Puritans have tried, and still try, [to act] against me and kill me; be that on the streets or with poison or by setting fire to the house during the night.' Despite rumours that the accident at Theobalds had been 'a premeditated case', the ambassador cautiously believed it to have been 'a natural affair'.[33]

To other foreign envoys, James's closeness to Gondomar supplied further evidence, as Lando put it, of James's determination 'to do everything against the grain', ignoring his Councillors' advice and the popular mood of the country. With James denying that his diplomatic alliance with Frederick's Protestant Evangelical Union necessitated English military intervention, a meeting with the Elector's envoy in London, Baron Achatius von Dohna, elicited only 'bitter and angry expressions against the Bohemians, his son-in-law and the princes themselves'. As Lando reported, James had declared 'I am an old king' who 'will not allow myself to be launched out by a young one', especially since 'the Spanish ambassador assures me that the Palatinate will not be attacked'.[34]

Unfortunately, Gondomar's assurances were misplaced. In August 1620, Habsburg forces invaded Frederick's patrimonial estates in the Lower Palatinate and conquered several towns, including Oppenheim and Alzey, that had been part of Elizabeth's marriage jointure. When Lando met James at Salisbury that month, the king 'seemed utterly weary of the affairs that are taking place all over the world'. Indeed, 'he hates being obliged every day to spend time over unpleasant matters and listen to nothing but requests and incitements to move in every direction, and to meddle with everything. He remarked: "I am not God Almighty."'[35] From Prague, however, Elizabeth wrote to Buckingham in September, imploring him to encourage her father to abandon futile diplomacy in favour of military action. He would thereby 'show himself a loving father to us, and not suffer his childrens' inheritance to be taken away', adding that 'the enemy will more regard his blows than his words.'[36] On the same day that Elizabeth petitioned Buckingham, Lando observed that, in London, 'the whole court is boiling over with rage at the news' of the Palatinate's invasion, but an audience between James and Dohna had only yielded 'a rigmarole of phrases and inconclusive promises'.[37]

Military defeat at the Battle of the White Mountain in November 1620 ended Frederick and Elizabeth's brief tenure as rulers of Bohemia. Placed under an Imperial Ban by Emperor Ferdinand, Frederick became a rebel and an outlaw. He and his family fled first to pro-Protestant

Silesia, while the Bohemian Estates sued for mercy soon afterwards. In a significant reversal for continental Protestantism, Bohemia's lands were occupied by Imperial troops and its inhabitants subjected to forcible re-Catholicization. As Protestant eyes turned expectantly to James, the army officer and former Governor of Utrecht Sir John Ogle acknowledged to a correspondent in England that 'the world stands at gaze to see what you in that great island will do in this important affair of Christendom.'[38] Ejected from Bohemia and unable to return to the Habsburg-occupied Palatinate, Elizabeth and her family's retinue – comprising around 200 individuals, fifty horses, and a menagerie of pet dogs and monkeys – arrived in The Hague in April 1621, having been deterred from travelling to England. Aware of the residual charisma attaching to his staunchly Protestant daughter and son-in-law, James had feared their perceived plight as embattled victims of Catholic Habsburg aggression could easily destabilize domestic politics.

At home, James's pacific inclinations became the target of increasingly excoriating criticism by pamphleteers including the Puritan polemicist Thomas Scott, whose *Vox Populi, or News from Spain* (1620) purported to report a meeting of the Spanish Council of State in which Gondomar confirmed that he had successfully duped England into passivity. Describing James as someone 'who otherwise is one of the most accomplished princes that ever reigned', 'Gondomar' explained that he also 'extremely hunts after peace' for which 'he will do or suffer anything'. While 'Gondomar' agreed that marriage between a Spanish Infanta and the heretic Stuarts was unthinkable, as Philip III's ambassador he had pursued the project as 'a cover for much intelligence, and a means to obtain whatsoever I desired', exploiting English hopes that a lucrative Spanish match was the means 'to settle peace, and fill the exchequer'.[39] Going through seven editions in 1620 alone, Scott's *Vox Populi* also appeared in a French translation, while the real Gondomar was so outraged by the temerity of the pamphlet's masquerade that he 'foams with wrath in every direction'.[40]

To foreign onlookers as much as his own subjects, James's reluctance to defend his daughter's interests against Austrian Habsburg incursion, while pursuing a Spanish Habsburg marriage for his son, seemed disastrous and incomprehensible. Circulating in manuscript in 1621, an anonymous libel entitled 'Tom Tell-Troth' warned the king that his foreign policy was 'not only inscrutable, but diametrically opposite to poor mens' understanding'. Rather than reassuring his subjects, James's (in)actions 'do already fulfil the utmost of our fears', with the only (ironic) inference being that his knowledge of current affairs must be superhuman, 'otherwise it could not be that your proceedings should so vary, as they do, from the whole current of human discourse'.[41] For his part, James firmly rejected his subjects' right to criticize, regarding foreign policy as *arcana imperii* and immune from scrutiny. As he had indicated in his poem on the 'great comet' in 1618:

> ... I wish the curious man to keep
> His rash imaginations till he sleep:
> Then let him dream of famine, plague, and war,
> And think the match with Spain hath raised this star:
> And let him think that I, their Prince, and minion
> Will shortly change or which is worse religion:[42]

Observing the eagerness with which his subjects 'walk Paul's, and meet the devil there', James knew that, as one pamphleteer later put it, St Paul's Cathedral had become 'the great exchange of all discourse . . . all turn merchants here, and traffic for news'.[43] A proclamation issued on Christmas Eve in 1620 sought to curb excessively 'lavish and licentious speech' and cautioned subjects not to 'intermeddle by pen, or speech, with causes of state, and secrets of empire, either at home or abroad'. The French ambassador, the sieur de Buisseaux, judged the popular mood disturbingly ominous, surmising that 'the hatred in which this king is held, in free speaking, cartoons, defamatory libels' usually constituted 'the ordinary precursors of civil war'.[44] Under pressure from James, the Dutch States-General issued a proclamation in January 1621 denouncing unlicensed publications in 'Latin, French, English, Scots, and various other languages' and prohibiting their overseas export, 'especially none against the King of Great Britain and his principal ministers'.[45]

*

Censure of James's pacifist policy also extended to criticism of his reliance on Buckingham, with some manuscript libels referring to the favourite as 'Ganymede': the Trojan boy loved by the Greek God, Zeus, and appointed as Zeus's cupbearer, which was a role Buckingham had once performed at court. Composed around 1619–23, one poem, entitled 'The War of the Gods', did not mention either James or Buckingham by name but invoked the Roman version of the myth to narrate how Jove's devotion to Ganymede provoked rage among the other gods, dismayed by:

> Great Jove that sways the imperial sceptre
> With his upstart love
> That makes him drunk with nectar
> They will remove.

The chaste goddess, Diana, vowed to remain unsatisfied until she witnessed those:

> Be quite disgraced,
> Or else displaced,
> For loving so against nature.

Meanwhile, the Roman fertility goddess, Proserpina, summoned 'twelve black furies' in a fiery coach and threatened:

> To have him burned
> That thus have turned
> Love's pleasure arse verse.[46]

Speculatively attributed to the Scots poet William Drummond of Hawthornden, another libel entitled 'The King's Five Senses' was presented in the form of a prayer to protect James's senses. The poet called for measures to prevent the king hearing 'Spanish treaties that may wound' or tasting 'the dangerous figs of Spain', while also needing to guard against James touching:

> . . . such a smooth and beardless chin
> As may provoke or tempt to sin.
> From such a hand whose moist palm may
> My sovereign lead out of the way
> From things polluted and unclean
> From all that's bestial or obscene.

Regarding the king's sense of smell, the poet likewise prayed:

> Thou wilt be pleased great God to save
> My sovereign from a Ganymede
> Whose whorish breath hath power to lead
> His excellence which way it list.[47]

Perhaps surprisingly, when shown this verse, James was reported to have jocularly observed of its anonymous author that 'this fellow wished good things for him'.[48] But when the English Parliament convened for the first time in seven years in January 1621, James was less sanguine in tolerating public criticism of his favourite. In April, the former Attorney-General Sir Henry Yelverton opined to a House of Lords committee investigating monopolies that Buckingham should have 'read the articles against Hugh Spencer in this place, for taking upon him to place and displace officers'. Executed for treason in 1326, Spencer (or Despencer) had been a notorious favourite of an earlier English king who had been deposed, Edward II. Learning of Yelverton's quip, James was outraged by the implied comparison, which was 'to esteem me a weak man, and I had rather be no king than such a one as King Edward II'.[49] Yelverton was imprisoned and fined; Buckingham remitted an additional fine due to him on account of the personal insult.

Within Parliament, peers and MPs heard increasingly bellicose demands for James to secure full restitution of Frederick's Palatinate territories and Electoral dignities through armed intervention. In November, Gondomar wrote to the Habsburg ruler of the Spanish Netherlands, Archduchess Isabella, relaying a recent *sotto voce* conversation with James in which the king had 'told me to feel sorry for him' as he faced pressures 'that the most wretched man in the world could not endure'. 'Making everything into one argument', James's advisers and critics alike were insisting that, either he deliberately sought 'the perdition of his daughter and grandchildren', or he needed to act 'to help her to recover and conserve the estate with which she was married'. But if MPs tried 'to meddle in any other matter' than providing financial subsidies for the Palatinate's restitution, James reassured Gondomar that he would immediately dissolve Parliament, having agreed a secret commission with Prince Charles and Buckingham 'that the three alone knew, and I, making four'. Buckingham had, moreover, admitted to advising James that 'we should not give the money that they give us to his son-in-law, but that we should join ourselves with Spain, and spend it against the common enemy', at which 'the king laughed a lot', surmising that Gondomar would assume that the 'common enemy' was the Ottoman Empire whereas Buckingham had meant 'the Estates of Holland'.[50]

Making good his threat, James dissolved Parliament in December 1621, after receiving a petition from MPs demanding that Prince

Charles marry a Protestant spouse. Denying that he was the victim of misinformation regarding Commons debates, James reminded MPs that he was 'an old and experienced king, needing no such lessons' in political communications. After ripping the offending 'Protestation' from the Commons record, James published a *Declaration* the following month, suggesting that his subjects 'should have given us great and hearty thanks' for maintaining peace across Britain at a time 'when all our neighbours about us are in a miserable combustion of war'. Moreover, the king reminded his subjects that 'this miserable war, which hath set all Christendom on fire, was not for religion following evil counsel, but only caused by our son-in-law, his hasty and rash resolution, to take to himself the crown of Bohemia'. Nor was it legitimate to cite the defence of Protestantism as 'a good pretext for dethroning of kings, and usurping their crowns'; such claims were, rather, traditional Jesuitical tenets.[51]

By June 1622, all territory in the Palatinate was under Habsburg Imperial control, except the cities of Frankenthal, Mannheim and Heidelberg, while an international peace conference convened in Brussels between May and September failed to end the conflict. Aware that the papacy had been preparing articles for the proposed Anglo-Spanish marriage, James took the unusual step of writing directly to Pope Gregory XV in September, addressing him as 'Most Holy Father' and confirming his distress at 'these calamitous discords and bloodsheds which, for these late years bypast, have so miserably rent the Christian world'. Ultimately, however, James's call for the pope to 'put your hand to so pious a work and so worthy of a Christian prince' by effecting a peaceful settlement fell on deaf ears, undermined by the papacy's support for Ferdinand's attempts to extirpate Protestantism in the Holy Roman Empire.[52]

At the same time, James still believed that a 'Spanish match' for Prince Charles offered a viable diplomatic solution on the grounds that Philip IV – who succeeded as king in March 1621 – would be obliged to persuade his Austrian Habsburg relations to resolve matters in the Palatinate, once his sister was married to the heir to the English throne. James was, however, unprepared for the sudden decision of Charles and Buckingham to travel incognito to Spain in February 1623 in an attempt to expedite the long-running marriage negotiations. Having informed only James and a few confidants of their plan, the prince and favourite donned wigs and false beards and adopted the alias names of 'Jack and Tom Smith' in an audacious move that defied every punctilio of diplomatic protocol. Shocked stupefaction was the general reaction to news that James's only son and heir had embarked on such a dangerous and risky overland journey.

To his baffled Privy Councillors, James lamely observed that, by venturing to woo the Infanta in person, Charles was simply following Stuart family tradition, since he himself had travelled to Denmark to bring Queen Anna to Scotland in 1589, while Charles's great-grandfather James V had voyaged to France to meet his first and second wives. The crucial difference was, however, that those royal journeys only took place *after* nuptial negotiations and proxy marriages had been concluded. Instinctively indulgent towards both Charles and Buckingham, James justified their impulsive actions in verse and, using their adopted aliases, recalled that:

> Thy grandsire, godsire, thy father too,
> Were thine examples, so to do;
> Their brave attempts in heat of love,
> France, Scotland and Denmark did approve.
> So Jack and Tom do nothing new,
> When love and fortune they pursue.[53]

Throughout what became Charles and Buckingham's six-month sojourn in Spain, James tellingly referred to his twenty-two-year-old son and heir as 'my baby' and additionally confirmed that 'I wear Steenie's picture in a blue ribbon under my waistcoat next to my heart'.[54] Although Frederick's former Electoral territories and dignities were in the process of being assigned by Emperor Ferdinand to Maximilian I of Bavaria, James continued to yoke military events in central Europe to his son's marriage plans. In early March, he reassured his Secretary of State, Sir George Calvert, that he would 'not abandon his son-in-law in recovering the Palatinate', but directed 'no ruffling words to be used to the ambassadors, till there comes news out of Spain'.[55] Writing to Charles and Buckingham three days later, James admitted the significant diplomatic stakes involved, fearing that 'if my baby's credit in Spain mend not these things, I will bid farewell to peace in Christendom during our times at least.' Four days later, however, the king had cheered himself with the thought that, in dynastic terms, the Spanish court 'have reason there, if they love themselves, to wish you and yours rather to succeed unto me than my daughter and her children'. Having already sent six letters to his 'sweet boys' by mid-March, James confirmed that he had also written 'five to Kate [Buckingham's wife], two to Sue [Buckingham's sister] and one to thy mother, Steenie, and all with my own hand'.[56]

From Madrid, Buckingham replied to the king's missives, describing himself 'now in a chamber alone, enjoying and reading over and over your sweet cordial letters'. In late April, he reassured the king that 'we will not be long before we get forth of this labyrinth, wherein we have been entangled these many years.'[57] But when Charles and Buckingham relayed a new stipulation requiring the Infanta to delay her departure from Spain for one year – to ensure fulfilment of all clauses in the marriage agreement regarding improved conditions for Catholics in England – James became alarmed and advised 'my sweet boys' to 'come speedily away if ye can get leave, and give over all treaty', admitting that 'I care for match nor nothing, so I may once have you in my arms again.' In July, the king reluctantly agreed to the revised marriage terms, but demanded that Charles and Buckingham 'forget not to make them keep their former conditions anent the portion [dowry], otherwise both my baby and I are bankrupts for ever'. James further reminded them to 'go as far as ye can before your parting upon the business of the Palatinate and Holland, that the world may see ye have thought as well upon the business of Christendom as upon the codpiece point'.[58]

Anticipating their imminent departure from Madrid, in late August 1623, Buckingham was signing himself off in letters to James with promises 'that when he once gets hold of your bedpost again', he would stay put 'never to quit it'. Ten days later, he was unable to 'think of giving thanks for friend, wife or child; my thoughts are only bent of having my dear dad and master's legs soon in my arms'.[59] Eventually returning to Portsmouth – *without* a Spanish wife – on 5 October, Charles and Buckingham encountered a spontaneous outburst of jubilation from a relieved populace. Elevated to a dukedom in his absence, Buckingham set about spearheading a diplomatic volte-face that championed military intervention in central Europe as the only viable means of securing the Palatinate's restitution to Frederick and Elizabeth.

*

Amid a bellicose popular mood, James summoned a new English Parliament in February 1624 and, in his opening speech, hinted to MPs and peers that he might finally be willing to abandon his long-standing pacifism. Despite repeated assurances regarding restitution of the Palatine territories and dignities from Habsburg control, he had 'found foul and empty performances, being fed only with delays', before Prince Charles's journey to Spain had served, 'as it were, [to] awake him out of a dream which his credulities had formerly brought him into'. Despite having dissolved Parliament three years earlier after disputing MPs' right to advise on foreign policy, James now styled himself 'your spouse' and Parliament 'my wife'. He was thus playing 'the part of a loving spouse' by not only having 'continual cherished' the assembly, but 'upon extraordinary occasions to communicate the secrets of his affairs unto her to have her best advice what is to be done therein'.[60] Responding to royal encouragement, MPs agreed a parliamentary subsidy of around £300,000, with provisos that the Spanish marriage negotiations be abandoned and that a Council of War, accountable to Parliament, approve any monies spent. But there were evidently limits to the king's uxoriousness. For while James undertook to abide by counsel from 'a secret and faithful Council of War', he would not tolerate royal intentions being 'ordered by a multitude' and would not be returning to ask MPs if he should 'send 20 or 10,000, by sea or land, east or west, by diversion or otherwise, by invasion upon the Bavarian or Emperor'.[61]

Angered by the reversal in royal policy, the Count of Gondomar's two replacements as Spanish ambassadors in London – Juan de Mendoza, Marquis of Inijosa, and Don Carlos Coloma – feared that James was being cynically misled. In a private meeting with James in April 1624, Coloma's religious confessor, Don Francisco de Carondolet, informed an aghast king that Buckingham had now taken Prince Charles's marriage into his own hands and authorized negotiations to start in Paris for a match with Louis XIII's younger sister, Henrietta Maria. Carondolet beseeched James to assert his authority and demonstrate that he was 'the oldest and wisest king in Europe'.[62] Several weeks later, Gondomar's former confessor, Diego de Lafuente, claimed that Buckingham was in fact intending to frustrate any marriage for Charles in order to advance an alternative match between his only daughter, Mary, and the Electress Elizabeth's oldest son (and James's grandson), Frederick Henry.[63] Although James demanded that all his Privy Councillors swear an oath denying knowledge of these allegations, an impasse was reached when the Spanish ambassadors refused to provide further substantiation of their charges against Buckingham.

In November 1624, terms of a Stuart-Bourbon marriage were formally agreed in Paris and thereafter ratified by James and Charles in Cambridge, facilitating a union between Charles and Henrietta Maria. The marriage treaty included religious concessions equally as stringent as those demanded by Spain, with Henrietta Maria granted total freedom of religion and control over the education of any children under thirteen. By a secret *écrit particulier*, James and Charles also undertook to release all Catholics imprisoned on religious grounds and to allow English Catholics to practise their religion peaceably.

Meanwhile, James's emotional dependence on Buckingham remained intact. In an undated letter to the duke, written in either December 1623 or December 1624, the king anticipated their making 'a new marriage ever to be kept hereafter' (see Plate 26). Proclaiming that 'I desire only to live in this world for your sake,' James vowed that he would 'rather live banished in any part of the earth with you than live a sorrowful widow's life without you'. Praying that Buckingham would 'ever be a comfort to your dear dad and husband', his wish would be fulfilled when, in March 1625, the duke attended the bedside of the dying king.[64]

Epilogue

THE DEATH OF KING JAMES

King James VI and I died on Sunday 27 March 1625 at his Theobalds residence in Hertfordshire. From early March he had been experiencing what contemporaries described as a 'tertian ague': a recurrent, usually non-fatal, malaria-like fever. On 25 March, however, he also suffered a stroke that affected his speech capacity, while the fever intensified. In the official Latin account of the king's final illness, royal physicians described how James had sustained 'both a long and horrible chill and a cruel fire'; eventually 'his speech failed him and so did his pulse, and with very many black ejections and a diaphoretic sweat' after a struggle 'endured for almost forty hours'.[1] The physicians' report was informed by the post-mortem examination undertaken on the day after the king's death, which had revealed a shrivelled kidney, putrid black liquid around his gall bladder, and layers of fatty tissue around his heart. As part of the autopsy procedure, James's body was also disembowelled and embalmed, with aromatic herbs stuffed into its hollowed cavities as a preservative, in order to facilitate an extended period of lying-in-state.[2]

The royal succession was assured. Directly upon James's death, Privy Councillors at Theobalds confirmed the twenty-four-year-old Charles I as king and dispatched copies of their proclamation for public announcement in Whitehall, Westminster and the City of London, before notifying the English shires, Scotland and the Royal Navy the following day. Constitutional calmness and clarity contrasted, however, with turbulent equinoctial storms. In a published elegy on James's death, the playwright Thomas Heywood lamented March as an 'ominous month' that had unleashed 'windy and obstreperous rage' and paired mourners' tears at their king's demise with 'strange varieties of stormy weather'.[3] In

Scotland, the Presbyterian chronicler David Calderwood later recalled how, the night before news of James's death was received, the country had been buffeted by 'a boisterous and vehement wind blowing in the night' with unusually high tides. Since 'the like of this tempest was not seen in our time, nor the like of it heard in this country in any age preceding', the storm had been 'taken by all men to be a forerunner of some great alteration'.[4]

Squalls also afflicted the torchlit procession accompanying transportation of James's body from Theobalds to London on 9 April. Involving around 3,600 individuals on horseback and in carriages, the convoy left Theobalds at 9 p.m. and, as John Chamberlain described, 'the show would have been solemn, but that it was marred by foul weather, so that there was nothing to be seen but coaches and torch.'[5] At Denmark House in the Strand, James's coffin was placed in the Privy Chamber on a large bed of state, and a wooden and wax effigy, five feet seven inches in length, was placed atop the coffin. Intended to underscore the immortality of royal authority, the effigy was dressed in royal robes, with its face fashioned from a death mask taken at Theobalds and fake hair, beard and eyebrows supplied by the court wigmaker. To one French dignitary paying his respects, James's effigy was 'so well fashioned ... that one would have said he was still alive', while the new Venetian ambassador, Zuane Pesaro, recorded how the effigy was attended with 'the customary vigil, thirty to forty noblemen and cavaliers being always present day and night'.[6] Despite Protestant unease at the use of torches and candles in funeral rituals – riskily resonant of Catholic intercessions for the dead – the corners of the late king's bed of state were illuminated by candles which, throughout each night of his lying-in-state, burned from silver candlesticks that James's son had acquired in Spain two years earlier.[7]

The first Prince of Wales to succeed as King of England since Henry VIII's accession in 1509, Charles I abandoned plans of travelling to Paris for his marriage to Henrietta Maria and instead broke with tradition by acting as the chief mourner at his father's funeral on 17 May. According to Pesaro, among observers of royal obsequies, 'it was especially remarked that, since William the Conqueror, the king had only thrice been present at the funeral celebrations' of their predecessor.[8] James himself had attended neither Prince Henry's funeral in 1612, nor that of Queen Anna seven years later. Despite parlous royal finances, Charles also approved funeral-related expenditure variously estimated to have exceeded £50,000 sterling; by comparison, Elizabeth I's funeral in 1603, and later construction of her marble tomb, had together cost £17,000. In 1625, much of the vast expenditure was consumed in acquiring sufficient funeral cloth to drape Denmark House, Westminster Abbey, funerary hearses and the thousands of mourners, with nineteen different cloth retailers receiving more than £28,000 for its supply.[9]

On the day of James's funeral, an extensive cortège set out from Denmark House at 10 a.m., comprising between 5,000 and 9,000 mourners, who processed over seven hours before the service started at Westminster Abbey at 5 p.m. One absentee was the Archbishop of St Andrews, John Spottiswoode, who initially succeeded in securing the right to proceed alongside the Archbishop of Canterbury, George Abbot, but who had then 'flatly refused' to don the same episcopal rochet, with billowing white sleeves, as his English counterpart. As one observer described, Spottiswoode had vehemently denied that he would 'do that scandal to the Church of Scotland' as to assume the Church of England's 'apparelling and forgo his own; whereupon he refused to be a mourner and appeared not'.[10]

Inside Westminster Abbey, the king's coffin – together with a second life-size effigy of James dressed in Parliament robes – was placed inside an ornate octagonal catafalque, designed by Inigo Jones and situated in the centre of the choir.[11] The funeral sermon was preached by the Lord Keeper, Bishop John Williams of Lincoln, deputizing for James's own nomination, Bishop Lancelot Andrewes of Winchester, who was ill. Taking as his text 1 Kings 11:41–3, Williams pursued an extended comparison of James and the Biblical King Solomon, venturing to the congregation that 'you never read in your lives, of two kings more fully paralleled amongst themselves, and better distinguished from all other kings besides themselves.' Aside from their extensive achievements, Williams noted that both kings had been only sons, both had been crowned as infant kings while their immediate predecessors were still alive and, just as the Book of Canticles described how 'Solomon was of complexion white, and ruddy . . . so was King James.' Extolling the latter's global influence, Williams marvelled that James VI & I's legacy now saw:

> . . . all kinds of learning highly improved, manufactures at home daily invented, trading abroad exceedingly multiplied, the Borders of Scotland

peaceably governed, the north of Ireland religiously planted, the Navy Royal magnificently furnished; Virginia, Newfoundland, and New England peopled; the East Indies well-traded; Persia, China and the Mogul visited; lastly, all the ports of Europe, Africa, Asia and America to our red crosses freed and opened.[12]

In the first royal funeral sermon to be published directly after its delivery, Williams also acknowledged the presence of the late king's life-size effigy, but explained that 'this artificial representation within the hearse ... shows no more than his outward body, or rather the body of his body, his clothes and ornaments.' Royal power now, however, resided in 'another statue' present within the Abbey, indeed 'a breathing statue of all his virtues': James's successor, Charles I.[13] After the two-hour service, James was laid to rest in Henry VII's Chapel, underneath Henry VII's tomb, in the vault that, back in 1606, he had reserved for his own interment by reassigning Elizabeth I's coffin a new location, atop that of her sister, Mary Tudor, in the chapel's north aisle.

James's final resting place symbolically confirmed his genealogical descent from Tudor royal predecessors. Above ground, his reign was most notably commemorated in the magnificently baroque ceiling decoration of Whitehall's Banqueting House, which Charles I commissioned from the Flemish artist Peter Paul Rubens around five years after James's death. Completed in 1634, the ceiling's central image presented the 'Apotheosis of King James' in a stylistic composition that combined counter-Reformation images of the 'Assumption of the Virgin' with classical features associated with a Roman emperor's deification. Rubens's depiction of James VI & I was thus similar in conception – but on a far grander and more ambitious scale – than earlier paintings he had completed imagining the apotheosis of Henri IV, painted for the French king's widow, Marie de' Medici, or the commission he accepted from James's favourite, George Villiers, Duke of Buckingham, to imagine the duke's own apotheosis. For the Banqueting House ceiling, Rubens presented King James being carried to heaven on the back of an eagle, holding a great orb, and assisted by a figure representing 'Justice', whose characteristic swiftness was confirmed by her grasp of a thunderbolt. Another figure personifying 'Religion' carried a Bible, while the winged figure of 'Peace' joined Minerva, the goddess of wisdom, in bestowing a laurel crown on the king's head.

Thus, as one modern commentator has described, 'into this whirling mythological heaven of acclamation and reward James serenely rises, great, good and just, sainted and deified.'[14]

*

In April 1626, several years before receiving Charles I's commission to decorate the Banqueting House ceiling, Rubens purchased a book entitled *Prodromus Vindictae in Ducem Buckinghamae* from an Antwerp bookseller. Published in Brussels under a false Frankfurt imprint, the anonymously issued tract was written by one of James's royal physicians, the Scots-born George Eglisham. The tract's breathtaking content was self-evident in its full English title: *The Forerunner of Revenge upon the Duke of Buckingham, for the Poisoning of the most Potent King James, of Happy Memory, of Great Britain, and the Lord Marquis of Hamilton, and others of the Nobility*. Crucial to Eglisham's case was his account of James, Marquis of Hamilton, who had died, aged thirty-five, on 2 March 1625, three weeks before the king. Before his death, Hamilton had repeatedly quarrelled with Buckingham, after the duke had opportunistically effected a marriage between his niece and Hamilton's eldest son and heir, the Earl of Arran, which Hamilton had opposed on account of the lower social origins of Buckingham's family. Having served as Hamilton's physician, Eglisham alleged that when the marquis became ill, he 'would not taste of any thing that was sent to him by any of Buckingham's friends', and when servants sampled such consignments, two died 'with manifest signs and symptoms of poison'. After the marquis's death, Eglisham confirmed that Hamilton's corpse had swelled alarmingly 'in such sort that his thighs were as big as six times their natural proportion', while large blisters spread across his skin, 'some white, some black, some red, some yellow, some green, some blue'.[15]

Thereafter – and contrary to the reassuringly serene account of James's death narrated in Williams's funeral sermon the previous year – Eglisham described scenes of confusion, heated argument and suspected malpractice during the king's final illness at Theobalds. As Eglisham recounted, six days before James's death, 'when all the king's doctors of physic were at dinner', Buckingham 'took his opportunity' and, without the doctors' knowledge, offered the king 'a white powder', which James initially refused but 'at length took it, drunk it in wine, and immediately became worse and worse, falling into many soundings and pains, and violent fluxes of the belly, so tormented, that his Majesty cried out aloud, "O this white powder! This white powder! Would to God I had never taken it, it will cost me my life."' In similar manner four days later, Buckingham's mother had intervened, also while the physicians were at dinner, and 'applied a plaster to the king's heart and breast, whereupon his Majesty grew faint, short-breathed, and in great agony'. When James died two days later, Eglisham further contended that 'Buckingham desired the physicians who attended the king, to sign with their handwriting a testimony that the powder which he gave the king was a good and safe medicine, which they refused to do.'[16]

Accordingly, Eglisham opened his anonymous tract by calling on Charles I to investigate the circumstances of his father's death. For the testimony of 'all histories' demonstrated that 'it is justice that makes kings, justice that maintains kings, and injustice that brings both kingdoms and kings to destruction, to fall in misery, to die like asses in ditches, or more beastly deaths, with eternal infamy after death.' With Buckingham now wielding greater political sway than ever, Charles had let himself 'so far to be led, that your best subjects are in doubt, whether he is your king, or you his'. To members of the English Parliament, Eglisham also acknowledged that Buckingham was 'so powerful that unless the whole body of a parliament lay hold upon him, no justice can be had of him'.[17]

Only ten days after James's death in March 1625, the Venetian ambassador, Pesaro, had observed Buckingham 'receiving the golden keys and the pass everywhere' that gave access to Charles I 'at all hours, even though shut in by triple keys'. But at the same time, Pesaro had noted that 'the common people speak differently, that Parliament will want to enquire into the rumours about poisonous applications to the disease of the defunct'.[18] Rumours of foul play and poisoning were not uncommon when prominent individuals died unexpectedly: similar allegations had, for example, surfaced at the time of Prince Henry's sudden demise in 1612. More ominously, however, James's erstwhile favourite, Robert Carr, Earl of Somerset, had indeed been convicted of poisoning the courtier Thomas Overbury in the Tower of London the following year.

When a new English Parliament opened in February 1626, MPs were indeed interested in pursuing allegations regarding Buckingham's conduct at the time of James's death, along with other instances of alleged misgovernment, including the duke's decision to approve a disastrous naval raid on the Spanish port of Cadiz the previous autumn. In late April, approval was given – by 228 votes to 168 – to a Commons select committee to investigate what one parliamentary diarist recorded as 'some violent attempt upon his late Majesty', and it subsequently received evidence from eight royal physicians and two royal surgeons in a three-day hearing.[19] Dr James Chambers, for example, recalled attending James five days before his death, when the king had objected to 'a posset with gillyflower' supplied by Buckingham and 'would say "Would you murder me and slay me?"'[20] Dr Alexander Ramsey also described how James had responded to a potion and plaster provided by Buckingham with 'panting, raving, swooning, uncertain beating of the pulse', while Dr John Craig – son of the Scots lawyer and union commissioner Thomas Craig – had insisted to his colleagues 'that which was given to the king, by the duke, was as bad as poison'.[21] Alone among his colleagues, Craig's refusal to accept the post-mortem findings after James's death had thereafter led to his exclusion from participation in the king's funeral procession.

While the dozen members of the select committee that met in 1626 did not receive definitive evidence of deliberate poisoning, they concluded that Buckingham's conduct in the royal sickroom had been an act of 'transcendent presumption of dangerous consequence' and sufficient to inform a broader range of impeachment charges.[22] In June, Buckingham sought to defend himself against the charges, but Commons MPs formulated a 'Remonstrance' formally requesting Charles 'graciously to remove this person from access to your sacred person'. With impeachment charges still being debated, and no financial subsidy approved, all discussions were terminated when Charles abruptly dissolved Parliament on 12 June 1626. Just over two years later, Buckingham's access to the king was permanently removed when the duke was assassinated in an inn in Portsmouth by an embittered demobilized soldier, John Felton, in August 1628.

Charles avoided calling an English Parliament for eleven years and resorted instead to 'Personal Rule' between 1629 and 1641. But when Scottish Covenanting opposition to the king's religious reforms escalated into armed warfare in the 'Bishops' Wars', Charles was obliged to reconvene the English Parliament in 1640 in an unsuccessful attempt to raise revenue. In 1642, up to six different versions of Eglisham's *The Forerunner of Revenge* were published, reminding readers of the dubious circumstances attaching to James's death seventeen years earlier. Gaining ground also was the charge that Charles I was complicit in his father's death by his precipitate dissolution of Parliament in 1626, in the midst of its investigations into Buckingham's conduct. By the late 1640s, Royalist forces had not only lost key battles of the civil wars, notably Marston Moor (1644) and Naseby (1645), but Charles's continued refusal to agree peace terms had provoked an even bloodier 'Second' civil war (1647–8). In February 1648, the English House of Commons issued a *Declaration* confirming that MPs were no longer prepared to negotiate with the defeated king, citing a litany of charges of misgovernment that included Charles's premature dissolution of Parliament in 1626 'before justice could be done'. Since 'there never was any legal enquiry made' into the former king's death, the MPs' *Declaration* concluded that 'we leave the world now to judge, where the guilt of this remains.'[23]

Later in 1648, MPs reversed their decision and reopened negotiations with Charles after Oliver Cromwell's victory at the Battle of Preston in August, while a plethora of Royalist pamphleteers sought to counter Parliamentarian invective and defend Charles. Returning to documentation produced in the immediate aftermath of James's death, Charles's supporters reminded readers that Buckingham had not been accused of deliberate poisoning, but of 'transcendent presumption' in offering the late king alternative medicines and remedies. Accordingly, as one modern account of events has observed, just as 'the English Revolution approached its climax, a confused and unsettled public was thus confronted not simply by the horrors of renewed civil war and the spectre of regicide, but also by a barrage of sophisticated, emotive polemic offering rival accounts of old parliamentary history and clashing expert opinion on agues and poisons, plasters, potions and autopsies'.[24]

In January 1649, Charles was put on trial for treason in a specially convened High Court of Justice. The king's refusal to recognize the court's authority and enter a plea removed the need for the chief prosecution barrister, John Cook, to present his case against the king in full. Cook's notes nevertheless indicated that he had intended including an aside about James's demise in order to venture that 'there is no Turk or Heathen but will say that if he [Charles] were any way guilty of his death, let him die for it.'[25]

*

After James's death in March 1625, an anonymous poet penned *A Funeral Elegy upon the Lamentable Loss of our late Liege and Royal King James*, acknowledging the deceased king as one 'who for his wisdom store / England did never show the like before'. The author trusted that James's memory would be assured through his prodigious published output, but also feared that the king's works might prove susceptible to posthumous perversion and 'lying, flying tales'. Left to make their own way in the world, James's writings no longer had their royal creator's protection:

> Methinks I see his books taking their leave
> Of him, from whom they Being did receive,
> And hear his Soul speaking, as it was flying,
> Being about to leave his body dying,
> 'Farewell, my works, but mayest though never die,
> Which dost detect papal apostasy.'

A committed Protestant, James had fought the papacy 'with that mighty sword / God's everlasting, undiminished Word'.[26] But by the 1630s, liturgical, ceremonial and other ecclesiastical reforms introduced by Charles I were generating widespread disquiet and sharp reproof from more Puritanically minded Protestants such as John Bastwick who, together with Henry Burton and William Prynne, was convicted of seditious libel in 1637. In a publication opposing church reform, Bastwick directed Charles to 'hear what the most learned king that ever was, (King James I mean)' had said in his speech to MPs and peers in the English Parliament in March 1610 when he had insisted 'that those that persuade kings to do contrary unto their laws, are vipers and pests, both against them and the commonwealth'. To Bastwick's mind, James had 'more policy in the paring of his nails, than all the grollish politicians that are now extant'. James remained a monarch 'whose dignity I shall never see trampled upon, though I suffer for my loyalty the whole fury of the prelates and their confederates'.[27]

Bastwick, together with Burton and Prynne, did indeed suffer, as the sentence attaching to their conviction for seditious libel entailed removal of both ears after being pilloried, a fine of £5,000, and life imprisonment. As opposition to Charles's rule intensified, an anonymous tract entitled *England's Complaint to Jesus Christ* appeared in 1640 and was later attributed to Bastwick's co-defendant Burton. Framed as a lamentation to Christ by a suffering populace, *England's Complaint* returned to the speech given by James to the English Parliament in 1610 to recall how the former king had contrasted 'an absolute monarchy, not bounded with laws' with polities such as England that was 'tempered, seasoned and conditioned with good laws', execution of which formed 'an essential part of the kingly office'.[28]

By the time civil war broke out in England in 1642, the former king's observations were being read more radically. Incorporating scattered Scotticisms, the anonymous author of *King James his Judgement of a King and Tyrant* (1642) opened by recalling the distinction made by James between lawful monarchy and tyranny in his parliamentary speech in 1610. The tract ended with twenty-eight questions, the first of which wondered why investigation into 'our geud King James's death' had been forestalled by Parliament's dissolution in 1626, while the final question asked whether Charles's 'setting up of the king's standard against the Parliament and best subjects of the kingdom be not an actual unkinging of him?' Since the tract breached the official Parliamentarian line that, in 1642, was justifying hostilities in terms of seeking to protect Charles from evil counsellors, *King James his Judgement* was ordered to be publicly burned. Arrested soon afterwards, Abigail Dexter tried to protect her husband – the printer and Parliamentarian dragoon Gregory Dexter – by claiming female 'imbecility' and 'ignorance'. In a deposition received by the House of Lords, Abigail Dexter maintained that, having found the text in her husband's workroom and 'knowing no other author thereof, but King James', she had approved its publication.[29] On their release, the Dexters emigrated to the new English plantation of Providence and Rhode Island.

Support for Parliamentarian opposition to Charles I could further be inferred via *The Duty of a King in his Royal Office*, published in late 1642. Bearing a frontispiece portrait of Charles I's late father, its title-page indicated that the tract was 'written by the High and Mighty Prince James'. *The Duty of a King* opened by reproducing the well-known part of James's speech to the English Parliament in 1610, which asserted the divinely ordained nature of royal authority, as well as the contrast between monarchy and tyranny, before silently switching to reproduce a substantial part of the king's earlier publication *Basilicon Doron*. Constructed to appear as a single, coherent work by James on kingship, it included his advice to Prince Henry to remember continually the 'true difference between a lawful good king, and a usurping tyrant'. On his peaceful death, a good king would be 'lamented by his subjects, and admired by his neighbours' whereas 'a tyrant's miserable and infamous life, arms in end his own subjects to become his burreaux [execution-ers]'. For although James insisted that 'rebellion be ever unlawful on their part, yet is the world so wearied of him, that his fall is little meaned by the rest of his subjects, and but smiled at by his neighbours'.[30]

As Charles struggled to assert his royal prerogative, his opponents continued to cite his father's words against him. Detained in New-castle in June 1646, for example, Charles exchanged a series of position papers with the Scots Presbyterian minister Alexander Henderson that were published three years later. To James's son, Henderson denied that the former king had ever endowed Episcopalianism with *iure divino* authority and, further, claimed that he had suspected Church of England 'prelates to savour of the popish hierarchy'. Accordingly, Henderson ventured that, 'could his ghost now speak to your Majesty', James would 'not advise your Majesty to run such hazards for those men who will choose rather to pull down your throne with their own ruin, than that they perish alone'. When Charles had retorted that, regarding his father, 'I had the happiness, to know him much better than you' and would 'dare say, should his ghost now speak, he would tell you, that a bloody Reformation was never lawful, as not warranted by God's word', Henderson responded by indicating that he 'did only produce what was professed by him [James], before the world'.[31]

Imaginatively ventriloquizing the thoughts of a dead king's ghost is one way of appraising a monarch. Four centuries after James's death, modern commentators routinely return to his speech to Parliament in 1610 to find a quintessential articulation of the theory known as the 'divine right of kings'. As James informed MPs, 'the state of monarchy is the supremist thing upon earth: for kings are not only God's lieuten-ants upon earth, and sit upon God's throne, but even by God himself, they are called Gods.' But as Parliamentarian critics of Charles I knew, selective quotation of the king's works permitted not only crude carica-ture, but also misleading impressions. As *The Mirror of Great Britain* has shown, James had a compulsive concern to communicate his think-ing, on a repeated basis if necessary. Indeed, he acknowledged in his speech in 1610 that 'I can say nothing at this time, whereof some of you that are here, have not at one time or other, heard me say the like already.' Conscientious discharge of his kingly duties nevertheless also rendered conversation with his subjects essential. In the same speech, James reiterated that since 'kings' actions (even in the secretest places) are as the actions of those that are set upon the stages, or on the tops of houses', he hoped 'never to speak that in private, which I shall not avow in public, and print it, if need be'.[32]

It was also in this speech in 1610 that James had presented English peers and MPs with a 'crystal mirror' as 'a great and a rare present', and he warned them not to damage that gift by regarding his mirror in 'a false light', seeking 'to soil it with a foul breath', or paying insufficient care 'to let it fall or break'.[33] But over the ensuing centuries, subsequent generations have – to invoke the Pauline metaphor from Scripture – been looking through a glass darkly and perceiving this king's reflection in too woefully a dim mirror. In both Scottish and English history, it was James's misfortune to succeed two monarchs – Mary, Queen of Scots and Elizabeth I – whose gender and rivalry understandably invites enduring scholarly and popular interest, and to precede Charles I, whose turbulent reign and calamitous end likewise attracts interest on a scale proportionate to the catastrophe he unleashed. James VI and I was indeed the first king of Great Britain; he was also, by far, its most interesting.

Notes

Anonymous, *Corona Regia*

Anonymous, *Corona Regia*, Winfried Schleiner and Tyler Fyotek (eds. and trans.) (Geneva, 2010).

Bacon, *Letters and Life*

The Letters and the Life of Francis Bacon including all his Occasional Works &c., James Spedding (ed.), 7 vols. (London, 1861–74).

Calderwood, *History of the Kirk*

David Calderwood, *The History of the Kirk of Scotland*, Thomas Thomson (ed.), 8 vols. (Edinburgh, 1842–9).

CSP *Foreign*

Calendar of the State Papers Foreign Series of the Reign of Elizabeth, Preserved in the Public Record Office, 25 vols. (London, 1863–1936).

CSP *Ireland*

Calendar of the State Papers Relating to Ireland, Preserved in the Public Record Office, 24 vols. (London, 1860–1910).

CSP *Scotland*

Calendar of the State Papers Relating to Scotland and Mary, Queen of Scotland, 1547–1603 &c., 13 vols. (Edinburgh/ Glasgow/London, 1898–1969).

CSP *Simancas*

Calendar of Letters and State Papers Preserved in, Or Originally Belonging to, the Archives of Simancas. Volume IV, Elizabeth 1587–1603, Martin A. S. Hume (ed.) (London, 1899).

CSP *Venice*

Calendar of State Papers and Manuscripts, relating to English Affairs, existing in the Archives and Collections of Venice, and in other Libraries of Northen Italy, 38 vols (London, 1864–1947).

Chamberlain, *Letters*

The Letters of John Chamberlain, Norman Egbert McClure (ed.), 2 vols. (Philadelphia, PA, 1939).

Elizabeth I and James VI, *Letters*

Letters of Queen Elizabeth and King James VI of Scotland, John Bruce (ed.) (London, 1849).

HMC *Downshire*

Historical Manuscripts Commission, *Report on the Manuscripts of the Marquis of Downshire, preserved at Easthampstead Park, Berkshire*, 6 vols. (London, 1924–95).

HMC *Salisbury*

Historical Manuscripts Commission, *Calendar of the Manuscripts of the Most Hon. The Marquis of Salisbury K.G. &c., Preserved at Hatfield House, Hertfordshire*, 21 vols. (London, 1883–1970).

James VI & I, *Letters*

Letters of King James VI & I, G. P. V. Akrigg (ed.) (Berkeley, CA, 1984).

James VI & I, *Poems*

The Poems of King James VI of Scotland, James Craigie (ed.), 2 vols. (Edinburgh, 1955–8).

James VI & I, *Political Writings*

James VI and I: Political Writings, Johann P. Sommerville (ed.) (Cambridge, 1994).

James VI & I, *Royal Correspondence*

The Royal Correspondence of King James I of England (VI of Scotland), to his Royal Brother-in-Law, King Christian IV of Denmark 1603–1625 &c., Ronald M. Meldrum (ed.) (Hassocks, 1977).

Nichols, *Progresses, Processions*

John Nichols, *The Progresses, Processions and Magnificent Festivities of James the*

First, his Royal Consort, Family and Court &c., 4 vols. (London, 1828).

Stuart Royal Proclamations, I   James F. Larkin and Paul L. Hughes (eds.), *Stuart Royal Proclamations. Volume 1: Royal Proclamations of King James 1603–1625* (Oxford, 1973).

I A MIRRORED LIFE

1. 'Speech to Parliament of 31 March 1607' in James VI & I, *Political Writings*, p. 177.
2. Ibid, p. 160.
3. See James Shapiro, *1606: Shakespeare and the Year of Lear* (London, 2015), p. 353. Uniquely in Shakespearean dramaturgy, the date, venue and royal audience of the play's first performance appeared on the title-page of *King Lear* when it was first published, in a quarto edition, in 1608.
4. 'Speech to Parliament of 31 March 1607' in James VI & I, *Political Writings*, p. 163.
5. 'Basilicon Doron' in ibid, p. 42.
6. 'Speech to Parliament of 19 March 1604', in ibid, p. 135.
7. James VI & I, *Royal Correspondence*, p. 1.
8. 'Speech to Parliament of 21 March 1610' in James VI & I, *Political Writings*, pp. 190–91.
9. 'Speech in Star Chamber of 20 June 1616' in ibid, p. 207.
10. John Morrill, 'Dynasties, Realms, Peoples and State Formation, 1500–1720' in Robert von Friedeburg and John Morrill eds., *Monarchy Transformed: Princes and their Elites in Early Modern Western Europe* (Cambridge, 2017), p. 39.
11. The Welsh devolution proposal was defeated by 80 to 20 per cent of voters, while the Scottish proposal was supported by a majority of 52 per cent of voters, but failed to satisfy an additional legislative threshold, having attracted a national turnout of only 33 per cent of the registered electorate.
12. Brendan O'Leary, *Making Sense of a United Ireland: Should It Happen? How Might It Happen?* (London, 2022), pp. 18–21.
13. 'Speech to Parliament of 31 March 1607' in James VI & I, *Political Writings*, p. 165.
14. Alex Salmond, 'Social Union and the Union of the Crowns', https://scottishgov-newsroom.prgloo.com/speeches-and-briefings/social-union-and-the-union-of-the-crowns [accessed 11 November 2024].
15. 'Speech to Parliament of 31 March 1607' in James VI & I, *Political Writings*, p. 169.
16. Tom Nairn, 'Sovereignty after the Election', *New Left Review*, 1:224 (July/August 1997), p. 6.

17. See Roy Strong, 'Three Royal Jewels: The Three Brothers, the Mirror of Great Britain and the Feather', *The Burlington Magazine*, 108:760 (1966), pp. 350–53.

18. John Donne, *A Sermon, Preached to the King's Majesty at Whitehall, 24 February 1625* [1626] (London, 1626), sig. A3v.

19. 'Speech to Parliament of 31 March 1607' in James VI & I, *Political Writings*, p. 162.

20. 'Speech to Parliament of 21 March 1610' in ibid, pp. 179, 203.

21. Maija Jansson ed., *Proceedings in Parliament, 1614* (Philadelphia, PA, 1988), p. 14.

22. Wallace Notestein, Frances Helen Relf and Hartley Simpson eds., *Commons Debates, 1621*, 7 vols. (New Haven, CT, 1935), II, p. 2. Adapting a verse from St Matthew's Gospel, James proceeded to reflect that 'I have often piped unto you, and you have not danced.' The Scriptural verse is Matthew 11:17: 'And saying, "We have piped unto you, and ye have not danced; we have mourned unto you, and ye have not lamented."' (King James Version)

23. J. P. Kenyon ed., *The Stuart Constitution 1603–1608: Documents and Commentary*, 2nd edition (Cambridge, 1986), p. 45.

24. Herbert Grabes, *The Mutable Glass: Mirror-Imagery in Titles and Texts of the Middle Ages and English Renaissance* (Cambridge, 1982), pp. 280–329 (Appendix: 'Mirror-titles in England, 1500–1700').

25. 'Basilicon Doron' in James VI & I, *Political Writings*, p. 34.

26. Quoted by Morna R. Fleming, '"Kin[g]es be the glas, the verie scoole, the booke, / Where priuate men do learne, and read, and looke" (Alexander Craig, 1604): The Translation of James VI to the Throne of England in 1603' in Theo van Heijnsbergen and Nicola Royan eds., *Literature, Letters and the Canonical in Early Modern Scotland* (East Linton, 2002), p. 102.

27. James VI & I, *Letters*, p. 338.

28. Rayna Kalas, *Frame, Glass, Verse: The Technology of Poetic Invention in the English Renaissance* (Ithaca, NY, 2007), pp. 107, 117–18.

29. 'House of Commons Journal Volume 1: 21 April 1604' in *Journal of the House of Commons: Volume 1, 1547–1629* (London, 1802), *British History Online* https://www.british-history.ac.uk/commons-jrnl/vol1/pp180–181 [accessed 9 September 2024].

30. Stuart Clark, *Vanities of the Eye: Vision in Early Modern European Culture* (Oxford, 2007), p. 22.

31. William Garter, 'Upon the Author and his Minerva' in Henry Peacham, *Minerva Britanna* [sic], *or A Garden of Heroical Devices furnished, and adorned with Emblems and Impresas of sundry natures, newly devised, moralised and published &c* (London, 1612), sig. B3r.

32. James VI, *Daemonologie in Form of a Dialogue, Divided into Three Books* (Edinburgh, 1597), p. 23.

33. Quoted by Iain Wright, '"Come like shadowes, so depart": The Ghostly Kings in *Macbeth*' in Peter Holbrook ed., *The Shakespearean International Yearbook. 6: Special Section, Shakespeare and Montaigne Revisited* (Aldershot, 2006), p. 225.

34. Vera Keller, *The Interlopers: Early Stuart Projects and the Undisciplining of Knowledge* (Baltimore, MD, 2023), pp. 86, 122, 124.

35. William Shakespeare, *Macbeth*, Act IV, Scene 1 (ll. 133–6).

36. Dedicatory epistle to Ben Jonson, 'Cynthia's Revels, or the Fountain of Self-Love' [1616)] in C. H. Herford and Percy Simpson eds., *Ben Jonson, Volume 4: Cynthia's Revels; Poetaster; Sejanus; Eastward Ho* (Oxford, 1932), p. 33.

37. Edward Forset, *A Comparative Discourse of the Bodies Natural and Politique &c.* (London, 1606), pp. 33, 32.

38. John Donne, *Devotions upon Emergent Occasions and Several Steps in my Sickness &c.* (London, 1624), p. 177.

39. See, for example, Steven J. Reid, *The Early Life of James VI: A Long Apprenticeship 1566–1585* (Edinburgh, 2023) which is the first of a two-volume biography of James concluding in 1603, and Alexander Courtney, *James VI, Britannic Prince: King of Scots and Elizabeth's Heir, 1566–1603* (Abingdon, 2024), the first of another two-volume account of James, with the next instalment covering the years 1603 to 1625.

2 A KING OF WORDS

1. See Charlotte Brewer, 'Setting a Standard: Authors and Sources in the *OED* ' in Linda Pillière, Wilfrid Andrieu, Valérie Kerfelec and Diana M. Lewis eds., *Standardising English: Norms and Margins in the History of the English Language* (Cambridge, 2018), pp. 127–43.

2. Steven J. Reid, 'Introduction' to Steven J. Reid and David McOmish eds., *Neo-Latin Literature and Literary Culture in Early Modern Scotland* (Leiden, 2017), p. 4.

3. Lori-Anne Ferrell, *Government by Polemic: James I, the King's Preachers and the Rhetorics of Conformity, 1603–1625* (Stanford, CA, 1998), p. 8.

4. 'Basilicon Doron' in James VI & I, *Political Writings*, p. 9.

5. James Craigie ed., *The Basilicon Doron of King James VI*, 2 vols. (Edinburgh, 1944–50), II, p. 20n.

6. James VI & I, *A Counterblaste to Tobacco* (London, 1604), sig. A3v

7. James VI & I, *A Remonstrance of the most Gracious King James I, King of Great Britain, France, and Ireland, Defender of the Faith, &c. For the Right of Kings, and the Independence of their Crowns* ([Cambridge], 1616), sig. A1v.

8. Quoted by Christopher R. Kyle, '"Wrangling Lawyers": Proclamations and the Management of the English Parliament of 1621', *Parliamentary History*, 34:1 (2015), p. 135.

9. Quoted by Susan Doran, *From Tudor to Stuart: The Regime Change from Elizabeth I to James I* (Oxford, 2024), p. 258.

10. Graham Rees and Maria Wakely, *Publishing, Politics and Culture: The King's Printers in the Reign of James I and VI* (Oxford, 2009), p. 94. The spring 1617 date is cited in James VI & I, *Political Writings*, p. xxxi.

11. John Donne, *Pseudo-Martyr. Wherein out of certain Propositions and Gradations, this conclusion is evicted. That those which are of the Roman religion in this Kingdom, may and ought to take the Oath of Allegiance* (London, 1610), sig. A3r.

12. Quoted by Sarah M. Dunnigan, 'Discovering Desire in the *Amatoria* of James VI' in Daniel Fischlin and Mark Fortier eds., *Royal Subjects: Essays on the Writings of James VI and I* (Detroit MI, 2002), p. 149.

13. James VI & I, *The Works of the most High and Mighty Prince, James, by the Grace of God, King of Great Britain, France and Ireland, Defender of the Faith &c.* (London, 1616 [1617]), sigs. B2v, C4v; regarding the shared etymology of 'author', 'authority' and 'authorship', see Jane Rickard, *Authorship and Authority: The Writings of James VI and I* (Manchester, 2007), pp. 8–9.

14. Queen Victoria, *Leaves from the Journal of Our Life in the Highlands, 1848 to 1861 and More Leaves from the Journal of a Life in the Highlands, from 1862 to 1882*, Margaret Homans, Joanna Marschner and Adrienne Munich eds. (Oxford, 2024), pp. 8, xiv.

15. 'Speech in Star Chamber of 20 June 1616' in James VI & I, *Political Writings*, p. 213.

16. James VI & I, *The Kings Majesty's Letter to the Lords Grace of Canterbury, touching Preaching, and Preachers* ([London, 1622]), sig. A2r.

17. [Thomas Scott], *Vox Regis* (['Utrecht'], 1624), 'To the Reader', sig. 2r. Scott's tendentious claim was that 'it expresses strength to have words sublimated into works, as the words of potent Princes used to be, or ought to be'.

18. John Milton, *Eikonoklastes in answer to a book entitled Eikon Basilike, the Portraiture of his Sacred Majesty in his Solitudes and Sufferings* (London, [1650]), sig. A2v. The passage does not appear in Milton's preface to the first edition in 1649.

19. 'The Epistle Dedicatory' in *The Holy Bible, containing the Old Testament, and the New, Newly Translated out of the Original Tongues &c.* (London, 1611), sig. A2v.

20. Philip Hensher, 'The Best Committee that Ever Sat', *The Spectator*, 5 April 2003.

21. Gordon Campbell, *Bible: The Story of the King James Version, 1611–2011* (Oxford, 2010), p. 275.

22. https://queenjamesbible.com/ [accessed 9 February 2024]; see R. Shannon Constantine, '"A Big, Fabulous Bible": The *Queen James Bible* and its Queering of Scripture', *Journal for Interdisciplinary Biblical Studies*, 2:2 (2021), pp. 95–117.

23. John S. Brewer ed., *The Court of King James the First; By Dr Godfrey Goodman, Bishop of Gloucester &c.*, 2 vols. (London, 1839), I, p. 18.

24. David M. Bergeron, *King James & Letters of Homoerotic Desire* (Iowa City, IA, 1999), p. 150.

25. Francis Osborne, *Historical Memoirs on the Reigns of Queen Elizabeth and King James* (London, 1658), sigs. G5v, M8v, M8r, M8v.

26. Quoted by David M. Bergeron, 'Writing King James's Sexuality' in Fischlin and Fortier eds., *Royal Subjects,* pp. 353, 354.

27. Lucy Hughes-Hallett, *The Scapegoat: The Brilliant Brief Life of the Duke of Buckingham* (London, 2024), p. 97.

28. Will Tosh, *Straight Acting: The Many Queer Lives of William Shakespeare* (London, 2024), pp. 239, 63, 233, 235, 240, 239. Such understandings also contextualize allegations of hypocritical double standards directed towards James, in light of his advice to Prince Henry that, as a king, there would be 'some horrible crimes that ye are bound in conscience never to forgive': namely witchcraft, wilful murder, incest, sodomy, poisoning and counterfeiting money ('Basilicon Doron' in James VI & I, *Political Writings*, p. 23).

29. 'Speech to Parliament of 31 March 1607' in James VI & I, *Political Writings*, pp. 164, 165, 164.

30. C. Sanford Terry ed., *De Unione Regnorum Britanniae Tractatus by Sir Thomas Craig* (Edinburgh, 1909), pp. 393, 356.

31. Julian Goodare, *State and Society in Early Modern Scotland* (Oxford, 1999), p. 98; another college founded at Fraserburgh in 1592 proved short-lived.

32. [Thomas Birch ed.], *The Court and Times of James the First; illustrated by authentic and confidential letters &c.*, 2 vols. (London, 1848), I, p. 37.

33. A. J. Loomie, *Guy Fawkes in Spain: The 'Spanish Treason' in Spanish Documents* (London, 1971), p. 62.

34. Quoted by Linda Levy Peck, *Court Patronage and Corruption in Early Stuart England* (London, 1993), p. 24.

35. Anonymous, *Corona Regia*, pp. 49, 79, 97. As its modern editors indicate, the counterfeit encomium was deemed by a French bibliography compiled in the 1860s to rank among the most scurrilous attacks ever directed at any prince in history, in any language (p. 11).

36. Timothy Peters, Peter Garrard, Vijeya Ganesan and John Stephenson, 'The Nature of King James VI/I's Medical Conditions: New Approaches to the Diagnosis', *History of Psychiatry*, 23:3 (2012), pp. 277–90.

37. [Sir Anthony Weldon], *The Court and Character of King James, Written and Taken by Sir A: W, Being an Eye and Ear Witness* (London, 1650), pp. 178–9, 186–7.

38. Isaac Disraeli, 'An Inquiry into the Literary and Political Character of James the First; including a Sketch of his Age' in *Literary Character of Men of Genius*, Benjamin Disraeli ed. (London, n.d.), p. 385.

39. Quoted by Marc L. Schwarz, 'James I and the Historians: Towards a Reconsideration', *Journal of British Studies*, 13:2 (1974), p. 115.

40. J. P. Kenyon, *The Stuarts: A Study in English Kingship* (London, 1956), p. 33.

41. Ann Uhry Abrams, *The Pilgrims and Pocahontas. Rival Myths of American Origin* (Builder, CO, 1959), p. 277; see also 'The Pageant at Plymouth', *The American Magazine of Art*, 12:10 (1921), pp. 354–5.

42. Bernard Norling, 'Tudor Willow and the Stuart Solomon', *The Review of Politics*, 19:2 (1957), pp. 245, 246.

43. Jenny Wormald, 'James VI and I (1566–1625), king of Scotland, England, and Ireland'. *Oxford Dictionary of National Biography* [accessed 16 September 2024].

44. Jenny Wormald, 'James VI and I: Two Kings or One?', *History*, 68:223 (1983), p. 187.

45. Walter Carruthers Sellar and Robert Julian Yeatman, *1066 And All That. A Memorable History of England, comprising all the parts you can remember, including 103 Good Things, 5 Bad Kings and 2 Genuine Dates* (London, 1990), p. 62.

46. Nigel Jones, 'A Phoenix from the Ashes: 17th-Century London Reborn', *The Spectator*, 6 February 2021.

47. Alison Herman, 'Mary & George: A Rollicking Family Affair', *Variety*, 5 April 2024.

48. Ina Ferris, 'The "Character" of James the First and Antiquarian Secret History', *The Wordsworth Circle*, 37:2 (2006), p. 75.

49. Elizabeth Read Foster ed., *Proceedings in Parliament, 1610*, 2 vols. (New Haven, CT, 1966), II, p. 105.

50. CSP *Simancas*, III, p. 518.

51. James VI & I, *Letters*, p. 309.

52. Maija Jansson ed., *Proceedings in Parliament, 1614 (House of Commons)* (Philadelphia, PA, 1988), p. xxii.

53. CSP *Scotland*, VI, pp. 26, 35.

54. Pierre Mathurin de L'Écluse des Loges ed., *Memoirs of the Duke of Sully; during his Residence at the English Court; to which he was sent Ambassador from Henry IV of France, upon the Accession of King James the First* (Dublin, 1751), pp. 123–4.

55. Quoted by R. Malcolm Smuts, 'Theological Polemics and James I's Diplomacy, 1604–1617', *Journal of Medieval and Early Modern Studies*, 50:3 (2020), pp. 517, 518.

56. CSP *Scotland*, VII, p. 275.

57. 'Basilicon Doron' in James VI & I, *Political Writings*, p. 18.

58. Quoted by John Cramsie, *Kingship and Crown Finance under James VI and I, 1603–1625* (Woodbridge, 2002), p. 134n.

59. HMC *Salisbury*, XIX, p. 11.

60. Emily V. Cole, 'The State Apartment in the Jacobean Country House, 1603–1625' (University of Sussex DPhil thesis, 2010), pp. 22, 24n.

61. HMC *Salisbury*, XVI, pp. 395–6.

62. Nichols, *Progresses, Processions*, III, p. 309.

63. Kenneth Fincham, *Prelate as Pastor: The Episcopate of James I* (Oxford, 1990), p. 39.

64. 'A Meditation upon the 27, 28, 29 Verses of the XXVII Chapter of Saint Matthew' in James VI & I, *Political Writings*, pp. 229, 231.

3 THE CRADLE KING

1. James Craigie, 'Last Poems of James VI', *Scottish Historical Review*, 29:108 Part 2 (1950), p. 139.

2. CSP *Foreign, 1566–1568*, p. 93.

3. Thomas Craig, 'On the Birth of James, most serene Prince of Scots, Duke of Rothesay, 1566' in Steven J. Reid and David McOmish eds., *Corona Borealis: Scottish Neo-Latin Poets on King James VI and his Reign, 1566–1603* (Glasgow, 2020), pp. 54, 55.

4. Queen Victoria, *Leaves from the Journal of Our Life in the Highlands, 1848 to 1861 and More Leaves from the Journal of a Life in the Highlands, from 1862 to 1882*, Margaret Homans, Joanna Marschner and Adrienne Munich eds. (Oxford, 2024), p. 23.

5. Lord Herries, *Historical Memoirs of the Reign of Mary, Queen of Scots, and of King James the Sixth* (Edinburgh, 1836), p. 79.

6. CSP *Scotland*, II, p. 218; Alexander Courtney, *James VI, Britannic Prince: King of Scots and Elizabeth's Heir, 1566–1603* (Abingdon, 2024), p. 9.

7. CSP *Scotland*, II, p. 268.

8. Herries, *Historical Memoirs*, p. 79.

9. Edward Seymour, Duke of Somerset, *An Epistle or Exhortation, to Unity [and] Peace sent from the Lord Protector &c* (London 1548), sigs. A3r, A3v, B3r.

10. See Steven Thiry, '"In Open Shew to the World": Mary's Stuart's Armorial Claim to the English Throne and Anglo-French Relations (1559–1561)', *English Historical Review*, 132:559 (2017), pp. 1405–39.

11. Regarding the French king's death, see Ibrahim Albert Srouji, 'Did One Ear Infection in France Change the History of Britain? The Illness and Death of Francis II (1544–1560)', *Journal of Medical Biography*, 17:4 (2009), pp. 231–4.

12. CSP *Scotland*, II, pp. 172, 171.

13. Thomas Thomson ed., *Memoirs of His Own Life by Sir James Melville of Halhill. MDLXIX–MDXCIII* (Edinburgh, 1827), pp. 158–9.

14. John Hill Burton ed., *The Register of the Privy Council of Scotland, Volume I: A. D. 1545–1569* (Edinburgh, 1877), p. 485.

15. Rayne Allinson, 'Queen Elizabeth I and the "Nomination" of the Young Prince of Scotland', *Notes and Queries*, 53:4 (2006), p. 425.

16. William C. Dickinson ed., *John Knox's History of the Reformation in Scotland*, 3 vols. (London, 1949), II, p. 192.

17. James VI & I, *An Apology for the Oath of Allegiance first set forth without a name, and now acknowledged by the Author, the Right High and Mighty Prince, James, by the Grace of God, King of Great Britain, France and Ireland, Defender of the Faith, &c.* (London, 1609), p. 33.

18. Patrick Adamson, 'A Birth-poem for the most serene Prince of Scotland, England and Ireland, James VI, son of Queen Mary' in Reid and McOmish eds., *Corona Borealis*, pp. 25, 29.

19. CSP *Scotland*, II, pp. 307–8.

20. Ibid, p. 316.

21. Steven J. Reid, *The Early Life of James VI: A Long Apprenticeship 1566–1585* (Edinburgh, 2023), p. 35.

22. Hill Burton ed., *Register of the Privy Council of Scotland, Volume I*, p. 519.

23. Mary raised over 5,000 crowns as a result; Allinson, 'Queen Elizabeth I and the "Nomination" of the Young Prince', p. 425n.

24. Quoted by Stephen Alford, *The Early Elizabethan Polity: William Cecil and the British Succession Crisis 1558–1569* (Cambridge, 1998), p. 158.

25. Robert Pitcairn ed., *Memorials of Transactions in Scotland, AD MDLXIX–AD MDLXXIII by Richard Bannatyne* (Edinburgh, 1836), p. 127.

26. CSP *Scotland*, II, p. 349.

27. Quoted by Claire Webb, 'The "Gude Regent"? A Diplomatic Perspective upon the Earl of Moray, Mary Queen of Scots and the Scottish Regency, 1567–1570' (University of St Andrews PhD thesis, 2008), p. 41.

28. CSP *Scotland*, II, p. 361.

29. Ibid, p. 366.

30. [George Buchanan], *A Detection of the Doings of Mary, Queen of Scots, Touching the Murder of her Husband, and her Conspiracy, Adultery and Pretended Marriage with the Earl of Bothwell &c.* [London, 1571], sig. O1r.

31. CSP *Scotland*, II, p. 365.

32. Quoted by Michael Lynch, 'Scotland's First Protestant Coronation: Revolutionaries, Sovereignty and the Culture of Nostalgia' in Luuk Houwen ed., *Literature and Religion in Late Medieval and Early Modern Scotland: Essays in Honour of Alasdair A. MacDonald* (Louvain, 2012), p. 198.

33. Reid, *The Early Life of James VI*, p. 34.

34. Quoted by Lynch, 'Scotland's First Protestant Coronation', p. 200.

35. Jane Dawson, *John Knox* (New Haven, CT, 2015), p. 273.

36. CSP *Simancas*, I, p. 673.

37. CSP *Scotland*, II, p. 408.

38. Ibid, p. 415.

39. Quoted by Lorna Hutson, *England's Insular Imagining: The Elizabethan Erasure of Scotland* (Cambridge, 2023), pp. 141, 142.

40. CSP *Scotland*, II, p. 595.

41. Ibid, p. 695.

42. CSP *Scotland*, III, p. 241.

43. Quoted by Hutson, *England's Insular Imagining*, p. 144.

44. Richard Bannatyne ed., *Journal of the Transactions in Scotland during the Contest between the Adherents of Queen Mary and those of her Son, 1570, 1571, 1572, 1573* (Edinburgh, 1806), pp. 247, 257; other accounts indicate that it was not a leaky roof that James spotted, but a hole in the cloth covering the main table; see, for example, Malcolm Laing ed., *The Historie and Life of King James the Sext: being an Account of the Affairs of Scotland, from the Year 1566 to the Year 1596* &c. (Edinburgh, 1825), p. 88.

45. CSP *Scotland*, IV, pp. 94, 96.

46. Ibid. p. 415.

47. Laing ed., *Historie and Life of King James the Sext*, p. 125.

48. CSP *Scotland*, IV, p. 569; p. 581 (for Cecil's abandoned visit).

4 SORE AND SHARP SCHOOLMASTERS

1. Anthony Nixon, *Oxford's Triumph in the Royal Entertainment of his most Excellent Majesty, the Queen, and the Prince, the 27 of August last, 1605 &c.* (London, 1605), sig. E2v; for James's wish to be detained in the library, see Robert Burton, *The Anatomy of Melancholy*, Nicolas K. Kiessling et al. eds., 6 vols. (Oxford, 1990), II, p. 88; see also Jennifer Summit, *Memory's Library: Medieval Books in Early Modern England* (Oxford, 2008), p. 219.

2. Nixon, *Oxford's Triumph in the Royal Entertainment of his most Excellent Majesty, the Queen, and the Prince, the 27 of August last, 1605 &c.*, sig. C4r–v.

3. Andrew Dalzel, *History of the University of Edinburgh from its Foundation*, David Laing ed., 2 vols. (Edinburgh, 1862), II, p. 67.

4. John Hacket, *Scrinia Reserata. A Memorial offered to the great Deservings of John Williams, DD, who some time held the Places of Lord Keeper of the Great Seal of England, Lord Bishop of Lincoln, and Lord Archbishop of York &c.* (London, 1693), p. 175.

5. William Barlow, *An Answer to a Catholic Englishman (so by himself entitled) who, without a name, passed his Censure upon the Apology made by the Right High and Mighty Prince James* (London, 1609), p. 105.

6. Jacques Davy Du Perron, *Les Diverses Œuvres de L'Illustrisime Cardinal Du Perron &c.* (Paris, 1633), p. 883 ('accomplir en sa personne le souhait de Platon, des philosophes regnants, ou des roys philosophants').

7. Quoted by Timothy Peters, Peter Garrard, Vijeya Ganesan and John Stephenson, 'The Nature of King James VI/I's Medical Conditions: New Approaches to the Diagnoses', *History of Psychiatry*, 23:3 (2012), p. 282.

8. Anonymous, *Corona Regia*, p. 37.

9. George Buchanan, 'A birth-poem for James VI, King of Scots' in Steven J. Reid and David McOmish eds., *Corona Borealis: Scottish Neo-Latin Poets on King James VI and his Reign, 1566–1603* (Glasgow, 2020), pp. 13, 15.

10. John Row, *The History of the Kirk of Scotland, from the year 1558 to August 1637* (Edinburgh, 1842), p. 34.

11. Aysha Pollnitz, *Princely Education in Early Modern Britain* (Cambridge, 2015), p. 270.

12. Quoted by ibid, p. 273.

13. Erasmus, *The Education of a Christine Prince*, Lisa Jardine ed. (Cambridge, 1997), pp. 9, 5, 6.

14. George F. Warner ed., 'The Library of James VI, 1573–1583 from a manuscript in the hand of Peter Young, his Tutor' in *Miscellany of the Scottish History Society* (Edinburgh, 1893), p. lxxii.

15. Ibid, pp. lxxii, lxxiii.

16. CSP *Scotland*, V, p. 13.

17. Robert Pitcairn ed., *The Autobiography and Diary of Mr James Melville* (Edinburgh, 1842), p. 48.

18. Quoted by David Harris Willson, *King James VI and I* (London, 1956), p. 23.

19. Gillian Sargent, '"Happy are they that read and understand": Reading for Moral and Spiritual Acuity in a Selection of Writings by King James' (University of Glasgow PhD thesis, 2013), p. 45.

20. Warner ed., 'Library of James VI', p. xviii.

21. I. D. McFarlane, *Buchanan* (London, 1981), p. 447n.

22. William Barker ed., *Richard Mulcaster's Positions concerning the Training Up of Children* (Toronto, 1994), p. 270.

23. Gordon Donaldson ed., *The Memoirs of Sir James Melville of Halhill &c.* (London, 1969), p. 103.

24. McFarlane, *Buchanan*, p. 448; Roger A. Mason, 'George Buchanan, James VI and the Presbyterians' in Mason ed., *Scots and Britons: Scottish Political Thought and the Union of 1603* (Cambridge, 1994), p. 115.

25. CSP *Simancas*, III, p. 289.

26. CSP *Venice*, XVII, *1621–1623*, pp. 444–5.

27. George Mackenzie, *The Lives and Characters of the most Eminent Writers of the Scots Nation &c.*, 3 vols. (Edinburgh, 1708–22), III, p. 180.

28. Steven Berkowitz ed., *A Critical Edition of George Buchanan's Baptistes and of its Anonymous Seventeenth-Century Translation Tyrannicall-Government Anatomized* (London, 1992), p. 351.

29. Roger A. Mason and Martin S. Smith eds., *A Dialogue on the Law of Kingship among the Scots: A Critical Edition and Translation of George Buchanan's De Iure Regni apud Scotos Dialogus* (Aldershot, 2004), p. 3.

30. Quoted by Mason and Smith, 'Introduction' to *A Dialogue on the Law of Kingship*, p. xxviii. Maitland also wrote to Mary to confirm that he was entirely uninvolved in Buchanan's fictional discussion of her deposition from power (see McFarlane, *Buchanan*, p. 393).

31. Mason and Smith eds., *A Dialogue on the Law of Kingship*, pp. 13, 55.

32. Ibid, pp. 103, 153, 155.

33. George Buchanan, 'Dedication of the History to James VI King of Scots' in W. A. Gatherer ed., *The Tyrannous Reign of Mary Stewart. George Buchanan's Account* (Edinburgh, 19858), p. 203.

34. Gatherer, 'Introduction: Buchanan as Historian' in Ibid., pp. 41–2.

35. Buchanan, 'Rerum Scoticarum Historia' in ibid, pp. 99, 153.

36. Mackenzie, *Lives and Characters*, III, p. 180.

37. George Lasry, Norbert Biermann and Satoshi Tomokiyo, 'Deciphering Mary Stuart's Lost Letters from 1578–1584', *Cryptologia*, 47:2 (2023), p. 65.

38. *The Records of the Parliaments of Scotland to 1707*, K. M. Brown et al. eds. (St Andrews, 2007–22), 1584/5/14 [accessed 17 December 2022].

39. Pollnitz, *Princely Education*, p. 265.

40. 'Trew Law of Free Monarchies' in James VI & I, *Political Writings*, p. 72.

41. 'Basilicon Doron' in ibid, p. 46.

42. 'Trew Law of Free Monarchies' in ibid, p. 83.

43. 'Basilicon Doron' in ibid, pp. 53–4, 55.

44. Quoted by W. B. Patterson, *King James VI and I and the Reunion of Christendom* (Cambridge, 1997), p. 126.

45. Mark Pattison, *Isaac Casaubon 1559–1614* (London, 1875), p. 322.

46. *A Brief Declaration of the Reasons that moved King James of Blessed Memory, and the State, to erect a College of Divines, and other Learned Men, at Chelsea* (London, 1645), p. 2.

47. Thomas Fuller, *The Church History of Britain from the Birth of Jesus Christ until the year M.DC.XLVIII* (London, 1655), pp. 51, 55; see D. E. Kennedy in 'King James I's College of Controversial Divinity at Chelsea' in D. E. Kennedy, Diana Robertson and Alexandra Walsham, *Grounds of Controversy: Three Studies in Late 16th and Early 17th Century English Polemics* (Melbourne, 1989), pp. 97–126.

48. Alice Crawford ed., *The Meaning of Libraries: A Cultural History* (Princeton, NJ, 2015), p. xv; regarding the royal donation of volumes in 1612, see https://special-collections.wp.st-andrews.ac.uk/2012/08/10/a-royal-foundation-400-years-of-the-king-james-library-a-new-exhibition-coming-soon/ [accessed 21 February 2024].

49. Isabel B. Taylor, *The Crown and Its Records: Archives, Access and the Ancient Constitution in Seventeenth-Century England* (Berlin, 2023), p. 340; since the grant stipulated as falling within the dispensation (patronage) of 'the Secretary of State', official royal recognition of the office was thereby conferred.

50. The National Archives, SP 14/94, f. 192; quoted by Alan Stewart, 'Familiar Letters and State Papers: The Afterlives of Early Modern Correspondence' in James Daybell and Andrew Gordon eds., *Cultures of Correspondence in Early Modern Britain* (Philadelphia, PA, 2015), p. 242.

51. Quoted by Kate Peters, '"Friction in the Archives": Access and the Politics of Record-Keeping in Revolutionary England' in Liesbeth Corens, Kate Peters and Alexandra Walsham eds., *Archives & Information in the Early Modern World* (Oxford, 2018), p. 165.

52. Ernesto Oyarbide Magaña, 'Collecting *"Toute l'Angleterre"*: English Books, Soft Power and Spanish Diplomacy at the *Casa del Sol* (1613–1622)' in Nina Lamal, Jamie Cumby and Helmer J. Helmers eds., *Print and Power in Early Modern Europe (1500–1800)* (Leiden, 2021), p. 328. See also Ernesto Eduardo Oyarbide Magaña, 'The First Count of Gondomar's Library and Diplomatic Practice (1613–1622)' (University of Oxford DPhil thesis, 2019).

53. Quoted by Ernesto E. Oyarbide Magaña, 'Between Love and Hate: Thomas Scott's Puritan Propaganda and his Interest in Spanish Culture' in Yolanda Rodríguez Pérez ed., *Literary Hispanophobia and Hispanophilia in Britain and the Low Countries (1550–1850)* (Amsterdam, 2020), p. 95.

54. Quoted by Oyarbide Magaña, 'The First Count of Gondomar's Library', p. 53.

55. Anthony Nixon, *Oxford's Triumph in the Royal Entertainment of his most Excellent Majesty, the Queen, and the Prince, the 27 of August last, 1605 &c.* (London, 1605), sig. Er.

56. Quoted by Summit, *Memory's Library*, p. 219.

57. Quoted by Catherine Cole, 'The Building of the Tower of Five Orders in the Schools' Quadrangle at Oxford', *Oxoniensis*, 33 (1968), p. 102.

5 THE NAKED SWORD

1. 'Speech to Parliament of 9 November 1605' in James VI & I, *Political Writings*, p. 148.

2. Ibid, pp. 148–9.

3. Robert Persons, *A Treatise of Three Conversions from Paganism to Christian Religion* ([St Omer], 1604), sig. *3.

4. Robert Appelbaum, *Terrorism Before the Letter: Mythography and Political Violence in England, Scotland, and France, 1559–1642* (Oxford, 2015), p. 3.

5. Stuart Carroll, 'The Rights of Violence', *Past & Present*, Supplement 7 (2012), p. 156.

6. Quoted by K. J. Kesselring, 'License to Kill: Assassination and the Politics of Murder in Elizabethan and Early Stuart England', *Canadian Journal of History*, 48 (2013), p. 428.

7. Antoine le Fèvre de la Boderie, *Ambassades de Monsieur de la Boderie en Angleterre sous le Règne d'Henri IV & la Minorité de Louis XIII depuis les années 1606 jusqu'à 1611*, 5 vols. (Paris, 1750), V, p. 268; 'qu'il devint plus blanc que la chemise'); CSP *Venice*, XI, *1607–1610*, p. 494.

8. Roger A. Mason and Martin S. Smith eds., *A Dialogue on the Law of Kingship among the Scots. A Critical Edition and Translation of George Buchanan's De Iure Regni apud Scotos Dialogus* (Aldershot, 2004), p. 153.

9. Quoted by Jamie A. Gianoutsos, *The Rule of Manhood: Tyranny, Gender and Classical Republicanism in England, 1603–1660* (Cambridge, 2020), p. 138n.

10. J. H. Burton ed., *Register of the Privy Council of Scotland. Volume II: A. D. 1569–1578* (Edinburgh, 1878), p. 683.

11. CSP *Scotland*, V, p. 283.

12. Ibid, p. 287. Bowes further confirmed that James's tutor, George Buchanan, was among those who hastily wrote to reassure the Privy Council that all 'the parties were well reconciled' and that plans to create a governing Council led by Morton should proceed as if 'no such matter had happened' (Ibid).

13. Quoted by Steven J. Reid, *The Early Life of James VI: A Long Apprenticeship 1566–1585* (Edinburgh, 2023), p. 100.

14. Quoted by ibid, p. 102.

15. Quoted by Elisabeth Rébeillé-Borgella, 'Esme Stuart d'Aubigny, First Duke of Lennox, c.1542–1583: A French Courtier in Scotland' (University of Edinburgh PhD thesis, 2022), p. 57.

16. Quoted by ibid, p. 81.

17. *The Correspondence of Robert Bowes, of Aske, Esquire, The Ambassador of Queen Elizabeth in the Court of Scotland* (London, [1843]), pp. 32, 70.

18. CSP *Scotland*, V, pp. 402, 426, 532.

19. Ibid, pp. 511, 514, 511.

20. *Correspondence of Robert Bowes, of Aske*, pp. 160–61.

21. CSP *Scotland*, V, pp. 633, 637.

22. J. H. Burton ed., *Register of the Privy Council of Scotland. Volume III: A. D. 1578–1585* (Edinburgh, 1880), p. 360; CSP *Scotland*, V, p. 679. In February 1581, Bowes drew up 'Intelligence to be used against d'Aubigny', compiling charges to be 'used and laid against d'Aubigny to prove him abusing the king, the nobility and that state' (CSP *Scotland*, V, pp. 608–10).

23. CSP *Scotland*, VI, p. 62.

24. Quoted by Rébeillé-Borgella, 'Esmé Stuart d'Aubigny, First Duke of Lennox, *c.* 1542–1583', p. 185 ('Je n'ay communicquer au Roy ces affairs pour cause du secret ; car il est anchore enfant').

25. Quoted by Alexander Courtney, *James VI, Britannic Prince: King of Scots and Elizabeth's Heir, 1566–1603* (Abingdon, 2024), pp. 55–6.

26. Quoted by Steven J. Reid, 'Of bairns and bearded men: James VI and the Ruthven Raid' in Miles Kerr-Peterson and Steven J. Reid eds., *James VI and Noble Power in Scotland, 1578–1603* (Abingdon, 2017), p. 32.

27. J. H. Burton ed., *Register of the Privy Council of Scotland. Volume III*, p. 508.

28. CSP *Simancas*, III, p. 396.

29. *Correspondence of Robert Bowes*, pp. 209, 228.

30. CSP *Simancas*, III, p. 444.

31. CSP *Scotland*, VI, p. 325.

32. Thomas Thomson ed., *Memoirs of His Own Life by Sir James Melville of Halhill MDXLIX–MDXCIII* (Edinburgh, 1827), pp. 285, 286, 289.

33. CSP *Scotland*, VI, p. 561.

34. 'Basilicon Doron' in James VI & I, *Political Writings*, p. 36.

35. Robert Ashton ed., *James I by his Contemporaries: An Account of his Career and Character as Seen by Some of his Contemporaries* (London, 1969), p. 2.

36. CSP *Scotland*, X, p. 531.

37. Ibid, p. 610.

38. James VI & I, *Poems*, II, p. 106; Robin G. MacPherson, 'Francis Stewart, 5th earl Bothwell, *c.* 1562–1612: Lordship and Politics in Jacobean Scotland' (University of Edinburgh PhD thesis, 1998), p. 392n.

39. Quoted by Keith M. Brown, *Bloodfeud in Scotland 1573–1625: Violence, Justice and Politics in an Early Modern Society* (Edinburgh, 1986), p. 159.

40. CSP *Scotland*, X, p. 653.

41. James VI & I, *Letters*, p. 118.

42. Joseph Bain ed., *Calendar of Letters and Papers relating to the Affairs of the Borders of England and Scotland &c.* 2 vols. (Edinburgh, 1894–6), I, pp. 407, 408.

43. CSP *Scotland*, X, pp. 756, 757.

44. CSP *Scotland*, XI, pp. 148, 149.

45. Ibid, pp. 145–6.

46. Elizabeth I and James VI, *Letters*, p. 101.

47. CSP *Scotland*, XIII, Part 2, p. 702; see Jenny Wormald, 'The Gowrie Conspiracy: Do we Need to Wait until the Day of Judgement?' in Miles Kerr-Peterson and Steven J. Reid eds., *James VI and Noble Power in Scotland 1578–1603* (London, 2017), pp. 194–206.

48. Philip Williamson and Natalie Mears, 'James I and Gunpowder Treason Day', *Historical Journal*, 64:2 (2021), p. 192.

49. Quoted by Peter E. McCullough, *Sermons at Court: Politics and Religion in Elizabethan and Jacobean Preaching* (Cambridge, 1998), p. 117.

50. 'Speech to Parliament of 9 November 1605' in James VI & I, *Political Writings*, pp. 148, 157.

51. Lancelot Andrewes, 'A Sermon preached before His Majesty on Sunday the Fifth of August last, at Holdenby, Anno. Dom. 1610' in Peter McCullough ed., *Lancelot Andrewes: Selected Sermons and Lectures* (Oxford, 2005), pp. 196, 204.

52. Brown, *Bloodfeud in Scotland*, pp. 5–6.

53. Quoted by ibid, p. 32.

54. Ibid, p. 20; the higher nobility comprised the Duke of Lennox, Lord Hamilton, and twenty-two earls.

55. James Dennistoun ed., *Memoirs of the Affairs of Scotland. By David Moysie. MDLXXVIII–MDCIII.* (Edinburgh, 1830), pp. 63–4.

56. Quoted by Calderwood, *History of the Kirk*, V, p. 390.

57. 'Basilicon Doron' in James VI & I, *Political Writings*, p. 28.

58. CSP *Scotland*, XIII, Part I, p. 228; see *The Records of the Parliaments of Scotland to 1707*, K. M. Brown et al. eds. (St Andrews, 2007–24), 1598/6/2 [accessed 20 September 2024].

59. Brown, *Bloodfeud in Scotland*, pp. 215, 218.

60. CSP *Scotland*, XIII, Part 2, p. 961.

61. 'Basilicon Doron' in James VI & I, *Political Writings*, p. 32.

62. *The Records of the Parliaments of Scotland to 1707*, K. M. Brown et al. eds. (St Andrews, 2007–23), 1600/11/33 [accessed 15 January 2023].

63. Markku Peltonen, *The Duel in Early Modern England: Civility, Politeness and Honour* (Cambridge, 2003), p. 82.

64. Henri IV, *An Edict or Statute lately set forth by the French King, concerning the Prohibition and Punishment of Single and Private Combats ... Newly translated out of French* (London, 1609), p. 1.

65. Quoted by K. J. Kesselring, *Making Murder Public: Homicide in Early Modern England, 1480–1680* (Oxford, 2019), p. 105.

66. *Historical Manuscripts Commission. Report on the Manuscripts of His Grace, the Duke of Portland preserved at Welbeck Abbey, Volume IX* (London, 1923), pp. 53, 55, 56.

67. *Stuart Royal Proclamations*, I, pp. 303, 304.

68. Francis Bacon, *The Charge of Sir Francis Bacon Knight, His Majesty's Attorney-General, Touching Duels upon an Information in the Star Chamber against Priest and Wright &c.* (London, 1614), pp. 9, 21.

69. Quoted by Ian Williams, 'James VI and I, *Rex et Iudex*: One King as Judge in Two Kingdoms' in William Eves, John Hudson, Ingrid Ivarsen and Sarah B. White eds., *Common Law, Civil Law and Colonial Law: Essays in Comparative Legal History from the Twelfth to the Twentieth Centuries* (Cambridge, 2019), pp. 107, 111.

70. Quoted by Kesselring, *Making Murder Public*, p. 110.
71. Quoted by Roger A. Mason, 'George Buchanan, James VI and the Presbyterians' in Roger A. Mason ed., *Scots and Britons: Scottish Political Thought and the Union of 1603* (Cambridge, 1994), p. 137.

6 THE APPRENTICE POET

1. 'Song: The first verses that ever the king made' in James VI & I, *Poems*, II, p. 133; two alternative versions are reproduced by Craigie with another from the Maitland Quarto MS, held in the Pepys Library, Magdalene College, Cambridge ('Since thought is free, think what thou will / O troubled heart to ease thy pain / Thought unrevealed can do no evil. / But words passed out, come not again / Be careful always for to invent / The way to get thine own intent').
2. The verses first appeared in John Pinkerton, *Ancient Scottish Poems, Never Before in Print*, 2 vols. (London, 1786), I, p. 177; the rejoinder is found among the manuscripts of one of James's most hostile Presbyterian critics, David Calderwood; see James VI & I, *Poems*, II, pp. 196–8.
3. This endorsement appears on a copy in papers formerly belonging to the lawyer Thomas Maitland in the National Records of Scotland (NRS RH 13/38), discovered by Sally Mapstone. The original reads 'thir maid in anno 1583, at ye duik of obiynnie his putting out of Scotland' (quoted by Roderick J. Lyall, 'James VI and the Sixteenth-Century Cultural Crisis' in Julian Goodare and Michael Lynch eds., *The Reign of James VI* (East Linton, 2000), p. 60).
4. Quoted by Sebastiaan Verweij, *The Literary Culture of Early Modern Scotland: Manuscript Production and Transmission, 1560–1625* (Oxford, 2015), p. 67.
5. See Joanna Summers, *Late-Medieval Prison Writing and the Politics of Autobiography* (Oxford, 2004), pp. 60–89.
6. See Peter C. Herman, *Royal Poetrie: Monarchic Verse and the Political Imaginary of Early Modern England* (Ithaca, NY, 2010), p. 3.
7. James VI & I, *Poems*, I, p. 7.
8. *The Records of the Parliaments of Scotland to 1707*, K. M. Brown et al. eds (St Andrews, 2007–23), 1584/5/13 [accessed 23 January 2023]. On 4 May 1584, William Ruthven, Earl of Gowrie, had been executed after being convicted of treason for his role in the attempted capture of James at Stirling Castle the previous month.
9. Quoted by Sebastiaan Verweij, '"Booke, go thy wayes": The Publication, Reading and Reception of James VI/I's Early Poetic Works', *Huntington Library Quarterly*, 77:2 (2014), p. 115.
10. Eleanor Relle, 'Some New Marginalia and Poems of Gabriel Harvey', *Review of English Studies*, 23:92 (1972), p. 405.

11. 'The Reulis and Cautelis to be Observit and Eschewit in Scottish Poesie' in James VI & I, *Poems*, I, pp. 74, 79.

12. Ibid, p. 78.

13. Quoted by Ruth Abraham, 'Appropriating James VI and I: Reading the King of Scotland/England from the 16th to the 21st Century' (Queen's University Belfast PhD thesis, 2011), p. 260.

14. 'An epitaphe on Montgomrie' in James VI & I, *Poems*, II, p. 107 ('prince of poets in our land'; 'sacred brethren of Castalian band').

15. For scepticism attaching to the notion of a 'Castalian band', see Priscilla Bawcutt, 'James VI's Castalian Band: A Modern Myth', *Scottish Historical Review*, 80:210 (2001), pp. 251–9.

16. 'Reulis and Cautelis' in James VI & I, *Poems*, I, p. 75; see David J. Parkinson, 'Alexander Montgomerie, James VI, and "Tumbling Verse"' in L. A. J. R. Houwen and A. A. MacDonald eds., *Loyal Letters: Studies in Mediaeval Alliterative Poetry and Prose* (Groningen, 1994), pp. 281–95, and Sally Mapstone, 'Invective as Poetic: The Cultural Context of Polwarth and Montgomerie's *Flyting*', *Scottish Literary Journal*, 26:2 (1999), pp. 18–40. In his *Defence*, Bellay had described rhythms 'tumblant en icelle' (falling over themselves).

17. 'Invectives Captain Alexander Montgomerie and Polwarth' and 'To Robert Hudson' in David J. Parkinson ed., *Alexander Montgomerie. Poems. Volume 1: Text* (Edinburgh, 2000), pp. 174, 173, 113.

18. Maurice Lee Jr., *Great Britain's Solomon: James VI and I in his Three Kingdoms* (Urbana, IL, 1990), p. 236; David M. Bergeron, *King James & Letters of Homoerotic Desire* (Iowa, IA, 1999), p. 64.

19. Quoted by Steven J. Reid, *The Early Life of James VI: A Long Apprenticeship 1566–1585* (Edinburgh, 2023), p. 132.

20. Amy L. Juhala, 'The Household and Court of King James VI of Scotland, 1567–1603' (University of Edinburgh PhD thesis, 2000), p. 33.

21. Joseph Bain ed., *Calendar of Letters and Papers relating to the Affairs of the Borders of England and Scotland &c.* 2vols (Edinburgh, 1894–6), II, p. 82; CSP *Scotland*, VI, p. 149.

22. CSP *Scotland*, VI, pp. 222, 223.

23. Arthur John Butler and Sophie Crawford Lomas eds., *Calendar of State Papers, Foreign Series of the Reign of Elizabeth, January–June 1583 and Addenda &c.* (London, 1913), p. 394.

24. 'Ane metaphoricall invention of a tragedie called Phœnix' in James VI & I, *Poems*, I, p. 41.

25. Ibid, pp. 42, 44 (ll. 26, 31 and 34).

26. Ibid, pp. 48, 50, 52 56 (ll. 120, 126, 146, 147, 162–8, 261–2).

27. Verweij, *Literary Culture of Early Modern Scotland*, p. 61.

28. Relle, 'Some New Marginalia', p. 404.

29. 'Reulis and Cautelis' in James VI & I, *Poems*, I, p. 79.

30. 'To the favourable Reader' in ibid, I, p. 16; see John Corbett, 'The Prentise and the Printer: James VI and Thomas Vautrollier' in Kevin J. McGinley and Nicola Royan eds., *The Apparelling of Truth: Literature and Literary Culture in the Reign of James VI* (Newcastle, 2010), pp. 80–93.

31. Steven W. May, *English Renaissance Manuscript Culture: The Paper Revolution* (Oxford, 2023), p. 42n.

32. Peter Auger, *Du Bartas' Legacy in England and Scotland* (Oxford, 2019), p. 17.

33. *The History of Judith in Form of A Poem. Penned in French, by the Noble Poet, G. Salluste, Lord of Bartas. Englished by Thomas Hudson* (Edinburgh, 1584), sigs. A2v, A3r, A3v.

34. Robert Appelbaum, 'Judith Dines Alone: From the Bible to Du Bartas', *Modern Philology*, 111:4 (2014), p. 691.

35. 'The Uranie translated' in James VI & I, *Poems*, I, pp. 17, 27 (ll. 153–60).

36. Auger, *Du Bartas' Legacy*, p. 32.

37. Quoted by Peter Auger, 'Du Bartas' Visit to England and Scotland in 1587', *Notes and Queries*, 59:4 (2012), p. 506.

38. Samuel F. Will, 'An Unpublished Letter of Du Bartas', *Modern Language Notes*, 49:3 (1934), p. 152.

39. Annie I. Cameron ed., *The Warrender Papers: Volume II* (Edinburgh, 1932), p. 96.

40. 'The Author to the Reader' and 'The Author's Preface to the Reader' in James VI & I, *Poems*, I, pp. 98, 198.

41. 'The Author's Preface to the Reader' in James VI & I, *Poems*, I, pp. 198, 200; see Robert Applebaum, 'War and Peace in *The Lepanto* of James VI and I', *Modern Philology*, 97:3 (2000), pp. 333–63.

42. Quoted by Verweij, '"Booke, Go Thy Wayes"', p. 117.

43. Quoted by Rebecca Jane Emmett, 'Networks of Print, Patronage and Religion in England and Scotland, 1580–1604: The Career of Robert Waldegrave' (Plymouth University PhD thesis, 2013), p. 238.

44. As Auger has shown, Du Bartas's 'Et leur ton ton-tonant erre, et prompt, rompt le rond / Du plancher estoillé' (*Lepanthe*, ll. 415–16) translated James's 'conspicuously Bartasian' lines: 'like thunder rearing rumling raue / With roares the highest Heauen' ('Lepanto', ll. 621–2) (Auger, *Du Bartas' Legacy*, pp. 43–4).

45. Ibid, p. 44.

46. Quoted by Astrid Stilma, *A King Translated: The Writings of King James VI & I and their Interpretation in the Low Countries, 1593–1603* (Farnham, 2012), p. 102.

47. Quoted by Jamie Reid-Baxter, '"Scotland will be the ending of all empires": Mr Thomas Murray and King James VI' in Steven Boardman and Julian Goodare eds., *Kings, Lords and Men in Scotland and Britain,*

1300–1625: Essays in Honour of Jenny Wormald (Edinburgh, 2014), pp. 327–8.

48. Michael Neill ed., *Othello, The Moor of Venice* (Oxford, 2006), p. 396 (V.2.352); 'The Lepanto' in James VI & I, *Poems*, I, p. 202 (line 11).

49. Jane Rickard, *Writing the Monarch in Jacobean England: Jonson, Donne, Shakespeare and the Works of King James* (Cambridge, 2015), p. 218.

50. Alexander Neville, *Academiae Cantabrigiensis Lachrymae Tumulo Nobilissimi Equitis &c.* (London, 1587), sig. K2v; Philip Sidney, *The Defence of Poesie, Astrophil and Stella and other Writings*, ed. Elizabeth Porges Watson (London, 1997), p. 118.

51. Samuel Rowlands, *Ave Cæsar. God Save the King. The Joyful Echoes of Loyal English Hearts, Rntertaining his Majesty's Late Arrival in England &c.* (London, 1603), sig. B3v.

52. 'A Vow or wish for the felicity & fertility of the owners of this house' in James VI & I, *Poems*, II, p. 177 ('the April of my days'; 'sat upon Parnassus's forked hill').

53. 'Epigrams', Colin Burrow ed., *The Cambridge Edition of the Works of Ben Jonson: Volume 5* (Cambridge, 2012), pp. 114–15; see Jennifer Brady, 'Jonson's "To King James": Plain Speaking in the "Epigrammes" and the "Conversations"', *Studies in Philology*, 82:3 (1985), pp. 380–98.

54. 'The Complaint of the Muses upon Sir William Alexander' in James Maidment ed., *A Miscellany of the Abbotsford Club: Volume First* (Edinburgh, 1837), p. 323; quoted by Peter Auger, 'Recreation and William Alexander's *Doomes-Day* (1637)', *Scottish Literary Review*, 2:2 (2010), pp. 1–21.

55. Jane Stevenson, 'Adulation and Admonition in *The Muses' Welcome*' in David J. Parkinson ed., *James VI and I: Literature and Scotland. Tides of Change, 1567–1625* (Leuven, 2013), p. 271.

56. Roger P. H. Green, 'The King Returns: *The Muses' Welcome* (1618)' in Steven J. Reid and David McOmish eds., *Neo-Latin Literature and Literary Culture in Early Modern Scotland* (Leiden, 2016), pp. 159–60.

57. Thomas Cogswell, 'Underground Verse and the Transformation of Early Stuart Political Culture', *Huntington Library Quarterly*, 60:3 (1997), pp. 310, 308.

58. *Stuart Royal Proclamations*, I, pp. 495, 496.

59. James Craigie, 'Last Poems of James VI', *Scottish Historical Review*, 29:108 Part 2 (1950), pp. 136, 137.

60. 'Basilicon Doron' in James VI & I, *Political Writings*, p. 49.

7 MARY, ELIZABETH – AND JAMES

1. Elizabeth I and James VI, *Letters*, p. 111.
2. CSP *Scotland*, III, p. 57.

3. Quoted by Carole Levin, 'All the Queen's Children: Elizabeth I and the Meanings of Motherhood', *Explorations in Renaissance Culture*, 30:1 (2004), p. 60.

4. CSP *Scotland*, V, p. 13.

5. Ibid, p. 269.

6. CSP *Simancas*, II, p. 581.

7. *The Correspondence of Robert Bowes, of Aske, Esquire, The Ambassador of Queen Elizabeth in the Court of Scotland* (London, [1843]), p. 143.

8. CSP *Scotland*, V, pp. 632, 648.

9. CSP *Simancas*, III, pp. 207–8.

10. CSP *Scotland*, VI, p. 65. I am grateful to Paulina Kewes for giving me prior sight of Susan Doran and Paulina Kewes, 'Inventing Iconography: Mary, Queen of Scots, James VI of Scotland and the Campaign for the Association, *c.* 1578–1584', in Yasmin Arshad and Chris Latouris eds., *Women and Cultures of Portraiture* (forthcoming).

11. CSP *Simancas*, III, p. 258.

12. CSP *Scotland*, VI, p. 115; for articles of proposed treaty 'for the Scottish Queen and her son', see ibid, pp. 116–17.

13. James VI & I, *Letters*, p. 46.

14. See Jayne Lewis, *Mary, Queen of Scots: Romance and Nation* (London, 1998), pp. 69–70.

15. CSP *Scotland*, VI, pp. 275, 278, 279.

16. Ibid, pp. 603, 605.

17. Quoted by Hannah Susan Coates, 'Sir Francis Walsingham and mid-Elizabethan Political Culture' (University of Leeds PhD thesis, 2017), pp. 219, 220; see also Kit Heyam, *The Reputation of Edward II, 1305–1697: A Literary Transformation of History* (Amsterdam, 2020), p. 191.

18. CSP *Scotland*, VII, p. 274.

19. Ibid, p. 389.

20. Quoted by Susan Doran, *Elizabeth I and her Circle* (Oxford, 2015), p. 101.

21. CSP *Scotland*, VIII, p. 23.

22. CSP *Simancas*, III, p. 502.

23. Elizabeth I and James VI, *Letters*, p. 50.

24. Ibid, p. 15.

25. Quoted by Rayne Allinson, *A Monarchy of Letters: Royal Correspondence and English Diplomacy in the Reign of Elizabeth I* (Basingstoke, 2012), p. 174.

26. CSP *Scotland*, VIII, p. 51. Variously a subject of the French, English and Scottish Crowns, Lennox had been 'quite possibly the first man to own land on both sides of the Anglo-Scottish border since the fourteenth century's wars of independence' (Marcus Merriman, 'Matthew Stewart, thirteenth or fourth Earl of Lennox (1516–1571), magnate and regent of Scotland', *Oxford Dictionary of National Biography*; accessed 4 March 2024).

27. Elizabeth I and James VI, *Letters*, pp. 31, 30, 32.

28. CSP *Scotland*, VIII, p. 415.

29. James VI & I, *Letters*, pp. 71–2.

30. See Peter C. Herman, *Royal Poetrie: Monarchic Verse and the Political Imaginary of Early Modern England* (Ithaca, NY, 2011), pp. 164–5.

31. CSP *Scotland*, VIII, pp. 281, 250.

32. Ibid, p. 622.

33. See Ruth Grant, 'The Making of the Anglo-Scottish Alliance of 1586' in Julian Goodare and Alasdair A. MacDonald eds., *Sixteenth-Century Scotland: Essays in Honour of Michael Lynch* (Leiden, 2008), pp. 211–35.

34. *By the Queen. A True Copy of the Proclamation lately published by the Queen's Majesty, under the Great Seal of England, for the Declaring of the Sentence, lately given against the Queen of Scots* (London, 1586), p. 2.

35. Robert Bell ed. and trans., *Extract from the Despatches of M. de Courcelles, French Ambassador at the Court of Scotland, 1586–1587* (Edinburgh, 1828), pp. 4, 18.

36. James VI & I, *Letters* pp. 74–5.

37. Elizabeth I and James VI, *Letters*, pp. 43, 42.

38. James VI & I, *Letters*, p. 82; see Susan Doran, 'Revenge her Foul and Most Unnatural Murder? The Impact of Mary Stewart's Execution on Anglo-Scottish Relations', *History*, 85:280 (2000), pp. 589–612.

39. Sir Walter Scott ed., *Memoirs of Robert Cary, Earl of Monmouth, Written by Himself* (Edinburgh, 1808), p. 12.

40. James VI & I, *Letters*, pp. 84–5.

41. Rev. M. Russell ed., *History of the Church of Scotland beginning the year of our Lord 203, and continued to the End of the Reign of King James VI by the Right Reverend John Spottiswoode &c.*, 3 vols. (Edinburgh, 1851), II, pp. 365, 367, 370, 368, 371.

42. CSP *Venice*, VIII, *1581–1591*, p. 330.

43. Joseph Bain ed., *Calendar of Letters and Papers relating to the Affairs of the Borders of England and Scotland &c.* 2 vols. (Edinburgh, 1894–6), II, p. 297.

44. Ibid, p. 311.

45. CSP *Scotland*, IX, p. 598.

46. James VI & I, *Letters*, p. 88.

47. CSP *Scotland*, IX, p. 666.

48. Ibid, p. 654.

49. Elizabeth I and James VI, *Letters*, pp. 162–3.

50. Ibid, pp. 72, 76, 91, 92.

51. CSP *Scotland*, XI, p. 248.

52. Elizabeth I and James VI, *Letters*, pp. 100–101.

53. Julian Goodare, 'James VI's English Subsidy' in Julian Goodare and Michael Lynch eds., *The Reign of James VI* (East Linton, 2000), p. 116.

54. Felicity Heal, 'Royal Gifts and Gift-Exchange in Sixteenth-Century Anglo-Scottish Politics' in Stephen I. Boardman, Julian Goodare and Jenny Wormald eds., *Kings, Lords and Men in Scotland and Britain, 1300–1625: Essays in Honour of Jenny Wormald* (Edinburgh, 2014), pp. 296.

55. Elizabeth I and James VI, *Letters*, pp. 68–9, 70.

56. Ibid, pp. 132, 133.

57. Quoted by Helen Georgia Stafford, *James VI of Scotland and the Throne of England* (New York, 1940), p. 223.

58. See John Bruce ed., *Correspondence of King James VI of Scotland with Sir Robert Cecil and others in England during the Reign of Queen Elizabeth &c.* (London, 1861).

59. Quoted by Alexander Courtney, 'The Scottish King and the English Court: The Secret Correspondence of James VI, 1601–1603' in Susan Doran and Paulina Kewes eds., *Doubtful and Dangerous: The Question of Succession in Late Elizabethan England* (Manchester, 2014),' p. 144.

60. Quoted by Peter Sherlock, 'The Monuments of Elizabeth Tudor and Mary Stuart: King James and the Manipulation of Memory', *Journal of British Studies*, 46:2 (2007), p. 270.

61. Ibid, p. 278, 275–6 ('*placida morte septuagenaria soluta*' and '*regno consortes & urna, hic obdormimus Elizabetha et Maria sorores in spe resurrectionis*').

62. Ibid, pp. 273, 278. The original, '*Ortu magna, viro major, sed maxima partu, / hic jacet Henrici filia, sponsa, parens*' ('Great by birth, greater by marriage, but greatest by offspring, / here lies the daughter, wife and mother of Henry'), was reworked to read '*Magna viro, maior natu, sed maxima partu; / conditur hic regum filia, sponsa, parens*' ('Great by marriage, greater by birth, but greatest by offspring, / Here is buried the daughter, wife, and mother of kings').

63. Ibid, pp. 278–9, 280 ('*infesto regibus exemplo, securi percutitur*') ('*Sit regis mactare nefas. / Ut sanguine posthac purpereo nunquam terra Britannia fluat*').

8 *PATERFAMILIAS*

1. 'Basilicon Doron' in James VI & I, *Political Writings*, pp. 41, 38, 40, 42.

2. James VI & I, *Letters*, p. 98.

3. 'Basilicon Doron' in James VI & I, *Political Writings*, p. 41.

4. James VI & I, *Royal Correspondence*, p. 11; this was Christian IV's third son; his first had been stillborn and a second survived less than a month.

5. 'Basilicon Doron' in James VI & I, *Political Writings*, pp. 39, 41, 39.

6. CSP *Simancas*, III, p. 320.

7. Ibid, p. 477; Mendoza added that, to placate Elizabeth, Leicester was now 'making great efforts to marry the girl to a private gentleman'. Mendoza had earlier reported rumours that were James to agree to marry Dorothy,

and confirm that he would not change his religion, 'they, Leicester and Wal-singham, will have him declared by the judges, to be the heir to the crown of England' (p. 451).

8. CSP *Venice*, VIII, *1581–1591*, p. 83. Having already refused to marry the widowed Philip II, Margaret became a nun and died in a Madrid monastery in 1633, aged sixty-six.

9. Annie I. Cameron ed., *The Warrender Papers: Volume II* (Edinburgh, 1932), p. 44.

10. Ibid, p. 37; As Young recalled, he and his fellow envoy, Sir Patrick Vaus of Barnbarroch, had denied that agreement over the islands' future was required for marriage discussions to progress, claiming 'that this was an answerless answer to their negotiation' (ibid, p. 37). Ironically, their answer echoed Elizabeth I's evasive attempts the previous autumn to delay confirm-ing a capital sentence after Mary's conviction for treason by insisting that her Privy Councillors must 'take in good part my answer answerless' (Leah Marcus, Janel Muller and Mary Beth Rose eds., *Elizabeth I: Collected Works* [Chicago, IL, 2000], pp. 197, 204).

11. Cameron ed., *Warrender Papers: Volume II*, pp. 68, 91, 99.

12. Thomas Thomson ed., *Memoirs of His Own Life by Sir James Melville of Halhill, M.D.XLIX–M.D.XCIII* (Edinburgh, 1827), p. 365.

13. CSP *Scotland*, IX, p. 655; X, p. 95.

14. CSP *Scotland*, X, pp. 87–8.

15. Ibid, pp. 103–5, 122.

16. Susan Doran, *From Tudor to Stuart: The Regime Change from Elizabeth I to James I* (Oxford, 2024), p. 43.

17. CSP *Scotland*, X, pp. 150, 157.

18. James VI & I, *Poems*, II, p. 68. ('No medicine my sickness may assuage / Nor cataplasm cure my wounds I see / Through deadly shott alive I daily die / I fry in flames of that envenomed dart'.) James's 'amatoria' (love poetry) was unpublished during his lifetime, but circulated in manuscript and evidently inspired ventriloquized imitations. A 'passionate sonnet' purportedly written by James 'upon the difficulties arising to cross his proceedings in love and marriage' was included in the commonplace book of an English Chancery clerk, Sir Stephen Powle. Attributing the lines of verse to Nicolas Breton, Powle noted that, although Breton claimed to have been in Scotland during James VI's reign, 'I rather think they were made by him in the person of the king' (Arthur F. Marotti, *Manuscript, Print and the English Renaissance Lyric* (Ithaca, NY, 1995), p. 14.

19. HMC *Salisbury*, III p. 438.

20. James VI & I, *Letters*, pp. 98, 99.

21. HMC *Salisbury*, III, p. 439.

22. CSP *Scotland*, X, p. 177.

23. James VI & I, *Poems*, II, p. 148 ('And lacking parents, brethren, bairns, or any near of king / In case of death, or absence to supply my place therein / And chiefly in so kitle a land, where few remember can / For to have seen governing there a king that was a man').

24. Cameron ed., *Warrender Papers: Volume II*, p. 111.

25. James Dennistoun ed., *Memoirs of the Affairs of Scotland. By David Moysie. MDLXXVII–MDCIII* (Edinburgh, 1830), p. 81.

26. Quoted by Lucinda H. S. Dean, '"richesse in fassone and in fairness": Marriage, Manhood and Sartorial Splendour for Sixteenth-Century Scottish Kings', *Scottish Historical Review*, 50:254 (2021), p. 393.

27. CSP *Scotland*, X, p. 188.

28. 'The Danish Account' in David Stevenson, *Scotland's Last Royal Wedding: The Marriage of James VI and Anne of Denmark* (Edinburgh, 1997), p. 96.

29. George Ritchie Kinloch ed., *The Diary of Mr James Melville, 1566–1601* (Edinburgh, 1829), p. 186.

30. James VI & I, *Letters*, p. 104. The Biblical text (Jeremiah 23:9–10) read 'I am like a drunken man, and like a man whom wine hath overcome, because of the Lord, and because of the words of his holiness. For the land is full of adulterers.'

31. 'The Danish Account' in Stevenson, *Scotland's Last Royal Wedding*, p. 99.

32. George F. Warner ed., 'The Library of James VI, 1573–1583 from a manuscript in the hand of Peter Young, his Tutor' in *Miscellany of the Scottish History Society* (Edinburgh, 1893), p. xlviii; see Matthias Skat Sommer, 'Niels Hemmingsen and the Construction of a Seventeenth-Century Protestant Memory', *Journal of Early Modern Christianity*, 4:1 (2017), pp. 149–50.

33. Quoted by I. D. McFarlane, *Buchanan* (London, 1981), p. 466.

34. James VI & I, *Poems*, II, p. 101 ('Then great is Tycho who by this his book / Commandment doth over these commanders brook').

35. CSP *Scotland*, X, p. 212.

36. Maureen M. Meikle, 'Anna of Denmark's Coronation and Entry into Edinburgh, 1590: Cultural, Religious and Diplomatic Perspectives' in Julian Goodare and Alasdair A. MacDonald eds., *Sixteenth-Century Scotland: Essays in Honour of Michael Lynch* (Leiden, 2008), p. 286.

37. Quoted and translated by Steven J. Reid, 'Andrew Melville and the Law of Kingship' in Roger A. Mason and Steven J. Reid eds., *Andrew Melville (1545–1622): Writings, Reception and Reputation* (Farnham, 2014), p. 56.

38. Meikle, 'Anna of Denmark's Coronation and Entry', p. 288.

39. *The Joyful Receiving of James the Sixth of that name King of Scotland and Queen Anne his wife into the Townes of Leith and Edinburgh. Together*

with the Triumphs shewed before the Coronation of the said Scottish Queen (London, 1590).

40. CSP *Scotland*, X, pp. 304–5.

41. Ibid, pp. 252, 591.

42. Ibid, p. 722.

43. Calderwood, *History of the Kirk*, V, p. 171.

44. Dennistoun ed., *Memoirs of the Affairs of Scotland. By David Moysie*, p. 113.

45. CSP *Scotland*, XI, p. 306.

46. Ibid, p. 410. As his godmother, Elizabeth insisted to James that 'I never counsel or advise you aught which tends not chiefly to your good', adding that not all kings were as fortunate in having 'so true espiers of their harm' (ibid).

47. Quoted by Esther Mijers, 'The Dutch in Scotland: The Diplomatic Visit of the States General upon the Baptism of Prince Henry' in Steven J. Reid ed., *Rethinking the Renaissance and Reformation in Scotland: Essays in Honour of Roger A. Mason* (Woodbridge, 2024), p. 269.

48. CSP *Scotland*, XI, p. 422; see See Rick Bowers, 'James VI, Prince Henry and "A True Reportarie" of the Baptism at Stirling, 1594', *Renaissance and Reformation / Renaissance et Réforme*, n.s., 29:4 (2005), pp. 3–22.

49. William Fowler, *A True Reportarie of the Most Triumphant, and Royal Accomplishment of the Baptism of the most Excellent, Right High, and Mighty Prince, Frederick Henry &c.* ([Edinburgh], 1594), sig. Dv.

50. CSP *Scotland*, XI, p. 280.

51. Ibid, pp. 626, 660, 662.

52. CSP *Scotland*, XIII, Part 2, p. 719.

53. James VI & I, *Letters*, p. 214.

54. Ibid, p. 257.

55. James VI & I, *Royal Correspondence*, p. 44.

56. Richard Turbet, 'Joyful Singing: Byrd's Music at a Royal Christening', *The Musical Times*, 145:1886 (2004), pp. 85–6.

57. James VI & I, *Letters*, p. 286.

58. HMC *Salisbury*, XIX, p. 209.

59. CSP *Venice*, XII, *1610–1613*, p. 227.

60. Maureen M. Meikle, 'Once a Dane, Always a Dane? Queen Anna of Denmark's Foreign Relations and Intercessions as a Queen Consort of Scotland and England, 1588–1619', *The Court Historian*, 24:2 (2019), p. 178.

61. John Florio, *Queen Anna's New World of Words, or Dictionary of the Italian and English Tongues, Collected and Newly Much Augmented &c.* (London, 1611), sig. ¶.

62. Jemma Field, *Anna of Denmark: The Material and Visual Culture of the Stuart Courts, 1589–1619* (Manchester, 2020), p. 46.

63. Ibid, p. 50.

64. The lines read: 'No more may I, than marigold by night / Bear blossoms when no sight of sun I have'; quoted by Morna R. Fleming, 'The *Amatoria* of James VI: Loving by the *Reulis*', in Daniel Fischlin and Mark Fortier eds., *Royal Subjects: Essays on the Writings of James VI and I* (Detroit, MI, 2002), p. 144.

65. James VI & I, *Poems*, II, p. 92.

66. Chamberlain, *Letters*, II, p. 216.

67. Quoted by Frances Teague, 'Makin [née Reginald], Bathsua (b. 1600, d. in or after 1675), scholar and teacher', *Oxford Dictionary of National Biography* [accessed 14 March 2024].

68. 'House of Lords Journal Volume 3: 8 March 1624' in *Journal of the House of Lords: Volume 3, 1620–1628* (London, 1767–1830), pp. 249–51. British History Online https://www.british-history.ac.uk/lords-jrnl/vol3/pp249-251 [accessed 21 March 2024].

69. James VI & I, *Letters*, pp. 440–41.

70. James VI & I, *Royal Correspondence*, p. 130.

71. See Catriona Murray, *Imaging Stuart Family Politics: Dynastic Crisis and Continuity* (Abingdon, 2017), pp. 109–10.

9 SLAVES OF THE DEVIL

1. CSP *Scotland*, X, pp. 523–4.

2. James VI & I, *Letters*, p. 114.

3. James VI, *Daemonologie in form of a Dialogue, Divided into Three Books* (Edinburgh, 1597), sigs. 2r, 2v.

4. James VI & I, 'The King's Answer' in *Cobbett's Complete Collection of State Trials and Proceedings for High Crimes and other Misdemeanours from the Earliest Period to the Present Time*, Volume II (London, 1809), p. 800.

5. James Sharpe, *The Bewitching of Anne Gunter: A Horrible and True Story of Deception, Witchcraft, Murder and the King of England* (London, 1999), p. 178.

6. *The Records of the Parliaments of Scotland to 1707*, K. M. Brown et al. eds. (St Andrews, 2007–24), A1563/6/9 [accessed 10 March 2024]; see Julian Goodare, 'The Scottish Witchcraft Act', *Church History*, 74:1 (2005), pp. 39–67.

7. CSP *Scotland*, II, p. 218; fearing that 'God is so offended with this nation', Randolph observed Mary beset by 'poverty, her country divided . . . misliked by her best subjects, guided by strangers with neither wits nor counsel, and other mad kind of fellows' (ibid).

8. Paraphrased in Glyn Parry, 'The Monarchical Republic and Magic: William Cecil and the Exclusion of Mary, Queen of Scots', *Reformation*, 17 (2012), p. 43.

9. 'G[eorge] B[uchanan]' [trans. Thomas Wilson], *A Detection of the Doings of Mary Queen of Scots touching the murder of her husband, and her conspiracy, adultery, and pretended marriage with the Earl Bothwell* ([London], 1571), sig. K3r; see Cathy Shrank, '"This fatal Medea", "this Clytemnestra": Reading and the Detection of Mary, Queen of Scots', *Huntington Library Quarterly*, 73:3 (2010), pp. 527–8.

10. CSP *Scotland*, X, p. 524.

11. Quoted by Liv Helene Willumsen, 'Witchcraft against Royal Danish Ships in 1589 and the Transnational Transfer of Ideas', *International Review of Scottish Studies*, 45 (2020), p. 70.

12. Thomas Thomson ed., *Memoirs of His Own Life by Sir James Melville of Halhill. MDLXIX–MDXCIII* (Edinburgh, 1827), p. 369.

13. 'Examinations and Confessions of Geilis Duncan and Agnes Sampson (?before December 1590)' in Lawrence Normand and Gareth Roberts eds., *Witchcraft in Early Modern Scotland: James VI's Demonology and the North Berwick Witches* (Exeter, 2000), pp. 136, 139.

14. 'Examination and Confession of Agnes Sampson, 4–5 December 1590' in Normand and Roberts eds., *Witchcraft in Early Modern Scotland*, pp. 144, 148, 146.

15. CSP *Scotland*, X, p. 430.

16. Ibid, pp. 467, 463.

17. 'News from Scotland' in Normand and Roberts eds., *Witchcraft in Early Modern Scotland*, p. 310.

18. Normand and Roberts eds., *Witchcraft in Early Modern Scotland*, p. 296.

19. 'News from Scotland' in Normand and Roberts eds., *Witchcraft in Early Modern Scotland*, p. 315.

20. Ibid, p. 314.

21. Ibid, pp. 317, 323, 324.

22. Normand and Roberts eds., *Witchcraft in Early Modern Scotland*, p. 293.

23. 'News from Scotland' in ibid, p. 316.

24. Jenny Wormald, 'The Witches, the Devil and the King' in Miles Kerr-Peterson ed., *James VI and I: Collected Essays by Jenny Wormald* (Edinburgh, 2021), p. 229.

25. 'Deposition of Janet Stratton' and 'Deposition of Janet Kennedy' in Normand and Roberts eds., *Witchcraft in Early Modern Scotland*, pp. 173, 175, 185.

26. CSP *Scotland*, X, p. 502.

27. Ibid, p. 505; see E. J. Cowan, 'The Darker Version of the Scottish Renaissance: The Devil and Francis Stewart' in I. B. Cowan and D. Shaw eds., *The Renaissance and Reformation in Scotland: Essays in Honour of Gordon Donaldson* (Edinburgh, 1983), pp. 125–40.

28. David Masson ed., *The Register of the Privy Council of Scotland. Volume IV: AD 1585–1592* (Edinburgh, 1881), pp. 644, 643, 644.

29. Annie I. Cameron ed., *The Warrender Papers: Volume* II. (Edinburgh, 1932), p. 157.

30. Ibid, p. 167.

31. Calderwood, *History of the Kirk*, V, p. 160.

32. Joseph Bain ed., *Calendar of Letters and Papers Relating to the Affairs of the Borders of England and Scotland &c.*, 2 vols. (Edinburgh, 1894), I, pp. 488, 486–7.

33. Wormald, 'The Witches, the Devil and the King', p. 232; for an alternative interpretation of events in 1597, see Julian Goodare, 'The Scottish Witchcraft Panic of 1597' in Goodare ed., *The Scottish Witch-Hunt in Context* (Manchester, 2002), pp. 51–72.

34. Quoted by Wormald, 'The Witches, the Devil and the King', p. 232.

35. CSP *Scotland*, XIII, Part I, p. 73.

36. Ibid, pp. 78, 78–9, 79.

37. James VI, *Daemonologie*, p. 42.

38. Normand and Roberts eds., *Witchcraft in Early Modern Scotland*, p. 328.

39. James VI, *Daemonologie*, sig. 2v.

40. Ibid, p. 55.

41. Ibid, sig. A4r, pp. 78, 43–4.

42. Ibid, pp. 22, 61–2.

43. James VI & I, *Letters*, p. 220.

44. Quoted by P. G. Maxwell-Stuart, 'King James's Experience of Witches and the 1604 English Witchcraft Act' in John Newton and Jo Bath eds., *Witchcraft and the Act of 1604* (Leiden, 2008), p. 43.

45. Brian P. Levack, *Witch-Hunting in Scotland: Law, Politics and Religion* (London, 2008), p. 2.

46. Samuel Harsnett, *A Declaration of Egregious Popish Impostures to withdraw the Hearts of her Majesty's Subjects from their Allegiance, and from the Truth of Christian Religion professed in England, under the Pretence of Casting out Devils &c.* (London, 1603), p. 166.

47. Quoted by Clive Holmes, 'Witchcraft and Possession at the Accession of James I: The Publication of Samuel Harsnett's *A Declaration of Egregious Popish Impostures*' in Newton and Bath eds., *Witchcraft and the Act of 1604*, p. 82.

48. James VI & I, *Letters*, p. 250; from James's former schoolroom classmate, the Earl of Mar, Cecil likewise learned that the king's party were 'continually busied either at hunting or examining of witches, and although I like the first better than the last, yet I must confess both uncertain sports' (HMC *Salisbury*, XVII p. 37).

49. Quoted by Henry N. Paul, *The Royal Play of Macbeth: When, Why, and How it was Written by Shakespeare* (New York, 1950), p. 117.

50. Quoted by Alexander Marr, 'Richard Haydocke's *Oneirologia*: A Manscript Treatise on Sleep and Dreams, including the "Arguments" of King James I', *Erudition and the Republic of Letters*, 2 (2017), pp. 155, 175, 177–8.

51. HMC *Salisbury*, XVII, p. 450.

52. William Barlow, *The Sermon Preached at Paul's Crosse, the Tenth Day of November, being the next Sunday after the Discovery of this Late Horrible Treason &c.* (London, 1606), sig. C3v.

53. Robert Stagg, *Shakespeare's Blank Verse: An Alternative History* (Oxford, 2022), pp. 75, 73; 'Reulis and Cautelis' in James VI & I, *Poems*, I, p. 71.

10 TEXTUARIES OF KINGSHIP

1. Quoted by James Craigie ed., *The Basilicon Doron of King James VI*, 2 vols. (Edinburgh, 1944–50), II, p. 4.

2. 'Basilicon Doron' in James VI & I, *Political Writings*, pp. 2–3.

3. Quoted by Craigie ed., *Basilicon Doron of King James VI*, II, p. 7.

4. Quoted by Alessandra Petrina, 'Translations Facing Inwards: James VI/I's *Basilikon Doron*' in Jean-Louis Fournel and Ivano Paccagnella eds., *Traduire – Tradurre – Translating. Vie des mots et voies does œuvres dans l'Europe de la Renaissance* (Geneva, 2022), p. 489.

5. 'Basilicon Doron' in James VI & I, *Political Writings*, pp. 4, 5, 10.

6. Chamberlain, *Letters*, I, p. 167.

7. CSP *Venice*, X, 1603–1607, p. 10; Jenny Wormald, 'James VI and I, *Basilicon Doron* and *The Trew Law of Free Monarchies*: The Scottish Context and the English Translation' in Linda Levy Peck ed., *The Mental World of the Jacobean Court* (Cambridge, 1991), p. 51.

8. 'Basilicon Doron' in James VI & I, *Political Writings*, pp. 11–12.

9. Jane Rickard, 'John Donne, James I and the Dilemmas of Publication' in Pete Langman ed., *Negotiating the Jacobean Printed Book* (Farnham, 2011), p. 92.

10. 'Basilicon Doron' in James VI & I, *Political Writings*, pp. 44, 20, 21.

11. Ibid, pp. 10, 9, 11.

12. The full title is 'The Trew Law of Free Monarchies: or, The Reciprock and Mutual Duetie betwixt a Free King and His Naturall Subjects' in James VI & I, *Political Writings*, pp. 62–3.

13. Ibid, pp. 62, 82.

14. Ibid, pp. 64, 75, 74.

15. Ibid, pp. 83, 65, 66.

16. Ibid, p. 68.

17. Jane Rickard, *Authorship and Authority: The Writings of James VI and I* (Manchester, 2007), p. 90.

18. 'Trew Law of Free Monarchies' in James VI & I, *Political Writings*, p. 64.

19. Ibid, pp. 71, 72.

20. James Aikman ed., George Buchanan, *The History of Scotland, translated from the Latin*, 4 vols. (Glasgow, 1827), I, pp. 156, 158.

21. 'Trew Law of Free Monarchies' in James VI & I, *Political Writings*, pp. 73, 74.

22. Steven J. Reid, *The Early Life of James VI: A Long Apprenticeship 1566–1585* (Edinburgh, 2023), pp. 114–15. In the event, production on the coin, with these mottoes, was paused until 1584.

23. Quoted by Linda Levy Peck, 'The Mentality of a Jacobean Grandee' in Peck ed., *The Mental World of the Jacobean Court*, p. 156.

24. ΤΑ ΤΩΝ ΜΟΥΣΩΝ ΕΙΣΟΔΙΑ: *The Muses Welcome to the High and Mighty Prince James by the Grace of God, King of Great Britain, France and Ireland, Defender of the Faith, &c. at His Majesty's Happy Return to his Old and Native Kingdom of Scotland &c.* (Edinburgh, 1618) p. 137.

25. John Lowrey, 'Sir William Bruce: Classicism and the Castle' in Louisa Humm, John Lowrey and Aonghas MacKechnie eds., *The Architecture of Scotland, 1660–1750* (Edinburgh, 2020), p. 80.

26. 'Trew Law of Free Monarchies' in James VI & I, *Political Writings*, pp. 80, 78, 79.

27. Quoted in ibid, p. 79; the quotation is from Du Bartas, *La Seconde Sepmaine*, troisième jour, 'Les Capitaines', ll. 1107–10.

28. 'Basilicon Doron' in James VI & I, *Political Writings*, p. 2.

29. Ibid, p. 15; 'Textuare *n.*'. *Dictionary of the Scots Language* (2004). Scottish Language Dictionaries Ltd. [accessed 18 Apr 2023] http://www.dsl.ac.uk/entry/dost/textuaire; see Gillian Sargent, '"Happy are they that read and understand": Reading for Moral and Spiritual Acuity in a Selection of Writings by King James VI and I' (University of Glasgow PhD thesis, 2013), pp. 136–7.

30. 'Basilicon Doron' in James VI & I, *Political Writings*, p. 16.

31. Ibid, pp. 25–6. As Roger Mason has shown, James added the phrase 'extraordinarily wrought by God' to the revised edition of *Basilicon Doron* prepared in 1603. The text of the first edition in 1599 had simply read 'But the reformation of religious in Scotland being made by a popular tumult and rebellion . . .' (Roger A. Mason, 'George Buchanan, James VI and the Presbyterians' in Mason ed., *Scots and Britons: Scottish Political Thought and the Union of 1603* (Cambridge, 1994), p. 121n).

32. 'Basilicon Doron' in James VI & I, *Political Writings*, pp. 27–8.

33. Ibid, p. 5.

34. Ibid, pp. 7, 5.

35. Roderick J. Lyall, 'The Marketing of James VI and I: Scotland, England and the Continental Book Trade', *Quærendo*, 32:3–4 (2002), p. 208.

36. Quoted by Craigie ed., *Basilicon Doron of King James VI*, II, pp. 33n, 34n.

37. French translations appeared in 1603, 1604, 1616 and 1617.

38. Craigie ed., *Basilicon Doron of King James VI*, II, p. 1.

39. See Hanna Orsolya Vincze, *The Politics of Translation and Transmission: Basilicon Doron in Hungarian Political Thought* (Newcastle, 2012).

40. Lyall, 'The Marketing of James VI and I', pp. 212–13.

41. Quoted by Craigie ed., *Basilicon Doron of King James VI*, II, p. 27.

42. See Antonio Rotondò, 'Sul "Basilikon Doron" di Giacomo Stuart', *Rivista Storica Italiana*, 75 (1963), pp. 877–80; this excerpt is as translated and quoted by Vincze, *The Politics of Translation*, p. 55.

43. 'Basilicon Doron' in James VI & I, *Political Writings*, p. 55. James offers a loose quotation from Horace's *Ars Poetica*; the original reads simply 'nescit vox missa reverti' to denote 'the word once sent out can never return'.

44. Sir John Harington, *A Tract on the Succession to the Crown (A.D. 1602)*, Clements R. Markham ed. (London, 1880), p. 50.

45. Richard Martin, *A Speech Delivered, To the Kings Most Excellent Majesty in the Name of the Sheriffs of London and Middlesex* (London, 1603), sig. B2r. As Martin continued, since the king had bound his own son to adhere to the principles set out in his works, he was confident that James would not 'follow other counsels or examples than your own'.

46. John Davies, *Microcosmos. The Discovery of the Little World, with the Government Thereof* (Oxford, 1603), pp. 18–19.

47. William Willymat, *A Prince's Looking-Glass, or A Prince's Direction, very requisite and necessary for a Christian Prince, to view and behold himself in containing sundry, wise, learned, godly, and princely Precepts and Instructions, excerpted and chosen out of that most Christian, and virtuous Basilikon Doron &c* (Cambridge 1603), sigs. A3r–v, p. 88. As the title-page confirmed, Willymat's work was published with 'His Majesty's Consent and Approbation being first had and obtained thereunto'.

48. Alan R. Young ed., *The English Emblem Tradition. Volume 5: Henry Peacham's Manuscript Emblem Books* (Toronto, 1998), p. 232.

49. Catharine Gray, *Women Writers and Public Debate in Seventeenth-Century Britain* (New York, 2007), p. 204, n. 1.

50. Dorothy Leigh, *The Mother's Blessing. Or, The Godly Counsel of a Gentlewoman not long since Deceased* &c. (London, 1616); Catharine Gray, 'Feeding on the Seed of the Woman: Dorothy Leigh and the Figure of Maternal Dissent', *English Literary History*, 68:3 (2001), pp. 563–4.

51. 'A Meditation upon the 27, 28, 29 Verses of the XXVII Chapter of Saint Matthew' in James VI & I, *Political Writings*, p. 232.

52. Charles I, *Eikon Basilike. The Portraiture of His Sacred Majesty in his Solitudes and Sufferings. Together with His Majesty's Prayers Delivered to Doctor Juxon immediately before his Death &c.* (London, 1649), pp. 173, 229, 221, 230, 226; regarding divergences between *Eikon Basilike*'s Royalist precepts and those of James's, see Jeffrey Collins, '*Eikon Basilike* in Context: The Intellectual History of a Martyrdom' in Paul D. Halliday, Eleanor Hubbard and Scott Sowerby eds., *Revolutionising Politics: Culture and Conflict in England, 1620–1660* (Manchester, 2021), pp. 95–120.

11 THIS TRIANGLE MONARCHY

1. Walter Scott ed., *Memoirs of Robert Carey, Earl of Monmouth, Written by Himself* (Edinburgh, 1808), pp. 118, 127, 128.

2. *Stuart Royal Proclamations*, I, pp. 2–3.

3. Chamberlain, *Letters*, I, p. 189.

4. Quoted by Susan Doran, '1603: A Jagged Succession', *Historical Research*, 93:261 (2020), p. 446.

5. HMC *Salisbury*, XII, p. 677.

6. G. R. Elton, *The Tudor Constitution: Documents and Commentary*, 2nd edition (Cambridge, 1982), p. 75.

7. Elizabeth I and James VI, *Letters*, pp. 132–3.

8. Thomas Birch, *Memoirs of the Reign of Queen Elizabeth from the Year 1581 till her Death*, 2 vols. (London, 1754), II, p. 512.

9. 'Basilicon Doron' in James VI & I, *Political Writings*, pp. 31, 42, 59.

10. See Susan Doran and Paulina Kewes, 'The Earlier Elizabethan Succession Question Revisited' in Susan Doran and Paulina Kewes eds., *Doubtful and Dangerous: The Question of Succession in Late Elizabethan England* (Manchester, 2014), pp. 20–44.

11. Paulina Kewes, '"The Idol of State Innovators and Republicans": Robert Persons's *A Conference About the Next Succession* (1594/5) in Stuart England' in Paulina Kewes and Andrew McRae eds., *Stuart Succession Literature: Moments and Transformations* (Oxford, 2019), p. 152.

12. Peter Lake, 'The King, (The Queen) and the Jesuit: James Stuart's *True Law of Free Monarchies* in Context/s', *Transactions of the Royal Historical Society*, 14 (2004), p. 245.

13. 'R. Doleman' [Robert Persons], *A Conference about the Next Succession to the Crown of England, divided into Two Parts &c.* ([Antwerp, 1595]), Part 2, pp. 263, 118.

14. Joseph Bain ed., *Calendar of Letters and Papers relating to the Affairs of the Borders of England and Scotland &c.* 2 vols. (Edinburgh, 1894–6), II p. 103.

15. CSP *Scotland*, XII, p. 193.

16. David Masson ed., *The Register of the Privy Council of Scotland. Volume V: AD 1592–1599* (Edinburgh, 1882), pp. 324–5.

17. CSP *Scotland*, XIII, Part 1, p. 136.

18. Walter Quin, 'Anagrammata in nomen Jacobi sexti (1595)' in John Flood ed., *The Works of Walter Quin: An Irishman at the Stuart Courts* (Dublin, 2014), pp. 59, 60.

19. Peter Wentworth, *A Pithy Exhortation to her Majesty for establishing her Successor to the Crown Whereunto is added a Discourse containing the Author's Opinion of the True and Lawful Successor to her Majesty* ([Edinburgh, 1598), p. 102.

20. Thomas Wilson, 'The State of England, Anno Dom. 1600', F. J. Fisher ed., *Camden Miscellany XVI* (London, 1936), p. 2.

21. James VI & I, *Letters*, pp. 173, 175–6.

22. Sir John Harington, *A Tract on the Succession to the Crown (A.D. 1602)*, Clements R. Markham ed. (London, 1880), pp. 50–51.

23. CSP *Simancas*, IV, p. 724.

24. Alexander Courtney, 'The Scottish King and the English Court: The Secret Correspondence of James VI, 1601–1603' in Doran and Kewes eds., *Doubtful and Dangerous*, p. 139.

25. John Bruce ed., *Correspondence of King James VI of Scotland with Sir Robert Cecil and others in England, During the Reign of Queen Elizabeth, with an Appendix containing Papers Illustrative of Transactions between King James and Robert, Earl of Essex* (London, 1861), pp. 13, 23.

26. Thomas Dekker, *The Wonderful Year 1603*, A. L. Rowse ed. (London, 1989), p. 31.

27. Quoted by Rei Kanemura, 'Kingship by Descent or Kingship by Election? The Contested Title of James VI and I', *Journal of British Studies*, 52:2 (2013), pp. 335–60.

28. Quoted by Alan MacColl, 'The Meaning of "Britain" in Medieval and Early Modern England', *Journal of British Studies*, 45:2 (2006), p. 264.

29. Quoted by Christopher Ivic, *The Subject of Britain, 1603–1625* (Manchester, 2020), p. 29.

30. CSP *Venice*, X, *1603–1607*, p. 5.

31. Quoted by Morna R. Fleming, '"Kin[g]es be the glas, the verie scoole, the booke, / Where priuate men do learne, and read, and looke" (Alexander Craig, 1604): The Translation of James VI to the Throne of England in 1603' in Theo van Heijnsbergen and Nicola Royan eds., *Literature, Letters and the Canonical in Early Modern Scotland* (East Linton, 2002), p. 107.

32. Calderwood, *History of the Kirk*, VI, p. 216.

33. James VI & I, *Letters*, p. 211.

34. Nichols, *Progresses, Processions*, I, p. 66.

35. Quoted by Diana Newton, *The Making of the Jacobean Regime: James VI and I and the Government of England, 1603–1605* (Woodbridge, 2005), p. 18.

36. Thomas Dekker, *The Magnificent Entertainment given to King James, Queen Anne his wife, and Henry Frederick the Prince &c.* (London, 1604), sig. A3r.

37. *Stuart Royal Proclamations*, I, pp. 18–19.

38. Quoted by Mark Nicholls, 'Treason's Reward: The Punishment of Conspirators in the Bye Plot of 1603', *Historical Journal*, 38:4 (1995), p. 826.

39. See Mark Brayshay, 'Long-distance Royal Journeys: Anne of Denmark's Journey from Stirling to Windsor in 1603', *Journal of Transport History*, 25:1 (2004), pp. 1–21.

40. *Stuart Royal Proclamations*, I, p. 37.

41. J. Wickham Legg, *The Coronation Order of King James I* (London, 1902), p. 11; see also Alice Hunt, 'The Bright Star of the North: James I and his English Coronation', *Medieval English Theatre*, 38 (2017), pp. 22–37, and Sybil M. Jack, '"A Pattern for a King's Inauguration": The Coronation of James I in England', *Pareregon*, 21:2 (2004), pp. 67–91.

42. Quoted by Ivic, *The Subject of Britain*, p. 6.

43. David Masson ed., *The Register of the Privy Council of Scotland. Volume VI: AD 1599–1604* (Edinburgh, 1884), p. 596.

44. 'Speech to Parliament of 19 March 1604' in James VI & I, *Political Writings*, pp. 134, 135, 137, 136.

45. 'House of Commons Journal Volume 1: 21 April 1604' in *Journal of the House of Commons: Volume 1, 1547–1629* (London, 1802) pp. 180–81, 193; *British History Online* https://www.british-history.ac.uk/commons-jrnl/vol1/pp180–181 and p193 [accessed 18 March 2024]; see also Sarah Waurechen, 'Imagined Polities, Failed Dreams, and the Beginnings of an Unacknowledged Britain: English Responses to James VI and I's Vision of Perfect Union', *Journal of British Studies*, 52:3 (2013), pp. 575–96.

46. Sir William Fraser ed., *The Elphinstone Family Book of the Lords Elphinstone, Balmerino and Coupar*, 2 vols. (Edinburgh, 1897), II, p. 170.

47. Quoted by Bruce Galloway, *The Union of England and Scotland 1603–1608* (Edinburgh, 1986), p. 22.

48. 'Speech in Star Chamber of 20 June 1616' in James VI & I, *Political Writings*, p. 208.

49. Chris R. Kyle ed., *Parliament, Politics and Elections, 1604–1648* (Cambridge, 2001), p. 30; J. P. Kenyon ed., *The Stuart Constitution 1603–1608: Documents and Commentary*, 2nd edition (Cambridge, 1986), pp. 29–35.

50. *Stuart Royal Proclamations*, I, pp. 95, 96, 97.

51. Quoted by B. J. Cook, '"Stamped with your own *Image*": The Numismatic Dimension of Two Stuart Successions' in Kewes and McRae eds., *Stuart Succession Literature*, p. 310; see also David Blaazer, *Forging Nations: Currency, Power and Nationality in Britain and Ireland since 1603* (Oxford, 2023), p. 38.

52. Quoted by Lorna Hutson, *England's Insular Imagining: The Elizabethan Erasure of Scotland* (Cambridge, 2023), p. 70.

53. C. Sanford Terry ed., *De Unione Regnorum Britanniæ Tractatus by Sir Thomas Craig* (Edinburgh, 1909), pp. 260, 391.

54. John Doddridge, 'A Brief Consideration of the Union' in Bruce R. Galloway and Brian P. Levack eds., *The Jacobean Union: Six Tracts of 1604* (Edinburgh, 1985), p. 146.

55. Paul J. McGinnis and Arthur H. Williamson eds., *The British Union: A Critical Edition and Translation of David Hume of Godscroft's De Unione Insulae Britannicae* (Aldershot, 2002), p. 127.

56. David Masson ed., *The Register of the Privy Council of Scotland. Volume VII: AD 1604–1607* (Edinburgh, 1885), p. 498.

57. David Harris Willson ed., *The Parliamentary Diary of Robert Bowyer, 1606–1607* (New York, 1971), p. 203n.

58. Simon Healy, 'Debates in the House of Commons, 1604–1648' in Kyle ed., *Parliaments, Politics and Elections 1604–1648*, p. 129. Piggott later protested that he had only intended to refer to 'the Scots that would have killed the King and not of the nation in general', but he was imprisoned in the Tower and a new MP selected in his place (ibid, p. 131).

59. Albert J. Loomie ed., *Spain and the Jacobean Catholics. Volume 1: 1603–1612* ([London], 1973), p. 97.

60. 'Speech to Parliament of 31 March 1607' in James VI & I, *Political Writings*, pp. 169, 177, 164, 163.

61. 'House of Commons Journal Volume 1: 02 May 1607' in *Journal of the House of Commons: Volume 1, 1547–1629* (London, 1802), *British History Online* https://www.british-history.ac.uk/commons-jrnl/vol1/pp366–368 [accessed 18 March 2024].

62. CSP *Venice*, X, *1603–1607*, p. 498.

63. Masson ed., *Register of the Privy Council of Scotland. Volume VII*, p. 536.

64. Quoted by Hiram Morgan, 'Francis Bacon and Policy-Making in Ireland under Elizabeth and James', *Proceedings of the Royal Irish Academy: Archaeology, Culture, History, Literature*, 119C (2019), p. 187.

65. 'Part Seven of the *Reports*' in Steve Sheppard ed., *The Selected Writings of Sir Edward Coke*, 3 vols. (Indianapolis, IN, 2003), I, p. 172.

66. [George Ridpath], *Considerations upon the Union of the Two Kingdoms: with An Account of the Methods taken by Ancient and Modern Governments to effect a Union, without endangering the Fundamental Constitutions of the United Countries* (?Edinburgh], 1706), p. 12.

12 BODILY CONSTITUTIONS

1. 'Speech to Parliament of 19 March 1604' in James VI & I, *Political Writings*, p. 132.

2. Thomas Dekker, *1603. The Wonderful Year. Wherein is showed the Picture of London Lying Sick of the Plague &c.* (London, 1603), sig. C3r.

3. James Godskall, *The Ark of Noah, for the Londoners that remain in the City &c.* (London, [1604]), sig. C3r.

4. Edmund Lodge ed., *Illustrations of British History: Biography and Manners in the Reigns of Henry VIII, Edward VI, Mary, Elizabeth and James 1*, 3 vols. (London, 1791), III, p. 186.

5. David Masson ed., *The Register of the Privy Council of Scotland. Volume III: AD 1578–1585* (Edinburgh, 1880), pp. 752–3.

6. J. F. D. Shrewsbury, *A History of Bubonic Plague in the British Isles* (Cambridge, 1970), p. 262.

7. 'Trew Law of Free Monarchies' in James VI & I, *Political Writings*, pp. 76, 77.

8. 'House of Commons Journal Volume 1: 02 May 1607' in *Journal of the House of Commons: Volume 1, 1547–1629* (London, 1802), *British History Online* https://www.british-history.ac.uk/commons-jrnl/vol1/pp366–368 [accessed 26 May 2024].

9. Quoted by Stephen Brogan, *The Royal Touch in Early Modern England: Politics, Medicine and Sin* (Woodbridge, 2015), pp. 71, 72–3.

10. Robert Pitcairn ed., *The Autobiography and Diary of Mr James Melvill . . . with a Continuation of the Diary* (Edinburgh, 1842), p. 657.

11. [James VI & I], *A Counterblaste to Tobacco* (London, 1604), sigs. A3r, Dv, D1r.

12. Ibid, sigs. D1v, Dv, C4r, C2r.

13. Todd Butler, 'Power in Smoke: The Language of Tobacco and Authority in Caroline England', *Studies in Philology*, 106:1 (2009), p. 102; Sandra J. Bell, '"Precious Stinke": James I's *A Counterblaste to Tobacco*' in Daniel Fischlin and Mark Fortier eds., *Royal Subjects: Essays on the Writings of James VI and I* (Detroit, MI, 2002), p. 323.

14. *Stuart Royal Proclamations*, I, p. 458.

15. David Masson ed., *The Register of the Privy Council of Scotland. Volume X: AD 1613–1616* (Edinburgh, 1891), p. 516.

16. Anthony R. Rowley, 'How England Learned to Smoke: The Introduction, Spread and Establishment of Tobacco Pipe Smoking in England before 1640' (University of York PhD thesis, 2003), p. 210n.

17. 'Basilicon Doron' in James VI & I, *Political Writings*, pp. 50, 51, 50, 56.

18. James VI & I, *Letters*, p. 246.

19. James VI & I, *Royal Correspondence*, pp. 52, 56.

20. James VI & I, *A Meditation upon the Lord's Prayer, written by the King's Majesty, for the Benefit of all his Subjects &c.* (London, 1619), p. 93.

21. B. J. Cook, '"Stampt with your Own *Image*": The Numismatic Dimension of Two Stuart Successions' in Paulina Kewes and Andrew McRae eds., *Stuart Succession Literature: Moments and Transformations* (Oxford, 2019), p. 308.

22. 'Basilicon Doron' in James VI & I, *Political Writings*, p. 53.

23. Arthur M. Hind, *Engraving in England in the Sixteenth and Seventeenth Centuries. Part II: The Reign of James I* (Cambridge, 1955), p. 50, Plates 20 and 21; see also Roderick J. Lyall, 'The Marketing of James VI and I: Scotland, England and the Continental Book Trade', *Quærendo*, 32:3–4 (2002), pp. 204–5.

24. Quoted by Kevin Sharpe, *Image Wars: Promoting Kings and Commonwealths in England, 1603–1660* (New Haven, CT, 2010), pp. 59, 64.

25. Duncan Thomson, 'On The Market: A New Portrait by Adam de Colone and its Context', *The British Art Journal*, 4:3 (2003), p. 96.

26. Caroline Rae and Aviva Burnstock, 'A Technical Study of Portraits of King James VI and I attributed to John Critz the Elder (d. 1642): Artist, Workshop and Copies' in Erma Hermens ed., *European Painting 15th to 18th Centuries: Copying, Emulating and Replicating* (London, 2014), pp. 58–66.

27. Roy Strong, 'Three Royal Jewels: The Three Brothers, the Mirror of Great Britain and the Feather', *The Burlington Magazine*, 108:760 (1966), p. 352.

28. Logan Pearsall Smith ed., *The Life and Letters of Sir Henry Wotton*, 2 vols. (Oxford, 1966), I, p. 314.

29. Quoted in CSP *Venice*, X, *1603–1607*, p. ix.

30. Ibid, p. 39.

31. 'Basilicon Doron' in James VI & I, *Political Writings*, pp. 52, 53; on the likely 'Cretan' signification of 'Candie soldier', see Daniel Fischlin, 'The "Candie-Souldier", Venice and James VI & I's Advice on Monarchic Dress in *Basilicon Doron*', *Notes & Queries*, 43:3 (1995), pp. 357–61.

32. *The Records of the Parliaments of Scotland to 1707*, K. M. Brown et al. eds (St Andrews, 2007–24), 1581/10/37 [accessed 26 May 2024].

33. *Fourth Report of the Royal Commission on Historical Manuscripts* (London, 1874), p. 527.

34. Maria Hayward, *Stuart Style: Monarchy, Dress and the Scottish Male Elite* (New Haven, CT, 2020), pp. 41, 42.

35. Ibid, pp. 48, 52.

36. Ibid, p. 50; Susan North, *Sweet and Clean? Bodies and Clothes in Early Modern England* (Oxford, 2020), p. 152.

37. Penelope Byrde and Peter Brears, 'A Pair of James I's Gloves', *Costume*, 24:1 (1990), p. 37.

38. Mary Bly, '"The Lure of a Taffeta Cloak": Middleton's Sartorial Seduction in *Your Five Gallants*' in Gary Taylor and Trish Thomas Henley eds., *The Oxford Handbook of Thomas Middleton* (Oxford, 2012), p. 591.

39. Quoted in ibid, pp. 591–2.

40. Quoted by Ann Rosalind Jones and Peter Stallybrass, *Renaissance Clothing and the Materials of Memory* (Cambridge, 2000), p. 1.

41. Maurice Lee Jr. ed., *Dudley Carleton to John Chamberlain, 1603–1624. Jacobean Letters* (New Brunswick, NJ, 1972), p. 55.

42. CSP *Venice*, XIV, *1617–1619*, pp. 111, 113–14.

43. CSP *Scotland*, VII, p. 274.

44. Quoted by Hugh Trevor-Roper, *Europe's Physician: The Various Life of Sir Theodore de Mayerne* (New Haven, CT, 2006), p. 269.

45. Quoted by Kenneth Fincham, *Prelate as Pastor: The Episcopate of James I* (Oxford, 1990), p. 38.

46. Trevor-Roper, *Europe's Physician*: pp. 270, 269. The full Latin 'Note on the Health of James I' is reproduced in Norman Moore, *The History of the Study of Medicine in the British Isles* (Oxford, 1908), pp. 162–76.

47. Trevor-Roper, *Europe's Physician*, p. 271; Sir Anthony Weldon, *The Court and Character of King James, whereunto is now added The Court of King Charles* &c. (London, 1651), p. 165.

48. Weldon, *Court and Character*, p. 165; Trevor-Roper, *Europe's Physician*, p. 270.

49. CSP *Scotland*, VII, p. 274.

50. James VI & I, *Letters*, p. 221.

51. Anonymous, *Corona Regia*, pp. 97, 87.

52. Alastair Bellany, 'Of Gods and Beasts: The Many Bodies of James VI and I' in William J. Bulman and Freddy C. Domínguez eds., *Political and Religious Practice in the Early Modern British World* (Manchester, 2022), p. 225.

53. Quoted by Algernon Cecil, *A Life of Robert Cecil, First Earl of Salisbury* (London, 1915), p. 373.

54. Quoted by Pauline Croft, 'The Reputation of Robert Cecil: Libels, Political Opinion and Popular Awareness in the Early Seventeenth Century', *Transactions of the Royal Historical Society*, 1 (1991), p. 55.

55. Chamberlain, *Letters*, I, p. 397.

56. Sir Francis Bacon, *The Essays of Sir Francis Bacon Knight, The King's Attorney-General, His Religious Meditations, Places of Persuasion and Dissuasion* (London, 1613), sigs. F6r–v.

57. Quoted by Neil Cuddy, 'The King's Chambers: The Bedchamber of James I in Administration and Politics, 1603–1625' (University of Oxford, DPhil thesis, 1987), p. 51.

58. HMC *Salisbury*, XXI, p. 255.

59. 'Note on the Health of James I' in Moore, *History of the Study of Medicine*, p. 166.

60. CSP *Scotland*, VIII, p. 364.

61. Anonymous, *Corona Regia*, p. 95.

62. Timothy Peters, Peter Garrard, Vijeya Ganesan and John Stephenson, 'The Nature of King James VI/I's Medical Conditions: New Approaches to the Diagnoses', *History of Psychiatry*, 23:3 (2012), pp. 277–90.

63. Ibid, p. 282.

64. Kristine Williams, Frederick Holmes, Susan Kemper and Janet Marquis, 'Written Language Clues to Cognitive Changes of Aging: An Analysis of the Letters of King James VI/I', *Journal of Gerontology Series B* (2003), pp. 42–4.

65. 'Basilicon Doron' in James VI & I, *Political Writings*, pp. 50, 52.

66. Smith ed., *Life and Letters of Sir Henry Wotton*, II, p. 315.

67. CSP *Scotland*, XIII, Part 1, p. 209.

68. Amy L. Juhala, 'An Advantageous Alliance: Edinburgh and the Court of James VI' in Julian Goodare and A. A. MacDonald eds., *Sixteenth-Century Scotland: Essays in Honour of Michael Lynch* (Leiden, 2008), pp. 357–8.

69. Peter Brears, *Cooking and Dining in Tudor and Early Stuart England* (London, 2015), p. 30.

70. Gabriel Heaton, *Writing and Reading Royal Entertainments from George Gascoigne to Ben Jonson* (Oxford, 2010), p. 141.

71. *Stuart Royal Proclamations*, I, p. 156.

72. Steve Hindle, 'Imagining Insurrection in Seventeenth-Century England: Representations of the Midland Rising of 1607', *History Workshop Journal*, 66 (2008), pp. 31, 32.

73. See William C. Carroll, *Fat King, Lean Beggar: Representations of Poverty in the Age of Shakespeare* (Ithaca, NY, 1996).

74. Nichols, *Progresses, Processions*, III, pp. 401–3.

75. E. L. McAdam Jr. and George Milne eds., *Johnson's Dictionary: A Modern Selection* (London, 1963), p. 378.

76. Nichols, *Progresses, Processions*, III, p. 495.

77. Trevor-Roper, *Europe's Physician*, p. 270.

78. William Brenchley Rye ed., *England as seen by Foreigners in the Days of Elizabeth and James the First* (London, 1865), pp. 119–20; Peter Kanelos, 'So Many Strange Dishes: Food, Love and Politics in *Much Ado About Nothing*' in David B. Goldstein and Amy L. Tigner eds., *Culinary Shakespeare: Staging Food and Drink in Early Modern England* (Philadelphia, PA, 2016), pp. 62–3.

79. James VI & I, *Letters*, p. 266; Alastair Bellany and Thomas Cogswell, *The Murder of James I* (New Haven, CT, 2016), p. 21.

80. Quoted by Brears, *Cooking and Dining*, p. 549.

81. Quoted by Trevor-Roper, *Europe's Physician*, p. 271.

82. James VI & I, *Meditation upon the Lord's Prayer*, p. 76.

13 THE REINS OF GOVERNMENT

1. CSP *Venice*, XVI, *1619–1621*, pp. 384, 412, 417, 415.

2. CSP *Venice*, XV, *1617–1619*, p. 260; XVI, *1617–1619*, p. 150.

3. CSP *Venice*, XVII, *1621–1623*, p. 428.

4. 'Basilicon Doron' in James VI & I, *Political Writings*, p. 56.

5. Ibid, p. 55.

6. Edmund Lodge ed., *Illustrations of British History, Biography and Manners, in the Reigns of Henry VIII, Edward VI, Mary, Elizabeth & James I*, 3 vols. (London, 1791), III, p. 247.

7. *Stuart Royal Proclamations*, I, p. 227.

8. Chamberlain, *Letters*, II, pp. 249, 566.

9. Quoted by Alan Stewart, 'Government by Beagle: The Impersonal Rule of James VI and I' in Erica Fudge ed., *Renaissance Beasts of Animals, Humans and other Wonderful Creatures* (Urbana, IL, 2004), p. 107.

10. Quoted by Robert Ashton ed., *James I by his Contemporaries: An Account of his Career and Character as seen by some of his Contemporaries* (London, 1969), pp. 2, 3.

11. Patrick Hume, *The Promine, Containing the Manner, Place and Time, of the Most Illustrious King James the Sixth, his first Passing to the Fields &c.* (Edinburgh, 1580), sig. A3v.

12. Quoted by Simon Adams, ' "The Queenes Majestie . . . is now become a great huntress": Elizabeth I and the Chase', *The Court Historian*, 18:2 (2013), p. 144.

13. John Robert Christianson, 'The Hunt of King Frederik II of Denmark: Structures and Rituals', *The Court Historian*, 18:2 (2013), p. 185.

14. Rebecca A. Calcagno, 'Publishing the Stuarts: Occasional Literature and Politics from 1603 to 1625' (Columbia University PhD thesis, 2011), p. 262. According to Calcagno, James and Christian hunted at Eltham on Saturday 19 July, Greenwich (Monday 21 July), Eltham (Tuesday 22 and Wednesday 23 July) and Waltham Forest (Friday 25 and Saturday 26 July).

15. Nichols, *Progresses, Processions*, II, pp. 61–2.

16. HMC *Salisbury*, XVI, p. 227.

17. Quoted by Nadine Akkerman, *Elizabeth Stuart: Queen of Hearts* (Oxford, 2021), p. 264.

18. [Edmund Sawyer ed.], *Memorials of Affairs of State in the Reigns of Q. Elizabeth and K. James I, collected chiefly from the Original Papers of the Right Honourable Sir Ralph Winwood Kt., sometime one of the Principal Secretaries of State*, 3 vols. (London, 1725), II, p. 150.

19. Nandini Das, *Courting India: England, Mughal India and the Origins of Empire* (London, 2023), p. 111.

20. K. G. Ponting ed., *Aubrey's Natural History of Wiltshire* (Newton Abbot, 1969), p. 60.

21. James VI & I, *Letters*, pp. 246, 247.

22. Quoted by Susan Doran, *From Tudor to Stuart: The Regime Change from Elizabeth I to James I* (Oxford, 2024), p. 256.

23. CSP *Venice*, X, *1603–1607*, p. 218.

24. Quoted by Alexander Courtney, 'Court Politics and the Kingship of James VI & I, c. 1615 to 1622' (Cambridge University PhD thesis, 2008), p. 91.

25. Quoted by Emily Cole, 'Theobalds, Hertfordshire: The Plan and Interiors of an Elizabethan Country House', *Architectural History*, 60 (2017), p. 115.

26. James VI & I, *Letters*, p. 265.

27. Shakespeare, *King Lear* (1.II.115); see David Levy, 'Shakespeare, *King Lear* and the Great Eclipse of 1605' in *David Levy's Guide to Eclipses, Transits, and Occultations* (Cambridge, 2010), pp. 9–16.

28. Peter E. McCullough, *Sermons at Court: Politics and Religion in Elizabethan and Jacobean Preaching* (Cambridge, 1998), p. 126. As McCullough noted, this was the first time that the English court had paid for preaching since Henry VIII's reign.

29. John Hacket, *Scrinia Reserata. A Memorial offered to the great Deservings of John Williams, DD, who some time held the Places of Lord Keeper of the Great Seal of England, Lord Bishop of Lincoln, and Lord Archbishop of York &c.* (London, 1693), pp. 227, 38, 88.

30. 'Speech to Parliament of 31 March 1607' in James VI & I, *Political Writings*, p. 166.

31. HMC *Salisbury* XIX, p. 291.

32. Quoted by Stewart, 'Government by Beagle', p. 105.

33. Quoted by ibid, pp. 101, 111; see also Frederick George Marcham, 'James I of England and the Little Beagle Letters' in *Persecution and Liberty: Essays in Honor of George Lincoln Burr* (New York, 1931), pp. 311–34.

34. Nichols, *Progresses, Processions*, II, pp. 203–4.

35. CSP *Scotland*, IX, p. 655.

36. CSP *Venice*, X, *1603–1607*, p. 70.

37. Quoted by Stewart, 'Government by Beagle', pp. 106–7.

38. CSP *Venice*, X, *1603–1607*, p. 353.

39. Ibid, p. 300.

40. Ibid, pp. 332–3.

41. CSP *Venice*, XI, *1607–1610*, p. 375; see also [Sawyer ed.], *Memorials of Affairs of State*, II, pp. 246–7.

42. CSP *Venice*, X, *1603–1607*, p. 39.

43. CSP *Venice*, XI, *1607–1610*, p. 276.

44. Chamberlain, *Letters*, I, 469; as Chamberlain added, 'love and kindness increases daily between them, and it is thought they were never in better terms'.

45. Tom Rose, 'Hunting, Sociability, and the Politics of Inclusion and Exclusion in Early Seventeenth-Century England' in Naomi Pullin and Kathryn Woods eds., *Negotiating Exclusion in Early Modern England, 1550–1800* (London, 2021), p. 161.

46. Lodge ed., *Illustrations of British History, Biography and Manners*, III, p. 245.

47. Quoted by Stewart, 'Government by Beagle', p. 106.

48. John Bruce ed., *Letters and Papers of the Verney Family Down to the End of the Year 1639 &c.* (London, 1853), p. 117.

49. Anonymous, *Corona Regia*, p. 91.

50. Quoted by Andrew McRae, *Literature, Satire and the Early Stuart State* (Cambridge, 2004), p. 170; McRae quotes variant versions of the poem, with different endings, potentially reworked after Buckingham's death in 1628.

51. *Cabala. Mysteries of State, in Letters of the Great Ministers of King James and King Charles* (London, 1654), p. 90.

52. Quoted by Alastair Bellany and Thomas Cogswell, *The Murder of King James I* (New Haven, CT, 2015), p. 21.

53. George F. Warner ed., 'The Library of James VI, 1573–1583 from a manuscript in the hand of Peter Young, his Tutor' in *Miscellany of the Scottish History Society* (Edinburgh, 1893), p. lxxiv.

54. Ian Stewart, 'Coinage and Propaganda: An Interpretation of the Coin-Types of James VI' in Anne O'Connor and D. V. Clarke eds., *From the Stone Age to the Forty-Five* (Edinburgh, 1983), pp. 456, 461.

55. Michael Bath, *Emblems in Scotland: Motifs and Meanings* (Boston, MA, 2018), pp. 93, 98.

56. Steven J. Reid, *The Early Life of James VI: A Long Apprenticeship 1566–1585* (Edinburgh, 2023), pp. 281–2.

57. 'Basilicon Doron' in James VI & I, *Political Writings*, p. 47.

58. 'House of Commons Journal Volume 1: 05 April 1604', in *Journal of the House of Commons: Volume 1, 1547–1629* (London, 1802), *British History Online* https://www.british-history.ac.uk/commons-jrnl/vol1/pp166–167 [accessed 1 October 2024].

59. Erasmus, *The Education of a Christine Prince*, Lisa Jardine ed. (Cambridge, 1997), p. 30.

60. Machiavelli, *The Prince*, Quentin Skinner ed. (Cambridge, 1988), p. 61.

61. Quoted by David Colclough, *Freedom of Speech in Early Stuart England* (Cambridge, 2005), p. 170.

62. CSP *Scotland*, IV, p. 577.

63. Reid, *Early Life of James VI*, p. 281.

64. HMC *Salisbury*, III, p. 165.

65. James VI & I, *Royal Correspondence*, pp. 17, 18.

66. Martin Goulding, *Wild Boar in Britain* (Stowmarket, 2003), p. 25.

67. Quoted by Lauren Working, *The Making of an Imperial Polity: Civility and America in the Jacobean Metropolis* (Cambridge, 2020), p. 36.

68. Chamberlain, *Letters*, II, p. 265.

69. HMC *Downshire*, III, p. 192.

70. Felicity Heal, *The Power of Gifts: Gift Exchange in Early Modern England* (Oxford, 2014), p. 157; CSP *Venice*, XVIII, *1623–1625*, p. 75.

71. Vera Keller, *The Interlopers. Early Stuart Projects and the Undisciplining of Knowledge* (Baltimore, MD, 2023), p. 208.

72. CSP *Venice*, XV, *1617–1619*, p. 258; Arthur MacGregor, 'The Household Out of Doors: The Stuart Court and the Animal Kingdom' in Eveline Cruickshanks ed., *The Stuart Courts* (Stroud, 2000), p. 104.

73. Quoted by Nicole Mennell, 'The Lion King: Shakespeare's Beastly Sovereigns' in Karen Raber and Holly Dugan eds., *The Routledge Handbook of Shakespeare and Animals* (London, 2020), p. 234.

74. Kristen Deiter, *The Tower of London in English Renaissance Drama: Icon of Opposition* (London, 2008), p. 61.

75. Nichols, *Progresses, Processions*, II, p. 259.

76. Calderwood, *History of the Kirk*, IV, p. 351.

77. Quoted by Erica Fudge, *Brutal Reasoning: Animals, Rationality and Humanity in Early Modern England* (Ithaca, NY, 2006), pp. 102–3.

78. Quoted by Anthony Grafton, 'Conrad Gessner and John Caius: The Meanings of Learned Friendship in Renaissance Europe' in Urs Leu and Peter Optiz eds., *Conrad Gessner (1516–1565): Die Renaissance der Wissenschaften / The Renaissance of Learning* (Munich, 2019), p. 358.

14 GOD'S SILLY VASSAL

1. 'To the right godly learned and his reverend good friend, Master John Johnston' in Robert Rollock, *A Treatise of God's Effectual Calling, written first in the Latin tongue . . . and now faithfully translated &c.* (London, 1603), unpaginated.

2. Robert Pitcairn ed., *The Autobiography and Diary of Mr James Melvill . . . with a Continuation of the Diary* (Edinburgh, 1842), pp. 370, 371.

3. 'Basilicon Doron' in James VI & I, *Political* Writings, p. 26.

4. William Croft Dickinson and Gordon Donaldson eds., *A Source Book of Scottish History*, 3 vols. (London, [1952–4]), III, p. 12.

5. Pitcairn ed., *Autobiography and Diary of Mr James Melvill*, p. 31.

6. Quoted by David George Mullan, *Episcopacy in Scotland: The History of an Idea, 1560–1638* (Edinburgh, 1986), p. 52.

7. K. M. Brown et al. eds., *The Records of the Parliaments of Scotland to 1707* (St Andrews, 2007–23), 1584/5/8 and 1584/5/10 [accessed 25 May 2023].

8. Ibid, 1584/5/75.

9. Pitcairn ed., *Autobiography and Diary of Mr James Melvill*, pp. 194, 192; see Alan R. Macdonald, 'The Subscription Crisis and Church-State Relations, 1584–1586', *Records of the Scottish Church History Society*, 25:2 (1994), pp. 222–55.

10. *Letters and Papers relating to Patrick, Master of Gray, afterwards seventh Lord Gray* (Edinburgh, 1885), p. 16.

11. Calderwood, *History of the Kirk*, IV, pp. 486–7. Gibson was thereafter detained in Edinburgh Castle.

12. CSP *Scotland*, IX, p. 166.

13. Richard Bancroft, *A Sermon preached at Paul's Cross, the 9 of February, being the first Sunday in the Parliament &c.* (London, 1589), p. 76.

14. Elizabeth I and James VI, *Letters*, pp. 63–4.

15. James VI & I, *Letters*, p. 111.

16. Owen Williams, 'The Blood of a Prophet and the Conscience of a King', *Reformation*, 22:1 (2017), p. 49n.

17. James VI, *A Fruitful Meditation containing a plain and facile Exposition of the 7, 8, 9 and 10 verses of the 20 chapter of the Revelation in form of a Sermon* (Edinburgh, 1588), title-page.

18. Quoted by Mullan, *Episcopacy*, p. 75.

19. Calderwood, *History of the Kirk*, V, pp. 102, 100.

20. See Alan R. Macdonald, 'The Parliament of 1592: A Crisis Averted?' in Keith Brown and Alastair J. Mann eds., *The History of the Scottish Parliament, Volume II: Parliament and Politics in Scotland, 1567–1707* (Edinburgh, 2005), pp. 57–81.

21. Pitcairn ed., *Autobiography and Diary of Mr James Melvill*, p. 329.

22. CSP *Scotland*, XI, p. 337.

23. Ibid, p. 517.

24. CSP *Scotland*, XII, p. 368.

25. Quoted by Julian Goodare, 'The Attempted Scottish *Coup* of 1596' in Julian Goodare and Alasdair A. MacDonald eds., *Sixteenth-Century Scotland: Essays in Honour of Michael Lynch* (Leiden, 2008), p. 318.

26. Quoted by ibid, p. 319.

27. Quoted by Julian Goodare, 'How Archbishop Spottiswoode became an Episcopalian', *Renaissance and Reform / Renaissance et Réforme*, 30:4 (2006–7), p. 90.

28. James VI & I, *Letters*, p. 148.

29. Calderwood, *History of the Kirk*, V, pp. 693–4.

30. James VI & I, *An Apology for the Oath of Allegiance first set forth without a name, and now acknowledged by the Author, the Right High and Mighty Prince James &c.* (London, 1609), p. 45.

31. 'Basilicon Doron' in James VI & I, *Political Writings*, pp. 26, 44.

32. For doubts as to the existence of a specific 'Millenary Petition', see William Craig, 'Hampton Court Again: The Millenary Petition and the Calling of the Conference', *Anglican and Episcopal History*, 77:1 (2008), pp. 46–70.

33. *Stuart Royal Proclamations*, I, p. 61.

34. William Barlow, *The Sum and Substance of the Conference which, it pleased his excellent Majesty to have with the Lords, Bishops, and other of his Clergy &c.* (London, 1604), p. 4.

35. Quoted by Alan Cromartie, 'King James and the Hampton Court Conference' in Ralph Houlbrooke ed., *James VI and I. Ideas, Authority and Government* (Aldershot, 2006), p. 67.

36. Barlow, *Sum and Substance*, p. 82.

37. Ibid, p. 77.

38. Quoted by Cromartie, 'King James and the Hampton Court Conference', p. 67.

39. James VI & I, *Letters*, p. 221.

40. 'Speech to Parliament of 19 March 1604' in James VI & I, *Political Writings*, p. 138.

41. HMC *Salisbury*, XVI, p. 363; see B. W. Quintrell, 'The Royal Hunt and the Puritans, 1604–1605', *Journal of Ecclesiastical History*, 31:1 (1980), pp. 41–58.

42. Quintrell, 'The Royal Hunt and the Puritans, 1604–1605', p. 57.

43. The precise number is unclear; see Kenneth Fincham, *Prelate as Pastor: The Episcopate of James I* (Oxford, 1990), pp. 323–6.

44. Henry Ellis ed., *Original Letters, Illustrative of English History &c.*, Second Series, 4 vols. (London, 1827), III, p. 216.

45. William Wilkes, *Obedience or Ecclesiastical Union. Treatised by William Wilkes, Doctor in Theology, and one of his Majesty's Chaplains-in-Ordinary* (London, 1605), pp. 19, 35.

46. Quoted by Richard Dutton, 'Marston wrote his father-in-law's preachings, and his father-in-law his comedies', *Early Theatre*, 23:2 (2020), pp. 60–61, 62. The lines quoted are from *The Malcontent* 4.III.127–30 and 2.V.118, 120–21.

47. Pitcairn ed., *Autobiography and Diary of Mr James Melvill*, pp. 663, 657, 659, 660.

48. Ibid, pp. 677–8, 679.

49. Calderwood, *History of the Kirk*, VI, p. 735.

50. Barlow, *Sum and Substance*, p. 71.

51. The records of the courts no longer survive; see G. I. R. McMahon, 'The Scottish Court of High Commission, 1610–1638', *Records of the Scottish Church History Society*, 15 (1963–5), pp. 193–209.

52. Quoted by Eric Platt, *Britain and the Bestandstwisten: The Causes, Course and Consequences of British Involvement in the Dutch Religious and Political Disputes of the Early Seventeenth Century* (Göttingen, 2015), p. 35.

53. Quoted by ibid, pp. 38, 51, 52.

54. Ian Atherton and David Como, 'The Burning of Edward Wightman: Puritanism and the Politics of Heresy in Early Modern England', *English Historical Review*, 120:489 (2005), pp. 1233, 1236.

55. Chamberlain, *Letters*, I, p. 337.

56. CSP *Venice*, XII, *1610–1613*, p. 294.

57. Quoted by Platt, *Britain and the Bestandstwisten*, p. 106.

58. Quoted by Simon Graham, 'Heresy as Treason: English "Ecclesiastical Diplomacy" in the United Provinces, 1610–1619', *Diplomacy & Statecraft*, 34:3 (2023), p. 380; see, more generally, Anthony Milton ed., *The British Delegation and the Synod of Dort (1618–1619)* (Woodbridge, 2005).

59. Calderwood, *History of the Kirk*, VII, p. 289.

60. James Maidment ed., 'Sermon preached … to the General Assembly holden at Perth, the 25th of August, 1618' in *The Spottiswoode Miscellany: A Collection of General Papers and Tracts, Illustrative Chiefly of the Ecclesiastical History of Scotland*, 2 vols. (Edinburgh, 1844–5), I, pp. 83, 66.

61. John Buckeridge, *A Sermon Preached before His Majesty at Whitehall, March 22. 1617 [1618] being Passion-Sunday … To which is added a Discourse Concerning Kneeling at the Communion* (London, 1618), p. 16.

62. 'A Meditation upon the 27, 28, 29 Verses of the Chapter XXVII of Saint Matthew' in James VI & I, *Political Writings*, p. 234.

63. 'A Meditation upon the Lord's Prayer' in *The Works of the most High and Mighty Prince, James, by the Grace of God, King of Great Britain, France and Ireland, Defender of the Faith &c.* (London, 1620), p. 578.

64. David Laing ed., *Original Letters Relating to the Ecclesiastical Affairs of Scotland, chiefly written by, or addressed to . . . King James the Sixth after his Accession to the English Throne*, 2 vols. (Edinburgh, 1861), II, p. 663.

65. Laura A. M. Stewart, 'The Political Repercussions of the Five Articles of Perth: A Reassessment of James VI and I's Religious Policies in Scotland', *Sixteenth Century Journal*, 38:4 (2007), p. 1035.

66. Calderwood, *History of the Kirk*, VII, p. 547.

15 THE KING JAMES VERSION

1. Philip Mason ed., *'Proofs of Holy Writ' by Rudyard Kipling* (Edinburgh, 1981), pp. 9, 19.

2. William Barlow, *The Sum and Substance of the Conference which, it pleased his excellent Majesty to have with the Lords, Bishops, and other of his Clergy &c.* (London, 1604), pp. 45–6.

3. John Spottiswood, *The History of the Church of Scotland beginning the year of our Lord 203, and continued to the end of the Reign of King James the VI &c.* (London, 1668), p. 465.

4. Barlow, *Sum and Substance*, pp. 20, 83, 84. As Lord Chancellor, Lord Ellesmere admitted that until he had observed James's interactions at Hampton Court, he had never previously 'seen the truth' of the maxim that *'rex est mixta persona cum sacerdote'* (ibid, p. 84).

5. Elizabeth I and James VI, *Letters*, p. 27.

6. James VI, *A Meditation upon the XXV, XVI, XVII, XVIII, and XXIV Verses of the XV Chapter of the First Book of the Chronicles of the Kings &c.* (Edinburgh, 1589), sig. A3v.

7. James VI, *A Fruitful Meditation containing a plain and facile Exposition of the 7, 8, 9 and 10 verses of the 20 chapter of the Revelation in form of a Sermon* (Edinburgh, 1588), sig. B2v.

8. Quoted by Kenneth Fincham, 'The King James Bible: Crown, Church and People', *Journal of Ecclesiastical History*, 17:1 (2020), pp. 79, 83.

9. Quoted by Mordechai Feingold, 'Birth and Early Reception of a Masterpiece: Some Loose Ends and Common Misconceptions' in Feingold ed., *Labourers in the Vineyard of the Lord: Scholarship and the Making of the King James Version of the Bible* (Leiden, 2018), p. 9.

10. HMC *Salisbury*, XVII p. 431.

11. Gordon Campbell, *Bible: The Story of the King James Version* (Oxford, 2011), p. 45.

12. 'Bishop Bancroft's Rules for the Revisers' in W. H. Stevenson ed., *King James Bible: A Selection* (London, 1994), p. 497.

13. Barlow, *Sum and Substance*, p. 46.

14. As Jane Rickard has shown, by inserting this marginal note, 'the attempt of ordinary people to interpret the Bible is literally marginalised, while the king occupies the central and divinely authorised position' ('The Word of God and the Word of the King: The Scriptural Exegeses of James VI and I and the King James Bible' in Ralph Houlbrooke ed., *James VI and I: Ideas, Authority and Government* (Aldershot, 2006), p. 143).

15. Quoted by Jan J. Martin, 'The Congregation and Church of England? William Tyndale's Approach to Lexical and Ecclesiological Reform between 1525 and 1535', *Moreana*, 59:1 (2022), p. 68.

16. Airay's letter is reproduced in Fincham, 'The King James Bible', p. 97.

17. Quoted by Feingold, 'Birth and Early Reception of a Masterpiece', p. 11.

18. Fincham, 'King James Bible', p. 81.

19. *The Holy Bible, containing the Old Testament, and the New: Newly Translated out of the Original Tongues &c.* (London, 1611), title-page. The exact date of publication remains uncertain; its classification as a revision of a previous text rather than an entirely fresh translation meant that no formal entry in the Stationers' Company Register was required. A copy held in Cambridge University Library (classmark Young.40) weighs 9.35kg.

20. 'The Epistle Dedicatory' in *The Holy Bible ... Newly Translated out of the Original Tongues &c.*, sig. A2v; Fincham regards the translators' claim regarding James's diligence in urging the project forward as 'highly questionable' ('The King James Bible', p. 81).

21. See Jane Rickard, 'Mover and Author: King James VI and I and the Political Use of the Bible' in Kevin Killeen, Helen Smith and Rachel Willie eds., *The Oxford Handbook of the Bible in Early Modern England, c. 1530–1700* (Oxford, 2015), pp. 371–83.

22. 'The Epistle Dedicatory' in *The Holy Bible ... Newly Translated out of the Original Tongues &c.*, sig. A2v.

23. 'The Translators to the Reader' in *The Holy Bible ... Newly Translated out of the Original Tongues &c.*, sigs. Bv, A6r, A4v.

24. Ibid, sigs. A4v, A4r, A6v.

25. Campbell, *Bible*, p. 104.

26. Fincham, 'King James Bible', pp. 85, 89.

27. Campbell, *Bible*, p. 2.

28. 'A Large Relation of the Puerto Rico Voyage; Written, as is Reported, by that Learned Man and Reverend Divine Doctor Layfield &c.' in Samuel Purchas,

Hakluytus Posthumus or, Purchas his Pilgrims, Volume 16 (Glasgow, 1906), pp. 96, 94.

29. Stephen Prickett, 'Language within Language. The King James Steamroller' in Hannibal Hamlin and Norman W. Jones eds., *The King James Bible after 400 Years: Literary, Linguistic, and Cultural Influences* (Cambridge, 2010), p. 33.

30. Naomi Tadmor, *The Social Universe of the English Bible: Scripture, Society, and Culture in Early Modern England* (Cambridge, 2010), pp. 121, 125.

31. Prickett, 'Language within Language', p. 38.

32. For other examples, see David Crystal, *Begat: The King James Bible and the English Language* (Oxford, 2010).

33. See 1 Samuel 25:22, 1 Samuel 25:34, 1 Kings 14:10, 1 Kings 16:11 ('a wall'), 1 Kings 21:21 and 2 Kings 9:8.

34. Quoted by David G. Whitla and Crawford Gribben, 'Preaching and Sermons in Post-Reformation Scotland' in William Ian P. Hazlett ed., *A Companion to the Reformation in Scotland, c. 1525–1638: Frameworks of Change and Development* (Leiden, 2022), p. 234.

35. James VI, *Fruitful Meditation*, title-page and sig. A2r.

36. Peter E. McCullough, *Sermons at Court: Politics and Religion in Elizabethan and Jacobean Preaching* (Cambridge, 1998), p. 155.

37. Quoted by ibid, p. 118.

38. Chamberlain, *Letters*, I, p. 295.

39. McCullough, *Sermons at Court*, p. 126.

40. T. S. Eliot, 'Lancelot Andrewes', *Times Literary Supplement*, 23 September 1926.

41. Quoted by Helen Wilcox, *1611: Authority, Gender and the Word in Early Modern England* (Oxford, 2014), p. 120.

42. Alexander Cooke, *The Abatement of Popish Brags, pretending Scripture to be Theirs &c.* (London, 1625), p. 49; see Patrick Collinson, *The Religion of Protestants: The Church in English Society 1559–1625* (Oxford, 1982), p. 49.

43. John Hacket, *Scrinia Reserata. A Memorial offered to the great Deservings of John Williams, DD, who some time held the Places of Lord Keeper of the Great Seal of England, Lord Bishop of Lincoln, and Lord Archbishop of York &c.* (London, 1693), p. 34.

44. Quoted by McCullough, *Sermons at Court*, p. 158.

45. James VI and I, *The Works of the most High and Mighty Prince, James, by the Grace of God, King of Great Britain, France and Ireland, Defender of the Faith &c.* (London, 1616 [1617]), p. 1.

46. Ibid, pp. 7, 2, 72.

47. Jane Rickard, *Authorship and Authority: The Writings of James VI and I* (Manchester, 2007), p. 84; italics in the original; see also Daniel Fischlin, '"To Eate the Flesh of Kings": James VI and I, Apocalypse,

Nation and Sovereignty' in Daniel Fischlin and Mark Fortier eds., *Royal Subjects: Essays on the Writings of James VI and I* (Detroit, MI, 2002), pp. 388–420.

48. *Stuart Royal Proclamations, I*, pp. 495, 521.

49. 'James VI & I, *Directions for Preachers* (1622)' in Peter McCullough, Hugh Adlington and Emma Rhatigan eds., *The Oxford Handbook of the Early Modern Sermon* (Oxford, 2011), pp. 558–9.

50. Quoted by Jeanne Shami, *John Donne and Conformity in Crisis in the Late Jacobean Pulpit* (Woodbridge, 2003), pp. 106, 108.

51. George R. Potter and Evelyn M. Simpson eds., *The Sermons of John Donne*, 10 vols. (Los Angeles, CA, 1959), IV, pp. 202, 208.

52. Ibid, pp. 105, 91, 92.

53. Quoted by Sonia Suman, '"A Most Notable Spectacle": Early Modern Easter Spital Sermons' in Thomas Cohen and Lesley Twomey eds., *Spoken Word and Social Practice: Orality in Europe (1400–1700)* (Leiden, 2015), p. 236.

54. John N. Wall, 'The Virtual Paul's Cross Project: Digital Modeling's Uneasy Approximation', *Educause Review* (26 October 2014); The website is at https://vpcross.chass.ncsu.edu/ [accessed 5 April 2024].

55. James VI, *Fruitful Meditation*, sigs. B3v–B4r.

56. James VI and I, *A Meditation upon the Lord's Prayer, written by the King's Majesty, for the benefit of all his Subjects, especially of such as follow the Court* (London, 1619), sigs. A2v, A3v, A3r. James's image is taken from Gregory the Great's commentary on the Book of Job that described Scripture as similar to a river 'broad and deep, shallow enough here for the lamb to go wading, but deep enough there for the elephant to swim'.

16 A 'CATHOLIC CHRISTIAN' KING

1. 'Speech to Parliament of 19 March 1604' in James VI & I, *Political Writings*, p. 138.

2. Ibid, pp. 138, 139.

3. Ibid, pp. 139, 140.

4. Quoted by W. B. Patterson, *King James VI and the Reunion of Christendom* (Cambridge, 1997), p. 348.

5. John Williams, *Great Britain's Salomon A Sermon preached at the Magnificent Funeral, of the Most High and Mighty King, James, the late King of Great Britain, France, and Ireland, Defender of the Faith*, &c. (London, 1625), pp. 69–70.

6. Quoted by T. H. Wadkins, 'The Percy-"Fisher" Controversies and the Ecclesiastical Politics of Jacobean Anti-Catholicism, 1622–1625', *Church History*, 57 (1988), p. 169.

7. Timothy H. Wadkins, 'King James meets John Percy SJ (25 May 1622). An Unpublished Manuscript from the Religious Controversies Surrounding the Countess of Buckingham's Conversion', *Recusant History*, 19 (1988), pp. 148, 153.

8. See Victor Houliston, Ginevra Crosignani and Thomas M. McCoog SJ eds., *The Correspondence and Unpublished Papers of Robert Persons SJ. Volume 1: 1574–1588* (Toronto, 2017), pp. 220, 221 and 228.

9. Quoted by Steven J. Reid, *The Early Life of James VI: A Long Apprenticeship 1566–1585* (Edinburgh, 2023), p. 134.

10. *A Short and General Confession of the True Christian Faith and Religion, according to God's Word and Acts of Parliament subscribed by the King's Majesty and his Household &c.* (Edinburgh, 1581), single-sheet.

11. R. Scott Spurlock, 'Catholicism in Scotland to 1603' in James E. Kelly and John McCafferty eds., *The Oxford History of British and Irish Catholicism, Volume 1: Endings and New Beginnings, 1530–1640* (Oxford, 2023), p. 86.

12. Calderwood, *History of the Kirk*, III, pp. 717–18.

13. CSP *Simancas*, III, pp. 519, 518.

14. Quoted by Ruth Grant, 'Friendship, Politics and Religion: George Gordon, Sixth Earl of Huntly, and King James VI, 1581–1595' in Miles Kerr-Peterson and Steven J. Reid eds., *James VI and Noble Power in Scotland 1578–1603* (London, 2017), p. 69; for more on the masque, see Roderick J. Lyall, 'James VI and the Sixteenth-Century Cultural Crisis' in Julian Goodare and Michael Lynch eds., *The Reign of James VI* (East Linton, 2000), pp. 66–9.

15. James VI, *A Fruitful Meditation containing a plain and facile Exposition of the 7, 8, 9 and 10 verses of the 20 Chapter of the Revelation in form of a Sermon* (Edinburgh, 1588), sigs. B2r, B2v.

16. CSP *Scotland*, IX, p. 693.

17. Annie I. Cameron ed., *The Warrender Papers. Volume II* (Edinburgh, 1932), p. 103.

18. James Dennistoun ed., *Memoirs of the Affairs of Scotland. By David Moysie. MDLXXVIII–MDCIII* (Edinburgh, 1830), p. 74.

19. CSP *Scotland*, IX, pp. 700, 701.

20. Anthony G. Petti ed., *The Letters and Dispatches of Richard Verstegan (c. 1550–1640)* (London, 1959), p. 196.

21. CSP *Scotland*, XI, p. 386.

22. CSP *Scotland*, XII, p. 118.

23. Petti ed., *Letters and Dispatches of Richard Verstegan*, p. 196; see, more generally, Maureen M. Meikle and Helen M. Payne, 'From Lutheranism to Catholicism: The Faith of Anna of Denmark (1574–619), *Journal of Ecclesiastical History*, 64:1 (2013), pp. 45–69.

24. CSP *Scotland*, XII, p. 151.

25. Quoted by Albert J. Loomie, 'King James I's Catholic Consort', *Huntington Library Quarterly*, 34:4 (1971), p. 305.

26. [Robert Abercrombie], 'The State of Scotland, 1601' in William Forbes-Leith SJ ed., *Narratives of Scottish Catholics under Mary Stuart and James VI* (London, 1889), p. 270; for divergent views on James's susceptibility to conversion, see Thomas M. McCoog, SJ, 'Converting a King: The Jesuit William Crichton and King James VI and I', *Journal of Jesuit Studies*, 7 (2020), pp. 11–33.

27. CSP *Venice*, X, *1603–1607*, pp. 21–2.

28. Quoted by Patterson, *Reunion of Christendom*, p. 41.

29. Quoted by ibid, pp. 55, 53.

30. *Stuart Royal Proclamations*, I, p. 71.

31. [John Colleton], *A Supplication to the King's Most Excellent Majesty wherein, several reasons of state and religion are briefly touched &c.* (n.p., 1604), pp. 4, 46.

32. Quoted by Michael C. Questier, *Dynastic Politics and the British Reformations, 1558–1630* (Oxford, 2019), p. 287.

33. HMC *Salisbury*, XVII, p. 254.

34. *Stuart Royal Proclamations*, I, p. 125.

35. 'Speech to Parliament of 9 November 1605' in James VI & I, *Political Writings*, p. 149.

36. James VI & I, *Letters*, p. 276.

37. CSP *Venice*, X, *1603–1607*, pp. 296.

38. 'An Act for the better Discovering and Repressing of Popish Recusants, 1606' in J. P. Kenyon ed., *The Stuart Constitution 1603–1608: Documents and Commentary*, 2nd edition (Cambridge, 1986), pp. 170, 171. Anyone who twice refused to swear the Oath of Allegiance risked imprisonment and loss of their goods.

39. 'The Trial of Henry Garnet, Superior of the Jesuits in England &c.' in *Cobbett's Complete Collection of State Trials and Proceedings for High Crimes and other Misdemeanours from the Earliest Period to the Present Time*, Volume II (London, 1809), p. 234.

40. William Shakespeare, *Macbeth*, II.3.7–10; see John Kerrigan, *Shakespeare's Binding Language* (Oxford, 2016), p. 324, and Máté Vince, 'The Porter and the Jesuits: *Macbeth* and the Forgotten History of Equivocation', *Renaissance Studies*, 35:5 (2021), pp. 837–55.

41. 'Triplici Nodo, Triplex Cuneus. Or, an Apology for the Oath of Allegiance' in James VI & I, *Political Writings*, pp. 103, 90.

42. [Edmund Sawyer ed.], *Memorials of Affairs of State in the Reigns of Q. Elizabeth and K. James I, collected chiefly from the Original Papers of the Right Honourable Sir Ralph Winwood Kt., sometime one of the Principal Secretaries of State*, 3 vols. (London, 1725), II, p. 282.

43. M. C. Questier, 'Loyalty, Religion and State Power in Early Modern England: English Romanism and the Jacobean Oath of Allegiance', *Historical*

Journal, 40:2 (1997), pp. 313, 314; for an alternative interpretation, see Johann P. Sommerville, 'Papalist Political Thought and the Controversy over the Jacobean Oath of Allegiance' in Ethan H. Shagan ed., *Catholics and the 'Protestant Nation': Religious Politics and Identity in Early Modern England* (Manchester, 2005), pp. 162–84.

44. Quoted by Stefania Tutino, *Law and Conscience: Catholicism in Early Modern England, 1570–1625* (Aldershot, 2007), p. 141.

45. HMC *Salisbury*, XIX p. 375.

46. 'Triplici Nodo, Triplex Cuneus' in James VI & I, *Political Writings*, pp. 116, 92, 110, 87. The title of James's tract echoed the woody metaphors of (im)perfect British union by providing a three-pronged polemical wedge to refute the triangular woody knot posed by the two papal breves and a letter to Blackwell from Bellarmine.

47. Quoted by David Harris Willson, 'James I and his Literary Assistants', *Huntington Library Quarterly*, 8:1 (1944), p. 43n.

48. Albert J. Loomie ed., *Spain and the Jacobean Catholics. Volume 1: 1603–1612* ([London], 1973), p. 121.

49. John King, *A Sermon preached at Whitehall, the 5 Day of November, Anno. 1608 &c.* (Oxford, 1608), p. 27.

50. John Hacket, *Scrinia Reserata. A Memorial offered to the great Deservings of John Williams, DD, who some time held the Places of Lord Keeper of the Great Seal of England, Lord Bishop of Lincoln, and Lord Archbishop of York &c.* (London, 1693), p. 227.

51. James VI & I, *Letters*, p. 302.

52. James VI & I, *An Apology for the Oath of Allegiance first set forth without a name, and now acknowledged by the Author, the Right High and Mighty Prince James &c.* (London, 1609), pp. 21, 19, 108.

53. Ibid, pp. 35, 46, 45.

54. Elisabeth Read Foster ed., *Proceedings in Parliament 1610*, 2 vols. (New Haven, CT, 1966), II, p. 106.

55. *Stuart Royal Proclamations*, I, p. 246.

56. Peter McCullough ed., *Lancelot Andrewes: Selected Sermons and Lectures* (Oxford, 2005), p. 185.

57. Quoted by Michael Questier, *Catholics and Treason: Martyrology, Memory and Politics in the Post-Reformation* (Oxford, 2022), p. 398.

58. Glyn Redworth ed., *The Letters of Luisa de Carvajal y Mendoza*, 2 vols. (London, 2012), II, pp. 157, 146, 145.

59. *Stuart Royal Proclamations*, I, p. 249.

60. Quoted by Michael Questier, 'Catholic Loyalism in Early Stuart England', *English Historical Review*, 123:504 (2008), pp. 1147, 1154.

61. Michael C. Questier ed., *Newsletters from the Archpresbyterate of George Birkhead* (Cambridge, 1998), p. 138.

62. Redworth ed., *Letters of Luisa de Carvajal*, II, pp. 272, 273, 272.

63. Quoted by J. Michael Hayden, *France and the Estates General of 1614* (Cambridge, 1974), p. 131.

64. Quoted by Ronald G. Asch, *Sacral Kingship between Disenchantment and Re-enchantment: The French and English Monarchies, 1587–1688* (Oxford, 2014), p. 193n ('[le serment] est venu par mer et à nagé d'Angleterre').

65. Sir Thomas Edmondes, *Remonstrances made by the King's Majesty's Ambassador, unto the French King and the Queen his Mother, June last past, 1615 &c.* (London, 1615), sigs. C2r, C2v, C3r–v.

66. Victoria and Albert Museum, accession number M.7-1931; see C. T. P. Bailey, 'A Royal Table Clock by David Ramsay', *The Connoisseur*, 87 (1931), pp. 238–9.

67. James VI & I, *The Works of the most High and Mighty Prince, James, by the Grace of God, King of Great Britain, France and Ireland, Defender of the Faith &c.* (London, 1616 [1617]), sig. D2r.

17 MORE ADO WITH IRELAND

1. Quoted by Isabel B. Taylor, *The Crown and its Records: Archives, Access and the Ancient Constitution in Seventeenth-Century England* (Berlin, 2023), p. 369.

2. Ibid.

3. Jane H. Ohlmeyer, '"Civilizinge of those Rude Partes": Colonization within Britain and Ireland, 1580s–1640s' in Nicholas Canny ed., *The Oxford History of the British Empire, Volume 1. The Origins of Empire: British Overseas Enterprise to the Close of the Seventeenth Century* (Oxford, 1998), pp. 139–40.

4. 'Basilicon Doron' in James VI & I, *Political Writings*, pp. 31–2.

5. Sir John Davies, *A Discovery of the True Causes why Ireland was never entirely subdued, nor brought under obedience of the crown of England, until the beginning of His Majesty's Happy Reign* (London, 1612), p. 259.

6. 'House of Common Journal Volume 1: 30 April 1621', in *Journal of the House of Commons: Volume 1, 1547–1629* (London, 1802), *British History Online* https://www. british-history.ac.uk/commons-jrnl/vol1/pp180–181 [accessed 20 September 2023].

7. Quoted by Victor Treadwell, *Buckingham and Ireland 1616–1628: A Study in Anglo-Irish Politics* (Dublin, 1998), p. 159.

8. Quoted by David Armitage, 'Making the Empire British: Scotland in the Atlantic World, 1542–1707', *Past & Present*, 155 (1997), p. 42.

9. Maurice Lee Jr., *Great Britain's Solomon: James VI and I in His Three Kingdoms* (Urbana, IL, 1990), p. 200.

10. Quoted by Hiram Morgan, 'Extradition and Treason Trial of a Gaelic Lord: The Case of Brian O'Rourke', *Irish Jurist*, 22:2 (1987), p. 287.

11. Annie I. Cameron ed., *The Warrender Papers. Volume II* (Edinburgh, 1932), p. 214.

12. CSP *Scotland*, XI, pp. 467, 466.

13. Ibid, p. 476.

14. Quoted by Alison Cathcart, 'Island Empire: James VI and I and the Isle of Man in an Archipelagic Context' in Neil McIntyre and Alison Cathcart eds., *Scotland and the Wider World: Essays in Honour of Allan I. Macinnes* (Martlesham, 2022), p. 41.

15. CSP *Ireland 1598, January–1599, March*, p. 142.

16. 'Basilicon Doron' in James VI & I, *Political Writings*, p. 32.

17. David Masson ed., *The Register of the Privy Council of Scotland. Volume VI: AD 1599–1604* (Edinburgh, 1884), p. 304.

18. Breandán Ó Buachalla, 'James our True King: The Ideology of Irish Royalism in the Seventeenth Century' in D. George Boyce, Robert Eccleshall and Vincent Geoghegan eds., *Political Thought in Ireland since the Seventeenth Century* (London, 1993), p. 11.

19. See Richard A. McCabe, 'Panegyric and its Discontents: The First Stuart Succession' in Paulina Kewes and Andrew McRae eds., *Stuart Succession Literature: Moments and Transformations* (Oxford, 2019), p. 32.

20. Quoted by John J. Silke, 'Peter Lombard and James I', *Irish Theological Quarterly*, 22 (1955), p. 128n.

21. Quoted by John Walter, 'The "Recusancy Revolt" of 1603 Revisited, Popular Politics and Civic Catholicism in Early Modern Ireland', *Historical Journal*, 65:2 (2022), pp. 259, 258.

22. CSP *Ireland, 1603–1606*, p. 29.

23. Norman Egbert McClure ed., *The Letters and Epigrams of Sir John Harington* (Philadelphia, PA, 1930), p. 107.

24. CSP *Ireland, 1603–1606*, p. 590.

25. Ibid, pp. 301–2.

26. Quoted by Keith Pluymers, *No Wood, No Kingdom: Political Ecology in the English Atlantic* (Philadelphia, PA, 2021), pp. 104–5.

27. CSP *Ireland, 1603–1606*, p. 389.

28. HMC *Salisbury*, XVIII, p. 255.

29. 'A Letter to the Earl of Salisbury on the State of Ireland, 1607' in Sir John Davies, *Historical Tracts: by Sir John Davies, Attorney-General, and Speaker of the House of Commons in Ireland &c.* (Dublin, 1787), pp. 256, 257.

30. *Stuart Royal Proclamations*, I, pp. 179, 178.

31. See Ciarán Brady, 'Pitying the Plumage: Commemorating the "Flight of the Earls" in Contemporary and Historical Contexts' in Mary Ann Lyons and Thomas O'Connor eds., *The Ulster Earls and Baroque Europe: Refashioning Irish Identities 1600–1800* (Dublin, 2010), pp. 362–79.

32. CSP *Ireland, 1606–1608*, pp. 277, 276.

33. CSP *Ireland, 1608–1610* p. 117.

34. No religious restrictions were imposed on the '*deserving natives*', but undertakers and servitors held their estates by free and common socage whereas the native Irish were granted estates by knight-service tenure. The implication for native landowners was that the heirs of original grantees would, in due course, need to take the Oath of Supremacy in order for their titles to their inheritance to receive crown approval.

35. CSP *Scotland*, XII, p. 291.

36. James VI, *Basilicon Doron. Divided into Three Books* (Edinburgh, 1599), pp. 42, 43.

37. 'Basilicon Doron' in James VI & I, *Political Writings*, p. 24.

38. CSP *Scotland*, XIII, Part I, p. 271; for the Lewis plantation, see Aonghas MacCoinnich, *Plantation and Civility in the North Atlantic World: The Case of the Northern Hebrides, 1570–1639* (Leiden, 2015), pp. 91–175.

39. Masson ed., *Register of the Privy Council of Scotland. Volume VI*, p. 420.

40. Sir Francis Bacon, 'Certain Considerations touching the Plantation in Ireland, presented to His Majesty' in Bacon, *Letters and Life*, IV, pp. 120, 122, 120.

41. Anonymous, *A Collection of such Orders and Conditions, as are to be Observed by the Undertakers, upon the Distribution and Plantation of the Escheated Lands of Ulster* (Edinburgh, 1609), sig. A2r.

42. Quoted by George Hill, *An Historical Account of the Plantation in Ulster at the Commencement of the Seventeenth Century, 1608–1620* (Belfast, 1877), p. 119.

43. Davies, *Discovery of the True Causes*, pp. 280, 282, 281, 284.

44. Barnaby Rich, *A New Description of Ireland wherein is Described the Disposition of the Irish whereunto they are Inclined* (London, 1610), sig. B4r.

45. CSP *Ireland, 1611–1614*, p. 310.

46. Ibid, p. 355; see John McCavitt, 'An Unspeakable Parliamentary Fracas: The Irish House of Commons, 1613', *Analecta Hibernica*, 37 (1998), pp. 223–35.

47. HMC *Downshire*, IV p. 124.

48. CSP *Ireland, 1611–1614*, p. 547.

49. Ibid, p. 462–3.

50. Quoted by James M. Smith, 'Effaced History: Facing the Colonial Contexts of Ben Jonson's *Irish Masque at Court*', *ELH: English Literary History*, 65:2 (1998), pp. 311, 309.

51. J. S. Brewer and William Bullen eds., *Calendar of the Carew Manuscripts, preserved in the Archiepiscopal Library at Lambeth [1600–1623]* (London, 1873), pp. 291, 290.

52. Mark Netzloff, 'Forgetting the Ulster Plantation: John Speed's *The Theatre of the Empire of Great Britain* (1611) and the Colonial Archive', *Journal of Medieval and Early Modern Studies*, 31:2 (2001), p. 331.

53. Brewer and Bullen eds., *Calendar of the Carew Manuscripts* ... *[1600–1623]*, pp. 306, 309.

54. David Heffernan ed., 'Three Surveys of the Londonderry Plantation, 1613–1616', *Analecta Hibernica*, 50 (2019), pp. 42–3.

55. Edward M. Hinton ed., 'Rych's Anothomy of Ireland, with an Account of the Author', *Proceedings of the Modern Language Association*, 55:1 (1940), pp. 84, 100, 91.

56. Brewer and Bullen eds., *Calendar of the Carew Manuscripts* ... *[1600–1623]*, p. 324.

57. Ian W. Archer, 'The City of London and the Ulster Plantation' in Éamonn Ó Ciardha and Micheál Ó Siochrú eds., *The Plantation of Ulster: Ideology and Practice* (Manchester, 2012), p. 83.

58. CSP *Venice*, XVI, *1619–1621*, p. 528.

59. Quoted by Taylor, *The Crown and its Records*, p. 370.

60. [Richard Hadsor], *Advertisements for Ireland: Being a Description of the State of Ireland in the Reign of James I contained in a Manuscript in the Library of Trinity College, Dublin*, George O'Brien ed. (Dublin, 1923), p. 22.

61. Quoted by M. Perceval-Maxwell, *The Scottish Migration to Ulster in the Reign of James I* (London, 1973), p. 211.

62. CSP *Venice*, XVII, *1621–1623*, p. 435.

18 THE KING IN PARLIAMENT

1. John Rushworth, *Historical Collections of Private Passages of State, Weighty Matters in Law, Remarkable Proceedings in Five Parliaments &c.*, 8 vols. (London, 1721), I, pp. 53–4.

2. 'His Majesty's Declaration, touching his proceedings in the late Assembly and Convention of Parliament' in James VI & I, *Political Writings*, pp. 255, 261.

3. Quoted by David Colclough, *Freedom of Speech in Early Stuart England* (Cambridge, 2005), p. 181.

4. Quoted by Andrew Thrush ed., *The House of Lords, 1604–1629*, 3 vols. (Cambridge, 2021), I, p. 2.

5. 'House of Commons Journal Volume 1: 02 May 1607' in *Journal of the House of Commons: Volume 1, 1547–1629* (London, 1802), *British History Online* https://www.british-history.ac.uk/commons-jrnl/vol1/pp366-368 [accessed 17 April 2024].

6. James VI & I, *Letters*, pp. 318–19. James recurrently invoked this metaphor. In 1615, he rejected the 'pernicious opinion; that the Pope may toss the French king his throne like a tennis ball' (*A Remonstrance of the most Gracious King James I, King of Great Britain, France & Ireland &c.* [Cambridge,

1616], sig. A2r). Regarding his son-in-law's decision to accept the Bohemian Crown, James insisted in January 1621, that he would not accept other monarchs disputing 'whether I be a lawful king or not and so to toss up and down crowns like tennis balls' (Wallace Notestein, Frances Helen Relf and Hartley Simpson eds., *Commons Debates, 1621*, 7 vols. [New Haven CT, 1935], II, p. 10). In March 1621, he addressed the House of Lords, hoping that Sir Edward Coke would not distract MPs with unhelpful precedents from turbulent reigns, including those of Henry VI, Richard II 'and such like princes and times when one house was up today, and another tomorrow, and the crown tossed up and down like a tennis ball' (Lady de Villiers ed., 'Hastings Journal of the Parliament of 1621', *Camden Miscellany XX*, 3rd series [1953], p. 27). The metaphor derives from Isaiah 22:18: 'He will surely roll and turn thee like a ball in a large country', potentially via a sermon on Job 1:9–12 by John Calvin that referred to God sporting with us 'as with a tennis' ball'; see Hannibal Hamlin, *The Bible in Shakespeare* (Oxford, 2013), p. 55.

7. Quoted by Alastair J. Mann, 'The Scottish Parliaments: The Role of Ritual and Procession in the pre-1707 Parliament and the New Parliament of 1999' in Emma Crewe and Marion G. Müller eds., *Rituals in Parliaments: Political, Anthropological and Historical Perspectives on Europe and the United States* (Oxford, 2006), p. 141.

8. Julian Goodare, 'The Scottish Parliament of 1621', *Historical Journal*, 38:1 (1995), p. 35.

9. Keith M. Brown and Alastair J. Mann, 'Introduction: Parliament and Politics in Scotland, 1567–1707' in Keith M. Brown and Alastair J. Mann eds., *The History of the Scottish Parliament. Volume II: Parliament and Politics in Scotland 1567–1707* (Edinburgh 2005), p. 18; see also Alan R. MacDonald, 'Consultation and Consent under James VI', *Historical Journal*, 54:2 (2011), pp. 287–306.

10. *The Records of the Parliaments of Scotland to 1707*, K. M. Brown et al. eds. (St Andrews, 2007–23), 1587/7/143 [accessed 20 September 2023].

11. See Julian Goodare, 'The Admission of Lairds to the Scottish Parliament', *English Historical Review*, 116:469 (2001), pp. 1103–33. As small shires, Clackmannan and Kinross were entitled to a single commissioner rather than two.

12. Julian Goodare, *State and Society in Early Modern Scotland* (Oxford, 1999), p. 74; *The Records of the Parliaments of Scotland to 1707*, Brown et al. eds; 1587/7/26 [accessed 17 April 2024].

13. CSP *Scotland*, X, pp. 681, 686.

14. Alan R. MacDonald, 'The Parliament of 1592: A Crisis Averted?' in Brown and Mann eds., *History of the Scottish Parliament. Volume II*, p. 63.

15. Calderwood, *History of the Kirk*, V, pp. 161, 162.

16. Julian Goodare, *The Government of Scotland 1560–1625* (Oxford, 2004), pp. 140, 131–2.

17. Quoted by Grant G. Simpson, 'The Personal Letters of James VI: A Short Commentary' in Julian Goodare and Michael Lynch eds., *The Reign of James VI* (East Linton, 2000), p. 141.

18. 'Trew Law of Free Monarchies' in James VI & I, *Political Writings*, p. 74.

19. 'Basilicon Doron' in ibid, p. 21.

20. Quoted by Goodare, 'The Admission of Lairds', p. 1126.

21. Maija Jansson ed., *Proceedings in Parliament 1614 (House of Commons)* (Philadelphia, PA, 1988), p. 140.

22. Quoted by Peter R. Roberts, 'The Tudor Origins of the Grant of Parliamentary Representation to English Universities in 1604', *Parliaments, Estates and Representation*, 26:1 (2006), p. 41.

23. David Harris Willson ed., *The Parliamentary Diary of Robert Bowyer, 1606–1607* (New York, 1971), p. 278n.

24. Alasdair Hawkyard, 'Inigo Jones, the Surveyors of the Works, and the "Parliament House"', *Parliamentary History*, 32:1 (2013), pp. 17, 22.

25. *Stuart Royal Proclamations*, I, pp. 67, 68.

26. Quoted by Brett F. Parker, 'Recasting England: The Varieties of Antiquarian Responses to the Proposed Union of Crowns, 1603–1607', *Journal of Medieval and Early Modern Studies*, 43:2 (2013), p. 406; see also Pauline Croft, 'Sir John Doddridge, King James I and the Antiquity of Parliaments', *Parliaments, Estates and Representation*, 12:2 (1992), pp. 95–107.

27. John Doddridge, 'The Union of Two Kingdoms' in Bruce R. Galloway and Brian P. Levack eds., *The Jacobean Union. Six Tracts of 1604* (Edinburgh, 1985), p. 146.

28. Quoted by Alexandra Gajda, 'The Society of Antiquaries and the Invention of the History of Parliament', *Huntington Library Quarterly*, 86:3 (2023), p. 531.

29. CSP *Venice*, X, 1603–7, p. 150.

30. James VI & I, 'Speech at the Prorogation of Parliament, 7 July 1604' in J. P. Kenyon ed., *The Stuart Constitution 1603–1688*, 2nd edition (Cambridge, 1986), pp. 36–7.

31. 'Speech to Parliament of 9 November 1605' in James VI & I, *Political Writings*, pp. 151, 155, 157.

32. Quoted by Michelle O'Callaghan, 'Performing Politics: The Circulation of the "Parliament Fart"', *Huntington Library Quarterly*, 69:1 (2006), p. 126–7, 128.

33. 'Speech to Parliament of 31 March 1607' in James VI & I, *Political Writings*, pp. 174, 173, 172.

34. Conrad Russell, *King James VI and I and his English Parliaments*, Richard Cust and Andrew Thrush eds. (Oxford, 2011), p. 63.

35. 'Speech to Parliament of 21 March 1610' in James VI & I, *Political Writings*, pp. 190–91, 197.

36. Elizabeth Read Foster ed., *Proceedings in Parliament, 1610*, 2 vols. (New Haven, CT, 1966), II, pp. 259, 102, 105.

37. Chamberlain, *Letters*, I, pp. 300, 301.

38. Read Foster ed., *Proceedings in Parliament, 1610*, II, p. 259.

39. Rudolph W. Heinze, 'Proclamations and Parliamentary Protest, 1539–1610' in Delloyd J. Guth and John W. McKenna eds., *Tudor Rule and Revolution: Essays for G. R. Elton from his American Friends* (Cambridge, 1982), p. 240.

40. Esther S. Cope, 'Sir Edward Coke and Proclamations, 1610', *American Journal of Legal History*, 15:3 (1971), p. 221.

41. *Stuart Royal Proclamations*, I, pp. 253–7.

42. Quoted by Russell, *King James VI and I and his English Parliaments*, p. 93.

43. Quoted by Bruce Galloway, *The Union of England and Scotland 1603–1608* (Edinburgh, 1986), p. 24; see *The Records of the Parliaments of Scotland to 1707*, K. M. Brown et al. eds. (St Andrews, 2007–23), 1604/4/21 [accessed 21 September 2023].

44. Thomas Hamilton, 'Memorial anent the Progress and Conclusion of the Parliament held at Edinburgh in October 1612' in *Miscellany of the Maitland Club consisting of Original Papers and other Documents illustrative of the History and Literature of Scotland. Volume III* (Edinburgh, 1843), p. 116; see Vaughan T. Wells, 'Constitutional Conflict after the Union of the Crowns: Contention and Continuity in the Parliaments of 1612 and 1621' in Brown and Mann eds., *History of the Scottish Parliament. Volume II*, pp. 82–100.

45. Bacon, *Letters and Life*, V, pp. 2, 26, 27.

46. Jansson ed., *Proceedings in Parliament 1614*, pp. 18, 19, 296, 433–4.

47. Ibid, pp. 316, 420.

48. Quoted by Stephen Clucas and Rosalind Davies in 'Introduction' to Stephen Clucas and Rosalind Davies eds., *The Crisis of 1614 and the Addled Parliament: Literary and Historical Perspectives* (Aldershot, 2003), p. 3.

49. Quoted by Ernesto Eduardo Oyarbide Magaña, 'The First Count of Gondomar's Library and Diplomatic Practice (1613–1622)' (University of Oxford DPhil thesis, 2019), pp. 122, 123.

50. HMC *Downshire*, VI, p. 219.

51. Nichols, *Progresses, Processions*, III, pp. 346–7.

52. 'House of Lords Journal Volume 3: 26 March 1621', in *Journal of the House of Lords: Volume 3, 1620–1628* (London, 1767–1830), *British History Online* https://www.british-history.ac.uk/lords-jrnl/vol3/pp68–72 [accessed 9 October 2024].

53. Quoted by Goodare, 'Scottish Parliament of 1621', pp. 31–2.

54. Pauline Croft, *King James* (Houndmills, 2003), p. 112.

55. 'House of Lords Journal Volume 3: 19 February 1624, 8 March 1624 and 25 March 1624' in *Journal of the House of Lords: Volume 3, 1620–1628* (London, 1767–1830), pp. 208–10, 249–51 and 281–3. *British*

History Online https://www.british-history.ac.uk/lords-jrnl/vol3/pp208–210 [accessed 12 April 2024].

56. James Alexander Manning ed., *Memoirs of Sir Benjamin Rudyerd Knt., Containing his Speeches and Poems* (London, 1841), pp. 79–80.

19 THIS CANKER OF WANT

1. CSP *Scotland*, X, p. 19.
2. James VI & I, *Letters*, p. 261.
3. Ibid, p. 291.
4. 'Speech to Parliament of 21 March 1610' in James VI & I, *Political Writings*, pp. 192–3.
5. CSP *Venice*, XVII, *1621–1623*, pp. 436–7.
6. Julian Goodare, 'Parliamentary Taxation in Scotland, 1560–1603', *Scottish Historical Review*, 68:185 (1989), pp. 24–8.
7. See M. Greengrass, 'Mary, Dowager Queen of France' in Michael Lynch ed., *Mary Stewart: Queen in Three Kingdoms* (Oxford, 1988), pp. 172–5.
8. Julian Goodare, *State and Society in Early Modern Scotland* (Oxford, 1999), p. 120.
9. CSP *Scotland*, VI, p. 300.
10. Julian Goodare, 'James VI's English Subsidy' in Julian Goodare and Michael Lynch eds., *The Reign of James VI* (East Linton, 2000), pp. 120–21.
11. Julian Goodare, 'The Debts of James VI of Scotland', *Economic History Review*, 62:4 (2009), p. 944; Alexander Montgomerie, 'King James VI's Tocher Gude and a Local Authorities Loan of 1590', *Scottish Historical Review*, 37 (1958), pp. 11–16.
12. Goodare, 'Parliamentary Taxation', pp. 50–51.
13. Richard Bruce Wernham ed., *List and Analysis of State Papers Foreign Series, Elizabeth I, preserved in the Public Record Office. Volume V: July 1593–December 1594* (London, 1989), p. 216.
14. Thomas Thomson ed., *Memoirs of His Own Life by Sir James Melville of Halhill* (Edinburgh, 1827), p. 413.
15. CSP *Scotland*, XII, p. 117.
16. Ibid, p. 291; see also Julian Goodare, 'The Octavians' in Miles Kerr-Peterson and Steven J. Reid eds., *James VI and Noble Power in Scotland 1578–1603* (London, 2017), pp. 176–93.
17. Julian Goodare, 'Thomas Foulis and the Scottish Fiscal Crisis of the 1590s' in W. Mark Ormrod, Margaret Bonney and Richard Bonney eds., *Crises, Revolutions and Self-Sustained Growth: Essays in European Fiscal History, 1130–1830* (Stanford, CA, 1999), p. 189.
18. Goodare, *State and Society*, p. 124.

19. 'Basilicon Doron' in James VI & I, *Political Writings*, p. 37.

20. John Maclean ed., *Letters from Sir Robert Cecil to Sir George Carew* (London, 1864), p. 147.

21. David L. Smith, *The Stuart Parliaments 1603–1689* (London, 1999), p. 51.

22. Tim Harris, *Rebellion: Britain's First Stuart Kings* (Oxford, 2014), pp. 119, 214.

23. Wallace Notestein, Frances Helen Relf and Hartley Simpson eds., *Commons Debates, 1621*, 7 vols. (New Haven, CT, 1935), II, p. 7.

24. Michael J. Braddick, *State Formation in Early Modern England, c. 1550–1700* (Cambridge, 2000), pp. 233–4.

25. *The Records of the Parliaments of Scotland to 1707*, K. M. Brown et al. eds. (St Andrews, 2007–23), 1592/4/63 [accessed 10 October 2023].

26. *Stuart Royal Proclamations*, I, p. 13.

27. Richard Martin, *A Speech Delivered, To the Kings Most Excellent Majesty in the Name of the Sheriffs of London and Middlesex* (London, 1603), sig. Br.

28. James VI & I, *Letters*, pp. 242–4.

29. *Stuart Royal Proclamations*, I, p. 7.

30. B. J. Cook, '"Stamped with your own *Image*": The Numismatic Dimension of Two Stuart Successions' in Paulina Kewes and Andrew McRae eds., *Stuart Succession Literature: Moments and Transformations* (Oxford, 2019), pp. 307, 309.

31. *Stuart Royal Proclamations*, I, p. 101, 99.

32. See David Fox, 'The Anglo-Scots Monetary Union of 1707', *Edinburgh Law Review*, 23:3 (2019), pp. 367–72.

33. Five months earlier, a report returned to Elizabeth's ministers had indicated that, alongside English and Irish currency, 'Spanish gold and silver is the coin that most abounds and is chiefest reckoned on in that realm' (CSP *Ireland, 1600, 1 November–1601, 31 July*, p. 127.

34. See David Blaazer, *Forging Nations: Currency, Power and Nationality in Britain and Ireland since 1603* (Oxford, 2023), pp. 23–31, and Michael Dolley, 'The Irish Coinage, 1534–1691' in F. X. Martin, F. J. Byrne and T. W. Moody eds., *A New History of Ireland: Early Modern Ireland 1534–1691* (Oxford, 1976), pp. 408–19.

35. See Pauline Croft, 'Purveyance and the City of London, 1589–1608', *Parliamentary History*, 4 (1985), pp. 9–34.

36. CSP *Venice*, X, *1603–7*, p. 353. The ambassador was Zorzi Giustinian.

37. John Cramsie, *Kingship and Crown Finance under James VI and I 1603–1625* (Woodbridge, 2002), p. 32.

38. [William Stallenge], *Instructions for the Increasing of Mulberry Trees, and the Breeding of Silkworms &c.* (London, 1609), sig. Br; see also Ben Marsh, *Unravelled Dreams: Silk and the Atlantic World, 1500–1840* (Cambridge, 2020), pp. 103–6.

39. David Harris Willson ed., *The Parliamentary Diary of Robert Bowyer 1606–1607* (New York, 1971), p. 75.

40. Thomas Craig, *The Jus Feudale by Sir [sic] Thomas Craig of Riccarton &c.*, J. A. Clyde ed., 2 vols. (Edinburgh, 1934), I, p. x.

41. Pauline Croft ed., 'A Collection of Several Speeches and Treatises of the late Lord Treasurer Cecil and of Several Observations of the Lords of the Council given to King James concerning his Estate and Revenue in the Years 1608, 1609, and 1610', *Camden Miscellany XXIX* (1987), pp. 275, 285, 284.

42. Eric Lindquist, 'The Failure of the Great Contract', *Journal of Modern History*, 57:4 (1985), p. 625.

43. Quoted by Micheline Kerney Walsh, *'Destruction by Peace': Hugh O'Neill after Kinsale: Glanconcadhain 1602–Rome 1616* ([Armagh], c. 1986), p. 220.

44. Elizabeth Read Foster ed., *Proceedings in Parliament, 1610*, 2 vols. (New Haven, CT, 1966), II, pp. 14, 15; I, pp. 6, 5; see Linda Levy Peck, ' "For a King not to be bountiful were a fault": Perspectives on Court Patronage in Early Stuart England', *Journal of British Studies*, 25:1 (1986), pp. 31–61.

45. 'Speech to Parliament of 21 March 1610' in James VI & I, *Political Writings*, p. 197.

46. Foster ed., *Proceedings in Parliament, 1610*, II, p. 106.

47. Quoted by Smith, *Stuart Parliaments*, p. 55.

48. Susan Doran, *From Tudor to Stuart: The Regime Change from Elizabeth I to James I* (Oxford, 2024), p. 220.

49. Foster ed., *Proceedings in Parliament, 1610*, II, p. 344.

50. Ibid, I p. 149.

51. Samuel Rawson Gardiner ed., *Parliamentary Debates in 1610. Edited from the Notes of a Member of the House of Commons* (London, 1862), pp. 11, 10.

52. James VI & I, *Letters*, p. 318.

53. Notestein, Relf and Simpson eds., *Commons Debates, 1621*, II, p. 12.

54. Thomas Cogswell, *Home Divisions: Aristocracy, the State and Provincial Conflict* (Manchester, 1998), p. 14.

55. See Pauline Croft, 'The Catholic Gentry, the Earl of Salisbury and the Baronets of 1611' in Peter Lake and Michael Questier eds., *Conformity and Orthodoxy in the English Church, c. 1560–1660* (Woodbridge, 2000), pp. 262–81; also Doran, *Tudor to Stuart*, p. 267.

56. Nichols, *Progresses, Processions*, II, p. 421; see Simon Wortham, 'Sovereign Counterfeits: The Trial of the Pyx', *Renaissance Quarterly*, 49:2 (1996), pp. 334–59.

57. *Stuart Royal Proclamations*, I, p. 263; six months later, another proclamation fixed gold prices in an attempt to correct global distortions whereby

'our gold at this time is more stirring abroad in parts beyond the seas, then here at home in our own island' (ibid., p. 272).

58. Quoted by Croft ed., 'Introduction' to 'Collection of Several Speeches', p. 259.

59. Chamberlain, *Letters*, I, p. 377.

60. Cramsie, *Kingship and Crown Finance*, p. 133.

61. Quoted by Ernesto Eduardo Oyarbide Magaña, 'The First Count of Gondomar's Library and Diplomatic Practice (1613–1622)' (University of Oxford DPhil thesis, 2019), p. 99.

62. Maija Jansson ed., *Proceedings in Parliament 1614 (House of Commons)* (Philadelphia, PA, 1988), p. 17.

63. Quoted by Isabel B. Taylor, *The Crown and its Records: Archives, Access and the Ancient Constitution in Seventeenth-Century England* (Berlin, 2023), pp. 79–80.

64. *Stuart Royal Proclamations*, I, pp. 312–14, 324–6.

65. Quoted by Cramsie, *Kingship and Crown Finance*, p. 147; Harris, *Rebellion*, p. 139.

66. Quoted by Simon Healy, 'Star Chamber and the Bullion Trade, 1618–1620' in K. J. Kesselring and Natalie Mears eds., *Star Chamber Matters: An Early Modern Court and its Records* (London, 2021), p. 180.

67. Chamberlain, *Letters*, II, pp. 249, 251.

68. Lady de Villiers ed., 'Hastings Journal of the Parliament of 1621', *Camden Miscellany XX*, 3rd series (1953), p. 26.

69. John Rushworth, 'Historical Collections: 1621' in *Historical Collections of Private Passages of State: Volume 1, 1618–29* (London, 1721), pp. 24–62. *British History Online* http://www.british-history.ac.uk/rushworth-papers/vol1/pp.24–62 [accessed 24 September 2023].

70. Quoted by Cramsie, *Kingship and Crown Finance*, p. 192.

71. 'House of Lords Journal Volume 3: 8 March 1624', in *Journal of the House of Lords: Volume 3, 1620–1688* (London, 1767–1830), *British History Online* https://www. british-history.ac.uk/lords-jrnl/vol3/ pp249–51 [accessed 24 September 2023].

72. Paul Douglas Lockhart, *Denmark 1513–1660: The Rise and Decline of a Renaissance Monarchy* (Oxford, 2007), p. 133.

20 DYNASTIC DIPLOMACY

1. CSP *Scotland*, X, p. 103.

2. Andrew Thrush, 'The French Marriage and the Origins of the 1614 Parliament' in Stephen Clucas and Rosalind Davies eds., *The Crisis of 1614 and the Addled Parliament. Literary and Historical Perspectives* (Aldershot, 2003), pp. 26–7.

3. 'Basilicon Doron' in James VI & I, *Political Writings*, p. 40.

4. Quoted by Michael Questier, *Dynastic Politics and the British Reformations 1558–1630* (Oxford, 2019), p. 1.

5. Robert Cross, "'The onely sovereign medecine": Religious Politics and Political Culture in the British-Spanish March, 1596–1625' in Valentina Caldari and Sara J. Wolfson eds., *Stuart Marriage Diplomacy. Dynastic Politics in their European Context, 1604–1630* (Woodbridge, 2018), p. 67.

6. *Memoirs of the Duke of Sully; During his Residence at the English Court; to which he was sent Ambassador from Henry IV. of France, Upon the Accession of King James the First &c.* (London, 1751), p. 162.

7. Melinda J. Gough, 'Dynastic Marriage, Diplomatic Ceremonial and the Treaties of London (1604–05) and Antwerp (1609)' in Caldari and Wolfson eds., *Stuart Marriage Diplomacy*, p. 289.

8. CSP *Venice*, X, *1603–1607*, p. 203.

9. [Edmund Sawyer ed.], *Memorials of Affairs of State in the Reigns of Q. Elizabeth and K. James I, Collected Chiefly from the Original Papers of the Right Honourable Sir Ralph Winwood, Kt &c.* 3 vols. (London, 1725), II, p. 90.

10. R. Malcolm Smuts, *Political Culture, the State, and the Problem of Religious War in Britain and Ireland, 1578–1625* (Oxford, 2023), p. 549.

11. Quoted by ibid.

12. Quoted by Berta Cano-Echevarría and Mark Hutchings, 'The Spanish Ambassador and Samuel Daniel's *Vision of the Twelve Goddesses*: A New Document' in *English Literary Renaissance*, 42:2 (2012), p. 246.

13. Quoted by Cross, 'The onely sovereign medecine' in Caldari and Wolfson eds., *Stuart Marriage Diplomacy*, pp. 74–5.

14. Quoted by Ellen R. Welch, *A Theater of Diplomacy: International Relations and the Performing Arts in Early Modern France* (Philadelphia, PA, 2017), p. 44.

15. See Pauline Croft, 'The Parliamentary Installation of Henry, Prince of Wales', *Historical Research*, 65:157 (1992), pp. 177–93.

16. Maria Shmygol, 'Jacobean Mock Sea-Fights on the River Thames: Nautical Theatricality in Performance and Print', *The London Journal*, 47:1 (2022), p. 14; for the Scottish precedent, see Pesala Bandara, 'Mary, Queen of Scots' Aquatic Entertainments for the Wedding of John Fleming, Fifth Lord of Fleming to Elizabeth Ross, May 1562' in Margaret Shewring and Linda Briggs eds., *Waterborne Pageants and Festivities in the Renaissance: Essays in Honour of J. R. Mulryne* (Farnham, 2013), pp. 199–209. The *naumachia* took place during a covert visit by Swedish diplomats to Mary's court to discuss a potential marriage between Mary and Eric XIV of Sweden.

17. Andrew Melville, 'Principis Scoti-Britannorum Natalia' in Paul J. McGinnis and Arthur H. Williamson eds., *George Buchanan: The Political Poetry* (Edinburgh, 1995), pp. 278, 280.

18. Sir Robert Cotton, *An Answer made by Command of Prince Henry to Certain Propositions of War and Peace delivered to His Highness by some of his Military Servants &c.* (London, 1655), pp. 3, 95.

19. [Sawyer ed.], *Memorials of Affairs of State*, II, p. 413.

20. George Marcelline, *The Triumphs of King James the First, of Great Britain, France, and Ireland, King; Defender of the Faith &c.* ([London], 1610), sig. A2r, pp. 65–6.

21. Robert Abbot, *The True Ancient Roman Catholic, Being an Apology or Counterproof against Doctor Bishop's Reproof of the Defence of the Reformed Catholic &c.* (London, 1611), 'The Epistle Dedicatory'.

22. 'Basilicon Doron' in James VI & I, *Political Writings*, p. 40.

23. Thrush, 'The French Marriage', p. 26.

24. HMC *Salisbury*, XXI p. 344.

25. J. H. Elliott, 'The Political Context of the 1612–1615 Franco-Spanish Treaty' in Margaret M. McGowan ed., *Dynastic Marriages, 1612/1615: A Celebration of the Habsburg and Bourbon Unions* (Farnham, 2013), p. 12.

26. Quoted by Smuts, *Political Culture, the State*, p. 571.

27. *Historical Manuscripts Commission Tenth Report on the Manuscripts of the Earl of Eglinton, Sir J. Stirling Maxwell Bart., C. S. H. Drummond Moray Esq., C. F. Weston Underwood Esq., and G. Wingfield Digby Esq.* (London, 1885), p. 556.

28. Quoted by Thomas Vernon Thoroughman, 'Some Political Aspects of Anglo-French Relations, 1610–1619' (University of North Carolina at Chapel Hill PhD thesis, 1968), p. 114.

29. Mary Anne Everett Green and S. C. Lomas, *Elizabeth Electress Palatine and Queen of Bohemia* (London, 1909), p. 33.

30. Thomas Birch, *The Life of Henry Prince of Wales, Eldest son of King James I. Compiled Chiefly from his own Papers, and other Manuscripts, never before Published* (Dublin, 1760), pp. 251–2; Nichols, *Progresses, Processions*, II, p. 460. For speculative attribution of these entertainments to the banquet at Woodstock in August 1612, see Anne Daye, ' "The Revellers are Entering": Shakespeare and Masquing Practice in Tudor and Stuart England' in Lynsey McCulloch and Brandon Shaw eds., *The Oxford Handbook of Shakespeare and Dance* (Oxford, 2019), p. 123.

31. 'W[illiam] H[aydone]', *The True Picture and Relation of Prince Henry, his Noble and Virtuous Disposition &c.* (Leiden, 1634), p. 9.

32. CSP *Venice*, XII, 1610–1613, p. 365; for the suggested dowry of a million crowns, see Thoroughman, 'Some Political Aspects', p. 161.

33. Birch, *Life of Henry Prince of Wales*, pp. 233, 235.

34. James VI & I, *Royal Correspondence*, p. 142.

35. CSP *Venice*, XII, *1610–1613*, p. 472.

36. Quoted by Jennifer Woodward, *The Theatre of Death: The Ritual Management of Royal Funerals in Renaissance England 1570–1625* (Woodbridge, 1997), p. 149.

37. HMC *Downshire*, III, p. 436.

38. Quoted by James Doelman, *The Daring Muse of the Early Stuart Funeral Elegy* (Manchester, 2021), p. 28.

39. CSP *Venice*, XII, *1610–1613*, pp. 450, 448.

40. Glyn Redworth ed., *The Letters of Luisa de Carvajal y Mendoza*, 2 vols. (London, 2012), II, p. 295.

41. Chamberlain, *Letters*, I, p. 391.

42. James VI & I, *Letters*, p. 329.

43. Nadine Akkerman, *Elizabeth Stuart, Queen of Hearts* (Oxford, 2021), pp. 71, 80.

44. Redworth ed., *Letters of Luisa de Carvajal y Mendoza*, II, pp. 295, 300.

45. Marie-Claude Canova-Green, '"Particularitez des Resjoyssances Publiques et Cérémonyes du Mariage de la Princesse": An Ambassadorial Account of the Palatine Wedding' in Sara Smart and Mara R. Wade eds., *The Palatine Wedding of 1613: Protestant Alliance and Court Festival* (Wiesbaden, 2013), p. 355.

46. John Taylor, *Heaven's Blessing and Earth's Joy; or, a True Relation of the supposed Sea-Fights and Fireworks as were accomplished before the Royal Celebration of the all-beloved Marriage of the two Peerless Paragons of Christendom, Frederick and Elizabeth &c.* (London, 1613) sig. A4r.

47. Redworth ed., *Letters of Luisa de Carvajal y Mendoza*, II, p. 300; see Stephen Farrell, 'The Armada Tapestries in the Old Palace of Westminster', *Parliamentary History*, 29:3 (2010), pp. 416–40.

48. Chamberlain, *Letters*, I, p. 424.

49. John Donne, 'An Epithalamion, or Marriage Song on the Lady Elizabeth, and Count Palatine being married on St. Valentines Day' in W. Milgate ed., *John Donne: The Epithalamions, Anniversaries and Epicedes* (Oxford, 1978), pp. 9, 10.

50. CSP *Venice*, XII, *1610–1613*, p. 526.

51. Nadine Akkerman ed., *The Correspondence of Elizabeth Stuart, Queen of Bohemia. Volume 1: 1603–1631* (Oxford, 2015), p. 114.

52. Maija Jansson ed., *Proceedings in Parliament 1614 (House of Commons)* (Philadelphia, PA, 1988), pp. 15, 16. The naturalization and succession bill passed the Commons and Lords but did not formally receive royal assent.

53. Quoted by Thrush, 'The French Marriage', p. 33, n. 1.

54. CSP *Venice*, XIII, *1613–1615*, pp. 64, 93.

55. Quoted by Thrush, 'The French Marriage', p. 29.

56. Sir Thomas Edmondes, *Remonstrances made by the King's Majesty's Ambassador, unto the French King and the Queen his Mother, June last past, 1615 &c.* (London, 1615), sigs. A3v–A4r, A4r, A4v.

57. See Elliott, 'The Political Context of the 1612–1615 Franco-Spanish Treaty', pp. 5–18.

58. 'Basilicon Doron' in James VI & I, *Political Writings*, pp. 40, 41.

59. CSP *Venice*, XIV, *1615–1617*, p. 510.

60. CSP *Venice*, XV, *1617–1619*, p. 206–7, 207.

61. Quoted by Nicholas Popper, *The Specter of the Archive: Political Practice and the Information State in Early Modern Britain* (Chicago, IL, 2024), pp. 116, 117.

62. CSP *Venice*, XVII, *1621–1623*, p. 132.

63. CSP *Venice*, XVIII, *1623–1625*, p. 308.

21 IT WILL CAUSE SCANDAL

1. William McElwee, *The Wisest Fool in Christendom: The Reign of King James I and VI* (London, 1958), p. 178.

2. James VI & I, *Letters*, pp. 337, 338.

3. CSP *Venice*, X, *1603–1607*, p. 33.

4. Christianna Floyd Kay, 'Royal Opportunity: Noble Marriages in the Reigns of Elizabeth and James VI/I, 1558–1625' (PhD thesis, Victoria University of Wellington, 2020), p. 108.

5. Mary Anne Everett Green ed., *Calendar of State Papers Domestic Series, of the Reign of James I &c., 1603–1610* (London, 1857), p. 417.

6. Francis Osborne, *Traditional Memoirs on the Reigns of Queen Elizabeth and King James* (London, 1658), pp. 84, 85 (2nd pagination).

7. Quoted by Alastair Bellany, *The Politics of Court Scandal in Early Modern England: News Culture and the Overbury Affair, 1603–1660* (Cambridge, 2002), p. 39.

8. Thomas Birch ed., *The Court and Times of James the First, Illustrated by Authentic and Confidential Letters, from Various Public and Private Collections*, 2 vols. (London, 1848), I, p. 191.

9. Hugh Trevor-Roper, *Europe's Physician: The Various Life of Sir Theodore de Mayerne* (New Haven, CT, 2006), p. 167.

10. Robert Cecil, Earl of Salisbury, *The State and Dignity of a Secretary of Estates Place, with the Care and Peril Thereof* (London, 1642), p. 3.

11. Chamberlain, *Letters*, I, p. 355.

12. Quoted by David Lindley, *The Trials of Frances Howard: Fact and Fiction at the Court of King James* (London, 1993), p. 85; Harold Spencer Scott ed., *The Journal of Sir Roger Wilbraham, Solicitor-General in Ireland and Master of Requests for the Years 1593 to 1616* (London, 1902), p. 116.

13. Chamberlain, *Letters*, I, p. 443; for the overseas mission, see Chester Dunning, 'The Fall of Sir Thomas Overbury and the Embassy to Russia in 1613', *Sixteenth Century Journal*, 22:4 (1991), pp. 695–704.

14. [Edmund Sawyer ed.], *Memorials of Affairs of State in the Reigns of Q. Elizabeth and K. James I, Collected Chiefly from the Original Papers of the Right Honourable Sir Ralph Winwood, Kt &c.* 3 vols. (London, 1725), III, p. 479.

15. James VI & I, 'The King's Answer' in *Cobbett's Complete Collection of State Trials and Proceedings for High Crimes and other Misdemeanours from the Earliest Period to the Present Time* (London, 1809), II, pp. 798, 800, 801.

16. Chamberlain, *Letters*, I, p. 475.

17. See Christine Adams, 'Francis Bacon's Wedding Gift of "A Garden of Glorious and Strange Beauty" for the Earl and Countess of Somerset', *Garden History*, 36:1 (2008), pp. 36–58.

18. James VI & I, *Letters*, p. 340.

19. S. R. Gardiner, 'On Certain Letters of Diego Sarmiento de Acuña, Count of Gondomar, giving an account of the affair of the Earl of Somerset, with remarks on the career of Somerset as a public man', *Archaeologia*, 41 (1867), pp. 159, 161.

20. 'Archbishop Abbot his Narrative' in John Rushworth ed., *Historical Collections of Private Passages of State, Weighty Matters in Law, Remarkable Proceedings in Five Parliaments &c.*, 8 vols. (London, 1721), I, p. 456.

21. 'Basilicon Doron' in James VI & I, *Political Writings*, p. 38.

22. James VI & I, *Letters*, pp. 338, 336, 337, 338, 339.

23. Anonymous, *Corona Regia*, pp. 89, 81.

24. Historical Manuscripts Commission, *Report on the Manuscripts of the Duke of Buccleuch and Queensberry, K.G.K.T., Preserved at Montagu House, Whitehall. Volume I* (London, 1899), p. 160.

25. Gardiner, 'On Certain Letters of Diego Sarmiento de Acuña', p. 170.

26. Mary Anne Everett Green ed., *Calendar of State Papers Domestic Series, of the Reign of James I &c., 1611–1618* (London, 1858), p. 293.

27. Gardiner, 'On Certain Letters of Diego Sarmiento de Acuña', p. 167.

28. James VI & I, *Letters*, pp. 343, 345, 343–4, 345.

29. Quoted by Bellany, *The Politics of Court Scandal*, p. 218.

30. Bacon, *Letters and Life*, V, p. 290.

31. William A. Shaw and G. Dyfnallt Owen eds., *Historical Manuscript Commission, Report on the Manuscripts of the Right Honourable Viscount De L'Isle V.C., Preserved at Penshurt Place, Kent, Volume V: Sidney Papers 1611–1626* (London, 1962), pp. 331, 332.

32. Bacon, *Letters and Life*, V, p. 211.

33. 'Inventories of the Earl of Somerset's Effects' in Alfred John Kempe ed., *The Loseley Manuscripts* (London, 1836), pp. 406–11.

34. James VI & I, *Letters*, p. 353.

35. Bacon, *Letters and Life*, V, pp. 295, 296.

36. Ibid, p. 299.

37. Ibid, pp. 307, 312–13.

38. HMC *Downshire*, V, p. 507.

39. Quoted by Lindley, *Trials of Frances Howard*, p. 178.

40. Chamberlain, *Letters*, II, p. 60. The new appellation has also been seen as a pro-Danish manoeuvre by James, following his involvement in brokering the Treaty of Stolbovo (1617) agreed between Denmark's traditional adversary, Sweden, and Russia (Jemma Field, *Anna of Denmark: The Material and Visual Culture of the Stuart Courts, 1589–1619* (Manchester, 2020), p. 55).

41. Quoted by Ernesto Eduardo Oyarbide Magaña, 'The First Count of Gondomar's Library and Diplomatic Practice (1613–1622)' (University of Oxford DPhil thesis, 2019), p. 136.

42. Bacon, *Letters and Life*, VI, p. 245.

43. Chamberlain, *Letters*, II, p. 100; see Johanna Luthman, *Love, Madness, and Scandal: The Life of Frances Coke Villiers, Viscountess Purbeck* (Oxford, 2017), Chapter 2.

44. Quoted by Johanna Luthman, *Family and Feuding at the Court of King James: The Lake and Cecil Scandals* (Oxford, 2023), pp. 51–2.

45. Quoted by ibid, p. 184.

46. Chamberlain, *Letters*, II, p. 144.

47. Andrew Thrush, 'The Fall of Thomas Howard, 1st earl of Suffolk and the Revival of Impeachment in the Parliament of 1621', *Parliamentary History*, 37:2 (2018), p. 202.

48. Quoted by Linda Levy Peck, *Court Patronage and Corruption in Early Stuart England* (London, 1990), pp. 184, 183.

49. Chamberlain, *Letters*, II, p. 274.

22 SITTING IN ROYAL JUDGEMENT

1. Ian Williams, 'James VI and I, *Rex et Iudex*: One King as Judge in Two Kingdoms' in William Eves, John Hudson, Ingrid Ivarsen and Sarah B. White eds., *Common Law, Civil Law and Colonial Law: Essays in Comparative Legal History from the Twelfth to the Twentieth Centuries* (Cambridge, 2019), p. 86.

2. Chamberlain, *Letters*, II, p. 213.

3. Johanna Luthman, *Family and Feuding at the Court of King James: The Lake and Cecil Scandals* (Oxford, 2023), p. 178.

4. HMC *Downshire*, VI, p. 596.

5. William Hudson, 'A Treatise of the Court of Star Chamber' in Francis Hargreaves ed., *Collectanea Juridica, consisting of Laws and Tracts relative to the Constitution of England. Volume II* (London, 1792), pp. 9, 8.

6. Chamberlain, *Letters*, II, p. 145.

7. 'Basilicon Doron' in James VI & I, *Political Writings*, p. 37.

8. Chamberlain, *Letters*, II, p. 211. Taken from 1 Kings 3:16–28, the Scriptural tale concerned a dispute between two women who lived together and each had a child, one of whom died after being smothered overnight. After both

women claimed the surviving child as theirs, Solomon pronounced that the child should be cut in half, only for one of the women then to demand that the sentence be stalled and that she would withdraw her claim. Solomon then awarded the child to that woman on the grounds that only the child's natural mother would act in such a way as to preserve its life above all other considerations.

9. For the allusion to Xantippe, see Chamberlain, *Letters*, I, p. 368; for Lady Lake's involvement in the case, see Williams, 'James VI and I: *rex et iudex*', p. 110.

10. Chamberlain, *Letters*, II, p. 214; Mary Anne Everett Green ed., *Calendar of State Papers Domestic Series, of the Reign of James I &c. 1619–1623* (London, 1858), p. 14.

11. CSP *Venice*, XIV, *1615–1617*, p. 597.

12. Chamberlain, *Letters*, II, p. 291.

13. Michael Lynch, 'Court Ceremony and Ritual during the Personal Reign of James VI' in Julian Goodare and Michael Lynch eds., *The Reign of James VI* (East Linton, 2000), p. 75.

14. See Ian Campbell and Aonghus MacKechnie, 'The "Great Temple of Solomon" at Stirling Castle', *Architectural History*, 54 (2011), pp. 91–118.

15. 'Basilicon Doron' in James VI & I, *Political Writings*, pp. 41, 15.

16. [John Hayward], *God's Universal Right Proclaimed. A Sermon preached at Paul's Cross, the 27 of March, 1603, being the next Sunday after Her Majesty's Departure* (London, 1603), sigs. D6v, D7r.

17. John Williams, *Great Britain's Salomon. A Sermon preached at the magnificent Funeral of the most High and Mighty King, James, the late King of Great Britaine, France, and Ireland, Defender of the Faith &c.* (London, 1625), p. 37.

18. HMC *Downshire*, VI, p. 626.

19. CSP *Scotland*, X, pp. 523, 524, 523.

20. Mark Godfrey, 'Control and the Constitutional Accountability of the College of Justice in Scotland, 1532–1626' in Ignacio Czeguhn, Jose Antonio López Nevot and Antonio Sanchez Aranda eds., *Control of Supreme Courts in Early Modern Europe* (Berlin, 2018), p. 128.

21. 'Basilicon Doron' in James VI & I, *Political Writings*, p. 45.

22. CSP *Scotland*, XIII, Part I, pp. 426–7. In his brief account of the case, Lord Cooper indicates that it should, more correctly, be referred as '*Auchterlonie & Others* v. *Bruce and Hamilton*'. Contrary to other accounts implying Bruce's stipend had been withheld by James, Cooper denied that the Crown was directly involved; see 'The King *versus* The Court of Session' in Lord Cooper of Culross, *Selected Papers 1922–1954* (Edinburgh, 1957), pp. 116–23.

23. CSP *Scotland*, XIII, Part I, pp. 428, 429.

24. Julian Goodare, *The Government of Scotland 1560–1625* (Oxford, 2004), p. 102.

25. Sir David Dalrymple of Hailes Bart., *Annals of Scotland from the Accession of Malcolm III . . . to the Accession of the House of Stewart &c.*, 3rd edition, 3 vols. (Edinburgh, 1819), III, p. 107.

26. Quoted by Williams, 'James VI and I: *rex et iudex*', p. 90.

27. 'Trew Law of Free Monarchies' in James VI & I, *Political Writings*, p. 75.

28. *The Actis and Constitutionis of the Realme of Scotland Made in Parliament &c.* (Edinburgh, 1566).

29. Quoted by Goodare, *The Government of Scotland*, p. 83. A similar view was reached by Thomas Craig of Riccarton (whose wife was Buchanan's niece) in his manuscript 'Jus Feudale', composed around 1607. From extensive legal research undertaken in his capacity as a parliamentary union commissioner, Craig concluded 'it has to be frankly admitted that the Scots acts are practically the only written source of genuine native law we have.' For Craig, 'customary precedent therefore ranks in authority after statute' (Thomas Craig, *The Jus Feudale by Sir [sic] Thomas Craig of Riccarton &c.*, J. A. Clyde ed., 2 vols. (Edinburgh, 1934), I, pp. 109, 110).

30. 'Trew Law of Free Monarchies' in James VI & I, *Political Writings*, pp. 73, 74, 73.

31. Thomas Park ed., *Nugae Antiquae: Being a Miscellaneous Collection of Original Papers in Prose and Verse &c.* (London, 1804), p. 180.

32. Williams, 'James VI and I: *rex et iudex*', p. 114.

33. Thomas Bilson, *A Sermon preached at Westminster before the King and Queen's Majesties, at their Coronations, on Saint James his day, being the 28 of July 1603* (London, 1603), sigs. A6r, C5r.

34. James S. Hart, *Justice upon Petition: The House of Lords and the Reformation of Justice, 1621–1675* (London, 1991), p. 33.

35. 'House of Commons Journal Volume 1: 13 April 1604 (2nd scribe)', in *Journal of the House of Commons: Volume 1, 1547–1629* (London, 1802), *British History Online* https://www.british-history.ac.uk/commons-jrnl/vol1/13-april-1604-2nd-scribe [accessed 3 November 2024].

36. Ibid, 26 April 1604 (second scribe).

37. *The Records of the Parliaments of Scotland to 1707*, K. M. Brown et al. eds. (St Andrews, 2007–24), 1604/4/20 [accessed 3 November 2024].

38. Bacon, *Letters and Life*, III, pp. 230, 231, 221, 233.

39. *Stuart Royal Proclamations*, I, p. 95.

40. HMC *Salisbury*, XVI, p. 363.

41. 'House of Commons Journal Volume 1: 24 February 1607 (2nd scribe)', in *Journal of the House of Commons: Volume 1, 1547–1629* (London, 1802), *British History Online* https://www.british-history.ac.uk/commons-jrnl/vol1/24-february-1607-2nd-scribe [accessed 4 November 2024].

42. 'Speech to Parliament of 31 March 1607' in James VI & I, *Political Writings*, pp. 162, 163, 162, 163.

43. Bacon, *Letters and Life*, VI, p. 59.

44. 'House of Commons Journal Volume 1: 14 February 1607', in *Journal of the House of Commons: Volume 1, 1547–1629* (London, 1802), *British History Online* https://www.british-history.ac.uk/commons-jrnl/vol1/pp334-335 [accessed 4 November 2024].

45. Bruce Galloway, *The Union of England and Scotland 1603–1608* (Edinburgh, 1986), p. 121.

46. Nicholas Fuller, *The Argument of Master Nicholas Fuller ... wherein it is plainly proved, that the Ecclesiastical Commissioners have no power, by virtue of their commission, to imprison, to put to the oath ex officio, or to fine any of his Majesty's subjects* (London, 1607), pp. 28, 23.

47. James VI & I, *Letters*, pp. 294–5.

48. 'Prohibitions del Roy (1607)' in Steve Sheppard ed., *The Selected Writings and Speeches of Sir Edward Coke. Volume I* (Indianapolis, IN, 2003), pp. 479, 480, 481.

49. HMC *Salisbury*, XIX, p. 345.

50. Quoted by Roland G. Usher, 'James I and Sir Edward Coke', *English Historical Review*, 18:72 (1903), p. 673.

51. 'Appendix II: The Epitaph of Sir Edward Coke' in Sheppard ed., *Selected Writings and Speeches ... Volume III*, p. 1337.

52. 'Sir Rafe Boswell to Dr Milborne', quoted by Usher, 'James I and Sir Edward Coke', p. 670. Although Usher presents this letter as a different account of the exchange in November 1607, Baker dates the letter to February 1609, recalling a separate incident (John H. Baker, *The Reinvention of Magna Carta 1216–1616* (Cambridge, 2017), p. 368, n. 172).

53. See Cressida Ryan, 'An Ignoramus about Latin? The Importance of Latin Literatures to George Ruggle's *Ignoramus*' in Philip Ford and Andrew Taylor eds., *The Early Modern Cultures of Neo-Latin Drama* (Leuven, 2013), pp. 159–74.

54. Chamberlain, *Letters*, I, pp. 597–8.

55. James VI & I, 'The True State of the Case, whether Peacham's Case be Treason or not. In the handwriting of King James' in *Cobbett's Complete Collection of State Trials and Proceedings for High Crimes and other Misdemeanours from the Earliest Period to the Present Time*, Volume II (London, 1809), pp. 871, 873; see also Todd Butler, 'The Cognitive Politics of Writing in Jacobean England: Bacon, Coke and the Case of Edmund Peacham', *Huntington Library Quarterly*, 78:1 (2015), pp. 21–39.

56. James VI & I, 'True State of the Case' in *Cobbett's Complete Collection of State Trials*, II, pp. 877, 880.

57. Quoted by Baker, *Reinvention of Magna Carta*, p. 411.

58. Quoted by Samuel E. Thorne, 'Præmunire and Sir Edward Coke', *Huntington Library Quarterly*, 2:1 (1938), p. 88.

59. 'Speech in Star Chamber of 20 June 1616' in James VI & I, *Political Writings*, pp. 217, 212. In Greek mythology, Ixion was expelled from Olympus after committing a murder and bound to a winged, fiery wheel for all eternity.

60. Ibid, pp. 214, 215, 228.

61. W. R. Prest ed., *The Diary of Sir Richard Hutton 1614–1639, with Related Texts* (London, 1991), p. 12.

62. Quoted by Baker, *Reinvention of Magna Carta*, p. 421.

63. Chamberlain, *Letters*, II, p. 34. Since James had thereafter commended Coke to his Privy Councillors as 'no way corrupt, but a good justiciar', Chamberlain inferred that the king 'meant to hang him with a silken halter' (ibid, p. 38).

64. *Stuart Royal Proclamations*, I, p. 494.

65. Lady de Villiers ed., 'Hastings Journal of the Parliament of 1621', *Camden Miscellany XX*, 3rd series (1953), p. 29.

66. See Bacon, *Letters and Life*, VII, pp. 252–62.

67. Chamberlain, *Letters*, II, p. 383.

68. 'Speech to Parliament of 31 March 1607' in James VI & I, *Political Writings*, p. 171.

69. Charles Dickens, *Bleak House*, Nicola Bradbury ed. (London, 2003), p. 16.

23 A NEW BRITAIN IN ANOTHER WORLD

1. 'A letter from R[ichard] F[errar] to ?', 5 December 1618, Ferrar Papers 93, Magdalene College, Cambridge; Virginia Company Archives Online [accessed 21 June 1624].

2. 'Laws Enacted by the First General Assembly of Virginia' in Donald S. Lutz ed., *Colonial Origins of the American Constitution: A Documentary History* (Indianapolis, IN, 1998), p. 328.

3. 'A letter from R[ichard] F[errar] to ?', 5 December 1618.

4. C. J. Ribton-Turner, *A History of Vagrants and Vagrancy and Beggars and Begging* (London, 1887), p. 143.

5. See Ken MacMillan, *Sovereignty and Possession in the English New World: The Legal Foundations of Empire, 1576–1640* (Cambridge, 2006), Introduction.

6. *A Declaration of the State of the Colony and Affairs in Virginia* (London, 1620), p. 8.

7. Quoted by Lauren Working, *The Making of an Imperial Polity: Civility and America in the Jacobean Metropolis* (Cambridge, 2020), p. 80.

8. Wesley Frank Craven, *Dissolution of the Virginia Company: The Failure of a Colonial Experiment* (Gloucester, MA, 1964), p. 54.

9. William Waller Hening ed., *The Statutes at Large; Being a Collection of all the Laws of Virginia from the first Session of the Legislation in the Year 1619*, 13 vols. (New York, 1814–23), I, pp. 57–8.

10. See Christopher J. Bilodeau, 'The Paradox of Sagadahoc: The Popham Colony, 1607–1608', *Early American Studies: An Interdisciplinary Journal*, 12:1 (2014), pp. 1–35.

11. Richard Crakanthorpe, *A Sermon at the Solemnising of the Happy Inauguration of our most Gracious and Religious Sovereign King James &c.* (London, 1609), sigs. B2v, D2v.

12. P. L. Barbour ed., *The Jamestown Voyages under the First Chapter, 1609–1609. Volume 1* (Cambridge, 1969), pp. 118, 119, 118, 120.

13. HMC *Salisbury*, XX, p. 185.

14. Quoted by Edmond Smith, 'Reinterpreting the Virginia Island Plantation, 1609–1618', *Journal of British Studies*, 61:4 (2022), p. 901.

15. Quoted by Michael J. Jarvis, *Isle of Devils, Isle of Saints: An Atlantic History of Bermuda, 1609–1684* (Baltimore, MD, 2022), p. 27.

16. [Francis Bacon], *A Declaration of the Demeanour and Carriage of Sir Walter Raleigh, Knight, as well in his Voyage, as in, and since his Return &c.* (London, 1618), sigs. Ar, A2v, A3v.

17. Agnes Latham and Joyce Youings eds., *The Letters of Sir Walter Ralegh* (Exeter, 1999), pp. 351, 350.

18. Quoted by Melissa N. Morris, 'Virginia and the Amazonian Alternative' in Paul Musselwhite, Peter C. Mancall and James Horn eds., *Virginia 1619: Slavery and Freedom in the Making of English America* (Chapel Hill, NC, 2019), pp. 276–7.

19. Joyce Lorimer ed., *English and Irish Settlement on the River Amazon, 1550–1646* (London, 1989), pp. 205, 206.

20. Ibid, pp. 209, 208, 211, 219.

21. Sir William Foster ed., *The Embassy of Sir Thomas Roe to India as Narrated in his Journal and Correspondence* (London, 1926), pp. 270, 378.

22. Ibid, p. 99.

23. Quoted by Nandini Das, *Courting India: England, Mughal India and the Origins of Empire* (London, 2023), pp. 37–8.

24. Quoted by Vera Keller, *The Interlopers: Early Stuart Projects and the Undisciplining of Knowledge* (Baltimore, MD, 2023), p. 129.

25. Quoted by Richmond Barbour, *The Loss of the 'Trades Increase': An Early Modern Maritime Catastrophe* (Philadelphia, PA, 2021), pp. 43, 44.

26. Rachel Peat ed., *Japan: Courts and Culture* (London, 2020), pp. 9, 14.

27. Quoted by Timon Screech, *The Shogun's Silver Telescope: God, Art, and Money in the English Quest for Japan, 1600–1625* (Oxford, 2020), pp. 151–2.

28. See Joseph Wagner, 'The Scottish East India Company of 1617: Patronage, Commercial Rivalry, and the Union of the Crowns', *Journal of British Studies*, 59:3 (2020), pp. 582–607.

29. Quoted by Jarvis, *Isle of Devils*, p. 100.

30. Quoted by Francis J. Bremer, *One Small Candle: The Story of the Plymouth Puritans and the Beginnings of English New England* (Oxford, 2020), p. 74.

31. 'Agreement between the Settlers at New Plymouth (The Mayflower Compact)' in Lutz ed., *Colonial Origins of the American Constitution*, p. 32.

32. Vernon A. Ives ed., *The Rich Papers: Letters from Bermuda, 1615–1646. Eyewitness Accounts sent by the early Colonists to Sir Nathaniel Rich* (Toronto, 1984), pp. 187, 186, 196–7, 196, 193.

33. Quoted by E. M. Rose, 'The "Bewitching Lotteries for Virginia", 1616–21: A List of Sites and Charitable Donations', *Huntington Library Quarterly*, 81:1 (2018), p. 110.

34. Quoted by E. M. Rose, 'The End of the Gamble: The Termination of the Virginia Lotteries in March 1621', *Parliamentary History*, 27:2 (2008), p. 182.

35. Quoted by Andrew Thrush, 'Sir Edwin Sandys' in Andrew Thrush ed., *The House of Commons 1604–1629*, 6 vols. (Cambridge, 2010), VI, pp. 186–7.

36. Susan Myra Kingsbury ed., *The Records of the Virginia Company of London*, 4 vols. (Washington DC, 1906–1935), III, p. 672.

37. Quoted by Alden T. Vaughan, *Roots of American Racism: Essays on the Colonial Experience* (New York, 2023), p. 297n.

38. E. M. Rose, 'Pocahontas's Trip to England: The View from London, 1616–1617' in Kathryn N. Gray and Amy M. E. Morris eds., *Matoaka, Pocahontas, Rebecca: Her Atlantic Identities and Afterlives* (Charlottesville, VA, 2024), p. 118.

39. John Smith, *The General History of Virginia, New England and the Summer Isles, with the Names of the Adventurers, Planters and Governors from their first Beginning, Anno 1584 to this present 1624* (London, 1624), pp. 122, 123.

40. Quoted by Charlotte Ickes, 'The Sartorial and the Skin: Portraits of Pocahontas and Allegories of English Empire', *American Art*, 29:1 (2015), p. 83.

41. Edward Waterhouse, *A Declaration of the State of the Colony and Affairs in Virginia, with a Relation of the Barbarous Massacre in the Time of Peace and League, treacherously executed by the Native Infidels upon the English, the 22 of March last* (London, 1622), p. 22; see Nicholas K. Mohlmann, 'Making a Massacre: The 1622 Virginia "Massacre", Violence, and the Virginia Company of London's Corporate Speech', *Early American Studies: An Interdisciplinary Journal*, 19:3 (2021), pp. 419–56.

42. John Donne, *A Sermon upon the VIII Verse of the First Chapter of the Acts of the Apostles preached to the Honourable Company of the Virginian Plantation, 13 November 1622* (London, 1622), sigs. A3r–v, p. 19.

43. Noel Malcolm, 'Hobbes, Sandys, and the Virginia Company' in Noel Malcolm, *Aspects of Hobbes* (Oxford, 2002), p. 60.

44. Donne, *A Sermon upon the VIII Verse*, pp. 12, 13.

45. Barbour ed., *Jamestown Voyages*, I, p. 115.

46. Cited in General Sir J. Henry Lefroy ed., *The History of the Bermudas or Summer Islands* (London, 1882), p. 296; see Jarvis, *Isle of Devils*, p. 85.

47. Kingsbury ed., *Virginia Company Records*, II, p. 376.

48. Ives ed., *The Rich Papers*, p. 259.

49. Peter Peckard ed., *Memoirs of the Life of Mr Nicholas Ferrar* (Cambridge, 1790), pp. 115–16.
50. Quoted by Craven, *Dissolution*, p. 272.
51. Jarvis, *Isle of Devils*, p. 105.
52. Chamberlain, *Letters*, II, p. 555.
53. Louis H. Roper, *The English Empire in America, 1602–1658: Beyond Jamestown* (London, 2009), p. 89.
54. Minnie G. Cook ed., 'Sir Thomas [sic] Wyatt, Governor: Documents, 1624–1626', *William and Mary College Quarterly Historical Magazine*, 8:3 (1928), p. 160.
55. Jonathan Barth, *The Currency of Empire: Money and Power in Seventeenth-Century English America* (Cornell, NY, 2022), p. 45.
56. *Stuart Royal Proclamations*, I, p. 601.
57. James F. Larkin ed., *Stuart Royal Proclamations. Volume 2: Royal Proclamations of King Charles I, 1625–1646* (Oxford, 1983), p. 28.

24 I AM AN OLD KING

1. Bacon, *Letters and Life*, VI, pp. 251, 252.
2. Quoted by Samuel Rawson Gardiner, *History of England from the Accession of James I to the Outbreak of Civil War 1603–1642*, Volume III (London, 1883), p. 98.
3. Quoted by Robert Zaller, *The Parliament of 1621: A Study in Constitutional Conflict* (Berkeley, CA, 1971), p. 70.
4. Bacon, *Letters and Life*, VI, pp. 27, 14, 15, 26, 14.
5. See Roger Lockyer, *Buckingham: The Life and Political Career of George Villiers, First Duke of Buckingham, 1592–1628* (Harlow, 1981), p. 155.
6. Quoted by Lucy Hughes-Hallett, *The Scapegoat: The Brilliant Brief Life of the Duke of Buckingham* (London, 2024), p. 158.
7. John Hacket, *Scrinia Reserata. A Memorial offered to the great Deservings of John Williams, DD, who some time held the Places of Lord Keeper of the Great Seal of England, Lord Bishop of Lincoln, and Lord Archbishop of York &c.* (London, 1693), p. 120.
8. See Christiane Hille, *Visions of the Courtly Body: The Patronage of George Villiers, first Duke of Buckingham, and the Triumph of Painting at the Stuart Court* (Berlin, 2012), pp. 197–213.
9. Henry Wotton, *Reliquiae Wottonianae, or, A Collection of Lives, Letters, Poems with Characters of Sundry Personages: and other incomparable pieces of Language and Art &c.* (London, 1672), p. 163.
10. P. R. Seddon ed., *Letters of John Holles, 1587–1637. Volume II* (Nottingham, 1983), II, p. 174.

11. James VI and I, *A Meditation upon the Lord's Prayer, written by the King's Majesty, for the Benefit of all his Subjects, especially of such as follow the Court* (London, 1619), sigs. A5v, A6r.

12. CSP *Venice*, XVIII, *1623–1625*, p. 438.

13. Elisabeth Bourcier ed., *The Diary of Sir Simonds D'Ewes (1622–1624)* (Paris, 1974), p. 87.

14. David M. Bergeron, *King James & Letters of Homoerotic Desire* (Iowa City, IA, 1999), pp. 180, 203, 49, 179.

15. James VI, *Demonology, in Form of a Dialogue, divided into Three Books* (Edinburgh, 1597), pp. 13, 14, 13.

16. Thomas Birch ed., *The Court and Times of James the First; illustrated by authentic and confidential letters &c.*, 2 vols. (London, 1838), II, p. 110.

17. James VI & I, *Poems*, II, p. 173.

18. Quoted by Isabel B. Taylor, *The Crown and its Records: Archives, Access and the Ancient Constitution in Seventeenth-Century England* (Berlin, 2023), pp. 355–6.

19. CSP *Venice*, XV, *1617–1619*, p. 366.

20. James VI & I, *Poems*, II, p. 175.

21. James VI & I, *Royal Correspondence*, pp. 197, 198.

22. Chamberlain, *Letters*, II, pp. 225, 227.

23. Nadine Akkerman ed., *The Correspondence of Elizabeth Stuart, Queen of Bohemia. Volume 1: 1603–1631* (Oxford, 2015), p. 195.

24. See Jemma Field, '"Orderinge Things according to His Majesties Comaundment": The Funeral of the Stuart Queen Consort, Anna of Denmark', *Women's History Review*, 30:5 (2021), pp. 835–55.

25. Chamberlain, *Letters*, II, p. 242.

26. Peter H. Wilson, 'Was the Thirty Years' War a "Total War"?' in Erica Charters, Eve Rosenhaft and Hannah Smith eds., *Civilians and War in Europe, 1618–1815* (Liverpool, 2012), p. 26.

27. Akkerman ed., *Correspondence of Elizabeth Stuart*, I, p. 202.

28. Samuel Rawson Gardiner ed., *Letters and other Documents illustrating the Relations between England and Germany at the Commencement of the Thirty Years Wars. Second Series* (London, 1868), pp. 40, 41, 42.

29. Quoted by Simon Adams, 'Foreign Policy and the Parliaments of 1621 and 1624' in Kevin Sharpe ed., *Faction and Parliament: Essays on Early Stuart History* (Oxford, 1978), p. 147.

30. [John Harrison], *A Short Relation of the Departure of the High and Mighty Prince Frederick, King-Elect of Bohemia: With His Royal & Virtuous Lady Elizabeth; And the Thrice Hopeful Young Prince Henry, From Heidelberg towards Prague &c.* (Dort, 1619), sigs. A3v, B4v.

31. CSP *Venice*, XVI, *1619–1621*, p. 76.

32. Samuel Rawson Gardiner trans. and ed., *El Hecho de Los Tratados del Matrimonio Pretendido por el Principe de Gales con La Serenissima Infante de España, Maria . . . Narrative of the Spanish Marriage Treaty* (London, 1869), pp. 313–14, 318.

33. Quoted by Ernesto Eduardo Oyarbide Magaña, 'The First Count of Gondomar's Library and Diplomatic Practice (1613–1622)' (University of Oxford DPhil thesis, 2019), p. 205.

34. CSP *Venice*, XVI, *1619–1621*, pp. 275, 274.

35. Ibid, p. 363.

36. Akkerman ed., *Letters of Elizabeth*, I, p. 254.

37. CSP *Venice*, XVI, *1619–1621*, p. 417.

38. Quoted by Adam Marks, *England and the Thirty Years' War* (Leiden, 2022), p. 84.

39. [Thomas Scott] *Vox Populi, or News from Spain, Translated according to the Spanish Copy. Which may Serve to Forewarn Both England and the United Provinces How Far to Trust to Spanish Pretences* ([London, 1620]), sig. Br.

40. CSP *Venice*, XVI, *1619–1621*, p. 491.

41. Quoted by David Coast, 'Speaking for the People in Early Modern England', *Past & Present*, 244 (2019), p. 79.

42. James VI & I, *Poems*, II, p. 173.

43. John Earle, *Microcosmographie, or A Piece of the world Discovered in Essays and Characters* (London, 1628), 'No. 53, 'Pauls Walke'.

44. *Stuart Royal Proclamations*, I, pp. 495, 496, 496n.

45. Quoted by Jayne E. E. Boys, *London's News Press and the Thirty Years War* (Woodbridge, 2011), p. 68.

46. Quoted by Curtis Perry, 'The Politics of Access and Representations of the Sodomite King in Early Modern England', *Renaissance Quarterly*, 53:4 (2000), pp. 1075, 1076. Etymologically, 'Ganymede' was the Latin root of 'catamite', denoting a young boy involved in a pederastic relationship with an older man.

47. Quoted by Paul Hammond, *Figuring Sex between Men from Shakespeare to Rochester* (Oxford, 2002), p. 142.

48. Quoted by Alastair Bellany, *The Politics of Court Scandal in Early Modern England: News Culture and the Overbury Affair, 1603–1660* (Cambridge, 2002), p. 258.

49. Samuel Rawson Gardiner ed., *Notes of the Debates in the House of Lords, Officially taken by Henry Elsing, Clerk of the Parliaments, AD 1621* (London, 1870), p. 48; quoted by Curtis Perry, 'Yelverton, Buckingham, and the Story of Edward II in the 1620s', *The Review of English Studies*, 54:215 (2003), pp. 314.

50. Brennan Pursell, 'War or Peace? Jacobean Politics and the Parliament of 1621' in Chris R. Kyle ed., *Parliament, Politics and Elections 1604–1648* (Cambridge, 2001), pp. 161, 162.

51. 'His Majesty's Declaration, touching his proceedings in the late Assembly and Convention of Parliament' in James VI & I, *Political Writings*, pp. 255, 257, 257–8, 258.

52. Quoted by W. P. Patterson, *King James VI and I and the Reunion of Christendom* (Cambridge, 1997), p. 313.

53. James Orchard Halliwell ed., *Letters of the Kings of England, Now first Collected from Royal Archives &c.*, 2 vols. (London, 1846), II, p. 172.

54. James VI & I, *Letters*, p. 392.

55. Quoted by Marks, *England and the Thirty Years' War*, p. 109.

56. James VI & I, *Letters*, pp. 394, 395, 396.

57. Bergeron, *Letters of Homoerotic Desire*, pp. 189, 190.

58. James VI & I, *Letters*, pp. 416, 417, 420.

59. Bergeron, *Letters of Homoerotic Desire*, pp. 197, 199.

60. '19th February 1624', in *Proceedings in Parliament 1624: The House of Commons*, ed. Philip Baker (2015–18), *British History Online* http://www.british-history.ac.uk/no-series/proceedings-1624-parl/feb-19 [accessed 3 September 2024].

61. '25th March 1624' and '1st April 1624' in *Proceedings in Parliament 1624: The House of Commons*, ed. Philip Baker (2015–18), *British History Online* http://www.british-history.ac.uk/no-series/proceedings-1624-parl/mar-25 [accessed 3 September 2024].

62. *Cabala. Mysteries of State, in Letters of the Great Ministers of King James and King Charles* (London, 1654), p. 91.

63. Robert E. Ruigh, *The Parliament of 1624: Politics and Foreign Policy* (Harvard, MA, 1971), pp. 279–81.

64. Bergeron, *Letters of Homoerotic Desire*, p. 175.

EPILOGUE

1 Quoted by Alastair Bellany and Thomas Cogswell, *The Murder of King James I* (New Haven, CT, 2015), p. 41; for the Latin account, see W. S. Munk, 'Marvodia: being an account of the last illness of James I and the Post-Mortem examination of his Body' in Walford D. Selby ed., *The Genealogist*, n.s., I (London, 1884), pp. 230–34.

2 Alastair Bellany, 'Writing the King's Death: The Case of James I' in Paulina Kewes and Andrew McRae eds., *Stuart Succession Literature: Moments and Transformations* (Oxford, 2018), p. 55–6.

3 Thomas Heywood, *A Funeral Elegy, upon the much lamented Death of the Trespuissant and Unmatchable King, King James, King of Great Britain, France and Ireland &c.* (London, 1625), sig B4r.

4 Calderwood, *History of the Kirk*, VII, p.632.

5 Chamberain, *Letters*, II, p. 609.

6 Quoted by Bellany, 'Writing the King's Death', pp. 43–4; CSP *Venice*, XIX, *1625–6*, p. 22.

7 Jennifer Woodward, 'The Ritual Management of Royal Death in Renaissance England: 1570–1625', 2 vols. (University of Warwick PhD thesis, 1994), I, p. 318.

8 CSP *Venice*, XIX, *1625–6*, p. 55.

9 Bellany and Cogswell, *Murder of King James I*, p. 46.

10 David Masson ed., *The Register of the Privy Council of Scotland. Second Series. Volume I: A. D. 1625–1627* (Edinburgh, 1899), p. 650.

11 See John Peacock, 'Inigo Jones's Catafalque for James I', *Architectural History*, 25 (1982), pp. 1–5.

12 John Williams, *Great Britain's Salomon. A Sermon preached at the Magnificent Funeral, of the most High and Mighty King, James, the Late King of Great Britain, France, and Ireland &c.* (London, 1625), pp. 37, 57.

13 Ibid, pp. 75–6.

14 Graham Parry, *The Golden Age Restor'd: The Culture of the Stuart Court, 1603–42* (Manchester, 1981), p. 36.

15 George Eglisham, *The Forerunner of Revenge upon the Duke of Buckingham, for the poisoning of the most potent King James of Happy Memory, King of Great Britan, and the Lord Marquis of Hamilton and others of the Nobility &c.* (Frankfurt [Brussels], 1626), pp. 13, 14, 15.

16 Ibid, p. 21.

17 Ibid, pp. 4, 10.

18 CSP *Venice*, XIX, *1625–6*, p. 19.

19 Quoted by Bellany and Cogswell, *Murder of James I*, p. 211.

20 J. J. Cartwright ed., *Historical Manuscripts Commission. Thirteenth Report, Appendix Part VII, The Manuscripts of the Earl of Lonsdale* (London, 1893), p. 5.

21 Quoted by Bellany and Cogswell, *Murder of James I*, p. 219.

22 Ibid, p. 228.

23 *A Declaration of the Commons of England in Parliament Assembled; Expressing their reasons and grounds of passing the late Resolutions touching No Further Address or Application to be made to the King &c.* (London, 1648), p. 17.

24 Bellany and Cogswell, *Murder of James I*, pp. 436–7.

25 Quoted by ibid, p. 449.

26 Anonymous, *A Funeral Elegy upon the lamentable Loss of our late Liege and Royal King James* (London, [1625]), single-sheet folio.

27 John Bastwick, *The Answer of John Bastwick, Doctor of Physic, to the Exceptions made against his Letany [sic] &c.* ([Leiden], 1637), sig. D2v, Br. 'Groll' was a Dutch term for an idiot.

28 Anonymous [?Henry Burton], *England's Complaint to Jesus Christ against the Bishops' Canons of the late Sinful Synod &c.* ([Amsterdam], 1640), sig. A4v.

29 Quoted by David R. Como, *Radical Parliamentarians and the English Civil War* (Oxford, 2018), p. 136. More generally, see Joseph Marshall, 'Reading King James VI and I in the Civil War' (University of Edinburgh PhD thesis, 1999).

30 'James I', *The Duty of a King in his Royal Office, showing how it is to be used in the Administration of Justice and Politic Government in his Kingdoms* (London, 1642), p. 5.

31 Charles I and Alexander Henderson, *The Papers which passed at Newcastle between His Sacred Majesty and Mr Al[expander] Henderson, Concerning the change of Church Government* (London, 1649), pp. 14, 20, 33–4.

32 'Speech to Parliament of 21 March 1610' in James VI & I, *Political Writings*, pp. 181, 179, 184.

33 Ibid, pp. 179, 203.

Select Bibliography

PRIMARY SOURCES

Anonymous, *Corona Regia*, Winfried Schleiner and Tyler Fyotek (eds. and trans.) (Geneva, 2010).

Robert Ashton (ed.), *James I by his Contemporaries: An Account of his Career and Character as seen by some of his Contemporaries* (London, 1969).

Francis Bacon, *The Letters and the Life of Francis Bacon including all his Occasional Works &c.*, James Spedding (ed.), 7 vols. (London, 1861–74).

Joseph Bain (ed.), *Calendar of Letters and Papers relating to the Affairs of the Borders of England and Scotland &c.*, 2 vols. (Edinburgh, 1894).

Richard Bancroft, *A Sermon preached at Paul's Cross, the 9 of February, being the first Sunday in the Parliament &c.* (London, 1589).

P. L. Barbour (ed.), *The Jamestown Voyages under the First Chapter, 1609–1609. Volume 1* (Cambridge, 1969).

William Barlow, *The Sum and Substance of the Conference which, it pleased his excellent Majesty to have with the Lords, Bishops, and other of his Clergy &c.* (London, 1604).

Thomas Birch, *The Life of Henry Prince of Wales, Eldest Son of King James I. Compiled Chiefly from his own Papers, and other Manuscripts, never before Published* (Dublin, [1760]).

[Thomas Birch ed.], *The Court and Times of James the First; illustrated by Authentic and Confidential letters from Various Public and Private Collections &c.*, 2 vols. (London, 1848).

Robert Bowes, *The Correspondence of Robert Bowes, of Aske, Esquire, The Ambassador of Queen Elizabeth in the Court of Scotland*, Joseph Stevenson (ed.) (London, [1843]).

Robert Bowyer, *The Parliamentary Diary of Robert Bowyer, 1606–1607*, David Harris Willson (ed.) (New York, 1971).

George Buchanan, *A Dialogue on the Law of Kingship among the Scots. A Critical Edition and Translation of George Buchanan's De Iure Regni apud Scotos Dialogus*, Roger A. Mason and Martin S. Smith (eds.) (Aldershot, 2004).

John Hill Burton (ed.), *The Register of the Privy Council of Scotland, Volume I: A. D. 1545–1569, Volume II: A. D. 1569–1578* and *Volume III: A. D. 1578–1585* (Edinburgh, 1877, 1878, 1880).

David Calderwood, *The History of the Kirk of Scotland*, Thomas Thomson (ed.), 8 vols. (Edinburgh, 1842–9).

Annie I. Cameron and Robert S. Rait (eds.), *The Warrender Papers*, 2 vols. (Edinburgh, 1931–2).

Luisa de Carvajal y Mendoza, *The Letters of Luisa de Carvajal y Mendoza*, Glyn Redworth (ed.), 2 vols. (London, 2012).

Robert Cary, *Memoirs of Robert Cary, Earl of Monmouth, Written by Himself*, Sir Walter Scott (ed.), (Edinburgh, 1808).

John Chamberlain, *The Letters of John Chamberlain*, Norman Egbert McClure (ed.), 2 vols. (Philadelphia, PA, 1939).

James Craigie, 'Last Poems of James VI', *Scottish Historical Review*, 29:108, Part 2 (1950), pp. 134–42.

Sir John Davies, *A Discovery of the True Causes why Ireland was never entirely subdued, nor brought under obedience of the crown of England, until the beginning of His Majesty's Happy Reign* (London, 1612).

Thomas Dekker, *1603. The Wonderful Year. Wherein is showed the Picture of London Lying Sick of the Plague &c.* (London, 1603).

George Eglisham, *The Forerunner of Revenge upon the Duke of Buckingham, for the poisoning of the most potent King James of Happy Memory, King of Great Britan, and the Lord Marquis of Hamilton and others of the Nobility &c.* (Frankfurt [Brussels], 1626).

Elizabeth Read Foster (ed.), *Proceedings in Parliament, 1610*, 2 vols. (New Haven, CT, 1966).

William Fowler, *A True Reportarie of the Most Triumphant, and Royal Accomplishment of the Baptism of the most Excellent, Right High, and Mighty Prince, Frederick Henry &c.* ([Edinburgh], 1594).

Bruce R. Galloway and Brian P. Levack (eds.), *The Jacobean Union: Six Tracts of 1604* (Edinburgh, 1985).

Godfrey Goodman, *The Court of King James the First; by Dr Godfrey Goodman, Bishop of Gloucester &c.*, John S. Brewer (ed.), 2 vols. (London, 1839).

John Hacket, *Scrinia Reserata. A Memorial offered to the great Deservings of John Williams, DD, who some time held the Places of Lord Keeper of the Great Seal of England, Lord Bishop of Lincoln, and Lord Archbishop of York &c.* (London, 1693).

Sir John Harington, *A Tract on the Succession to the Crown (A.D. 1602)*, Clements R. Markham (ed.), (London, 1880).

James VI, *A Fruitful Meditation containing a plain and facile Exposition of the 7, 8, 9 and 10 verses of the 20 chapter of the Revelation in form of a Sermon* (Edinburgh, 1588).

James VI, *Daemonologie in form of a Dialogue, Divided into Three Books* (Edinburgh, 1597).

[James VI & I], *A Counterblaste to Tobacco* (London, 1604).

James VI & I, *His Majesty's Speech in this last session of Parliament as near his very Words as could be Gathered at the Instant. Together with a Discourse of the Manner of the Discovery of this late intended Treason, joined with the Examination of some of the Prisoners* (London, 1605).

James VI & I, *An Apology for the Oath of Allegiance first set forth without a name, and now acknowledged by the Author, the Right High and Mighty Prince, James, by the Grace of God, King of Great Britain, France and Ireland, Defender of the Faith, &c.* (London, 1609).

James VI & I, *A Remonstrance of the most gracious King James I, King of Great Britain, France, and Ireland, Defender of the Faith, &c. For the right of Kings, and the Independence of their Crowns* ([Cambridge], 1616).

James VI & I, *The Works of the most High and Mighty Prince, James, by the Grace of God, King of Great Britain, France and Ireland, Defender of the Faith &c.* (London, 1616 [1617]).

James VI & I, *A Meditation upon the Lord's Prayer, written by the King's Majesty, for the Benefit of all his Subjects &c.* (London, 1619).

James VI & I, *The Kings Majesty's Letter to the Lords Grace of Canterbury, touching Preaching, and Preachers* ([London, 1622]).

James VI & I, *Letters of Queen Elizabeth and King James VI of Scotland*, John Bruce (ed.) (London, 1849).

James VI & I, *The Basilicon Doron of King James VI, with an Introduction, Notes, Appendices, and Glossary*, James Craigie (ed.), 2 vols. (Edinburgh, 1944–50).

James VI & I, *The Poems of King James VI of Scotland*, James Craigie (ed.), 2 vols. (Edinburgh, 1955–8).

James VI & I, *The Royal Correspondence of King James I of England (VI of Scotland), to his Royal Brother-in-Law, King Christian IV of Denmark 1603–1625 &c.*, Ronald M. Meldrum (ed.) (Hassocks, 1977).

James VI & I, *Minor Prose Works of King James VI and I*, James Craigie (ed.) (Edinburgh, 1982).

James VI & I, *Letters of King James VI & I*, G. P. V. Akrigg (ed.), (Berkeley, CA, 1984).

James VI & I, *James VI and I: Political Writings*, Johann P. Sommerville (ed.) (Cambridge, 1994).

Maija Jansson (ed.), *Proceedings in Parliament, 1614* (Philadelphia, PA, 1988).

Susan Myra Kingsbury (ed.), *The Records of the Virginia Company of London*, 4 vols. (Washington DC, 1906–35).

James F. Larkin and Paul L. Hughes (eds.), *Stuart Royal Proclamations. Volume 1: Royal Proclamations of King James 1603–1625* (Oxford, 1973).

George Marcelline, *The Triumphs of King James the First, of Great Britain, France, and Ireland, King; Defender of the Faith &c.* ([London], 1610).

David Masson (ed.), *The Register of the Privy Council of Scotland, Volume IV: AD 1585–1592, Volume V: AD 1592–1599, Volume VI: AD 1599–1604, Volume VII: AD 1604–1607* and *Volume X: AD 1613–1616* (Edinburgh, 1881, 1882, 1774, 1885, 1891).

Sir James Melville, *Memoirs of His Own Life by Sir James Melville of Halhill. MDLXIX–MDXCIII*, Thomas Thomson (ed.) (Edinburgh, 1827).

James Melville, *The Autobiography and Diary of Mr James Melvill ... with a Continuation of the Diary*, Robert Pitcairn (ed.) (Edinburgh, 1842).

David Moysie, *Memoirs of the Affairs of Scotland. By David Moysie. MDLXXVII–MDCIII*, James Dennistoun (ed.) (Edinburgh, 1830).

John Nichols, *The Progresses, Processions and Magnificent Festivities of James the First, his Royal Consort, Family and Court &c.*, 4 vols. (London, 1828).

Anthony Nixon, *Oxford's Triumph in the Royal Entertainment of his most Excellent Majesty, the Queen, and the Prince, the 27 of August last, 1605 &c.* (London, 1605).

Lawrence Normand and Gareth Roberts (eds.), *Witchcraft in Early Modern Scotland: James VI's Demonology and the North Berwick Witches* (Exeter, 2000).

Wallace Notestein, Frances Helen Relf and Hartley Simpson (eds.), *Commons Debates, 1621*, 7 vols. (New Haven, CT, 1935).

Henry Peacham, *Minerva Britanna* [sic]*, or A Garden of Heroical Devices furnished, and adorned with Emblems and Impresas of sundry natures, newly devised, moralised and published &c* (London, 1612).

[Robert Persons], *A Conference about the Next Succession to the Crown of England, divided into Two Parts &c.*, ([Antwerp, 1595]).

Walter Quin, *The Works of Walter Quin: An Irishman at the Stuart Courts*, John Flood (ed.) (Dublin, 2014).

Steven J. Reid and David McOmish (eds.), *Neo-Latin Literature and Literary Culture in Early Modern Scotland* (Leiden, 2017).

The Holy Bible, containing the Old Testament, and the New, Newly Translated out of the Original Tongues &c. (London, 1611).

Andrew Thrush (ed.), *The House of Lords, 1604–1629*, 3 vols. (Cambridge, 2021).

George F. Warner (ed.), 'The Library of James VI, 1573–1583 from a Manuscript in the Hand of Peter Young, his Tutor' in *Miscellany of the Scottish History Society* (Edinburgh, 1893).

John Williams, *Great Britain's Salomon. A Sermon preached at the Magnificent Funeral, of the Most High and Mighty King, James, the late King of Great Britain, France, and Ireland, Defender of the Faith*, &c. (London, 1625).

SECONDARY SOURCES

Rayne Allinson, *A Monarchy of Letters: Royal Correspondence and English Diplomacy in the Reign of Elizabeth I* (Basingstoke, 2012).

Peter Auger, *Du Bartas' Legacy in England and Scotland* (Oxford, 2019).

Alastair Bellany, *The Politics of Court Scandal in Early Modern England: News Culture and the Overbury Affair, 1603–1660* (Cambridge, 2002).

Alastair Bellany and Thomas Cogswell, *The Murder of James I* (New Haven, CT, 2016).

Alastair Bellany, 'Of Gods and Beasts: The Many Bodies of James VI and I' in William J. Bulman and Freddy C. Domínguez (eds.), *Political and Religious Practice in the Early Modern British World* (Manchester, 2022), pp. 220–40.

David M. Bergeron, *King James & Letters of Homoerotic Desire* (Iowa City, IA, 1999).

Stephen I. Boardman, Julian Goodare and Jenny Wormald (eds.), *Kings, Lords and Men in Scotland and Britain, 1300–1625: Essays in Honour of Jenny Wormald* (Edinburgh, 2014).

Rick Bowers, 'James VI, Prince Henry and "A True Reportarie" of the Baptism at Stirling, 1594', *Renaissance and Reformation/Renaissance et Réforme*, n.s., 29:4 (2005), pp. 3–22.

Keith M. Brown, *Bloodfeud in Scotland 1573–1625: Violence, Justice and Politics in an Early Modern Society* (Edinburgh, 1986).

Valentina Caldari and Sara J. Wolfson (eds.), *Stuart Marriage Diplomacy: Dynastic Politics in their European Context, 1604–1630* (Woodbridge, 2018).

Gordon Campbell, *Bible: The Story of the King James Version, 1611–2011* (Oxford, 2010).

Stephen Clucas and Rosalind Davies (eds.), *The Crisis of 1614 and the Addled Parliament: Literary and Historical Perspectives* (Farnham, 2003).

Thomas Cogswell, 'Underground Verse and the Transformation of Early Stuart Political Culture', *Huntington Library Quarterly*, 60:3 (1997), pp. 303–26.

David Colclough, *Freedom of Speech in Early Stuart England* (Cambridge, 2005).

Alexander Courtney, 'The Scottish King and the English Court: The Secret Correspondence of James VI, 1601–1603' in Susan Doran and Paulina Kewes (eds.), *Doubtful and Dangerous: The Question of Succession in Late Elizabethan England* (Manchester, 2014), pp. 134–51.

Alexander Courtney, *James VI, Britannic Prince: King of Scots and Elizabeth's Heir, 1566–1603* (Abingdon, 2024).

John Cramsie, *Kingship and Crown Finance under James VI and I, 1603–1625* (Woodbridge, 2002).

Nandini Das, *Courting India: England, Mughal India and the Origins of Empire* (London, 2023).

Susan Doran, *From Tudor to Stuart: The Regime Change from Elizabeth I to James I* (Oxford, 2024).

J. H. Elliott and L. W. B. Brockliss (eds.), *The World of the Favourite* (New Haven, CT, 1999).

Lori-Anne Ferrell, *Government by Polemic: James I, the King's Preachers and the Rhetorics of Conformity, 1603–1625* (Stanford, CA, 1998).

Jemma Field, *Anna of Denmark: The Material and Visual Culture of the Stuart Courts, 1589–1619* (Manchester, 2020).

Kenneth Fincham, *Prelate as Pastor: The Episcopate of James I* (Oxford, 1990).

Kenneth Fincham, 'The King James Bible: Crown, Church and People', *Journal of Ecclesiastical History*, 17:1 (2020), pp. 77–97.

Daniel Fischlin and Mark Fortier (eds.), *Royal Subjects: Essays on the Writings of James VI and I* (Detroit, MI, 2002).

Bruce Galloway, *The Union of England and Scotland 1603–1608* (Edinburgh, 1986).

Julian Goodare, *State and Society in Early Modern Scotland* (Oxford, 1999).

Julian Goodare, *The Government of Scotland 1560-1625* (Oxford, 2004).

Julian Goodare, 'The Debts of James VI of Scotland', *Economic History Review*, 62:4 (2009), pp. 926–52.

Julian Goodare and Alasdair A. MacDonald (eds.), *Sixteenth-Century Scotland: Essays in Honour of Michael Lynch* (Leiden, 2008).

Julian Goodare and Michael Lynch (eds.), *The Reign of James VI* (East Linton, 2000).

Hannibal Hamlin and Norman W. Jones (eds.), *The King James Bible after 400 Years: Literary, Linguistic, and Cultural Influences* (Cambridge, 2010).

Maria Hayward, *Stuart Style: Monarchy, Dress and the Scottish Male Elite* (New Haven, CT, 2020).

Peter C. Herman, *Royal Poetrie: Monarchic Verse and the Political Imaginary of Early Modern England* (Ithaca, NY, 2010).

Christiane Hille, *Visions of the Courtly Body: The Patronage of George Villiers, First Duke of Buckingham, and the Triumph of Painting at the Stuart Court* (Berlin, 2012).

Ralph Houlbrooke (ed.), *James VI and I: Ideas, Authority and Government* (Aldershot, 2006).

Lucy Hughes-Hallett, *The Scapegoat: The Brilliant Brief Life of the Duke of Buckingham* (London, 2024).

Lorna Hutson, *England's Insular Imagining: The Elizabethan Erasure of Scotland* (Cambridge, 2023).

Christopher Ivic, *The Subject of Britain, 1603–1625* (Manchester, 2020).

Lisa Jardine and Alan Stewart, *Hostage to Fortune: The Troubled Life of Francis Bacon* (London, 1998).

Rei Kanemura, 'Kingship by Descent or Kingship by Election? The Contested Title of James VI', *Journal of British Studies*, 52:2 (2013), pp. 317–42.

Rei Kanemura, 'Historical Perspectives on the Anglo-Scottish Union Debate: Re-reading the Norman Conquest in the 1610s', *History of European Ideas*, 40:2 (2014), pp. 155–76.

Vera Keller, *The Interlopers: Early Stuart Projects and the Undisciplining of Knowledge* (Baltimore, MD, 2023).

Miles Kerr-Peterson and Steven J. Reid (eds.), *James VI and Noble Power in Scotland, 1578–1603* (Abingdon, 2017).

Paulina Kewes and Andrew McRae (eds.), *Stuart Succession Literature: Moments and Transformations* (Oxford, 2019).

Peter Lake, 'The King, (The Queen) and the Jesuit: James Stuart's *True Law of Free Monarchies* in Context/s', *Transactions of the Royal Historical Society*, Sixth series, 14 (2004), pp. 243–60.

Pete Langman (ed.), *Negotiating the Jacobean Printed Book* (Farnham, 2011).

George Lasry, Norbert Biermann and Satoshi Tomokiyo, 'Deciphering Mary Stuart's Lost Letters from 1578–1584', *Cryptologia*, 47:2 (2023), pp. 101–202.

Maurice Lee Jr., *Great Britain's Solomon: James VI and I in His Three Kingdoms* (Urbana, IL, 1990).

Brian P. Levack, *Witch-Hunting in Scotland: Law, Politics and Religion* (London, 2008).

Roger Lockyer, *Buckingham: The Life and Political Career of George Villiers, First Duke of Buckingham, 1592–1628* (Harlow, 1981).

Johanna Luthman, *Family and Feuding at the Court of King James: The Lake and Cecil Scandals* (Oxford, 2023).

Roderick J. Lyall, 'The Marketing of James VI and I: Scotland, England and the Continental Book Trade', *Quærendo*, 32:3-4 (2002), pp. 204–17.

Michael Lynch, 'Scotland's First Protestant Coronation: Revolutionaries, Sovereignty and the Culture of Nostalgia' in Luuk Houwen (ed.), *Literature and Religion in Late Medieval and Early Modern Scotland: Essays in Honour of Alasdair A. MacDonald* (Louvain, 2012), pp. 177–208.

Aonghas MacCoinnich, *Plantation and Civility in the North Atlantic World: The Case of the Northern Hebrides, 1570–1639* (Leiden, 2015).

Alan R. MacDonald, *The Jacobean Kirk, 1567–1625: Sovereignty, Polity and Liturgy* (Aldershot, 1998).

Alan R. MacDonald, 'Consultation and Consent under James VI', *Historical Journal*, 54:2 (2011), pp. 287–306.

Peter E. McCullough, *Sermons at Court: Politics and Religion in Elizabethan and Jacobean Preaching* (Cambridge, 1998).

I. D. McFarlane, *Buchanan* (London, 1981).

Kevin J. McGinley and Nicola Royan (eds.), *The Apparelling of Truth: Literature and Literary Culture in the Reign of James VI* (Newcastle, 2010).

Andrew McRae, *Literature, Satire and the Early Stuart State* (Cambridge, 2004).

Roger A. Mason, 'George Buchanan, James VI and the Presbyterians' in Roger A. Mason (ed.), *Scots and Britons: Scottish Political Thought and the Union of 1603* (Cambridge, 1994), pp. 112–38.

Maureen M. Meikle and Helen M. Payne, 'From Lutheranism to Catholicism: The Faith of Anna of Denmark (1574–619)', *Journal of Ecclesiastical History*, 64:1 (2013), pp. 45–69.

Catriona Murray, *Imaging Stuart Family Politics: Dynastic Crisis and Continuity* (Abingdon, 2017).

Paul Musselwhite, Peter C. Mancall and James Horn (eds.), *Virginia 1619: Slavery and Freedom in the Making of English America* (Chapel Hill, NC, 2019).

Diana Newton, *The Making of the Jacobean Regime: James VI and I and the Government of England, 1603–1605* (Woodbridge, 2005).

John Newton and Jo Bath (eds.), *Witchcraft and the Act of 1604* (Leiden, 2008).

Éamonn Ó Ciardha and Micheál Ó Siochrú (eds.), *The Plantation of Ulster: Ideology and Practice* (Manchester, 2012).

Brett F. Parker, 'Recasting England: The Varieties of Antiquarian Responses to the Proposed Union of Crowns, 1603–1607', *Journal of Medieval and Early Modern Studies*, 43:2 (2013), pp. 393–417.

David J. Parkinson ed., *James VI and I, Literature and Scotland: Tides of Change, 1567–1625* (Leuven, 2013).

W. B. Patterson, *King James VI and I and the Reunion of Christendom* (Cambridge, 1997).

Linda Levy Peck, *Court Patronage and Corruption in Early Stuart England* (London, 1993).

Michael Perceval-Maxwell, *The Scottish Migration to Ulster in the Reign of James I* (London, 1990).

Timothy Peters, Peter Garrard, Vijeya Ganesan and John Stephenson, 'The Nature of King James VI/I's Medical Conditions: New Approaches to the Diagnosis', *History of Psychiatry*, 23:3 (2012), pp. 277–90.

Aysha Pollnitz, *Princely Education in Early Modern Britain* (Cambridge, 2015).

Michael C. Questier, *Dynastic Politics and the British Reformations, 1558–1630* (Oxford, 2019).

Michael C. Questier, 'The Reputation of James VI and I Revisited', *Journal of British Studies*, 61:4 (2022), pp. 949–69.

Graham Rees and Maria Wakely, *Publishing, Politics and Culture: The King's Printers in the Reign of James I and VI* (Oxford, 2009).

Steven J. Reid, *The Early Life of James VI: A Long Apprenticeship 1566–1585* (Edinburgh, 2023).

Steven J. Reid (ed.), *Rethinking the Renaissance and Reformation in Scotland: Essays in Honour of Roger A. Mason* (Woodbridge, 2024).

Jane Rickard, *Authorship and Authority: The Writings of James VI and I* (Manchester, 2007).

Jane Rickard, *Writing the Monarch in Jacobean England: Jonson, Donne, Shakespeare and the Works of King James* (Cambridge, 2015).

Jane Rickard, 'Mover and Author: King James VI and I and the Political Use of the Bible' in Kevin Killeen, Helen Smith and Rachel Willie (eds.), *The Oxford Handbook of the Bible in Early Modern England, c. 1530–1700* (Oxford, 2015), pp. 371–83.

Conrad Russell, *King James VI and I and his English Parliaments*, Richard Cust and Andrew Thrush (eds.) (Oxford, 2011).

Marc L. Schwarz, 'James I and the Historians: Towards a Reconsideration', *Journal of British Studies*, 13:2 (1974), pp. 114–34.

Calvin F. Senning, *Spain, Rumor, and Anti-Catholicism in Mid-Jacobean England: The Palatine Match, Cleves, and the Armada Scares of 1612–1613 and 1614* (London, 2019).

James Sharpe, *The Bewitching of Anne Gunter: A Horrible and True Story of Deception, Witchcraft, Murder and the King of England* (London, 1999).

Peter Sherlock, 'The Monuments of Elizabeth Tudor and Mary Stuart: King James and the Manipulation of Memory', *Journal of British Studies*, 46:2 (2007), pp. 263–89.

Sara Smart and Mara R. Wade (eds.), *The Palatine Wedding of 1613: Protestant Alliance and Court Festival* (Wiesbaden, 2013).

R. Malcolm Smuts, 'Theological Polemics and James I's Diplomacy, 1604–1617', *Journal of Medieval and Early Modern Studies*, 50:3 (2020), pp. 515–40.

R. Malcolm Smuts, *Political Culture, the State, and the Problem of Religious War in Britain and Ireland, 1578–1625* (Oxford, 2023).

David Stevenson, *Scotland's Last Royal Wedding: The Marriage of James VI and Anne of Denmark* (Edinburgh, 1997).

Alan Stewart, *The Cradle King: A Life of James VI & I* (London, 2003).

Alan Stewart, 'Government by Beagle: The Impersonal Rule of James VI and I' in Erica Fudge (ed.), *Renaissance Beasts: Of Animals, Humans and Other Wonderful Creatures* (Urbana, IL, 2004), pp. 101–15.

Astrid Stilma, *A King Translated: The Writings of King James VI & I and their Interpretation in the Low Countries, 1593–1603* (Farnham, 2012).

Isabel B. Taylor, *The Crown and Its Records: Archives, Access and the Ancient Constitution in Seventeenth-Century England* (Berlin, 2023).

Simon Thurley, *Palaces of Revolution: Life, Death and Art at the Stuart Court* (London, 2021).

Will Tosh, *Straight Acting: The Many Queer Lives of William Shakespeare* (London, 2024).

Victor Treadwell, *Buckingham and Ireland 1616–1628: A Study in Anglo-Irish Politics* (Dublin, 1998).

Hugh Trevor-Roper, *Europe's Physician: The Various Life of Sir Theodore de Mayerne* (New Haven, CT, 2006).

Sebastiaan Verweij, '"Booke, go thy wayes": The Publication, Reading and Reception of James VI/I's Early Poetic Works', *Huntington Library Quarterly*, 77:2 (2014), pp. 111–31.

Sebastiaan Verweij, *The Literary Culture of Early Modern Scotland: Manuscript Production and Transmission, 1560–1625* (Oxford, 2015).

Hanna Orsolya Vincze, *The Politics of Translation and Transmission: Basilicon Doron in Hungarian Political Thought* (Newcastle, 2012).

Sarah Waurechen, 'Imagined Polities, Failed Dreams, and the Beginnings of an Unacknowledged Britain: English Responses to James VI and I's Vision of Perfect Union', *Journal of British Studies*, 52:3 (2013), pp. 575–96.

Ian Williams, 'James VI and I, *Rex et Iudex*: One King as Judge in Two Kingdoms' in William Eves, John Hudson, Ingrid Ivarsen and Sarah B. White (eds.), *Common Law, Civil Law and Colonial Law: Essays in Comparative Legal History from the Twelfth to the Twentieth Centuries* (Cambridge, 2019), pp. 86–119.

Jennifer Woodward, *The Theatre of Death: The Ritual Management of Royal Funerals in Renaissance England 1570–1625* (Woodbridge, 1997).

Lauren Working, *The Making of an Imperial Polity: Civility and America in the Jacobean Metropolis* (Cambridge, 2020).

Jenny Wormald, 'James VI and I: Two Kings or One?', *History*, 68:223 (1983), pp. 187–209.

Jenny Wormald, 'James VI and I, *Basilicon Doron* and *The Trew Law of Free Monarchies*: The Scottish Context and the English Translation' in Linda Levy Peck (ed.), *The Mental World of the Jacobean Court* (Cambridge, 1991), pp. 36–54.

Michael B. Young, *King James and the History of Homosexuality*, 2nd edition ([Oxford], 2016).

UNPUBLISHED THESES

Ruth Abraham, 'Appropriating James VI and I: Reading the King of Scotland/England from the 16th to the 21st Century' (Queen's University Belfast PhD thesis, 2011).

Rebecca A. Calcagno, 'Publishing the Stuarts: Occasional Literature and Politics from 1603 to 1625' (Columbia University PhD thesis, 2011).

Emily V. Cole, 'The State Apartment in the Jacobean Country House, 1603–1625' (University of Sussex DPhil thesis, 2010).

Alexander Courtney, 'Court Politics and the Kingship of James VI & I, *c.* 1615 to 1622' (University of Cambridge PhD thesis, 2008).

Neil Cuddy, 'The King's Chambers: The Bedchamber of James I in Administration and Politics, 1603–1625' (University of Oxford DPhil thesis, 1987).

Amy L. Juhala, 'The Household and Court of King James VI of Scotland, 1567–1603' (University of Edinburgh PhD thesis, 2000).

Robin G. MacPherson, 'Francis Stewart, 5th earl Bothwell, *c.* 1562–1612: Lordship and Politics in Jacobean Scotland' (University of Edinburgh PhD thesis, 1998).

Ernesto Eduardo Oyarbide Magaña, 'The First Count of Gondomar's Library and Diplomatic Practice (1613–1622)' (University of Oxford DPhil thesis, 2019).

Joseph Marshall, 'Reading King James VI and I in the Civil War' (University of Edinburgh PhD thesis, 1999).

Elisabeth Rébeillé-Borgella, 'Esme Stuart d'Aubigny, First Duke of Lennox, *c.* 1542–1583: A French Courtier in Scotland' (University of Edinburgh PhD thesis, 2022).

Anthony R. Rowley, 'How England Learned to Smoke: The Introduction, Spread and Establishment of Tobacco Pipe Smoking in England before 1640' (University of York PhD thesis, 2003).

Gillian Sargent, '"Happy are they that read and understand": Reading for Moral and Spiritual Acuity in a Selection of Writings by King James' (University of Glasgow PhD thesis, 2013).

Acknowledgements

Anniversaries mattered to James. As king of Scotland, he defied Kirk distaste for festival celebrations by instituting the country's first religious anniversary for a royal event: 'Gowrie Day'. From the early years of his English reign, he ordered the annual observation of three anniversaries – Gowrie Day, Gunpowder Treason Day and his own Accession Day – with the second date still celebrated each year on 5 November. As James knew, anniversaries focus minds and offer occasions for reflection. To this end, I'm grateful to Simon Winder at Allen Lane, and to Hayley Bracken at Liveright, for embracing the opportunity to revisit the life of this extraordinary king in the quatercentenary year of his death. From the outset, Simon's joyous enthusiasm has been immensely galvanizing, accompanied by instantaneous responses to queries and incisive advice. I cannot imagine a more encouraging or supportive editor. I am likewise indebted to Hayley for her thoughtful and careful editorial interventions, and to my agent, Natasha Fairweather, for the regular supply of sage counsel and warm reassurance in equal measure. Working with Cecilia Mackay on illustrations for this book has, once again, been hugely pleasurable and, for overseeing its production and publicity, I'm grateful to Rosie Brown, Nick Curley, Richard Duguid, Clio Hamilton, Kadiatou Keita, Olivia Kumar, Jodie Lewis, Richard Mason, Peter Miller, Luke Swann and Kim Walker.

In Cambridge, colleagues at Trinity Hall have supplied stimulation via countless lunchtime conversations, with particular thanks to David Cowan, Tim Harvey-Samuel, Mary Hockaday, Pedro Ramos Pinto, Jan-Melissa Schramm and James Wood. Ana Calzada Sanchez's regular encouragement in the Aula Bar has likewise been a valuable spur, while expert assistance has also been provided by Alexandra Browne, Jenni Lecky-Thompson and Sophie Pittock in the Jerwood Library and by Kathryn Martin-Chambers in the Alumni and Development Office. I remain deeply appreciative of the University Library's phenomenal holdings and am especially indebted to the knowledgeable and obliging staff in the Rare Books Room, as well as Rebecca Gower in the Collections Development and Academic Liaison Department.

For reading draft chapters of *The Mirror of Great Britain*, I am grateful for the expertise of Paul Cavill, Sally Mapstone, Anthony Milton, Nicola Padfield and David Smith. I am indebted to Kieran Owens for inviting me to speak about James at Farmleigh House in Dublin, to Naomi Pullin for a similar invitation to the University of Warwick and to Brendan Simms and the Centre of Geopolitics in Cambridge for co-hosting an event at Trinity Hall. A chance conversation with Carrie Gracie sharpened my initial thinking about how to write this book and was followed by fruitful discussions with, among others, Alexander Courtney, Steven Reid and Anna Whitelock. For generous hospitality in Edinburgh, warm thanks are due to Amy Blakeway, Patricia Glennie and Celia Joicey. On Islay, Margaret Storrie has been keenly interested in the book's progress, while numerous friends in Cambridge have maintained my momentum, with especial thanks to Leah Loughnane and Julie McCrae for encouraging regular exercise.

My greatest debt, however, is owed to Mark Goldie and our son, Julius. As James insisted to his English Privy Councillors in November 1617, 'No worldly thing is so precious as time'. Mark and Julius have not only readily tolerated my prolonged preoccupation with James, but also filled the time spent away from my desk with laughter, purpose and love.

Index